2006

PRESIDENTIAL PROFILES
THE
GEORGE H. W. BUSH
YEARS

PRESIDENTIAL PROFILES
THE
GEORGE H. W. BUSH
YEARS

John Robert Greene

An imprint of Infobase Publishing

Presidential Profiles: The George H. W. Bush Years

Facts On File, Inc.
An imprint of Infobase Publishing
132 West 31st Street
New York NY 10001

Library of Congress Cataloging-in-Publication Data

Greene, John Robert, 1955–
    The George H. W. Bush years / John Robert Greene.
        p. cm. — (Presidential profiles)
    Includes bibliographical references and index.
    ISBN 0-8160-5279-4 (hardcover : alk. paper)
    1. Politicians—United States—Biography. 2. United States—Politics and government—1981–1989. 3. United States—Politics and government—1989–1993. 4. Bush, George, 1924—Friends and associates. 5. United States—History—1969—Biography. 6. United States—Biography. I. Title. II. Presidential profiles (Facts on File, Inc.)

    E840.6.G74 2005
    973.928′092—dc22   2005000687

Text design by Mary Susan Ryan-Flynn
Cover design by Nora Wertz
Maps by Jeremy Eagle
All photographic reproductions are from the George Bush Presidential Library.

Printed in the United States of America

VB Hermitage 10 9 8 7 6 5 4 3 2 1

This book is printed on acid-free paper.

For
Patty, T. J., Christopher, and Mary Rose

CONTENTS

CONTRIBUTORS   IX

PREFACE AND ACKNOWLEDGMENTS   XI

INTRODUCTION   XIII

BIOGRAPHICAL DICTIONARY A–Z   1

APPENDICES   91
Maps   93
Chronology   97
Principal U.S. Government Officials of the George H. W. Bush Years   108
Selected Primary Documents   168

SELECTED BIBLIOGRAPHY   485

INDEX   493

CONTRIBUTORS

Kari Cadrette   Cazenovia College

Brandon Clark   Cazenovia College

Sarah Davison   Cazenovia College

Amber Farr   Cazenovia College

Jennifer Hartwell   Cazenovia College

Marcie Palmer   Cazenovia College

Karen Sinnott   Cazenovia College

Shirley Anne Warshaw   Gettysburg College

Kaleb Wilson   Cazenovia College

StephanieWoodcock   Cazenovia College

Alea Wratten   Cazenovia College

PREFACE AND ACKNOWLEDGMENTS

*All of us who have written on the modern presidency over the past several decades know the value of having the relevant volume of the *Presidential Profiles* series on their desk as they write. These volumes offer all the relevant material from any of the covered presidential administrations, in a format that is both easy to use and factually trustworthy. I was pleased to have been asked to contribute this volume on the presidency of George H. W. Bush to this prestigious series. Leaner than the original series by design, this volume nevertheless keeps all the features of the original series. Profile entries on all the relevant political players, world leaders, leaders of Congress, Supreme Court appointees, and cabinet members are included. The vast majority of these entries were written by myself; those written by colleagues are identified at the end of the entry (if there is no author identification, it was written by myself). Also included are detailed appendices, including a chronology. In addition, this volume adds to the series a collection of primary source documents relevant to the Bush years. These documents were drawn from George H. W. Bush, *Public Papers of the President: 1989–1993*, available at http://bushlibrary. tamu.edu/research/paper.html.

To date, there has been all too little serious scholarly analysis of the first Bush administration (see the bibliography at the end of this vol-ume for a complete list). Largely due to government regulations and the understandable backlog of work, is has been a slow process for the George H. W. Bush Presidential Library (College Station, TX) to release the documents of the Bush administration for scholarly review. Yet several studies are available. As I worked on this volume, several books were always within arm's reach: Rick Atkinson, *Crusade: The Untold Story of the Persian Gulf War*; George Bush and Brent Scowcroft, *A World Transformed*; George Bush, *All the Best: My Life in Letters and Other Writings*; Michael Duffy and Dan Goodgame, *Running in Place: The Status Quo Presidency of George Bush*; John Robert Greene, *The Presidency of George Bush*; David Mervin, *George Bush and the Guardianship Presidency*; and Herbert Parmet, *George Bush: The Life of a Lone Star Yankee*. Arthur L. Galub and George J. Lankevich's *The Rehnquist Court: 1986–1994* is not only a worthy collection of documents on its subject but also provides an outstanding chronology of the Bush years that was used with great profit in developing my own chronology. These books form the core of the research material for entries in this volume, and, as such, they are not cited as references for each entry.

No one writes alone. At Cazenovia College, I particularly thank President Mark Tierno and Academic Dean Donald McCrimmon for their support. Stanley Kozaczka and his staff at the Cazenovia College Library offered assistance, without which this project would not have gone forward. Jenna Hartwell, Marcie Palmer, and Brian Kuntz provided outstanding research help, and Carol "Lolly" Kuntz provided invaluable support assistance.

My usual thanks are reserved for my writing colleague, Shirley Anne Warshaw at Gettysburg College. Owen Lancer at Facts On File is an outstanding and prescient editor—a true writer's editor. And, as noted in the dedication, nothing is written from this desk without the support of my family.

INTRODUCTION

THE PRESIDENTIAL ELECTION OF 1988

Few politicians have come to the White House as well prepared as George Herbert Walker Bush. Successful businessman, congressman, ambassador to the United Nations, chairman of the Republican Party, minister to the People's Republic of China—Bush was justifiably christened the "résumé candidate" when he ran for the presidency in 1980. However, the juggernaut that was Ronald Reagan ended Bush's campaign before the convention, and many were surprised when Reagan chose Bush as his vice presidential running mate. During Reagan's first term, Bush showed his loyalty and served with particular distinction and discretion during the period immediately following the April 1981 attempt on Reagan's life. In the election of 1984, Reagan's popularity, a resurgence of American patriotism, and a strong economy made the Republican team virtually unbeatable. On November 6, 1984, the Reagan-Bush ticket was reelected by one of the largest pluralities in American history.

Immediately following the 1984 landslide, the press christened Bush the front-runner for the 1988 presidential race. However, the Iran-contra scandal and stories of Bush's involvement in the White House planning of the arms for hostages deal served to dull his edge. Many Republican challengers subsequently appeared. Former automobile executive Lee Iacocca, former Delaware governor Pierre "Pete" DuPont, former secretary of state Alexander Haig, former secretary of defense Donald Rumsfeld, and former senator Howard Baker all challenged Bush, and all had dropped out of the race in the early primaries. Bush's main competition came from Senate Majority Leader Bob Dole (R-Kans.), New York congressman Jack Kemp, and evangelist Pat Robertson. Any of these three candidates stood to tap into the large number of conservatives who had become disenchanted with the Reagan administration. Indeed, Robertson's strong showing in the May 1986 Michigan delegate convention was indicative of the depth of this support. Bush's loss in the Iowa primary—placing third behind Dole and Robertson—underscored this.

Three individuals were largely responsible for Bush's comeback victory in 1988. Harvey Leroy Atwater, a former political director in the Reagan White House, brought a hard edge and the courage of a riverboat gambler to the Bush campaign. Atwater encouraged Bush to take a hard line during an interview with CBS anchor Dan Rather (charging that Rather had changed the ground rules on the interview by talking about the Iran-contra scandal, Bush

President Ronald Reagan and Vice President George Bush, accompanied by wives Nancy and Barbara, join hands after the president endorses Bush's run for the presidency during the President's dinner, Washington, D.C., May 12, 1988.

stormed: "I don't think its fair . . . to judge a whole career . . . by a rehash on Iran. How would you like it if I judged your career by those seven minutes when you walked off the set in New York?"—referring to the time when Rather, angry that a tennis match had delayed the start of his newscast, stormed off the set). Atwater thought it was the perfect pitch, and while it came too late to save Bush in the Iowa primary, Atwater's combative tone rubbed off on both Bush and the campaign. It would become the tone for the rest of the campaign.

The second key individual was John Sununu, governor of New Hampshire. It was Sununu—whose prickly personality took a back seat to no one, not even Atwater—who mobilized the local Republican machinery in the Granite State, and it was he who effectively engineered Bush's victory in the New Hampshire primary. Atwater, Sununu, and Roger Ailes—a former television producer then serving as the director of advertising for the Bush campaign, the third most important person in that campaign—designed a proactive, attack operation against Dole that effectively negated the momentum which Dole has earned from his Iowa victory. A series of ads were designed in which Dole was dubbed "Senator Straddle" to imply that he favored a tax hike. These were the leading factors in Bush's victory on February 16; Bush won with 38 percent of the vote to Dole's 28 percent. Dole pushed his own knife in deeper when interviewed election night. Asked what message he had for Bush, he snarled: "Tell him to quit lying about my record." The momentum had shifted. On Super Tuesday, Bush won every state but Washington. At the Republican National Convention in New Orleans, Bush delivered a thundering acceptance address, written by former Reagan speechwriter Peggy Noonan, in which he pounded the podium and promised, "Read my lips. No new taxes."

The only unanswered question at the convention remained Bush's choice of a running mate. Brushing aside several suggestions by his staff (including Atwater's proposal that Bush choose Reagan cabinet member Elizabeth Dole), Bush chose J. Danforth Quayle, the junior senator from Indiana. Quayle brought a great deal to the ticket that Bush lacked—youth, strong conservative credentials, and a Midwestern charm. However, Quayle's exuberance (when announced to the press, he literally squealed with delight, pumped his fist in the air, and grabbed the more solemn Bush's hand to jointly raise their arms in a victory salute—a gesture that clearly caught Bush by surprise) made him the immediate butt of jokes. More important, however, the vetting process within the Bush campaign had neglected to see a potential problem in Quayle's tenure in the National Guard during the Vietnam War, with evidence emerging that his family had pulled strings to keep him from being drafted. The press had a field day with Quayle, and Bush's running mate was effectively kept out of sight for the rest of the campaign.

Bush's cause was aided by the man whom Democrats chose as his opponent. The two strongest candidates—Senator Edward Kennedy of Massachusetts and Governor Mario Cuomo of New York—refused to run. In the end, Massachusetts governor Michael Dukakis emerged from a crowded field. A brilliant policy strategist, Dukakis's command of the issues was overshadowed by his flat, almost lifeless delivery and

his often cold demeanor. Unwilling to play Atwater's game, Dukakis spent the entirety of the fall campaign serving as a target for Bush campaign attacks. Bush's depiction of Dukakis as an ultraliberal went virtually unchallenged. Bush also co-opted the American flag as a symbol of the Republican Party by hammering at Dukakis's veto of a Massachusetts bill requiring the Pledge of Allegiance to be recited in every Massachusetts classroom. Yet the most memorable symbol of the campaign was Willie Horton, who, while on a furlough from a Massachusetts prison where he was serving a sentence for murder, broke into a home in Maryland, pistol whipped the owner, and raped his wife. Dukakis had supported the furlough program, and the Bush campaign made it the crux of a devastatingly effective advertisement, which showed convicts going in and out of prison through a revolving door.

In November, Bush handily defeated Dukakis. He won 54 percent of the popular vote and 426 electoral votes to Dukakis's 112. But the election by no means marked a political realignment. For the first time in 28 years, the Democrats gained seats in both houses of Congress while losing the presidency. The Democrats controlled both houses of Congress and thus Bush's challenge would be to find a way to advance a legislative agenda through a Congress that would be prone to react adversely to his proposals.

THE BUSH TEAM

Bush's choices for his White House staff offered pundits some surprises. For his chief of staff, he bypassed Craig Fuller, his vice presidential chief of staff, and Robert Teeter, his chief pollster. Instead, the position went to John Sununu, one of the architects of the all-important New Hampshire primary victory. Instead of keeping his vice presidential press secretary, Sheila Tate,

Bush kept Reagan's press secretary. In an unprecedented move, Bush chose to keep the highly respected Marlin Fitzwater, who had served as Reagan's press secretary for seven years of his presidency, at that position. Also kept from the Reagan White House was Richard Darman, who had been a deputy secretary of the Treasury under Reagan, and who was now made the director of the Office of Management and Budget. Yet not all his vice presidential loyalists were jettisoned. C. Boyden Gray, who had been a close adviser to Bush throughout the vice presidential years, was named White House counsel and, for his role in the campaign, Lee Atwater was named to head the Republican National Committee. Despite grumblings about an unfriendly transition, and Reagan staffers being asked to leave their offices by January 20, 1989, so that Bush appointees could take their places, there were significant holdovers from the Reagan administration.

This observation applied to the majority of Bush's cabinet appointments as well. Seven Reagan cabinet members were kept on into the Bush cabinet, either retained in their old department or reassigned. Within 12 hours of his election, Bush announced—to no one's surprise—the appointment of James A. Baker III as his secretary of state. Baker, who was perhaps Bush's closest friend in government, served as a political adviser to Gerald R. Ford during the 1976 campaign. He had also served as Ronald Reagan's secretary of the Treasury, before becoming that administration's chief of staff. Bush also kept Nicholas Brady at Treasury, Lauro Cavasos at Education, and Richard Thornburgh as Attorney General. Three others were reassigned—Elizabeth Dole was moved from Transportation to Labor; Clayton Yeutter was moved from U.S. Trade Representative to Agriculture, and William Bennett was moved from Education to the position of director of the Office of National Drug Control Policy. Rounding out the cabinet appointees were Jack Kemp at Housing and Urban Development, John Tower at Defense, Robert Mosbacher at Commerce, Samuel Skinner at Transportation, Edward Derwinski at Veteran's Affairs, Louis Sullivan at Health and Human Services, and Admiral James Watkins at the Department of Energy.

In a league by itself was Bush's appointment of his special assistant for national security. Brent Scowcroft, who had held that position under Ford, had been a reliable critic of Reagan's foreign policy. Consistently warning that the Soviet Union was not as weak as events in the 1980s might suggest (the "Sleeping Bear" viewpoint), Scowcroft was one of the most hawkish of Bush's advisers, and, by the time of the Persian Gulf War, the most influential. Foreign policy would, in the Bush administration, be formed in the National Security Council.

However, one appointment led to the most significant crisis of the early Bush administration. Anxious to exploit any weaknesses to avenge what they perceived to be the unfair tactics of the Bush campaign, Democrats in Congress zeroed in on the Tower nomination. Tower presented an easy target. Rumors of his excessive drinking and his womanizing had circulated on Capitol Hill for decades. Indeed, a story appeared soon after his nomination charging that, while serving as the nation's chief arms control negotiator, Tower had had an affair with a woman who was actually a KGB agent. Tower also maintained business relations with several key defense contractors, thus leaving himself open to claims of conflict of interest. Perhaps most important, the brusque Tower had never been a well-liked member of the Senate "club." As a result of all these factors, his nomination met serious scrutiny. As reports from the FBI on Tower's personal life began to leak, it was clear that there would not be a consensus in either the Senate Foreign Relations Committee or on the floor of the Senate, whose members would be called upon to confirm Tower. On February 23, 1989, on a straight party-line vote, the Armed Services Committee voted 11-9 against the nomination. And yet, despite pressure from his staff to find another nominee, Bush stuck with his appointee. The nomination went to the floor of the Senate, where on March 9, 1989, it was defeated by a vote of 53 to 47.

Bush's second choice for defense, like Baker and Bush himself, cut his political teeth in the administration of Gerald Ford. Richard B. Cheney had served as both deputy chief of staff and then chief of staff, to Ford. He was subsequently elected to the U.S. House of Representatives from Wyoming. Respected on both sides of the aisle, Cheney's nomination was approved by the full Senate on March 17, 1989, by a vote of 92-0. However, the political bloodletting did not end with Cheney's confirmation. Wounded Republicans immediately set their sights on James B. Wright, then serving as the Speaker of the House of Representatives. Like Tower, Wright was vulnerable to attack, having taken monies for a book he had written outside the limits of the honorarium system set for congressmembers and also having been charged with taking $145,000 in improper gifts from a Texas congressman. Besieged in the media, Wright finally resigned his office on May 31, 1989. He was replaced as Speaker by Thomas Foley of Washington.

DOMESTIC POLICIES

On January 20, 1989, Bush delivered his inaugural address to the nation. In a rather slow, plodding delivery, the new president noted that "a new breeze is blowing" and that "there is much to do." He also pointedly observed that "we have more will than wallet, but will is what we need." To the Reaganites in the audience, this smacked of nothing less than heresy; and, in fact, the inaugural foreshadowed a Bush administration that would do its level best to separate its policies from that of its predecessor. Still, the inaugural words reflected the political reality. The Democrats had a 10 vote majority in the Senate and an 89 vote majority in the House. For the administration's policies to have any hope of passage, they would have to appeal to moderate Democrats. Thus, Bush was faced throughout his administration with a situation that would soon be labeled "Gridlock Government."

Early on, the administration tried to tone down expectations on domestic policies. Sununu touted Bush's plans as a "limited agenda." Even the catch phrase "Investing in America's Future" sounded bland. Bush was largely seen by the press to be a man who was trying to "wing" it, an assessment he fed by playfully drawing a parallel between himself and the last vice president to assume the presidency: "This is the Martin van Buren analogy. We didn't come in here throwing the rascals out to try to do something—correct all the ills of the world in 100 days. . . . I'm methodically, I think pragmatically, moving forward on these."

But lines were soon drawn, as Democratic congressmembers gleefully reminded the public of Bush's pledge during the campaign not to raise taxes and opined that *no* domestic policy package could succeed without new revenue to support those plans. To no one's surprise, the administration thus tried to use the veto as a tool to affect legislation. Indeed, in this strategy, the numbers favored the administration. Bush needed to keep only 34 of his 43 Republican votes to sustain a veto in the Senate. Overall, Bush vetoed 44 bills during his tenure, and his veto was upheld 43 times. This allowed Bush to put his mark on legislation. For example, in June 1989 he vetoed a bill that raised the minimum wage from $3.35 to $4.55. In 1990 he vetoed the Amtrak Reauthorization and Improvement Act.

The use of the veto strategy, while spun by Bush's aides as a positive initiative that allowed the president to affect legislation, served to show how difficult it was for the administration to have a domestic policy of its own with a Democratic Congress and high budget deficits. One way to deal with the problem was to try to offer initiatives that were funded so cheaply that it would be impossible for Congress not to pass them. This approach stood at the heart of Bush's education package. Few could argue that the American education system needed a drastic overhaul: 33.5 percent of the nation's youth did not finish four years of high school; yet, during the years 1980–85 spending for precollegiate education in the United States had declined precipitously. In his final budget, Reagan had proposed a freeze on all education spending. Bush showed his resolve to face the issue of education by delivering a speech to a joint session of Congress devoted entirely to the issue. On February 9, 1989, the president proposed a new $500 million program to reward what he called "Merit Schools" as well as to promote the use of magnet schools to allow parents in the public system more choice on where they sent their children. These two proposals formed the heart of the Educational Excellence Act, proposed that April. However, the money infused into the act was simply too little. Bush was attacked by Democrats and educators for proposing education reform on the cheap and by conservative Republicans for proposing education reform that cost anything at all. To jump-start his campaign for the bill, Bush held an innovative conference of the nation's governors on September 27–28, 1989, to discuss the issue. (One of the key players at that conference was Governor Bill Clinton of Arkansas, who received a personal thank you note from the president.) But the plan now had too many enemies. As Bush attempted to regain the initiative, he fired Secretary of Education Lauro Cavasos, replacing him with former Tennessee governor Lamar Alexander. Alexander became the administration front man for a proposal

dubbed "America 2000," which placed the burden of improving the nation's schools on the local communities without an influx of funds—indeed, the proposed budget for FY 1992 cut education spending.

Yet gridlock and budget deficits were not the only domestic policy problems Bush faced. He was also being pushed hard by the right flank of his own party to advance shifts in policy that conservatives felt were long overdue. Confusion surrounded the fight against illicit drugs because the nation had, in effect, two drug czars with two differing points of view on how to win the war—drug czar William Bennett and the president himself. A true evangelist for his program, the quotable Bennett was a darling of the press; most observers assumed that he harbored presidential ambitions himself. He was also well-liked by the conservative right, particularly when he advocated invading Bolivia and taking back the streets of Washington, D.C., as immediate solutions to the drug policy. Bush, however, was more circumspect, calling for the expansion of the criminal justice system to deal with offenders and strengthening border-interdiction patrols. It may well have been the private grumbling of Bennett that led Bush to deliver a nationally televised address on September 5, 1989. During the speech, Bush held up as a prop a bag of cocaine that he claimed had been "seized a few days ago in a park across the street from the White House." The next day it was revealed that while the bag did, indeed, contain crack cocaine, it had been purchased from a dealer who had been enticed to leave his territory in southeast Washington to the area directly across from the White House. Undeterred, Bush continued to push forward with his proposals; in November 1990 Bennett left the administration, replaced by former Florida governor Bob Martinez. In February 1991 the administration took a new tack in proposing an 11 percent increase in the budget for health incentives that would include monies for the drug problem.

To overcome the congressional stalemate and advance his policies, Bush was not above glomming on to a piece of legislation already germinating in Congress and adopting it as his own in order to gain a victory. The Americans with Disabilities Act (ADA) was a prime example. The nation's disabled had not been fully covered by the Civil Rights Act of 1964, and during the Reagan administration legislation had begun to be drafted to change this inequity. The bill as proposed called for an end to employment discrimination for those with disabilities and required businesses to provide access to their places of business for those patrons with disabilities. Bush had always been in favor of the legislation, and he had spoken out in favor of it in his inaugural address. He immediately pledged his support for the bill, and he quickly signed it upon passage.

Clearly, Bush "adopted" the ADA as his own. However, without the support of the administration the amendments to the Clean Air Act of 1970, stuck on Capitol Hill at the time of his inauguration, might well not have passed. The original act, largely the work of Senator Edmund Muskie (D-Maine), required the automobile industry to implement a 90 percent reduction in total emissions by January 1, 1975, and directed the Environmental Protection Agency (EPA) to set limits on toxic pollutants and air-quality standards for industry. Those requirements were several times extended, and the next time they would be up for discussion was 1987. By 1988 a bill had been drafted but was stuck in committee, facing opposition from representatives of states such as Michigan (automobile industry) and West Virginia (bituminous coal). While Bush clearly understood the needs of those constituencies, there was also a need for him to create a strong environmental package that would help Republicans win in California in 1990 and 1992. Bush

emerged as an early supporter of the amendments to the 1970 act, a stand that was inadvertently helped by the March 24, 1989, breakup of the oil tanker *Exxon Valdez*, which ran aground in Alaska's Prince William Sound, spilling more than 10 million gallons of oil into the water. The accident galvanized the public, and, despite opposition from both Capitol Hill and inside his own White House (Budget director Darman and Energy secretary Watkins argued that the amendments were too costly), Bush combined his own threats of a veto with the skillful maneuvering of Senate Majority Leader George Mitchell (D-Maine) and a compromise measure was signed into law on November 15, 1990. The bill enumerated provisions that would bring cities into compliance with clean air standards, called for an acid rain program, and created a program that would reduce industrial emissions of air pollutants. It also set standards for tailpipe emissions and detailed the nation's first steps for dealing with ozone depletion.

THE SUPREME COURT AND CIVIL RIGHTS

To the outside observer, it seemed as if the Supreme Court could be counted on to help Bush in his quest to advance conservative policy initiatives. However, the opposite turned out to be the case, as the Court, led by Chief Justice William Rehnquist, proved to be an unexpected foe of policies the administration held dear.

During the 1984 Republican National Convention, held in Dallas, Texas, Gregory Lee Johnson had joined a demonstration against the policies of the Reagan administration. In so doing, he participated in the act of burning an American flag, for which he was arrested and charged with violating a Texas statute that made the desecration of the flag a criminal act.

President Bush signs the Americans with Disabilities Act in the Rose Garden, White House, July 26, 1990.

On June 21, 1989, the Court issued its ruling in *Texas v. Johnson*. In its 5-4 ruling, the justices declared that burning an American flag was a form of symbolic speech, protected by the First Amendment. The ruling thus invalidated all state flag desecration laws. A furious Bush announced that he would seek an amendment to the Constitution which protected the flag from any desecration. However, the Flag Burning Amendment was opposed by Speaker of the House Thomas Foley, who called the amendment "unnecessary." Suspecting that the White House might well be trying to make hay out of a political issue, Foley instead supported a congressional measure, the Flag Protection Act of 1989, that closely matched Bush's constitutional amendment. The bill passed both houses of Congress, but, on June 11, 1989, it was declared unconstitutional by the Supreme Court (*U.S. v. Eichmann*). The Court's actions renewed a cry for a constitutional amendment, but a proposal for such an amendment was defeated in the Senate.

Nowhere, however, was the clash between Court and administration as marked as it was over the issue of abortion. Conservatives had long hoped for a case that would allow the Court to overturn *Roe v. Wade* (1973), which had legalized abortions throughout the first six months of pregnancy. Indeed, conservatives counted on action by the Court as Bush remained suspect in their eyes. He had changed his views on abortion several times in the years prior to his election to the presidency until he settled on the position advanced by most moderate Republicans, namely, that, although he was pro-life, he believed that abortion was a matter best left up to the states. Thus, while his public statements on abortion were true to the pro-life cause, there was good reason in the conservative community to believe that the president was not wedded to their cause. Bush's stand mirrored public opinion; only 9 percent of Americans in 1988 wanted a complete overturning of *Roe*. On July 3, 1989, the Court seemed to side with Bush when, in *Webster v. Reproductive Health Services of Missouri*, it gave states the right to impose new restrictions on abortions but stopped short of completely overturning *Roe*. While the White House publicly praised the decision, in reality Bush was furious. Despite his public pronouncements, Bush's Solicitor General had worked hard in an attempt to get the court to use the *Webster* case to completely overturn *Roe*, and had failed. Immediately following the decision, the administration let it be known that it would favor an anti-abortion amendment to the Constitution, but the proposal had no traction on Capitol Hill. Thus, Bush used his veto to affect the direction of abortion legislation—10 of his 44 vetoes were wielded against abortion-related legislation, and all 10 of those vetoes were upheld.

In one area of civil rights the Court did indeed support the president, but the administration was unable to harness that support. In 1989, the Court handed down two key decisions regarding racial discrimination. In *Patterson v. McLean Credit Union*, the Court limited the extent to which the Civil Rights Act of 1966 could be used to sue for private acts of racial discrimination. And in *Wards Cove v. Atonio* the Court made it clear that plaintiffs could not charge discrimination by saying that a business work group did not represent the demographics of the local workforce. Incensed, the Democratic Congress proposed the Civil Rights Bill of 1990, which provided for significant monetary damages from businesses that violated the existing civil rights statutes. Businesses were up in arms against the bill, and, immediately following its October 17, 1990, passage, Bush vetoed the measure, a veto that was upheld. Yet Congress continued to press for the measure, and it was clear that as the presidential election season crept closer, Bush would have to settle for a compromise bill. On November 21, 1991, Bush signed the Civil Rights Bill of 1991, which stated that any business practice that led to a racial disparity automatically made the employer guilty of discrimination unless the employer could prove a valid "business necessity." This was the best that Bush could hope for from the Democratic Congress, but it did little to improve his standing among his party's conservative wing.

In the shadow of the decisions taken in *Webster, Patterson,* and *Ward's Cove*, Bush was presented with the opportunity to make his first appointment to the Supreme Court. Indeed, with the resignation of liberal icon William Brennan on July 19, 1990, Bush was presented with an opportunity to turn the Court further toward the right. Instead, he chose to nominate a jurist whose policies, because they were neither black nor white but gray, could be easily confirmed. David H. Souter, a New Hampshire jurist then sitting on the Circuit Court for the District of Columbia, so carefully guarded his views during the confirmation hearings that the press dubbed him the "stealth candidate." But the strategy proved a success as Souter was unanimously confirmed by the Senate.

THE ECONOMY AND THE CONGRESSIONAL ELECTIONS OF 1990

The $2.7 trillion budget deficit inherited from the Reagan administration was, as noted above, a driving factor behind the lack of coherence in the Bush domestic agenda. Closing the budget gap thus became an issue of its own, one that Bush and his advisers badly mishandled. Essentially a social moderate, Bush could not bring himself to make the spending cuts necessary to bring the budget closer in balance. Indeed, his plan to deal with the crisis of the American banking industry, where Savings and Loans continued to close at a precipitous rate into the first months of his presidency, promised to further worsen the deficit by necessitating spending to bail out the banks. To manage the crisis, Bush created the Office of Thrift Supervision in February 1989. However, even this new office would not be enough, and the administration was forced to announce that federal aid to bail out the Thrifts would exceed $39.9 billion over the next 10 years. Indeed, the government would have to spend an additional $24 billion to liquidate all the Thrifts that *would* be closed into the 1990s.

Bush had also painted himself into a political corner with his 1988 promise not to raise taxes. On the surface, this seemed to be a philosophical imperative for Bush. In fact, in the early months of his administration, Bush had argued for a 50 percent *cut* in the capital gains tax. And during his first year, Bush was able to get a budget through Congress without raising taxes or significantly cutting spending. The budget for FY 1990 estimated federal spending at $1.16 trillion, with an adjusted budget deficit of $91.1 billion. The plan was brokered through Dan Rostenkowski (D-Ill.), a friend of Bush and chairman of the House Ways and Means Committee, who essentially gave the administration a free pass on the budget for its first year. However, no observer believed that the Democrats would allow the administration to get through one more budget cycle without publicly facing up to its promise not to raise taxes.

Bush's hopes for a second brokered budget deal were further darkened by a worsening economy. Constrained by a Federal Reserve System that continued to pursue a tight money policy, the economy was lurching toward a recession. Inflation had hit 4.8 percent by 1989. On October 13, 1989, the stock market took its worst plunge in several years, dropping 190 points in one day. All evidence pointed to a nasty budget showdown the following year.

On January 29, 1990, Bush submitted his FY 1991 budget to the Congress. It called for a total of $1.23 trillion in spending and a reduction of the deficit to $64 billion. However, the proposal included some $14 billion in revenues from what was called "users fees." The congressional counterproposal called for a cost-of-living freeze in all spending categories, as well as an increase of 15 cents per gallon in the gasoline tax. Clearly, there would be no reconciliation without Bush agreeing to some form of tax increases, which he did during a negotiating session on June 26. Bush quickly paid the political price as the media excoriated him for his flip-flop (the *New York Post* headline: "Read My Lips: I Lied."). Conservatives within his own party, led by a furious minority whip, Newt Gingrich (R-Ga.), publicly criticized the president for caving in on taxes. As a result of the split in his own party, Bush went into the final stage of the budget negotiations with a severely weakened hand. The president tried to strengthen his position by linking the budget negotiations to the situation in the Persian Gulf. After the August 2, 1990, invasion of Kuwait by Iraq, Bush announced that "domestic policy was inexorably tied to foreign affairs . . . we must address our budget deficit—not after election day, not next year, but *now*. . . . This is no time to risk America's ability to defend her vital interests."

On September 26 a negotiated settlement to the budget was announced. The White House agreed to cut a total of $301 billion in spending and to increase tax revenues by $134 billion—revenues that would largely be created by a phased-in tax on gasoline over a five-year period. Furious, conservative Republicans now openly abandoned the budget process—Gingrich refused to appear at the White House for the announcement of the agreement. Conservatives held up the vote on the package on Capitol Hill through two continuing resolutions and a three-day mandatory government shutdown. In the end, the Omnibus Budget Reconciliation Act of 1990 dispensed with the gasoline tax and replaced it with a tax on the upper-income bracket.

All in all, the budget crisis marked an embarrassing defeat for Bush, and, as conservatives continued to keep their distance from the president, contributed to GOP losses that fall in the off-year elections. Despite the nation's ramp-up in patriotism following the beginning of Operation Desert Shield, Republicans lost 10 Senate seats, 25 House seats, and two governorships.

FOREIGN POLICY: SOVIET UNION, PANAMA, AND CHINA

Many from the Conservative right had quietly seethed as Ronald Reagan opened a détente with Mikhail Gorbachev, and they were quietly hopeful when, at the outset of his term, Bush refused to rush into a continuation of that dialogue. Counseled by such hard-liners as James Baker, Brent Scowcroft, and Robert Gates, Scowcroft's deputy at the NSC, Bush initially chose to slow down the Soviet-American relationship by instigating a lengthy internal "policy review" on the relationship. The Soviets called it the *pauza*. Gorbachev tried to use British prime minister Margaret Thatcher as his broker at the White House to help thaw the freeze, but to no avail. Unlike Reagan, who Bush believed had raced into a relationship with the Soviet Union, Bush would not be rushed.

The first two steps taken toward the Soviets came in May 1989. At a commencement address delivered at Texas A&M University on May 12, Bush proposed a plan that he called "Open Skies," which gave both the United States and the Soviet Union the right to fly over each other's territory on reconnaissance missions. However, in an age of satellite spying, the offer was of little substance; it did, however, serve to signal the first thaw in the administration's attitude toward its relationship with the Soviets. Two weeks later, on May 28, at a meeting of NATO ministers in Brussels, Bush proposed that both NATO and the Warsaw Pact nations slash their conventional forces to about 275,000 per side. Because the United States would bear the brunt of this cutback (to get to the levels Bush proposed, the United States would have to cut some 350,000 troops), this proposal showed Bush's desire to finally move the Soviet-American relationship along the lines of détente begun by Reagan.

This progress was immediately threatened by events in the People's Republic of China (PRC). Gorbachev's promises of glasnost and perestroika had inadvertently opened a window for Chinese dissidents, believing they might be able to force their own Communist government in the same direction. On May 15, 1989, Gorbachev arrived in China for a state visit. That same day, hundreds of thousands of Chinese students descended upon Tiananmen Square, their protest sparked by the death of a student leader one month before. After Gorbachev left, Chinese troops cleared the square. On June 4 some 3,000 protesters were killed and 10,000 more were wounded as the army opened fire on the demonstrators. Torn by a personal revulsion that was clearly articulated in private, nonetheless Bush could not bring himself to destroy a growing relationship with the PRC—and possibly, by default, the Soviet Union. Thus, Bush's reaction to the Tiananmen Square massacre was a measured one that offered no real public protest from the United States. Indeed, on May 24, 1990, Bush extended China's most favored nation trade status. This response only served to further anger conservatives, who felt that Bush had come perilously close to condoning another Communist atrocity.

If nothing else, the Tiananmen Square massacre gave hope to those European dissidents who, for decades, had fought for their freedom from the Soviet Union. By 1989, from the Soviet republics of Latvia, Lithuania, and Estonia to Poland, Yugoslavia, and East Germany there were strong nationalist movements in place in most countries behind the Iron Curtain. Abhorring instability more than communism, Bush made a half-hearted attempt to slow the pace of nationalism in these nations, most notably in Poland, where he encouraged Communist general Wojciech Jaruzelski to run for the Polish presidency. He also quickened the pace of détente with the Soviet Union, giving to Gorbachev a badly needed public relations coup by announcing a summit with Gorbachev in Malta for December 1989, several months ahead of schedule.

But even before the summit could assemble, communism fell in Eastern Europe. It began in East Germany in early October, with thousands of demonstrators trying to leave the country. The decision by the East German government to close all its borders only led to more rioting, and Gorbachev decided that the satellite nation was not worth defending. Announcing on October 7 that East German policy was made "not in Moscow, but in Berlin," Gorbachev effectively ended Communist Party dominance in East Germany. The government immediately fell, and, on October 18, the new government opened the gates to the west. Crowds dashed for West Berlin, and Germans from both sides scaled the Berlin Wall, chipping off pieces for souvenirs.

True to his character, Bush refused to gloat about what was now touted as the "fall of communism." Neither to the press in the days following the collapse of the East German regime nor during the December 1–3, 1989, summit with Gorbachev did Bush rejoice in Gorbachev's travails. Such prudence brought more criticism for the president, particularly, once again, from conservatives who felt vindicated by the events in Europe. However, Bush's careful posture would keep Gorbachev as a useful ally, and, as events in the Middle East would soon show, this would be of immense value to the United States.

In Europe and in China, Bush believed that a cautious approach toward communism would reap the widest benefits for the United States. Not so in Latin America. Bush reacted to Panamanian strongman Manuel Noriega with the single-minded rage that his generation had once reserved for Adolf Hitler. Clearly, Noriega's character and tactics deserved antipathy. A paid informant for the CIA, the Panamanian strongman was also a key player in the Latin American drug trade. When on May 7, 1989, Noriega nullified the results of an election that had ousted him from power and had his henchmen publicly beat the victorious vice presidential candidate with an iron bar until his shirt was blood-soaked, Bush ordered his Chairman of the Joint Chiefs of Staff, Admiral William Crowe, to put together a plan that would oust the dictator from power.

On October 3, 1989—less than a day after General Colin Powell had been sworn in as the new chairman of the Joint Chiefs of Staff (replacing Crowe, who had resigned)—a coup, planned by a cadre within the Panamanian army, began. The administration was asked to help the coup leadership by blocking several entrances to the Panama Canal. They did so, but, not knowing enough about the coup plans, they gave no further help. Indeed, the rebellion was poorly planned and its leadership was quickly arrested, tortured, and executed. But Bush's national security team had reacted sluggishly to the opportunity, operating in informal, rather than formal, strategy sessions. They also failed to devise an adequate plan of reaction. In the days after the botched coup, the press played up a picture of a rudderless administration; a fuming Bush told his staff that "amateur hour is over." When the next opportunity came, it would find a White House, thanks to several steps put in place that restructured national security decision making, better prepared to react.

On December 16, 1989, four American soldiers were stopped at a roadblock by Panamanian soldiers. Once stopped, a crowd encircled the car; speeding away, the checkpoint guards fired, killing one American officer. That same evening, a U.S. Navy lieutenant and his wife were detained at the same checkpoint. Both were blindfolded and badly beaten. Bush invoked the brutality to order that the plan created by Crowe be put into action. Now codenamed Operation Just Cause, American paratroopers invaded Panama City. The country was in American hands by 9:00 a.m. the following morning, but it took another three weeks to capture Noriega, who finally surrendered from his sanctuary at the home of the papal nuncio on January 3, 1990.

The Persian Gulf War

Saddam Hussein, Iraq's leader since 1979, commanded the fourth-largest army in the world. His eight-year war with neighboring Iran had

Presidents Bush and Gorbachev at the Malta Summit, December 2, 1989

cost some $250 billion, thus devastating his nation's economy. The Bush administration had tried to help stabilize the economy of its erstwhile ally by increasing the number of agricultural credits available to that nation. However, suspicious of the intentions of his neighbors—particularly after the fall of communism in Europe—Saddam began to rattle his saber, publicly threatening Israel with annihilation if the Israelis should attack Iraq. He also began to develop a nuclear ability for his nation, a program that in 1989 was in its final stages. As a result of these developments, in May 1989 the Bush administration decided to cancel the next payment of its agricultural credits to Iraq.

Saddam saw a possible solution to his financial difficulties as well as a means to solidify his stature in the Middle East in the oil fields of the neighboring Emirate of Kuwait. A longtime feud marked the relations between the two nations. Iraq had only grudgingly accepted Kuwait's right to exist in 1963. Baghdad fumed that Kuwaiti actions had kept the price of oil artificially low and that its neighbor had sanctioned "slant drilling" into the Rumaylah oil field, the majority of which lay in Iraqi territory. Add to this the fact that Saddam owed Kuwait $10 billion borrowed during his war with Iran, and the scene was set. On August 2, 1990, some 140,000 Iraqi troops invaded Kuwait. Within 12 hours, Kuwait had fallen.

While the United States had a plan in place to counter Iraqi aggression, a plan developed by General Norman Schwarzkopf, the commander in chief of the Central Command, Washington assumed that Saddam intended to make a quick, surgical strike against Kuwait followed by a rapid withdrawal. This misreading of Saddam's intentions was fed by the allies of the United States in the Middle East, which informed Bush that, following so closely on the heels of the war with Iran, Saddam would never commit large forces to such an invasion. Yet whereas the United States was initially caught

off guard by the invasion, once it had occurred it was immediately assumed that Saddam intended to push through Kuwait and into Saudi Arabia—thus posing an even greater threat to American oil supplies. With this in mind, Bush acted quickly and decisively in the days following the invasion. Within hours of the invasion he signed an executive order freezing the approximately $100 billion in Iraqi assets and property both in the United States and overseas. He also immediately moved the *Independence* carrier battle group into the Persian Gulf.

Bush also began a round of personal diplomacy that was designed to isolate Saddam. He telephoned every major world leader and 11 nations, including the United Kingdom, France, Germany, and Japan, joined the United States in freezing Iraqi assets. Thanks largely to American prodding, the United Nations approved, in its strongest show of unanimity since its founding, passage of Resolution 660, denouncing the Iraqi invasion, calling for a complete withdrawal, and promising sanctions should that withdrawal not be accomplished.

The key to this "coalition" was the Soviet Union. Moscow joined in the majority of the UN resolutions. However, Gorbachev did this at great political risk as his right flank was pushing him to support Saddam. Bush helped in this regard by flying to Helsinki, Finland, on September 5 for another summit, one at which the United States agreed to a Soviet presence in the Middle East. Indeed, Bush's patient diplomacy during the events surrounding the fall of the Berlin Wall and his understanding of Gorbachev's needs in fall 1990 now paid dividends. On October 3 Gorbachev joined the United States in calling for an international embargo on arms sales to Iraq.

It bears repeating that for Bush, the key issue in the Persian Gulf conflict was always Saudi Arabia and its oil reserves. In the hours after Saddam's invasion, Bush began to court the Saudi royal family, lobbying King Fahd for his approval to station a large American military contingent in his country. Despite the very real possibility of an Iraqi threat to their nation, the Saudis were initially opposed to any American presence on their soil. But Bush would not be deterred. On August 5 Bush sent the Saudis a message, announcing as he stepped off his helicopter at the White House that "This will not stand—this aggression." Bush had now promised that Saudi Arabia's own protection depended on evicting the Iraqis from Kuwait. The king quickly gave his approval to the president, and, on August 8, Bush told the nation that the 82nd Airborne Division as well as two squadrons of F-15 fighters had been deployed to Saudi Arabia. By the end of August, there were 80,000 coalition forces in Saudi Arabia, and both the United States and Iraq proceeded to increase their manpower commitment. By September 1, it was costing the United States $28.9 million a day to keep its troops in Saudi Arabia. On September 11, in a speech to a joint session of Congress, Bush vigorously stated: "Iraq will not be permitted to annex Kuwait. That's not a threat or a boast. That's just the way it's going to be."

During this period of buildup—now called Operation Desert Shield—Bush worked hard to keep the Israelis *out* of the conflict. The possibility of Israel joining the coalition, or even attacking the Iraqi flank, held great appeal to Saddam—he could then declare a pan-Arab war against Israel, and Bush's coalition might well fall apart. Yet once again Bush's personal diplomacy prevailed. Despite overwhelming opposition in his cabinet, Prime Minister Yitzhak Shamir promised that even if attacked, Israel would refrain from retaliation. This was, in retrospect, Bush's greatest diplomatic coup of his presidency; it did no less than keep his anti-Iraq coalition together.

Nowhere in any of the public statements, or presently available private memorandum gen-

erated during the crisis, did the United States call for the overthrow of Saddam from power in Iraq. This simply was not a war aim. For Bush, the "Vietnam Syndrome" drove all military considerations. Afraid of a quagmire that would engulf the United States and require a long-term presence in the region that the American people simply would not support, Bush made it clear that his goal was nothing more than the liberation of Kuwait. However, the means by which that liberation was to be effected was hotly debated in the Bush White House. Some, most notably Powell, argued that the economic sanctions had to be given a satisfactory period with which to work. It was affirmed that, once isolated, Saddam would have control of a massive oil supply that he would not be able to sell, and would have to back down. However, equally influential voices, led by Richard Cheney and Brent Scowcroft, argued for an offensive military strike to expel Saddam from Kuwait at the earliest possible opportunity. This point of view contended that the sanctions might not work, and any delay in expelling Saddam allowed him to strengthen his hand for an invasion of Saudi Arabia.

Whether Bush was in favor of an offensive option from the beginning or whether his thinking evolved toward that option throughout the fall is still an open question, with principals from Bush's team taking various stands on the issue. However, what cannot be debated is that by late fall Bush had had enough of the economic sanctions and was wedded to expelling Saddam from Kuwait. A plan for a counterstrike against Iraqi forces in Kuwait had been developed immediately after the invasion; it called for an intensive air bombardment followed by a ground invasion. Bush immediately ordered reinforcing of the ground troops, recognizing that he needed an increased ground contingent in order to make an aerial bombardment viable. Immediately after the 1990 off-year elections, on November 8, Bush announced that he was

President Bush meets with his National Security Council to discuss Iraq's invasion of Kuwait, August 2, 1990.

doubling the American force in Saudi Arabia, to total some 500,000 troops. On November 29 the United Nations voted to support the use of "all necessary means" by the coalition forces to expel Saddam from Kuwait if he did not withdraw his forces by January 15, 1991.

These developments brought a spate of antiwar feeling at home and grumbling from Capitol Hill. Indeed, Bush was opposed, once again, by conservatives from within his own party, who, like television commentator Pat Buchanan, warned of getting involved in a conflict with which there was no stated or implied exit strategy. Indeed, as Bush became immersed in the 1991 budget fight, popular support for the war waned. It thus became important for Bush to seek and receive a statement of con-

gressional support for his actions. While dispatching Baker for a last, very public round of negotiations with the Iraqis, Bush encouraged (despite the advice of several of his advisers, including Cheney) a congressional debate on the president's authority to send troops into combat. In the Senate, an antiwar resolution had been sponsored by Majority Leader George Mitchell; both the House and the Senate voted on January 12, 1991. In the House, the vote was 250-183 against an antiwar resolution; in the Senate, the vote was 52-47 against Mitchell's resolution. Despite these actions, Bush would later tell *Time* magazine's Hugh Sidey that even if Congress had not supported him, he would have gone to war against Iraq without congressional authorization.

On January 17, 1991, at 3:00 a.m. Iraqi time, the air war began—Operation Desert Shield morphed into Operation Desert Storm. Apache attack helicopters flew into Iraq to destroy early warning systems and F117A "Stealth Bombers," supported by Tomahawk missiles, struck targets in Baghdad. After five and a half weeks of near constant bombardment, and some 100,000 sorties flown, the ground war began on February 24. An amphibious Marine landing just outside Kuwait City was merely a diversion; the First and Second Marine Divisions and the Tiger Brigade of the 22nd Armored Division lunged into the heart of the Iraqi defenses while the XVIII and VII Corps swept in a flanking action around the Iraqis to their rear. This "Left Hook" effectively encircled the Iraqis, cutting off their retreat back toward Baghdad.

Badly outnumbered, Saddam's strategy had been to entrench his soldiers. This turned out to be a fatal error—the coalition forces knew that the Iraqi lines were stable, and thus they became easy targets for aerial bombardment. In one battle lasting 40 minutes, 300 Iraqi tanks were lost at a cost of one American. Furthermore, when the Left Hook movement came, the Iraqi soldiers found themselves virtually immobile. Indeed, they were often run over in their trenches by advancing American tanks. Outmaneuvered, Saddam began to lob Scud missiles into populated areas of Israel, hoping to prod that nation into the war (total death toll from this action—31 dead and 400 injured). However, true to his word, Shamir held off the hawks in his cabinet and did not retaliate. As a result, the Americans were able to fight the limited war they desired.

This is not to say that there were no American errors in the war. Indeed, the greatest single loss of American life in the war—28 American soldiers killed when an Iraqi Scud missile hit their barracks—was caused by an American computer failure, which allowed the missile to pierce coalition defenses. The most famous coalition blunder took place on February 13, when American missiles destroyed a bunker in the Al Firdos area of Baghdad that was believed to be a camouflaged command-and-control bunker. Instead, it was an air-raid shelter, and the attack killed 204 civilians, many of them children.

A cease-fire was declared on February 28 and signed by the warring parties at Safwan, Iraq, on March 3. In an error of gigantic proportions, Schwarzkopf, who was given carte blanche by the White House to negotiate the terms of surrender, allowed the Iraqis to continue to fly armed helicopters over their territory. Saddam would use this favor to turn his attack helicopters on Kurdish dissidents, thus tightening his postwar control over Iraq. American dead totaled 293 soldiers; the rest of the coalition lost 65. The total cost to the United States was estimated at $57 billion. While precise figures of Iraqi dead are still elusive, the most credible total is 22,000, with some 80,000 Iraqi prisoners of war captured.

THE PRESIDENTIAL ELECTION OF 1992

On March 6, 1991, Bush spoke to a joint session of Congress; he turned to the Kuwaiti ambassador, sitting in the balcony, and declared to a standing ovation: "Ambassador Al-Sabah—Kuwait is free." The following weeks would see a resurgence of patriotism, as American troops, fresh from duty in Iraq, paraded down the streets of Washington, and members of Bush's cabinet—and Schwarzkopf himself—were touted as presidential material. But for Bush, this celebration would be short-lived. The rest of the year 1991 saw a series of events unfold that, when taken together, would greatly weaken a president who had just won a war and was enjoying a 67 percent approval rating—events that would weaken him to the point where his reelection was no longer assured.

Indeed, by December 1991, his approval ratings had dropped to 51 percent, and, by spring 1992, the figures bottomed out at 42 percent.

The first—and in many ways most devastating—blow to the Bush campaign came on March 5, 1990, when, speaking at a fund-raising dinner, Lee Atwater collapsed in agony on stage. He was diagnosed with a brain tumor, and he died almost exactly one year later, on March 29, 1991. Atwater's death deprived the Bush campaign of the one strategic voice who best understood the political feel of the country; an adequate replacement was never found.

The spring of 1991 also saw the Bush White House buffeted by scandal. John Sununu, Bush's imperious chief of staff, was charged in the press with having taken 99 taxpayer-financed flights on air force jets for his own personal use, at a cost of nearly $500,000. It was also reported that Sununu had traveled to New York City in his government limousine to purchase at auction stamps for his collection. Sununu refused to resign, and Bush initially supported his chief of staff. However, the press coverage became blistering, and, on December 3, 1991, on the eve of the Iowa caucuses, Sununu resigned. He was replaced by former secretary of transportation Samuel Skinner, who had difficulty in serving as the type of abrupt decisionmaker that Sununu had been. Skinner left the administration in August 1992, replaced by former secretary of state James Baker.

But before Sununu resigned, the administration was buffeted over its second choice to the Supreme Court. On June 28, 1991, after 24 years on the Court, Justice Thurgood Marshall retired. On July 1 Bush announced that he would nominate Clarence Thomas of the District of Columbia Court of Appeals to replace Marshall. Prior to his appointment by Bush to the circuit court, Thomas had worked at the Department of Education, had been chair of the Equal Employment Opportunity Commission (EEOC), and had a scanty judicial record.

It seemed that the "stealth strategy" used in the nomination of David Souter would work again, as Thomas sailed through the preliminary hearings before the Senate Judiciary Committee.

However, toward the end of the hearings, staffers leaked an FBI interview with Anita Hill, formerly Thomas's assistant at the EEOC and then a professor of law at the University of Oklahoma. Hill charged that Thomas had sexually harassed her, and, in her testimony before the Judiciary Committee, provided graphic detail to support her allegations. In the media circus that followed, both Thomas and Hill were pilloried. The Republicans on the Judiciary Committee, led by Wyoming's Alan Simpson, charged that Hill's allegations were made in bad faith since she had made no attempt to cease contact with Thomas following his advances. Incensed, Thomas made a return appearance before the committee, calling the process a "lynching" and "Kafka-esque." Thomas was ultimately confirmed by the Senate, but not before the dysfunctional process had taken a substantial toll on Bush—his standing in the African-American community plummeted, as did his already low standing among women, who accused him of harboring a harasser.

Foreign affairs also conspired against Bush in 1991. Early in the year, Gorbachev had cracked down on dissidents in Lithuania. This served only to exacerbate the tension in that Soviet republic. Gorbachev found himself losing the support of his Communist hard-liners, but Bush continued to back his partner in the Gulf War coalition—to the consternation of Republican conservatives, who joined in the clamor supporting independence for the Baltic states. Despite Bush's support, Gorbachev finally lost his grasp on power. On August 18, 1991, he was put under house arrest in his dacha on the Black Sea. The coup was poorly planned and it ultimately failed; three days after Gorbachev's return, the Communist Party was voted out of existence in the Soviet Union. On December 21, 11 former republics formed the Commonwealth of Independent States, and Russian authorities accepted Gorbachev's resignation—even though it had yet to be offered. Liberals skewered Bush for abandoning Gorbachev and conservatives skewered him for standing by the Soviet leader past the point of rational hope for his survival.

Most important for the long run, by late 1990 the promised recession had finally arrived. The big three automobile manufacturers had fired 60,000 workers and layoffs were a fact of life in virtually every business. Cutbacks in the defense industry, and the subsequent base closings that were carried out by Cheney, were the most visible—and politically potent—signs of the recession. By June 1991 the national unemployment rate had risen to 7.8 percent, the highest in eight years. For his part, Bush was initially loath to even admit that there *was* a recession, feeding Democratic criticism about his competence; furthermore, Bush gave the impression throughout 1991 that he believed that the economic downturn would be short-lived and that it would not become a serious electoral issue.

By the end of 1991, the goodwill that Bush had earned through his successful prosecution of the Gulf War had evaporated. As the economy went from bad to worse, voter anger—not just at Bush but at *any* "politician as usual"—grew. This rising sentiment fed the presidential ambitions of Texas billionaire H. Ross Perot, who utilized talk television and lengthy infomercials to organize a grassroots third-party campaign. But Bush was also challenged from within his own party. Conservative television pundit and former Nixon speechwriter Pat Buchanan mounted a primary challenge to Bush. After finishing in the New Hampshire primary with an astonishing 34 percent of the vote, Buchanan vowed to keep his campaign going right through to the convention—which he did, at a tremendous cost to Bush both in time and in money.

Mistakes within the Bush campaign itself, nowhere near as well organized as in 1988, kept Buchanan afloat. In May 1992, riots followed the acquittal of four Los Angeles policemen charged with beating a suspect, Rodney King—a beating caught on videotape. It took the administration an agonizingly long time to react to the riots in south central Los Angeles, and, when it did, Buchanan zeroed in on the high amount of federal monies given to Los Angeles ($1.5 billion) to rebuild itself. Bush also angered Buchanan's followers when he said in June that there would be no "litmus test" on sexual orientation imposed on his cabinet appointees. After their renomination, the Bush-Quayle ticket, bloodied from the primary, found itself running behind a newcomer to the national stage, a candidate who told the American people that he "felt their pain."

Like Bush, Bill Clinton had survived his own brutal primary season. Stories of his womanizing and his choices regarding Vietnam-era military service were daily media fodder. But with a skillful southern strategy, Clinton had ended his primary campaign much earlier than Bush, bound some of those wounds by choosing a former rival, Tennessee senator Al Gore as his running

President Bush gestures from the back of a train car during his campaign whistlestop in Bowling Green, Ohio, September 26, 1992.

President Bush and the 1992 cabinet

mate, and had begun to craft a message—"It's the Economy, Stupid"—while Bush was still battling Buchanan. Adaptable and telegenic where Bush was neither, Clinton struck a chord with a country that was sick of business as usual. As Perot's campaign self-destructed, Clinton zeroed in on the economy, and Bush did not fight back in kind (à la Atwater) until the very last debate. Clinton's victory was complete: he won 370 electoral votes to Bush's 168, and the Arkansas governor garnered 43 percent of the popular vote to Bush's 38 percent and Perot's 19 percent.

Bush's last two months in office were unusually active. In December, after Saddam Hussein had violated the Gulf War armistice by flying in the no-fly zone, Bush responded with air strikes. On December 17, 1992, the North American Free Trade Agreement (NAFTA) was signed. Bush also sent 25,000 American troops to Somalia to aid UN peacekeepers in getting food and other supplies into that African nation, paralyzed by tribal warfare.

On January 20, 1993, Bill Clinton was inaugurated president of the United States, and George Bush returned to Texas. He entered into a lucrative speaking career and was a hands-on manager in the planning and opening of his presidential library, located on the campus of Texas A&M University in College Station, Texas. In 2001 he saw his son, George W. Bush, inaugurated as Bill Clinton's successor.

BIOGRAPHICAL
DICTIONARY A–Z

Ailes, Roger
(1940–) *media adviser, George Bush presidential campaign*

Born in Warren, Ohio, Roger Ailes graduated from Ohio University with a B.A. in 1962. Ailes began his broadcast career in Cleveland, Ohio, as a prop boy. He then moved up to produce a local television show, *The Mike Douglas Show*, for KYW-TV. When the show went national, Ailes won two Emmys for his production work. After a discussion with a 1968 guest on the show, Richard Nixon, Ailes was hired to do the television advertising for Nixon's presidential campaign that year. Following Nixon's victory, Ailes founded Ailes Communications, Inc., in New York, a media consulting firm. From 1970 to 1988, Ailes consulted for many political candidates, including Ronald Reagan in 1984, where he came onto the campaign and coached Reagan to two clear-cut debate victories, after a first debate defeat to challenger Walter Mondale. He also worked on Indiana senator DAN QUAYLE's 1986 reelection campaign.

Recruited by LEE ATWATER, in 1988, Ailes served as senior director for marketing for the presidential campaign of George H. W. Bush. Ailes's major contribution to Bush's campaign was to get Bush's advertisements to focus largely on visual symbols, rather than on issue statements. He also encouraged Bush to take the offensive in the primaries—it was Ailes who was largely responsible for Bush's performance during a January 25 interview with Dan Rather (when Rather asked Bush about his role in Iran-contra, Bush snapped: "How would you like it if I judged your career by those seven minutes when you walked off the set in New York?"). Ailes and his wife also produced an ad that showed primary opponent BOB DOLE (R-Kans.) as a two-faced "Senator Straddle"; the ad ran heavily in the last days of the New Hampshire primary, and for many observers provided the impetus that gave Bush his primary victory in that state. Ailes also lobbied hard for Quayle as the choice for the vice presidential nod, and he argued in favor of Bush's declaration of "read my lips: no new taxes" in his acceptance speech to the Republican National Convention. Alienated by the intrigue of the Bush White House, Ailes decided not to join the Bush campaign in 1992, a decision that many observers have credited as a factor in Bush's eventual defeat by BILL CLINTON.

In 1993, Ailes became president of CNBC Cable Network. In 1996, he became the chairman, chief executive officer, and president of Fox Television News.

Alexander, Lamar
(1940–) *secretary of education*

Born in Maryville, Tennessee, Lamar Alexander took a B.A. from Vanderbilt University in 1962, then a law degree from New York University in 1965. He clerked for a federal judge in New Orleans from 1965 to 1966.

In 1967, Alexander joined the staff of Senator Howard Baker (R-Tenn.); two years later, he went to work for the Nixon White House as an assistant to Bryce Harlow, then the executive assistant to the president. In 1970, he returned to Nashville, where he practiced law and managed the campaign of a successful gubernatorial candidate. In 1974, Alexander ran for governor of Tennessee and was defeated; in 1978, however, he won election. Alexander served as governor from 1979 to 1987 and was best known for his success in attracting new industry to his state and in creating a merit-based compensation package for teachers. After a trip abroad, Alexander was named the president of the University of Tennessee in 1987. There, he served as a member of President George H. W. Bush's Education Advisory Committee. It was from this position that Bush chose him to be his secretary of education in 1991, replacing LAURO CAVASOS.

As secretary, Alexander touted the administration's education plan, "America 2000," announced in June 1991. The plan returned the responsibility for the improvement of schools to the states. It also called for voluntary national standards for education and requested business leaders to raise $150 million to fund 535 "break the mold" schools. However, no new budget funds were requested to help pay for the plan, and it languished, despite Alexander's constant advocacy of the program. Also, the White House refused to back down from its belief that college aid linked to race should be ended—the decision that had caused the firestorm in the press that led to Cavasos's resignation.

Mentioned as a possible presidential candidate as early as his governorship, Alexander ran unsuccessfully for the Republican nomination in 1996. One of his key planks was abolishing the Department of Education and transferring that power to the states. From 2001 to 2002, Alexander was a visiting professor at Harvard University's John F. Kennedy School of Government. In 2002, he was elected to his first term as a U.S. senator from Tennessee.

Aquino, Maria Corazon Cojuangco
(1933–) *president, Republic of the Philippines*

Born in Manila, Corazon ("Cory") Aquino attended the Assumption Convent in the Philippines and then traveled to the United States, finishing her secondary school studies at the Notre Dame Convent School in New York. She earned her B.A. from Mount St. Vincent College in New York (where she worked for the presidential campaign of Thomas E. Dewey). Returning to the Philippines, Aquino began to study law, but she stopped her studies after her 1954 marriage to Benigno S. "Ninoy" Aquino, Jr. A leader of the opposition to the regime of General Ferdinand Marcos, Benigno Aquino was one of the first opposition leaders jailed when Marcos declared martial law in 1972. He was imprisoned until 1980, when he entered into a three-year political exile in the United States (he was allowed to travel out of the country to undergo heart surgery, but the government proclaimed a death sentence on him should he return), where he was joined by his wife. Despite the death sentence, Ninoy returned to Manila on August 21, 1983, and he was assassinated immediately upon his return.

For several years following Aquino's death, the opposition forces were in disarray. Many tried to push his widow into accepting the mantle of leadership from her fallen husband. In 1985, Marcos called for an election, believing that the opposition was so discouraged that it could never mount a true challenge to his authority. Aquino declared herself a candidate for the presidency in the fall of 1985. The election reeked of fraud (Marcos men destroyed ballots in full view of foreign journalists), and both Marcos and Aquino declared themselves the winner. In response to the confusion, several of Marcos's key military advisers came out against the government. Marcos responded by sending tanks into Manila, but thousands of Filipinos thwarted the government's position by swarming into the streets and halting the tanks. However, the rebels succeeded in dislodging Marcos; on February 25, 1986, Marcos proclaimed himself president, and he and his wife Imelda left for exile in Hawaii. That day, Aquino was inaugurated president of the Philippines. As president, she advocated the spread of democracy in her nation and pushed for its economic recovery; in December 1986, she was named *Time* magazine's "Woman of the Year."

On November 30, 1989, the first of what would be seven coup attempts against Aquino was initiated. When Aquino requested help from the United States, President George H. W. Bush was in Europe, meeting with MIKHAIL GORBACHEV at Malta. While both Vice President DAN QUAYLE and Chairman of the Joint Chiefs of Staff COLIN POWELL have taken credit for managing the crisis, it was Bush's order—no use of U.S. troops but U.S. planes were ordered to fly low and buzz the rebel aircraft on the tarmac—that kept the planes on the ground and effectively dismantled the coup.

In 1992, Aquino was succeeded by Fidel Ramos, one of the military leaders who sparked the 1985 rebellion. She now serves as chairperson of the Benigno S. Aquino Foundation in the Philippines.

Arens, Moshe
(1925–) *foreign minister, Israel; defense minister, Israel*

Born in 1925 in Lithuania, Moshe Arens's family moved to the United States in 1938. In 1948, Arens emigrated to Israel. He returned to the United States, spent two years (1944–46) in the U.S. Armed Forces, then studied mechanical engineering at the Massachusetts Institute of Technology and aeronautical engineering at the California Institute of Technology. Returning to Israel, from 1962 to 1971 he was the deputy director general of Israel Aircraft Industries. In 1974, he was elected to the Knesset as a member of the Likud Party, where he served on that body's Finance Committee and Committee on Foreign Affairs and Security. In 1983, Prime Minister Menachem Begin named Arens Israel's ambassador to the United States, and, in 1983, he was named minister of defense. The following year he was named minister without portfolio, and from 1988 to 1990, he was minister of foreign affairs. From 1990 to 1992, Arens served as minister of defense.

Immediately following the August 1990 invasion of Kuwait by SADDAM HUSSEIN, Arens was one of the first among world statesmen to publicly compare the Iraqi leader to Adolf Hitler. Following the first of Hussein's Scud missile attacks against Israel, Arens immediately called Secretary of Defense DICK CHENEY to obtain U.S. shipment of Patriot missiles to Israel and begin plans for an Israeli counterattack. However, President George H. W. Bush asked Prime Minister YITZHAK SHAMIR not to retaliate against the attacks so as not to alienate Arab allies and embroil the entire region in the war. Shamir prevailed over Arens in the cabinet, and, for the entirety of the war, Israel kept her patience in the face of Iraqi attacks.

In a 1995 book, *Broken Covenant: American Foreign Policy and the Crisis between the U.S. and*

Israel, Arens accused the Bush administration, notably the president and Secretary of State JAMES BAKER, of conspiring to overthrow Shamir's Likud government by manufacturing government crises that led to Likud's 1992 defeat at the polls. According to Arens, the Bush administration sought to secure the election of a Labor government, which Washington believed would be more amenable to the U.S. stance in the Middle East peace process.

Arens retired from politics in 1992, only to return in 1999 when he was once again named minister of defense.

Atwater, Harvey Leroy "Lee"
(1951–1991) *political consultant; chairman, Republican National Committee*

Born in Columbia, South Carolina, Lee Atwater took his B.A. from Newberry College (South Carolina) in 1973 and his M.A. from the University of South Carolina. While at Newberry, he interned twice in the office of Senator Strom Thurmond. In 1972, he attended the Republican National Convention as a delegate, and he served as the youngest presidential elector from South Carolina. Following his graduation from Newberry, Atwater worked on the campaign of Karl Rove to become chairman of the College Republicans National Committee (CRNC)—a full-time paid job. Rove won, and he appointed Atwater to his old job—the executive director of CRNC. From 1974 to 1978, Atwater was involved with a series of 28 winning Republican campaigns for local races, including his work in Strom Thurmond's 1978 successful reelection bid to the U.S. Senate and the election of Carroll Campbell to the South Carolina State Senate—an election that featured Atwater's use of anti-Semitism as a wedge issue against Campbell's opponent.

Atwater would become known—fairly, and by his own admission—as a master of attack politics. His chief biographer quotes him as saying, "the contest, the winning, the losing thing is big for me." For example, during a 1980 congressional campaign in South Carolina, Atwater, then a consultant for the Republican incumbent, planted a story saying that the Democratic challenger Tom Turnipseed, who had received electroshock therapy for adolescent depression at the age of 16, was "hooked up to jumper cables" and "mentally ill."

It was Atwater's work as regional political director in the 1980 South Carolina primary that was largely responsible for delivering the state to Reagan. He did little during the fall campaign, but, as a quid pro quo for Thurmond, he was appointed to Reagan's Office of Political Affairs in 1981. From that post, Atwater became a successful—if somewhat covert—fund-raiser for the Republican Party. In 1982, he was promoted to the post of deputy assistant to the president for political affairs; that same year, the United States Jaycees recognized him as one of the Ten Outstanding Young Men of America (one of the other awardees: Senator DAN QUAYLE of Indiana).

Introduced to George H. W. Bush by Rove in 1973, the relationship between Atwater and Bush survived even Atwater's support of Ronald Reagan in that year's primaries. As a Reagan supporter, the Bush family never fully trusted Atwater. However, Bush recognized his need for both a southerner and an attack-style politico on his staff. Thus, in 1988, he turned his primary campaign largely over to Atwater. However, Bush's son GEORGE W. BUSH was brought onto Atwater's staff, largely to keep an eye on the impetuous young South Carolinian. Working closely with ROGER AILES, Atwater sharpened his candidate's tone, exulting in the January 25, 1988, Bush interview with Dan Rather (where Bush snapped at the reporter, who was asking a question about the vice president's role in Iran-contra: "How would you like it if I judged your career by those seven

President Bush and Lee Atwater play guitar at the Celebration for Young Americans, DC Armory, Washington, D.C., January 21, 1989.

minutes when you walked off the set in New York?") as "the most important event of the primary campaign." Moreover, Atwater was largely responsible for convincing Bush—beginning as early as 1986—that to win the nomination he had to position himself as the rightful heir to the party's right wing, which was the core of Ronald Reagan's support.

Atwater introduced many of the techniques that are today a part of modern politics. He invented "bounce polling," and he is largely credited with coining the phrase "spin." He also introduced the concept of the primary "fire-

wall"—a primary that would deliver a victory to his candidate if needed between the New Hampshire primary and the multistate "Super Tuesday" primaries, held early in March. In the summer, Atwater sharpened the Bush campaign, then trailing MICHAEL DUKAKIS by 17 points. He approved a series of "soft money" advertisements that tied the Bush campaign to what was then perceived as years of prosperity under Reagan ("Why Go Back Seven Years?"). Most important, Atwater wanted to paint Dukakis as a far-left liberal—he coined the phrase "Taxachusetts"; emphasized the fact that he was a "card-carrying member" of the American Civil Liberties Union (ACLU); and co-opted the American flag for his candidate, as Bush wore a small flag in his lapel. Atwater railed against Dukakis's veto of a 1977 bill passed by the Massachusetts legislature requiring that teachers lead their class in the Pledge of Allegiance.

It was also Atwater who, along with others in the campaign, advocated the use of the case of Willie Horton—a convicted murderer who, while away from his Massachusetts prison participating in a furlough program, broke into a home, pistol-whipped the owner, and raped his wife. (Atwater reportedly said: "if I can make Willie Horton a household name, we'll win the election.") The advertisement: "Revolving Door," became the most famous of the campaign, and it strengthened Bush's stock with conservative Republicans who rated law and order as their most important concern. Immediately following the election, Atwater served on a transition team (the "Scrub Team"), chaired by George W. Bush, which was responsible for vetting all administration appointments.

For his efforts, Atwater was rewarded with the chairmanship of the Republican National Committee (many around the president counseled against giving the volatile Atwater a job inside the White House). However, this hardly muted the South Carolinian. As he prepared for the 1990 congressional elections, Atwater once again went on the attack. He is universally credited with approving a committee memo that charged Speaker of the House TOM FOLEY with being a homosexual ("Tom Foley: Out of the Liberal Closet"); for this, Atwater was formally reprimanded by the president, who wanted to keep the lines of communication open with Foley.

On March 5, 1989, while speaking at a fund-raiser for Texas senator Phil Gramm, Atwater collapsed. Diagnosed with a brain tumor, Atwater was eventually replaced at the Republican National Committee by WILLIAM BENNETT. Immediately prior to his death on March 29, 1992, Atwater sent out letters of apologies to those whom he felt he had wronged in his career. Most observers have argued that Atwater's absence from the 1992 campaign was a major reason why Bush lost to BILL CLINTON. Many of those same observers have noted that George W. Bush utilized most of Atwater's techniques in the 2000 presidential campaign.

B

Baker, James A(ddison), III
(1930–) *secretary of state, White House chief of staff*

James Baker graduated from Princeton University in 1952 with a degree in the classics. He served two years in the U.S. Marine Corps and returned to earn his law degree from the University of Texas, Austin, in 1957. That year, he joined Andrews and Kurth, a Houston law firm, where he worked until 1975. During that period, he managed George H. W. Bush's unsuccessful 1970 campaign for the U.S. Senate. One of Bush's oldest friends, Bush is godfather to one of Baker's daughters.

In 1975, Baker was named undersecretary of commerce in the Ford administration. In May 1976, he left his position at Commerce to serve as a chairman for delegate operations in the Ford campaign against Ronald Reagan for the Republican nomination for president. In August, he was named the national chairman of the President Ford Committee, and he managed Ford's unsuccessful fall campaign against Jimmy Carter.

In 1978, Baker ran for attorney general of Texas and was defeated. From 1979 to 1980, Baker directed Bush's unsuccessful campaign to win the Republican presidential nomination. Ronald Reagan won the nomination and Bush was chosen as his running mate. Baker was brought aboard the Reagan/Bush presidential campaign as a senior adviser. Baker served the entirety of the Reagan administration in several different capacities. He began as Reagan's chief of staff, and he was widely given credit for securing the passage of Reagan's 1981 tax reform bill. At the beginning of Reagan's second term, from 1985 to 1988, he served as secretary of the Treasury; while at Treasury, he also chaired the President's Economic Policy Council. Baker resigned near the end of Reagan's second term in order to once again chair Bush's presidential campaign. Following Bush's election, Baker was the president-elect's first cabinet appointment, as he was nominated to be secretary of state.

In several areas, Baker made significant contributions to foreign relations during the Bush era. He formed a close working relationship with Soviet foreign minister Eduard Shevardnadze, with whom he worked to ease the tension caused by the fall of the Iron Curtain and the crumbling of the Soviet Union. He was also influential in the planning of the Madrid Conference of 1991, which took significant steps forward toward a discussion of the Palestinian-Israeli conflict, and he was instrumental in placing the North American Free Trade Agreement (NAFTA) on the congressional fast track, which facilitated its signing in December 1992.

During the events leading up to the Persian Gulf War, Baker's friendship with Shevardnadze bore fruit, as the two leaders worked together to gain MIKHAIL GORBACHEV's overt support for the joint U.S./UN policy requiring SADDAM HUSSEIN's retreat from Kuwait. A member of Bush's war cabinet, Baker, along with Chairman of the Joint Chiefs of Staff COLIN POWELL, argued for economic sanctions against Iraq, and then for an extension of the period of time allotted to give those sanctions time to work. However, they failed to win approval for their approach in losing to others in the cabinet, most notably National Security Advisor BRENT SCOWCROFT and Secretary of Defense DICK CHENEY, who argued for a rapid armed intervention so as to expel Hussein from Kuwait.

Yet in many ways, Baker's political contributions to Bush's tenure were as important as his diplomatic efforts. Along with his service as Bush's 1988 campaign manager, Baker served as a valuable bridge to the conservative wing of the Republican Party, which became increasingly restless at some of Bush's domestic policies. In August 1992, in an effort to jump start Bush's faltering reelection effort, Baker was returned to the White House, where he was named chief of staff (replacing SAMUEL SKINNER) and counselor to the president (he was succeeded as secretary of state by LAWRENCE EAGLEBURGER).

Following his service in the Bush administration, Baker returned to his position as senior

President Bush meets with Secretary of State James Baker III.

partner of Baker and Botts, a law firm with offices in Houston and Washington. He received the Presidential Medal of Freedom in 1991, and, in 2000, he served as chief legal adviser for the GEORGE W. BUSH presidential campaign in Florida, where he oversaw the recount of the vote in that state.

Barr, William P(elham)
(1950–   ) *U.S. Attorney General*

William Barr was born in Virginia, earning both his B.A. (1971) and his M.A. (1973) from Columbia University, and his law degree from George Washington University in 1977. While attending law school, he served as an analyst for the Central Intelligence Agency. Upon graduation from Columbia, he worked as an assistant legislative counsel for the CIA in 1977, then clerked on the U.S. Court of Appeals for the District of Columbia from 1977 to 1978. From 1978 to 1982, Barr was with Shaw, Pittman, Potts, and Trowbridge, a Washington law firm. From 1982 to 1983, he served in the Reagan White House as deputy assistant director for legal policy in the White House Office of Legal Policy. In 1982, he rejoined his law practice.

A friendship with C. BOYDEN GRAY, President George Bush's chief counsel, led to Barr's joining the Justice Department in 1989 as Assistant U.S. Attorney General for the Office of Legal Counsel. In 1990, he was named Deputy U.S. Attorney General, and, in 1991, following the resignation of RICHARD THORNBURGH, served as acting U.S. Attorney General. Nominated by Bush to succeed Thornburgh, Barr was confirmed by the Senate and served as Attorney General until the end of the Bush administration.

Following the Bush administration, Barr returned to his law practice. He was elected senior vice president and general counsel of GTE in 1994. Following the Bell Atlantic/GTE merger that created Verizon, Barr became executive vice president and general counsel for the new company. He is also senior adviser to Americans for Victory over Terrorism, an organization chaired by WILLIAM BENNETT.

Bennett, William J.
(1943–   ) *director, Office of National Drug Control Policy*

Born in Brooklyn, New York, William Bennett earned his B.A. from Williams College (1965), his Ph.D. from the University of Texas (1970), and his J.D. from Harvard University (1971). Following his graduation from Harvard, he joined the faculty of Boston University, where he taught philosophy and served as an associate dean and an assistant to the president, John Silber. Bennett left Boston University in 1976 to become the executive director of the National Humanities Center for scholarly research in North Carolina.

Bennett served as chairman of the National Endowment for the Humanities from 1981 to 1985. He then served as secretary of education (1985–88) in the administration of Ronald Reagan—a position that Reagan had promised to eliminate. Joining in the call for the department's elimination, Bennett advocated returning responsibility for education to the states and he was soon a leading voice in the new conservative movement.

In 1989, in a nod to the right wing of his party, George H. W. Bush named Bennett the nation's first drug policy director. Quickly dubbed the "Drug Czar" by the press, three days after he was sworn in, Bennett—always blunt and often abrasive—declared that the streets of the nation's capital would soon belong to him. On CNN's *Larry King Live*, when asked by a caller about the Saudi Arabian practice of beheading drug dealers, Bennett replied: "Morally, I don't have a problem with it." He feuded with the Justice Department over who was actually going to control drug policy, and he angered Attorney General RICHARD THORNBURGH when, without vetting his plan through the Justice Department, he told a news conference that he was going to send a special narcotics team into Washington, D.C., to clean up the city. He also angered Secretary of State JAMES A. BAKER III when he announced that he supported withholding foreign aid to any Latin American countries that did not crack down on drug dealing. Outsiders also saw slights to Bennett from Bush himself— no cabinet rank, an office outside the White House itself—possibly because of Bennett's well-known presidential ambitions. And yet his proposals to solve the drug problem, such as sending drug offenders to boot camps, enhanced his already high standing within the right wing of the Republican Party. In November 1990, Bennett resigned; he was replaced by Bob Martinez, the former governor of Florida.

In 1996, Bennett was offered the Republican vice presidential nomination by ROBERT DOLE (R-Kans.); he declined. Presently, he is a fellow at the Heritage Foundation, the chairman of K-12, an Internet-based elementary and secondary school, a co-director of Empower America, a combination think tank and conservative lobbying group, and chairman of Americans for Victory over Terrorism.

Bentsen, Lloyd M(illard), Jr.
(1921–) *member of the Senate, Democratic Party vice presidential candidate*

Lloyd Bentsen was born in Mission, Texas, received his law degree from the University of Texas (1942), and served in the U.S. Army Air Corps during World War II. From 1946 to 1948, he served as county judge of Hidalgo County. He was elected as a Democrat to the House of Representatives in 1949 and served until 1957, when he left public office to start an insurance business. In 1970, he defeated George H. W. Bush and was elected to the U.S. Senate. From 1987 to 1993, he was chairman of the influential Senate Finance Committee. In 1976, he ran unsuccessfully for the Democratic nomination for the presidency. In 1988, Democratic presidential nominee MICHAEL DUKAKIS chose Bentsen as his running mate. In one of the more memorable moments of the campaign, during the vice presidential debate against Republican DAN QUAYLE, Bentsen responded to Quayle's claim that he had more experience than did John F. Kennedy when he ran for president with the quip: "Senator, I served with Jack Kennedy. I knew Jack Kennedy. Jack Kennedy was a friend of mine. Senator, you are no Jack Kennedy."

Bentsen resigned from the Senate in 1993 to serve as President BILL CLINTON's secretary of the Treasury, a position he resigned for health reasons in 1994.

Bond, Richard N.
(?–) *chairman, Republican National Committee*

Born in New York City, Richard Bond earned a B.A. in English and philosophy from Fordham University and a M.A. in government from Georgetown University. He worked at the Republican National Committee under Presidents Ford and Reagan. He then became a political operative for then presidential candidate George H. W. Bush. In 1979, Bond moved his family to Iowa and organized the state for Bush. It was he who was largely responsible for creating the "Bush Brigades" that criss-crossed the state, and he himself made some 300 personal appearances—all of which contributed to Bush's upset victory over Ronald Reagan in the 1980 Iowa caucuses. He continued to work for Bush throughout the 1980 primaries, and he stayed close to Bush throughout his vice presidency. As Bush geared up to run for the presidency in 1988, Bond once again played a key role, working for campaign manager JAMES A. BAKER III. One of Bond's key contributions came in Michigan where he helped defuse a challenge by Pat Robertson for control of that state's delegation to the Republican National Convention.

In 1992, Bond replaced CLAYTON YEUTTER as the head of the Republican National Committee. During the 1992 primary season, Bond made little pretense of impartiality, calling challenger PAT BUCHANAN a "David Duke in a jacket and tie." Buchanan called on Bush to dismiss Bond, but no dismissal was forthcoming.

Bond is presently the president of Bond and Company, a Washington, D.C., consulting company.

Boskin, Michael J.
(1945–) *chairman, Council of Economic Advisers*

Michael Boskin received his B.A. (1967), M.A. (1968), and Ph.D. (1971) from the University of California, Berkeley. A doctrinaire conservative and an international expert on world economic growth and tax and budget theory, Boskin taught at Stanford, the University of California, Harvard University, and Yale University.

In 1989, Boskin was chosen to head the Council of Economic Advisors (CEA) in the new administration of George H. W. Bush. After a period of reduced influence in the Reagan White House, Boskin rejuvenated the CEA under Bush, making it a true center of policy power. Indeed, Boskin became a Bush favorite, often joining the president on the tennis court. It was widely reported that Boskin continually warned Bush that the economy was

headed toward a recession, only to have his warnings ignored until 1991. Boskin was also one of the economic advisers who suggested that Bush break his "read my lips" pledge and raise taxes as a response to the recession. In an effort to show that Bush understood the gravity of the economic situation, three weeks before the 1992 election, his campaign announced that many members of his economic team, including Boskin, would not be reappointed to their positions should the president win a second term.

Following his tenure in the Bush White House, Boskin chaired a blue-ribbon congressional commission on the consumer price index from 1995 to 1997. He worked as an adviser to the presidential campaign of ROBERT DOLE (1996) and GEORGE W. BUSH (2000). Often mentioned in press reports as a possible successor to Alan Greenspan as chairman of the Federal Reserve, Boskin is currently a senior fellow at the Hoover Institution and the Tully M. Friedman Professor of Economics at Stanford University.

Brady, Nicholas F.
(1930–) *secretary of Treasury*

Born in New York City, Nicholas Brady received his B.A. from Yale University in 1952 and his M.B.A. from Harvard Business School in 1954. He subsequently moved into a career in investment banking. In 1954, he joined Dillon, Read and Company in New York, becoming its chairman of the board. In 1982, he was appointed to the U.S. Senate representing New Jersey to fill the unexpired term of Harrison Williams. However, Brady declined to run for election in his own right. During the Reagan administration, Brady chaired several commissions, most notably the Presidential Task Force on Market Mechanisms ("The Brady Commission") in 1987. A close friend

President Bush at a meeting with Secretary of the Treasury Nicholas Brady

of George H. W. Bush, he was named secretary of the Treasury in 1989.

At Treasury, Brady oversaw the response of the Bush administration to the meltdown of the savings and loan (S&L) industry that had occurred during the Reagan years. In so doing, Brady proposed sweeping changes to the banking industry, changes that affected the banking sector in ways not seen since the reforms of the New Deal. Brady was also a key player in the negotiations with Congress that led to the Omnibus Budget Reconciliation Act of 1990, in which the administration accepted new revenue enhancers in direct contradiction of its campaign promises not to raise taxes. Brady also faced the crisis of debt in developing countries with the creation of what became known as "Brady Bonds"—defaulted loans that were converted into bonds using U.S. zero-coupon Treasury Bonds as collateral. The bonds aided

restructuring of the debt of developing nations, particularly in Latin America, which helped strengthen the economics of these countries. Brady also was the leading proponent within the administration for free trade, and he advocated measures designed to ease the economies of the newly independent former republics of the Soviet Union into the world marketplace.

Brady is currently the president of Dillon, Read and Company in New York City.

Buchanan, Patrick J.

(1938–   ) *presidential speechwriter, journalist, candidate for the Republican nomination for president*

Patrick Buchanan was born in Washington, D.C., received his B.A. from Georgetown University (1961) and his M.A. in journalism from

Columbia University (1962). He was an editorial writer and assistant editorial page editor for the *St. Louis Globe-Democrat* from 1962 to 1965. In 1965 he joined the staff of Richard M. Nixon, who was then in New York, and he helped plan his 1968 run for the presidency. Following Nixon's election, Buchanan joined the White House speechwriting staff, where he served until 1974. Universally seen as Nixon's most conservative speechwriter, Buchanan nonetheless refused a request from H. R. Haldeman and John Ehrlichman to spearhead the "Plumbers" Unit, designed to ferret out leaks from the Nixon White House. After leaving the White House following Nixon's August 1974 resignation, Buchanan wrote a nationally syndicated newspaper column, and he was a charter member (along with liberal Tom Braden) of the CNN political talk show *Crossfire*. Buchanan returned to active politics in 1989, when he joined Ronald Reagan's White House speechwriting team. However, Buchanan's persistent attempts to get Reagan to voice a staunchly conservative line led to tension within the White House, and Buchanan resigned in 1987. Now the most public voice of the far-right wing of the Republican Party, Buchanan was an early and frequent critic of the George H. W. Bush administration, even to the point of taking the then unpopular stance against intervention in the Persian Gulf War, and he publicly referred to the president as "King George."

In 1992, Buchanan ran against Bush for the Republican nomination. In the New Hampshire primary, he finished a surprising second to Bush, garnering 34 percent of the vote. Defying the party regulars who pled with him to withdraw from the race so as to unify the party, Buchanan stayed in the race until the convention, hammering away at Bush's drifting away from a conservative social and economic agenda, particularly castigating the president over his support for free trade. While he would never again come as close to

victory as he had in New Hampshire, Buchanan eventually garnered 3 million primary votes, forcing Bush to spend valuable time and money in the primary campaigns. Moreover, his histrionic speech to the Republican National Convention in Houston—where, before a primetime television audience, he pilloried homosexuals and called the Democratic ticket "the most pro-gay and pro-lesbian ticket in history"—served to further polarize the Republican Party. Many observers thus give Buchanan a significant amount of the credit for BILL CLINTON's defeat of Bush in the fall election.

In February 1993, Buchanan founded The American Cause. Buchanan ran again, also unsuccessfully, for the presidency in 1996. Buchanan has since been active as a newspaper columnist and media pundit.

Bush, Barbara Pierce
(1925–) *first lady*

Born in Rye, New York, Barbara Pierce was the granddaughter of an Ohio Supreme Court justice and her father was distantly related to Franklin Pierce, the 14th president of the United States. Her father later became president of McCall Corporation. She attended boarding school at Ashley Hall in South Carolina. When she was 16, Barbara met her future husband George H. W. Bush at a dance on Christmas vacation. In 1945, Barbara left Smith College in Northampton, Massachusetts, after only two years of study, to marry Bush. Following Bush's World War II service and his undergraduate education at Yale University, the couple moved to Texas, where he went into the oil business and she raised their five children—George, John (Jeb), Neil, Marvin, and Dorothy. In 1953, another daughter, Robin, died of leukemia at the age of three. Mrs. Bush lived in 17 different cities before she became first lady. These included Houston, Texas, Washington, D.C., and Peking, China.

While her husband served as both vice president and president, Barbara Bush selected the promotion of literacy as her particular cause. She continued this work as first lady, calling it the "most important issue we have." In 1989, she established the Barbara Bush Foundation for Family Literacy. The profits earned by her first book *C. Fred's Story* (1984), a narrative about the Bush family told through the voice of their cocker spaniel, were donated to literacy charities. Barbara also donated the nearly $1 million earned by *Millie's Book* (1990), written while she was first lady, about the Springer Spaniel that she took to the White House, to the same charities.

President and Mrs. Bush with Millie at Walker's Point, Kennebunkport, Maine, July 11, 1991

Barbara Bush's humor and style earned her many admirers, and she was noted for her charitable and humanitarian efforts. As first lady, Barbara Bush was also a strong advocate of volunteerism. Through volunteerism, she promoted many causes, including the homeless, AIDS, the elderly, and school volunteer programs. Barbara Bush became one of the most popular first ladies; she consistently ranked in the top three most-admired women in America. Much of this popularity stems from the image she calls "everybody's grandmother."

As first lady, Barbara Bush was not only popular but also courageous. In 1988, shortly after becoming first lady, she was diagnosed with Graves' disease. While undergoing therapy, she continued to perform her official duties. And yet, she also had her detractors. At a commencement ceremony at Wellesley College in June 1990, she confronted students who thought that she did not represent the type of independent women that their college wanted to graduate. However, she pleased the audience with a speech in which she predicted that someone from the graduating class could one day follow in her footsteps, ending with the phrase—"and I wish him well."

After her husband's defeat for reelection in 1992, Barbara and George Bush retired to Texas. In retirement, Barbara remained active in promoting literacy, but her main interest centered on her family. This commitment led her to play an active role in the successful campaigns of her sons Jeb and GEORGE W. BUSH for the governorships of Florida and Texas, respectively, and in her son George's subsequent quest for the presidency in 2000.

—MP

Bush, George H(erbert) W(alker)
(1924–   ) *president of the United States*

On June 12, 1924, George Herbert Walker Bush was born in Milton, Massachusetts, to Prescott

Sheldon Bush and Dorothy Walker Bush. The senior Bush was partner in a global bank house and, in 1952, became U.S. senator from the state of Connecticut. Dorothy was the daughter of an affluent investor. George was the couple's second son and was named after his grandfather on his mother's side.

After his family moved to Greenwich, Connecticut, Bush was taught exclusively in private schools, including Phillips Academy in Andover, Massachusetts. Though he would later be criticized for his affluent upbringing, Bush's parents made sure he grew up in a strictly controlled environment. Boastful, showy, and pretentious behavior was forbidden in the Bush household. Bush graduated from Phillips Academy on his 18th birthday on June 12, 1942. Though already accepted at Yale University, the day he graduated he chose to join the U.S. Navy as seaman, second class.

Bush launched his military service in Chapel Hill, North Carolina. There he underwent preflight training. From North Carolina he went on to Minnesota to train as a pilot, then to Corpus Christi, Texas, for training in instrument flying and navigation. In July 1943, Bush received his wings and became the youngest pilot in the navy to that point. In 1944, Bush traveled around the country practicing carrier landings and flying Grumman's three-man torpedo bombers. Bush was posted to the Pacific theater, where he flew torpedo bombers off the USS *San Jacinto;* he flew 58 combat missions. In September 1944, his plane was shot down while making a bombing run. Bush finished his mission before flying out to sea to bail out of his plane. He was later rescued by a navy submarine. For his service he was honored with the Distinguished Flying Cross and three other air medals.

On January 6, 1945, Bush married BAR-BARA PIERCE BUSH of Rye, New York. Together they parented five children; George Walker (1946), Pauline Robinson ("Robin"

1949–53), John Ellis "Jeb," (1953), Neil Mallon (1955), Marvin (1956), and Dorothy Walker ("Doro," 1959). Shortly after Jeb's birth, Robin was diagnosed with leukemia already in its advanced stages; she died in October 1953.

Returning home from the service in 1945, Bush entered Yale University. He was one of the many veterans to go back to school in a group described as the "GI Bulge." Bush was very active on campus. A member of the restricted "Skull and Bones" society, Bush was also the captain of the baseball team. His fielding at first base was good enough for major league scouts to take an interest in his talent. Bush graduated Phi Beta Kappa in 1948 with a degree in economics—acquiring the degree had taken Bush only two years.

After his graduation, Bush decided to try his hand in the oil business. His father had been on the board of directors of Dresser Industries, and he was friends with the president of the company, Neil Mallon. Mallon took Bush on as the company's only trainee in 1948. That year he moved to western Texas, beginning his career at IDECO (International Derrick and Equipment Company). Bush initially earned $375 a month and became a member of the United Steelworker's Union. From Texas he was transferred to Pacific Pumps in California to work as a salesman. This however, did not satisfy Bush's goals. Joining forces with a friend, John Overby, Bush created an oil development company in Midland, Texas. In 1952, Bush and Overby merged with a firm run by William and Hugh Liedke to develop Zapata Petroleum. By 1954, business was booming and Bush became the president of a subsidiary of Zapata, Zapata Offshore, and he relocated his family to Houston, Texas. By the time he was 41, Bush was a millionaire.

Bush's father was elected in 1952 to the U.S. Senate from Connecticut. This seems to have been the spark that ignited Bush's political interests. Though defeated in a run for the

Starting at the top left-hand corner clockwise: George H. W. Bush, naval aviator cadet; Bush in his Yale baseball uniform; Bush in the oil fields of Midland, Texas; Congressman Bush and his family in front of the U.S. Capitol, Washington, D.C.

U.S. Senate from Texas in 1964, two years later Bush became the first Republican to represent Houston in the House of Representatives, where he served two terms. In 1970, Bush ran against LLOYD M. BENTSEN for the Senate and was defeated.

This defeat was the catalyst that began a different kind of government service for Bush. In return for his loyalty and effort in the Senate race, President Richard Nixon named Bush ambassador to the United Nations; Bush served in that post from 1971 to 1973. Nixon then named him chairman of the Republican National Committee, chief of the U.S. Liaison office in the People's Republic of China in 1974. President Gerald Ford named him director of the Central Intelligence Agency in 1976.

In 1980, Bush sought the Republican nomination for president. Though he lost the nomination, he became Ronald Reagan's running mate and served two terms as vice president from 1980 to 1988. As vice president, Bush was given high marks for his loyalty to the president, both in public and in private. However, Bush was tainted by the Iran-contra affair, when it was charged that, as a statutory member of the National Security Council and as a member of Reagan's inner circle, he must have known more than he admitted about the plans that led to the scandal.

In 1988, upon the conclusion of Reagan's second term, Bush won the Republican nomination for president, with Senator DAN QUAYLE of Indiana as his running mate. The Democrats nominated Massachusetts governor MICHAEL DUKAKIS. Running a campaign that painted Dukakis as being far to the left of his actual position on issues, Bush was able to hold together the coalition of voters who had supported Reagan, and he overcame Dukakis's double-digit lead, giving him on election day 54 percent of the popular vote and 426 electoral votes. On January 20, 1989, George Herbert Walker Bush was elected the 41st president of the United States of America.

Bush confronted difficulties in making policy decisions on domestic issues early in his term. Facing a Democratic majority of 10 votes in the Senate and 89 votes in the House, Bush decided that the best tactic would be to promote issues by means of small isolated campaigns rather then offering one thematic domestic policy (what his first chief of staff, JOHN SUNUNU, labeled a "limited agenda"). For example, in 1989 Bush created a $500-million plan to reward the best of American schools. This proposal also included an award for each state's finest teachers, the creation of a program of National Science Scholars, and magnet schools. Though the plan ultimately failed to pass the Congress due to its cost, the endeavor was considered a partial success because of the positive interactions between Bush and other politicians. However, Bush's domestic agenda counted several more successful proposals, including the passage of the Americans with Disabilities Act (1990) and the Clean Air Act (1990).

Bush had also inherited from Reagan a weak and mismanaged economy. By 1989, the

President-elect Bush and President Reagan shake hands in the Oval Office, January 19, 1989.

budget deficit stood at $2.7 trillion—three times its 1980 level. Bush held the belief that income levels and the standard of living would never increase if the foundation of the economy remained mired in debt. However, Bush had also pledged during the campaign not to raise the country's taxes. His attempt in 1990 to convince Congress to pass his budget was thus extremely difficult as the Democrats and Republicans were unable to compromise. Democrats held that tax increases for the rich would solve the problem; Republicans, on the other hand, believed substantial cuts in domestic spending would provide the cure. Bush's solution amounted to a combination of increased taxes and expenditure cuts that would decrease the deficit by $500 billion over five years. Conservative Republicans, who had rejoiced over Bush's "no new taxes" pledge, felt deceived and took vengeance by defeating the bill in the House. To succeed with a budget plan, Bush had to try to win a majority and to do so he had to agree to several of the Democrat's requests, which included raising taxes and increased expenditures.

As president, Bush oversaw two major military actions. In 1989, he sent 24,000 American troops to Panama to overthrow General MANUEL NORIEGA. In 1988, Noriega had been charged with drug trafficking in the United States, and, in May 1989, he annulled a presidential vote after American poll watchers had claimed he had lost. The assault lasted less than one week, and left 23 American soldiers and between 500 and 600 Panamanian civilians and armed forces dead, with Noriega being captured by American troops several months later. The conflict also drew attention to President Bush's fight against trade of illegal narcotics.

One year later, on August 2, 1990, Iraqi president SADDAM HUSSEIN invaded Kuwait and threatened to enter Saudi Arabia. Within hours of the attack Bush's talent for diplomacy took over. On August 3, Bush spoke with every principal leader in the Western alliance to create a coalition that was later used to defend the Iraqi invaders. The coalition included the Soviet Union, which was crucial, bearing in mind the past tensions between the two nations. On August 21, Bush sent 425,000 American troops and 118,000 troops from coalition allies to the Persian Gulf to secure Saudi Arabia and remove the Iraqi army from Kuwait in a maneuver dubbed Operation Desert Shield. Tensions continued as Saddam Hussein refused to move his troops out of Kuwait and told Iraqi citizens to get ready for "the mother of all battles." By November 28, the United Nations had had enough, and members passed Security Council Resolution 678, which set the deadline of January 15, 1991, for Hussein to remove his troops from Kuwait. He failed to do so. On January 17, 1991, Operation Desert Storm commenced. Bush ordered immense bombing followed by a ground assault beginning on February 24. Iraqi soldiers laid down their arms four days later. Bush did not seek to remove Hussein, his objective limited to removing him from Kuwait. In the end, 358 coalition soldiers perished, 513 were wounded, and thousands of Iraqis died in the conflict.

Bush also oversaw the end of the cold war during his presidency. After the spring 1989 collapse of the Berlin Wall, Bush refused to gloat, believing that such behavior might hurt future opportunities to bargain with the Soviet Union. In July 1991, President Bush and Soviet president MIKHAIL GORBACHEV signed the Strategic Arms Reduction Treaty (START). START involved a limitation on nuclear arms initially designed by Ronald Reagan, and the treaty put limits on an assortment of vehicles and weapons. Five months after START was enacted the Soviet Union collapsed and Gorbachev was overthrown.

Despite Bush's military victories and foreign achievements, throughout 1991 and 1992 discontent with his administration continued at home. With his vetoing of a bill to raise the minimum wage to $4.55 an hour as well as the Civil Rights Act of 1990 (vetoed because he was concerned it would create hiring quotas), and his agreement to raise taxes despite his promise to the contrary, Bush's approval ratings in January 1992 had tumbled to half of what they had been a year before.

In 1992, after weathering a tough challenge from PATRICK BUCHANAN (a conservative political columnist), Bush received the Republican nomination for the presidential race. However, in the fall election, he was beaten by Arkansas governor BILL CLINTON.

Currently, George H. W. Bush is a resident of Houston, Texas, and he summers in Kennebunkport, Maine. He sits on the board of visitors of MD Anderson Hospital and on the board of the Episcopal Church Foundation, and he serves on the vestry of St. Ann's Episcopal Church in Maine. He is the grandfather of 14 children and father of the 43rd president, GEORGE W. BUSH.

—JH

Bush, George W(alker)
(1946–)   *general managing partner, Texas Rangers; adviser to the president*

The firstborn son of George H. W. Bush and BARBARA PIERCE BUSH, George W. Bush was born in New Haven, Connecticut. He received his B.A. from Yale University (1968) and his M.B.A. from Harvard University (1975). From 1968 to 1975, Bush served as a pilot in the Texas Air National Guard. From 1975 through the late 1980s, Bush worked in the Texas energy business. In 1978, he ran unsuccessfully for the U.S. House of Representatives from Texas's 19th Congressional District. From 1987 to 1988, Bush left his business activities to work on his father's campaign for the presidency.

Following his father's victory, Bush's career shifted gears. After forming an investing group that bought the Texas Rangers' professional baseball team, in 1989 Bush became the team's managing general partner. However, despite his obligations to the Rangers, Bush served as an important "minister without portfolio" during his father's presidency. Bush chaired a transition team known to insiders as the "Scrub Team," which vetted potential administration appointments for their loyalty to the senior Bush and the Bush family in general. There is some evidence that when the time came in 1991 to fire White House chief of staff JOHN SUNUNU, it was George W. Bush who actually delivered the news to Sununu. In April 1992, he was called upon to help steady his father's reelection campaign, a campaign that had been buffeted by the challenge of conservative columnist PAT BUCHANAN.

In 1994, Bush defeated incumbent Ann Richards, winning 53.5 percent of the vote, to become governor of Texas. In 2000, Bush won the presidency of the United States in a close election that was decided by the U.S. Supreme Court. Notable events during his presidency included the terrorist attacks on the United States on September 11, 2001, the national response to those attacks as armed invasions of Afghanistan (2001) and Iraq (2003), and the struggle over a declining economy. In 2004, Bush was reelected to a second term in office.

Byrd, Robert C(arlyle)
(1917–)   *member of the Senate*

Robert Byrd was born in North Wilkesboro, North Carolina. He attended Beckley College, Concord College, Morris Harvey College, and Marshall College. In 1963 he graduated from The American University.

Byrd served in the West Virginia House of Delegates from 1947 to 1950 and in the West

Virginia Senate from 1951 to 1952. In 1953, Byrd began service in the U.S. House of Representatives. He was elected to the U.S. Senate from West Virginia in 1958, where he continues to serve. He has served as a member of the Appropriations Committee for the majority of his tenure. From 1971 to 1977, he was the Democratic Whip; he served as his party's majority leader from 1977 to 1980 and 1987 to 1988, and its Minority Leader from 1981 to 1986. During the Bush administration, he served as President Pro Tempore of the Senate (1989–95).

Byrd was a consistent opponent of the amendments to the Clean Air Act of 1970, which were supported both by the Bush administration and many Democrats in Congress, and he argued against the bill to protect the coal-mining interests so important to the economy of West Virginia. Byrd was also one of the leading congressional opponents of the use of American troops in the Persian Gulf following the August 1989 invasion of Kuwait by SADDAM HUSSEIN. Byrd argued that such a commitment would lead to a quagmire and "mounting casualties"; he also argued that, from a constitutional standpoint, the president needed to secure a declaration of war from Congress—a declaration that Byrd insisted would never pass because of the revulsion the American people felt toward the governments of many coalition members, most notably Saudi Arabia.

Byrd served once again as President Pro Tempore of the Senate from 2001 to 2003. He publicly criticized the administration of GEORGE W. BUSH regarding its 2003 invasion if Iraq, stating that "I do question the motives of a deskbound president who assumes the garb of a warrior for the purposes of a speech." In 2004, Byrd became the longest-serving member of Congress.

Card, Andrew
(1947–) *White House assistant chief of staff, secretary of transportation*

Andrew Card was born in Brockton, Massachusetts. He attended the U.S. Merchant Marine Academy (1966–67), and took his B.S. from the University of South Carolina (1971) in engineering. A structural design engineer, Card worked in that capacity until 1975, when he was elected to the Massachusetts House of Representatives. He served in the state legislature until 1985. Card chaired the presidential campaign of George H. W. Bush in Massachusetts in 1980. In 1982, he ran for governor, and was defeated. He then returned to the private sector, working as vice president of CMIS Corporation from 1983 until employed by the Reagan administration, serving first as special assistant for intergovernmental affairs (to 1987) and then director of intergovernmental affairs until 1988.

In 1988, Card once again managed Bush's primary campaign, this time in New Hampshire. This put him in close contact with JOHN SUNUNU, governor of that state, and, in 1989, Card was chosen White House assistant chief of staff under Sununu. Card worked in that capacity until 1991, when, after Sununu's resignation, he worked briefly for his successor, SAMUEL SKINNER. Skinner had come to the White House from his service as secretary of transportation; in 1992, Card was confirmed as Skinner's successor at transportation.

The major issue during Card's tenure at the Transportation Department concerned the devastation caused to South Florida by Hurricane Andrew. Card was put in charge of the government relief effort, for which he received sharp criticism from then presidential candidate BILL CLINTON about the slow pace of the relief efforts. Card also led the administration's fight for the privatization of airport policy. After Clinton's victory in the fall 1992 election, Card chaired the White House transition team.

From 1993 to 1998, Card was president and CEO of the American Automobile Manufacturer's Association, and from 1998 to 2000, he was the vice president of governmental relations—the chief lobbyist—for General Motors. In 2000, he was named White House chief of staff for President GEORGE W. BUSH.

Cavasos, Lauro F(red), Jr.
(1927–) *secretary of education*

Born in South Texas, Lauro Cavasos earned his undergraduate degrees from Texas Tech University (a B.A. in 1949 and an M.A. in 1951), and earned his Ph.D. in physiology from Iowa State University in 1954. Cavasos taught at the Medical College of Virginia from 1954 to 1964, and he served as professor and then dean of the Tufts School of Medicine from 1964 to 1980. From 1980 to 1988, he served as the president of Texas Tech University.

In 1988, Ronald Reagan nominated Cavasos to succeed WILLIAM J. BENNETT as secretary of education. The first Hispanic-American to hold a cabinet post, Cavasos was confirmed at the end of the Reagan tenure, and George H. W. Bush asked him to stay on at that post during the new administration. An advocate of school choice, Cavasos was instrumental in planning the National Summit on Education with the nation's governors, held in September 1989. However, early in December 1989, the Department of Education ruled that scholarships that were awarded only to minorities were illegal. In the ensuing firestorm in the press, Cavasos was forced to resign; he was succeeded by LAMAR ALEXANDER.

Following his tenure in the Bush administration, Cavasos returned to his professorial chair at Tufts University.

Ceauşescu, Nicolae
(1918–1989) *Communist Party leader of Romania*

Born in Oltenia, Romania, Nicolae Ceauşescu was imprisoned during World War II for his Communist activities. After 1945, as Romania entered the Communist orbit, Ceauşescu served as secretary of the Union of Communist Youth, minister of agriculture, and deputy minister of the armed forces. During the leadership of Gheorghe Gheorghui-Dej, Ceauşescu was the second-leading official in Romania.

After the death of Gheorghui-Dej in 1965, Ceauşescu became the leader of the Romanian Communist Party. An independent, he regu-

larly criticized the Soviet Union; in 1968, he publicly condemned Moscow's invasion of Czechoslovakia. This led Richard Nixon to believe that he was a Communist leader with whom he could deal; he used Ceauşescu as a secret diplomatic entrée to both North Vietnam and the People's Republic of China (PRC).

However, despite the fact that he was palatable to many Western leaders, Ceauşescu's iron control over his people, as well as his maintenance of a brutal secret police force, made him both hated and feared at home. In 1989, Ceauşescu became one of the most grotesque symbols of the fall of European communism. On December 17, 1989, he ordered his forces to fire upon anticommunist demonstrators. However, within days the army was siding with the demonstrators. Ceauşescu and his wife attempted to flee Bucharest, but they were captured, and, on December 25, they were both executed by a firing squad.

Cheney, Richard ("Dick") B.
(1941–) *secretary of defense*

Born in Lincoln, Nebraska, Dick Cheney attended Yale University and Casper College before taking his B.A. (1965) and M.A. (1966) from the University of Wyoming. Without obtaining a degree, Cheney did additional graduate-level work at the University of Wisconsin, and he was awarded a Congressional Fellowship for 1968–69. Immediately following his fellowship, Cheney became a special assistant to Donald Rumsfeld, then the director of the Office of Economic Opportunity. Cheney moved up in the Nixon White House in 1971 when he became a White House staff assistant, then director of the Cost of Living Council, where he served until 1973.

Upon the resignation of Nixon in August 1974, Cheney served as a member of a short-lived transition team in the Ford White House,

President Bush meets with Richard Cheney in the Oval Office, March 12, 1990.

headed by Donald Rumsfeld. When Rumsfeld became Ford's White House chief of staff in 1974, Cheney became his deputy; when Rumsfeld was chosen secretary of defense in November 1975, Cheney was promoted to serve as Ford's chief of staff, a position he held to the end of the Ford administration in 1977.

In 1978, Cheney was elected to the House of Representatives as the at-large congressman from Wyoming. He served in that capacity until 1989. While in Congress, Cheney voted for every attempt to increase military spending. He was also an outspoken supporter of the Nicaraguan contras. He served as chairman of the Republican Policy Committee, chairman of the House Republican Conference, and minority whip.

Immediately following his election to the presidency, George H. W. Bush nominated Texas senator JOHN TOWER to serve as secretary of defense. However, Tower's nomination stalled on Capitol Hill as information surfaced regarding his financial and personal indiscretions. When he finally abandoned Tower, Bush searched for a replacement candidate who was both knowledgeable and quickly confirmable. Cheney was both. On March 17, 1989, one week after Bush submitted his name to the U.S. Senate, he was unanimously confirmed by that body; three days later he was sworn in as secretary of defense.

Unwilling to be a passive bureaucrat, Cheney saw himself more in the mold of a staffer, saying to one reporter, "I am the president's man." Cheney ceded the day-to-day operational details of the Pentagon to his deputies, and instead he concentrated upon becoming a force in national security policy making in the Bush administration. This goal began with Cheney's efforts to reemphasize his civilian control of the military. Only days after being sworn in at defense, Cheney moved to show his authority. Air Force chief of staff General Lawrence Welch had visited Capitol Hill, ostensibly to break a deadlock over appropriations for Midgetman missiles and the deployment of 50 MX missiles. During a press conference, Cheney issued a stinging rebuke of the general's actions, accusing him of "freelancing"—leading many to conclude that Welch's true offense had been in acting without the approval of the secretary of defense. In another instance that arose during the crisis in the Persian Gulf, Cheney dismissed U.S. Air Force chief of staff General Michael Dugan, who had been on the Joint Chiefs of Staff for only three months, for telling reporters on a plane trip back from Saudi Arabia that the proposed ground war was doomed to failure and that the United States needed to use air power in the Persian Gulf.

Many observers noted that of all Bush's advisers, Cheney was the most hawkish. Of MIKHAIL GORBACHEV, the reform-minded president of the Soviet Union, Cheney was quoted as saying "I would guess he would ultimately fail." Bush distanced himself from Cheney over this statement ("I made it clear to Mr. Gorbachev . . . when we met, that we wanted to see perestroika succeed"), but, on most matters, the president agreed with his defense secretary. Before the May 1990 NATO meeting, a proposal had been floated that recommended that both the United States and the Soviet Union unilaterally withdraw all their troops from Europe; Cheney argued against the proposal, and the statement was eventually softened. After the Soviet Union fell in 1991, Cheney was one of the clearest voices in the administration warning against the dangers of permitting the newly independent republics to retain control of their nuclear stockpiles, argu-

ing that mishandling those weapons could have disastrous consequences.

Ironically, for a defense hawk like Cheney, financial exigencies compelled him to make severe cutbacks in the nation's defense infrastructure. As soon as he had taken office, Bush announced that the defense budget had to be cut by $6.3 billion. Cheney accomplished this for FY 1990 and, except for FY 1991 (the year of the Persian Gulf War), defense department budgetary allocations dropped each year of the Bush presidency (a 2.9 percent drop in FY 1990, a 9.8 percent drop in FY 1992, and an 8.1 percent drop in FY 1993). Indeed, an enduring portrait of Cheney for this period depicts him having to oversee base closures all around the country to help meet budget constraints; these closures were used effectively against the administration in the 1992 campaign.

On August 6, 1990, four days after the Iraqi invasion of Kuwait, Cheney joined other members of the administration on an unprecedented mission to convince KING FAHD of Saudi Arabia to grant permission to launch Operation Desert Shield from within his borders; a mission that was ultimately successful. Cheney was one of the voices within Bush's inner circle who argued for a military option that would expel SADDAM HUSSEIN from Kuwait. During Iraq's Scud bombings of Israel, Cheney also spoke up in sympathy with the desires of the Israelis to retaliate. Cheney also argued against asking Congress for authorization for the president under the War Powers Act to commit troops to Kuwait; on December 3, 1990, Cheney shared this feeling before a congressional committee: "I do not believe the president requires any additional authorization from the Congress before committing U.S. forces to achieve our objectives in the Gulf." During the war, Cheney took a direct and active role in operations.

Immediately following the end of the Bush administration, Cheney became a senior fellow at the American Enterprise Institute. In

1995, he explored the idea of a run for the presidency, but he finally dismissed it (most reporters cited Cheney's health—to that point, he had had three heart attacks). Later that year, Cheney was named chief executive officer of the Halliburton Company, a leader in energy service products. In 2001, after a challenge to the vote in Florida, Cheney was elected vice president of the United States on a ticket headed by GEORGE W. BUSH.

Clinton, William (Bill) Jefferson
(1946–) *president of the United States*

President Clinton was born on August 19, 1946, in Hope, Arkansas. His mother, Virginia Cassidy, married William Blythe, but Blythe died in an automobile accident before his son's birth. The son, William Jefferson Blythe IV, was later adopted by Roger Clinton, Virginia Blythe's second husband. Bill Blythe took Clinton's surname and became William Jefferson Clinton when he was 15 years old.

Clinton graduated from Georgetown University with a degree in international affairs in 1968, after serving as an intern during college for Senator J. William Fulbright (D-Ark.). After winning a Rhodes scholarship, Clinton attended Oxford University from 1968 to 1970. He returned to the United States and entered Yale Law School, graduating in 1973. While at Yale, Clinton met another law student, Hillary Rodham, whom he married on October 11, 1975.

After graduating from law school, Clinton returned to Arkansas to teach law at the University of Arkansas at Fayetteville (1974–76). In 1974, he made his first run for public office by challenging Republican incumbent John Paul Hammerschmidt for a seat in the U.S. House of Representatives. He successfully ran for state attorney general in 1978 and for governor in 1980.

Bill Clinton served as the 42nd president of the United States from 1993 to 2001. Clinton defeated President George H. W. Bush on November 3, 1992, garnering 43 percent of the vote. Bush received 38 percent of the vote and third party challenger ROSS PEROT received an unprecedented 19 percent of the vote. Clinton was reelected on November 5, 1996, for a second term, garnering 49 percent of the popular vote. The Republican challenger, Senator BOB DOLE, received 41 percent of the vote and Ross Perot, again in the race, received 8 percent of the vote.

When he ran for president in 1992, Clinton was the governor of Arkansas, where he had been the nation's longest serving governor. Clinton first ran for governor in 1978, after having served as Arkansas Attorney General for two years (1976–78). He was governor for only two years, losing the election in 1980 but recapturing the governor's office in 1982. He was then reelected for five consecutive terms.

During his tenure as governor of Arkansas from 1982 to 1993, Clinton served as chairman of the Democratic Leadership Council (1990–91), an organization that he had helped to create; chairman of the National Governors' Association (1986–87); chairman of the Educational Commission of the States (1986–87); and chairman of the Mississippi Delta Development Commission (1988–90). In addition he co-chaired the National Governors' Association Task Force on Health Care (1990–91).

In 1988, Clinton led a major effort by the nation's governor's to restructure national welfare laws and to secure congressional support for the Family Support Act. The Family Support Act proposed to change the welfare system to require that welfare recipients work while receiving support from the federal government. The act was finally passed, in a somewhat altered form, during his first term as president.

Clinton announced his candidacy for president on October 3, 1991, while President George H. W. Bush was still receiving strong public support after defeating Iraq in the Persian Gulf War. As a result of Bush's high polling numbers, many Democratic contenders chose not to enter the 1992 presidential race.

Convinced that he could win the presidency, Clinton actively sought the Democratic nomination and began to enter the 1992 Democratic primary elections. He focused his fledgling campaign around the nation's economy, constantly using the state of the economy as the theme of his campaign. He hired political strategists James Carville and Paul Begala to manage his campaign. The major setback to the campaign came when Gennifer Flowers asserted that she had had a 12-year relationship with Clinton, which he denied. Clinton and his wife, Hillary Rodham Clinton, chose to be interviewed on the national news program *60 Minutes*, during which he fervently denied Flowers's assertions. When she sold her story to a national tabloid, her credibility was further diminished.

By June 1992, the Clinton campaign had won enough primary states to secure the Democratic Party's nomination. In mid-July, at the Democratic National Convention in New York City, Clinton was elected the party's candidate and he then chose Senator AL GORE (D-Tenn.) as his running mate. On Tuesday, November 3, 1992, Clinton was elected president and he was sworn into office on January 20, 1993.

After leaving office in January 2001, President Clinton moved into spacious offices in Manhattan, but the cost of the offices drew fire from Republicans. Since his wife had just been elected to the U.S. Senate from New York, President Clinton chose to move to less expensive quarters. At the suggestion of Representative Charles Rangel (D-N.Y.), who represented Harlem, President Clinton moved his official offices to Harlem. President and Mrs. Clinton also purchased a home in Chappaqua, New York, and a home in Washington, D.C.

—SAW

Coelho, Anthony
(1942–) *member of the House of Representatives*

Born in Los Banos, California, Tony Coelho took his B.A. from Loyola University (California) in 1964. In 1965, Coelho began his political career as an intern—and then later as an administrative assistant—for California congressman B. F. Sisk. When Sisk retired in 1978, Coelho ran for his seat, and he was elected. From 1981 to 1986, he served as chairperson of the Democratic Congressional Campaign Committee. In 1987, Coelho was elected majority whip, a position he held until his resignation from the House.

Coelho earned a reputation as one of the Democratic Party's most prolific fund-raisers. In 1986, he called Thomas Spiegel, CEO of a Beverly Hills savings and loan, for investment advice. Spiegel helped Coelho arrange a $100,000 junk-bond investment that, when discovered, raised eyebrows because of Spiegel's personal contacts in Washington. While there was no evidence that Coelho helped Spiegel on any legislative matters, or on matters of regulation regarding S&L's, the scandal precipitated Coelho's resignation from the House of Representatives on June 15, 1989.

From 1989 to 1995, Coelho served as the managing director of Wertheim Schroder and Company, a New York investment banking firm. In 1995, he formed ETC w.TCI, a technology training company (it was sold in 1997). In 1999, Coelho served as the chairman of AL GORE's campaign for the Democratic presidential nomination.

D

Darman, Richard G(ordon)
(1943–) *director, Office of Management and Budget*

Born in Charlotte, North Carolina, Richard Darman earned a B.A. from Harvard University in 1964 and an M.B.A. from the Harvard Business School in 1967. From 1971 to 1973 he served the Nixon administration in positions in the Department of Health, Education, and Welfare, Department of Defense, and Department of Justice. After serving as a fellow at the Woodrow Wilson International Center for Scholars (1974–75) and as director of ICF Incorporated (1974–75 and 1977–80), Darman joined the Ford administration as assistant secretary of commerce for policy. Following Ford's 1976 reelection defeat, Darman returned to Harvard, where he joined the faculty of the John F. Kennedy School of Government. In 1981, Darman returned to government, joining the Reagan administration as deputy to the chief of staff (1981–85), where he played a key role in the passage of the 1981 tax reform bill, and deputy secretary of the Treasury (1985–87), where he was a key player in the 1986 tax reform measure. After leaving the Reagan administration, Darman served as a managing director in the investment banking group of Shearson Lehman Hutton in New York until December 1988.

In 1988, George H. W. Bush appointed Darman head of the Office of Management and Budget, a position in which Darman served for the entirety of the Bush administration. Known equally for his abrasive personality and for his belief in fiscal integrity, Darman's appointment sent a strong signal that Bush was ready to reconsider his "no new taxes" pledge made during the campaign. This appraisal turned out to be correct. As the problems of Reagan's deficits loomed large on the political and economic horizon, Darman counseled Bush that spending cuts would not be enough to make up the gap and make the deficit at least workable. After substantial meetings with the congressional leadership, on June 26, 1990, Bush announced that he was now supporting the need for "tax revenue increases" to help close the deficit gap. While this breaking of the famous "read my lips" pledge would ultimately cost Bush politically—particularly from within his own party, as conservatives were upset that he had reneged on his promise not to raise taxes—the decision laid the groundwork for both the economic recovery and the budget surpluses that would transpire during the tenure of Bush's successor.

On leaving the Bush administration, Darman became a partner at the Carlyle Group, an investment firm, and he returned to the faculty of Harvard University.

Derwinski, Edward J(oseph)
(1926–) *secretary of veterans affairs*

Born in Chicago, Illinois, Edward Derwinski served in the U.S. Army in 1945 as a member of the occupation force in Japan. Following his service, he took a B.A. in history from Loyola University in 1952. Later that year, Derwinski was elected to the first of two terms in the Illinois House of Representatives. In 1958, he was elected to the U.S. House of Representatives, where he served until 1980, when, in that year's election, handicapped by the fact that his district was reapportioned into five new districts, Derwinski lost reelection. During his congressional tenure, Derwinski served as a delegate to the United Nations, where he served with then ambassador to the United Nations George H. W. Bush. He then became a counselor to Secretary of State George Shultz, rising to the position of under secretary of state for security assistance, science, and technology (1983–86).

Created by the Reagan administration, the Department of Veterans Affairs did not secure official status until March 15, 1989. Derwinski served as secretary of the department for the entirety of the Bush administration. Following the end of Bush's term in office, Derwinski served as legislative consultant to Morrill and Associates.

Dole, Elizabeth Hanford
(1936–) *secretary of labor; president, American Red Cross*

Born in Salisbury, North Carolina, Elizabeth Dole took a B.A. from Duke University (1958).

She did postgraduate work at Oxford University, and then took an M.A. in education and political science from Harvard University (1960) and a law degree from Harvard School of Law (1965). In 1967 (as a Democrat—she would change her party membership to Republican after marrying BOB DOLE in 1975) she joined the Johnson administration's Department of Health, Education, and Welfare as a staff assistant. In 1968, she joined the Committee for Consumer Interests, where she rose to executive director, a post she kept when that committee became the Office of Consumer Affairs during the Nixon administration. In 1974, Nixon appointed her to the Federal Trade Commission, a position she resigned in order to campaign with her husband—both in his unsuccessful bid for the vice presidency in 1976 and then his unsuccessful bid for the presidency in 1980. However, in 1981, Ronald Reagan appointed her as assistant to the president for public liaison, and, in 1983, he appointed her his secretary of transportation—his first woman cabinet member and the first woman to hold that position.

Dole kept her secretaryship until 1987, when she once again resigned to campaign for her husband; this time, Bob Dole was defeated for the Republican nomination by George H. W. Bush. Once again, her husband's opponent named Elizabeth Dole to his cabinet, as Bush tapped her to be his secretary of labor. Important for her high profile—in 1988 a Gallup poll listed her as one of the world's top 10 influential women—Dole was also a key figure in the resolution of an 11-month Pittston coal strike in Virginia.

Dole resigned in 1990 (being replaced by LYNN MARTIN), and took the position of president of the American Red Cross (during her first year, she volunteered her time, accepting no salary). In 1995, she took a leave of absence from that position to once again campaign for her husband in yet another unsuccessful run for the presidency, this time against BILL CLIN-TON. In January 1999, she resigned her position at the Red Cross and began her own campaign for the presidency. However, after finishing third in the Iowa straw poll she withdrew from the race—published reports claimed that she had difficulty with the necessary fund-raising. In November 2002, she was elected to her first term as U.S. senator from North Carolina.

Dole, Robert

(1923–   ) *member of the Senate, Republican Party presidential candidate*

Robert Dole was born in Russell, Kansas. During World War II he served with the U.S. Army's 10th Mountain Division. He was wounded during the Italian campaign and, despite nine operations, never regained the full use of his right arm. For his service, Dole was awarded two Purple Hearts and the Bronze Star.

Returning to Kansas following the war, Dole took his B.A. degree from Washburn Municipal University and his law degree from the same school in 1952. In 1951, he was elected to the Kansas state legislature, and, in 1952, he was elected to the first of four terms as Russell County attorney. In 1960 he was elected to the U.S. House of Representatives from Kansas's Sixth Congressional District; he would serve four terms in the House. In 1968, Dole was elected to the U.S. Senate; he would serve in that body until his resignation in 1996.

In 1971, President Richard Nixon tapped Dole to serve as chairman of the Republican National Committee (RNC); Dole would serve in that position, defending the White House from Watergate-related charges, until 1973. In 1976, President Gerald Ford chose Dole as his running mate, but the ticket was defeated that fall by Democrats Jimmy Carter and Walter Mondale. In 1984, Dole was elected Senate Majority Leader, a position he kept for two

years, until the Republicans lost control of the Senate in the 1986 off-year election; then Dole was elected to the post of Senate Minority Leader. Dole served as Minority Leader until the off-year elections of 1994, when the Republicans regained control of the Senate. Reelected Senate Majority Leader, Dole would hold that position until his resignation.

In 1980, Dole made his first run for the Republican nomination for president, being defeated by Ronald Reagan. In 1988, Dole ran again; this time his strongest challenger was then vice president George H. W. Bush. Dole's often sarcastic personality was offset by his distance from the final troubled years of the Reagan presidency—his was a formidable candidacy, which began by hammering Bush about his links to the Iran-contra scandal. Dole won the Iowa caucuses, but then he came in second to Bush in New Hampshire thanks largely to the effect of an ad written by Bush adviser ROGER AILES that depicted Dole as "Senator Straddle" on the issues. Following his defeat, Dole lashed out at Bush rather than offering a courteous concession ("Tell him to stop lying about my record"), and his campaign progressed slowly downhill, with Bush emerging as the eventual victor.

Following his defeat by Bush, Dole returned to his leadership role in the Senate. Observers were astounded at how quickly he seemed to repair his hurt feelings from the campaign, and he become an indispensable part of the administration's efforts to push its legislation through Congress. He was an important part of the negotiating team on the 1991 budget, and he helped shepherd that agreement through Congress. He was also a vocal administration supporter of the Persian Gulf War and was primarily responsible for passage of the Senate resolution supporting the sending of U.S. troops to the gulf.

Dole continued his leadership service in the Senate until 1996, when he resigned in order to devote his full attention to his run for the presidency. That year, he won the Republican nomination but was defeated by BILL CLINTON in the fall election. Following his defeat, Dole formed Bob Dole Enterprises, which monitors his business affairs. He has also been a member of the International Commission on Missing Persons, and he was influential in the planning of a World War II memorial, dedicated in Washington, D.C., in 2004.

Dukakis, Michael
(1933–) *governor, Massachusetts; Democratic Party presidential candidate*

Michael Dukakis was born in Brookline, Massachusetts. His parents were first-generation Greek immigrants who had worked in the mill towns surrounding Boston. Dukakis took his B.A. (Phi Beta Kappa) from Swarthmore College in 1955 and then his law degree from Harvard Law School in 1960. After serving two years in the U.S. Army, Dukakis began his political career. First elected as a member from the town of Brookline, he was elected to the Massachusetts state legislature in 1962 for the first of four terms. While in the state legislature, Dukakis earned a reputation as an anti-establishment individualist. In 1970, he ran for lieutenant governor on a ticket headed by Boston mayor Kevin White. Although the ticket lost, Dukakis came back two years later, running for governor and defeating incumbent Frank Sargeant. Dukakis was then defeated for reelection in 1978 by Edward King. Stunned, he spent the next four years planning his political comeback. In 1982, Dukakis defeated King, and he was reelected to a third term as governor in 1986. During those years, Dukakis was given the lion's share of the credit for turning his state around from the recession of the early 1980s. Dubbed the "Massachusetts Miracle," it was his reputation as a fixer of

weak economies that propelled him into the 1988 presidential race.

In the primaries, Dukakis met with success by positioning himself as a centrist Democrat. He easily outmaneuvered a field that included former senator Gary Hart, Senator Joseph Biden of Delaware, Senator ALBERT GORE, JR., and Reverend JESSE JACKSON. For his part, Jackson stayed in the race to the end, long after Dukakis had sewn up the nomination, but Dukakis kept him at arm's length, thus solidifying his image as a moderate. Indeed, he strengthened this image, as well as addressed the charge that he had no federal experience, by choosing Senator LLOYD BENTSEN as his running mate.

As the fall campaign began, Dukakis led George H. W. Bush by 16 points. His early fall campaign looked as if it could maintain that lead, as Dukakis pounded Bush before farm and labor audiences as a cold, aloof patrician. However, as Bush began to call Dukakis "the man from Harvard," the populist momentum shifted and the Bush campaign portrayed Dukakis as a cold, almost lifeless technocrat. His background offered tidbits that Bush campaign adviser LEE ATWATER could grab hold of as he pursued a strategy of painting Dukakis as a far-left liberal Democrat. Dukakis had vetoed a bill, passed by the Massachusetts legislature, making it mandatory that all public school teachers lead their classes in the Pledge of Allegiance; in response, Atwater advised Bush to wear a flag in his lapel. The Bush campaign also castigated Dukakis for not fulfilling his pledge to obey the provisions of the Clean Water Act and clean up Boston harbor; Bush arrived for a speech on the environment in Boston via that same harbor. Most damning for the Dukakis campaign, however, was the case of Willie Horton, a convicted murderer who, while released from a Massachusetts prison on a furlough program initiated by Dukakis, entered a home, pistol-whipped the owner, and raped his wife. The fallout from the Horton affair led to the famous "Revolving Door" advertisement, which implicated Dukakis not only for his initial support of the program but also implied that he was a racist.

But, as Atwater stated, "we couldn't have done it without them." Dukakis seemed to be uninterested in answering Bush's attack ads, sticking to his campaign theme, "good jobs at good wages." He also refused to craft a campaign around tightly defined issues. Rather, he criss-crossed the country at a frenzied pace in an attempt to connect with as many voters as possible. Indeed, the decision to contest Bush in every state, rather than targeting funds and effort into those states with a larger number of electoral votes, was, for many, the key strategic

mistake of the Dukakis campaign. While this narrowed the gap that had been created by Bush's attack-style campaign, it did not offer a sufficiently focused message to resonate with the majority of voters. There were also other memorable blunders. The governor allowed himself to be photographed driving an M-1 tank; the resulting photo, with Dukakis wearing a tank commander's helmet, made him look for all the world like the cartoon character Snoopy. And then in the second presidential debate, Dukakis was asked by moderator Bernard Shaw of CNN if his wife, Kitty, "were raped or murdered, would you favor an irrevocable death penalty for the killer," Dukakis gave a cold, almost bureaucratic answer that made him seem as if he simply did not care.

Immediately following his defeat in the November election, Dukakis announced that he would not run for reelection as governor. Following his leaving office in 1991, Dukakis entered higher education. He has served as a visiting professor of political science at the University of Hawaii and at Boston's Northeastern University. Dukakis's research has centered on national health care policy. In 1998, Dukakis was nominated by President BILL CLINTON for a five-year term as a member of the Board of Directors of Amtrak. At present, he holds the position of vice chairman on the Amtrak Reform Board.

Vice President Bush debates Michael Dukakis, Los Angeles, California, October 13, 1988.

Durenberger, David F(erdinand)
(1934–   ) *member of the Senate*

David Durenberger was born in St. Cloud, Minnesota. He graduated from St. John's University (B.A. in political science) in 1955 and from the University of Minnesota Law School (1959). After serving in the U.S. Army (1956–63) Durenberger practiced law in Minneapolis from 1963 to 1966. From 1967 to 1971, he served as executive secretary to Governor

Harold LeVander. From 1971 to 1978, he was the counsel for legal and community affairs for the H. B. Fuller Company. In November 1978 he was elected to the U.S. Senate in a special election to complete the unexpired term of Hubert H. Humphrey, who had died in office. He was reelected in 1982 and 1988, serving most notably as chairman of the Select Committee on Intelligence.

In May 1990, Durenberger was charged with exceeding the honoraria limits set by the Senate (40 percent of salary during any one year), altering campaign contributions for his personal use, and violating the Senate's rules on personal travel. Durenberger allegedly transformed speaking fees into promotional fees for two books he wrote; he was also charged with participating in a financial scheme to lease a condominium he owned in order to secure travel reimbursements from the Senate. On July 25, he was unanimously denounced by the Senate (the vote was 96-0), becoming only the ninth senator in history to receive a formal denunciation.

Durenberger was not a candidate for reelection in 1994. From 1995, he served as a senior counselor with APCO Associates, a consulting firm in Washington, D.C.

E

Eagleburger, Lawrence S(idney)

(1930–) *deputy secretary of state, secretary of state*

Born in Milwaukee, Wisconsin, Lawrence Eagleburger earned a B.S. from the University of Wisconsin (1952). After spending two years in the U.S. Army, he returned to the University of Wisconsin to take his M.S. (1957). In 1957 Eagleburger began what would be a decade's tenure in the U.S. Foreign Service. For two years, he served at the U.S. embassy in Honduras. From 1959 to 1961, he was a political analyst for Cuba in the Bureau of Intelligence and Research; from 1961 to 1965, he served at the U.S. embassy in Yugoslavia, where he worked for the economic section. In 1966, he joined the Johnson administration, first as a member of the National Security Council (NSC) staff and then as special assistant to the under secretary of state, a position he kept through 1969. He then transited to the Nixon administration, where for several months he served as executive assistant to Henry Kissinger, then Nixon's head of the National Security Council. Also during the Nixon administration, Eagleburger served as the chief of the political section of the U.S. Mission to NATO (1969–71), and deputy assistant secre-

tary of defense (1971–73). Under President Ford, he was once again executive assistant to Henry Kissinger, then serving as secretary of state. In 1977, President Carter nominated Eagleburger as ambassador to Yugoslavia, a post he filled until 1981, when he returned home to join the Reagan administration. During Reagan's first term, Eagleburger served as assistant secretary of state for European affairs (1981–82), and undersecretary of state for political affairs (1982–84). Eagleburger left the Reagan White House in 1984 and became president of Kissinger Associates (1984–89).

Following the 1988 victory of George H. W. Bush, Eagleburger was named deputy secretary of state, a position he would hold for all but one month of the Bush administration. On August 23, 1992, Secretary of State JAMES A. BAKER III resigned to become head of Bush's reelection campaign. Eagleburger was named acting secretary of state. On December 8, 1992, following the resignation of Baker, Eagleburger was sworn in as secretary of state, a position he held for seven weeks, until the end of the administration.

After his service to the Bush administration, Eagleburger joined the law firm of Baker, Donelson, Bearrnan, and Caldwell as a senior foreign policy adviser.

F

Fahd ibn Abdul Aziz, King
(1921–2005) *king of Saudi Arabia*

King Fahd ibn Abdul Aziz was born in Riyadh, the capital of Saudi Arabia, in 1921 as the 11th son of King Abdul Aziz bin Abdulrahman Al-Saud, the founder of the Saudi kingdom. In 1932, at nine years of age, Fahd watched his father establish the Saudi kingdom. Fahd was educated at the Princes' School in Riyadh, a school founded by King Abdulaziz. In 1953, Fahd represented Saudi Arabia at the coronation of Great Britain's Queen Elizabeth II, which gave him the chance to meet many heads of state from around the world. Also in 1953, at the age of 30, his father appointed Fahd as his education minister.

Fahd's brother, King Kahlid, died in 1957, and Fahd became crown prince and prime minister. In 1959, he headed the Arab League of States after his term of education minister was completed. In 1962, Fahd was appointed interior minister of Saudi Arabia. After being appointed to the post, and not long after the 1973 Yom Kippur War, Fahd made an official visit to the United States. During the visit he had many discussions with President Richard Nixon and Secretary of State Henry Kissinger. The two nations agreed to establish a U.S.-Saudi Joint Commission on Economic Coop-

eration. Five years later he became second deputy prime minister. In 1981, as prime minister, Fahd introduced a plan, the Gulf Cooperation Council, which called for peace in the Middle East and demanded that Israel withdraw its forces and remove all Jewish settlements from the occupied areas. His plan was eventually adopted and became the basis of the Arab League's position on resolution of the Israeli-Palestinian conflict.

In 1982, Fahd became the fifth king to rule Saudi Arabia. As king his first act was to supervise a massive project to expand Islam's two holiest sites, the Holy Mosque in Mecca and the Prophets Mosque in Medina. He also promoted facilitation of improved means of transportation for the millions of pilgrims who worship in Saudi Arabia and better education and health measures. On the world scene, he supported efforts, in cooperation with President Reagan, to help Afghan freedom fighters during the Soviet occupation of their country. In 1992, factional fighting between Afghan leaders broke out. King Fahd stepped in and hosted a peace conference held in Mecca. The conference resulted in an accord signed on March 12, 1993.

During the presidency of George H. W. Bush, King Fahd and several other world leaders were given assurances by SADDAM HUSSEIN that he would not invade Kuwait. Regardless,

President Bush and King Fahd, at the Royal Pavilion in Saudi Arabia, discuss the situation in Iraq, November 21, 1990.

on August 2, 1990, the Iraqi leader invaded, shocking the Arab world. President Bush and the UN Security Council were well briefed on Saddam's activities. The CIA and other intelligent experts were receiving information that the Iraqis were on the brink of developing a nuclear capability and possibly possessed biological weapon capabilities. The Security Council passed Resolution 660, which condemned the invasion and ordered Iraqi forces to withdraw from Kuwait. Iraqi troops were also threatened with possible military action from the United States. Fahd supported the UN resolution, sent troops to the Kuwait border, and endorsed an Arab League resolution that condemned Iraq. However, that resolution failed to pass. Saddam then tried to settle the issue by telling the Israelis to withdraw from Arab lands—then, and only then, would he pull out of Kuwait. King Fahd invited U.S. troops to Saudi Arabia both to defend his monarchy and to use Saudi territory as a staging ground for action to launch a strike to drive the Iraqis from Kuwait. He did so after an initial period of hesitation, reluctant to allow large numbers of foreign, non-Muslim troops into the kingdom. Following Fahd's decision to allow entry of foreign forces, the coalition sent more than 500,000 troops, who served as the centerpiece for Operation Desert Shield.

Fahd retained the throne in Saudi Arabia until his death in August 2005 of complications following a stroke.

—BC

Foley, Thomas S(tephen)
(1929–) *member of the House of Representatives*

Born in Spokane, Washington, Thomas Foley received his B.A. (1951) from the University of Washington. Following two years of graduate study in international affairs, Foley entered the law school at the University of Washington, taking his degree in 1957.

Foley practiced law in Spokane for one year, then became deputy prosecutor for Spokane County in 1958 and assistant state attorney general in 1960. Then, in 1961, he moved to Washington to join the staff of newly elected Democratic senator Henry "Scoop" Jackson (D-Wash.). Jackson would become Foley's political mentor. In 1964, Jackson convinced Foley to return to Washington and run against the Republican incumbent from Spokane for a seat in the House of Representatives. Foley did so, and he won the election. In 1974, as part of a post-Watergate uprising against the entrenched committee system, Foley was chosen chair of the Agriculture Committee, becoming one of the youngest committee chairs in many years. In 1981, he was chosen as Democratic whip, a position he filled until 1987 when he was chosen as his party's Majority Leader. As Majority Leader, Foley served on the Permanent Select Committee on Intelligence, the Committee on the Budget, and the Select Committee to Investigate Covert Arms Transactions with Iran.

Foley stood next in line to Speaker JAMES WRIGHT (D-Tex.), who found himself under fire in 1989 from charges of ethical misconduct. However, Foley's reputation for fairness allowed him to assume the position of "honest broker" between Wright and the Ethics Committee, which was pushing for the Speaker's resignation. Following Wright's resignation, on June 6, 1989, Foley was elected the 49th Speaker of the House of Representatives.

Foley soon earned a reputation for being fair to both sides of the aisle—one of the stories most told by the astounded opposition was the time early in his speakership when Foley found in favor of the Republicans on a voice vote. This characteristic was utilized most notably during the Bush administration when he maintained for himself once again the role of "honest broker" during the acrimonious 1990 budget negotiations.

Following his defeat in the congressional election of 1994, Foley became a partner in Akin, Gump, Strauss, Hauer, and Feld, a Washington D.C., law firm. From 1997 to 2001, he served as U.S. ambassador to Japan.

Franklin, Barbara Hackman
(1940–) *alternate representative to the United Nations General Assembly, secretary of commerce*

Born in Lancaster County, Pennsylvania, Barbara Franklin earned her bachelor's degree from Pennsylvania State University in 1962, and, in 1964, she was a member of the second class of women to receive their M.B.A. from the Harvard Business School. From 1971 to 1973, Franklin served as a staff assistant to President Richard Nixon, a position from where she worked to recruit more women into the administration. She then served as commissioner of the U.S. Product Safety Commission from 1973 to 1979. From 1979 to 1988, she was a senior fellow and director of the government and business program at the Wharton School. While in that position, she also served two terms as a member of the Advisory Committee for Trade Policy and Negotiations under Ronald Reagan (1982–84), and she opened Barbara Franklin Enterprises, a private investment and counseling firm, in 1980.

During the George H. W. Bush administration, Franklin served as an alternate representative to the 44th General Assembly of the United Nations. In December 1991, she was nominated by Bush to serve as his second secretary of commerce (replacing ROBERT MOSBACHER, who had recently resigned). Despite Franklin's experience, the press speculated that she was chosen either to aid Bush's standing with women in the following year's election or to reward her for years of service as a significant donor to the Republican Party. In December 1992, immediately following Bush's defeat,

Franklin became the first cabinet secretary to visit the People's Republic of China (PRC) since the 1989 Tiananmen Square massacre. As a result of that trip, contracts totalling $1 billion were signed between the United States and the People's Republic of China, and the Joint Commission on Commerce and Trade was reconvened.

Following her tenure in the Bush administration, Franklin returned to head Barbara Franklin Enterprises.

G

Gates, Robert

(1943–) *assistant to the president and deputy National Security Advisor; director, Central Intelligence Agency*

Born in Wichita, Kansas, Robert Gates earned his bachelor's degree from the College of William and Mary, his master's degree in history from Indiana University, and his doctorate in Russian and Soviet history from Georgetown University. Beginning his career as a Sovietologist, in 1971 he joined the Central Intelligence Agency's (CIA) support staff on arms control issues. BRENT SCOWCROFT brought Gates into the National Security Council as a junior staffer during the Ford administration, and Gates continued to serve at the NSC under Jimmy Carter. Gates returned to the CIA, where he served throughout the Reagan administration. In July 1982, he was named to the top CIA analytical post, that of deputy director of intelligence. He was named deputy director of the CIA by President Ronald Reagan in 1986, at the height of what became known as the Iran-contra affair. Persistent questions about his role in the scandal led Gates to withdraw his name after Reagan nominated him as his director of central intelligence in 1987.

In January 1989, Gates was chosen by George H. W. Bush as special assistant to the president and deputy to National Security Advisor Brent Scowcroft. He would ultimately wield more power than any previous NSC deputy, thanks to one of Bush's first moves as president. On the day of his inauguration, Bush issued a National Security Directive (NSD-1) that created two new subcommittees of the NSC—the Principals Committee and the Deputies Committee. Gates chaired the latter committee, which was charged with the development of policy options. Gates attended the morning briefing of the president on national security affairs and often attended NSC meetings with Scowcroft. He was also in charge of the day-to-day management of the NSC, leaving Scowcroft to become Bush's closest foreign policy adviser. Gates also headed an interdepartmental group, the European Strategy Steering Group, and in that role was one of Bush's chief emissaries to European capitals to sell arms control. A hawk, Gates opposed cooperation with MIKHAIL GORBACHEV, a position that brought him into some conflict with Secretary of State JAMES A. BAKER III, who preferred a more conciliatory approach to the Soviet Union.

During the Persian Gulf War, Gates served as a member of what was dubbed the "Gang of Eight," advisers to whom Bush turned for his wartime counsel. Along with Scowcroft and

Chief of Staff JOHN SUNUNU, Gates advocated an offensive option that would expel SADDAM HUSSEIN from Kuwait, once again putting him into conflict with Baker. Gates also argued vociferously against a lengthy U.S. presence in Iraq after the war.

Gates was nominated by Bush for the post of director of central intelligence in May 1991. While his nomination was once again held up by questions regarding his role in Iran-contra, Gates was confirmed in November 1991. Thus, he became the first former director of the agency's directorate of intelligence to ascend to the top position. Gates served in that post until the end of the Bush administration (a position that, as under his predecessor William Webster, did not carry with it cabinet rank).

Following his tenure in the Bush administration, Gates served as the dean of the George Bush School of Government and Public Service at Texas A&M University from 1999 to 2001. In 2002, he was named president of Texas A&M.

Gingrich, Newton ("Newt") Leroy
(1943–   ) *member of the House of Representatives*

Newt Gingrich was born in Harrisburg, Pennsylvania, and received his B.A. degree from Emory University and his M.A. (1968) and Ph.D. (1971) degrees from Tulane University. From 1970 to 1978, he taught history and environmental studies at West Georgia College in Carrollton, Georgia.

In 1974 and 1976, Gingrich lost in his first two attempts to be elected to Congress. In 1978, however, he was elected into the GOP minority in Congress as a Republican representative. During his first term in office, Gingrich was one of the first of a new breed of congressmembers to use television to enhance his constituent service and to build for himself

a national reputation. He encouraged other Republicans to take his lead and, as a result, he created a strategy that outraged Democratic members of Congress. He helped both Republican challengers to win elections and incumbents to keep their seats in Congress. Gingrich brought a deep concern to improve the health system for all Americans. He provided leadership in helping to save Medicare from bankruptcy and motivating the reform of the FDA to help seriously ill citizens. A new focal point was created for the agency based on research, prevention, and wellness for the nation's citizens. His contributions brought him accolades, including receiving the highest nonmedical award from the American Diabetes Association and being named the 1995 Georgia Citizen of the Year by the March of Dimes.

During the presidency of George H. W. Bush, Gingrich, now serving as House minority whip, was the most recognizable face among the new conservative wing of the party, which felt that, through his economic policies, Bush was undoing the gains made by Ronald Reagan. Gingrich was especially incensed at the 1990 decision by the administration to raise taxes, even after Bush promised during the campaign (saying "read my lips") that he would not. Gingrich led the fight against the budget package in Congress, thus putting him at odds with his own president. Indeed, he led the opposition to the point that, in October 1990, no budget had yet been passed and for three days the government shut down. When the Omnibus Budget Reconciliation Bill was finally passed, Gingrich had effectively positioned himself as an enemy of the administration.

Following the Bush administration, Gingrich increased his public exposure through a campaign, spearheaded by him, centered on a "Contract with America," a statement listing 10 steps toward moving power out of Washington's hands and back to the American people. The campaign proved very popular and guided the Republican Party to victory in the congressional elections of 1994 in capturing a majority in the U.S. House for the first time in 40 years. The following year, Gingrich was elected Speaker of the U.S. House of Representatives. However, Gingrich was subsequently tainted by a book publishing scandal that resulted in the House voting for the first time in its history to discipline a House Speaker by giving him a $300,000 fine. In 1999, Gingrich resigned from the Speakership and refused to run for reelection. He founded the Gingrich Group, an Atlanta-based communications and management-consulting firm that he serves as CEO. He is also a political analyst for the Fox News Channel.

—KS

Gorbachev, Mikhail Sergeyevich

(1931–) *general secretary of the Communist Party of the Soviet Union, president of the Soviet Union*

Mikhail Gorbachev was born into a peasant family in Privolnoye, in the Stavropol district of Russia. He joined the Communist Party in 1952, and, the following year, he received a law degree from Moscow University. In the early 1960s he became the head of the Agriculture Department in the Stavropol area. He was elected to the Central Committee in 1971 with the help of Yuri Andropov. Gorbachev became a member of the Politburo in 1980. Under Andropov's mentoring, Gorbachev came to realize that the collective system was flawed in many ways. On March 11, 1985, after the death of Communist Party chairman Constantine Chernenko, Gorbachev was elected general secretary of the Communist Party.

President-elect George H. W. Bush first met Gorbachev in a meeting with outgoing president Ronald Reagan on Governor's Island in New York harbor on December 7, 1988. To outside observers, it appeared to be a warm, friendly encounter. Bush said of Gorbachev that he was a leader different from all of his Soviet predecessors. Both Bush and Gorbachev stated publicly that they sought to continue the friendly atmosphere, but the meeting, in fact, was rather formal and personal relations quite frigid. In their discussions, Gorbachev lost his temper. Their initial meeting set the stage for what the Soviets came to call *pauza*, a "pause" that was sought by Bush to allow both sides to take a look at where the United States and Soviet Union were headed with their relations.

Gorbachev sought to bring about many significant reforms in Soviet society. They included, most notably, the concepts of glasnost ("openness") and perestroika ("restructuring"), both encompassing attempts to help rejuvenate the Soviet system and economy. Gorbachev also began to actively seek to put an end to the arms race between the Soviet Union and Western countries. In December 1988, Gorbachev announced that the Soviet Union would cut its troop strength by 500,000 and reduce the number of its tanks by 10,000. The late 1980s saw the end of Soviet influence in Eastern Europe. In 1988–89, Gorbachev relinquished virtually all control of the Eastern European nations and many of the Communist governments in the region began to fall. Communist governments in Yugoslavia and Bulgaria fell in late 1988. The opening of the Berlin Wall in November 1989 marked the end of the 40-year division of Germany's capital city. By 1990 the Soviet Union itself began to break up. Lithuania declared its independence in March 1990. With the Soviet Union's influence diminishing across the world, Gorbachev announced that Moscow would carry out a complete withdrawal from Afghanistan. By February 15, 1989, the last Soviet troop had departed Afghanistan. While these events contributed directly to the "end of the cold war," his actions cost Gorbachev dearly at home as opposition to his policies by hard-line Communists began to coalesce.

After the collapse of Eastern Europe, Gorbachev and Bush met at Malta in December 1989. Gorbachev, realizing that Soviet control over the satellite nations was slipping away, told Bush that he recognized the importance of the U.S. presence in Europe and that the two countries should henceforth work together. At this encounter, Bush and Gorbachev got along well together. The two leaders announced a new era in American-Soviet relations had begun. Despite opposition from among his own advisers, Bush soon came to believe that good relations with the Soviet Union depended on maintaining support for Gorbachev.

On May 29, 1990, Gorbachev came to the United States and met with Bush in Washington, D.C. The Soviet leader wanted limits placed on German power in NATO and in the military strength of the Western powers. He also strongly wanted a trade agreement with the United States so that he could return home to his strife-torn nation with a political victory. Bush told Gorbachev that he would not send a trade agreement to Congress unless Moscow lifted its embargo against Lithuania. Gorbachev withdrew Soviet objections to a unified Germany, and Bush was able to negotiate major concessions without harming U.S.-Soviet relations.

When SADDAM HUSSEIN invaded Kuwait in 1990, the UN Security Council met to discuss the crisis. The council unanimously denounced the invasion and called for sanctions against Iraq. Bush knew that the key to maintaining UN solidarity was the Soviet Union. For its part, Moscow cooperated in announcing

Presidents Bush and Gorbachev hold a press conference at the Helsinki Summit, Finland, September 9, 1990.

that it would not ship arms to Hussein. This was the first time since the end of World War II that the Soviet Union and the United States presented a united front in a pending international crisis. In return, Bush promoted Gorbachev's prestige in extending opportunities to share the world stage. On September 9, Bush and Gorbachev met in Helsinki, Finland, where they agreed that the Soviets would have a presence in Middle Eastern affairs.

But strife within the Soviet Union did not abate. While he survived one coup attempt, Gorbachev had unleashed forces of reform and nationalism in his own nation that he could not rein in. In December 1991, eight republics seceded from the Soviet Union. The Communist Party was also voted out of existence by Soviet legislators. On December 25, 1991, Mikhail Gorbachev resigned his position and the Soviet Union ceased to exist. Bush, although angering many members of the Republican Party, stood by Gorbachev until the very end.

Following his resignation, Gorbachev remained on the international scene. In 1993, he created the Green Cross International, an environmental organization designed to help clean up military toxins and promote enactment of laws to protect the environment. Gorbachev is also the founder and president of the Gorbachev Foundation, which focuses on major socioeconomic and political issues. He ran for president of Russia in 1996, receiving less than 1 percent of the vote. He currently lives in Moscow.

—KW

Gore, Albert A(rnold), Jr.

(1948–   ) *member of the Senate, vice president of the United States*

Al Gore was born in Washington, D.C. His early years were spent on the family farm, near the small town of Carthage, Tennessee. When his father, Albert Gore, Sr., became a U.S. senator, he moved his family to Washington, D.C., where they took up residence at the Fairfax Hotel. During the summer and on holidays, Gore and his family would travel back to the family farm in Tennessee. After graduating from St. Albans Preparatory School in 1965, Gore enrolled at Harvard University. There he received a bachelor's degree in government, graduating cum laude in 1969 after writing a senior thesis about the impact of television on the conduct of the president.

On August 7, 1969, after graduation, Gore volunteered for the army. He enlisted at the Newark, New Jersey, recruiting office. By the end of August, he shipped out to Fort Dix, New Jersey, for eight weeks of basic training. In October 1969, Gore was sent to Fort Rucker in Alabama, were he stayed until December 1970 for on-the-job training at the Army's *Flier* newspaper. A month later, in January 1971, he was sent to Vietnam as a field reporter for *Stars and Stripes.* Gore never saw frontline action and served only five months in Vietnam. On May 24, 1971, Gore's request for an early discharge (by only three months) to attend graduate school was granted.

After his discharge, Gore enrolled at the Vanderbilt University School of Religion, where he attended graduate school from 1971 to 1972. He then attended the Vanderbilt University School of Law from 1974 to 1976. While at the university, he worked as an investigative reporter for the *Nashville Tennessean* from 1971 to 1976. In 1976, Gore decided to quit law school to begin a career in politics. That year, he was elected as a Democrat to the 95th Congress, where he served three successive terms.

During his tenure in Congress, Gore was very interested in learning about arms control. He asked the chairman of the Committee on Intelligence for a tutor on the subject; in

November 1980, Leon Fuerth and Gore began meeting once or twice a week. Fuerth was the arms control expert on the staff of the House Permanent Select Committee on Intelligence. Gore placed before Congress in March 1982 a proposal that if the United States positioned only one warhead on each missile and spread them farther apart, the Soviet Union would not have enough warheads to take out an American land-based arsenal. The idea failed to secure backing as President Ronald Reagan wanted to fund the MX missile, which would hold 10 independently targetable warheads. The *Congressional Quarterly* also published Gore's first comprehensive report dealing with arms control in its February 1982 issue.

Two years later, in 1984, Gore was elected to the U.S. Senate from Tennessee, winning 61 percent of the vote. In 1988 he was unsuccessful as he tried to gain the Democratic nomination for the presidency (the nod eventually went to Massachusetts governor MICHAEL DUKAKIS). In 1990, he was reelected to the Senate with 70 percent of the vote.

In 1992, Gore was asked by Arkansas governor BILL CLINTON, who was challenging the incumbent president, George H. W. Bush, to serve as his running mate, and Gore accepted. During a televised debate, Gore easily defeated his two opponents, incumbent vice president DAN QUAYLE, and Admiral James Stockdale, the running mate of Reform Party candidate ROSS PEROT. Clinton and Gore were elected as the 45th president and vice president of the United States in November.

During Gore's vice presidency, he continued his advocacy for environmental conservation, which had been outlined in his book titled *Earth in the Balance* in 1992. Also as vice president, Gore formulated policies for reducing the cost and size of the federal government, and he was an ardent proponent of expansion of computer technology. In 1996, Clinton and Gore were reelected for a second term in the White House. In 2000, Gore was once again a candidate for his party's nomination for the presidency. He won the nomination as well as the popular vote in that fall's election against GEORGE W. BUSH. However, due largely to faulty electoral practices in Florida, Gore lost both the electoral vote and a Supreme Court appeal, thus giving Bush the presidency. Following his defeat, he began teaching at Columbia University, Fisk University, Middle Tennessee State University, and the University of California in Los Angeles. Gore also took a position as vice chairman for Metropolitan West Financial, where he developed investment strategies in the biotechnology and information technology fields, and he accepted a consulting job with a Los Angeles law firm, where he served as adviser to Google.

—SD

Gray, C(layland) Boyden

(1943–) *counsel to Vice President George H. W. Bush, counsel to the president*

Son of Gordon Gray, who had served as special assistant to the president for national security under Dwight Eisenhower, and heir to the Reynolds tobacco fortune, C. Boyden Gray earned his A.B. from Harvard University in 1964 and his law degree from the University of North Carolina in 1968, where he graduated first in his class and edited the law review. Following his graduation, Gray clerked for Chief Justice Earl Warren for a year. In 1969, he joined Wilmer, Cutler, and Pickering, a Washington, D.C., law firm, becoming a partner in 1976. From 1981 to 1989, Gray served as counsel to then vice president George H. W. Bush, notably serving on the Presidential Task Force on Regulatory Relief, a committee chaired by Bush.

Following Bush's 1988 election to the presidency, Gray was Bush's first appointee, joining the administration in the same capacity as he

President Bush signs the Executive Order Ethics Package as C. Boyden Gray looks on in the Oval Office of the White House, April 12, 1989.

had served the vice president. Gray also joined the transition team, holding responsibility for checking the ethical record of each new appointee. More than with previous transfers of power, the transition was a particularly volatile period for the incoming administration, largely because Bush had publicly promised that his administration would be an ethically upright one (drawing a marked contrast to the Iran-contra affair that plagued the final days of his predecessor). In a rather public spat, Gray requested that JAMES A. BAKER III, secretary of state–designate, sell a large block of stock he held in a bank that made loans to developing countries. Gray also took a hit regarding his own ethical portfolio, coming under fire for failing to put his own money in a blind trust and

for keeping his salary as a director of his family's Summit Communication Group, which owned 16 radio stations and had 130,000 cable television subscribers throughout the South (Gray eventually put his holdings into a blind trust). He played a quieter role in the failed nomination of JOHN TOWER as secretary of defense. In his memoirs, Tower claimed that Gray helped to scuttle his nomination by telling members of the committee that he, Tower, was possessed of a "Napoleon complex."

Gray's influence ran deep in the Bush administration. When the press got word of JOHN SUNUNU's misappropriation of funds for travel in early 1991, Gray's office produced a 21-page internal review of Sununu's trips, and pronounced them acceptable. When the scandal grew too hot to handle, Bush ordered that Sununu approve all his travel plans with Gray. Immediately following Iraq's invasion of Kuwait in 1990, Gray was also responsible for seeking the legal justification necessary to deploy military power without congressional approval. Perhaps Gray's most long-lasting accomplishment lay in the role he played in choosing CLARENCE THOMAS as an associate justice of the Supreme Court in 1991. Gray's office oversaw judicial selections, and, after the appearance of ANITA HILL's charges of sexual harassment against Thomas, Gray defended the nominee with zeal.

Several scholars have observed that Gray initiated a change in the Office of the Counsel to the President by actively participating in policy decisions. Others have opined that Gray was actually Bush's closest adviser on issues of domestic policy. He was, by most accounts, largely responsible for crafting the 1991 amendments to the Clean Air Act. He was also largely responsible for framing the Americans with Disabilities Act; a bill described by Gray to one scholar as "the greatest welfare reform ever pulled off." Bush also put Gray in charge of dealing with Congress regarding the passage of the 1991 Civil Rights Act. Gray maintained an interest in deregulation, begun during his service in the Reagan administration. He headed the Council on Competitiveness, a working group on deregulation.

Gray currently is a partner with Wilmer, Cutler, and Pickering in Washington, D.C. In 2000, he served as a member of the transition team in planning the incoming administration of GEORGE W. BUSH.

Greenspan, Alan
(1926–   ) *chairman, Board of Governors of the Federal Reserve System*

Born on March 6, 1926, Alan Greenspan received his B.S. in economics, summa cum laude, from New York University (1948) and his M.A. in economics from New York University (1950). He began his Ph.D. studies at Columbia University but left Columbia when he ran out of money and took a job as an economist for the National Industrial Conference Board. He eventually received his Ph.D. from New York University in 1977. Although most of his career was spent in the public sector, Greenspan worked for 20 years as chief executive office and president of Townsend-Greenspan and Company, Inc., in New York City (1954–74). Greenspan's firm offered economic forecasts to large companies and financial institutions. Few corporations had their own professional staff economists at this time, making Greenspan's company very profitable.

Greenspan had been briefly involved in politics in 1968, when he served as director of domestic policy research for Richard M. Nixon's successful presidential campaign. Though he turned down a permanent position in the Nixon administration, he served on the presidential transition team and advised President Nixon informally from his Townsend-Greenspan Company. In 1974, President Nixon named Greenspan to the position of chairman of the Council of Economic Advisers. Greenspan accepted the position, to deal with the rising inflation rate during the mid-1970s. He did not, however, take office until September 1, 1974, nearly one month after President Nixon had resigned and President Ford had been sworn into office.

As chairman of the Council of Economic Advisers in a period of economic downturn, Greenspan extended to President Ford economic advice on wage and price controls and the oil crisis. Frequently called to testify in hearings on Capitol Hill, Greenspan learned how to deal with members of Congress. When he served as chairman of the Council of Economic Advisers, he had not yet received his Ph.D. He completed the degree in 1977.

With the election of Jimmy Carter in 1977, Greenspan returned to New York City to his consulting firm of Townsend-Greenspan. Following the 1981 election, President Reagan then named Greenspan to serve as chairman of the National Commission on Social Security Reform (1981–83). During the Reagan administration, Greenspan was also appointed to the President's Economic Policy Advisory Board (1981–87) and the President's Foreign Intelligence Advisory Board (1983–85).

When Paul Volcker, the chairman of the Federal Reserve Board, unexpectedly announced his retirement in June 1987, President Reagan nominated Greenspan to the Board of Governors of the Federal Reserve Board. Greenspan accepted the nomination and was confirmed by the Senate on August 11, 1987. In 1988, Reagan named Greenspan chairman. After his appointment to the Federal Reserve Board, Greenspan dissolved the Townsend-Greenspan firm when a suitable buyer could not be found. He was reappointed chairman of the board by President George H. W. Bush in 1992. Greenspan was reappointed chairman by President BILL CLINTON to four-year terms in 1996 and 2000.

The Federal Reserve Board is composed of seven members, each appointed by the president, confirmed by the Senate. Each member serves a 14-year term. The board features a chairman and a vice chairman, each appointed by the president for a four-year term, which can be renewed. As chairman of the Federal Reserve, Greenspan oversaw two committees: the Board of Governors, which handles regulation and administrative matters, and the Federal Open Market Committee, which sets the interest rates charged by the government for loans to banks.

Throughout his tenure at the Federal Reserve Board, Greenspan pursued a tight-money policy in order to combat inflation and encourage full employment. When the Dow Jones Industrial average fell by 508 points on October 19, 1987, Greenspan reassured the financial markets that the Federal Reserve Board would provide rate changes to spur the economy.

Greenspan married NBC news reporter Andrea Mitchell in 1997 after a 12-year relationship.

—SAW

H

Hill, Anita F.
(1956–) *staff member, Department of Education and Equal Employment Opportunity Commission; professor of law*

Anita Hill was born in Lone Tree, Oklahoma. She earned her bachelor's degree from Oklahoma State University in 1977. She then entered Yale University, taking her law degree in 1980. Upon her graduation from Yale, Hill joined Ward, Hardraker, and Rose (Washington, D.C.). In 1981, she left the practice of law, and became assistant to CLARENCE THOMAS, then the assistant secretary for civil rights at the U.S. Department of Education. When Thomas was named chairman of the Equal Employment Opportunity Commission (EEOC), Hill followed him to that post as a member of his legal staff. In January 1983, Hill left the EEOC for a faculty position at Oral Roberts University; subsequently, she joined the law faculty at the University of Oklahoma.

On October 23, 1991, President George H. W. Bush nominated Thomas to the Supreme Court. In corroborating depositions to the FBI, Hill charged that Thomas had, at both the Department of Education and the EEOC, sexually harassed her. Portions of those depositions were leaked to the press by Democratic staffers on the Senate Judiciary Committee, and the ensuing media firestorm brought the hearings to a halt. On October 11, 1991, Hill testified before the Judiciary Committee. In her testimony, Hill claimed that Thomas had asked her to go out socially with him, when he engaged in what she termed as "vivid" sexual conversations. Hill was questioned rigorously about her decision, despite her claims of harassment, to follow Thomas from the Education Department to the EEOC; Hill explained her actions, saying that she had "faced the realistic fact that [I] had no alternative job." Despite her testimony, Thomas was confirmed by the Senate on October 15, 1991.

Hill is presently a member of the law faculty at Brandeis University, and she has written a memoir of her role in the Thomas confirmation battle, *Speaking Truth to Power* (1997).

Hills, Carla
(1934–) *U.S. trade representative*

Carla Hills was born in Los Angeles, California, earned her bachelor's degree from Stanford University and her law degree in 1958 from Yale University. In 1962, she cofounded the law firm of Munger, Tolles, and Hills (Los Angeles), where she was a partner until 1974. From 1974 to 1975, she served as assistant attorney general in the Civil Division. In 1975, Hills was chosen by Gerald Ford to serve as secretary of housing and urban development, becoming only the third woman to hold a cabinet position. During the Reagan administration, Hills held a number of key committee positions, including service as the vice chairman of Reagan's Commission on Housing (1981–82) and as a member of the President's Commission on Defense Management (1985–86).

In 1989, George H. W. Bush appointed Hills to the post of U.S. Trade Representative (USTR), with cabinet rank. In this position, Hills became the administration's lead negotiator of the North American Free Trade Agreement (NAFTA).

Hills is presently the chairman and CEO of Hills and Company, an international consulting firm.

Hussein, Saddam
(1937–   ) *president of Iraq*

Saddam Hussein was born on April 28, 1937. He spent his childhood living in a mud hut in the village of Al-Awja in the District of Iraq. Hussein never knew his father; his mother remarried a man named Ibrahim al Hassan, who treated Hussein harshly and forced him to participate in stealing. In 1947, at the age of 10, Saddam moved to Baghdad to live with his uncle, Khairallah Tulfah, whose hatred of British imperialism rubbed off on Saddam. Saddam finished intermediate school at the age of 16 and sought admission to the prestigious Baghdad Military Academy, but he was rejected because of poor grades.

In 1956, Hussein participated in an unsuccessful coup attempt against the monarchy of King Faisal II. Joining the Ba'ath Party, a radical nationalist movement, Hussein earned his reputation for brutality; his first murder was reportedly at the age of 19. Hussein was also involved in a plot against the Iraqi prime minister in 1959. The assassination plot failed and Hussein fled to Syria and then to Cairo, Egypt, where he finished high school and continued his higher education at the University of Cairo Law School. He would later be granted a degree in law from the University of Baghdad in 1968.

Hussein rose quickly through the ranks of the radical nationalist movement. When the Ba'athist Party split in 1963, Hussein was appointed a member of the Ba'ath regional command, but he was soon arrested for his revolutionary activities. Escaping a jail term for life, in 1966 Hussein created the Ba'athist internal party security system. In 1968, the Ba'athists seized the government and Hussein was made the deputy chairman of the Revolutionary Command Council, in charge of internal security. He slowly began to consolidate his power over Iraqi's government and the Ba'ath Party structure. By the age of 31, he had risen to the second highest position of authority in the Ba'athist party, a position he held for a decade, appointing numerous family members to important posts in the Iraqi government.

On July 16, 1979, the president of the Nationalist Party either resigned or was eliminated by Hussein. In either case, Hussein was now the supreme leader of the country. In 1980, Hussein ordered a surprise cross-border attack on Iran. Intended as a swift operation to capture the Shatt al Arab waterway leading to the Persian Gulf, Iranian resistance was far stronger than Hussein had imagined. After eight years of bloodshed the battle ended with a cease-fire between Iraq and Iran. During the war, Iraq borrowed a great deal of money from Western powers, including the United States, and other Arab states. Indeed, Hussein felt that the war had been fought for the benefit of other Arab states in the region as much as for Iraq; consequently, all Iraqi debts should be forgiven. In the late 1980s, neighboring

Kuwait began drilling oil from wells that Iraq considered within its borders. In 1990, Hussein complained to the U.S. Department of State about Kuwait's land drilling, but to no avail. Hussein ordered troops to the Iraqi/Kuwait border. American officials indicated that they would not interfere in any border disputes between the two nations, and Hussein understood this to mean that America would not oppose an invasion of Kuwait. Hussein subsequently ordered the invasion of his small neighbor on August 2, 1990.

President George H. W. Bush surprised Hussein by calling for a coalition of world leaders to oppose Iraqi aggression. By the end of August some 80,000 coalition troops had assembled in Saudi Arabia, an operation known as Desert Shield. On September 2, Hussein urged Iraqi citizens to prepare for the "mother of all wars." The United Nations responded to the crisis in passing Security Council Resolution 678, which denounced the Iraqi invasion and called for an immediate evacuation of Iraqi troops from Kuwait, to be completed by January 15, 1991. On November 19, 1990, Hussein added another 250,000 troops; his total military contingent now stood at 680,000 troops. When Hussein missed the UN-imposed deadline, Bush initiated Operation Desert Storm, starting with an aerial bombardment of Iraqi targets and following with use of ground troops. Within 100 hours of moving in ground troops, Kuwait was liberated and the Iraqi military stood in ruins. Hussein, however, remained in power.

Following the Persian Gulf War, Hussein used helicopters—allowed under the terms of the cease-fire—to brutally repress revolts within his nation, particularly among the Kurds in northern Iraq. Hussein spent almost a decade of blunting UN demands to inspect and, if found, have destroyed, any weapons of mass destruction held by the regime. After the September 11, 2001, terrorist attack against the United States, President GEORGE W. BUSH accused Hussein's Iraq of being a "terrorist state." Determined to combat terrorism and convinced the dictator posed a threat, the United States invaded Iraq in March 2003. About three weeks after the beginning of the invasion, the Iraqi government collapsed, and, by April 19, Hussein disappeared. He was captured in what was called Operation Red Dawn by coalition forces on December 14, 2003, in an underground "spider hole" at a farmhouse in al-Dawn near his hometown. At the time of his capture he was armed with a pistol but offered no resistance. He awaits trial.

—AW

J

Jackson, Jesse
(1941–) *director, Rainbow Coalition; Democratic Party candidate for president*

Born in Greenville, South Carolina, Jesse Jackson attended the University of Illinois from 1959 to 1960 on a football scholarship. He then transferred to North Carolina A&T State University at Greensboro, where he took his B.A. in sociology in 1964 and, as a senior, began to take an active part in the civil rights movement in the South. He then enrolled at Chicago Theological Seminary and was ordained a Baptist minister in 1968. But he delayed his full-time studies to work full-time in the movement (he would receive a Master's of Divinity degree from Chicago Theological Seminary in 2000). In 1965, Jackson joined the Southern Christian Leadership Conference (SCLC), where he worked closely with Reverend Martin Luther King. In 1966, Jackson founded the Chicago branch of Operation Breadbasket—the economic wing of SCLC. While some controversy still exists as to whether or not Jackson was the last man to talk to King alive, it is certain that he was with King in Memphis, Tennessee, at the time of King's assassination on April 4, 1968.

In 1971, Jackson was suspended from the SCLC when its leaders claimed he was using that organization as a platform for his own ambitions. Later that year, Jackson founded Operation PUSH (People United to Save Humanity) in Chicago, and, in 1984, he founded the National Rainbow Coalition in Washington, D.C., an organization wedded to reform within the Democratic Party. The two organizations merged in 1996 to form the Rainbow/PUSH Coalition.

Jackson's first campaign for the Democratic nomination for the presidency in 1984 was credited with registering over 1 million new voters. However, he lost that campaign; he made several fatal mistakes, including his reference to New York City as "Hymietown." In 1988, another million voters were registered, as Jackson once again sought the presidency. After scoring several impressive early victories, Jackson lost ground to MICHAEL DUKAKIS, the eventual nominee. Nevertheless, Jackson did not withdraw from the race until the convention.

Following the 1988 election, Jackson redirected his political energies toward the District of Columbia. In 1989, he floated some trial balloons in advance of a possible run for mayor of Washington, but he later decided against the race. In 1991, Jackson became one of two "shadow senators" for the District of Columbia, in effect, a lobbyist for statehood. In 1992, he supported BILL CLINTON for the presidency. From 1992 to 2000, he hosted *Both Sides with Jesse Jackson* on CNN. In 1999, he helped get the release of three American military prisoners in Yugoslavia. In 2000, Clinton awarded Jackson the Presidential Medal of Freedom.

K

Kemp, Jack F.

(1935–) *Republican Party candidate for president, secretary of housing and urban development*

Born in Los Angeles, Jack Kemp earned his B.A. in physical education from Occidental College in 1957. From 1958 to 1962, he served in the U.S. Army Reserve. From 1960 to 1962, Kemp was the quarterback and team captain of the San Diego Chargers of the American Football League (AFL). In 1962, he was traded to the Buffalo Bills of the AFL. He led his team to the league championship in 1964 and 1965, and, in 1965, he was named the league's Most Valuable Player. In 1970, Kemp was elected to the U.S. House of Representatives from Buffalo, where he served until 1989. During his tenure, Kemp served seven years as chairman of the House Republican Leadership Conference.

In 1988, Kemp ran for the Republican nomination for the presidency, but he lost to George H. W. Bush. In 1989, Bush chose Kemp to serve as his secretary of housing and urban development (HUD). At HUD, Kemp emerged as the administration's leading advocate for the creation of Enterprise Zones, an innovative concept designed to foster inner-city economic development.

In 1996, Kemp ran unsuccessfully as ROBERT DOLE's running mate on the Republican ticket. Kemp presently serves on the board of directors of Empower America, a public policy organization cofounded in 1993 by Kemp and WILLIAM BENNETT, Jeane Kirkpatrick, and Vin Weber.

King, Glen ("Rodney")

(1965–)

Glen King was born in Sacramento, California. (Although his given name is Glen, during the 1991–92 events he was mistakenly identified in the press as Rodney King, and the name stuck.) A former usher at Dodger Stadium, King had an extensive list of run-ins with the law, including a robbery conviction for which, in 1991, he was on probation.

On March 3, 1991, after being observed driving erratically, King was pulled over by members of the Los Angeles Police Department (LAPD) after a 7.8-mile car chase. Later tests would show that King had both alcohol and marijuana in his blood. When ordered to get out of the car, King refused; he then charged the officers. The police attempted to subdue King with stun guns, but they were twice unsuccessful. They then struck him 56 times with their nightsticks. Three officers administered the beatings while some 24 other officers either watched or assisted. The beatings were captured on videotape by George Holliday, an amateur photographer, and the 68-second tape (the entire incident was 81 seconds long) was soon released nationwide. Many denounced the action as an example of police brutality by the LAPD.

On March 15, 1992, four officers (Laurence Powell, Stacey Koon, Theodore Briseno, and Timothy Wind) were charged with assault and with filing false police reports. After a trial that received national attention (during his testimony, King claimed that he did not believe that the officers beat him because he was black), on April 29 a jury of 10 whites, one Hispanic, and one Asian found the officers innocent on all charges.

President Bush, clearly as astounded at the verdict as were many others, released a statement saying that the decision "has left us all with a deep sense of personal frustration and anguish." That anguish exploded in the streets of Los Angeles within hours of the verdict. Four days of rioting in South Central Los Angeles left 55 people dead, 2,383 injured, 8,000 arrested, and $1 billion in property damages. King pleaded on live television for the rioting to stop, uttering the now-famous plea, "Can't we all just get along?" In an attempt to quell the riots, Bush announced that he would charge the officers with a violation of King's civil rights. King was eventually awarded $3.8 million in the civil suit that ensued, and two of the officers spent 30 months in federal prison.

In 1997, King started a record label, "Straight Alta Pazz." In 1999, he was convicted of spousal abuse and sentenced to 90 days in jail. In 2001, he plead guilty to several counts of drug use and indecent exposure, and he was ordered to undergo counseling treatments. In 2003, he was once again charged with domestic abuse.

L

Lujan, Manuel, Jr.
(1928–) *secretary of the interior*

Born in San Idlefonso, New Mexico, Manuel Lujan earned a B.A. from the College of Santa Fe in 1950. For the next decade, he worked in the insurance business. In 1964, Lujan was defeated for election as a state senator. Four years later, however, he was elected a member of the U.S. House of Representatives. Lujan retained his seat in the House for 21 years, serving on, among other committees, the Interior and Insular Affairs Committee. As a result, Lujan became the longest serving Republican House member in New Mexico's history.

In 1978, Lujan was one of the first congressmen to declare his support for George H. W. Bush for president. Given the appointment of WILLIAM K. REILLY, a professional environmentalist, as director of the Environmental Protection Agency, conservatives wanted a more doctrinaire conservative for secretary of the interior. This may well have been the deciding factor in Bush's choice of Lujan for that position.

From the beginning of his tenure, Lujan was criticized for his lack of engagement in, and surprisingly weak knowledge of, environmental issues. As a rule, the administration preferred to dispatch Secretary of Transportation SAMUEL SKINNER as its frontline representative to environmental crises, such as the *Exxon Valdez* oil spill in Alaska.

Following his tenure in the Bush White House, Lujan founded Manuel Lujan Associates, a consulting firm.

M

Madigan, Edward
(1936–1994) *secretary of agriculture*

Edward Madigan was born in Lincoln, Illinois. In 1955, he earned an A.A. degree in business from Lincoln Junior College, and, for the next decade, he managed the family business, a cab company. In 1966, he was elected to the Illinois House of Representatives; in 1972, he was elected to the U.S. House of Representatives. During his tenure in the House, he served as the ranking Republican member of the Agriculture Committee. In March 1991, Madigan resigned from the House when George H. W. Bush appointed him to serve as his second secretary of Agriculture (replacing CLAYTON YEUTTER). Madigan's short tenure in the cabinet was highlighted by his role in negotiating several trade agreements for the administration. Madigan died in Springfield, Illinois, on December 7, 1994.

Malek, Frederic
(1936–) *director, 1988 Republican National Convention (New Orleans); director, Economic Summit of Industrialized Nations; campaign manager for George H. W. Bush*

Born in Berwyn, Illinois, Fred Malek graduated from the U.S. Military Academy in 1959, fol-

lowing which he served as an airborne ranger officer with the Special Forces (Green Berets) in Vietnam. He also received his M.B.A. from Harvard University in 1964. From 1975 to 1988, Malek worked for Marriott Hotels, becoming its president in 1982. Malek entered the Nixon administration as deputy under secretary of health, education, and welfare. In 1970, he became a special assistant to Nixon, with responsibility for recruiting positions in the executive office. In 1972, he served as deputy campaign manager for the Committee to Reelect the President. He then served as deputy director of the Office of Management and Budget under President Nixon and President Ford.

In 1988, Malek served as the director of the Republican National Convention in New Orleans. Immediately following the convention, Malek was named as Frank Fahrenkopf's deputy at the Republican National Committee. However, he was forced to resign after it was revealed that, while in the Nixon White House, upon the request of the president, he had made a list of the number of Jews who were then working at the Bureau of Labor Statistics. In July 1990, Malek directed the Economic Summit of Industrialized Nations (the G-7 meeting), for which service he earned the rank of ambassador. From 1989 to 1991, he served as president and vice chairman of Northwest Airlines. In 1992, Malek

President Bush meets with Frederic Malek in the Oval Office, February 1, 1990.

once again returned to national politics as a campaign manager for the unsuccessful reelection campaign of George H. W. Bush.

Following his service to the Bush administration, Malek founded Thayer Capital Partners, a merchant bank in Washington, D.C., where he serves as its president and CEO. He was also a former partner in the Texas Rangers Major League Baseball Team with GEORGE W. BUSH, and he spearheaded a successful effort to bring major league baseball back to the Washington, D.C., area.

Martin, Lynn (Morley)
(1939–) *secretary of labor*

Born in Evanston, Illinois, Lynn Martin took her bachelor's degree from the University of Illinois in 1960. She then worked as a high school teacher of economics, government, and English. In 1972, she was elected to the Winnebago County Board, where she served until 1976. That year, she was elected to the Illinois House of Representatives. In 1979, she was elected to the Illinois State Senate, and, in 1980, she was elected to the U.S. House of Representatives. When she was elected vice chair of the House Republican Conference, she became the first woman elected to a congressional leadership post. In 1990, she did not stand for reelection to the House; rather, she ran an unsuccessful campaign for the Republican nomination for the U.S. Senate.

In February 1991, George H. W. Bush nominated Martin to serve as his second secretary of labor (replacing ELIZABETH DOLE in the post). In her short tenure at the Department of Labor, Martin developed "Job Training 2000," a youth employment program. She also championed efforts to place women into nontraditional jobs, and she established a commission to investigate attitudes toward women in the modern workplace.

Presently residing in Chicago, Martin is the chair of Deloitte and Touche's Council on the Advancement of Women.

Michel, Robert H(enry)
(1923–) member of the House of Representatives

Robert Michel was born in Peoria, Illinois. He graduated from Bradley University in 1948, then served in the European theater with the U.S. Army during World War II, winning two Bronze Stars, a Purple Heart, and four battle stars. From 1948 to 1956, Michel served as an administrative aide to Congressman Harold Velde. In 1956, he was elected to the U.S. House of Representatives from Illinois's 18th Congressional District, where he would serve for the next 39 years. In 1975, he was elected House minority whip. During that period, from 1972 to 1974, he served as the chairman of the Republican Congressional Campaign Committee. In 1981, he was elected House Minority Leader. As leader of the minority during the Bush administration, Michel was a consistent loyalist, particularly effective in gaining support and passage for the congressional resolution in support of the Persian Gulf War.

In 1995, rather than risk a divisive public battle with NEWT GINGRICH (R-Ga.) for the House leadership, Michel retired from Congress. He joined Hogan and Hartson, a Washington, D.C., law firm, as a senior adviser on corporate and governmental affairs. In 1994, he was presented with the Presidential Medal of Freedom by President BILL CLINTON.

Mitchell, George
(1925–) member of the Senate

Born in Waterville, Maine, George Mitchell took his B.A. from Bowdoin College in 1954. After a two-year stint in the U.S. Army, he earned his law degree from Georgetown University Law Center in 1960. From 1960 to 1962, Mitchell worked for the U.S. Attorney General's office in the Antitrust Department, and, from 1962 to 1965, he was the chief aide to Senator Edmund Muskie (D-Maine). From 1965 to 1977, Mitchell practiced law in Maine. During that time, he served as the state chairman for the Maine Democratic Party, and he also served as a Democratic national committeeman from 1969 to 1977. In 1974, Mitchell was defeated in a race for governor of Maine. In 1977, he was appointed U.S. attorney for Maine, and, in 1979, he was appointed a U.S. district judge.

In 1980, when President Jimmy Carter chose Muskie to serve as his secretary of state, Mitchell was appointed to complete Muskie's unexpired term in the Senate. In 1982, Mitchell was elected to the seat in his own right. Propelled into the national limelight by his service on the Select Committee on the Iran-contra affair in 1987 (where he held a national viewing audience spellbound as he reminded Oliver North that "God does not take sides in American politics"), Mitchell was chosen Senate Majority Leader in January 1989.

Mitchell began his relationship with the George H. W. Bush administration by leading the fight to deny JOHN TOWER Senate approval as the new secretary of defense. Yet Mitchell would be key to the passage of many of the administration's legislative successes, including the Clean Air Act Amendments (1990) and the Americans with Disabilities Act (1990). He was also instrumental in stewarding the Omnibus Budget Reconciliation Act of 1990 (which called for new revenue measures that reversed Bush's pledge—"read my lips"—not to raise taxes) through Congress. However, following the invasion of Kuwait by SADDAM HUSSEIN, Mitchell sponsored an antiwar resolution in the Senate, only to see it defeated 52 to 47.

For six consecutive years, congressional aides voted Mitchell the "most respected member" of the Senate. In 1994, following the retirement of Justice Harry A. Blackmun, President BILL CLINTON attempted to convince Mitchell to accept a nomination to the U.S. Supreme Court; Mitchell, however, declined. Following his retirement from the Senate in 1995, Mitchell joined the law firm of Verner, Liipfert, Bernhard, McPherson, and Hand (Washington, D.C.). In 1995, Clinton chose Mitchell to chair peace negotiations in Northern Ireland, culminating in the "Good Friday" peace accord of 1998, which was approved by a vote of the Irish people, both North and South. His honors include the Presidential Medal of Freedom.

Mosbacher, Robert A(dam)
(1927–   ) *secretary of commerce*

Born in White Plains, New York, Robert Mosbacher earned his bachelor's degree from Washington and Lee University (Virginia) in 1947. Immediately upon graduation, he left for Texas, became an oil and gas wildcatter, and, in 1954, found a field of natural gas in southern Texas that made him a millionaire. He founded and chaired the Mosbacher Energy Company of Houston, Texas, and he served as both a member and a chairman (1984–85) of the National Petroleum Council.

Mosbacher was also deeply involved in Republican Party politics as well as one of the party's leading fund-raisers. A close friend of George H. W. Bush, he served as the national finance chairman for the President Ford Committee (1976), general chairman of the Repub-

lican National Committee, and both the general chairman and the national finance chairman for the George Bush for President Committee in 1988. In that position, he raised some $75 million for his friend.

In December 1988, George H. W. Bush appointed Mosbacher to the post of secretary of commerce, where he was instrumental in negotiations to secure the North American Free Trade Agreement (NAFTA). In December 1991, Mosbacher resigned in order to chair, along with Robert Teeter and FRED MALEK, the unsuccessful Bush reelection effort (he was succeeded at the Department of Commerce by BARBARA HACKMAN FRANKLIN).

Following his tenure in the Bush administration, Mosbacher returned to the private sector to chair both the Mosbacher Energy Company and the Mosbacher Power Group (both in Houston, Texas).

Mubarak, Muhammad Hosni
(1928–   ) *president of Egypt*

Hosni Mubarak was born in Kafr-al Mehelsa in the Delta region of Egypt; his father was an inspector in the Egyptian Ministry of Justice. Mubarak graduated from the Egyptian Military Academy in 1949 (taking a B.A. in military science). In 1950, he took a second bachelor's degree from the Egyptian Air Force Academy in aviation sciences. Mubarak rose through the ranks of the Egyptian air force, serving first as a flight instructor, then as the director of the Air Force Academy, and finally as air force chief of staff from 1969 to 1972. He then became the commander of the air force, and he emerged a national hero for his tactical expertise during the 1973 Yom Kippur War against Israel. In 1975, he was named vice president of Egypt, serving under President Anwar Sadat. Following Sadat's 1981 assassination, Mubarak became president of Egypt.

In 1990, immediately prior to Iraq's invasion of Kuwait, Mubarak stood in the forefront of efforts to achieve a negotiated settlement to differences between Iraq and the United States. Following Iraq's invasion of Kuwait, Mubarak continued to try to broker a peaceful end to the crisis, believing SADDAM HUSSEIN's goal to be a quick surgical strike for public relations purposes, and then an equally quick withdrawal. Mubarak withdrew from that process when Hussein offered Egypt a share of Kuwait's oil and the treasure that was looted from that country in return for Egypt's support for the invasion. Mubarak refused, and he became one of the Arab world's most vocal supporters of UN sanctions against Iraq. He was instrumental in coordinating a condemnation of the invasion by the Arab League, one that committed a pan-Arab force to defend Saudi Arabia. For its part, Egypt sent some 38,500 troops to fight in Operation Desert Storm. Mubarak was also instrumental in arranging a meeting between George H. W. Bush and Syrian president Hafez al-Assad in Geneva, Switzerland, in November 1991.

Following the war, Mubarak emerged as an outspoken, persistent voice in favor of a long-term peace accord in the Middle East. He survived a June 1995 assassination attempt, and he was subsequently accused of suppressing

President and Mrs. Bush with President and Mrs. Hosni Mubarak of Egypt at the White House, April 4, 1989

opposition to his government by the Muslim Brotherhood, a fundamentalist Islamic group. In 1999, Mubarak was reelected to a fourth six-year term.

N

Noonan, Margaret "Peggy"
(1950–) *head speechwriter*

Born in New York City, Peggy Noonan worked her way through Fairleigh Dickenson University as a waitress while earning her bachelor's degree in English, cum laude. She was the editor of the student newspaper in college, and she began her professional career as a writer at WEEI-AM in Boston (CBS), where she soon became its editorial and public affairs director. She then moved to CBS News in New York, where she worked as a producer and a writer for Dan Rather's daily radio show.

In 1984, Noonan began a two-year stint as special assistant to President Ronald Reagan, where she became widely known as Reagan's favorite speechwriter. She was perhaps best known for her writing of Reagan's 1986 eulogy of the *Challenger* astronauts (they had "slipped the surly bonds of earth to touch the face of God"). In 1986, she resigned, later citing differences with Chief of Staff Donald Regan.

Technically in retirement, Noonan worked with then vice president George H. W. Bush on the 1987 speech that announced his candidacy for the Republican nomination for the presidency. She then joined the campaign full-time during the New Hampshire primary. Noonan penned Bush's acceptance speech to the Republican National Convention, which included the memorable phrases a "thousand points of light" and a "kinder, gentler nation" (Noonan remembered in her memoir of the period that the phrase came to her after reading a note from Bush describing his motivation in politics as being "I know what drives me . . . everyone matters"), and "read my lips—no new taxes" (a phrase that Noonan defended as "definite. It's not subject to misinterpretation. It means, 'I mean this'."). Noonan penned Bush's inaugural address, but she did not choose to join the White House speechwriting staff. However, she was the primary author of Bush's 1992 State of the Union Address, and she came back to the Bush reelection campaign as a speechwriter in April 1992.

Noonan presently lives in Brooklyn, New York, and she continues to be a frequent guest on political talk shows as well as an adviser to NBC's *The West Wing*. She is also a contributing editor to the *Wall Street Journal* and was nominated for an Emmy Award for her writing of a post-9/11 television special.

Noriega, Manuel Antonio
(1934–) *military leader of Panama*

Noriega was born in Panama City, and briefly educated at the Military School de Chorrillos in Peru. When he returned to his native country in 1967, he joined the Panamanian National Guard, and he participated in the 1968 coup that overthrew the government of Arnulfo Arias and placed in power Omar Torrijos, whom Noriega served as head of Panamanian Intelligence. Noriega oversaw the office in charge of dealing with opponents of the government, and he performed the task with gusto, brutalizing and imprisoning any of the regime's opponents—particularly peasant guerrillas in western Panama. By the time of Torijos's 1981 death in a plane crash, Noriega had emerged as the de facto military leader of Panama; after free elections were held in 1984, he saw to it that the winner of the Panamanian presidency, an outspoken opponent of Noriega, was removed from power. Carried out over the protest of the United States, the U.S. opposition would later smack of hypocrisy when it was learned that, since his college years, Noriega had been in the employ of the Central Intelligence Agency and the U.S. Army as well as other foreign powers, particularly Cuba, supplying them with information for hire (he had been paid some $322,000 in cash and gifts). It was also well known that he was active in the international drug trade. In 1983, Noriega assumed command of the Panamanian military, and, by 1988, Reagan administration officials were pushing for Noriega to step down, even to the point of securing an indictment against him by the Drug Enforcement Agency (DEA) on February 4, 1988, on drug charges, and placing economic sanctions against Panama.

On May 7, 1989, Noriega nullified yet another election—this time, one in which the voters had ousted him from power. President George H. W. Bush called for Noriega to step down, but the Panamanian leader responded by sending his personal guard—the "Dignity Battalions"—to beat and bloody his deposed opponent in the street. Outraged, Bush immediately ordered an additional 2,000 troops to the Canal Zone, and he ordered the formation of a military plan to oust Noriega from power. At the same time, Bush prepared American public opinion for an invasion, charging in a May 14 speech at Mississippi State University that "the will of the people should not be thwarted by this man and his Doberman thugs." For his part, Noriega was quietly defiant—he labeled a target on his pistol range "Bush," and he was seen shooting several bullets through the human form on the target.

However, at this point, the Bush national security machinery was not yet equipped to deal effectively with Noriega; the administration handled the October 2, 1989, attempted coup against Noriega, headed by Major Moises Giroldi Vega, tentatively, eventually refusing to send in military help and sacrificing Giroldi, who was tortured and killed as the coup disintegrated. Learning a bitter lesson about both Noriega's intentions and the lack of administration preparedness to overthrow his government, the Bush White House weathered the storm of criticism that appeared in the press following the aborted coup and fine-tuned an invasion scenario, codenamed Operation Blue Spoon. Reacting to the pressure, on December 15, 1989, Noriega publicly declared that a state of war existed between Panama and the United States.

The next day, December 16, 1989, a U.S. Navy lieutenant and his wife, stationed in Panama City, were detained by Noriega's soldiers; both were blindfolded, kicked, and beaten. Less than an hour later, at the same checkpoint, four soldiers were detained by the same soldiers. One, Lieutenant Robert Paz, was shot, and he died soon after arriving at a nearby hospital. Bush ordered the invasion scenario—now codenamed Operation Just Cause—to commence. On December 20, Guillermo Endara was sworn in as president;

15 minutes later, American paratroopers descended on Panama City; 24,000 troops would follow. By the next morning, the city was in American hands. However, it took several more weeks to capture the wily Noriega, who, on Christmas Eve, took refuge in the home of the papal nuncio, the official representative of the pope in Panama. It took two weeks to dislodge Noriega, using a mixture of negotiation and threat, and employing such means as playing loud volume rock and roll music outside the nunciature. He surrendered to the Americans on January 2, 1990.

Noriega was whisked to Miami to stand trial on his 1988 indictment for racketeering, drug trafficking, and money laundering. In April 1992, he was convicted on all eight counts, and he is serving a 40-year sentence at a federal penitentiary in Miami. He is eligible for parole in 2006.

P

Perot, H(enry) Ross

(1930–) *Reform Party candidate for president*

Born on June 27, 1930, in Texarkana, Texas, Ross Perot was raised in Texarkana and attended Texarkana Junior College. In 1949 he entered the U.S. Naval Academy and graduated in 1953. After graduation, Perot served at sea for four years on a destroyer and an aircraft carrier.

In 1962, Perot founded a data processing company, using a $1,000 loan from his wife. He had been a salesman for IBM (1957–62) when he founded his data processing company. The company, Electronic Data Systems (EDS), became a multibillion-dollar business employing 70,000 people. Perot sold his company to General Motors in 1984 for $2.5 billion. The ownership that he retained in the business made him the largest individual stockholder in General Motors and gave him a seat on the board of directors. Perot resigned from the board in 1986 in a dispute, and General Motors subsequently bought out Perot's stock for $700 million. In 1988, Perot founded another computer service company, Perot Systems. He became involved with the Department of Defense in 1969, when he joined a project on securing the release of prisoners of war in Vietnam. Perot received the Medal for Distinguished Public Service from the Department of Defense for his efforts. Ten years later he again became involved in a military issue, this time in financing a private rescue mission for two EDS employees taken hostage by the Iranian government in 1979. The mission was led by retired Green Beret colonel Arthur "Bull" Simons. Perot went into Iran with the rescue mission and pulled the two EDS employees from prison. The rescue was later chronicled in a book, *On Wings of Eagles*, by Ken Follett.

Perot began a presidential campaign early in 1992 as an unaffiliated candidate who pledged to remain independent and to personally finance his campaign. Reportedly, Perot disliked President George H. W. Bush, because he believed that Bush, as vice president under Ronald Reagan, had not done enough to support efforts to find missing POWs in Vietnam. Perot, a native Texan, also believed that Bush was actually a resident of Washington, D.C., whose claim of residency in Texas was made solely on the basis of a rented hotel suite in Houston.

Perot had been unhappy that George H. W. Bush had won the 1988 presidential election and decided in 1992 to challenge Bush in the general election. Perot went on a nationally televised program, *Larry King Live*, and asked that volunteers around the country get signatures to put his name on the ballot. He eventually was placed on enough ballots to run for president and poured $37 million of his own money into the race, receiving 19 percent of the vote in the November election.

Perot might have had a stronger showing in the November election had he not left the race in July 1992 believing that he could not win. He also claimed that the Democratic Party had been revitalized and could win the election. Perot reentered the race in October 1992 after polls showed that voters liked Perot's status as an "outsider." Clinton chose not to mount an active campaign against Perot, opting instead to stress his own status as an "outsider" but noting that unlike Perot, who lacked a legislative base, he would have the

backing of the Democratic Party to achieve his goals in Congress.

After Bush's loss to Clinton in the 1992 election, Republicans derided Perot for his candidacy. They accused Perot of costing them the election since many Perot voters were conservative Republicans who liked his message of fiscal austerity. But once Clinton took office, Perot shifted his attacks from Bush to Clinton. In 1993, Perot established a watchdog organization called United We Stand to monitor the federal government and the performance of both national parties.

Perot remained highly visible during the first term of the Clinton administration, seeking to maintain a national image for a run for president in 1996. He regularly attacked President Clinton during his first term, most notably in leading an effort to stop the passage of the North American Free Trade Agreement (NAFTA).

In 1995, Perot founded a new political party, the Reform Party, to serve as a springboard for his 1996 presidential election campaign. In 1996, at the Reform Party's national convention, Perot was nominated as the party's candidate for president and won 8 percent of the vote in the November election.

During the 1996 campaign, Perot directed his efforts against President Clinton. Perot often made unpleasant comments about the president, suggesting that he was too corrupt to serve as president and that he couldn't be trusted to babysit one's children. He often commented about President Clinton's personal life, including references to the Paula Corbin Jones allegations of sexual harassment.

After two failed attempts at capturing the Oval Office, it was unclear whether Perot would try again in the 2000 elections. Perot's political party, the Reform Party, had been splintered in the intervening years, with a number of popular politicians seeking to keep Perot out of the national limelight. Minnesota

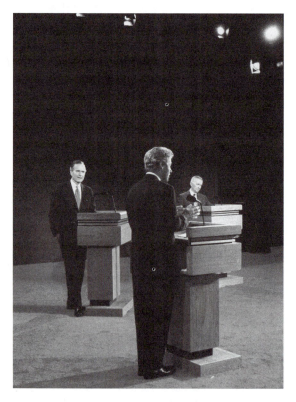

Presidential debate—President Bush, Governor Bill Clinton, and H. Ross Perot, October 19, 1992

governor Jesse Ventura, a member of the Independent Party/Reform Party, became a leader of the anti-Perot wing of the party. After significant internal fighting, the party nominated former Republican activist and Nixon speechwriter Patrick Buchanan as its candidate in 2000. Perot distanced himself from the party at this point. He did not employ another political vehicle to run in 2000 and simply dropped out of the public limelight through the election cycle.

—SAW

Powell, Colin L(uther)
(1937–   ) *chairman, Joint Chiefs of Staff*

Colin Powell was born in Harlem, New York, and grew up in the South Bronx. He entered the City College of New York, where he joined that school's Reserve Officer Training Corps (ROTC), and graduated in 1958 with a bachelor of science degree in geology, and the rank of cadet colonel. Later that year, after completing Officer Candidate School at Fort Benning, Georgia, Powell was commissioned a second lieutenant. He was among the 16,000 military "advisers" sent to Vietnam in 1962 by President John F. Kennedy. He served two tours of duty in Vietnam, was wounded in combat in 1963, and was awarded the Purple Heart and Bronze Star. In his second tour of duty, he survived a helicopter crash in which he pulled his comrades from the wreck. For this act of heroism he was awarded the Soldier's Medal. From 1968 to 1969, he served as the executive officer of a battalion. Following his service in Vietnam, Powell was given several diverse assignments, including command of an infantry battalion in South Korea.

Powell returned to the United States and earned his master's in business administration at George Washington University in 1971. The following year, Powell was given a White House Fellowship, during which he worked at the Office of Management and Budget until 1973. Following the completion of his fellowship, he served as a battalion commander in Korea and as a staffer at the Pentagon. After graduating from the Army War College in 1976 with a promotion to colonel, he commanded a brigade of the 101st Airborne Division at Fort Campbell, Kentucky. Called once again to service in Washington, Powell served as an assistant to both the secretaries of defense and energy under President Jimmy Carter. Following the 1980 victory of Ronald Reagan, Powell once again left Washington—this time to serve as assistant and then deputy commander of infantry divisions in Fort Carson, Colorado, and Fort Leavenworth, Kansas—and once again was recalled to Washington. Powell became senior military assistant to Secretary of Defense Caspar Weinberger. From 1986 to 1987, Powell served as the commander of the U.S. Army Fifth Corps in Europe, but he was once again recalled to Washington in 1987 to join the staff of the National Security Council. When NSC head Frank Carlucci was appointed as secretary of defense, Powell was named Reagan's National Security Advisor, a position he held until 1988. In 1979, he was promoted to Brigadier General; in 1983 to Lieutenant General; and in 1989 to General.

Following his election in 1988, George H. W. Bush offered Powell the post of either director of the Central Intelligence Agency or deputy secretary of state; Powell opted instead to become the commander of U.S. Forces Command, responsible for all field forces in the United States. However, when Admiral William Crowe chose not to seek another term as the Chairman of the Joint Chiefs of Staff (JCS), Secretary of Defense DICK CHENEY and National Security Advisor BRENT SCOWCROFT lobbied hard for Powell. In August 1989 Bush named Powell the chairman of the JCS, the first African American to serve at that post.

Colin Powell *(Library of Congress)*

In the first three months of his chairmanship, Powell dealt with two attempted coups and directed an American military invasion. Powell's chairmanship was only one day old when he learned of an attempted military coup against Panamanian strongman MANUEL NOR-IEGA. Caught off guard, the administration did nothing to help the coup, and its leaders were captured and killed. Facing intense media and political criticism, the administration was loath to refuse to react during the next crisis, which came in November 1989 with the attempted coup against CORAZON AQUINO in the Philippines. Powell took active command of the situation (Bush was at the Malta Summit with Soviet leader MIKHAIL GORBACHEV) and ordered U.S. planes to fly low and buzz the rebel planes on the ground—a show of force that helped quell the revolt.

The following month, matters once again came to a head in Panama, as Noriega invalidated the results of a free election, had members of the opposing party publicly beaten, detained and abused American soldiers and their wives, and oversaw the killing of an American soldier by his personal guard. Powell, who allegedly had argued earlier against the use of military power in Panama, believing such action would fail to dislodge Noriega and would cost the Panamanian citizenry too many lives, now recommended implementing the previously planned Operation Blue Spoon (renamed Operation Just Cause). Bush ordered the invasion plan to begin on December 20. Within 24 hours, Noriega had been chased from power; he was captured by American forces on January 3, 1990.

Following the August 2, 1990, invasion of Kuwait by Iraqi dictator SADDAM HUSSEIN, Powell argued in council against the administration's predilection for evicting Hussein by force from Kuwait in favor of giving economic sanctions an opportunity to work. However, following the successful completion of Operation Desert Storm, he became a national hero. Indeed, as the 1992 election approached, Democrats quietly approached him to see if he was interested in running as a Democrat—he refused.

Following his service in the Bush White House, Powell stayed on as head of the JCS, publicly disagreeing with President BILL CLIN-TON over his plan to allow gay men and gay women to serve in the military. Powell stepped down from the JCS in 1993, and was consistently listed in the press as a potential front-runner for the Republican presidential nomination in 1996. However, after testing the waters, he refused to allow his name to be submitted as a candidate, citing family obligations. In 2000, he was chosen by President GEORGE W. BUSH to serve as his secretary of state; in November 2004, he resigned that position.

Q

Quayle, J. Danforth (Dan)
(1947–) *vice president of the United States*

Born in Indianapolis, Indiana, Dan Quayle graduated from DePauw University (Greencastle, Indiana) in 1969, and he took his law degree from the University of Indiana in 1974. While attending law school, Quayle served in the Indiana National Guard. Quayle also began his public career while still a student in law school. In 1971 he became an investigator for the Consumer Protection Division of the Indiana Attorney General's Office. He then served as an administrative assistant to the governor of Indiana, and as the director of the Inheritance Tax Division of the Indiana Department of Revenue. Upon graduation from law school, rather than practice law he became associate publisher of the *Huntington Herald Press*, his family's newspaper. In 1976, Quayle was elected to the U.S. House of Representatives, where he served until 1981. In 1980, he rode Ronald Reagan's coattails to victory, and he was elected to the U.S. Senate from Indiana, defeating three-term incumbent Birch Bayh. He was reelected to that office in 1986.

In 1988, George H. W. Bush chose Quayle as his vice presidential running mate—a position for which Quayle had actively lobbied. He filled several significant gaps in Bush's electoral needs—he was young, a true movement conservative, and a Midwesterner. He had also voted against his party an average of only 10 percent of the time while in Congress—a record of party loyalty that impressed Bush. However, Quayle's youthful energy initially worked against him; when Bush introduced his running mate to the press, an all-too-gleeful Quayle put his arm around Bush, pumped his fist in the air, and shouted "Go get 'em!" While this public display of vigor might have simply drawn a few guffaws in the press, when the media probed Quayle's career, they found problems of substance, including evidence that Quayle's joining of the National Guard was simply to avoid going to Vietnam. They also found evidence that Quayle's father had bought his way into law school. When these stories broke, the Bush campaign was at a loss for how to deal with them—they had not properly vetted Quayle, and thus they chose to slide him quietly into the background during the campaign. During the vice presidential debate with Senator LLOYD BENTSEN (D-Tex.), Quayle's perceived lack of maturity was captured by his opponent when Quayle attempted to compare his youth to that of John F. Kennedy ("Senator, I served with Jack Kennedy. I knew Jack Kennedy. Jack Kennedy was a friend of mine. Senator, you are no Jack Kennedy.").

President Bush and Vice President Quayle walk along the colonnade at the White House, March 20, 1992.

While serving as vice president, Quayle made visits to 47 countries. He also chaired the President's Council on Competitiveness and the National Space Council. But his largest contribution to the administration was during the Persian Gulf War. Bush kept his vice president completely in the decision-making loop during the entire conflict, and, by all accounts, Quayle's counsel was both moderate and steady. Bush kept Quayle on the ticket in 1992, and Quayle attempted to carve out a niche for the campaign with those conservative Republicans who had come to feel that they had been abandoned by the Bush administration. In a notable moment, Quayle publicly castigated the fictional television character Murphy Brown for having a baby out of wedlock; to Quayle, this amounted to one more example of the decline of American family values. However, the issue never really caught fire during the campaign, and Quayle's contribution to the defeat of the ticket was negligible.

Following his tenure as vice president, Quayle was mentioned several times as a possible presidential candidate. However, in 1995, facing health issues and encountering difficulty raising the money needed to pursue the nomination, he took himself out of contention.

R

Rehnquist, William H.
(1924–2005) *associate justice of the Supreme Court, chief justice of the Supreme Court*

William Rehnquist was born and raised in Milwaukee, Wisconsin. When World War II began, he enlisted in the U.S. Army Air Corps as a weather observer, serving in North Africa. After the war Rehnquist entered Stanford University and earned his bachelor's degree and his master's degree in political science in 1948. He continued his education at Harvard University where he earned another master's degree in Government in 1950. Rehnquist returned to Stanford Law School in 1950. He earned his law degree and graduated first in his class in 1952. During his two years in law school Rehnquist established himself as a brilliant legal thinker. A professor at Stanford set up a private interview between Rehnquist and Supreme Court justice Robert Jackson in 1952; that same year, Justice Jackson selected Rehnquist for a clerkship. In 1953, Rehnquist moved to Phoenix, Arizona, to work for a law firm.

During his practice of law Rehnquist concentrated mainly on civil litigation. He also took an interest in politics. Following the advice of Justice Felix Frankfurter, Rehnquist joined the Republican Party. He quickly became a party official and established himself as a strong opponent of liberal initiatives. During the 1964 presidential election, he campaigned for Barry Goldwater. He also befriended Richard Kleindienst, a Phoenix lawyer who would be chosen deputy attorney general in the Nixon administration. In 1969 Kleindienst appointed Rehnquist as his deputy attorney general in the Justice Department's Office of Legal Counsel.

In 1971, Supreme Court justice John Marshall Harlan retired from his position, and Nixon nominated Rehnquist for the seat. Rehnquist was affirmed by a 68 to 26 Senate vote. On January 7, 1972, Rehnquist was sworn in as an associate justice. In his early years as a justice on the Supreme Court, Rehnquist often found himself the lone dissenting voice among even the justices. In his most famous dissent, against the majority in *Roe v. Wade* (1973), Rehnquist questioned the use of the definition of privacy as applied by the majority.

On September 25, 1986, President Ronald Reagan nominated Rehnquist to succeed Warren Burger as chief justice of the Supreme Court. Rehnquist was affirmed by a 65 to 33 Senate vote. In the landmark cases that came before the Court during the presidency of

George H. W. Bush, Rehnquist could be counted on as a reliable conservative voice. In *Bethel School District v. Fraser* (1986), for example, Rehnquist, along with five other justices, reversed a ruling of the Washington state court. The state decision held that the First Amendment protects explicit sexual metaphors spoken in public during a school assembly. In a reversal, the Supreme Court affirmed that explicit sexual metaphors spoken in public during a school assembly violate the First Amendment. Chief Justice Rehnquist concurred with this decision.

In *Texas v. Johnson* (1989), the Court ruled that burning an American flag during a protest amounted to a form of symbolic speech protected by the First Amendment. The decision was upheld by a 5 to 4 vote, with Rehnquist voting in opposition. Rehnquist stated in his dissenting opinion that the flag stood as an important symbol of the country and the country's history. He affirmed: "No American symbol has been as universally honored as the flag." For his part, Bush was outraged and called for passage of the Flag Protection Act, which was enacted in 1989. However, the Court held in the case of the *United States v. Eichmann* (1989) that the legislation was unconstitutional in that it violated the right to freedom of expression. Again, Rehnquist dissented.

On the issue of abortion, in 1989, the Court found itself presented with an opportunity to overturn *Roe v. Wade*. Nevertheless, in its decision in *Webster v. Reproductive Health Services of Missouri* (1989), the Court did not fully overturn *Roe*. This particular case revealed Rehnquist's capacity to compromise. The majority ruling, in which Rehnquist concurred, gave the states the right to impose new restrictions on abortion, but it did not reverse the decision that the right of privacy included abortion. Rehnquist pointed out that "states do not have to remain in the business or practice of abortions," in supporting the majority opinion that the *Roe* decision

not be overturned. The ruling—a compromise between liberal and conservative justices—drew the ire of antiabortion activists.

In 1989, the Supreme Court upheld six judicial decisions limiting the rights of employees in the workplace. In *Patterson v. McLean Credit Union* (1989), the Court approved placing limitations on the Civil Rights Act of 1866, which had been used to sue for private acts of racial discrimination. Rehnquist concurred with the decision of the Court. In *Wards Cove Packing Co. v. Atonio* (1989), the Court reversed a decision of the lower court that the employer had to present rebutting evidence of no discrimination in hiring and promotion. All employment records, such as test records for promotion and advancement, must be made available for public use.

After the Bush administration left office, Rehnquist continued his tenure as chief justice. He died in September 2005 from complications of thyroid cancer, becoming the first Supreme Court chief justice to die in office since the 1950s.

—AF

Reilly, William K(ane)
(1940–) *administrator, U.S. Environmental Protection Agency*

Born in Decatur, Illinois, and raised in Massachusetts, William Reilly earned his bachelor's degree in history from Yale University and his law degree from Harvard University in 1965. After two years (1966–67) in the U.S. Army, Reilly took a master's degree in urban planning from Columbia University in 1968.

From 1968 to 1970, Reilly served as associate director of the Urban Policy Center and the National Urban Coalition. In 1970, Reilly was appointed to the staff of the President's Council on Environmental Quality. Two years later,

President Bush signs the Clean Air Act as William Reilly (right) and Secretary of Energy James D. Watkins look on in the Rose Garden of the White House, July 21, 1989.

he was appointed director of the Rockefeller Task Force on Land Use and Urban Growth.

In 1973, he became the president of the Conservation Foundation, a research group that merged with the World Wildlife Fund in 1985, keeping Reilly as its president.

In 1989, George H. W. Bush appointed Reilly to serve as the seventh administrator of the Environmental Protection Agency (EPA). Reilly was the first professional environmentalist to serve at the post. He played a key role in revising the Clean Air Act of 1970, which led to passage of the Clean Air Act Amendments of 1990. He also placed the issue of protection of natural systems—particularly the nation's waterways—at the forefront of the environmental agenda. He oversaw a rapid cleanup at Superfund sites—in 1992 alone, the agency completed a cleanup at a Superfund site every five days. Reilly also led the administration's efforts to spearhead a worldwide environmental plan; he headed the U.S. delegation to the June 1992 Earth Summit in Brazil, and he was an active proponent for the North American Free Trade Agreement (NAFTA). Reilly also urged the business community to find ways to provide emission protections beyond voluntary control standards.

Reilly is presently president and CEO of Aqua International Partners, a firm that invests in water projects and companies in developing countries. He has also continued his work as chairman of the board of the World Wildlife Fund.

Schwarzkopf, Herbert Norman

(1934–) *commander in chief, U.S. Army Central Command*

Norman Schwarzkopf was born in Trenton, New Jersey. His father had attended West Point and served in World Wars I and II. During World War II, Schwarzkopf's father was stationed in Iran, helping to instruct and organize the national police force. The rest of the family joined him there in 1946.

After returning to the United States, Schwarzkopf began to follow in his father's footsteps. First, he attended Valley Forge Military Academy before acceptance into the U.S. Military Academy at West Point. He graduated from West Point in 1956 with a bachelor of science degree in mechanical engineering and was commissioned a second lieutenant. Next, he received advanced infantry and airborne training as an executive officer at the 2nd Airborne Battle Group at Fort Benning, Georgia. He held assignments in the United States and also in Germany, including the 101st Airborne Division in Kentucky, the 6th Infantry Division in West Germany, and as an aide-de-camp to the Berlin command in 1960 and 1961.

Upon returning to the United States, Schwarzkopf resumed his education. He attended the University of Southern California

and earned a master's degree in mechanical engineering. In 1965 he returned to West Point to teach. Volunteering for service in Vietnam, Schwarzkopf earned a Purple Heart. After his return he served on the West Point faculty for another two years. In 1969, after earning an early promotion to lieutenant colonel, he returned for another tour of duty in Vietnam. Winning three Silver Stars and having been wounded several times, Schwarzkopf returned to the United States in 1971 in a hip-to-shoulder body cast.

Schwarzkopf earned for himself a series of in-the-field and Washington assignments, which culminated in his 1983 promotion to brigadier general. That same year, Schwarzkopf commanded all U.S. ground forces in the successful invasion of Grenada. In 1988, he was promoted to full general and appointed commander in chief of the U.S. Army Central Command, with responsibility for the African and Middle Eastern theaters.

In late July 1990, U.S. intelligence spotted SADDAM HUSSEIN moving his forces close to the border of Kuwait, in full invasion mode. Schwarzkopf met with George H. W. Bush to discuss the situation, and he presented the president with a two-pronged plan of response. The first was to penalize Saddam with a petty infraction for crossing the borders while the second was to use American military force to expel Saddam from Kuwait. The second phase was code-named Operations Plan 1002-90. Bush and Schwarzkopf both thought Saddam had no intention of engaging his troops in armed confrontation, but rather was using the threat of an invasion to win bribes from countries to back down. To the surprise of analysts, on August 2, 1990, Saddam sent troops into Kuwait, gaining control of 21 percent of the world's oil supply. Immediately following the attack, the United Nations passed Resolution 660, calling for Iraq's immediate withdrawal and authorizing, in the event of noncompliance, member nations to launch an attack to eject Hussein's forces.

After the UN decision, Bush's attention shifted to protecting Saudi Arabia, as U.S. intelligence believed Saddam Hussein's next assault would be there. Bush increased the number of troops that Schwarzkopf had originally requested to 80,000, and he christened the plan Operation Desert Shield. Between the months of August and January, Schwarzkopf assembled over 765,000 combat forces from 28 countries (541,000 were American) as well as hundreds of ships and thousands of planes and tanks to dislodge the Iraqi invaders.

On February 27, 1991, Bush gave the order to initiate offensive strikes against Hussein to expel him from Kuwait—Operation Desert Storm. Schwarzkopf led U.S. troops and those of allied countries in a brilliant campaign that accomplished objectives with a minimal number of casualties, all in record time. Strategic attacks to disrupt enemy communi-

President Bush riding in an armored jeep with General Schwarzkopf in Saudi Arabia, November 22, 1990

cations and supply lines constituted the key to the allied victory. When advanced tactics allowed the Allied troops to quickly cut through enemy lines, destroying communications along with their supply lines, the Iraqis soon started to retreat. After the initiation of the 42-day airborne battles, the ground war led to less than 400 American casualties, compared to 8,000 to 15,000 Iraqis.

Schwarzkopf returned home to a hero's welcome, and he was considered in some quarters a possible contender for the Republican nomination for the presidency. He retired from the army in 1992.

—SW

Scowcroft, Brent

(1925–) *National Security Advisor*

Brent Scowcroft was born in Ogden, Utah, and took his B.S. from the U.S. Military Academy in 1947. In 1947, he was commissioned a second lieutenant in the U.S. Army Air Corps, and the following year he earned his fighter pilot's wings, although he never saw combat. He took his M.A. (1953) and Ph.D. (1957) in international relations from Columbia University. From 1953 to 1957, he taught Russian history at the U.S. Military Academy. From 1957 to 1959, he entered the Strategic Intelligence School in Washington, D.C., and, from 1959 to 1961, Scowcroft served at the U.S. embassy in Belgrade, Yugoslavia. He then entered the Armed Forces Staff College, and, in 1962, he joined the political science department of the U.S. Air Force Academy as its chair.

In 1964, Scowcroft began seven years of service in the Pentagon. From 1964 to 1967, he served as a member of the long-range planning division of the Office of the Deputy Staff for Plans and Operations. From 1968 to 1969, he worked for the assistant secretary of defense for international security affairs, and, from 1969 to 1971, he served as a staff member to the Joint Chiefs of Staff.

In 1971, Scowcroft moved to the White House. In November 1971, he was made chief military aide to the president. In this role, he headed the advance team for President Richard Nixon's 1972 visit to the Soviet Union. In 1973, when Alexander Haig left his position as deputy to Henry Kissinger, then the National Security Advisor (Kissinger was serving concurrently as National Security Advisor and secretary of state), Scowcroft was promoted to that position, where he served until 1975; his service carried over into the administration of Gerald R. Ford.

In 1975, President Ford promoted Scowcroft to the position of National Security Advisor (following Ford's decision to separate Kissinger from the position and give him the exclusive portfolio at State). In this role, Scowcroft became Ford's chief adviser on national security issues. He was largely responsible for the 1975 evacuation of American forces from Vietnam, and he was closest to the president regarding the decision making surrounding the freeing of the hostages from the merchant ship *Mayaguez*. After Ford's 1976 defeat for reelection, from 1982 to 1989, Scowcroft was the vice chairman of Kissinger Associates, Inc., a consulting firm. In 1987 he was once again called to government service, this time as a member of the President's Special Review Board on Iran Contra (the Tower Commission).

In 1988, president-elect George H. W. Bush offered Scowcroft the position of National Security Advisor. Although Scowcroft later remembered in his memoirs that he had hoped to be named secretary of defense, he accepted the position. Scowcroft's appointment signaled a significant break between the Bush and the Reagan administrations on the cold war. Scowcroft had supported neither the "evil empire" rhetoric of the early Reagan years nor the seemingly speedy pursuit of détente with MIKHAIL GORBACHEV that signaled the end of the Reagan years. Wary of Soviet intentions, he termed the Soviet Union the "clever bear," and he advocated vigilance in U.S. dealings with Moscow. It was Scowcroft who coined the phrase the "New World Order" to describe the world after the fall of communism, and it was Scowcroft who counseled that the United States initiate a period of distance from the Soviet Union (the *pauza*) following the implosion of Eastern Europe to await developments in internal Soviet affairs as to whether Gorbachev could survive. Following the June 1989 massacre at Tiananmen Square, Scowcroft, along with Assistant Secretary of State LAWRENCE EAGLEBURGER, was sent to China to persuade Beijing to ameliorate its repression. Following the August 1990 invasion of Kuwait by SADDAM HUSSEIN, Scowcroft was one of the strongest advocates for writing off the economic sanctions as a failure and initiating an offensive option designed to expel Hussein's forces from Kuwait.

In 1991, President Bush presented Scowcroft with the Medal of Freedom Award. In 1998, he coauthored a volume of memoirs with Bush, *A World Transformed.* Scowcroft is the founder and president of the Scowcroft Group, a consulting firm. He is also the founder and president of the Forum for International Policy.

Shamir, Yitzhak
(1915–) *prime minister of Israel*

Born in Ruzinoy, Poland, Yitzhak Shamir began the study of law in Warsaw. However, in 1935, he emigrated to Palestine, then a British mandate, where he continued his studies at the Hebrew University in Jerusalem. Soon after his emigration, Shamir joined the youth movement dedicated to expelling Britain from Pales-

tine (Lohamei Herut Yisrael). In 1941, he was imprisoned by the British, only to escape two years later and emerge as a primary leader of the youth movement. Imprisoned once again in 1946, Shamir once again escaped in 1947 and was given political asylum in France. He stayed in France until the 1948 creation of Israel when he returned to the Middle East. After several business ventures, Shamir joined Israel's security forces. By the 1960s he was active in the movement that would evolve into the Likud Party. In 1973, Shamir was elected to the Knesset; reelected in 1977, he became that body's Speaker. In 1980, he joined the cabinet of Prime Minister Menachem Begin as foreign minister, and, in 1983, he succeeded Begin as prime minister. During the Persian Gulf War (1990–91), Shamir proved to be a moderate voice within his own cabinet. He acceded to George H. W. Bush's request not to respond to SADDAM HUSSEIN's missile attacks on Israel—a reaction that would have surely widened the war. In return, the White House sponsored a Middle East peace conference in Madrid in October 1991. After a 1990 vote of no confidence in the Knesset, Shamir's government fell. However, with no one else able to form a viable government, Shamir assembled a coalition government. Defeated in 1992, Shamir relinquished his party leadership. In 1996, he retired from the Knesset.

Simpson, Alan K(ooi)
(1931–) *member of the Senate*

Alan Simpson was born in Cody, Wyoming. He attended the University of Wyoming, earning a bachelor's of science degree in law in 1954. From 1954 to 1956, Simpson served in the U.S. Army, stationed in Germany. After his discharge from the army, he returned to the University of Wyoming, where he took his law degree in 1958. From 1958 to 1964, Simpson practiced law in Cody with the firm of Simpson, Kepler, and Simpson. During that period, he served as city attorney (1959–69) and Wyoming assistant attorney general (1958–59).

In 1964, Simpson was elected to the Wyoming House of Representatives, where he served for the next 13 years. In 1978, Simpson was elected to the U.S. Senate. While in the Senate, Simpson served on the Judiciary Committee, Finance Committee, Environment and Public Works Committee, and chaired the Veterans Affairs Committee. In 1984, he was elected Republican whip, a position he held until 1994.

On the short list for Bush's choice of a running mate in 1988, Simpson led the charge against the allegations of ANITA HILL in the fall of 1989. Countering Hill's claim that Supreme Court nominee CLARENCE THOMAS had sexually harassed her, Simpson appeared on television with Hill's telephone records, showing that she had actually stayed in close touch with Thomas even after she left his employ at the Equal Opportunity Employment Commission.

Simpson retired from Congress in 1997. From 1998 to 2000, he was a visiting lecturer at Harvard University's John F. Kennedy School of Government. In 2000, he returned to the University of Wyoming as a lecturer. He is also a partner in Burg, Simpson, Eldridge, and Hersh, a Cody and Denver law firm. Simpson continued his feud with the press in authoring *Right in the Old Gazoo: A Lifetime of Scrapping with the Press* (1997).

Skinner, Samuel K(nox)

(1938–) *secretary of transportation, White House chief of staff*

Born in Springfield, Illinois, Samuel Skinner took an accounting degree from the University of Illinois at Urbana-Champaign in 1960. He spent the following year in the U.S. Army and then began work at IBM as a salesman in 1961, where he stayed for eight years. During that time, he took night classes toward his law degree from DePaul University, completing that degree in 1966.

In 1968, with the help of IBM general counsel Burke Marshall (who had run the Civil Rights Division of the Justice Department during the Kennedy administration), Skinner was named an assistant U.S. attorney. Skinner became close with James Thompson, who became U.S. attorney in 1968. When Thompson resigned from the position to run for Illinois governor in 1975 (an election he won), Skinner was appointed to Thompson's former position. Skinner's tenure in office ended in 1977 when Jimmy Carter was elected president, and he joined the law firm of Sidney and Austin, using that platform to work as a close political adviser to Thompson. In 1988, Thompson, who had been instrumental in George H. W. Bush's primary victory in Illinois, pushed hard for Skinner's inclusion in the cabinet. Skinner also campaigned hard for the position, and he was rewarded with his choice of secretary of transportation.

Skinner immediately distinguished himself in a cabinet that, apart from those who dealt with national security issues, numbered few stars. Indeed, Skinner stepped in as the administration's representative in several crises, including, most notably, the Eastern Airlines strike, the *Exxon Valdez* catastrophe (1989), Hurricane Hugo (1989), and a major earthquake in California.

In 1991, following the resignation of JOHN SUNUNU, Bush asked Skinner to move into the White House to serve as his chief of staff. Observers largely rate Skinner a weak chief of staff, who was ill-prepared to deal with the turf battles waged within the West Wing. His role during the riots in Los Angeles (April 1992) has been frequently cited, in which a seeming inability to assign speech writing assignments in a timely manner cost the White House precious time in getting in front of the issue. In August 1992, Skinner was replaced as chief of staff by then secretary of state JAMES A. BAKER III.

Following his tenure at the White House from 1992 to 1998, Skinner served as president of Commonwealth Edison Company in Chicago. He currently serves on several boards and is a partner in Hopkins and Sutter, a Chicago law firm.

Souter, David H(ackett)

(1939–   ) *associate justice, U.S. Supreme Court*

David Souter was born in Melrose, Massachusetts. He took his B.A. in philosophy from Harvard University in 1961 (writing his undergraduate thesis on Oliver Wendell Holmes, Jr.). He then spent two years at Oxford University as a Rhodes Scholar, and earned a second bachelor's degree in jurisprudence in 1962 and a master's degree in 1989. Returning to the United States, he reentered Harvard and earned his law degree in 1966. From 1966 to 1968, Souter was in private practice in New Hampshire, working at the firm of Orr and Reno. In 1968, he was named that state's assistant attorney general, a post he filled until 1971, when the then attorney general for New Hampshire, Warren Rudman, appointed Souter to be his deputy. In 1976, Souter was promoted once again, to the position of attorney general for New Hampshire. In 1978, Souter was appointed to the New Hampshire Superior Court; in 1983 he was named justice of the New Hampshire Supreme Court. Souter remained on the New Hampshire bench until 1990, when President George H. W. Bush named him to the U.S.

Court of Appeals for the District of Columbia on May 25, 1990.

Souter had served at the Court of Appeals for only two months when, on July 15, 1990, Bush nominated him to a seat on the U.S. Supreme Court to fill the vacancy left by the retirement of Associate Justice William Brennan. Remembering the firestorm caused by the most recent Supreme Court nomination— Ronald Reagan's 1987 failed nomination of Robert Bork—Bush resolved that his first choice to the nation's highest court would receive a smooth confirmation hearing on Capitol Hill. Souter did—indeed, so little was known about his views on controversial subjects, and so little criticism was weighed against his candidacy, that the press nicknamed him the "stealth candidate." The Senate approved his nomination by a vote of 90 to 9 and Souter was sworn in on October 9, 1990.

In the years since his appointment, Souter, who began his tenure voting with the Court's conservative members, has evolved into a moderate voice. He dissented in *Bush v. Gore*, the decision that decided the outcome of the presidential election of 2000.

Sullivan, Louis W(ade)

(1933–   ) *secretary of health and human services*

Born in Atlanta, Louis Sullivan took his B.S. from Morehouse University in 1954 and his M.D. from Boston University Medical School in 1958. He served as a fellow at the Massachusetts General Hospital from 1960 to 1961 and a fellow at the Thorndike Medical Research Laboratories from 1964 to 1966. From 1966 to 1975, Sullivan taught medicine at Boston University. In 1975, he took a position at his alma mater, teaching biology and medicine at Morehouse University until 1985, when he became the first president of that institution's School of Medicine.

In 1989, George H. W. Bush nominated him to the post of secretary of health and human services. However, his nomination met trouble initially after he told a reporter that women should be able to have abortions. Later, he corrected himself, saying that he opposed abortion except in cases of incest, rape, or a threat to the woman's life. His tenure, which lasted the entirety of the Bush administration, was a rocky one, as he focused his energies on battling the tobacco companies over advertising directed at children and the administration itself over its lack of funding for AIDS research.

In 1993, Sullivan returned to his position as president of the Morehouse School of Medicine.

Sununu, John H.
(1939–) *governor of New Hampshire, White House chief of staff, counselor to the president*

John Sununu took his bachelor's degree (1961), master's degree (1962), and doctorate (1966) from the Massachusetts Institute of Technology. From 1963 to 1989 he served as the president of JHS Engineering and Thermal Research, Inc. He also helped found Astro Dynamics, Inc., and served as its chief engineer from 1960 to 1965. From 1963 to 1978, he served as the associate dean of the College of Engineering at Tufts University as well as associate professor of mechanical engineering.

In 1973, Sununu was elected to the New Hampshire House of Representatives. He served in that body for one year. In 1983, he was elected governor of New Hampshire. While governor, Sununu chaired three influential groups—the Coalition of Northeast-

ern Governors, the Republican Governor's Association, and the National Governor's Association. Sununu was an instrumental figure in George H. W. Bush's 1988 victory over BOB DOLE in the New Hampshire Republican primary.

For his service in the campaign, Sununu was named White House chief of staff. Sununu's brusque, take-no-prisoners personality (his assistant, ANDREW CARD, observed that Sununu was "very tough in driving policy from concept to reality") was an irritant to many, but it naturally complimented Bush's easygoing managerial style. As a doctrinaire conservative and an outspoken anti-Soviet hard-liner, Sununu's choice also appealed to the right wing of the Republican Party, which Bush needed to court.

Clearly, Bush had complete faith in his chief of staff. In a significant restructuring of his national security staff, Bush made sure that Sununu was included on the NSC. This gave Sununu more input into foreign and security policy than any of his predecessors. Sununu was also a member of the White House inner circle during the Persian Gulf War, and he was instrumental in the choice of both DAVID SOUTER and CLARENCE THOMAS to the Supreme Court. And yet his prickly demeanor made him many enemies. This was clearly apparent during the 1990 budget summit. Sununu and RICHARD DARMAN were largely responsible for the planning of the negotiations between the White House and Capitol Hill that ended in the Omnibus Budget Reconciliation Act of 1990. However, his heavy handed style of negotiating (saying to the press, for example, that Republican senator Trent Lott of Mississippi "has become an insignificant member in this process") left him with few friends in high places.

In May 1991, stories began to leak regarding Sununu's use of an air force jet to take 99

President Bush talks on the telephone regarding Operation Just Cause in Panama with Lt. General Brent Scowcroft (left) and Governor John Sununu nearby, December 20, 1989.

personal flights at taxpayer expense—at a cost of nearly $500,000. Dubbed "Air Sununu," the story grew in magnitude until calls were being made for the chief of staff's resignation. Bush moved slowly, more than likely because he was loath to part with a member of his team who had been instrumental in reaching out to conservatives. But when Sununu publicly blamed Bush for flubbing a line in a speech, thus calling his boss's judgment into question, his service was effectively at an end. Sununu resigned on December 3, 1991, and was replaced by Secretary of Transportation SAMUEL K. SKINNER.

From 1992 to 1998, Sununu cohosted *Crossfire*, a political talk show broadcast on CNN. Presently, he is president of JHS Associates, Ltd., and a partner in Trinity International Partners.

T

Thatcher, Margaret H(ilda)
(1925–) *prime minister of Great Britain*

Margaret Hilda Thatcher was born Margaret Hilda Roberts on October 13, 1925, in Grantham, England. She was educated at the University of Oxford, studying and earning degrees in chemistry. She received her bachelor of arts in 1946, bachelor of science in 1949, and master of arts in 1950. Thatcher became the first woman president of the Oxford University Conservative Association. From 1947 to 1951, she worked as a research chemist. In 1951, she married Denis Thatcher. She studied law and became a tax lawyer in 1953.

Thatcher first stood for Parliament in 1950 but was unsuccessful in securing a seat. She later joined the Conservative Party in 1953 and was elected to the House of Commons in 1959. From 1961 to 1964, she served as joint parliamentary secretary to the Ministry of Pensions and National Insurance. She was also secretary of state for education and science in the cabinet of Prime Minister Edward Heath from 1970 to 1974. After two defeats in the general elections, she was elected the Conservative Party's first woman leader in 1975.

In 1975, Thatcher challenged Edward Heath for leadership of the Conservative Party. She was successful, and, in 1979, she became prime minister. She vowed to reverse Britain's declining economic standing and to lessen the role of government in economic and social affairs. She reduced the influence of trade unions and combated inflation in carrying out an economic policy based on introducing broad changes along free-market lines. Thatcher's government controlled the money

Prime Minister Margaret Thatcher and President Bush in London, June 1, 1989

supply and sharply reduced public spending. She also taxed higher-income individuals. During her first two terms in office, unemployment virtually tripled, jumping from 1.1 to 3 million. Business losses and bankruptcies also increased as her government strove to reduce inflation.

In foreign policy, Thatcher proved to be a hawk, particularly with regard to the Soviet Union. She counseled maintaining a wary eye in relationships with the Soviet bloc and, although she affirmed that Soviet leader MIKHAIL GORBACHEV was a man with whom the West could do business, she initially opposed German reunification. She believed that a reunited Germany would once again seek to dominate Europe. BRENT SCOWCROFT, President George H. W. Bush's National Security Advisor, took Thatcher's side, but Secretary of State JAMES A. BAKER III convinced Bush to support the reunification of the country.

Following the August 1990 invasion of Kuwait by Iraq, the United Kingdom, France, West Germany, Japan, and seven other countries met in the United States to decide whether they should jointly freeze Iraqi assets. Bush and Thatcher met in Aspen, Colorado, where, in a joint press conference, the two leaders announced that the invasion of Kuwait amounted to a blatant violation of international law. She said further that she felt the West was compelled to take action as part of a defensive posture to protect Saudi Arabia's integrity. When she arrived back in London, she talked on the telephone with KING FAHD of Saudi Arabia and received his formal request to station aircraft and possible ground forces from Western nations in the kingdom. Contemporary reports claim that it was Thatcher who urged the United States to mount an offensive campaign to expel SADDAM HUSSEIN from Iraq and it was her arguments that proved pivotal in Bush's decision-making process.

In 1992, following a split in her cabinet over the issue of Britain's participation in the European Union and after imposition of a widely unpopular poll tax, Thatcher resigned as prime minister. Later that year, as the baroness Thatcher of Kesteven, she entered the House of Lords.

—KC

Thomas, Clarence
(1948–) *associate justice, U.S. Supreme Court*

Clarence Thomas was born in Pin Point, Georgia. After his father abandoned his family, Thomas's mother moved her children to Philadelphia, and then back to Savannah. Originally intending to train for the Catholic priesthood, Thomas attended Immaculate Conception Seminary in Georgia from 1967 to 1968, only to leave because of what he claimed to be racism. He entered Holy Cross College, where he took his bachelor's degree in English in 1971. He earned his law degree from Yale University in 1974, concentrating in antitrust law.

Thomas served as assistant attorney general of Missouri from 1974 to 1977, where he worked for then state attorney general John Danforth. He specialized in tax cases. Thomas left state government in 1979 to become an attorney with the Monsanto Company, where he worked until 1979. He then rejoined Danforth, now serving in the U.S. Senate, as his legislative assistant from 1979 to 1981. While at this post he was spotted by the Reagan administration. Appointed assistant secretary for civil rights at the Department of Education, he served in this position from 1981 to 1982. From 1982 to 1990, he was chairman of the U.S. Equal Employment Opportunity Commission (EEOC).

In 1990, President George H. W. Bush nominated Thomas to the U.S. Court of Appeals for the District of Columbia. Thomas served in that position until October 23, 1991, when, following the retirement of Thurgood Marshall, Bush nominated him to be associate justice of the U.S. Supreme Court. Thomas's confirmation hearings were contentious as he was assailed by feminist organizations for his statement that he had not yet had time to formulate an opinion on *Roe v. Wade* (1973). He was also criticized under questioning for his outspoken criticism of affirmative action, even though he himself had been admitted to Yale University under an affirmative action program. But it was clear that his nomination would be voted upon favorably by the Senate Judiciary Committee. However, on the final day of testimony, Democratic staffers leaked to the media an FBI report that claimed that a former colleague of Thomas's, ANITA HILL, then a professor of law at the University of Oklahoma, had been sexually harassed by Thomas when he had been her direct supervisor, both at the Department of Education and later at the EEOC. Hill was called to testify before the committee, and her graphic testimony riveted the nation, forcing the Judiciary Committee to reopen its hearings. Thomas was the last to appear before the extended hearings, when he emotionally labeled the proceedings a "high tech lynching for uppity blacks" and made it clear that "I am not going to allow myself to be further humiliated in order to be confirmed." Senate supporters claimed no compelling evidence had been found to support Hill's testimony, and Thomas was approved by the Judiciary Committee and by the full Senate on October 15 by a vote of 52-48. He was sworn in as an associate justice on October 23, 1991.

Since taking his seat on the bench, Thomas has consistently allied himself with the conservative wing of the Court; indeed, his voting record mirrors that of his colleague, Antonin Scalia.

Thornburgh, Richard L(ewis)
(1932–　) *U.S. Attorney General*

Dick Thornburgh was born in Pittsburgh and received his B.S. in engineering from Yale University in 1954 and his law degree from the University of Pittsburgh in 1957. After practicing law, Thornburgh was named attorney general for Western Pennsylvania in 1969. In 1975, he was named assistant U.S. Attorney General, Criminal Division. In 1979, Thornburgh was elected to the first of two terms as governor of Pennsylvania.

In 1988, President Ronald Reagan appointed Thornburgh U.S. Attorney General. Later that year, president-elect George H. W. Bush retained Thornburgh in the post. Thornburgh resigned from the cabinet in 1990 to run for the U.S. Senate from Pennsylvania; he was defeated by Harris Wofford.

Following his tenure in the Bush administration, Thornburgh served as undersecretary general at the United Nations (1992–93) and then as director of the Institute of Politics at Harvard's John F. Kennedy School of Government. He later joined Kirkpatrick and Lockhart, a Washington, D.C., law firm.

Tower, John G(oodwin)
(1925–1991) *member of the Senate*

John Tower was born in Houston, Texas. In 1942, he began his studies at Southwestern University, only to have them interrupted by World War II. In 1943, he joined the U.S. Navy. He served on an amphibious gunboat in the Pacific theater and was discharged in 1946. Tower then returned to Southwestern, where he received a bachelor of arts degree in political science in 1948. Tower put himself through graduate school working as a radio announcer and selling insurance. In 1951, after completing his graduate coursework in political science at Southern Methodist University (SMU), Tower was given an associate professorship at Midwestern University. He served on the political science faculty of Midwestern until 1960; in 1952, he studied at the London School of Economics and Political Science, and, in 1953, he earned his master's of arts from SMU.

Tower's interest in politics ran concurrent to his teaching career. In 1954, he made an unsuccessful run for the Texas state legislature, and, in 1960, he challenged Lyndon B. Johnson, the incumbent U.S. senator, for the seat Johnson was trying to win at the same time he was running for vice president (on a Democratic ticket headed by John F. Kennedy). Johnson won both races, resigned his Senate seat in January 1961, and, in the special election held that year, Tower became the first Republican elected to the Senate from Texas since 1870; at 36, he was also the youngest man in the Senate. Tower's two main interests were banking and national defense; he served on the Armed Services Committee from 1965 until his retirement. As chairman of that committee, Tower consistently championed measures to promote the buildup of the nation's armed forces.

In 1985, Tower retired from his Senate seat, choosing instead to work as a defense consultant. Two weeks after his retirement, President Ronald Reagan called him back into service as the chief negotiator at the Strategic Arms Reduction Talks in Geneva. The following year, Reagan asked Tower to chair the committee charged with investigating the Iran-contra affair. Known popularly as the "Tower Commission," the investigation found fault with virtually every member of the president's national security team; nor did committee members wholly exonerate the president himself.

In 1988, Tower was one of the first to support the presidential candidacy of George H. W. Bush. Following the election Bush reciprocated by choosing Tower as his secretary of defense designate. Most observers believed that as a former senator, Tower would be quickly confirmed. However, the nomination stalled amid allegations of Tower's womanizing, drinking, and unacceptably close relationship with key defense contractors. Bush decided not to withdraw the nomination, and it was defeated on the floor of the Senate by a vote of 53-47—the first defeat of a cabinet nomination since 1959.

In 1990, Bush appointed Tower chairman of the President's Foreign Intelligence Advisory Board (PFIAB). The next year, Tower wrote his memoirs, *Consequences: A Personal and Political Memoir*. On April 5, 1991, Tower and his daughter Marian were killed in an airplane crash near New Brunswick, Georgia.

Watkins, James D(avid)
(1927–) *secretary of energy*

Born in California, James Watkins graduated with his bachelor's degree from the U.S. Naval Academy in 1949 and from the Naval Submarine School in 1951, and he took his master's degree from the Naval Postgraduate School in Monterey, California, in 1958. His service in the U.S. Navy spanned almost four decades. During that period, he served as commander of the Sixth Fleet, vice chief of naval operations, and commander of the Pacific Fleet, earning the rank of admiral.

In 1989, George H. W. Bush nominated Watkins to serve as his secretary of energy, a post he held for the entirety of the Bush administration. His efforts to shape a national energy policy acceptable to both the administration and Congress were largely met with frustration.

Following his tenure in the Bush administration, Watkins became president of the Joint Oceanographic Institutions (JOI), where he established the Consortium for Oceanographic Research and Education (CORE).

Webster, William H.
(1924–) *director of central intelligence*

William Webster was born in St. Louis, Missouri, took his B.A. from Amherst College in 1947, and his J.D. from Washington University Law School in 1949. He served in the U.S. Navy during both World War II and the Korean War. From 1949 to 1959, Webster practiced law in St. Louis. In 1960, he was named U.S. attorney for the Eastern District of Missouri. He served in that position for a year, and then returned to private practice. In 1970, he became a justice for the U.S. District Court for the Eastern District of Missouri; in 1973, he was elevated to the U.S. Court of Appeals for the Eighth Circuit.

Webster served on the bench until 1978, when he was chosen by President Jimmy Carter to head the Federal Bureau of Investigation (FBI). Upon the recommendation of Vice President George H. W. Bush, Webster was moved from the FBI to become the 14th director of central intelligence in 1987. Even before he was elected president in 1988, Bush told officials that he had decided to keep Webster as a sign that he intended to have a depoliticized CIA. Webster had specifically asked not to have cabinet rank, so as to maintain the impartial character of his post. Many sources suggest that Webster was not a true member of Bush's inner circle, despite the daily intelligence briefings that Webster usually delivered to the president personally. While director, Webster moved to repair the rifts with Congress that had been created under his predecessor, William Casey, and which had become further exacerbated during the period of disclosure of Iran-contra–related abuses of power. Webster also moved to hire more women and minorities at the CIA, and he pushed for improvements in the handling of defectors.

By the end of 1989, however, stories in the press described Webster as a disengaged director. Some contemporary reports suggest that there was talk within the administration during the first coup attempt against Panamanian strongman MANUEL NORIEGA in 1989 that the CIA was deficient in its intelligence gathering abilities. With the fall of the Soviet Union in 1990, there were calls to scale back intelligence-gathering operations in the United States. Webster, however, called for an increase in economic intelligence work; others advocated use of the CIA to help fight the drug war.

Criticism against both Webster and the CIA mounted during the Persian Gulf War. Throughout 1989, the intelligence community stuck to findings that claimed SADDAM HUS-SEIN was unlikely to take any military action in the Middle East because Iraqi forces had been so badly mauled in the Iran-Iraq War. After the Iraqi invasion of Kuwait, Webster seemed to waffle on whether or not he supported economic sanctions or military actions against Hussein, giving the impression that the CIA was not up to speed on events transpiring in the Persian Gulf. During the war, the agency overestimated the number of Iraqi soldiers in Kuwait; it also did not know that the Al Firdos bunker—a command post by day that was bombed by U.S. fighter planes—was packed with women and children at night.

On May 8, 1991, Webster left the administration and returned to practicing law (he was replaced by RICHARD GATES). Webster became a senior partner in the firm of Milbank, Tweed, Hadley, and McCloy in Washington, D.C., heading the litigation department. In 1991, President Bush awarded him the Presidential Medal of Freedom, the nation's highest civilian award.

Y

Yeltsin, Boris Nikolayevich
(1931–) *president of Russia*

Born on February 1, 1931, in Sverdlovsk (now Yekaterinburg), Boris Yeltsin graduated from Ural Polytechnic Institute (1955) majoring in construction. He was an engineer and builder by profession. Yeltsin worked on various construction projects from 1955 to 1968 and became chief engineer for a large housing construction plant. He joined the Communist Party in 1961 during former premier Nikita Khrushchev's anti-Stalinist reforms. In 1976, Yeltsin became first chairman of the Sverdlovsk party committee.

While chairman of the party committee in Sverdlovsk, Yeltsin met Mikhail Gorbachev, who held the same position in Stavropol. When Gorbachev took power in 1985, he brought Yeltsin to Moscow to reform the corrupt Moscow party hierarchy. Yeltsin became dissatisfied with Gorbachev's slow-moving reforms and resigned from the party leadership in 1987 and from the Politburo in 1988. Yeltsin was demoted to the post of deputy construction minister.

When Gorbachev instituted free elections in 1989, Yeltsin won a landslide victory for a seat in the Congress of People's Deputies and was later elected speaker of the Congress of People's Deputies in May 1990. In July 1990, Yeltsin resigned from the Communist Party as tensions increased between Gorbachev, who was president of the USSR, and Yeltsin, who was president of one member state, Russia.

In the nation's first democratic elections, held on June 12, 1991, Yeltsin was elected president of Russia. When a coup sought to remove Gorbachev from power on August 18, 1991, and confined Gorbachev to house arrest at his summer residence in the Crimea, Yeltsin delivered a speech from the top of an armored vehicle in Moscow denouncing the coup. The coup failed, its leaders fled, and Gorbachev returned briefly to power. A week later, the presidents of Russia, Ukraine, and Belarus signed a treaty to create the Commonwealth of Independent States. On December 24, 1991, Russia took over the Soviet Union's seat in the United Nations. The next day, Gorbachev resigned.

Yeltsin ran into problems over his leadership when the Congress of People's Deputies voted to impeach him on March 26, 1993. In a national referendum held on April 25, 1993, he won 58 percent of the vote to retain his presidency. He sought and achieved, on December 12, 1993, passage of a referendum to approve a new Constitution, which increased his presidential powers.

A year later, Yeltsin began his attempt to crush the three-year-old Chechen rebellion by

President Bush and President Boris Yeltsin, January 3, 1993

sending Russian troops to Chechnya. By spring 1995, Russian troops controlled the capital, Grozny. Months of bombings in Grozny led to thousands of deaths of Chechen civilians and hundreds of thousands became refugees.

President BILL CLINTON met with Yeltsin in March 1997 in Helsinki, Finland, to discuss the North Atlantic Treaty Organization's (NATO) decisions on enlargement of NATO and to consider a Russian request for membership in the Group of 7 (G-7) economic meetings. Russia sought full membership in the group, but President Clinton failed to extend such an offer at the time. By 1999, Yeltsin had succeeded in securing Russia's inclusion in the annual economic meetings, thus expanding the membership to form the Group of 8 (G-8).

In November 1999, relations between the United States and Russia deteriorated over the demand by the United States that Russia stop bombing in Chechnya, which was seeking independence from Russia. Yeltsin protested the U.S. position, insisting to Pres-

ident Clinton at a summit in Istanbul, Turkey: "You have no right to criticize Russia for Chechnya. There will be no negotiations with bandits and murderers." Yeltsin accused NATO and the United States of carrying out bombing in Kosovo and so had no moral grounds for denouncing Russia for bombing in Chechnya.

The Chechen bombing issue may have arisen in response to Yeltsin's anger at being marginalized during NATO's activities in the Balkans in its dealing with Slobodan Milošević. Russia was given a limited role in dealing with the crises in Bosnia and Kosovo.

In 1995, Yeltsin suffered two heart attacks, and his health continued to deteriorate over the next four years. At times, he was absent from his job for weeks without any public bulletins on where he was or the state of his health.

In 1996, Yeltsin ran for reelection, facing stiff opposition from Gennady Zyuganov. Yeltsin won the election in July. However, in November 1996, Yeltsin underwent quadruple heart bypass surgery and remained in the hospital for months. His health continued to deteriorate for the next three years, leading to his abrupt resignation on New Year's Eve, 1999. Vladimir Putin served as acting president until national elections were held in March 2000.

—SAW

Yeutter, Clayton K.
(1930–   ) *secretary of agriculture; chairman, Republican National Committee; counselor to the president*

Clayton Yeutter was born in Eustis, Nebraska. He earned his B.S. in animal husbandry (1952) and his J.D. (1963) and Ph.D. in agricultural economics (1966) from the University of Nebraska. He served in the U.S. Air Force from 1952 to 1957, when he returned to Nebraska to manage his 2,500 acre farm. From 1960 to 1966, he served as a college professor. He practiced law, then served as the executive assistant to the governor of Nebraska from 1966 to 1968, and twice served as director of the University of Nebraska mission to Colombia in 1968 and 1970.

Yeutter joined the Nixon administration in 1970 as an assistant secretary of agriculture. He then became a regional director for the Committee to Re-Elect the President. Under Gerald Ford, Yeutter served as assistant secretary of marketing and consumer services, assistant secretary for international affairs from 1974 to 1975, and deputy special trade representative from 1975 to 1977. In 1977, he returned to his law practice (Nelson, Harding, Yeutter, and Leonard in Lincoln, Nebraska), but in 1978 he accepted the position of president of the Chicago Mercantile Exchange. In 1985, as a member of the Reagan administration, Yeutter served as special trade representative from 1985 to 1989.

In 1989, Yeutter was nominated to serve as George H. W. Bush's secretary of agriculture. His nomination sparked a small tempest from Democratic circles—concerns were raised about his lack of experience. Another source of opposition stemmed from Yeutter's status as a Reagan holdover, an outsider among a tightly knit circle of Bush supporters who distrusted their predecessors. Yeutter's tenure at the Department of Agriculture was an active one. In May 1989, the administration was criticized for approving a subsidy of approximately 1.5 million metric tons of wheat for Soviet sales, reversing the previous public stand of the administration against such subsidies. Yeutter opposed such subsidies, but he lost the battle to advisers, particularly RICHARD DARMAN, who supported the measure. Yeutter also was instrumental in the planning of the July 1990 G-7 meeting at Houston, led the American negotiating team for the U.S.-Canada Free Trade Agreement, and helped launch the 100-nation Uruguay Round of GATT negotiations. In 1991, Yeutter left the Department of Agriculture to become chairman of the Republican National Committee. He succeeded LEE ATWATER, who had resigned in the wake of treatment for a brain tumor.

President Bush at a press conference with Secretary Clayton Yeutter, April 24, 1990

In 1992, Yeutter once again moved into the White House, now serving as counselor to the president for domestic policy (he was replaced as RNC chair by RICH BOND). He took the post with the understanding that he would gain control of the Domestic Policy Council and the Economic Policy Council. Yeutter then abolished both councils, replacing them with the Policy Coordinating Group (PRG). This created a new layer of administrative control, one that bred resentment among many within the White House. In August 1992, when JAMES A. BAKER III was moved from his position as secretary of state to that of White House chief of staff (replacing SAM SKINNER as part of a thinly veiled effort to have Baker take control of Bush's faltering reelection effort), Yeutter resigned.

Yeutter is presently a member of Hogan and Hartson, a Washington, D.C., law firm.

APPENDICES

MAPS

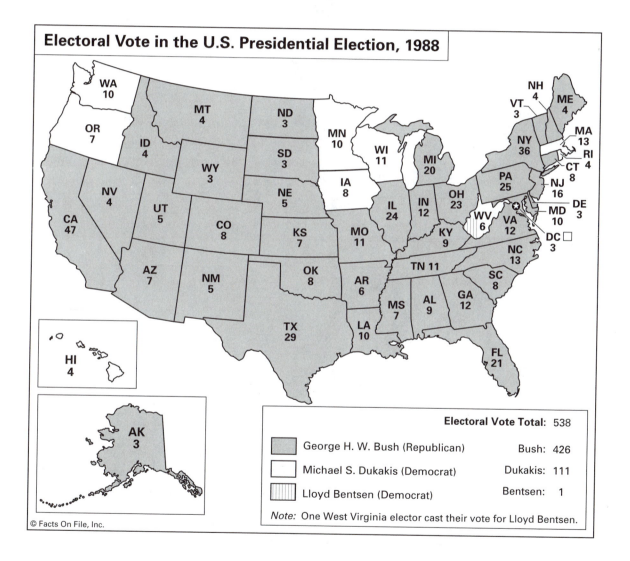

Electoral Vote in the U.S. Presidential Election, 1988

WA 10
MT 4
ND 3
MN 10
WI 11
MI 20
NH 4
VT 3
ME 4
NY 36
MA 13
RI 4
CT 8
PA 25
NJ 16
DE 3
MD 10
OH 23
IN 12
IL 24
WV 6
VA 12
DC 3
NC 13
SC 8
GA 12
FL 21
OR 7
ID 4
WY 3
SD 3
NE 5
IA 8
NV 4
UT 5
CO 8
KS 7
MO 11
KY 9
TN 11
AR 6
OK 8
NM 5
AZ 7
CA 47
TX 29
LA 10
MS 7
AL 9
HI 4
AK 3

Electoral Vote Total: 538

George H. W. Bush (Republican) — Bush: 426

Michael S. Dukakis (Democrat) — Dukakis: 111

Lloyd Bentsen (Democrat) — Bentsen: 1

Note: One West Virginia elector cast their vote for Lloyd Bentsen.

© Facts On File, Inc.

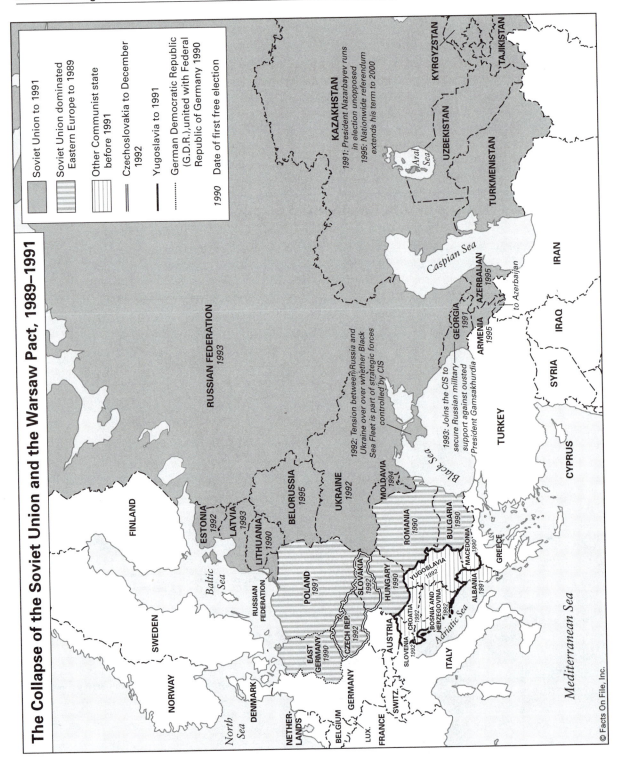

The Collapse of the Soviet Union and the Warsaw Pact, 1989–1991

Legend:

- Soviet Union to 1991
- Soviet Union dominated Eastern Europe to 1989
- Other Communist state before 1991
- Czechoslovakia to December 1992
- Yugoslavia to 1991
- German Democratic Republic (G.D.R.),united with Federal Republic of Germany 1990
- *1990* Date of first free election

KAZAKHSTAN
1991: President Nazarbayev runs in election unopposed 1995: Nationwide referendum extends his term to 2000

KYRGYZSTAN

TAJIKISTAN

UZBEKISTAN

TURKMENISTAN

Aral Sea

Caspian Sea

IRAN

RUSSIAN FEDERATION
1993

1992: Tension between Russia and Ukraine over over whether Black Sea Fleet is part of strategic forces controlled by CIS

1993: Joins the CIS to secure Russian military support against ousted President Gamsakhurdia

GEORGIA 1991

AZERBAIJAN 1995
to Azerbaijan

ARMENIA 1995

TURKEY

SYRIA

IRAQ

CYPRUS

Black Sea

FINLAND

ESTONIA 1992
LATVIA 1993
LITHUANIA 1990

BELORUSSIA 1995

UKRAINE 1992

MOLDAVIA 1994

ROMANIA 1990

BULGARIA 1990

MACEDONIA 1990

GREECE

Baltic Sea

SWEDEN

RUSSIAN FEDERATION

POLAND 1991

SLOVAKIA 1992

HUNGARY 1990

YUGOSLAVIA 1992

NORWAY

DENMARK

NETHER-LANDS

BELGIUM

LUX.

FRANCE

SWITZ.

GERMANY

EAST GERMANY 1990

CZECH REP. 1992

AUSTRIA

SLOVENIA 1992

CROATIA 1992

BOSNIA AND HERZEGOVINA 1992

ALBANIA 1991

ITALY

Adriatic Sea

Mediterranean Sea

North Sea

© Facts On File, Inc.

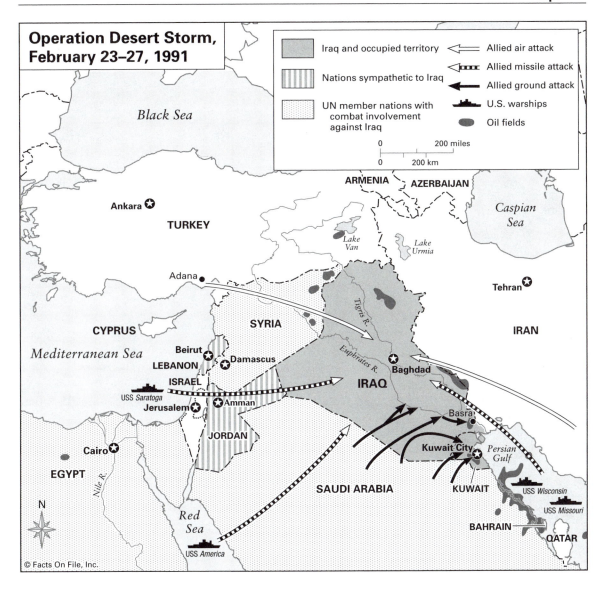

Operation Desert Storm, February 23–27, 1991

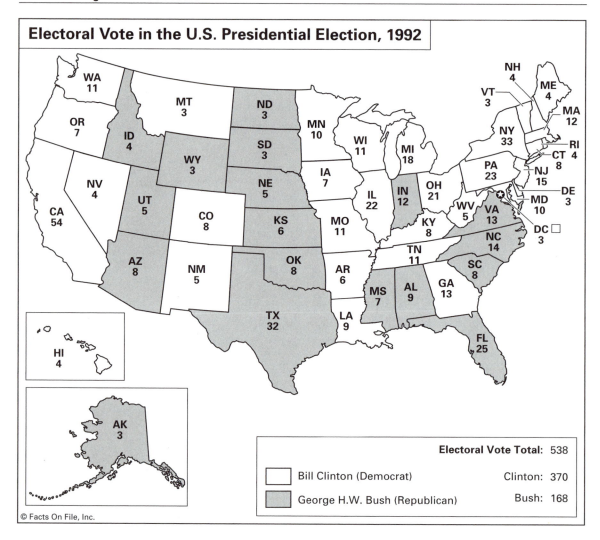

Electoral Vote in the U.S. Presidential Election, 1992

WA 11
OR 7
MT 3
ND 3
MN 10
ID 4
SD 3
WI 11
WY 3
NE 5
IA 7
MI 18
NV 4
UT 5
CO 8
KS 6
IL 22
IN 12
OH 21
CA 54
AZ 8
NM 5
OK 8
MO 11
KY 8
WV 5
VA 13
NC 14
AR 6
TN 11
SC 8
TX 32
LA 9
MS 7
AL 9
GA 13
FL 25
HI 4
AK 3

NH 4
VT 3
ME 4
NY 33
MA 12
PA 23
RI 4
CT 8
NJ 15
DE 3
MD 10
DC 3

Electoral Vote Total: 538

☐ Bill Clinton (Democrat)

▨ George H.W. Bush (Republican)

Clinton: 370

Bush: 168

© Facts On File, Inc.

CHRONOLOGY

1924

June 12—George Herbert Walker Bush is born in Milton, Massachusetts.

1925

June 8—Barbara Pierce is born in Rye, New York.

1938

Bush enters Philips Andover Academy.

1941

December 7—Japanese surprise attack on the U.S. naval base at Pearl Harbor leads to U.S. entry into World War II.

1942

June 12—Bush enlists in the U.S. Navy.

August 6—Bush ordered to active duty as an aviation cadet; reports for training to Chapel Hill, North Carolina.

1943

July 9—Bush earns his aviator wings and is promoted to ensign.

December 15—Bush is assigned to the aircraft carrier *San Jacinto*.

1944

June—Bush and his crew participate in the Battle of the Marianas and the invasion of the island of Saipan.

September 2—While flying a bombing run near Chichi Jima, Bush's plane is shot down. He parachutes into the ocean, but his two crewmates are killed. Bush is picked up by the submarine USS *Finback* about a half hour later. For heroism under fire, Bush will be awarded the Distinguished Flying Cross.

1945

January 6—Bush marries Barbara Pierce.

Fall—Bush enters Yale University.

1946

July 6—Son George W. Bush is born.

1949

The Bush family relocates to Texas, and Bush begins a career in the oil business.

December 20—Daughter Robin Bush is born.

1953

February 11—Son John ("Jeb") Bush is born.

October 11—Robin Bush dies after a battle with leukemia.

1955

January 22—Son Neil Bush is born.

1956

October 22—Son Marvin Bush is born.

1959

August 18—Dorothy ("Doro") Bush is born.

1964

Bush wins the Republican primary for a U.S. Senate seat from Texas. However, he does not win a majority of the votes cast, thus forcing a runoff. In the Republican Party's runoff election for the Senate, Bush (49,751 votes for 62%) defeats Jack Cox (30,333 votes for 38%).

November—In the general election, Ralph Yarborough (1,463,958 votes for 56%) defeats Bush (1,134,337 votes for 44%) for the Senate.

1966

November—In the general election in Texas's Seventh Congressional District, Bush (53,756 votes for 56%) defeats Frank Briscoe (39,958 votes for 42%) and is elected to the House of Representatives (Bush had been unopposed in that year's Republican Party primary).

1968

November—Bush is reelected to Congress without opposition.

1970

In the Republican primary for a U.S. Senate seat from Texas, Bush (96,806 votes for 88%) defeats Robert Morris (13,659 votes for 12%).

November—In the general election for the U.S. Senate, Lloyd Bentsen (1,194,069 votes for 54%) defeats Bush (1,035,794 votes for 46%).

1971

December 11—President Richard M. Nixon appoints Bush U.S. ambassador to the United Nations.

1973

January—Nixon appoints Bush as the chairman of the Republican National Committee (RNC).

1974

August 9—Richard Nixon resigns as president of the United States. Gerald R. Ford is sworn in as the 38th president.

August—Ford appoints Bush the American envoy to the People's Republic of China (PRC).

1975

Ford appoints Bush director of the Central Intelligence Agency (CIA).

1979

May 1—Bush announces that he is a candidate for the Republican nomination for the presidency.

1980

May 31—After losing in the New Hampshire primary to Ronald Reagan, Bush withdraws from the race.

Bush chosen as Reagan's running mate.

The ticket of Ronald Reagan and George Bush (43,642,539 votes for 50.69%) defeat incumbents Jimmy Carter and Walter Mondale (35,480,948 votes for 41.06%).

1981

January 20—Reagan and Bush sworn in as president and vice president of the United States.

March 3—Reagan is seriously wounded by a gunman's bullet in Washington, D.C. At the time of the attack, Bush is returning from Fort Worth, Texas, on Air Force Two.

1985

July 13—Reagan undergoes surgery for intestinal cancer. Before receiving anesthesia, he signs a letter temporarily transferring power to Bush (when he regained consciousness the same day, he signed a letter to reclaim his power).

1987

February 26—The report of the "Tower Commission," charged by President Reagan to investigate the Iran-contra scandal, is released.

March 3—Director of the Federal Bureau of Investigation (FBI) William Webster is nominated by Reagan to become the director of central intelligence. (He is confirmed on May 1.)

March 16—Governor Michael Dukakis (D-Mass.) announces he will seek his party's nomination for president.

June 11—Margaret Thatcher is reelected to her third term as prime minister of Great Britain.

July 24—Reagan nominates Judge William Sessions to head the FBI.

September 7—Jesse Jackson announces he will seek his party's nomination for the presidency.

October 12—Bush announces that he is a candidate for the Republican presidential nomination.

1988

January 25—During a live interview, Bush argues with CBS anchorman Dan Rather when questioned about his role in the Iran–contra affair.

February 5—The Justice Department indicts General Manuel Noriega of Panama for involvement in the drug trade and for taking bribes.

February 16—Bush defeats Senator Robert Dole (R-Kans.) in the New Hampshire primary.

May 11—Reagan endorses Bush for the presidency.

June 10—The House Ethics Committee votes to investigate the finances of Speaker Wright.

July 21—The Democratic National Convention nominates Michael Dukakis for the presidency and Lloyd Bentsen of Texas for the vice presidency.

August 5—James Baker resigns as secretary of the Treasury in order to become Bush's campaign manager.

August 18—The Republican National Convention nominates Bush for the presidency and J. Danforth ("Dan") Quayle of Indiana for the vice presidency.

October 1—Mikhail Gorbachev becomes president of the Union of Soviet Socialist Republics (USSR).

October 25—The Department of Veteran's Affairs is added to the cabinet.

November 8—The ticket of George Bush and Dan Quayle (48,881,278 votes for 53.38%) defeat Michael Dukakis and Lloyd Bentsen (41,805,374 votes for 45.65%).

November 29—George Mitchell (D-Maine) is named Majority Leader of the U.S. Senate.

December 6–7—Gorbachev visits the United Nations and holds a summit in New York with Reagan and Bush.

December 16—Bush nominates John Tower (R-Tex.) as his secretary of defense.

December 21—A terrorist bomb destroys Pan Am flight 103 over Lockerbie, Scotland, killing 270 people.

1989

January 4—American jets destroy two Libyan fighters over international waters.

January 7—Emperor Hirohito of Japan dies after a reign of 62 years; his successor is Crown Prince Akihito.

January 20—Bush and Quayle sworn in as president and vice president of the United States.

February 1—Kenneth Starr is nominated as the administration's Solicitor General, and William Bennett is named the administration's "Drug czar."

February 8—The Federal Deposit Insurance Corporation (FDIC) assumes control over the banking crisis.

February 19—David Duke is elected to the Louisiana legislature.

February 21—Oliver North begins his trial for Iran–contra crimes.

March 9—By a vote of 53-47, the Senate rejects the nomination of Tower to be secretary of defense.

March 14—Bennett declares a "war on crime" in the District of Columbia.

March 24—The tanker *Exxon Valdez* runs aground in Prince William Sound, Alaska, causing the biggest oil spill in the nation's history.

March 26—Boris Yeltsin is elected to the Russian Congress of Deputies.

April 12—Speaker of the House Jim Wright (D-Tex.) is accused of ethical violations.

April 19—An explosion on the USS *Iowa* kills 47 sailors.

April 19–27—Student demonstrations engulf the city of Beijing.

May 4—Oliver North is found guilty on three of 12 charges.

May 8—William Rehnquist becomes the first chief justice of the Supreme Court to testify before Congress as he calls for higher pay for the federal judiciary.

May 19—The Dow Jones Industrial Average passes 2500 for the first time since the stock market crash of October 1987.

May 26—House Majority Whip Tony Coelho (D-Calif.) resigns amid a financial scandal.

May 28–29—Bush attends a meeting of NATO leaders in Brussels, where he proposes that the United States and USSR reduce their troop strengths in Europe to 275,000 men each.

May 31—Jim Wright resigns as Speaker of the House. Thomas Foley (D-Wash.) assumes the Speaker's chair.

June 4—Thousands of protesters die as Chinese troops remove student protesters from Beijing's Tiananmen Square.

June 4—The Solidarity Union, reinstated by the Communist government in April as a legal political movement, wins major gains in a free Polish election.

June 13—Bush vetoes a rise in the minimum wage and an override vote fails.

June 20—In the wake of the Tiananmen Square massacre, the United States suspends high-level relations with the PRC.

July 13–14—Bush attends the 15th G-7 summit in Paris.

July 13—Surgeon General Everett Koop resigns his position. He had become vulnerable as a result of his call for AIDS education, as well as his public statements claiming that abortions do not hurt women physically.

July 20—Bush calls for an American Moon base and a mission to Mars.

August 5—Congress authorizes the Resolution Trust Corporation to spend $166 billion to bail out failing savings and loans.

September 5—Bush's first national TV address highlights the drug crisis "sapping our strength as a nation." However, the impact of the president's display of a bag of crack cocaine during the speech is lessened when it is announced that the sample was obtained illegally.

September 28—At a summit of the nation's governors on education, Bush pledges to eliminate illiteracy, improve teacher standards, and create national performance goals.

October 3—Noriega routs a U.S.-supported coup attempt.

October 3—Televangelist Jim Bakker is found guilty on 24 counts of fraud and conspiracy.

October 17—A devastating earthquake hits San Francisco, killing 75 people, causing more than $1 billion in damage, and delaying baseball's World Series.

October 19—The Senate rejects an administration-sponsored constitutional amendment to protect the flag from desecration.

October 21—Bush vetoes a measure allowing the government to pay for abortions in the case of rape or incest.

October 31—Congress passes, with administration support, a new minimum wage: $3.80 for 1990 and $4.25 in 1991.

November 9—East Germany opens its borders to the West. Cheering crowds begin to dismantle the Berlin Wall.

November 21—Bush is formally presented with a piece of the Berlin Wall by West German foreign minister Hans Dietrich Genscher.

December 1–3—Bush and Gorbachev meet in a summit off the coast of Malta.

December 20—U.S. forces invade Panama, executing Operation Just Cause. Panama City is taken within eight hours and Noriega takes refuge in the Vatican consulate.

December 22—President Nicolae Ceaușescu of Romania attempts to flee Bucharest, but he is captured and executed.

December 28–29—In Czechoslovakia, Alexander Dubček becomes the new leader of parliament and Vaclav Havel becomes the nation's president.

1990

January 3—General Noriega surrenders to the United States; he is extradited to Florida the next day.

January 10—President Bush lifts U.S. restrictions on China after it ends its martial law.

January 18—Health and Human Services secretary Louis Sullivan accuses the tobacco industry of creating a "culture of cancer" for blacks.

January 31—Bush delivers his second State of the Union address.

February 11—Nelson Mandela is freed from a South African prison.

February 15—Bush attends a drug summit of North and South American nations in Colombia; the attendees agree to cooperate together to end the drug trade.

February 25—Smoking is banned on all domestic flights of six hours or less.

March 11—Lithuania declares itself independent of the USSR.

April 28—More than 200,000 antiabortion activists march in Washington. They are addressed by both Bush and Quayle.

May 29—Boris Yeltsin is elected president of Russia.

May 31–June 3—Bush and Gorbachev meet in Washington for their third summit. They agreed to cut long-range nuclear missiles as well as the production of chemical weapons.

June 26—After a meeting with the congressional leadership, Bush announce the need for "tax revenue increases," thus reversing his "no new taxes" promise of 1988.

July 11—Economic summit held in Houston, Texas.

July 12—Yeltsin resigns from the Communist Party.

July 22—Bush nominates David Souter of New Hampshire to replace Justice William Brennan on the Supreme Court (Brennan had retired on July 20).

July 25—David Durenberger (R-Minn.) is censured by a 96-0 vote of the full Senate.

July 26—The House formally reprimands Barney Frank (D-Mass.) for ethics violations.

July 27—Over the objection of the administration, Congress imposes sanctions on Iraq for its humans rights violations.

August 2—Iraq invades Kuwait.

August 13—Jordan's King Hussein supports Iraq, but other Arab states join the Washington-led coalition.

August 15—Iraq settles its eight-year conflict with Iran.

September 9—Bush meets Gorbachev in Helsinki, Finland. Gorbachev promises to cooperate with the United States against Iraq.

September 14—The administration announces the largest arms sale in the nation's history, $20 billion in arms to Saudi Arabia.

September 30—After Bush drops his demand for a cut in the capital gains tax, a budget compromise is achieved.

October 1—Bush addresses the United Nations, and says he is still searching for a diplomatic solution to the crisis in Kuwait.

October 2—Souter is confirmed in the Senate by a vote of 90-9.

October 6—Bush vetoes a stopgap budget and the government begins to shut down. Bush would sign a revised budget on October 19.

October 15—Mikhail Gorbachev is awarded the Nobel Peace Prize.

October 26—The administration announces that FY90 produced a $220 billion deficit—second largest in history.

November 6—In the off-year elections, the Democrats retain control of Congress.

November 15—Bush signs into law the Clean Air Act of 1990.

November 22—Following a rebellion in her own party, Margaret Thatcher is forced to resign as Britain's prime minister. John Major succeeds her in the office.

November 29—The UN passes Security Council Resolution 678, which authorizes the use of force against Iraqi forces to free Kuwait, and gives Saddam Hussein a January 15, 1991, deadline to withdraw from that nation.

December 2—A coalition led by Chancellor Helmut Kohl wins the first free elections in a unified Germany since 1932.

December 6—Saddam Hussein announces he will permit all hostages to leave Kuwait; over 1,000 are immediately released.

December 9—Slobodan Miloševic wins the presidency of Yugoslavia.

December 12—Secretary of Education Lauro Cavazos resigns.

December 12—Bush approves up to $1 billion in food loan guarantees for the USSR.

December 18—The Federal Reserve admits that the economy is indeed in recession.

December 20—USSR foreign minister Eduard Shevardnadze resigns.

December 23—Slovenia declares itself independent from Yugoslavia.

December 25—Six Arab states warn Iraq that it must withdraw from Kuwait or face attack by a coalition of forces, led by the United States.

1991

January 12—Congress authorizes the president to use U.S. forces in the Persian Gulf to implement Security Council Resolution 678. The vote is 52-47 in the Senate and 250-183 in the House.

January 13—Martial law is proclaimed in Lithuania, after Russian forces kill 11 protesters.

January 16—At 7:00 p.m. EST (3:00 a.m., January 17, Iraqi time), U.S. forces begin Operation Desert Storm, bombing targets in Kuwait and Iraq.

January 17—Beginning a counterattack, Iraq attacks Israel with a Scud missile bombardment.

January 22–25—Iraqi troops set fire to Kuwaiti oil fields and release oil into the Persian Gulf.

February 2—President de Klerk of South Africa asks his legislature to repeal the apartheid laws.

February 24—The ground war begins, as coalition forces attack Iraqi emplacements in Kuwait and Iraq.

February 26—Kuwait City is liberated.

February 28—Cease-fire is declared.

March 3—At Safwan, Iraq, cease-fire terms are announced at a meeting of the Iraqi and coalition military leadership.

Casualties: U.S. and Coalition Forces: 148 dead, 458 wounded; Iraqi: 22,000 dead.

March 3—Latvia and Estonia hold plebiscites, which declare in favor of independence from the USSR.

March 6—A videotape showing Los Angeles police beating Rodney King during his arrest is broadcast nationwide.

March 15—Four members of the Los Angeles Police Department are indicted in the Rodney King incident.

March 21—Congress approves an additional $30 billion for S&L bailouts.

April 4—Senator John Heinz (R-Pa.) dies in a plane crash.

April 6—The Gulf War formally ends as Saddam Hussein accepts all UN demands.

April 9—The Republic of Georgia declares itself independent of the USSR.

April 12—The U.S. military assumes responsibility for 700,000 Kurdish refugees in a "safe zone" of northern Iraq.

April 12—Secretary of Defense Dick Cheney announces plans to close 31 military bases.

April 17—The Dow Jones Industrial Average closes above 3,000 points for the first time.

April 18—Bush announces a plan, entitled "America 2000," to revitalize American education by national testing, more student aid, and the creation of model schools.

May 15—Bush asks Congress to renew "most favored nation" trade status with the PRC.

May 21—Campaigning for reelection, former Indian prime minister Rajiv Gandhi is assassinated.

June 13—Boris Yeltsin becomes the first popularly elected leader of Russia.

June 20—Bush meets with Yeltsin in New York City.

June 25—Slovenia and Croatia leave Yugoslavia.

June 28—Thurgood Marshall announces his retirement from the Supreme Court.

July 1—President nominates Clarence Thomas of the Circuit Court of Appeals for the District of Columbia to succeed Marshall.

July 8—Iraq admits that it produced enriched uranium for a nuclear program.

July 9—Bush approves the Defense Department program to close or consolidate military installations around the nation.

July 11—The Congressional Black Caucus approves the Thomas nomination (19-1).

July 22—Daryl Gates, chief of the Los Angeles Police Department, announces his retirement.

July 30–31—At a summit in Moscow, Bush and Gorbachev sign the START treaty.

August 16—Bush orders the cancellation of an AIDS conference in the United States, using as his rationale the fact that American policy prohibits carriers of the HIV virus to enter the country.

August 18—A coup begins against Gorbachev, who is detained by plotters at his dacha on the Black Sea.

August 19—Yeltsin denounces the coup and calls for a general strike.

August 21—Coup collapses.

August 22–23—Riots explode in Crown Heights, Brooklyn, when a black child is struck and killed by a car driven by a Hasidic Jew.

August 27—The European Community recognizes the independence of Lithuania, Latvia, and Estonia.

August 27—An American Bar Association (ABA) panel gives Thomas its lowest rating, stating that he is only "qualified" to be named an associate justice of the Supreme Court.

September 6—The USSR confirms that Lithuania, Latvia, and Estonia are independent republics.

September 10—Judiciary Committee hearings on Thomas begin.

September 16—Federal courts drop all charges against Oliver North.

September 23—In a speech to the United Nations, Bush declares that the organization must renounce its 1975 declaration that equated Zionism with racism.

September 27—Following a 7-7 vote, the Judiciary Committee sends the Thomas nomination to the full Senate floor.

October 6—Charges of sexual harassment are raised against Thomas; a second round of hearings is immediately scheduled.

October 11–13—The second round of the Thomas hearings produce accusations from law professor Anita Hill about her alleged harassment at the hands of Thomas while they were both employed by the Equal Employment Opportunity Commission, which Thomas angrily denies.

October 15—The full Senate approves the Thomas nomination by a vote of 52 to 48.

October 29—Bush and Gorbachev meet in Spain to attend a conference on peace in the Middle East.

November 3—The FY91 deficit is announced as being $268.7 billion.

November 4—For the first time, five living presidents (Nixon, Carter, Ford, Reagan, and Bush) gather to dedicate the Reagan Presidential Library in Simi Valley, California.

November 5—Robert Gates is confirmed by the Senate as CIA director.

November 14—With little hope of extradition, the United States indicts two Libyans in the bombing of Pan Am flight 103.

November 21—The Civil Rights Act of 1991 is signed.

November 27—Another $100 billion is approved by Congress for the S&L bailout.

December 1—The Ukraine votes its independence from the USSR.

December 3—After the appearance of a scandal involving his misuse of Executive Office travel funds, White House chief of staff John Sununu resigns.

December 8—A Commonwealth of Independent States is proclaimed, replacing the USSR. Gorbachev refuses to accept the proclamation.

December 9—The 12 nations of the European Community sign the Maastricht Treaty mandating greater political and economic unity.

December 16—The UN repeals its "Zionism Equals Racism" resolution.

December 18—General Motors announces the closing of another 21 plants, forcing the layoff of some 70,000 workers.

December 25—Gorbachev announces his resignation, effective December 31.

1992

January 8—During a trip to Japan, Bush becomes ill at a state dinner and vomits on Prime Minister Kiichi Miyazawa of Japan.

January 22—For a second time, Bush addresses antiabortion marchers convened in Washington.

January 28—Bush delivers his fourth State of the Union Address.

February 18—North and South Korea begin talks for the inspection of possible nuclear sites.

February 27—Bush meets with Latin American leaders in a second drug summit.

March 12—Speaker of the House Thomas Foley admits that 335 members overdrew their accounts in the House bank. Names of 303 offenders would be made public on April 16.

March 29—Governor Bill Clinton (D-Ark.), the front-runner for the Democratic nomination, admits he tried marijuana in the 1960s but "didn't inhale."

April 9—Manuel Noriega is convicted on drug trafficking and money laundering charges.

April 29—A California jury finds four policemen in the Rodney King beating not guilty. Rioting immediately breaks out in South-Central Los Angeles; 58 persons will die before May 2.

July 13–16—The Democratic National Convention nominates Clinton for the presidency and Senator Al Gore of Tennessee for the vice presidency.

July 16—Billionaire Ross H. Perot of Texas temporarily withdraws from the presidential race.

August 12—The United States, Mexico, and Canada announce their plans to negotiate a North American Free Trade Agreement (NAFTA).

August 20—The Republican National Convention renominates Bush for the presidency and Quayle for the vice presidency.

August 24—Hurricane Andrew strikes South Florida. Thirty are killed and thousands are left homeless.

August 27—U.S. planes begin to enforce the "no-fly" zone over southern Iraq.

October 1—Perot reenters the presidential campaign.

October 11—First presidential debate.

October 15—Second presidential debate.

October 19—Third presidential debate.

November 3—The ticket of Bill Clinton and Al Gore (44,908,233 votes for 42.98%) defeats George Bush and Dan Quayle (39,102,282 votes for 37.37%) and Ross Perot and Admiral James Stockdale (19,721,433 votes for 18.88%).

December 24—Pardons are granted by Bush to six participants in the Iran-contra affair.

1993

January 17—U.S. missiles destroy an industrial complex in Iraq.

January 20—Bill Clinton inaugurated as 42nd president of the United States; Bush returns to Houston, Texas.

PRINCIPAL U.S. GOVERNMENT OFFICIALS OF THE GEORGE H. W. BUSH YEARS

⌇

UNITED STATES SUPREME COURT: 1989–1993

Last Name	First Name	Appointed by	Year of Appointment	Year of Retirement
Brennan, Jr.	William J.	Eisenhower	1956	1990
Marshall	Thurgood	Johnson	1967	1991
Blackmun	Harry A.	Nixon	1970	1994
Rehnquist	William R.	Nixon (as associate)	1972–1986 (associate)	
		Reagan (as Chief Justice)	1986–2005 (Chief Justice)	
Stevens	John Paul	Ford	1975	
O'Connor	Sandra Day	Reagan	1981	
Scalia	Antonin	Reagan	1986	
Kennedy	Anthony	Reagan	1988	
Souter	David	Bush	1990	
Thomas	Clarence	Bush	1991	

EXECUTIVE DEPARTMENTS: 1989–1993

Secretary of State
    James A. Baker, III (1989–1992)
    Lawrence S. Eagleburger (1992–1993)
Secretary of the Treasury
    Nicholas F. Brady (1989–1993)
Secretary of Defense
    Richard B. Cheney (1989–1993)
Attorney General
    Dick Thornburgh (1989–1991)
    William P. Barr (1991–1993)

Secretary of the Interior
    Manuel Lujan (1989–1993)
Secretary of Agriculture
    Clayton Yeutter (1989–1991)
    Edward R. Madigan (1991–1993)
Secretary of Commerce
    Robert Mosbacher (1989–1992)
    Barbara H. Franklin (1992–1993)
Secretary of Labor
    Elizabeth H. Dole (1989–1990)
    Lynn Morley Martin (1990–1993)

Secretary of Health and Human Services
  Louis W. Sullivan (1989–1993)
Secretary of Housing and Urban Development
  Jack Kemp (1989–1993)
Secretary of Transportation
  Samuel Skinner (1989–1991)
  Andrew H. Card (1992–1993)

Secretary of Energy
  James Watkins (1989–1993)
Secretary of Education
  Lauro F. Cavazos, Jr. (1989–1991)
  Lamar Alexander (1991–1993)
Secretary of Veterans Affairs
  Edward J. Derwinski (1989–1992)

SENATE LEADERSHIP: 1989–1993[1]

I. 101st Congress (1989–1991)

Total Membership
  100 Senators
Party Divisions
  45 Republican; 55 Democrat
President Pro Tempore
  Robert C. Byrd (D-W.Va.;
    Term: 1989–1995)
Majority Leader
  George L. Mitchell (D-Maine)
Minority Leader
  Robert Dole (R-Kans.)
Republican Whip
  Alan K. Simpson (R-Wyo.;
    Term: 1985–1995)
Democratic Whip
  Alan Cranston (D-Calif.;
    Term: 1977–1991)

II. 102nd Congress (1991–1993)

Total Membership
  100 Senators
Party Divisions
  44 Republican; 56 Democrat
President Pro Tempore
  Robert C. Byrd (D-W.Va.;
    Term: 1989–1995)
Majority Leader
  George L. Mitchell (D-Maine)
Minority Leader
  Robert Dole (R-Kans.)
Republican Whip
  Alan K. Simpson (R-Wyo.;
    Term: 1985–1995)
Democratic Whip
  Wendell H. Ford (D-Ky.;
    Term: 1991–1999)

U.S. CONGRESS: 101ST SENATE[2]

(ARRANGED BY STATE)

State	Last Name	First Name	Party	Date Service Begins	Date Service Ends
AK	Murkowski	Frank	R	1980	2002 (Dec.)
	Stevens	Ted	R	1968	
AL	Heflin	Howell	D	1979	1997

(continued)

[1] http://www.senate.gov/artandhistory/history/common/briefing/Majority_Minority_Leaders.htm;
http://www.senate.gov/artandhistory/history/common/briefing/Party_Whips.htm
[2] See *Senators of the United States, 1789–2003: A Chronological List of Senators from the First Congress to the 108th Congress.* Prepared under the direction of Gary Sisco, Secretary of the Senate, by the Senate Historical Office.

State	Last Name	First Name	Party	Date Service Begins	Date Service Ends
AL	Shelby	Richard	D/R	1987	
AR	Bumpers	Dale	D	1975	1999
	Pryor	David	D	1979	1997
AZ	DeConcini	Dennis	D	1977	1995
	McCain	John	R	1987	
CA	Cranston	Alan	D	1969	1993
	Wilson	Pete	R	1983	1991
CO	Armstrong	William	R	1979	1991
	Wirth	Timothy	D	1987	1993
CT	Dodd	Christopher	D	1981	
	Lieberman	Joseph	D	1989	
DE	Biden	Joseph	D	1973	
	Roth	William	R	1971	2001
FL	Graham	Bob	D	1987	
	Mack	Connie	R	1989	2001
GA	Fowler	Wyche	D	1987	1993
	Nunn	Samuel	D	1972	1997
HI	Akaka	Daniel	D	1989	
	Matsunaga	Spark	D	1977	1990
IA	Grassley	Charles	R	1981	
	Harkin	Tom	D	1985	
ID	McClure	James	R	1973	1991
	Symms	Steven	R	1981	1993
IL	Dixon	Alan	D	1981	1993
	Simon	Paul	D	1985	1997
IN	Coats	Daniel P.	R	1987	1999
	Lugar	Richard	R	1977	
KS	Dole	Robert	R	1969	1996 (June)
	Kassebaum	Nancy	R	1978	1997
KY	Ford	Wendell	D	1974	1999
	McConnell	Mitch	R	1985	
LA	Breaux	John	D	1987	2005
	Johnston	J. Bennett, Jr.	D	1972	1997
MA	Kennedy	Edward ("Ted")	D	1962	
	Kerry	John	D	1985	
MD	Mikulski	Barbara	D	1987	
	Sarbanes	Paul	D	1977	
ME	Cohen	William	R	1979	1997
	Mitchell	George	D	1979	1995
MI	Levin	Carl	D	1979	
	Riegle	Donald	D	1976	1995
MN	Boschwitz	Rudy	R	1978	1991
	Durenberger	David	R	1978	1995

State	Last Name	First Name	Party	Date Service Begins	Date Service Ends
MO	Bond	Kit	R	1987	
	Danforth	John H., Jr.	R	1976	1995
MS	Cochran	Thad	R	1978	
	Lott	Trent	R	1989	
MT	Baucus	Max	D	1978	
	Burns	Conrad	R	1989	
NC	Helms	Jesse	R	1973	2003
	Sanford	Terry	D	1986	1993
ND	Burdick	Quentin	D	1960	1992 (Sept.)
	Conrad	Kent	D	1987	
NE	Exon	J. James	D	1979	1997
	Kerrey	Bob	D	1989	2001
NH	Humphrey	Gordon	R	1979	1990
	Rudman	Warren	R	1980	1993
	Smith	Robert	R	1990	2003
NJ	Bradley	Bill	D	1979	1997
	Lautenberg	Frank	D	1982–2001; 2003	
NM	Bingaman	Jeff	D	1983	
	Domenici	Pete	R	1973	
NV	Bryan	Richard	D	1989	2001
	Reid	Harry	D	1987	
NY	D'Amato	Alfonse	R	1981	1999
	Moynihan	Daniel P.	D	1977	2001
OH	Glenn	John H., Jr.	D	1974	1999
	Metzenbaum	Howard	D	1974, 1976	1995
OK	Boren	David	D	1979	1994 (Nov.)
	Nickles	Donald	R	1981	
OR	Hatfield	Mark	R	1967	1997
	Packwood	Robert	R	1969	1995 (Oct.)
PA	Heinz	H. John, III	R	1977	1991
	Specter	Arlen	R	1981	
RI	Chafee	John H., Jr.	R	1976	1999
	Pell	Claiborne	D	1961	1997
SC	Hollings	Ernest	D	1965	
	Thurmond	Strom	D/R	1954	2003
SD	Daschle	Tom	D	1987	
	Pressler	Larry	R	1979	1997
TN	Gore	Albert, Jr.	D	1985	1993
	Sasser	James	D	1977	1995
TX	Bentsen	Lloyd	D	1971	1993
	Gramm	Phil	R	1985	2003
UT	Garn	E. J. "Jake"	R	1974	1993
	Hatch	Orrin	D/R	1977	

(continued)

State	Last Name	First Name	Party	Date Service Begins	Date Service Ends
VA	Robb	Charles	D	1989	2001
	Warner	John	R	1979	
VT	Leahy	Patrick	D	1975	
	Jeffords	Jim	R/I	1989	
WA	Adams	Brock	D	1987	1993
	Gorton	Thomas (Slade), III	R	1981–1987; 1989	
WI	Kasten	Robert	R	1981	1993
	Kohl	Herbert	D	1989	
WV	Byrd	Robert	D	1959	
	Rockefeller	John D., IV	D	1985	
WY	Simpson	Alan	R	1979	1997
	Wallop	Malcolm	R	1977	1995

U.S. Congress: 101st Senate[3]

(Arranged by Senator's Name)

Last Name	First Name	State	Party	Date Service Begins	Date Service Ends
Adams	Brock	WA	D	1987	1993
Akaka	Daniel	HI	D	1989	
Armstrong	William	CO	R	1979	1991
Baucus	Max	MT	D	1978	
Bentsen	Lloyd	TX	D	1971	1993
Biden	Joseph	DE	D	1973	
Bingaman	Jeff	NM	D	1983	
Bond	Kit	MO	R	1987	
Boren	David	OK	D	1979	1994 (Nov.)
Boschwitz	Rudy	MN	R	1978	1991
Bradley	Bill	NJ	D	1979	1997
Breaux	John	LA	D	1987	2005
Bryan	Richard	NV	D	1989	2001
Bumpers	Dale	AR	D	1975	1999
Burdick	Quentin	ND	D	1960	1992 (Sept.)
Burns	Conrad	MT	R	1989	
Byrd	Robert	WV	D	1959	
Chafee	John H., Jr.	RI	R	1976	1999
Coats	Daniel P.	IN	R	1987	1999
Cochran	Thad	MS	R	1978	

[3] See *Senators of the United States, 1789–2003: A Chronological List of Senators from the First Congress to the 108th Congress.* Prepared under the direction of Gary Sisco, Secretary of the Senate, by the Senate Historical Office.

Last Name	First Name	State	Party	Date Service Begins	Date Service Ends
Cohen	William	ME	R	1979	1997
Conrad	Kent	ND	D	1987	
Cranston	Alan	CA	D	1969	1993
D'Amato	Alfonse	NY	R	1981	1999
Danforth	John H., Jr.	MO	R	1976	1995
Daschle	Tom	SD	D	1987	
DeConcini	Dennis	AZ	D	1977	1995
Dixon	Alan	IL	D	1981	1993
Dodd	Christopher	CT	D	1981	
Dole	Robert	KS	R	1969	1996 (June)
Domenici	Pete	NM	R	1973	
Durenberger	David	MN	R	1978	1995
Exon	J. James	NE	D	1979	1997
Ford	Wendell	KY	D	1974	1999
Fowler	Wyche	GA	D	1987	1993
Garn	E. J. "Jake"	UT	R	1974	1993
Glenn	John H., Jr.	OH	D	1974	1999
Gore	Albert, Jr.	TN	D	1985	1993
Gorton	Thomas (Slade), III	WA	R	1981–1987; 1989	
Graham	Bob	FL	D	1987	
Gramm	Phil	TX	R	1985	2003
Grassley	Charles	IA	R	1981	
Harkin	Tom	IA	D	1985	
Hatch	Orrin	UT	R	1977	
Hatfield	Mark	OR	R	1967	1997
Heflin	Howell	AL	D	1979	1997
Heinz	H. John, III	PA	R	1977	1991
Helms	Jesse	NC	R	1973	2003
Hollings	Ernest	SC	D	1965	
Humphrey	Gordon	NH	R	1979	1990
Jeffords	Jim	VT	R/I	1989	
Johnston	J. Bennett, Jr.	LA	D	1972	1997
Kassebaum	Nancy	KS	R	1978	1997
Kasten	Robert	WI	R	1981	1993
Kennedy	Edward ("Ted")	MA	D	1962	
Kerrey	Bob	NE	D	1989	2001
Kerry	John	MA	D	1985	
Kohl	Herbert	WI	D	1989	
Lautenberg	Frank	NJ	D	1982–2001; 2003	
Leahy	Patrick	VT	D	1975	
Levin	Carl	MI	D	1979	

(continued)

Last Name	First Name	State	Party	Date Service Begins	Date Service Ends
Lott	Trent	MS	R	1989	
Lieberman	Joseph	CT	D	1989	
Lugar	Richard	IN	R	1977	
Mack	Connie	FL	R	1989	2001
Matsunaga	Spark	HI	D	1977	1990
McCain	John	AZ	R	1987	
McClure	James	ID	R	1973	1991
McConnell	Mitch	KY	R	1985	
Metzenbaum	Howard	OH	D	1974, 1976	1995
Mikulski	Barbara	MD	D	1987	
Mitchell	George	ME	D	1979	1995
Moynihan	Daniel P.	NY	D	1977	2001
Murkowski	Frank	AK	R	1980	2002 (Dec.)
Nickles	Donald	OK	R	1981	
Nunn	Samuel	GA	D	1972	1997
Packwood	Robert	OR	R	1969	1995 (Oct.)
Pell	Claiborne	RI	D	1961	1997
Pressler	Larry	SD	R	1979	1997
Pryor	David	AR	D	1979	1997
Reid	Harry	NV	D	1987	
Riegle	Donald	MI	D	1976	1995
Robb	Charles	VA	D	1989	2001
Rockefeller	John D., IV	WV	D	1985	
Roth	William	DE	R	1971	2001
Rudman	Warren	NH	R	1980	1993
Sanford	Terry	NC	D	1986	1993
Sarbanes	Paul	MD	D	1977	
Sasser	James	TN	D	1977	1995
Shelby	Richard	AL	D/R	1987	
Simon	Paul	IL	D	1985	1997
Simpson	Alan	WY	R	1979	1997
Smith	Robert	NH	R	1990	2003
Specter	Arlen	PA	R	1981	
Stevens	Ted	AK	R	1968	
Symms	Steven	ID	R	1981	1993
Thurmond	Strom	SC	D/R	1954	2003
Wallop	Malcolm	WY	R	1977	1995
Warner	John	VA	R	1979	
Wilson	Pete	CA	R	1983	1991
Wirth	Timothy	CO	D	1987	1993

U.S. Congress: 102nd Senate[4]
(Arranged by State)

State	Last Name	First Name	Party	Date Service Begins	Date Service Ends
AK	Murkowski	Frank	R	1980	2002 (Dec.)
	Stevens	Ted	R	1968	
AL	Heflin	Howell	D	1979	1997
	Shelby	Richard	D/R	1987	
AR	Bumpers	Dale	D	1975	1999
	Pryor	David	D	1979	1997
AZ	DeConcini	Dennis	D	1977	1995
	McCain	John	R	1987	
CA	Cranston	Alan	D	1969	1993
	Seymour	John	R	1991	1992 (Nov.)
	Feinstein	Dianne	D	1992	
CO	Brown	George Hanks (Hank)	R	1991	1997
	Wirth	Timothy	D	1987	1993
CT	Dodd	Christopher	D	1981	
	Lieberman	Joseph	D	1989	
DE	Biden	Joseph	D	1973	
	Roth	William	R	1971	2001
FL	Graham	Bob	D	1987	
	Mack	Connie	R	1989	2001
GA	Fowler	Wyche	D	1987	1993
	Nunn	Samuel	D	1972	1997
HI	Akaka	Daniel	D	1989	
	Matsunaga	Spark	D	1977	1990
IA	Grassley	Charles	R	1981	
	Harkin	Tom	D	1985	
ID	Craig	Larry	R	1991	
	Symms	Steven	R	1981	1993
IL	Dixon	Alan	D	1981	1993
	Simon	Paul	D	1985	1997
IN	Coats	Daniel P.	R	1987	1999
	Lugar	Richard	R	1977	
KS	Dole	Robert	R	1969	1996 (June)
	Kassebaum	Nancy	R	1978	1997
KY	Ford	Wendell	D	1974	1999
	McConnell	Mitch	R	1985	
LA	Breaux	John	D	1987	2005
	Johnston	J. Bennett, Jr.	D	1972	1997

(continued)

[4] See *Senators of the United States, 1789–2003: A Chronological List of Senators from the First Congress to the 108th Congress.* Prepared under the direction of Gary Sisco, Secretary of the Senate, by the Senate Historical Office.

State	Last Name	First Name	Party	Date Service Begins	Date Service Ends
MA	Kennedy	Edward ("Ted")	D	1962	
	Kerry	John	D	1985	
MD	Mikulski	Barbara	D	1987	
	Sarbanes	Paul	D	1977	
ME	Cohen	William	R	1979	1997
	Mitchell	George	D	1979	1995
MI	Levin	Carl	D	1979	
	Riegle	Donald	D	1976	1995
MN	Wellstone	Paul	D	1991	2002 (Oct.)
	Durenberger	David	R	1978	1995
MO	Bond	Kit	R	1987	
	Danforth	John H., Jr.	R	1976	1995
MS	Cochran	Thad	R	1978	
	Lott	Trent	R	1989	
MT	Baucus	Max	D	1978	
	Burns	Conrad	R	1989	
NC	Helms	Jesse	R	1973	2003
	Sanford	Terry	D	1986	1993
ND	Burdick	Quentin	D	1960	1992 (Sept.)
	Burdick	Jocelyn	D	1992	1992 (Dec.)
	Conrad	Kent	D	1987	
	Dordan	Byron	D	1992	
NE	Exon	J. James	D	1979	1997
	Kerrey	Bob	D	1989	2001
NH	Humphrey	Gordon	R	1979	1990
	Rudman	Warren	R	1980	1993
	Smith	Robert	R	1990	2003
NJ	Bradley	Bill	D	1979	1997
	Lautenberg	Frank	D	1982–2001; 2003	
NM	Bingaman	Jeff	D	1983	
	Domenici	Pete	R	1973	
NV	Bryan	Richard	D	1989	2001
	Reid	Harry	D	1987	
NY	D'Amato	Alfonse	R	1981	1999
	Moynihan	Daniel P.	D	1977	2001
OH	Glenn	John H., Jr.	D	1974	1999
	Metzenbaum	Howard	D	1974, 1976	1995
OK	Boren	David	D	1979	1994 (Nov.)
	Nickles	Donald	R	1981	
OR	Hatfield	Mark	R	1967	1997
	Packwood	Robert	R	1969	1995 (Oct.)
PA	Wofford	Harris	D	1991	1995
	Specter	Arlen	R	1981	

State	Last Name	First Name	Party	Date Service Begins	Date Service Ends
RI	Chafee	John H., Jr.	R	1976	1999
	Pell	Claiborne	D	1961	1997
SC	Hollings	Ernest	D	1965	
	Thurmond	Strom	D/R	1954	2003
SD	Daschle	Tom	D	1987	
	Pressler	Larry	R	1979	1997
TN	Gore	Albert, Jr.	D	1985	1993
	Sasser	James	D	1977	1995
TX	Bentsen	Lloyd	D	1971	1993
	Gramm	Phil	R	1985	2003
UT	Garn	E. J. "Jake"	R	1974	1993
	Hatch	Orrin	R	1977	
VA	Robb	Charles	D	1989	2001
	Warner	John	R	1979	
VT	Leahy	Patrick	D	1975	
	Jeffords	Jim	R/I	1989	
WA	Adams	Brock	D	1987	1993
	Gorton	Thomas (Slade), III	R	1981–1987; 1989	
WI	Kasten	Robert	R	1981	1993
	Kohl	Herbert	D	1989	
WV	Byrd	Robert	D	1959	
	Rockefeller	John D., IV	D	1985	
WY	Simpson	Alan	R	1979	1997
	Wallop	Malcolm	R	1977	1995

U.S. Congress: 102nd Senate[5]

(Arranged by Senator's Name)

Last Name	First Name	State	Party	Date Service Begins	Date Service Ends
Adams	Brock	WA	D	1987	1993
Akaka	Daniel	HI	D	1989	
Baucus	Max	MT	D	1978	
Bentsen	Lloyd	TX	D	1971	1993
Biden	Joseph	DE	D	1973	
Bingaman	Jeff	NM	D	1983	
Bond	Kit	MO	R	1987	
Boren	David	OK	D	1979	1994 (Nov.)
Bradley	Bill	NJ	D	1979	1997

(continued)

[5] See *Senators of the United States, 1789–2003: A Chronological List of Senators from the First Congress to the 108th Congress.* Prepared under the direction of Gary Sisco, Secretary of the Senate, by the Senate Historical Office.

Last Name	First Name	State	Party	Date Service Begins	Date Service Ends
Breaux	John	LA	D	1987	2005
Brown	George Hanks (Hank)	CO	R	1991	1997
Bryan	Richard	NV	D	1989	2001
Bumpers	Dale	AR	D	1975	1999
Burdick	Quentin	ND	D	1960	1992 (Sept.)
Burdick	Jocelyn	ND	D	1992	1992 (Dec.)
Burns	Conrad	MT	R	1989	
Byrd	Robert	WV	D	1959	
Chafee	John H., Jr.	RI	R	1976	1999
Coats	Daniel P.	IN	R	1987	1999
Cochran	Thad	MS	R	1978	
Cohen	William	ME	R	1979	1997
Conrad	Kent	ND	D	1987	
Craig	Larry	ID	R	1991	
Cranston	Alan	CA	D	1969	1993
D'Amato	Alfonse	NY	R	1981	1999
Danforth	John H., Jr.	MO	R	1976	1995
Daschle	Tom	SD	D	1987	
DeConcini	Dennis	AZ	D	1977	1995
Dixon	Alan	IL	D	1981	1993
Dodd	Christopher	CT	D	1981	
Dole	Robert	KS	R	1969	1996 (June)
Domenici	Pete	NM	R	1973	
Dordan	Byron	ND	D	1992	
Durenberger	David	MN	R	1978	1995
Exon	J. James	NE	D	1979	1997
Feinstein	Dianne	CA	D	1992	
Ford	Wendell	KY	D	1974	1999
Fowler	Wyche	GA	D	1987	1993
Garn	E. J. "Jake"	UT	R	1974	1993
Glenn	John H., Jr.	OH	D	1974	1999
Gore	Albert, Jr.	TN	D	1985	1993
Gorton	Thomas (Slade), III	WA	R	1981–1987; 1989	
Graham	Bob	FL	D	1987	
Gramm	Phil	TX	R	1985	2003
Grassley	Charles	IA	R	1981	
Harkin	Tom	IA	D	1985	
Hatch	Orrin	UT	R	1977	
Hatfield	Mark	OR	R	1967	1997
Heflin	Howell	AL	D	1979	1997
Helms	Jesse	NC	R	1973	2003
Hollings	Ernest	SC	D	1965	

Last Name	First Name	State	Party	Date Service Begins	Date Service Ends
Humphrey	Gordon	NH	R	1979	1990
Jeffords	Jim	VT	R/I	1989	
Johnston	J. Bennett, Jr.	LA	D	1972	1997
Kassebaum	Nancy	KS	R	1978	1997
Kasten	Robert	WI	R	1981	1993
Kennedy	Edward ("Ted")	MA	D	1962	
Kerrey	Bob	NE	D	1989	2001
Kerry	John	MA	D	1985	
Kohl	Herbert	WI	D	1989	
Lautenberg	Frank	NJ	D	1982–2001; 2003	
Leahy	Patrick	VT	D	1975	
Levin	Carl	MI	D	1979	
Lieberman	Joseph	CT	D	1989	
Lott	Trent	MS	R	1989	
Lugar	Richard	IN	R	1977	
Mack	Connie	FL	R	1989	2001
Matsunaga	Spark	HI	D	1977	1990
McCain	John	AZ	R	1987	
McConnell	Mitch	KY	R	1985	
Metzenbaum	Howard	OH	D	1974, 1976	1995
Mikulski	Barbara	MD	D	1987	
Mitchell	George	ME	D	1979	1995
Moynihan	Daniel P.	NY	D	1977	2001
Murkowski	Frank	AK	R	1980	2002 (Dec.)
Nickles	Donald	OK	R	1981	
Nunn	Samuel	GA	D	1972	1997
Packwood	Robert	OR	R	1969	1995 (Oct.)
Pell	Claiborne	RI	D	1961	1997
Pressler	Larry	SD	R	1979	1997
Pryor	David	AR	D	1979	1997
Reid	Harry	NV	D	1987	
Riegle	Donald	MI	D	1976	1995
Robb	Charles	VA	D	1989	2001
Rockefeller	John D., IV	WV	D	1985	
Roth	William	DE	R	1971	2001
Rudman	Warren	NH	R	1980	1993
Sanford	Terry	NC	D	1986	1993
Sarbanes	Paul	MD	D	1977	
Sasser	James	TN	D	1977	1995
Seymour	John	CA	R	1991	1992 (Nov.)
Shelby	Richard	AL	D/R	1987	
Simon	Paul	IL	D	1985	1997
Simpson	Alan	WY	R	1979	1997

(continued)

Last Name	First Name	State	Party	Date Service Begins	Date Service Ends
Smith	Robert	NH	R	1990	2003
Specter	Arlen	PA	R	1981	
Stevens	Ted	AK	R	1968	
Symms	Steven	ID	R	1981	1993
Thurmond	Strom	SC	D/R	1954	2003
Wallop	Malcolm	WY	R	1977	1995
Warner	John	VA	R	1979	
Wellstone	Paul	MN	D	1991	2002 (Oct.)
Wirth	Timothy	CO	D	1987	1993
Wofford	Harris	PA	D	1991	1995

HOUSE LEADERSHIP: 1989–1993[6]

I. 101st Congress (1989–1991)
Total Membership
   435 Representatives, 4 delegates, 1 Resident Commissioner
Party Divisions
   175 Republicans; 260 Democrats
Speaker of the House
   James C. Wright, Jr. (D-Tex.; resigned June 6, 1989)
   Thomas S. Foley (D-Wash.)
Majority Leader
   Thomas S. Foley (D-Wash.; served until June 6, 1989)
   Richard A. Gephardt (D-Mo.)
Republican Leader
   Robert H. Michel (R-Ill.)
Majority Whip
   Tony Coelho (D-Calif.; resigned from the House, September 10, 1991)
   William H. Gray, III (D-Pa.)
Republican Whip
   Dick Cheney (R-Wyo.; resigned from House on March 17, 1989 to become Secretary of
      Defense)
   Newt Gingrich (R-Ga.)

II. 102nd Congress (1991–1993)
Total Membership
   435 Representatives, 4 delegates, 1 Resident Commissioner
Party Divisions
   167 Republicans; 267 Democrats; 1 Independent

[6] See http://clerk.house.gov/histHigh/Congressional_History/index.php

Speaker of the House
Thomas S. Foley (D-Wash.)
Majority Leader
Richard A. Gephardt (D-Mo.)
Republican Leader
Robert H. Michel (R-Ill.)
Majority Whip
William H. Gray, III (D-Pa.; resigned from House September 11, 1991)
David E. Bonior (D-Mich.)
Republican Whip
Newt Gingrich (R-Ga.)

U.S. Congress: 101st House of Representatives
(Arranged by State)

State	Last Name	First Name	District	Party
AK	Young	Don	At Large	R
AL	Bevill	Tom	4th	D
	Browder	Glen	3rd	D
	Callahan	Sonny	1st	R
	Dickenson	William L.	2nd	R
	Erdreich	Ben	6th	D
	Flippo	Ronnie G.	5th	D
	Harris	Claude	7th	D
AR	Anthony	Beryl, Jr.	4th	D
	Alexander	Bill	1st	D
	Hammerschmidt	John Paul	3rd	R
	Robinson	Tommy	2nd	R
AS	Faleomavaega	Eni F. H.	Delegate	D
AZ	Kolbe	Jim	5th	R
	Kyl	Jon L.	4th	R
	Rhodes	John J., III	1st	R
	Stump	Bob	3rd	R
	Udall	Morris K.	2nd	D
CA	Anderson	Glenn M.	32nd	D
	Bates	Jim	44th	D
	Beilenson	Anthony C.	23rd	D
	Berman	Howard L.	26th	D
	Bosco	Douglas H.	1st	D
	Boxer	Barbara	6th	D
	Brown	George E., Jr.	36th	D
	Campbell	Tom	12th	R

(continued)

State	Last Name	First Name	District	Party
CA	Condit	Gary L.	15th	D
	Cox	C. Christopher	40th	R
	Dannemeyer	William E.	39th	R
	Dellums	Ronald V.	8th	D
	Dixon	Julian C.	28th	D
	Dornan	Robert K.	38th	R
	Dreier	David	33rd	R
	Dymally	Mervyn M.	31st	D
	Edwards	Don	10th	D
	Fazio	Vic	4th	D
	Gallegly	Elton	21st	R
	Hawkins	Augustus F.	29th	D
	Herger	Wally	2nd	R
	Hunter	Duncan	45th	R
	Lagomarsino	Robert J.	19th	R
	Lantos	Tom	11th	D
	Lehman	Richard H.	18th	D
	Levine	Mel	27th	D
	Lewis	Jerry	35th	R
	Lowery	Bill	41st	R
	McCandless	Alfred A.	37th	R
	Martinez	Matthew G.	30th	D
	Matsui	Robert T.	3rd	D
	Miller	George	7th	D
	Mineta	Norman	13th	R
	Moorhead	Carlos	22nd	R
	Packard	Ron	43rd	R
	Panetta	Leon	16th	D
	Pashayan	Charles, Jr.	17th	R
	Pelosi	Nancy L.	5th	D
	Rohrabacher	Dana	42nd	R
	Roybal	Edward	25th	D
	Shumway	Norman	14th	D
	Stark	Fortney Pete	9th	D
	Thomas	William	20th	R
	Torres	Esteban Edward	34th	D
	Waxman	Henry	24th	D
CO	Brown	Hank	4th	R
	Campbell	Ben Nighthorse	3rd	D
	Hefley	Joel	5th	R
	Schaefer	Dan	6th	R
	Schroeder	Patricia F.	1st	D
	Skaggs	David	2nd	D

State	Last Name	First Name	District	Party
CT	Gejdenson	Sam	2nd	D
	Johnson	Nancy L.	6th	R
	Kennelly	Barbara B.	1st	D
	Morrison	Bruce	3rd	D
	Rowland	John	5th	R
	Shays	Christopher	4th	R
DC	Fauntroy	Walter E.	Delegate	D
DE	Carper	Thomas R.	At Large	D
FL	Bennett	Charles E.	3rd	D
	Bilirakis	Michael A.	9th	R
	Fascell	Dante	19th	D
	Gibbons	Sam	7th	D
	Goss	Porter J.	13th	R
	Grant	Bill	2nd	R
	Hutto	Earl	1st	D
	Ireland	Andy	10th	R
	James	Craig T.	4th	R
	Johnston	Harry	14th	D
	Lehman	William	17th	D
	Lewis	Tom	12th	R
	McCollum	Bill	5th	R
	Nelson	Bill	11th	D
	Ros-Lehtinen	Ileana	18th	R
	Shaw	E. Clay, Jr.	15th	R
	Smith	Lawrence, Jr.	16th	D
	Stearns	Cliff	6th	R
	Young	C. W. Bill	8th	R
GA	Barnard	Doug, Jr.	10th	D
	Darden	George (Buddy)	7th	D
	Gingrich	Newt	6th	R
	Hatcher	Charles	2nd	D
	Jenkins	Edward F.	9th	D
	Jones	Ben	4th	D
	Lewis	John	5th	D
	Ray	Richard	3rd	D
	Rowland	J. Roy	8th	D
	Thomas	Lindsay	1st	D
GU	Blaz	Ben Garrido	Delegate	R
HI	Mink	Patsy	2nd	D
	Saiki	Patricia F.	1st	R
IA	Grandy	Fred	6th	R
	Leach	Jim	1st	R
	Lightfoot	Jim	5th	R

(continued)

State	Last Name	First Name	District	Party
IA	Nagle	David	3rd	D
	Smith	Neal	4th	D
	Tauke	Thomas	2nd	R
ID	Craig	Larry E.	1st	R
	Stallings	Richard	2nd	D
IL	Annunzio	Frank	11th	D
	Bruce	Terry L.	19th	D
	Collins	Cardiss	7th	D
	Costello	Jerry F.	21st	D
	Crane	Philip M.	12th	R
	Durbin	Richard J.	20th	D
	Evans	Lane	17th	D
	Fawell	Harris W.	13th	R
	Hastert	J. Dennis	14th	R
	Hayes	Charles A.	1st	D
	Hyde	Henry	6th	R
	Lipinski	William O.	5th	D
	Madigan	Edward R.	15th	R
	Martin	Lynn	16th	R
	Michel	Robert	18th	R
	Porter	John Edward	10th	R
	Poshard	Glenn M.	22nd	D
	Rostenkowski	Dan	8th	R
	Russo	Marty	3rd	D
	Sangmeister	George	4th	D
	Savage	Gus	2nd	D
	Yates	Sidney	9th	D
IN	Burton	Dan	6th	R
	Hamilton	Lee H.	9th	D
	Hiler	John	3rd	R
	Jacobs	Andrew, Jr.	10th	D
	Jontz	Jim	5th	D
	Long	Jill L.	4th	D
	McCloskey	Frank	8th	D
	Myers	John T.	7th	R
	Sharp	Philip	2nd	D
	Visclosky	Peter	1st	D
KS	Glickman	Dan	4th	R
	Meyers	Jan	3rd	R
	Roberts	Pat	1st	R
	Slattery	Jim	2nd	D
	Whittaker	Bob	5th	R
KY	Bunning	Jim	4th	R

State	Last Name	First Name	District	Party
KY	Hopkins	Larry	6th	R
	Hubbard	Carroll, Jr.	1st	D
	Mazzoli	Romano	3rd	D
	Natcher	William H., III	2nd	D
	Perkins	Carlos	7th	D
	Rogers	Harold E.	5th	R
LA	Baker	Richard H.	6th	R
	Boggs	Lindy	2nd	D
	Hayes	James A.	7th	D
	Holloway	Clyde	8th	R
	Huckaby	Jerry	5th	D
	Livingston	Bob	1st	R
	McCrery	Jim	4th	R
	Tauzin	W. J.	3rd	D
MA	Atkins	Chester G.	5th	D
	Conte	Silvio O.	1st	R
	Donnelly	Brian J.	11th	D
	Early	Joseph D.	3rd	D
	Frank	Barney	4th	D
	Kennedy	Joseph P., II	8th	D
	Markey	Edward J.	7th	D
	Mavroules	Nicholas	6th	D
	Moakley	John Joseph	9th	D
	Neal	Richard	2nd	D
	Studds	Gerry	10th	D
MD	Bentley	Helen Delich	2nd	R
	Byron	Beverly B.	6th	D
	Cardin	Benjamin L.	3rd	D
	Dyson	Roy	1st	D
	Hoyer	Steny H.	5th	D
	McMillen	C. Thomas	4th	D
	Mfume	Kweisi	7th	D
	Morella	Constance	8th	R
MI	Bonior	David E.	12th	D
	Broomfield	William S.	18th	R
	Carr	Bob	6th	D
	Conyers	John, Jr.	1st	D
	Crockett	George W., Jr.	13th	D
	Davis	Robert W.	11th	R
	Dingell	John D.	16th	D
	Ford	Wiliam D.	15th	D
	Henry	Paul B.	5th	R
	Hertel	Dennis M.	14th	D

(continued)

State	Last Name	First Name	District	Party
MI	Kildee	Dale E.	7th	D
	Levin	Sander M.	17th	D
	Pursell	Carlos	2nd	R
	Schuette	Bill	10th	R
	Traxler	Bob	8th	D
	Upton	Frederick	4th	R
	Vander Jagt	Guy	9th	R
	Wolpe	Howard	3rd	D
MN	Brennan	Joseph E.	1st	D
	Frenzel	Bill	3rd	R
	Oberstar	James L.	8th	D
	Penny	Timothy	1st	D
	Sabo	Martin Olav	5th	D
	Sikorski	Gerry	6th	D
	Snowe	Olympia	2nd	R
	Stangeland	Arlan	7th	R
	Vento	Bruce	4th	D
	Weber	Vin	2nd	R
MO	Buechner	Jack	2nd	R
	Clay	William	1st	D
	Coleman	E. Thomas	6th	R
	Emerson	Bill	8th	R
	Gephardt	Richard A.	3rd	D
	Hancock	Mel	7th	R
	Skelton	Ike	4th	D
	Volkmer	Harold E.	9th	D
	Wheat	Alan	5th	D
MS	Espy	Mike	2nd	D
	Montgomery	G. V. (Sonny)	3rd	D
	Parker	Mike	4th	D
	Taylor	Gene	5th	D
	Whitten	Jamie	1st	D
MT	Marlenee	Ron	2nd	R
	Williams	Pat	1st	D
NC	Clarke	James McClure	11th	D
	Coble	Howard	6th	R
	Hefner	W. G. (Bill)	8th	D
	Jones	Walter B.	1st	D
	Lancaster	H. Martin	3rd	D
	McMillan	J. Alex	9th	R
	Neal	Stephen	5th	D
	Price	David	4th	D
	Rose	Charles	7th	D

State	Last Name	First Name	District	Party
NC	Valentine	Tim	2nd	D
ND	Dorgan	Byron L.	At Large	D
NE	Bereuter	Doug	1st	R
	Hoagland	Peter A.	2nd	D
	Smith	Virginia	3rd	R
NH	Douglas	Chuck	2nd	R
	Smith	Robert C.	1st	R
NJ	Andrews	Robert E.	1st	D
	Courter	Jim	12th	R
	Dwyer	Bernard J.	6th	D
	Gallo	Dean	11th	R
	Guarini	Frank J.	14th	D
	Hughes	William J.	2nd	D
	Pallone	Frank Jr.	3rd	D
	Payne	Donald E.	10th	D
	Rinaldo	Matthew	7th	R
	Roe	Robert	8th	D
	Roukema	Marge	5th	R
	Saxton	Jim	13th	R
	Smith	Christopher	4th	R
	Torricelli	Robert	9th	D
NM	Richardson	Bill	3rd	D
	Schiff	Steven	1st	R
	Skeen	Joe	2nd	R
NV	Bilbray	James H.	1st	D
	Vucanovich	Barbara B.	2nd	R
NY	Ackerman	Gary L.	7th	D
	Boehlert	Sherwood L.	25th	R
	Downey	Thomas J., Jr.	2nd	D
	Engel	Eliot L.	19th	D
	Fish	Hamilton, Jr.	21st	R
	Flake	Floyd H.	6th	D
	Gilman	Benjamin A.	22nd	R
	Green	Bill	15th	R
	Hochbrueckner	George	1st	D
	Horton	Frank	29th	R
	Houghton	Amo	34th	R
	LaFalce	John J., Jr.	32nd	D
	Lent	Norman F.	4th	R
	Lowey	Nita M.	20th	D
	McGrath	Raymond J.	5th	R
	McHugh	Matthew F.	28th	D
	McNulty	Michael R.	23rd	D

(continued)

State	Last Name	First Name	District	Party
NY	Manton	Thomas J., Jr.	9th	D
	Martin	David O'Brien	26th	R
	Molinari	Susan	14th	R
	Mrazek	Robert J.	3rd	D
	Nowak	Henry J.	33rd	D
	Owens	Major	12th	D
	Paxon	Bill	31st	R
	Rangel	Charles	16th	D
	Scheuer	James	8th	D
	Schumer	Charles	10th	D
	Serrano	Jose E.	18th	D
	Slaughter	Louise McIntosh	30th	D
	Solarz	Stephen	13th	D
	Solomon	Gerald	24th	R
	Towns	Edolphus	11th	D
	Walsh	James	27th	R
	Weiss	Ted	17th	D
OH	Applegate	Douglas	18th	D
	DeWine	Michael	7th	R
	Eckart	Dennis E.	11th	D
	Feighan	Edward F.	19th	D
	Gillmor	Paul E.	5th	R
	Gradison	Willis D., Jr.	2nd	R
	Hall	Tony P.	3rd	D
	Kaptur	Marcy	9th	D
	Kasich	John R.	12th	R
	Luken	Thomas	1st	D
	Lukens	Donald E.	8th	R
	McEwen	Bob	6th	R
	Miller	Clarence	10th	R
	Oakar	Mary Rose	20th	D
	Oxley	Michael	4th	D
	Pease	Donald E.	13th	D
	Regula	Ralph	16th	R
	Sawyer	Thomas	14th	D
	Stokes	Louis	21st	D
	Traficant	James A., Jr.	17th	D
	Wylie	Chalmers	15th	R
OK	Edwards	Mickey	5th	R
	English	Glenn M.	6th	D
	Inhofe	James M.	1st	R
	McCurdy	Dave	4th	D
	Synar	Mike	2nd	D

State	Last Name	First Name	District	Party
OK	Watkins	Wes	3rd	D
OR	AuCoin	Les	1st	D
	DeFazio	Peter A.	4th	D
	Smith	Denny	5th	R
	Smith	Robert F.	2nd	R
	Wyden	Ron	3rd	D
PA	Borski	Robert A.	3rd	D
	Clinger	William F., Jr.	23rd	R
	Coughlin	Lawrence	13th	R
	Coyne	William J.	14th	D
	Foglietta	Thomas M.	1st	D
	Gaydos	Joseph M.	20th	D
	Gekas	George W., Jr.	17th	R
	Goodling	William F., Jr.	19th	R
	Gray	William H., III	2nd	R
	Kanjorski	Paul E.	11th	D
	Kolter	Joe	4th	D
	Kostmayer	Peter H.	8th	D
	McDade	Joseph M.	10th	R
	Murphy	Austin	22nd	D
	Murtha	John P.	12th	D
	Ridge	Thomas	21st	R
	Ritter	Don	15th	R
	Schulze	Richard	5th	R
	Shuster	Bud	9th	R
	Walgren	Doug	18th	D
	Walker	Robert	16th	R
	Weldon	Curt	7th	R
	Yatron	Gus	6th	D
PR	Fuster	Jaime B.	Resident Commissioner	D
RI	Machtley	Ronald K.	1st	R
	Schneider	Claudine	2nd	R
SC	Derrick	Butler	3rd	D
	Patterson	Elizabeth J.	4th	D
	Ravenel	Arthur, Jr.	1st	R
	Spence	Floyd H.	2nd	R
	Spratt	John M., Jr.	5th	D
	Tallon	Robin	6th	D
SD	Johnson	Tim	At Large	D
TN	Clement	Bob	5th	D
	Cooper	Jim	4th	D
	Duncan	John J., Jr.	2nd	R
	Ford	Harold E.	9th	D

(continued)

State	Last Name	First Name	District	Party
	Gordon	Bart	6th	D
	Lloyd	Marilyn	3rd	D
	Quillen	James H.	1st	R
	Sundquist	Don	7th	R
	Tanner	John S.	8th	D
TX	Andrews	Michael A.	25th	D
	Archer	Bill	7th	R
	Armey	Richard K.	26th	R
	Bartlett	Steve	3rd	R
	Barton	Joe	6th	R
	Brooks	Jack	9th	D
	Bryant	John	5th	D
	Bustamante	Albert G.	23rd	D
	Chapman	Jim	1st	D
	Coleman	Ronald D.	16th	D
	Combest	Larry	19th	R
	de la Garza	Eligio, II	15th	D
	DeLay	Tom	22nd	R
	Fields	Jack	8th	R
	Frost	Martin	24th	D
	Geren	Pete	12th	D
	Gonzalez	Henry B.	20th	D
	Hall	Ralph M.	4th	D
	Laughlin	Greg	14th	D
	Leath	Marvin	11th	D
	Ortiz	Solomon P.	27th	D
	Pickle	J. J.	10th	D
	Sarpalius	Bill	13th	D
	Smith	Lamar	21st	R
	Stenholm	Charles W.	17th	D
	Washington	Craig	18th	D
	Wilson	Charles	2nd	D
UT	Hansen	James V.	1st	R
	Nielson	Howard	3rd	R
	Owens	Wayne	2nd	D
VA	Bateman	Herbert H.	1st	R
	Bliley	Thomas J., Jr.	3rd	R
	Boucher	Rick	9th	D
	Olin	Jim	6th	D
	Parris	Stan	8th	R
	Payne	Lewis F., Jr.	5th	D
	Pickett	Owen	2nd	D
	Sisisky	Norman	4th	D

State	Last Name	First Name	District	Party
VA	Slaughter	D. French, Jr.	7th	R
	Wolf	Frank	10th	R
VI	de Lugo	Ron	Delegate	D
VT	Smith	Peter	At Large	R
WA	Chandler	Rod	8th	R
	Dicks	Norman D.	6th	D
	Foley	Thomas S.	5th	D
	McDermott	Jim	7th	D
	Miller	John	1st	R
	Morrison	Sid	4th	R
	Swift	Al	2nd	D
	Unsoeld	Jolene	3rd	D
WI	Aspin	Les	1st	D
	Gunderson	Steve	3rd	R
	Kastenmeier	Robert W.	2nd	D
	Kleczka	Gerald D.	4th	D
	Moody	Jim	5th	D
	Obey	David	7th	D
	Petri	Thomas	6th	R
	Roth	Toby	8th	R
	Sensenbrenner	F. James	9th	R
WV	Mollohan	Alan	1st	D
	Rahall	Nick Joe, II	4th	D
	Staggers	Harley O., Jr.	2nd	D
	Wise	Robert E., Jr.	3rd	D
WY	Thomas	Craig T.	At Large	R

U.S. Congress: 101st House of Representatives

(Arranged by Last Name of Member)

Last Name	First Name	State	District	Party
Ackerman	Gary L.	NY	7th	D
Alexander	Bill	AR	1st	D
Anderson	Glenn M.	CA	32nd	D
Andrews	Robert E.	NJ	1st	D
Andrews	Michael A.	TX	25th	D
Annunzio	Frank	IL	11th	D
Anthony	Beryl, Jr.	AR	4th	D
Applegate	Douglas	OH	18th	D

(continued)

Last Name	First Name	State	District	Party
Archer	Bill	TX	7th	R
Armey	Richard K.	TX	26th	R
Aspin	Les	WI	1st	D
Atkins	Chester G.	MA	5th	D
AuCoin	Les	OR	1st	D
Baker	Richard H.	LA	6th	R
Barnard	Doug, Jr.	GA	10th	D
Bartlett	Steve	TX	3rd	R
Barton	Joe	TX	6th	R
Bateman	Herbert H.	VA	1st	R
Bates	Jim	CA	44th	D
Beilenson	Anthony C.	CA	23rd	D
Bennett	Charles E.	FL	3rd	D
Bentley	Helen Delich	MD	2nd	R
Bereuter	Doug	NE	1st	R
Berman	Howard L.	CA	26th	D
Bevill	Tom	AL	4th	D
Bilbray	James H.	NV	1st	D
Bilirakis	Michael A.	FL	9th	R
Blaz	Ben Garrido	GU	Delegate	R
Bliley	Thomas J., Jr.	VA	3rd	R
Boehlert	Sherwood L.	NY	25th	R
Boggs	Lindy	LA	2nd	D
Bonior	David E.	MI	12th	D
Borski	Robert A.	PA	3rd	D
Bosco	Douglas H.	CA	1st	D
Boucher	Rick	VA	9th	D
Boxer	Barbara	CA	6th	D
Brennan	Joseph E.	MN	1st	D
Brooks	Jack	TX	9th	D
Broomfield	William S.	MI	18th	R
Browder	Glen	AL	3rd	D
Brown	George E., Jr.	CA	36th	D
Brown	Hank	CO	4th	R
Bruce	Terry L.	IL	19th	D
Bryant	John	TX	5th	D
Buechner	Jack	MO	2nd	R
Bunning	Jim	KY	4th	R
Burton	Dan	IN	6th	R
Bustamante	Albert G.	TX	23rd	D
Byron	Beverly B.	MD	6th	D
Callahan	Sonny	AL	1st	R
Campbell	Tom	CA	12th	R

Last Name	First Name	State	District	Party
Campbell	Ben Nighthorse	CO	3rd	D
Cardin	Benjamin L.	MD	3rd	D
Carper	Thomas R.	DE	At Large	D
Carr	Bob	MI	6th	D
Chandler	Rod	WA	8th	R
Chapman	Jim	TX	1st	D
Clarke	James McClure	NC	11th	D
Clay	William	MO	1st	D
Clement	Bob	TN	5th	D
Clinger	William F., Jr.	PA	23rd	R
Coble	Howard	NC	6th	R
Coleman	E. Thomas	MO	6th	R
Coleman	Ronald D.	TX	16th	D
Collins	Cardiss	IL	7th	D
Combest	Larry	TX	19th	R
Condit	Gary L.	CA	15th	D
Conte	Silvio O.	MA	1st	R
Conyers	John Jr.	MI	1st	D
Cooper	Jim	TN	4th	D
Costello	Jerry F.	IL	21st	D
Coughlin	Lawrence	PA	13th	R
Courter	Jim	NJ	12th	R
Cox	C. Christopher	CA	40th	R
Coyne	William J.	PA	14th	D
Craig	Larry E.	ID	1st	R
Crane	Philip M.	IL	12th	R
Crockett	George W., Jr.	MI	13th	D
Dannemeyer	William E.	CA	39th	R
Darden	George (Buddy)	GA	7th	D
Davis	Robert W.	MI	11th	R
de la Garza	Eligio, II	TX	15th	D
de Lugo	Ron	VI	Delegate	D
DeFazio	Peter A.	OR	4th	D
DeLay	Tom	TX	22nd	R
Dellums	Ronald V.	CA	8th	D
Derrick	Butler	SC	3rd	D
DeWine	Michael	OH	7th	R
Dickenson	William L.	AL	2nd	R
Dicks	Norman D.	WA	6th	D
Dingell	John D.	MI	16th	D
Dixon	Julian C.	CA	28th	D
Donnelly	Brian J.	MA	11th	D
Dorgan	Byron L.	ND	At Large	D

(continued)

Last Name	First Name	State	District	Party
Dornan	Robert K.	CA	38th	R
Douglas	Chuck	NH	2nd	R
Downey	Thomas J., Jr.	NY	2nd	D
Dreier	David	CA	33rd	R
Duncan	John J., Jr.	TN	2nd	R
Durbin	Richard J.	IL	20th	D
Dwyer	Bernard J.	NJ	6th	D
Dymally	Mervyn M.	CA	31st	D
Dyson	Roy	MD	1st	D
Early	Joseph D.	MA	3rd	D
Eckart	Dennis E.	OH	11th	D
Edwards	Don	CA	10th	D
Edwards	Mickey	OK	5th	R
Emerson	Bill	MO	8th	R
Engel	Eliot L.	NY	19th	D
English	Glenn M.	OK	6th	D
Erdreich	Ben	AL	6th	D
Espy	Mike	MS	2nd	D
Evans	Lane	IL	17th	D
Faleomavaega	Eni F. H.	AS	Delegate	D
Fascell	Dante	FL	19th	D
Fauntroy	Walter E.	DC	Delegate	D
Fawell	Harris W.	IL	13th	R
Fazio	Vic	CA	4th	D
Feighan	Edward F.	OH	19th	D
Fields	Jack	TX	8th	R
Fish	Hamilton, Jr.	NY	21st	R
Flake	Floyd H.	NY	6th	D
Flippo	Ronnie G.	AL	5th	D
Foglietta	Thomas M.	PA	1st	D
Foley	Thomas S.	WA	5th	D
Ford	Wiliam D.	MI	15th	D
Ford	Harold E.	TN	9th	D
Frank	Barney	MA	4th	D
Frenzel	Bill	MN	3rd	R
Frost	Martin	TX	24th	D
Fuster	Jaime B.	PR	Resident Commissioner	D
Gallegly	Elton	CA	21st	R
Gallo	Dean	NJ	11th	R
Gaydos	Joseph M.	PA	20th	D
Gejdenson	Sam	CT	2nd	D
Gekas	George W., Jr.	PA	17th	R

Last Name	First Name	State	District	Party
Gephardt	Richard A.	MO	3rd	D
Geren	Pete	TX	12th	D
Gibbons	Sam	FL	7th	D
Gillmor	Paul E.	OH	5th	R
Gilman	Benjamin A.	NY	22nd	R
Gingrich	Newt	GA	6th	R
Glickman	Dan	KS	4th	R
Gonzalez	Henry B.	TX	20th	D
Goodling	William F., Jr.	PA	19th	R
Gordon	Bart	TN	6th	D
Goss	Porter J.	FL	13th	R
Gradison	Willis D., Jr.	OH	2nd	R
Grandy	Fred	IA	6th	R
Grant	Bill	FL	2nd	R
Gray	William H., III	PA	2nd	R
Green	Bill	NY	15th	R
Guarini	Frank J.	NJ	14th	D
Gunderson	Steve	WI	3rd	R
Hall	Tony P.	OH	3rd	D
Hall	Ralph M.	TX	4th	D
Hamilton	Lee H.	IN	9th	D
Hammerschmidt	John Paul	AR	3rd	R
Hancock	Mel	MO	7th	R
Hansen	James V.	UT	1st	R
Harris	Claude	AL	7th	D
Hastert	J. Dennis	IL	14th	R
Hatcher	Charles	GA	2nd	D
Hawkins	Augustus F.	CA	29th	D
Hayes	Charles A.	IL	1st	D
Hayes	James A.	LA	7th	D
Hefley	Joel	CO	5th	R
Hefner	W. G. (Bill)	NC	8th	D
Henry	Paul B.	MI	5th	R
Herger	Wally	CA	2nd	R
Hertel	Dennis M.	MI	14th	D
Hiler	John	IN	3rd	R
Hoagland	Peter A.	NE	2nd	D
Hochbrueckner	George	NY	1st	D
Holloway	Clyde	LA	8th	R
Hopkins	Larry	KY	6th	R
Horton	Frank	NY	29th	R
Houghton	Amo	NY	34th	R
Hoyer	Steny H.	MD	5th	D

(continued)

Last Name	First Name	State	District	Party
Hubbard	Carroll, Jr.	KY	1st	D
Huckaby	Jerry	LA	5th	D
Hughes	William J.	NJ	2nd	D
Hunter	Duncan	CA	45th	R
Hutto	Earl	FL	1st	D
Hyde	Henry	IL	6th	R
Inhofe	James M.	OK	1st	R
Ireland	Andy	FL	10th	R
Jacobs	Andrew, Jr.	IN	10th	D
James	Craig T.	FL	4th	R
Jenkins	Edward F.	GA	9th	D
Johnson	Nancy L.	CT	6th	R
Johnson	Tim	SD	At Large	D
Johnston	Harry	FL	14th	D
Jones	Ben	GA	4th	D
Jones	Walter B.	NC	1st	D
Jontz	Jim	IN	5th	D
Kanjorski	Paul E.	PA	11th	D
Kaptur	Marcy	OH	9th	D
Kasich	John R.	OH	12th	R
Kastenmeier	Robert W.	WI	2nd	D
Kennedy	Joseph P., II	MA	8th	D
Kennelly	Barbara B.	CT	1st	D
Kildee	Dale E.	MI	7th	D
Kleczka	Gerald D.	WI	4th	D
Kolbe	Jim	AZ	5th	R
Kolter	Joe	PA	4th	D
Kostmayer	Peter H.	PA	8th	D
Kyl	Jon L.	AZ	4th	R
LaFalce	John J., Jr.	NY	32nd	D
Lagomarsino	Robert, J.	CA	19th	R
Lancaster	H. Martin	NC	3rd	D
Lantos	Tom	CA	11th	D
Laughlin	Greg	TX	14th	D
Leach	Jim	IA	1st	R
Leath	Marvin	TX	11th	D
Lehman	Richard H.	CA	18th	D
Lehman	William	FL	17th	D
Lent	Norman F.	NY	4th	R
Levin	Sander M.	MI	17th	D
Levine	Mel	CA	27th	D
Lewis	Jerry	CA	35th	R
Lewis	Tom	FL	12th	R

Last Name	First Name	State	District	Party
Lewis	John	GA	5th	D
Lightfoot	Jim	IA	5th	R
Lipinski	William O.	IL	5th	D
Livingston	Bob	LA	1st	R
Lloyd	Marilyn	TN	3rd	D
Long	Jill L.	IN	4th	D
Lowery	Bill	CA	41st	R
Lowey	Nita M.	NY	20th	D
Luken	Thomas	OH	1st	D
Lukens	Donald E.	OH	8th	R
Machtley	Ronald K.	RI	1st	R
Madigan	Edward R.	IL	15th	R
Manton	Thomas J., Jr.	NY	9th	D
Markey	Edward J.	MA	7th	D
Marlenee	Ron	MT	2nd	R
Martin	Lynn	IL	16th	R
Martin	David O'Brien	NY	26th	R
Martinez	Matthew G.	CA	30th	D
Matsui	Robert T.	CA	3rd	D
Mavroules	Nicholas	MA	6th	D
Mazzoli	Romano	KY	3rd	D
McCandless	Alfred A.	CA	37th	R
McCloskey	Frank	IN	8th	D
McCollum	Bill	FL	5th	R
McCrery	Jim	LA	4th	R
McCurdy	Dave	OK	4th	D
McDade	Joseph M.	PA	10th	R
McDermott	Jim	WA	7th	D
McEwen	Bob	OH	6th	R
McGrath	Raymond J.	NY	5th	R
McHugh	Matthew F.	NY	28th	D
McMillan	J. Alex	NC	9th	R
McMillen	C. Thomas	MD	4th	D
McNulty	Michael R.	NY	23rd	D
Meyers	Jan	KS	3rd	R
Mfume	Kweisi	MD	7th	D
Michel	Robert	IL	18th	R
Miller	George	CA	7th	D
Miller	Clarence	OH	10th	R
Miller	John	WA	1st	R
Mineta	Norman	CA	13th	R
Mink	Patsy	HI	2nd	D
Moakley	John Joseph	MA	9th	D

(continued)

Last Name	First Name	State	District	Party
Molinari	Susan	NY	14th	R
Mollohan	Alan	WV	1st	D
Montgomery	G. V. (Sonny)	MS	3rd	D
Moody	Jim	WI	5th	D
Moorhead	Carlos	CA	22nd	R
Morella	Constance	MD	8th	R
Morrison	Bruce	CT	3rd	D
Morrison	Sid	WA	4th	R
Mrazek	Robert J.	NY	3rd	D
Murphy	Austin	PA	22nd	D
Murtha	John P.	PA	12th	D
Myers	John T.	IN	7th	R
Nagle	David	IA	3rd	D
Natcher	William H., III	KY	2nd	D
Neal	Richard	MA	2nd	D
Neal	Stephen	NC	5th	D
Nelson	Bill	FL	11th	D
Nielson	Howard	UT	3rd	R
Nowak	Henry J.	NY	33rd	D
Oakar	Mary Rose	OH	20th	D
Oberstar	James L.	MN	8th	D
Obey	David	WI	7th	D
Olin	Jim	VA	6th	D
Ortiz	Solomon P.	TX	27th	D
Owens	Major	NY	12th	D
Owens	Wayne	UT	2nd	D
Oxley	Michael	OH	4th	D
Packard	Ron	CA	43rd	R
Pallone	Frank, Jr.	NJ	3rd	D
Panetta	Leon	CA	16th	D
Parker	Mike	MS	4th	D
Parris	Stan	VA	8th	R
Pashayan	Charles, Jr.	CA	17th	R
Patterson	Elizabeth J.	SC	4th	D
Paxon	Bill	NY	31st	R
Payne	Donald E.	NJ	10th	D
Payne	Lewis F., Jr.	VA	5th	D
Pease	Donald E.	OH	13th	D
Pelosi	Nancy L.	CA	5th	D
Penny	Timothy	MN	1st	D
Perkins	Carlos	KY	7th	D
Petri	Thomas	WI	6th	R
Pickett	Owen	VA	2nd	D

Last Name	First Name	State	District	Party
Pickle	J. J.	TX	10th	D
Porter	John Edward	IL	10th	R
Poshard	Glenn M.	IL	22nd	D
Price	David	NC	4th	D
Pursell	Carlos	MI	2nd	R
Quillen	James H.	TN	1st	R
Rahall	Nick Joe, II	WV	4th	D
Rangel	Charles	NY	16th	D
Ravenel	Arthur, Jr.	SC	1st	R
Ray	Richard	GA	3rd	D
Regula	Ralph	OH	16th	R
Rhodes	John J., III	AZ	1st	R
Richardson	Bill	NM	3rd	D
Ridge	Thomas	PA	21st	R
Rinaldo	Matthew	NJ	7th	R
Ritter	Don	PA	15th	R
Roberts	Pat	KS	1st	R
Robinson	Tommy	AR	2nd	R
Roe	Robert	NJ	8th	D
Rogers	Harold E.	KY	5th	R
Rohrabacher	Dana	CA	42nd	R
Rose	Charles	NC	7th	D
Ros-Lehtinen	Ileana	FL	18th	R
Rostenkowski	Dan	IL	8th	R
Roth	Toby	WI	8th	R
Roukema	Marge	NJ	5th	R
Rowland	John	CT	5th	R
Rowland	J. Roy	GA	8th	D
Roybal	Edward	CA	25th	D
Russo	Marty	IL	3rd	D
Sabo	Martin Olav	MN	5th	D
Saiki	Patricia F.	HI	1st	R
Sangmeister	George	IL	4th	D
Sarpalius	Bill	TX	13th	D
Savage	Gus	IL	2nd	D
Sawyer	Thomas	OH	14th	D
Saxton	Jim	NJ	13th	R
Schaefer	Dan	CO	6th	R
Scheuer	James	NY	8th	D
Schiff	Steven	NM	1st	R
Schneider	Claudine	RI	2nd	R
Schroeder	Patricia F.	CO	1st	D
Schuette	Bill	MI	10th	R

(continued)

Last Name	First Name	State	District	Party
Schulze	Richard	PA	5th	R
Schumer	Charles	NY	10th	D
Sensenbrenner	F. James	WI	9th	R
Serrano	Jose E.	NY	18th	D
Sharp	Philip	IN	2nd	D
Shaw	E. Clay, Jr.	FL	15th	R
Shays	Christopher	CT	4th	R
Shumway	Norman	CA	14th	D
Shuster	Bud	PA	9th	R
Sikorski	Gerry	MN	6th	D
Sisisky	Norman	VA	4th	D
Skaggs	David	CO	2nd	D
Skeen	Joe	NM	2nd	R
Skelton	Ike	MO	4th	D
Slattery	Jim	KS	2nd	D
Slaughter	Louise McIntosh	NY	30th	D
Slaughter	D. French, Jr.	VA	7th	R
Smith	Lawrence, Jr.	FL	16th	D
Smith	Neal	IA	4th	D
Smith	Virginia	NE	3rd	R
Smith	Robert C.	NH	1st	R
Smith	Christopher	NJ	4th	R
Smith	Denny	OR	5th	R
Smith	Robert F.	OR	2nd	R
Smith	Lamar	TX	21st	R
Smith	Peter	VT	At Large	R
Snowe	Olympia	MN	2nd	R
Solarz	Stephen	NY	13th	D
Solomon	Gerald	NY	24th	R
Spence	Floyd H.	SC	2nd	R
Spratt	John M., Jr.	SC	5th	D
Staggers	Harley O., Jr.	WV	2nd	D
Stallings	Richard	ID	2nd	D
Stangeland	Arlan	MN	7th	R
Stark	Fortney Pete	CA	9th	D
Stearns	Cliff	FL	6th	R
Stenholm	Charles W.	TX	17th	D
Stokes	Louis	OH	21st	D
Studds	Gerry	MA	10th	D
Stump	Bob	AZ	3rd	R
Sundquist	Don	TN	7th	R
Swift	Al	WA	2nd	D
Synar	Mike	OK	2nd	D

Last Name	First Name	State	District	Party
Tallon	Robin	SC	6th	D
Tanner	John S.	TN	8th	D
Tauke	Thomas	IA	2nd	R
Tauzin	W. J.	LA	3rd	D
Taylor	Gene	MS	5th	D
Thomas	William	CA	20th	R
Thomas	Lindsay	GA	1st	D
Thomas	Craig T.	WY	At Large	R
Torres	Esteban Edward	CA	34th	D
Torricelli	Robert	NJ	9th	D
Towns	Edolphus	NY	11th	D
Traficant	James A., Jr.	OH	17th	D
Traxler	Bob	MI	8th	D
Udall	Morris K.	AZ	2nd	D
Unsoeld	Jolene	WA	3rd	D
Upton	Frederick	MI	4th	R
Valentine	Tim	NC	2nd	D
Vander Jagt	Guy	MI	9th	R
Vento	Bruce	MN	4th	D
Visclosky	Peter	IN	1st	D
Volkmer	Harold E.	MO	9th	D
Vucanovich	Barbara B.	NV	2nd	R
Walgren	Doug	PA	18th	D
Walker	Robert	PA	16th	R
Walsh	James	NY	27th	R
Washington	Craig	TX	18th	D
Watkins	Wes	OK	3rd	D
Waxman	Henry	CA	24th	D
Weber	Vin	MN	2nd	R
Weiss	Ted	NY	17th	D
Weldon	Curt	PA	7th	R
Wheat	Alan	MO	5th	D
Whittaker	Bob	KS	5th	R
Whitten	Jamie	MS	1st	D
Williams	Pat	MT	1st	D
Wilson	Charles	TX	2nd	D
Wise	Robert E., Jr.	WV	3rd	D
Wolf	Frank	VA	10th	R
Wolpe	Howard	MI	3rd	D
Wyden	Ron	OR	3rd	D
Wylie	Chalmers	OH	15th	R
Yates	Sidney	IL	9th	D
Yatron	Gus	PA	6th	D

(continued)

Last Name	First Name	State	District	Party
Young	Don	AK	At Large	R
Young	C. W. Bill	FL	8th	R

U.S. CONGRESS: 102ND HOUSE OF REPRESENTATIVES
(ARRANGED BY STATE)

State	Last Name	First Name	District	Party
AK	Young	Don	At Large	R
AL	Bevill	Tom	4th	D
	Browder	Glen	3rd	D
	Callahan	Sonny	1st	R
	Cramer	Robert E.	5th	D
	Dickenson	William L.	2nd	R
	Erdreich	Ben	6th	D
	Harris	Claude	7th	D
AR	Alexander	Bill	1st	D
	Anthony	Beryl, Jr.	4th	D
	Hammerschmidt	John Paul	3rd	R
	Thornton	Raymond J.	2nd	D
AS	Faleomavaega	Eni F. H.	Delegate	D
AZ	Kolbe	Jim	5th	R
	Kyl	Jon L.	4th	R
	Pastor	Ed	2nd	D
	Rhodes	John J., III	1st	R
	Stump	Bob	3rd	R
CA	Anderson	Glenn M.	32nd	D
	Beilenson	Anthony C.	23rd	D
	Berman	Howard L.	26th	D
	Boxer	Barbara	6th	D
	Brown	George E., Jr.	36th	D
	Campbell	Tom	12th	R
	Condit	Gary L.	15th	D
	Cox	C. Christopher	40th	R
	Cunningham	Randy	44th	R
	Dannemeyer	William E.	39th	R
	Dellums	Ronald V.	8th	D
	Dixon	Julian C.	28th	D
	Dooley	Calvin	17th	D
	Doolittle	John	14th	R
	Dornan	Robert K.	38th	R
	Dreier	David	33rd	R

State	Last Name	First Name	District	Party
CA	Dymally	Mervyn M.	31st	D
	Edwards	Don	10th	D
	Fazio	Vic	4th	D
	Gallegly	Elton	21st	R
	Herger	Wally	2nd	R
	Hunter	Duncan	45th	R
	Lagomarsino	Robert J.	19th	R
	Lantos	Tom	11th	D
	Lehman	Richard H.	18th	D
	Levine	Mel	27th	D
	Lewis	Jerry	35th	R
	Lowery	Bill	41st	R
	Martinez	Matthew G.	30th	D
	Matsui	Robert T.	3rd	D
	McCandless	Alfred A.	37th	R
	Miller	George	7th	D
	Mineta	Norman	13th	R
	Moorhead	Carlos	22nd	R
	Packard	Ron	43rd	R
	Panetta	Leon	16th	D
	Pelosi	Nancy L.	5th	D
	Riggs	Frank	1st	R
	Rohrabacher	Dana	42nd	R
	Roybal	Edward	25th	D
	Stark	Fortney Pete	9th	D
	Thomas	William	20th	R
	Torres	Esteban Edward	34th	D
	Waters	Maxine	29th	D
	Waxman	Henry	24th	D
CO	Allard	Wayne	4th	R
	Campbell	Ben Nighthorse	3rd	D
	Hefley	Joel	5th	R
	Schaefer	Dan	6th	R
	Schroeder	Patricia F.	1st	D
	Skaggs	David	2nd	D
CT	deLauro	Rosa	3rd	D
	Franks	Gary L.	5th	R
	Gejdenson	Sam	2nd	D
	Johnson	Nancy L.	6th	R
	Kennelly	Barbara B.	1st	D
	Shays	Christopher	4th	R
DC	Norton	Eleanor Holmes	Delegate	D
DE	Carper	Thomas R.	At Large	D

(continued)

State	Last Name	First Name	District	Party
FL	Bacchus	Jim	11th	D
	Bennett	Charles E.	3rd	D
	Bilirakis	Michael A.	9th	R
	Fascell	Dante	19th	D
	Gibbons	Sam	7th	D
	Goss	Porter J.	13th	R
	Hutto	Earl	1st	D
	Ireland	Andy	10th	R
	James	Craig T.	4th	R
	Johnston	Harry	14th	D
	Lehman	William	17th	D
	Lewis	Tom	12th	R
	McCollum	Bill	5th	R
	Peterson	Douglas	2nd	D
	Ros-Lehtinen	Ileana	18th	R
	Shaw	E. Clay, Jr.	15th	R
	Smith	Lawrence, Jr.	16th	D
	Stearns	Cliff	6th	R
	Young	C. W. Bill	8th	R
GA	Barnard	Doug, Jr.	10th	D
	Darden	George (Buddy)	7th	D
	Gingrich	Newt	6th	R
	Hatcher	Charles	2nd	D
	Jenkins	Edward F.	9th	D
	Jones	Ben	4th	D
	Lewis	John	5th	D
	Ray	Richard	3rd	D
	Rowland	J. Roy	8th	D
	Thomas	Lindsay	1st	D
GU	Blaz	Ben Garrido	Delegate	R
HI	Abercrombie	Neil	1st	D
	Mink	Patsy	2nd	D
IA	Grandy	Fred	6th	R
	Leach	Jim	1st	R
	Lightfoot	Jim	5th	R
	Nagle	David	3rd	D
	Nussle	Jim	2nd	R
	Smith	Neal	4th	D
ID	LaRocco	Larry	1st	D
	Stallings	Richard	2nd	D
IL	Annunzio	Frank	11th	D
	Bruce	Terry L.	19th	D
	Collins	Cardiss	7th	D

State	Last Name	First Name	District	Party
IL	Costello	Jerry F.	21st	D
	Cox	John W., Jr.	16th	D
	Crane	Philip M.	12th	R
	Durbin	Richard J.	20th	D
	Evans	Lane	17th	D
	Ewing	Thomas	15th	R
	Fawell	Harris W.	13th	R
	Hastert	J. Dennis	14th	R
	Hayes	Charles A.	1st	D
	Hyde	Henry	6th	R
	Lipinski	William O.	5th	D
	Michel	Robert	18th	R
	Porter	John Edward	10th	R
	Poshard	Glenn M.	22nd	D
	Rostenkowski	Dan	8th	R
	Russo	Marty	3rd	D
	Sangmeister	George	4th	D
	Savage	Gus	2nd	D
	Yates	Sidney	9th	D
IN	Burton	Dan	6th	R
	Hamilton	Lee H.	9th	D
	Jacobs	Andrew, Jr.	10th	D
	Jontz	Jim	5th	D
	Long	Jill L.	4th	D
	McCloskey	Frank	8th	D
	Myers	John T.	7th	R
	Roemer	Tim	3rd	D
	Sharp	Philip	2nd	D
	Visclosky	Peter	1st	D
KS	Glickman	Dan	4th	R
	Meyers	Jan	3rd	R
	Nichols	Dick	5th	R
	Roberts	Pat	1st	R
	Slattery	Jim	2nd	D
KY	Bunning	Jim	4th	R
	Hopkins	Larry	6th	R
	Hubbard	Carroll, Jr.	1st	D
	Mazzoli	Romano	3rd	D
	Natcher	William H., III	2nd	D
	Perkins	Carlos	7th	D
	Rogers	Harold E.	5th	R
LA	Baker	Richard H.	6th	R
	Hayes	James A.	7th	D

(continued)

State	Last Name	First Name	District	Party
LA	Holloway	Clyde	8th	R
	Huckaby	Jerry	5th	D
	Jefferson	William	2nd	D
	Livingston	Bob	1st	R
	McCrery	Jim	4th	R
	Tauzin	W. J.	3rd	D
MA	Atkins	Chester G.	5th	D
	Donnelly	Brian J.	11th	D
	Early	Joseph D.	3rd	D
	Frank	Barney	4th	D
	Kennedy	Joseph P., II	8th	D
	Markey	Edward J.	7th	D
	Mavroules	Nicholas	6th	D
	Moakley	John Joseph	9th	D
	Neal	Richard	2nd	D
	Olver	John	1st	D
	Studds	Gerry	10th	D
MD	Bentley	Helen Delich	2nd	R
	Byron	Beverly B.	6th	D
	Cardin	Benjamin L.	3rd	D
	Gilchrest	Wayne	1st	R
	Hoyer	Steny H.	5th	D
	McMillen	C. Thomas	4th	D
	Mfume	Kweisi	7th	D
	Morella	Constance	8th	R
MI	Bonior	David E.	12th	D
	Broomfield	William S.	18th	R
	Camp	Dave	10th	R
	Carr	Bob	6th	D
	Collins	Barbara-Rose	13th	D
	Conyers	John, Jr.	1st	D
	Davis	Robert W.	11th	R
	Dingell	John D.	16th	D
	Ford	Wiliam D.	15th	D
	Henry	Paul B.	5th	R
	Hertel	Dennis M.	14th	D
	Kildee	Dale E.	7th	D
	Levin	Sander M.	17th	D
	Pursell	Carlos	2nd	R
	Traxler	Bob	8th	D
	Upton	Frederick	4th	R
	Vander Jagt	Guy	9th	R
	Wolpe	Howard	3rd	D

State	Last Name	First Name	District	Party
MN	Andrews	Thomas	1st	D
	Oberstar	James L.	8th	D
	Penny	Timothy	1st	D
	Peterson	Collin	7th	D
	Ramstad	Jim	3rd	R
	Sabo	Martin Olav	5th	D
	Sikorski	Gerry	6th	D
	Snowe	Olympia	2nd	R
	Vento	Bruce	4th	D
	Weber	Vin	2nd	R
MO	Clay	William	1st	D
	Coleman	E. Thomas	6th	R
	Emerson	Bill	8th	R
	Gephardt	Richard A.	3rd	D
	Hancock	Mel	7th	R
	Horn	Joan Kelly	2nd	D
	Skelton	Ike	4th	D
	Volkmer	Harold E.	9th	D
	Wheat	Alan	5th	D
MS	Espy	Mike	2nd	D
	Montgomery	G. V. (Sonny)	3rd	D
	Parker	Mike	4th	D
	Taylor	Gene	5th	D
	Whitten	Jamie	1st	D
MT	Marlenee	Ron	2nd	R
	Williams	Pat	1st	D
NC	Ballenger	Cass	10th	R
	Clayton	Eva	1st	D
	Coble	Howard	6th	R
	Hefner	W. G. (Bill)	8th	D
	Lancaster	H. Martin	3rd	D
	McMillan	J. Alex	9th	R
	Neal	Stephen	5th	D
	Price	David	4th	D
	Rose	Charles	7th	D
	Taylor	Charles H.	11th	R
	Valentine	Tim	2nd	D
ND	Dorgan	Byron L.	At Large	D
NE	Barrett	Bill	3rd	R
	Bereuter	Doug	1st	R
	Hoagland	Peter A.	2nd	D
NH	Swett	Dick	2nd	D
	Zeliff	William	1st	R

(continued)

State	Last Name	First Name	District	Party
NJ	Andrews	Robert E.	1st	D
	Dwyer	Bernard J.	6th	D
	Gallo	Dean	11th	R
	Guarini	Frank J.	14th	D
	Hughes	William J.	2nd	D
	Pallone	Frank, Jr.	3rd	D
	Payne	Donald E.	10th	D
	Rinaldo	Matthew J.	7th	R
	Roe	Robert	8th	D
	Roukema	Marge	5th	R
	Saxton	Jim	13th	R
	Smith	Christopher	4th	R
	Torricelli	Robert	9th	D
	Zimmer	Dick	12th	R
NM	Richardson	Bill	3rd	D
	Schiff	Steven	1st	R
	Skeen	Joe	2nd	R
NV	Bilbray	James H.	1st	D
	Vucanovich	Barbara B.	2nd	R
NY	Ackerman	Gary L.	7th	D
	Boehlert	Sherwood L.	25th	R
	Downey	Thomas J., Jr.	2nd	D
	Engel	Eliot L.	19th	D
	Fish	Hamilton, Jr.	21st	R
	Flake	Floyd H.	6th	D
	Gilman	Benjamin A.	22nd	R
	Green	Bill	15th	R
	Hochbrueckner	George	1st	D
	Horton	Frank	29th	R
	Houghton	Amo	34th	R
	LaFalce	John J., Jr.	32nd	D
	Lent	Norman F.	4th	R
	Lowey	Nita M.	20th	D
	Manton	Thomas J., Jr.	9th	D
	Martin	David O'Brien	26th	R
	McGrath	Raymond J.	5th	R
	McHugh	Matthew F.	28th	D
	McNulty	Michael R.	23rd	D
	Molinari	Susan	14th	R
	Mrazek	Robert J.	3rd	D
	Nadler	Jerrold	17th	D
	Nowak	Henry J.	33rd	D
	Owens	Major	12th	D

State	Last Name	First Name	District	Party
NY	Paxon	Bill	31st	R
	Rangel	Charles	16th	D
	Scheuer	James	8th	D
	Schumer	Charles	10th	D
	Serrano	Jose E.	18th	D
	Slaughter	Louise McIntosh	30th	D
	Solarz	Stephen	13th	D
	Solomon	Gerald	24th	R
	Towns	Edolphus	11th	D
	Walsh	James	27th	R
OH	Applegate	Douglas	18th	D
	Boehner	John	8th	R
	Eckart	Dennis E.	11th	D
	Feighan	Edward F.	19th	D
	Gillmor	Paul	5th	R
	Gradison	Willis D., Jr.	2nd	R
	Hall	Tony P.	3rd	D
	Hobson	David	7th	R
	Kaptur	Marcy	9th	D
	Kasich	John R.	12th	R
	Luken	Thomas	1st	D
	McEwen	Bob	6th	R
	Miller	Clarence	10th	R
	Oakar	Mary Rose	20th	D
	Oxley	Michael	4th	D
	Pease	Donald E.	13th	D
	Regula	Ralph	16th	R
	Sawyer	Thomas	14th	D
	Stokes	Louis	21st	D
	Traficant	James A., Jr.	17th	D
	Wylie	Chalmers	15th	R
OK	Brewster	Bill	3rd	D
	Edwards	Mickey	5th	R
	English	Glenn M.	6th	D
	Inhofe	James M.	1st	R
	McCurdy	Dave	4th	D
	Synar	Mike	2nd	D
OR	AuCoin	Les	1st	D
	DeFazio	Peter A.	4th	D
	Kopetski	Michael	5th	D
	Smith	Robert F.	2nd	R
	Wyden	Ron	3rd	D
PA	Blackwell	Lucien	2nd	D

(continued)

State	Last Name	First Name	District	Party
PA	Borski	Robert A.	3rd	D
	Clinger	William F., Jr.	23rd	R
	Coughlin	Lawrence	13th	R
	Coyne	William J.	14th	D
	Foglietta	Thomas M.	1st	D
	Gaydos	Joseph M.	20th	D
	Gekas	George W., Jr.	17th	R
	Goodling	William F., Jr.	19th	R
	Kanjorski	Paul E.	11th	D
	Kolter	Joe	4th	D
	Kostmayer	Peter H.	8th	D
	McDade	Joseph M.	10th	R
	Murphy	Austin	22nd	D
	Murtha	John P.	12th	D
	Ridge	Thomas	21st	R
	Ritter	Don	15th	R
	Santorum	Rick	18th	R
	Schulze	Richard	5th	R
	Shuster	Bud	9th	R
	Walker	Robert	16th	R
	Weldon	Curt	7th	R
	Yatron	Gus	6th	D
PR	Colorado	Antonio	Resident Commissioner	D
RI	Machtley	Ronald K.	1st	R
	Reed	Jack	2nd	D
SC	Derrick	Butler	3rd	D
	Patterson	Elizabeth J.	4th	D
	Ravenel	Arthur, Jr.	1st	R
	Spence	Floyd H.	2nd	R
	Spratt	John M., Jr.	5th	D
	Tallon	Robin	6th	D
SD	Johnson	Tim	At Large	D
TN	Clement	Bob	5th	D
	Cooper	Jim	4th	D
	Duncan	John J., Jr.	2nd	R
	Ford	Harold E.	9th	D
	Gordon	Bart	6th	D
	Lloyd	Marilyn	3rd	D
	Quillen	James H.	1st	R
	Sundquist	Don	7th	R
	Tanner	John S.	8th	D
TX	Andrews	Michael A.	25th	D
	Archer	Bill	7th	R

State	Last Name	First Name	District	Party
TX	Armey	Richard K.	26th	R
	Barton	Joe	6th	R
	Brooks	Jack	9th	D
	Bryant	John	5th	D
	Bustamante	Albert G.	23rd	D
	Chapman	Jim	1st	D
	Coleman	Ronald D.	16th	D
	Combest	Larry	19th	R
	de la Garza	Eligio, II	15th	D
	DeLay	Tom	22nd	R
	Edwards	Chet	11th	D
	Fields	Jack	8th	R
	Frost	Martin	24th	D
	Geren	Pete	12th	D
	Gonzalez	Henry B.	20th	D
	Hall	Ralph M.	4th	D
	Johnson	Sam	3rd	R
	Laughlin	Greg	14th	D
	Ortiz	Solomon P.	27th	D
	Pickle	J. J.	10th	D
	Sarpalius	Bill	13th	D
	Smith	Lamar	21st	R
	Stenholm	Charles W.	17th	D
	Washington	Craig	18th	D
	Wilson	Charles	2nd	D
UT	Hansen	James V.	1st	R
	Orton	Bill	3rd	D
	Owens	Wayne	2nd	D
VA	Allen	George	7th	R
	Bateman	Herbert H.	1st	R
	Bliley	Thomas J., Jr.	3rd	R
	Boucher	Rick	9th	D
	Moran	James	8th	D
	Olin	Jim	6th	D
	Payne	Lewis F., Jr.	5th	D
	Pickett	Owen	2nd	D
	Sisisky	Norman	4th	D
	Wolf	Frank	10th	R
VI	de Lugo	Ron	Delegate	D
VT	Sanders	Bernard	At Large	I
WA	Chandler	Rod	8th	R
	Dicks	Norman D.	6th	D
	Foley	Thomas S.	5th	D

(continued)

State	Last Name	First Name	District	Party
WA	McDermott	Jim	7th	D
	Miller	John	1st	R
	Morrison	Sid	4th	R
	Swift	Al	2nd	D
	Unsoeld	Jolene	3rd	D
WI	Aspin	Les	1st	D
	Gunderson	Steve	3rd	R
	Kleczka	Gerald D.	4th	D
	Klug	Scott	2nd	R
	Moody	Jim	5th	D
	Obey	David	7th	D
	Petri	Thomas	6th	R
	Roth	Toby	8th	R
	Sensenbrenner	F. James	9th	R
WV	Mollohan	Alan	1st	D
	Rahall	Nick Joe, II	4th	D
	Staggers	Harley O., Jr.	2nd	D
	Wise	Robert E., Jr.	3rd	D
WY	Thomas	Craig T.	At Large	R

U.S. Congress: 102nd House of Representatives

(Arranged by Last Name of Member)

Last Name	First Name	State	District	Party
Abercrombie	Neil	HI	1st	D
Ackerman	Gary L.	NY	7th	D
Alexander	Bill	AR	1st	D
Allard	Wayne	CO	4th	R
Allen	George	VA	7th	R
Anderson	Glenn M.	CA	32nd	D
Andrews	Thomas	MN	1st	D
Andrews	Robert E.	NJ	1st	D
Andrews	Michael A.	TX	25th	D
Annunzio	Frank	IL	11th	D
Anthony	Beryl, Jr.	AR	4th	D
Applegate	Douglas	OH	18th	D
Archer	Bill	TX	7th	R
Armey	Richard K.	TX	26th	R
Aspin	Les	WI	1st	D
Atkins	Chester G.	MA	5th	D

Last Name	First Name	State	District	Party
AuCoin	Les	OR	1st	D
Bacchus	Jim	FL	11th	D
Baker	Richard H.	LA	6th	R
Ballenger	Cass	NC	10th	R
Barnard	Doug, Jr.	GA	10th	D
Barrett	Bill	NE	3rd	R
Barton	Joe	TX	6th	R
Bateman	Herbert H.	VA	1st	R
Beilenson	Anthony C.	CA	23rd	D
Bennett	Charles E.	FL	3rd	D
Bentley	Helen Delich	MD	2nd	R
Bereuter	Doug	NE	1st	R
Berman	Howard L.	CA	26th	D
Bevill	Tom	AL	4th	D
Bilbray	James H.	NV	1st	D
Bilirakis	Michael A.	FL	9th	R
Blackwell	Lucien	PA	2nd	D
Blaz	Ben Garrido	GU	Delegate	R
Bliley	Thomas J., Jr.	VA	3rd	R
Boehlert	Sherwood L.	NY	25th	R
Boehner	John	OH	8th	R
Bonior	David E.	MI	12th	D
Borski	Robert A.	PA	3rd	D
Boucher	Rick	VA	9th	D
Boxer	Barbara	CA	6th	D
Brewster	Bill	OK	3rd	D
Brooks	Jack	TX	9th	D
Broomfield	William S.	MI	18th	R
Browder	Glen	AL	3rd	D
Brown	George E., Jr.	CA	36th	D
Bruce	Terry L.	IL	19th	D
Bryant	John	TX	5th	D
Bunning	Jim	KY	4th	R
Burton	Dan	IN	6th	R
Bustamante	Albert G.	TX	23rd	D
Byron	Beverly B.	MD	6th	D
Callahan	Sonny	AL	1st	R
Camp	Dave	MI	10th	R
Campbell	Tom	CA	12th	R
Campbell	Ben Nighthorse	CO	3rd	D
Cardin	Benjamin L.	MD	3rd	D
Carper	Thomas R.	DE	At Large	D

(continued)

Last Name	First Name	State	District	Party
Carr	Bob	MI	6th	D
Chandler	Rod	WA	8th	R
Chapman	Jim	TX	1st	D
Clay	William	MO	1st	D
Clayton	Eva	NC	1st	D
Clement	Bob	TN	5th	D
Clinger	William F., Jr.	PA	23rd	R
Coble	Howard	NC	6th	R
Coleman	E. Thomas	MO	6th	R
Coleman	Ronald D.	TX	16th	D
Collins	Cardiss	IL	7th	D
Collins	Barbara-Rose	MI	13th	D
Colorado	Antonio	PR	Resident Commissioner	D
Combest	Larry	TX	19th	R
Condit	Gary L.	CA	15th	D
Conyers	John, Jr.	MI	1st	D
Cooper	Jim	TN	4th	D
Costello	Jerry F.	IL	21st	D
Coughlin	Lawrence	PA	13th	R
Cox	C. Christopher	CA	40th	R
Cox	John W., Jr.	IL	16th	D
Coyne	William J.	PA	14th	D
Cramer	Robert E.	AL	5th	D
Crane	Philip M.	IL	12th	R
Cunningham	Randy	CA	44th	R
Dannemeyer	William E.	CA	39th	R
Darden	George (Buddy)	GA	7th	D
Davis	Robert W.	MI	11th	R
de la Garza	Eligio, II	TX	15th	D
de Lugo	Ron	VI	Delegate	D
DeFazio	Peter A.	OR	4th	D
deLauro	Rosa	CT	3rd	D
DeLay	Tom	TX	22nd	R
Dellums	Ronald V.	CA	8th	D
Derrick	Butler	SC	3rd	D
Dickenson	William L.	AL	2nd	R
Dicks	Norman D.	WA	6th	D
Dingell	John D.	MI	16th	D
Dixon	Julian C.	CA	28th	D
Donnelly	Brian J.	MA	11th	D
Dooley	Calvin	CA	17th	D
Doolittle	John	CA	14th	R

Last Name	First Name	State	District	Party
Dorgan	Byron L.	ND	At Large	D
Dornan	Robert K.	CA	38th	R
Downey	Thomas J., Jr.	NY	2nd	D
Dreier	David	CA	33rd	R
Duncan	John J., Jr.	TN	2nd	R
Durbin	Richard J.	IL	20th	D
Dwyer	Bernard J.	NJ	6th	D
Dymally	Mervyn M.	CA	31st	D
Early	Joseph D.	MA	3rd	D
Eckart	Dennis E.	OH	11th	D
Edwards	Don	CA	10th	D
Edwards	Mickey	OK	5th	R
Edwards	Chet	TX	11th	D
Emerson	Bill	MO	8th	R
Engel	Eliot L.	NY	19th	D
English	Glenn M.	OK	6th	D
Erdreich	Ben	AL	6th	D
Espy	Mike	MS	2nd	D
Evans	Lane	IL	17th	D
Ewing	Thomas	IL	15th	R
Faleomavaega	Eni F. H.	AS	Delegate	D
Fascell	Dante	FL	19th	D
Fawell	Harris W.	IL	13th	R
Fazio	Vic	CA	4th	D
Feighan	Edward F.	OH	19th	D
Fields	Jack	TX	8th	R
Fish	Hamilton, Jr.	NY	21st	R
Flake	Floyd H.	NY	6th	D
Foglietta	Thomas M.	PA	1st	D
Foley	Thomas S.	WA	5th	D
Ford	Wiliam D.	MI	15th	D
Ford	Harold E.	TN	9th	D
Frank	Barney	MA	4th	D
Franks	Gary L.	CT	5th	R
Frost	Martin	TX	24th	D
Gallegly	Elton	CA	21st	R
Gallo	Dean	NJ	11th	R
Gaydos	Joseph M.	PA	20th	D
Gejdenson	Sam	CT	2nd	D
Gekas	George W., Jr.	PA	17th	R
Gephardt	Richard A.	MO	3rd	D
Geren	Pete	TX	12th	D
Gibbons	Sam	FL	7th	D

(continued)

Last Name	First Name	State	District	Party
Gilchrest	Wayne	MD	1st	R
Gillmor	Paul	OH	5th	R
Gilman	Benjamin A.	NY	22nd	R
Gingrich	Newt	GA	6th	R
Glickman	Dan	KS	4th	R
Gonzalez	Henry B.	TX	20th	D
Goodling	William F., Jr.	PA	19th	R
Gordon	Bart	TN	6th	D
Goss	Porter J.	FL	13th	R
Gradison	Willis D., Jr.	OH	2nd	R
Grandy	Fred	IA	6th	R
Green	Bill	NY	15th	R
Guarini	Frank J.	NJ	14th	D
Gunderson	Steve	WI	3rd	R
Hall	Tony P.	OH	3rd	D
Hall	Ralph M.	TX	4th	D
Hamilton	Lee H.	IN	9th	D
Hammerschmidt	John Paul	AR	3rd	R
Hancock	Mel	MO	7th	R
Hansen	James V.	UT	1st	R
Harris	Claude	AL	7th	D
Hastert	J. Dennis	IL	14th	R
Hatcher	Charles	GA	2nd	D
Hayes	Charles A.	IL	1st	D
Hayes	James A.	LA	7th	D
Hefley	Joel	CO	5th	R
Hefner	W. G. (Bill)	NC	8th	D
Henry	Paul B.	MI	5th	R
Herger	Wally	CA	2nd	R
Hertel	Dennis M.	MI	14th	D
Hoagland	Peter A.	NE	2nd	D
Hobson	David	OH	7th	R
Hochbrueckner	George	NY	1st	D
Holloway	Clyde	LA	8th	R
Hopkins	Larry	KY	6th	R
Horn	Joan Kelly	MO	2nd	D
Horton	Frank	NY	29th	R
Houghton	Amo	NY	34th	R
Hoyer	Steny H.	MD	5th	D
Hubbard	Carroll, Jr.	KY	1st	D
Huckaby	Jerry	LA	5th	D
Hughes	William J.	NJ	2nd	D
Hunter	Duncan	CA	45th	R

Last Name	First Name	State	District	Party
Hutto	Earl	FL	1st	D
Hyde	Henry	IL	6th	R
Inhofe	James M.	OK	1st	R
Ireland	Andy	FL	10th	R
Jacobs	Andrew, Jr.	IN	10th	D
James	Craig T.	FL	4th	R
Jefferson	William	LA	2nd	D
Jenkins	Edward F.	GA	9th	D
Johnson	Nancy L.	CT	6th	R
Johnson	Tim	SD	At Large	D
Johnson	Sam	TX	3rd	R
Johnston	Harry	FL	14th	D
Jones	Ben	GA	4th	D
Jontz	Jim	IN	5th	D
Kanjorski	Paul E.	PA	11th	D
Kaptur	Marcy	OH	9th	D
Kasich	John R.	OH	12th	R
Kennedy	Joseph P., II	MA	8th	D
Kennelly	Barbara B.	CT	1st	D
Kildee	Dale E.	MI	7th	D
Kleczka	Gerald D.	WI	4th	D
Klug	Scott	WI	2nd	R
Kolbe	Jim	AZ	5th	R
Kolter	Joe	PA	4th	D
Kopetski	Michael	OR	5th	D
Kostmayer	Peter H.	PA	8th	D
Kyl	Jon L.	AZ	4th	R
LaFalce	John J., Jr.	NY	32nd	D
Lagomarsino	Robert J.	CA	19th	R
Lancaster	H. Martin	NC	3rd	D
Lantos	Tom	CA	11th	D
LaRocco	Larry	ID	1st	D
Laughlin	Greg	TX	14th	D
Leach	Jim	IA	1st	R
Lehman	Richard H.	CA	18th	D
Lehman	William	FL	17th	D
Lent	Norman F.	NY	4th	R
Levin	Sander M.	MI	17th	D
Levine	Mel	CA	27th	D
Lewis	Jerry	CA	35th	R
Lewis	Tom	FL	12th	R
Lewis	John	GA	5th	D
Lightfoot	Jim	IA	5th	R

(continued)

Last Name	First Name	State	District	Party
Lipinski	William O.	IL	5th	D
Livingston	Bob	LA	1st	R
Lloyd	Marilyn	TN	3rd	D
Long	Jill L.	IN	4th	D
Lowery	Bill	CA	41st	R
Lowey	Nita M.	NY	20th	D
Luken	Thomas	OH	1st	D
Machtley	Ronald K.	RI	1st	R
Manton	Thomas J., Jr.	NY	9th	D
Markey	Edward J.	MA	7th	D
Marlenee	Ron	MT	2nd	R
Martin	David O'Brien	NY	26th	R
Martinez	Matthew G.	CA	30th	D
Matsui	Robert T.	CA	3rd	D
Mavroules	Nicholas	MA	6th	D
Mazzoli	Romano	KY	3rd	D
McCandless	Alfred A.	CA	37th	R
McCloskey	Frank	IN	8th	D
McCollum	Bill	FL	5th	R
McCrery	Jim	LA	4th	R
McCurdy	Dave	OK	4th	D
McDade	Joseph M.	PA	10th	R
McDermott	Jim	WA	7th	D
McEwen	Bob	OH	6th	R
McGrath	Raymond J.	NY	5th	R
McHugh	Matthew F.	NY	28th	D
McMillan	J. Alex	NC	9th	R
McMillen	C. Thomas	MD	4th	D
McNulty	Michael R.	NY	23rd	D
Meyers	Jan	KS	3rd	R
Mfume	Kweisi	MD	7th	D
Michel	Robert	IL	18th	R
Miller	George	CA	7th	D
Miller	Clarence	OH	10th	R
Miller	John	WA	1st	R
Mineta	Norman	CA	13th	R
Mink	Patsy	HI	2nd	D
Moakley	John Joseph	MA	9th	D
Molinari	Susan	NY	14th	R
Mollohan	Alan	WV	1st	D
Montgomery	G. V. (Sonny)	MS	3rd	D
Moody	Jim	WI	5th	D
Moorhead	Carlos	CA	22nd	R

Last Name	First Name	State	District	Party
Moran	James	VA	8th	D
Morella	Constance	MD	8th	R
Morrison	Sid	WA	4th	R
Mrazek	Robert J.	NY	3rd	D
Murphy	Austin	PA	22nd	D
Murtha	John P.	PA	12th	D
Myers	John T.	IN	7th	R
Nadler	Jerrold	NY	17th	D
Nagle	David	IA	3rd	D
Natcher	William H., III	KY	2nd	D
Neal	Richard	MA	2nd	D
Neal	Stephen	NC	5th	D
Nichols	Dick	KS	5th	R
Norton	Eleanor Holmes	DC	Delegate	D
Nowak	Henry J.	NY	33rd	D
Nussle	Jim	IA	2nd	R
Oakar	Mary Rose	OH	20th	D
Oberstar	James L.	MN	8th	D
Obey	David	WI	7th	D
Olin	Jim	VA	6th	D
Olver	John	MA	1st	D
Ortiz	Solomon P.	TX	27th	D
Orton	Bill	UT	3rd	D
Owens	Major	NY	12th	D
Owens	Wayne	UT	2nd	D
Oxley	Michael	OH	4th	D
Packard	Ron	CA	43rd	R
Pallone	Frank, Jr.	NJ	3rd	D
Panetta	Leon	CA	16th	D
Parker	Mike	MS	4th	D
Pastor	Ed	AZ	2nd	D
Patterson	Elizabeth J.	SC	4th	D
Paxon	Bill	NY	31st	R
Payne	Donald E.	NJ	10th	D
Payne	Lewis F., Jr.	VA	5th	D
Pease	Donald E.	OH	13th	D
Pelosi	Nancy L.	CA	5th	D
Penny	Timothy	MN	1st	D
Perkins	Carlos	KY	7th	D
Peterson	Douglas	FL	2nd	D
Peterson	Collin	MN	7th	D
Petri	Thomas	WI	6th	R
Pickett	Owen	VA	2nd	D

(continued)

Last Name	First Name	State	District	Party
Pickle	J. J.	TX	10th	D
Porter	John Edward	IL	10th	R
Poshard	Glenn M.	IL	22nd	D
Price	David	NC	4th	D
Pursell	Carlos	MI	2nd	R
Quillen	James H.	TN	1st	R
Rahall	Nick Joe, II	WV	4th	D
Ramstad	Jim	MN	3rd	R
Rangel	Charles	NY	16th	D
Ravenel	Arthur, Jr.	SC	1st	R
Ray	Richard	GA	3rd	D
Reed	Jack	RI	2nd	D
Regula	Ralph	OH	16th	R
Rhodes	John J., III	AZ	1st	R
Richardson	Bill	NM	3rd	D
Ridge	Thomas	PA	21st	R
Riggs	Frank	CA	1st	R
Rinaldo	Matthew J.	NJ	7th	R
Ritter	Don	PA	15th	R
Roberts	Pat	KS	1st	R
Roe	Robert	NJ	8th	D
Roemer	Tim	IN	3rd	D
Rogers	Harold E.	KY	5th	R
Rohrabacher	Dana	CA	42nd	R
Rose	Charles	NC	7th	D
Ros-Lehtinen	Ileana	FL	18th	R
Rostenkowski	Dan	IL	8th	R
Roth	Toby	WI	8th	R
Roukema	Marge	NJ	5th	R
Rowland	J. Roy	GA	8th	D
Roybal	Edward	CA	25th	D
Russo	Marty	IL	3rd	D
Sabo	Martin Olav	MN	5th	D
Sanders	Bernard	VT	At Large	I
Sangmeister	George	IL	4th	D
Santorum	Rick	PA	18th	R
Sarpalius	Bill	TX	13th	D
Savage	Gus	IL	2nd	D
Sawyer	Thomas	OH	14th	D
Saxton	Jim	NJ	13th	R
Schaefer	Dan	CO	6th	R
Scheuer	James	NY	8th	D
Schiff	Steven	NM	1st	R

Last Name	First Name	State	District	Party
Schroeder	Patricia F.	CO	1st	D
Schulze	Richard	PA	5th	R
Schumer	Charles	NY	10th	D
Sensenbrenner	F. James	WI	9th	R
Serrano	Jose E.	NY	18th	D
Sharp	Philip	IN	2nd	D
Shaw	E. Clay, Jr.	FL	15th	R
Shays	Christopher	CT	4th	R
Shuster	Bud	PA	9th	R
Sikorski	Gerry	MN	6th	D
Sisisky	Norman	VA	4th	D
Skaggs	David	CO	2nd	D
Skeen	Joe	NM	2nd	R
Skelton	Ike	MO	4th	D
Slattery	Jim	KS	2nd	D
Slaughter	Louise McIntosh	NY	30th	D
Smith	Lawrence, Jr.	FL	16th	D
Smith	Neal	IA	4th	D
Smith	Christopher	NJ	4th	R
Smith	Robert F.	OR	2nd	R
Smith	Lamar	TX	21st	R
Snowe	Olympia	MN	2nd	R
Solarz	Stephen	NY	13th	D
Solomon	Gerald	NY	24th	R
Spence	Floyd H.	SC	2nd	R
Spratt	John M., Jr.	SC	5th	D
Staggers	Harley O., Jr.	WV	2nd	D
Stallings	Richard	ID	2nd	D
Stark	Fortney Pete	CA	9th	D
Stearns	Cliff	FL	6th	R
Stenholm	Charles W.	TX	17th	D
Stokes	Louis	OH	21st	D
Studds	Gerry	MA	10th	D
Stump	Bob	AZ	3rd	R
Sundquist	Don	TN	7th	R
Swett	Dick	NH	2nd	D
Swift	Al	WA	2nd	D
Synar	Mike	OK	2nd	D
Tallon	Robin	SC	6th	D
Tanner	John S.	TN	8th	D
Tauzin	W. J.	LA	3rd	D
Taylor	Gene	MS	5th	D
Taylor	Charles H.	NC	11th	R

(continued)

Last Name	First Name	State	District	Party
Thomas	William	CA	20th	R
Thomas	Lindsay	GA	1st	D
Thomas	Craig T.	WY	At Large	R
Thornton	Raymond J.	AR	2nd	D
Torres	Esteban Edward	CA	34th	D
Torricelli	Robert	NJ	9th	D
Towns	Edolphus	NY	11th	D
Traficant	James A., Jr.	OH	17th	D
Traxler	Bob	MI	8th	D
Unsoeld	Jolene	WA	3rd	D
Upton	Frederick	MI	4th	R
Valentine	Tim	NC	2nd	D
Vander Jagt	Guy	MI	9th	R
Vento	Bruce	MN	4th	D
Visclosky	Peter	IN	1st	D
Volkmer	Harold E.	MO	9th	D
Vucanovich	Barbara B.	NV	2nd	R
Walker	Robert	PA	16th	R
Walsh	James	NY	27th	R
Washington	Craig	TX	18th	D
Waters	Maxine	CA	29th	D
Waxman	Henry	CA	24th	D
Weber	Vin	MN	2nd	R
Weldon	Curt	PA	7th	R
Wheat	Alan	MO	5th	D
Whitten	Jamie	MS	1st	D
Williams	Pat	MT	1st	D
Wilson	Charles	TX	2nd	D
Wise	Robert E., Jr.	WV	3rd	D
Wolf	Frank	VA	10th	R
Wolpe	Howard	MI	3rd	D
Wyden	Ron	OR	3rd	D
Wylie	Chalmers	OH	15th	R
Yates	Sidney	IL	9th	D
Yatron	Gus	PA	6th	D
Young	Don	AK	At Large	R
Young	C. W. Bill	FL	8th	R
Zeliff	William	NH	1st	R
Zimmer	Dick	NJ	12th	R

GOVERNORS

(ARRANGED BY NAME OF GOVERNOR)[7]

Last Name	First Name	State	Party	Years of Service
Ada	Joseph F.	Guam	R	1987–1995
Andrus	Cecil D.	Idaho	D	1987–1995
Ashcroft	John	Missouri	R	1989–1993
Baliles	Gerald L.	Virginia	D	1986–1990
Bangerter	Norman H.	Utah	R	1985–1993
Bayh	Evan	Indiana	D	1988–1996
Bellmon	Henry	Oklahoma	R	1963–1967; 1987–1991
Blanchard	James Johnston	Michigan	D	1983–1991
Branstad	Terry	Iowa	R	1983–1999
Campbell	Carroll A.	South Carolina	R	1987–1995
Caperton	Gaston	West Virginia	D	1989–1997
Carruthers	Garrey E.	New Mexico	R	1987–1990
Casey	Robert P.	Pennsylvania	D	1987–1995
Castle	Michael Newbold	Delaware	R	1985–1993
Celeste	Richard	Ohio	D	1983–1991
Chiles	Lawton	Florida	D	1991–1998
Clements	William P.	Texas	R	1979–1983; 1987–1991
Clinton	William Jefferson	Arkansas	D	1979–1981; 1983–1991
Coleman	Peter Tali	American Samoa	R	1957–1961; 1978–1985; 1988–1993
Cowper	Steve	Alaska	D	1986–1990
Cuomo	Mario	New York	D	1983–1995
De leon Guerrero	Lorenzo I.	Northern Mariana Islands	R	1990–1994
Deukmejian	George	California	R	1983–1991
DiPrete	Edward D.	Rhode Island	R	1985–1991
Dukakis	Michael S.	Massachusetts	D	1975–1979; 1983–1991
Edwards	Edwin W.	Louisiana	D	1972–1980; 1992–1996
Engler	John	Michigan	R	1991–2003
Farrelly	Alexander A.	Virgin Islands	D	1987–1995
Finney	Joan	Kansas	D	1991–1995
Florio	Jim	New Jersey	D	1990–1994
Gardner	Booth	Washington	D	1985–1993
Goldschmidt	Neil	Oregon	D	1987–1991
Gregg	Judd	New Hampshire	R	1989–1993
Harris	Joseph Frank	Georgia	D	1983–1991
Hayden	John Michael	Kansas	R	1987–1991

(continued)

---

[7] http://www.nga.org/governors/1,1169,C_PAST_GOV,00.html

Last Name	First Name	State	Party	Years of Service
Hernandez-Colon	Rafael	Puerto Rico	Popular Democrat	1973–1977; 1985–1993
Hickel	Walter J.	Alaska	I/R	1966–1969; 1990–1994
Hunt	Guy	Alabama	R	1987–1993
Jones	Brereton C.	Kentucky	D	1992–1996
Kean	Thomas H.	New Jersey	R	1982–1990
Kunin	Madeleine M.	Vermont	D	1985–1991
Mabus	Ray	Mississippi	D	1988–1992
Martin	James G.	North Carolina	R	1985–1993
Martinez	Robert	Florida	D, R	1987–1991
McKernan	John R., Jr.	Maine	R	1987–1995
McWhirter	Ned Ray	Tennessee	D	1987–1995
Mickelson	George S.	South Dakota	R	1991–1995
Miller	Zell	Georgia	D	1990–1998
Miller	Bob	Nevada	D	1989–1999
Mofford	Rose	Arizona	D	1988–1991
Nelson	E. Benjamin	Nebraska	D	1990–1998
O'Neill	William A.	Connecticut	D	1980–1991
Orr	Kay A.	Nebraska	R	1987–1991
Perpich	Rudolph	Minnesota	Democratic-Farmer-Labor	1976–1979; 1983–1991
Richards	Ann W.	Texas	D	1991–1995
Roberts	Barbara	Oregon	D	1991–1995
Romer	Roy	Colorado	D	1987–1999
Schaefer	William Donald	Maryland	D	1987–1995
Sinner	George A.	North Dakota	D	1984–1992
Snelling	Richard A.	Vermont	R	1977–1991
Stephens	Stan	Montana	R	1989–1993
Sullivan	Michael J.	Wyoming	D	1987–1995
Sundlun	Bruce G.	Rhode Island	D	1991–1995
Symington	J. Fife	Arizona	R	1991–1997
Tenorio	Pedro P.	Northern Mariana Islands	R	1982–1990; 1998–2002
Thompson	James Robert	Illinois	R	1977–1991
Thompson	Tommy G.	Wisconsin	R	1987–2001
Tucker	Jim Guy	Arkansas	D	1991–1996
Voinovich	George V.	Ohio	R	1991–1998
Waihee	John	Hawaii	D	1986–2000
Walters	David	Oklahoma	D	1991–1995
Weicker	Lowell P., Jr.	Connecticut	I	1991–1995
Weld	William F. R.	Massachusetts	R	1991–1997
Wilder	L. Douglas	Virginia	D	1990–1994
Wilkinson	Wallace G.	Kentucky	D	1987–1991
Wilson	Pete	California	R	1991–1999

GOVERNORS
(ARRANGED BY STATE)[8]

State	Last Name	First Name	Party	Dates of Service
Alabama	Hunt	Guy	R	1987–1993
Alaska	Cowper	Steve	D	1986–1990
	Hickel	Walter J.	I/R	1966–1969; 1990–1994
American Samoa	Coleman	Peter Tali	R	1957–1961; 1978–1985; 1988–1993
Arizona	Mofford	Rose	D	1988–1991
	Symington	J. Fife	R	1991–1997
Arkansas	Clinton	William Jefferson	D	1979–1981; 1983–1991
	Tucker	Jim Guy	D	1991–1996
California	Deukmejian	George	R	1983–1991
	Wilson	Pete	R	1991–1999
Colorado	Romer	Roy	D	1987–1999
Connecticut	O'Neill	William A.	D	1980–1991
	Weicker	Lowell P., Jr.	I	1991–1995
Delaware	Castle	Michael Newbold	R	1985–1993
Florida	Chiles	Lawton	D	1991–1998
	Martinez	Robert	D, R	1987–1991
Georgia	Harris	Joseph Frank	D	1983–1991
	Miller	Zell	D	1990–1998
Guam	Ada	Joseph F.	R	1987–1995
Hawaii	Waihee	John	D	1986–2000
Idaho	Andrus	Cecil D.	D	1987–1995
Illinois	Thompson	James Robert	R	1977–1991
Indiana	Bayh	Evan	D	1988–1996
Iowa	Branstad	Terry	R	1983–1999
Kansas	Finney	Joan	D	1991–1995
	Hayden	John Michael	R	1987–1991
Kentucky	Jones	Brereton C.	D	1992–1996
	Wilkinson	Wallace G.	D	1987–1991
Louisiana	Edwards	Edwin W.	D	1972–1980; 1992–1996
Maine	McKernan	John R., Jr.	R	1987–1995
Maryland	Schaefer	William Donald	D	1987–1995
Massachusetts	Dukakis	Michael S.	D	1975–1979; 1983–1991
	Weld	William F.	R	1991–1997

(continued)

[8] http://www.nga.org/governors/1,1169,C_PAST_GOV,00.html

State	Last Name	First Name	Party	Dates of Service
Michigan	Blanchard	James Johnston	D	1983–1991
	Engler	John	R	1991–2003
Minnesota	Perpich	Rudolph	Democratic-Farmer-Labor	1976–1979; 1983–1991
Mississippi	Mabus	Ray	D	1988–1992
Missouri	Ashcroft	John	R	1989–1993
Montana	Stephens	Stan	R	1989–1993
Nebraska	Nelson	E. Benjamin	D	1990–1998
	Orr	Kay A.	R	1987–1991
Nevada	Miller	Bob	D	1989–1999
New Hampshire	Gregg	Judd	R	1989–1993
New Jersey	Florio	Jim	D	1990–1994
	Kean	Thomas H.	R	1982–1990
New Mexico	Carruthers	Garrey E.	R	1987–1990
New York	Cuomo	Mario	D	1983–1995
North Carolina	Martin	James G.	R	1985–1993
North Dakota	Sinner	George A.	D	1984–1992
Northern Mariana Islands	De leon Guerrero	Lorenzo I.	R	1990–1994
	Tenorio	Pedro P.	R	1982–1990; 1998–2002
Ohio	Celeste	Richard	D	1983–1991
	Voinovich	George V.	R	1991–1998
Oklahoma	Bellmon	Henry	R	1963–1967; 1987–1991
	Walters	David	D	1991–1995
Oregon	Goldschmidt	Neil	D	1987–1991
	Roberts	Barbara	D	1991–1995
Pennsylvania	Casey	Robert P.	D	1987–1995
Puerto Rico	Hernandez-Colon	Rafael	Popular Democrat	1973–1977; 1985–1993
Rhode Island	DiPrete	Edward D.	R	1985–1991
	Sundlun	Bruce G.	D	1991–1995
South Carolina	Campbell	Carroll A.	R	1987–1995
South Dakota	Mickelson	George S.	R	1991–1995
Tennessee	McWhirter	Ned Ray	D	1987–1995
Texas	Clements	William P.	R	1979–1983; 1987–1991
	Richards	Ann W.	D	1991–1995
Utah	Bangerter	Norman H.	R	1985–1993
Vermont	Kunin	Madeleine M.	D	1985–1991
	Snelling	Richard A.	R	1977–1991
Virgin Islands	Farrelly	Alexander A.	D	1987–1995

State	Last Name	First Name	Party	Dates of Service
Virginia	Baliles	Gerald L.	D	1986–1990
	Wilder	L. Douglas	D	1990–1994
Washington	Gardner	Booth	D	1985–1993
West Virginia	Caperton	Gaston	D	1989–1997
Wisconsin	Thompson	Tommy G.	R	1987–2001
Wyoming	Sullivan	Michael J.	D	1987–1995

SELECTED PRIMARY DOCUMENTS

﹡

All documents are taken from *Public Papers of the President: George Bush*, and are located at http://bushlibrary.tamu.edu/research/paper.html

1. Inaugural Address, January 20, 1989

2. Address on Administration Goals before a Joint Session of Congress, February 9, 1989

3. Interview with Chinese Television Journalists in Beijing, February 26, 1989

4. Statement on the Failure of the Senate to Approve the Nomination of John Tower as Secretary of Defense, March 9, 1989

5. Message to the Congress Transmitting Proposed Legislation on Educational Excellence, April 5, 1989

6. Statement on the Chinese Government's Suppression of Student Demonstrations, June 3, 1989

7. Remarks Announcing Proposed Legislation to Amend the Clean Air Act, June 12, 1989

8. White House Fact Sheet on the Points of Light Initiative, June 22, 1989

9. Address to the Nation on the National Drug Control Strategy, September 5, 1989

10. Joint Statement on the Education Summit with the Nation's Governors in Charlottesville, Virginia, September 28, 1989

11. Statement on the Flag Protection Act of 1989, October 26, 1989

12. Remarks of the President and Soviet Chairman Gorbachev and a Question-and-Answer Session with Reporters in Malta, December 3, 1989

13. Address to the Nation Announcing United States Military Action in Panama, December 20, 1989

14. The President's News Conference, December 21, 1989

15. Address before a Joint Session of the Congress on the State of the Union, January 31, 1990

16. Remarks at a White House Briefing for Conservative Leaders, April 26, 1990

17. Remarks and an Exchange with Reporters on the Soviet–United States Summit, May 31, 1990

18. Statement on Signing the Americans with Disabilities Act of 1990, July 26, 1990

19. Remarks and an Exchange with Reporters on the Iraqi Invasion of Kuwait, August 2, 1990

20. Remarks and an Exchange with Reporters on the Iraqi Invasion of Kuwait, August 5, 1990

21. Address to the Nation Announcing the Deployment of U.S. Armed Forces to Saudi Arabia, August 8, 1990

22. Order for Emergency Deficit Control Measures for Fiscal Year 1991, August 25, 1990

23. Soviet Union–United States Joint Statement on the Persian Gulf Crisis, September 9, 1990

24. Address before a Joint Session of the Congress on the Persian Gulf Crisis and the Federal Budget Deficit, September 11, 1990

25. Address to the People of Iraq on the Persian Gulf Crisis, September 16, 1990

26. Remarks Announcing a Federal Budget Agreement, September 30, 1990

27. The President's News Conference on the Federal Budget Crisis, October 6, 1990

28. Message to the Senate Returning without Approval the Civil Rights Act of 1990, October 22, 1990

29. Statement on Signing the Omnibus Budget Reconciliation Act of 1990, November 5, 1990

30. President's News Conference on the Persian Gulf Crisis, November 8, 1990

31. Radio Address to the Nation on the Persian Gulf Crisis, January 5, 1991

32. Address to the Nation Announcing Allied Military Action in the Persian Gulf, January 16, 1990

33. Address before a Joint Session of the Congress on the State of the Union, January 29, 1991

34. Address to the Nation Announcing Allied Military Ground Action in the Persian Gulf, February 23, 1991

35. Address to the Nation on the Suspension of Allied Offensive Combat Operations in the Persian Gulf, February 27, 1991

36. Address before a Joint Session of the Congress on the Cessation of the Persian Gulf Conflict, March 6, 1991

37. White House Statement on Weapons of Mass Destruction, March 7, 1991

38. Remarks at Maxwell Air Force Base War College in Montgomery, Alabama, April 13, 1991

39. Address to the Nation on the National Education Strategy, April 18, 1991

40. Remarks at the University of Michigan Commencement Ceremony in Ann Arbor, May 4, 1991

41. The President's News Conference with Soviet President Mikhail Gorbachev in Moscow, July 31, 1991

42. The President's News Conference in Kennebunkport, Maine, on the Attempted Coup in the Soviet Union, August 20, 1991

43. The President's News Conference in Kennebunkport, Maine, on the Attempted Coup in the Soviet Union, August 21, 1991

44. Remarks at the Swearing-In Ceremony for Supreme Court Designate Clarence Thomas, October 18, 1991

45. Remarks at the Welcoming Ceremony for President Vaclav Havel of Czechoslovakia, October 22, 1991

46. The President's News Conference with President Gorbachev of the Soviet Union in Madrid, Spain, October 29, 1991

47. Remarks on the Civil Rights Act of 1991, November 21, 1991

48. Letter Accepting the Resignation of John H. Sununu as Chief of Staff to the President, December 3, 1991

49. Statement on the Resignation of Mikhail Gorbachev as President of the Soviet Union, December 25, 1991

50. Remarks at the Annual Convention of the National Religious Broadcasters, January 27, 1992

51. Address before a Joint Session of the Congress on the State of the Union, January 28, 1992

52. Remarks to the United Nations Security Council in New York City, January 31, 1992

53. Remarks Announcing the Bush-Quayle Candidacies for Reelection, February 12, 1992

54. Declaration of San Antonio [Following International Drug Summit], February 27, 1992

55. Remarks to the American Society of Newspaper Editors, April 9, 1992

56. Address to the Nation on the Civil Disturbances in Los Angeles, California, May 1, 1992

57. White House Fact Sheet: The North American Free Trade Agreement, August 12, 1992

58. Remarks Accepting the Presidential Nomination at the Republican National Convention in Houston, August 20, 1992

59. Address to the Nation on Hurricane Andrew Disaster Relief, September 1, 1992

60. Presidential Debate in St. Louis, October 11, 1992

61. Presidential Debate in Richmond, Virginia, October 15, 1992

62. Presidential Debate in East Lansing, Michigan, October 19, 1992

63. Remarks in Houston on the Results of the Presidential Election, November 3, 1992

64. Address to the Nation on the Situation in Somalia, December 4, 1992

1. Inaugural Address
January 20, 1989

Mr. Chief Justice, Mr. President, Vice President Quayle, Senator Mitchell, Speaker Wright, Senator Dole, Congressman Michel, and fellow citizens, neighbors, and friends:

There is a man here who has earned a lasting place in our hearts and in our history. President Reagan, on behalf of our nation, I thank you for the wonderful things that you have done for America.

I've just repeated word for word the oath taken by George Washington 200 years ago, and the Bible on which I placed my hand is the Bible on which he placed his. It is right that the memory of Washington be with us today not only because this is our bicentennial inauguration but because Washington remains the Father of our Country. And he would, I think, be gladdened by this day; for today is the concrete expression of a stunning fact: our continuity, these 200 years, since our government began.

We meet on democracy's front porch. A good place to talk as neighbors and as friends. For this is a day when our nation is made whole, when our differences, for a moment, are suspended. And my first act as President is a prayer. I ask you to bow your heads.

Heavenly Father, we bow our heads and thank You for Your love. Accept our thanks for the peace that yields this day and the shared faith that makes its continuance likely. Make us strong to do Your work, willing to heed and hear Your will, and write on our hearts these words: "Use power to help people." For we are given power not to advance our own purposes, nor to make a great show in the world, nor a name. There is but one just use of power, and it is to serve people. Help us remember, Lord. Amen.

I come before you and assume the Presidency at a moment rich with promise. We live in a peaceful, prosperous time, but we can make it better. For a new breeze is blowing, and a world refreshed by freedom seems reborn. For in man's heart, if not in fact, the day of the dictator is over. The totalitarian era is passing, its old ideas blown away like leaves from an ancient, lifeless tree. A new breeze is blowing, and a nation refreshed by freedom stands ready to push on. There is new ground to be broken and new action to be taken. There are times when the future seems thick as a fog; you sit and wait, hoping the mists will lift and reveal the right path. But this is a time when the future seems a door you can walk right through into a room called tomorrow.

Great nations of the world are moving toward democracy through the door to freedom. Men and women of the world move toward free markets through the door to prosperity. The people of the world agitate for free expression and free thought through the door to the moral and intellectual satisfactions that only liberty allows.

We know what works: Freedom works. We know what's right: Freedom is right. We know how to secure a more just and prosperous life for man on Earth: through free markets, free speech, free elections, and the exercise of free will unhampered by the state.

For the first time in this century, for the first time in perhaps all history, man does not have to invent a system by which to live. We don't have to talk late into the night about which form of government is better. We don't have to wrest justice from the kings. We only have to summon it from within ourselves. We must act on what we know. I take as my guide the hope of a saint: In crucial things, unity; in important things, diversity; in all things, generosity.

America today is a proud, free nation, decent and civil, a place we cannot help but love. We know in our hearts, not loudly and proudly but as a simple fact, that this country has meaning beyond what we see, and that our strength is a force for good. But have we changed as a nation even in our time? Are we enthralled with material things, less appreciative of the nobility of work and sacrifice?

My friends, we are not the sum of our possessions. They are not the measure of our lives. In our hearts we know what matters. We cannot hope only to leave our children a bigger car, a bigger bank account. We must hope to give them a sense of what it means to be a loyal friend; a loving parent; a citizen who leaves his home, his neighborhood, and town better than he found it. And what do we want the men and women who work with us to say when we're no longer there? That we were more driven to succeed than anyone around us? Or that we stopped to ask if a sick child had gotten better and stayed a moment there to trade a word of friendship?

No President, no government can teach us to remember what is best in what we are. But if the man you have chosen to lead this government can help make a difference; if he can celebrate the quieter, deeper successes that are made not of gold and silk but of better hearts and finer souls; if he can do these things, then he must.

America is never wholly herself unless she is engaged in high moral principle. We as a people have such a purpose today. It is to make kinder the face of the Nation and gentler the face of the world. My friends, we have work to do. There are the homeless, lost and roaming. There are the children who have nothing, no love and no normalcy. There are those who cannot free themselves of enslavement to whatever addiction—drugs, welfare, the demoralization that rules the slums. There is crime to be conquered, the rough crime of the streets. There are young women to be helped who are about to become mothers of children they can't care for and might not love. They need our care, our guidance, and our education, though we bless them for choosing life.

The old solution, the old way, was to think that public money alone could end these problems. But we have learned that that is not so. And in any case, our funds are low. We have a deficit to bring down. We have more will than wallet, but will is what we need. We will make the hard choices, looking at what we have and perhaps allocating it differently, making our decisions based on honest need and prudent safety. And then we will do the wisest thing of all. We will turn to the only resource we have that in times of need always grows: the goodness and the courage of the American people.

And I am speaking of a new engagement in the lives of others, a new activism, hands-on and involved, that gets the job done. We must bring in the generations, harnessing the unused talent of the elderly and the unfocused energy of the young. For not only leadership is passed from generation to generation but so is stewardship. And the generation born after the Second World War has come of age.

I have spoken of a Thousand Points of Light, of all the community organizations that are spread like stars throughout the Nation, doing good. We will work hand in hand, encouraging, sometimes leading, sometimes being led, rewarding. We will work on this in the White House, in the Cabinet agencies. I will go to the people and the programs that are the brighter points of light, and I'll ask every member of my government to become involved. The old ideas are new again because they're not old, they are timeless: duty, sacrifice, commitment, and a patriotism that finds its expression in taking part and pitching in.

We need a new engagement, too, between the Executive and the Congress. The challenges before us will be thrashed out with the House and the Senate. And we must bring the Federal budget into balance. And we must ensure that America stands before the world united, strong, at peace, and fiscally sound. But of course things may be difficult. We need to compromise; we've had dissension. We need harmony; we've had a chorus of discordant voices.

For Congress, too, has changed in our time. There has grown a certain divisiveness. We have seen the hard looks and heard the statements in which not each other's ideas are challenged but each other's motives. And our great parties have too often been far apart and untrusting of each other. It's been this way since Vietnam. That war cleaves us still. But, friends, that war began in earnest a quarter of a century ago, and surely the statute of limitation has been reached. This is a fact: The final lesson of Vietnam is that no great nation can long afford to be sundered by a memory. A new breeze is blowing, and the old bipartisanship must be made new again.

To my friends, and, yes, I do mean friends—in the loyal opposition and, yes, I mean loyal—I put out my hand. I am putting out my hand to you, Mr. Speaker. I am putting out my hand to you, Mr. Majority Leader. For this is the thing: This is the age of the offered hand. And we can't turn back clocks, and I don't want to. But when our fathers were young, Mr. Speaker, our differences ended at the water's edge. And we don't wish to turn back time, but when our mothers were young, Mr. Majority Leader, the Congress and the Executive were capable of working together to produce a budget on which this nation could live. Let us negotiate soon and hard. But in the end, let us produce. The American people await action. They didn't send us here to bicker. They ask us to rise above the merely partisan. "In crucial things, unity"—and this, my friends, is crucial.

To the world, too, we offer new engagement and a renewed vow: We will stay strong to protect the peace. The offered hand is a reluctant fist; once made—strong, and can be used with great effect. There are today Americans who are held against their will in foreign lands and Americans who are unaccounted for. Assistance can be shown here and will be long remembered. Good will begets good will. Good faith can be a spiral that endlessly moves on.

Great nations like great men must keep their word. When America says something, America means it, whether a treaty or an agreement or a vow made on marble steps. We will always try to speak clearly, for candor is a compliment; but subtlety, too, is good and has its place. While keeping our alliances and friendships around the world strong, ever strong, we will continue the new closeness with the Soviet Union, consistent both with our security and with progress. One might say that our new relationship in part reflects the triumph of hope and strength over experience. But hope is good, and so is strength and vigilance.

Here today are tens of thousands of our citizens who feel the understandable satisfaction of those who have taken part in democracy and seen their hopes fulfilled. But my thoughts have been turning the past few days to those who would be watching at home, to an older fellow who will throw a salute by himself when the flag goes by and the woman who will tell her sons the words of the battle hymns. I don't mean this to be sentimental. I mean that on days like this we remember that we are all part of a continuum, inescapably connected by the ties that bind.

Our children are watching in schools throughout our great land. And to them I say, Thank you for watching democracy's big day. For democracy belongs to us all, and freedom is like a beautiful kite that can go higher and higher with the breeze. And to all I say, No matter what your circumstances or where you are, you are part of this day, you are part of the life of our great nation.

A President is neither prince nor pope, and I don't seek a window on men's souls. In fact, I yearn for a greater tolerance, and easygoingness about each other's attitudes and way of life.

There are few clear areas in which we as a society must rise up united and express our intolerance. The most obvious now is drugs. And when that first cocaine was smuggled in on a ship, it may as well have been a deadly bacteria, so much has it hurt the body, the soul of our country. And there is much to be done and to be said, but take my word for it: This scourge will stop!

And so, there is much to do. And tomorrow the work begins. And I do not mistrust the future. I do not fear what is ahead. For our problems are large, but our heart is larger. Our challenges are great, but our will is greater. And if our flaws are endless, God's love is truly boundless.

Some see leadership as high drama and the sound of trumpets calling, and sometimes it is that. But I see history as a book with many pages, and each day we fill a page with acts of hopefulness and meaning. The new breeze blows, a page turns, the story unfolds. And so, today a chapter begins, a small and stately story of unity, diversity, and generosity—shared, and written, together.

Thank you. God bless you. And God bless the United States of America.

2. Address on Administration Goals before a Joint Session of Congress February 9, 1989

Mr. Speaker, Mr. President, and distinguished Members of the House and Senate, honored guests, and fellow citizens: Less than 3 weeks ago, I joined you on the West Front of this very building and, looking over the monuments to our proud past, offered you my hand in filling the next page of American history with a story of extended prosperity and continued peace. And tonight I'm back to offer you my plans as well. The hand remains extended; the sleeves are rolled up; America is waiting; and now we must produce. Together, we can build a better America.

It is comforting to return to this historic Chamber. Here, 22 years ago, I first raised my hand to be sworn into public life. So, tonight I feel as if I'm returning home to friends. And I intend, in the months and years to come, to give you what friends deserve: frankness, respect, and my best judgment about ways to improve America's future. In return, I ask for an honest commitment to our common mission of progress. If we seize the opportunities on the road before us, there'll be praise enough for all. The people didn't send us here to bicker, and it's time to govern.

And many Presidents have come to this Chamber in times of great crisis: war and depression, loss of national spirit. And 8 years ago, I sat in that very chair as President Reagan spoke of punishing inflation and devastatingly high interest rates and people out of work—American confidence on the wane. And our challenge is different. We're fortunate—a much changed landscape lies before us tonight. So, I don't propose to reverse direction. We're headed the right way, but we cannot rest. We're a people whose energy and drive have fueled our rise to greatness. And we're a forward-looking nation—generous, yes, but ambitious, not for ourselves but for the world. Complacency is not in our character—not before, not now, not ever.

And so, tonight we must take a strong America and make it even better. We must address some very real problems. We must establish some very clear priorities. And we must make a very substantial cut in the Federal budget deficit. Some people find that agenda impossible, but I'm presenting to you tonight a realistic plan for tackling it. My plan has four broad features: attention to urgent priorities, investment in the future, an attack on the deficit, and no new taxes. This budget represents my best judgment of how we can address our priorities. There are many areas in which we would all like to spend more than I propose; I understand that. But we cannot until we get our fiscal house in order.

Next year alone, thanks to economic growth, without any change in the law, the Federal Government will take in over $80 billion more than it does this year. That's right—over $80 billion in new revenues, with no increases in taxes. And our job is to allocate those new resources wisely. We can afford to increase spending by a modest amount, but enough to invest in key priorities and still cut the deficit by almost 40 percent in 1 year. And that will allow us to meet the targets set forth in the Gramm-Rudman-Hollings law. But to do that, we must recognize that growth above inflation in Federal programs is not preordained, that not all spending initiatives were designed to be immortal.

I make this pledge tonight: My team and I are ready to work with the Congress, to form a special leadership group, to negotiate in good faith, to work day and night—if that's what it takes—to meet the budget targets and to produce a budget on time.

We cannot settle for business as usual. Government by continuing resolution, or government by crisis, will not do. And I ask the Congress tonight to approve several measures which will make budgeting more sensible. We could save time and improve efficiency by enacting 2-year budgets. Forty-three Governors have the line-item veto. Presidents should have it, too. And at the very least, when a President proposes to rescind Federal spending, the Congress should be required to vote on that proposal instead of killing it by inaction. And I ask the Congress to honor the public's wishes by passing a constitutional amendment to require a balanced budget. Such an amendment, once phased in, will discipline both the Congress and the executive branch.

Several principles describe the kind of America I hope to build with your help in the years ahead. We will not have the luxury of taking the easy, spendthrift approach to solving problems because higher spending and higher taxes put economic growth at risk. Economic growth provides jobs and hope. Economic growth enables us to pay for social programs. Economic growth enhances the security of the Nation, and low tax rates create economic growth.

I believe in giving Americans greater freedom and greater choice. And I will work for choice for American families, whether in the housing in which they live, the schools to which they send their children, or the child care they select for their young. You see, I believe that we have an obligation to those in need, but that government should not be the provider of first resort for things that the private sector can produce better. I believe in a society that is free from discrimination and bigotry of any kind. And I will work to knock down the barriers left by past discrimination and to build a more tolerant society that will stop such barriers from ever being built again.

I believe that family and faith represent the moral compass of the Nation. And I'll work to make them strong, for as Benjamin Franklin said: "If a sparrow cannot fall to the ground without His notice, can a great nation rise without His aid?" And I believe in giving people the power to make their own lives better through growth and opportunity. And together, let's put power in the hands of people.

Three weeks ago, we celebrated the bicentennial inaugural, the 200th anniversary of the first Presidency. And if you look back, one thing is so striking about the way the Founding Fathers looked at America. They didn't talk about themselves. They talked about posterity. They talked about the future. And we, too, must think in terms bigger than ourselves. We must take actions today that will ensure a better tomorrow. We must extend American leadership in technology, increase long-term investment, improve our educational system, and boost productivity. These are the keys to building a better future, and here are some of my recommendations:

I propose almost 2.2 billion for the National Science Foundation to promote basic research and keep us on track to double its budget by 1993.

I propose to make permanent the tax credit for research and development.

I've asked Vice President Quayle to chair a new Task Force on Competitiveness.

And I request funding for NASA [National Aeronautics and Space Administration] and a strong space program, an increase of almost .4 billion over the current fiscal year. We must have a manned space station; a vigorous, safe space shuttle program; and more commercial development in space. The space program should always go "full throttle up." And that's not just our ambition; it's our destiny.

I propose that we cut the maximum tax rate on capital gains to increase long-term investment. History on this is clear—this will increase revenues, help savings, and create new jobs. We won't be competitive if we leave whole sectors of America behind. This is the year we should finally enact urban enterprise zones and bring hope to the inner cities.

But the most important competitiveness program of all is one which improves education in America. When some of our students actually have trouble locating America on a map of the world, it is time for us to map a new approach to education. We must reward excellence and cut through bureaucracy. We must help schools that need help the most. We must give choice to parents, students, teachers, and principals; and we must hold all concerned accountable. In education, we cannot tolerate mediocrity. I want to cut that dropout rate and make America a more literate nation, because what it really comes down to is this: The longer our graduation lines are today, the shorter our unemployment lines will be tomorrow.

So, tonight I'm proposing the following initiatives: the beginning of a $500 million program to reward America's best schools, merit schools; the creation of special Presidential awards for the best teachers in every State, because excellence should be rewarded; the establishment of a new program of National Science Scholars, one each year for every Member of the House and Senate, to give this generation of students a special incentive to excel in science and mathematics; the expanded use of magnet schools, which give families and students greater choice; and a new program to encourage alternative certification, which will let talented people from all fields teach in our classrooms. I've said I'd like to be the "Education President." And tonight, I'd ask you to join me by becoming the "Education Congress."

Just last week, as I settled into this new office, I received a letter from a mother in Pennsylvania who had been struck by my message in the Inaugural Address. "Not 12 hours before," she wrote, "my husband and I received word that our son was addicted to cocaine. He had the world at his feet. Bright, gifted, personable—he could have done anything with his life. And now he has chosen cocaine." "And please," she wrote, "find a way to curb the supply of cocaine. Get tough with the pushers. Our son needs your help."

My friends, that voice crying out for help could be the voice of your own neighbor, your own friend, your own son. Over 23 million Americans used illegal drugs last year, at a staggering cost to our nation's well-being. Let this be recorded as the time when America rose up and said no to drugs. The scourge of drugs must be stopped. And I am asking tonight for an increase of almost a billion dollars in budget outlays to escalate the war against drugs. The war must be waged on all fronts. Our new drug czar, Bill Bennett, and I will be shoulder to shoulder in the executive branch leading the charge.

Some money will be used to expand treatment to the poor and to young mothers. This will offer the helping hand to the many innocent victims of drugs, like the thousands of babies born addicted or with AIDS because of the mother's addiction. Some will be used to cut the waiting time for treatment. Some money will be devoted to those urban schools where the emergency is now the worst. And much of it will be used to protect our borders, with help from the Coast Guard and the Customs Service, the Departments of State and Justice, and, yes, the U.S. military.

I mean to get tough on the drug criminals. And let me be clear: This President will back up those who put their lives on the line every single day—our local police officers. My budget asks for beefed-up prosecution, for a new attack on organized crime, and for enforcement of tough sentences—and for the worst kingpins, that means the death penalty. I also want to make sure that when a drug dealer is convicted there's a cell waiting for him. And he should not go free because prisons are too full. And so, let the word go out: If you're caught and convicted, you will do time.

But for all we do in law enforcement, in interdiction and treatment, we will never win this war on drugs unless we stop the demand for drugs. So, some of this increase will be used to educate the young about the dangers of drugs. We must involve the parents. We must involve the teachers. We must involve the communities. And, my friends, we must involve ourselves, each and every one of us in this concern.

One problem related to drug use demands our urgent attention and our continuing compassion, and that is the terrible tragedy of AIDS. I'm asking for 1.6 billion for education to prevent the disease and for research to find a cure.

If we're to protect our future, we need a new attitude about the environment. We must protect the air we breathe. I will send to you shortly legislation for a new, more effective Clean Air Act. It will include a plan to reduce by date certain the emissions which cause acid rain, because the time for study alone has passed, and the time for action is now. We must make use of clean coal. My budget contains full funding, on schedule, for the clean coal technology agreement that we've made with Canada. We've made that agreement with Canada, and we intend to honor that agreement. We must not neglect our parks. So, I'm asking to fund new acquisitions under the Land and Water Conservation Fund. We must protect our oceans. And I support new penalties against those who would dump medical waste and other trash into our oceans. The age of the needle on the beaches must end.

And in some cases, the gulfs and oceans off our shores hold the promise of oil and gas reserves which can make our nation more secure and less dependent on foreign oil. And when those with the most promise can be tapped safely, as with much of the Alaska National Wildlife Refuge, we should proceed. But we must use caution; we must respect the environment. And so, tonight I'm calling for the indefinite postponement of three lease sales which have raised troubling questions, two off the coast of California and one which could threaten the Everglades in Florida. Action on these three lease sales will await the conclusion of a special task force set up to measure the potential for environmental damage.

I'm directing the Attorney General and the Administrator of the Environmental Protection Agency to use every tool at their disposal to speed and toughen the enforcement of our laws against toxic-waste dumpers. I want faster cleanups and tougher enforcement of penalties against polluters.

In addition to caring for our future, we must care for those around us. A decent society shows compassion for the young, the elderly, the vulnerable, and the poor. Our first obligation is to the most vulnerable—infants, poor mothers, children living in poverty—and my proposed budget recognizes this. I ask for full funding of Medicaid, an increase of over 3 billion, and an expansion of the program to include coverage of pregnant women who are near the poverty line. I believe we should help working families cope with the burden of child care. Our help should be aimed at those who need it most: low-income families with young children. I support a new child care tax credit that will aim our efforts at exactly those families, without discriminating against mothers who choose to stay at home.

Now, I know there are competing proposals. But remember this: The overwhelming majority of all preschool child care is now provided by relatives and neighbors and churches and community groups. Families who choose these options should remain eligible for help. Parents should have choice. And for those children who are unwanted or abused or whose parents are deceased, we should encourage adoption. I propose to reenact the tax deduction for adoption expenses and to double it to $3,000. Let's make it easier for these kids to have parents who love them.

We have a moral contract with our senior citizens. And in this budget, Social Security is fully funded, including a full cost-of-living adjustment. We must honor our contract.

We must care about those in the shadow of life, and I, like many Americans, am deeply troubled by the plight of the homeless. The causes of homelessness are many; the history is long. But the moral imperative to act is clear. Thanks to the deep well of generosity in this great land, many organizations already contribute, but we in government cannot stand on the sidelines. In my budget, I ask for greater support for emergency food and shelter, for health services and measures to prevent substance abuse, and for clinics for the mentally ill. And I propose a new initiative involving the full range of government agencies. We must confront this national shame.

There's another issue that I've decided to mention here tonight. I've long believed that the people of Puerto Rico should have the right to determine their own political future. Personally, I strongly favor statehood. But I urge the Congress to take the necessary steps to allow the people to decide in a referendum.

Certain problems, the result of decades of unwise practices, threaten the health and security of our people. Left unattended, they will only get worse. But we can act now to put them behind us.

Earlier this week, I announced my support for a plan to restore the financial and moral integrity of our savings system. I ask Congress to enact our reform proposals within 45 days. We must not let this situation fester. We owe it to the savers in this country to solve this problem. Certainly, the savings of Americans must remain secure. Let me be clear: Insured depositors will continue to be fully protected, but any plan to refinance the system must be accompanied by major reform. Our proposals will prevent such a crisis from recurring. The best answer is to make sure that a mess like this will never happen again. The majority of thrifts in communities across the Nation have been honest. They've played a major role in helping families achieve the dream of home ownership. But make no mistake, those who are corrupt, those who break the law, must be kicked out of the business; and they should go to jail.

We face a massive task in cleaning up the waste left from decades of environmental neglect at America's nuclear weapons plants. Clearly, we must modernize these plants and operate them safely. That's not at issue; our national security depends on it. But beyond that, we must clean up the old mess that's been left behind. And I propose in this budget to more than double our current effort to do so. This will allow us to identify the exact nature of the various problems so we can clean them up, and clean them up we will.

We've been fortunate during these past 8 years. America is a stronger nation than it was in 1980. Morale in our Armed Forces has been restored; our resolve has been shown. Our readiness has been improved, and we are at peace. There can no longer be any doubt that peace has been made more secure through strength. And when America is stronger, the world is safer.

Most people don't realize that after the successful restoration of our strength, the Pentagon budget has actually been reduced in real terms for each of the last 4 years. We cannot tolerate continued real reduction in defense. In light of the compelling need to reduce the deficit, however, I support a 1-year freeze in the military budget, something I proposed last fall in my flexible freeze plan. And this freeze will apply for only 1 year, and after that, increases above inflation will be required. I will not sacrifice American preparedness, and I will not compromise American strength.

I should be clear on the conditions attached to my recommendation for the coming year: The savings must be allocated to those priorities for investing in our future that I've spoken about tonight. This defense freeze must be a part of a comprehensive budget agreement which meets the targets spelled out in Gramm-Rudman-Hollings law without raising taxes and which incorporates reforms in the budget process.

I've directed the National Security Council to review our national security and defense policies and report back to me within 90 days to ensure that our capabilities and resources meet our commitments and strategies. I'm also charging the Department of Defense with the task of developing a plan to improve the defense procurement process and management of the Pentagon, one which will fully implement the Packard commission report. Many of these changes can only be made with the participation of the Congress, and so, I ask for

your help. We need fewer regulations. We need less bureaucracy. We need multiyear procurement and 2-year budgeting. And frankly—and don't take this wrong—we need less congressional micromanagement of our nation's military policy. I detect a slight division on that question, but nevertheless—[laughter].

Securing a more peaceful world is perhaps the most important priority I'd like to address tonight. You know, we meet at a time of extraordinary hope. Never before in this century have our values of freedom, democracy, and economic opportunity been such a powerful and intellectual force around the globe. Never before has our leadership been so crucial, because while America has its eyes on the future, the world has its eyes on America.

And it's a time of great change in the world, and especially in the Soviet Union. Prudence and common sense dictate that we try to understand the full meaning of the change going on there, review our policies, and then proceed with caution. But I've personally assured General Secretary Gorbachev that at the conclusion of such a review we will be ready to move forward. We will not miss any opportunity to work for peace. The fundamental facts remain that the Soviets retain a very powerful military machine in the service of objectives which are still too often in conflict with ours. So, let us take the new openness seriously, but let's also be realistic. And let's always be strong.

There are some pressing issues we must address. I will vigorously pursue the Strategic Defense Initiative. The spread, and even use, of sophisticated weaponry threatens global security as never before. Chemical weapons must be banned from the face of the Earth, never to be used again. And look, this won't be easy. Verification—extraordinarily difficult, but civilization and human decency demand that we try. And the spread of nuclear weapons must be stopped. And I'll work to strengthen the hand of the International Atomic Energy Agency. Our diplomacy must work every day against the proliferation of nuclear weapons.

And around the globe, we must continue to be freedom's best friend. And we must stand firm for self-determination and democracy in Central America, including in Nicaragua. It is my strongly held conviction that when people are given the chance they inevitably will choose a free press, freedom of worship, and certifiably free and fair elections.

We must strengthen the alliance of the industrial democracies, as solid a force for peace as the world has ever known. And this is an alliance forged by the power of our ideals, not the pettiness of our differences. So, let's lift our sights to rise above fighting about beef hormones, to building a better future, to move from protectionism to progress.

I've asked the Secretary of State to visit Europe next week and to consult with our allies on the wide range of challenges and opportunities we face together, including East-West relations. And I look forward to meeting with our NATO partners in the near future.

And I, too, shall begin a trip shortly to the far reaches of the Pacific Basin, where the winds of democracy are creating new hope and the power of free markets is unleashing a new force. When I served as our representative in China 14 or 15 years ago, few would have predicted the scope of the changes we've witnessed since then. But in preparing for this trip, I was struck by something I came across from a Chinese writer. He was speaking of his country, decades ago, but his words speak to each of us in America tonight. "Today," he said, "we're afraid of the simple words like 'goodness' and 'mercy' and 'kindness.' " My friends, if we're to succeed as a nation, we must rediscover those words.

In just 3 days, we mark the birthday of Abraham Lincoln, the man who saved our Union and gave new meaning to the word "opportu-

nity." Lincoln once said: "I hold that while man exists, it is his duty to improve not only his own condition but to assist in ameliorating that of mankind." It is this broader mission to which I call all Americans, because the definition of a successful life must include serving others.

And to the young people of America, who sometimes feel left out, I ask you tonight to give us the benefit of your talent and energy through a new program called YES, for Youth Entering Service to America.

To those men and women in business, remember the ultimate end of your work: to make a better product, to create better lives. I ask you to plan for the longer term and avoid that temptation of quick and easy paper profits.

To the brave men and women who wear the uniform of the United States of America, thank you. Your calling is a high one: to be the defenders of freedom and the guarantors of liberty. And I want you to know that this nation is grateful for your service.

To the farmers of America, we appreciate the bounty you provide. We will work with you to open foreign markets to American agricultural products.

And to the parents of America, I ask you to get involved in your child's schooling. Check on the homework, go to the school, meet the teachers, care about what is happening there. It's not only your child's future on the line, it's America's.

To kids in our cities, don't give up hope. Say no to drugs; stay in school. And, yes, "Keep hope alive."

To those 37 million Americans with some form of disability, you belong in the economic mainstream. We need your talents in America's work force. Disabled Americans must become full partners in America's opportunity society.

To the families of America watching tonight in your living rooms, hold fast to your dreams because ultimately America's future rests in your hands.

And to my friends in this Chamber, I ask your cooperation to keep America growing while cutting the deficit. That's only fair to those who now have no vote: the generations to come. Let them look back and say that we had the foresight to understand that a time of peace and prosperity is not the time to rest but a time to press forward, a time to invest in the future.

And let all Americans remember that no problem of human making is too great to be overcome by human ingenuity, human energy, and the untiring hope of the human spirit. I believe this. I would not have asked to be your President if I didn't. And tomorrow the debate on the plan I've put forward begins, and I ask the Congress to come forward with your own proposals. Let's not question each other's motives. Let's debate, let's negotiate; but let us solve the problem.

Recalling anniversaries may not be my specialty in speeches— [laughter]—but tonight is one of some note. On February 9th, 1941, just 48 years ago tonight, Sir Winston Churchill took to the airwaves during Britain's hour of peril. He'd received from President Roosevelt a hand-carried letter quoting Longfellow's famous poem: "Sail on, O Ship of State! Sail on, O Union, strong and great! Humanity with all its fears, With all the hopes of future years, Is hanging breathless on thy fate!" And Churchill responded on this night by radio broadcast to a nation at war, but he directed his words to Franklin Roosevelt. "We shall not fail or falter," he said. "We shall not weaken or tire. Give us the tools, and we will finish the job."

Tonight, almost half a century later, our peril may be less immediate, but the need for perseverance and clear-sighted fortitude is just as great. Now, as then, there are those who say it can't be done. There are voices who say that America's best days have passed, that we're bound by constraints, threatened by problems, surrounded by troubles which limit our ability

to hope. Well, tonight I remain full of hope. We Americans have only begun on our mission of goodness and greatness. And to those timid souls, I repeat the plea: "Give us the tools, and we will do the job."

Thank you. God bless you, and God bless America.

3. Interview with Chinese Television Journalists in Beijing February 26, 1989

China-U.S. Relations

Q. Mr. President, I'm sure millions of Chinese people are watching this program now. I wonder if you would like to say a few words to them first.

The President. Well, I do have an opening statement, but first let me thank you for this unique opportunity. It's a great honor for me to be the first American President to speak to the Chinese people in a live broadcast. And I feel as if I were talking to old friends who, while out of sight, have never, never been out of heart and mind.

Fourteen years ago, Barbara and I came to your beautiful land when I was, as you said, Chief of the United States Liaison Office. And for us, returning to Beijing is a homecoming. Our work here was a source of great personal satisfaction, a happy, challenging time in our lives. And we actually went to church here; indeed, our daughter was baptized in our faith here. And we rode bicycles down the hutongs [narrow streets] of Beijing and came to have a general feeling of affection for the Chinese people. And we knew then that the relationship that we would establish between our two nations would be a special one indeed.

And we were right. Today the bridges that started with the Shanghai communique years ago—today that relationship has joined our peoples together in friendship and respect. And our two countries continue to weave an increasingly rich fabric of relations through our expanding trade and cultural and scientific exchange. American students study at many of your finest universities, and we welcome thousands of Chinese students and researchers to educational institutions in the United States. The understanding and friendship that these students have developed will only help to improve and deepen relations between our two countries in the years ahead.

I've spoken to the American people about a new breeze blowing in the world today. And there's a worldwide movement toward greater freedom: freedom of human creativity and freedom of economic opportunity. And we've all begun to feel the winds of change sweep us toward an exciting and challenging new century. These winds—new, sometimes gentle, sometimes strong and powerful. China was one of the first nations to feel this new breeze, and like a tree in a winter wind, you've learned to bend and adapt to new ways and new ideas and reform.

Many challenges lie before our two nations. And together, we must find political solutions to regional conflicts. We must foster global growth. And together, in order to make life better for future generations, we must seek solutions to worldwide concerns, such as our planet's environment, the threat to all people from international terror, the use and spread of chemical and biological weapons, and international drug trafficking. I know your leaders share with me a determination to solve these and other problems, and as President of the United States, I look forward to continuing to work closely with them as I have done in the past.

The Americans and Chinese share many things, but perhaps none is more important than our strong sense of family. Just a few weeks ago, Barbara and I were blessed by a new grandchild. And when I think of her and I think of the beautiful children of China, my commitment to peace is renewed and reaffirmed.

I am confident that when future generations of Chinese and Americans look back upon this time they'll say that the winds of change blew favorably upon our lands. Thank you for your friendship, your hospitality, and the many warm memories of this wonderful country that Barbara and I take with us as we return tomorrow to the United States. Thank you all.

Q. Mr. President, you've been in office for just a month, and many people are probably surprised that you've decided to come to China so soon. Why now?

The President. Now because, you see, I view the relationship between China and the United States as highly significant, as one of the very most important relationships that we have. And so, it has a lot to do with bilateralism, with our trade and our cultural exchanges and what I said here about the children. But it's more than that. It really has, because of China's importance and ours, a lot to do with world peace. And so, before much time went by, I wanted to reaffirm the importance that the United States places on this bilateral relationship, and I wanted to pledge to the Chinese leaders—and I've met the top four leaders in the last day and a half—that this relationship will grow and it will prosper. And we have economic problems, and China has some. But together we're going to solve them, and we're going to move forward.

Q. Well, this is your second day in China. How do you assess your time here? What specifically have you achieved on this trip?

The President. Well, really it's been a period to—just in that short period of time—to visit with the Chinese leadership and Chairman Deng Xiaoping and others—Zhao Ziyang and Li Peng, Chairman Yang—all of these men giving a lot of their time to explain the reforms in China, the new directions that China is taking in world affairs. We had an interesting exchange on the forthcoming visit of General Secretary Gorbachev coming here. And it is important that they understand what I'm thinking in terms of the Middle East or the subcontinent or our relations with the Soviet Union on arms control, and it's important I understand theirs. So, it hasn't been a visit that has three points on an agenda. It's a visit with a much broader perspective and a reaffirmation of a relationship that's strong.

Q. Mr. President, you know perhaps as well as anyone about the development of relations between your country and China. How would you say that relationship contributes to world peace and development?

The President. Well, I think it contributes a lot, because in the first place, we in the United States have a disproportionate responsibility for discussions on strategic weapons, for example, and we want to go forward with the Soviet Union, in this instance, on negotiations. But we don't want to do that in a way that would jeopardize the interests of any other country. And so, in that one area, we can have discussions with the Chinese, just as our Secretary of State, Jim Baker, had with the European leaders.

Another area is the economy. And we have some economic problems at home, and I wanted to assure the Chinese leaders that I am going to do my level best to get our deficit down. The Chinese people might say, Well, what in the world does that have to do with me living in Beijing or down in Shanghai or out further in the countryside? Well, the economies of the world are interlocked in a way. And if I can do my job properly, that might mean lower interest rates. And what does that mean to the average man on the street in China? That might mean that eventually his goods come to him at a lower price. So, I just come back to the fact that the visit is a chance to explore in depth the complicated international relationships and to build on this bilateral relationship.

China-U.S. Trade

Q. Well, it's said there's vast potential in strengthening both the economic and technological cooperation between China and the United States. How do we best tap that potential, and how do we overcome problems such as the restrictions on the transfer of technology?

The President. Well, in the first place, I had an opportunity just a minute ago—I was almost late for your program because I was talking to Zhao Ziyang, a very impressive leader, about the economy and about reforms. We congratulate the Chinese leaders in the steps they've taken towards economic reform.

Now, in terms of something technical like technological exchange, I made clear to the Chinese leaders, particularly in a conversation with Li Peng, that we are prepared to go the extra mile in terms of investment, in terms of business, exports and imports. You know, when I was here in China 15 years ago, total trade was $800 million. And now, depending on how one accounts for it, we would say we would use a figure of $14 billion. So, we're going to move forward. We will advance technology to China as much as we possibly can under what is known as the COCOM [Coordinating Committee for Multilateral Export Security Controls] arrangement. There are some highly sensitive, highly sophisticated military technologies that I'm not even sure China is interested in, but that we are prohibited from exporting under the law. Having said that, we have exported some highly sophisticated technology to China, and as President, I want to continue to do that. And that will benefit the life of the average Chinese citizen.

We're in an information society in many ways in the United States, and clearly that is going to come to China—computer knowledge and education techniques that are coming to the average Chinese kid from computers. And we've been blessed by advanced technology, and now we want to share it as much as we can.

Q. Well, you know there are reforms in China right now—

The President. I know it.

Q.—and the Chinese Government is trying to attract more foreign investment. So, does your administration have or plan to have any specific measures to encourage American businesses to invest in China?

The President. Well, we had a chance to talk about that here today with the Chinese leaders, and I did point out to them that there are certain things that we'd like to see China move forward on that would enhance further investment here. I'd like to see an investment treaty between the two countries of some sort—an agreement, not a treaty but a bilateral agreement on trade. We—like we do not just with China but many other countries—talk about copyright and patent protection, and yet I find on this visit that

China is moving forward with a new patent code and now drafting copyright legislation, which would be very helpful.

So, there are some artificial barriers. And the good thing about a visit like this is we can sit and talk to the leaders in a dispassionate way. And where they disagree with me, they will tell me, and where I disagree with them, I'm obliged to tell them. And that's what a good frank relationship can do.

But I told them that I must work to get the budget deficit in the United States down, because that does have an adverse impact on international interest rates. So, there are things that we can do, and there were things that I've asked China to do in terms of facilitating business. Sometimes I think your country is as bad as mine is on red tape. And to get the best flow of investment, China needs to do better on red tape, and so do we. It's a two-way street.

Q. Well, I've got more questions—

The President. Go ahead.

Q.—but the time is up.

The President. Oh, dear.

Q. And I'm afraid you have another important activity right after this, so we have to end this interview right now.

Thank you very much, Mr. President. It's been a pleasure to have you here.

The President. Well, this has been a unique opportunity. And let me just conclude my part of your broadcast by again saying as President of the United States, the growing relationship between China and the United States is vital to my country. It is important to my country. And I hope it will benefit the people in China. I am confident that it will, and I know it will benefit world peace as well.

Q. Thank you very much, Mr. President.

The President. Thank you, ma'am.

Note: The interview began at 6:02 p.m. at the CCTV Studios. In his remarks, the president referred to Zhao Ziyang, general secretary of the Chinese Communist Party; Deng Xiaoping, chairman of the Central Military Commission; Li Peng, premier of the State Council, and Yang Shangkun, president of China. Following his remarks, the president traveled to Seoul, Republic of Korea.

4. Statement on the Failure of the Senate to Approve the Nomination of John Tower as Secretary of Defense
March 9, 1989

John Tower has devoted his life to service of country. Whether in the U.S. Senate, at the arms control negotiating table, or in the privacy of his counsel to Presidents, he has always held the interests of this nation above all else. John Tower has been steadfast in his advocacy of a strong defense and consistent in support of the many principles for which he fought throughout his career. He is and will remain my friend.

I have read Senator Tower's statement regarding the decision of the Senate and find its dignity and lack of rancor to be typical of the man whose leadership, knowledge, and experience would have benefited the Department of Defense and the Nation.

Instead of the recompense of a grateful nation, John Tower's lot in the past weeks has been a cruel ordeal. For this, I am truly sorry for both him and his family.

The Senate has made its determination. I respect its role in doing so, but I disagree with the outcome. I am also concerned by the way in which perceptions based on groundless rumor seemed to be the basis on which at least some

made up their minds in judging a man well-qualified to be my Secretary of Defense. Now, however, we owe it to the American people to come together and move forward.

5. Message to the Congress Transmitting Proposed Legislation on Educational Excellence
April 5, 1989

To the Congress of the United States:
I am pleased to transmit today for your immediate consideration and enactment the "Educational Excellence Act of 1989," a bill to provide incentives to attain a better-educated America. I believe that greater educational achievement promotes sustained economic growth, enhances the Nation's competitive position in world markets, increases productivity, and leads to higher incomes for everyone. The Nation must invest in its young people, giving them the knowledge, skills, and values to live productive lives. The "Educational Excellence Act of 1989" would move us toward this goal.

The initiatives included in this bill embody four principles central to my Administration's policies on education and essential for further education reform. These principles are:

1) Recognition of excellence. Excellence and achievement in education should be recognized and rewarded.

2) Addressing need. Federal dollars should be targeted to help those most in need.

3) Flexibility and choice. Greater flexibility and choice in education—both for parents in selecting schools for their children and local school systems' choice of teachers and principals—are essential.

4) Accountability. I support educational accountability, and toward this end, I am committed to measuring and rewarding progress toward quality education.

This legislation builds on the accomplishments of the last Congress, which enacted into law the Augustus F. Hawkins–Robert T. Stafford Elementary and Secondary School Improvement Amendments of 1988. That law took significant steps toward improving elementary and secondary education by improving program accountability, reauthorizing the magnet school program and expanding parental choice, providing greater flexibility to local school districts in the implementation of bilingual education programs, enhancing parental involvement in programs for disadvantaged children, and stimulating education innovation and reform. My proposals have distinct differences from current law, but complement in numerous ways the important work of the 100th Congress in pursuing educational excellence.

The Educational Excellence Act of 1989 includes seven specific legislative initiatives aimed at fulfilling these important principles:

(1) The Presidential Merit Schools program would reward public and private elementary and secondary schools that have made substantial progress in raising students' educational achievement, creating a safe and drug-free school environment, and reducing the dropout rate. This program would provide a powerful incentive for all schools to improve their educational performance.

(2) A new Magnet Schools of Excellence program would support the establishment, expansion, or enhancement of magnet schools, without regard to the presence of desegregation plans in applicant districts.

Magnet schools have been highly successful at increasing parental choice and improving educational quality.

(3) The Alternative Certification of Teachers and Principals program would assist States interested in broadening the pool of talent from which to recruit teachers and principals. Funds would assist States to develop and implement, or expand and improve, flexible certification systems, so that talented professionals who have demonstrated their subject area competence or leadership qualities in fields outside education might be drawn into education.

(4) President's Awards for Excellence in Education would be given to teachers in every State who meet the highest standards of excellence. Each award would be for $5,000.

(5) Drug-Free Schools Urban Emergency Grants would provide special assistance to urban school districts that are disproportionately affected by drug trafficking and abuse. These funds would be used for a comprehensive range of services appropriate to the needs of individual communities.

(6) A National Science Scholars program would provide scholarships to high school seniors who have excelled in the sciences and mathematics. These scholarships, of up to $10,000 a year, would recognize recipients' academic achievement and encourage them to continue their education in science, mathematics, and engineering. The President would select recipients after considering recommendations made by Senators and Members of the House of Representatives.

(7) I am proposing to provide additional endowment matching grants for Histori-

cally Black Colleges and Universities, institutions that occupy a unique position and have a major responsibility in the structure of American higher education.

I urge the Congress to take prompt and favorable action on this legislation. Taken together, these seven initiatives, for which I have proposed adding $422.6 million in the 1990 budget, would help us advance toward the goal of a better-educated Nation.

In addition to these initiatives, I have proposed a budget amendment for $13 million in new funds for experiments and data collection in support of education reform. I am also asking the Congress to fund fully the authorization in the Stewart McKinney Homeless Assistance Act. This includes $2.5 million to fund for the first time the Exemplary Grants program and $2.7 million in additional funding for literacy programs for homeless adults.

George Bush
The White House,
April 5, 1989

6. Statement on the Chinese Government's Suppression of Student Demonstrations
June 3, 1989

It is clear that the Chinese Government has chosen to use force against Chinese citizens who were making a peaceful statement in favor of democracy. I deeply deplore the decision to use force against peaceful demonstrators and the consequent loss of life. We have been urging—and continue to urge—nonviolence, restraint, and dialog. Tragically, another course has been chosen. Again, I urge a return to nonviolent means for dealing with the current situation.

The United States and People's Republic of China over the past two decades have built up

through great efforts by both sides a constructive relationship beneficial to both countries. I hope that China will rapidly return to the path of political and economic reform and conditions of stability so that this relationship, so important to both our peoples, can continue its growth.

7. Remarks Announcing Proposed Legislation to Amend the Clean Air Act
June 12, 1989

Well, in this room are Republicans and Democrats, leaders from both sides of the aisle in Congress, Governors, executives from some of the most important companies and business organizations in America, leading conservationists, and people who have devoted their lives to creating a cleaner and safer environment. And I've invited you here today to make a point. With the leadership assembled in this room, we can break the stalemate that has hindered progress on clean air for the past decade; and with the minds, the energy, the talent assembled here, we can find a solution.

So, let me tell you the purposes of this morning's gathering. First, I'd like to lay on the table my proposals to curb acid rain and cut urban smog and clean up air toxics. And second, I want to call upon all of you to join me in enacting into law a new Clean Air Act this year. But first, we should remember how far we've come and recognize what works. The 1970 Clean Air Act got us moving in the right direction with national air quality standards that were strengthened by amendments in 1977. Since 1970, even though we have 55 percent more cars going 50 percent farther, in spite of more utility output and more industrial production, we've still made progress. Lead concentrations in the air we breathe are down 98 percent. Sulfur dioxide and carbon monoxide cut by over a third. Particulate matter cut 21 percent; even ozone-causing emissions have been cut by 17 percent. And still, over the last decade, we have not come far enough.

Too many Americans continue to breathe dirty air. And political paralysis has plagued further progress against air pollution. We have to break this logjam by applying more than just Federal leverage. We must take advantage of the innovation, energy, and ingenuity of every American.

The environmental movement has a long history here in this country. It's been a force for good, for a safer, healthier America. And as a people, we want and need that economic growth, but now we must also expect environmental responsibility and respect the natural world. And this will demand a national sense of commitment, a new ethic of conservation. And I reject the notion that sound ecology and a strong economy are mutually exclusive. So, last week I outlined five points of a new environmental philosophy: one, to harness the power of the marketplace; two, to encourage local initiative; three, to emphasize prevention instead of just cleanup; four, to foster international cooperation; and five, to ensure strict enforcement—polluters will pay.

We know more now than we did just a few years ago. New solutions are close at hand. It's time to put our best minds to work; to turn technology and the power of the marketplace to the advantage of the environment; to create; to innovate; to tip the scales in favor of recovery, restoration, and renewal. Every American expects and deserves to breathe clean air, and as President, it is my mission to guarantee it—for this generation and for the generations to come. If we take this commitment seriously, if we believe that every American expects and deserves clean air, and then we act on that belief, then we will set an example for the rest of the world to follow.

Today I am proposing to Congress a new Clean Air Act and offering a new opportunity. We've seen enough of this stalemate; it's time to clear the air. And you know, I think we will. We touched a lot of bases as we prepared this bill, and we've had the benefit of some good thinking on the Hill. And we've met with business leaders who see environmental protection as essential to long-term economic growth, and we've talked with environmentalists who know that cost-effective solutions help build public support for conservation. And we've worked with academics and innovative thinkers from every quarter who have laid the groundwork for this approach. And just this morning I spoke by phone with Prime Minister Mulroney of Canada. I believe he's excited about the prospect, too. I have no pride of authorship. Let me commend Project 88 and groups like the Environmental Defense Fund for bringing creative solutions to longstanding problems, for not only breaking the mold but helping to build a new one.

And we've had to make some tough choices. And some may think we've gone too far, and others not far enough; but we all care about clean air. To the millions of Americans who still breathe unhealthy air, let me tell you, I'm concerned—I'm concerned about vulnerable groups like the elderly and asthmatics and children, concerned about every American's quality of life; and I'm committed to see that coming generations receive the natural legacy they deserve.

We seek reforms that make major pollution reductions where we most need them. First, our approach is reasonable deadlines for those who must comply. It has compelling sanctions for those who don't. It accounts for continued economic growth and expansion; offers incentives, choice, and flexibility for industry to find the best solutions; and taps the power of the marketplace and local initiative better than any previous piece of environmental legislation.

This legislation will be comprehensive. It will be cost-effective; but above all, it will work. We will make the 1990's the era for clean air. And we have three clear goals and three clear deadlines. First, we will cut the sulfur dioxide emissions that cause acid rain by almost half, by 10 million tons, and we will cut nitrogen oxide emissions by 2 million tons, both by the year 2000. We have set absolute goals for reductions and have emphasized early gains. And that means 5 million tons will be cut by 1995, and the degradation caused by acid rain will stop by the end of this century. To make sure that coal continues to play a vital role in our energy future, we've provided an extension of 3 years and regulatory incentives for the use of innovative, clean-coal technology. We've set an ambitious reduction target, and applying market forces will be the fastest, most cost-effective way to achieve it. So, we're allowing utilities to trade credits among themselves for reductions they make, to let them decide how to bring aggregate emissions down as cost-effectively as possible. Cleaner fuels, better technologies, energy conservation, improved efficiency—in any combination, just as long as it works.

There's a wisdom to handing work to those most qualified to do it. Four hundred years ago Montaigne wrote: "Let us permit nature to have her way. She understands her business better than we do." Well, it's true. Acid rain must be stopped, and that's what we all care about. But it's also true that business understands its business better than we do. So, we're going to put that understanding to work on behalf of clean air and a sound environment. We've provided the goals, but we won't try to micromanage them. We will allow flexibility in how industry achieves these goals, but we stand firm on what must be achieved.

Second, this Federal proposal will cut the emissions that cause urban ozone, smog, virtually in half. This will put the States well on the road to meeting the standard. Twenty years ago, we started on the job. And if Congress will act on the clean air reforms that I'm offering today, 20 years from now, every American in every city in America will breathe clean air. Today 81 cities don't meet Federal air quality standards. This legislation will bring clean air to all but about 20 cities by 1995, and within 20 years, even Los Angeles and Houston and New York will be expected to make it.

In the nine urban areas with the greatest smog problems, we propose bold new initiatives to reconcile the automobile to the environment, ensuring continued economic growth without disruptive driving controls. We'll accomplish this through alternative fuels and clean-fueled vehicles. We propose to put up to a million clean-fueled vehicles a year on the road by 1997. But we're also proposing flexibility on the means, even as we remain firm on the goals. A city can either request inclusion in the program or, if they show they can achieve these ambitious reductions through other measures, we will scale back the clean-fuel vehicle requirements accordingly. Also, we're sensitive to the problems of smaller cities, whose own ozone problems are due largely to pollutants that are generated in other areas, other regions, other cities. They will not be penalized for pollution problems outside their control.

Our program incorporates a mix of cost-effective measures to cut emissions from cars, fuels, factories, and other sources. But I'm asking the EPA to develop rules like those we're employing on acid rain to allow auto and fuel companies to trade required reductions in order to meet the standard in the most cost-effective way. Our challenge is to develop an emissions trading plan; their challenge is to meet the standards.

The third leg of our proposal is designed to cut all categories of airborne toxic chemicals by three-quarters within this decade. Our best minds will apply the most advanced industrial technology available to control these airborne poisons. The very best control technology we have will determine the standard we set for those plants. And until now, because of an unworkable law, the EPA has been able to regulate only 7 of the 280 known air toxics. The bill I am proposing today will set a schedule for regulating sources of air toxics by dates certain. In addition, it will give the dedicated people of the EPA the right tools for the job, and it will make state-of-the-art technology an everyday fact of doing business. And that's the way it should be.

In its first phase, this initiative should eliminate about three-quarters of the needless deaths from cancer that have been caused by toxic industrial air emissions. And we plan a second phase to go after any remaining unreasonable risk. People who live near industrial facilities should not have to fear for their health.

And for 10 years, we've struggled to engage a united effort on behalf of clean air, and we're now on the edge of real change. Nineteen eighty-nine could be recorded as the year when business leaders and environmental advocates began to work together, when environmental issues moved out of the courts, beyond conflict, into a new era of cooperation. And this can be known as the year we mobilized leadership, both public and private, to make environmental protection a growth industry and keep our ecology safe for diversity. The wounded winds of north, south, east, and west can be purified and cleansed, and the integrity of nature can be made whole again. Ours is a rare opportunity to reverse the errors of this generation in the service of the next; and we cannot, we must not, fail. We must prevail. I ask for your support. We need your support to make all of this into a reality.

Thank you all, and God bless you, and thank you very much for coming.

8. White House Fact Sheet on the Points of Light Initiative June 22, 1989

Challenge

Though America is at peace and more Americans are enjoying a greater degree of prosperity than ever before in our history, we still have work to do. As long as millions of Americans are illiterates, dropouts, drug abusers, pregnant teens, delinquent or suicidal young people, AIDS victims, and among the homeless and hungry, America has not yet fulfilled its promise. Our challenge is to overcome the disintegration of communities, large and small. While the Government's role is critical, government cannot overcome this challenge alone.

Mission

The President believes in the readiness and ability of every individual and every institution in America to initiate action as "a point of light." Meaningful one-to-one engagement in the lives of others is now required to overcome our most serious national problems. The growth and magnification of "points of light" must now become an American mission.

Strategy
i. claim problems as your own

A. The President's Call for Action

The President calls on all Americans and all American institutions, large and small, to make service of central value in our daily life and work. The President calls on the heads of businesses and professional firms to include community service among the factors considered in making hiring, compensation, and promotion decisions. The President calls on newspapers, magazines, radio and television stations, cable systems, and other media institutions to identify service opportunities, spotlight successful service initiatives, and profile outstanding community leaders regularly. The President calls on State and local education boards to uphold the value of service and to encourage students, faculty, and personnel to serve others. The President calls on college and university presidents to recognize the value of community service in considering applicants; to uphold the value of community service; and to encourage students, faculty, and personnel to serve others. The President calls on not-for-profit service organizations to build the capacity to absorb increasing numbers of volunteers in purposeful roles. The President challenges all young people to lead the nation in this movement of community service through the YES (Youth Engaged in Service) to America Initiative. The President will call all young people to help overcome society's challenges by serving others through existing organizations or new initiatives.

He will also challenge:

leaders from all institutions to engage their organizations in the development of young people;

community leaders and students to reach out to alienated young people and develop community service opportunities which redirect their lives in a positive way;

community service organizations to build the capacity to absorb large numbers of young people in purposeful community service.

Through the foundation, the President will:

select the President's National Service Youth Representatives, who will lead other young people in community service in their regions, suggest ways that other young peo-

ple can engage in community service, and assist in developing and implementing local programs;

initiate the President's National Service Youth Leadership Forums; and

present the President's National Service Youth Leadership Awards to honor outstanding youth community leaders.

YES to America is not a Federal Government program, but a nationwide service movement. It is:

a movement that is grassroots and community-based rather than devised in and imposed from Washington;

a movement that does not compensate people with Federal dollars for what should be an obligation of citizenship;

a movement that integrates service into young people's normal life and career pattern, developing in them a lifelong commitment to service rather than a temporary, 1- or 2-year involvement.

B. One-to-One Problem Solving

Every individual should "connect" with his or her institution—businesses, professional firms, the media, labor, education, religion, civic groups, associations of all kinds, and not-for-profit service organizations—and engage in the lives of others in need on a one-to-one basis. Examples of the kinds of engagement the President calls for include:

starting a literacy program to teach every employee or member who wants to learn to read;

adopting a school, class, or single student, providing tutoring, computers and other learning aids, food, clothing, or shelter for each student who needs them;

adopting a nursing home, offering comfort and cheer;

starting a one-to-one mentoring program for needy young people;

forming a consortium to make decent, affordable housing available to the homeless;

contributing and distributing surplus food to soup kitchens each day to feed the hungry.

Individuals wishing to help another in any of the above ways independently of an institution are encouraged to establish a one-to-one relationship with an individual in need.

ii. identify, enlarge and replicate what is working

The President will serve as Honorary Chairman of a foundation called the Points of Light Initiative. The President will convene an advisory committee to make recommendations (within 45 days of its first meeting) on the structure and composition of the foundation and the legislation most appropriate to accomplish the purpose of the President's national service initiative.

The President will seek a congressional appropriation of $25 million annually for the foundation, which will, in turn, seek to match that amount from private sector contributions.

The President will challenge each Governor to replicate this initiative in each State and encourage State and local leaders to develop Points of Light Working Groups composed of community leaders. These groups will marshal resources within their communities and deploy them to overcome local problems.

The President believes that virtually every problem in America is being solved somewhere. There are already countless service initiatives working successfully throughout America. However, these successful initiatives are too often isolated and unknown to others. These initiatives must be replicated over and over again by individuals and teams until everyone is connected to someone, one to one.

A. Peer-to-Peer Working Groups

Through a foundation initiative to be called the ServNet Project, corporations, professional firms, unions, schools, religious groups, civic groups, and not-for-profit service organizations will be asked to donate the services of some of their most talented and promising people for a period of time. These extraordinary individuals will form and lead peer-to-peer working groups, e.g., lawyers going to fellow lawyers, teachers to fellow teachers, union members to fellow union members, bringing examples of successful initiatives and providing training, technical assistance, and other support to enable other institutions to devise similar initiatives.

B. Linking Servers to Needs

One of the foundation's objectives is to help to improve existing methods of matching would-be volunteers with purposeful service opportunities. Over time, through an initiative called the ServLink Project, the foundation will stimulate the development through private-sector resources of technology links between those who wish to serve and those who need service, e.g., telephone calls, interactive computers, etc.

Volunteer centers should be easily accessible to all Americans in their neighborhoods, matching people with service opportunities. Such contact points may be in a place of worship, union hall, library, fire station, business building, service group headquarters or neighborhood home. In addition, every bank, credit card issuer, telephone and utility company will be asked to include in billing and statement envelopes printed information about how people and their institutions can become engaged in serving others.

C. Recognition and Awards

In order to encourage others to engage in service, every newspaper, magazine, radio and television station will be asked to identify service opportunities, spotlight successful service initiatives and profile outstanding community leaders regularly.

The President's Build a Community Awards will honor those people and institutions who have worked together to rebuild families or to revitalize communities. Through the foundation, the President will recognize and present awards and other forms of commendation to talented community leaders and successful initiatives that are solving the Nation's most critical social problems.

iii. discover and encourage new leaders

America's community service movement must have the strongest, most creative leadership, nationally and locally. Such leadership must be constantly recruited. The foundation, with the help of existing organizations, will identify the most promising new leaders in all walks of life who are not now engaged in community service and encourage them to devote part of their talent and energy to community service. The foundation will give special attention to young people and to those who have not had the opportunity to fulfill their leadership potential.

iv. conclusion

The President's national service initiative focuses on the most critical domestic challenges facing the Nation today. These problems were long in coming and cannot be solved overnight. But if each American citizen and each American institution responds to the President's call to engage "one to one" in the life of another person in need, this initiative will be the most comprehensive and inclusive movement of our time. This movement can dramatically reverse negative trends on many fronts and ensure the fulfillment of America's promise.

9. Address to the Nation on the National Drug Control Strategy September 5, 1989

Good evening. This is the first time since taking the oath of office that I felt an issue was so important, so threatening, that it warranted talking directly with you, the American people. All of us agree that the gravest domestic threat facing our nation today is drugs. Drugs have strained our faith in our system of justice. Our courts, our prisons, our legal system, are stretched to the breaking point. The social costs of drugs are mounting. In short, drugs are sapping our strength as a nation. Turn on the evening news or pick up the morning paper and you'll see what some Americans know just by stepping out their front door: Our most serious problem today is cocaine, and in particular, crack.

Who's responsible? Let me tell you straight out—everyone who uses drugs, everyone who sells drugs, and everyone who looks the other way.

Tonight, I'll tell you how many Americans are using illegal drugs. I will present to you our national strategy to deal with every aspect of this threat. And I will ask you to get involved in what promises to be a very difficult fight.

This is crack cocaine seized a few days ago by Drug Enforcement agents in a park just across the street from the White House. It could easily have been heroin or PCP. It's as innocent-looking as candy, but it's turning our cities into battle zones, and it's murdering our children. Let there be no mistake: This stuff is poison. Some used to call drugs harmless recreation; they're not. Drugs are a real and terribly dangerous threat to our neighborhoods, our friends, and our families.

No one among us is out of harm's way. When 4-year-olds play in playgrounds strewn with discarded hypodermic needles and crack vials, it breaks my heart. When cocaine, one of the most deadly and addictive illegal drugs, is available to school kids—school kids—it's an outrage. And when hundreds of thousands of babies are born each year to mothers who use drugs—premature babies born desperately sick—then even the most defenseless among us are at risk.

These are the tragedies behind the statistics, but the numbers also have quite a story to tell. Let me share with you the results of the recently completed household survey of the National Institute on Drug Abuse. It compares recent drug use to 3 years ago. It tells us some good news and some very bad news. First, the good. As you can see in the chart, in 1985 the Government estimated that 23 million Americans were using drugs on a "current" basis; that is, at least once in the preceding month. Last year that number fell by more than a third. That means almost 9 million fewer Americans are casual drug users. Good news.

Because we changed our national attitude toward drugs, casual drug use has declined. We have many to thank: our brave law enforcement officers, religious leaders, teachers, community activists, and leaders of business and labor. We should also thank the media for their exhaustive news and editorial coverage and for their air time and space for antidrug messages. And finally, I want to thank President and Mrs. Reagan for their leadership. All of these good people told the truth: that drug use is wrong and dangerous.

But as much comfort as we can draw from these dramatic reductions, there is also bad news, very bad news. Roughly 8 million people have used cocaine in the past year. Almost 1 million of them used it frequently—once a week or more. What this means is that, in spite of the fact that overall cocaine use is down, fre-

quent use has almost doubled in the last few years. And that's why habitual cocaine users, especially crack users, are the most pressing, immediate drug problem.

What, then, is our plan? To begin with, I trust the lesson of experience: No single policy will cut it, no matter how glamorous or magical it may sound. To win the war against addictive drugs like crack will take more than just a Federal strategy: It will take a national strategy, one that reaches into every school, every workplace, involving every family.

Earlier today, I sent this document, our first such national strategy, to the Congress. It was developed with the hard work of our nation's first Drug Policy Director, Bill Bennett. In preparing this plan, we talked with State, local, and community leaders, law enforcement officials, and experts in education, drug prevention, and rehabilitation. We talked with parents and kids. We took a long, hard look at all that the Federal Government has done about drugs in the past—what's worked and, let's be honest, what hasn't. Too often, people in government acted as if their part of the problem—whether fighting drug production or drug smuggling or drug demand—was the only problem. But turf battles won't win this war; teamwork will.

Tonight, I'm announcing a strategy that reflects the coordinated, cooperative commitment of all our Federal agencies. In short, this plan is as comprehensive as the problem. With this strategy, we now finally have a plan that coordinates our resources, our programs, and the people who run them. Our weapons in this strategy are the law and criminal justice system, our foreign policy, our treatment systems, and our schools and drug prevention programs. So, the basic weapons we need are the ones we already have. What's been lacking is a strategy to effectively use them.

Let me address four of the major elements of our strategy. First, we are determined to enforce the law, to make our streets and neighborhoods safe. So, to start, I'm proposing that we more than double Federal assistance to State and local law enforcement. Americans have a right to safety in and around their homes. And we won't have safe neighborhoods unless we're tough on drug criminals—much tougher than we are now. Sometimes that means tougher penalties, but more often it just means punishment that is swift and certain. We've all heard stories about drug dealers who are caught and arrested again and again but never punished. Well, here the rules have changed: If you sell drugs, you will be caught. And when you're caught, you will be prosecuted. And once you're convicted, you will do time. Caught—prosecuted—punished.

I'm also proposing that we enlarge our criminal justice system across the board—at the local, State, and Federal levels alike. We need more prisons, more jails, more courts, more prosecutors. So, tonight I'm requesting—all together—an almost .5 billion increase in drug-related Federal spending on law enforcement.

And while illegal drug use is found in every community, nowhere is it worse than in our public housing projects. You know, the poor have never had it easy in this world. But in the past, they weren't mugged on the way home from work by crack gangs. And their children didn't have to dodge bullets on the way to school. And that's why I'm targeting $50 million to fight crime in public housing projects— to help restore order and to kick out the dealers for good.

The second element of our strategy looks beyond our borders, where the cocaine and crack bought on America's streets is grown and processed. In Colombia alone, cocaine killers have gunned down a leading statesman, murdered almost 200 judges and 7 members of their supreme court. The besieged governments of the drug-producing countries are fighting back, fighting to break the international drug rings. But you and I agree with the courageous President of Colombia, Virgilio Barco, who said that if Americans use cocaine, then Americans are paying for murder. American cocaine users need to understand that our nation has zero tolerance for casual drug use. We have a responsibility not to leave our brave friends in Colombia to fight alone.

The million emergency assistance announced 2 weeks ago was just our first step in assisting the Andean nations in their fight against the cocaine cartels. Colombia has already arrested suppliers, seized tons of cocaine, and confiscated palatial homes of drug lords. But Colombia faces a long, uphill battle, so we must be ready to do more. Our strategy allocates more than a quarter of a billion dollars for next year in military and law enforcement assistance for the three Andean nations of Colombia, Bolivia, and Peru. This will be the first part of a 5-year, billion program to counter the producers, the traffickers, and the smugglers.

I spoke with President Barco just last week, and we hope to meet with the leaders of affected countries in an unprecedented drug summit, all to coordinate an inter-American strategy against the cartels. We will work with our allies and friends, especially our economic summit partners, to do more in the fight against drugs. I'm also asking the Senate to ratify the United Nations antidrug convention concluded last December.

To stop those drugs on the way to America, I propose that we spend more than a billion and a half dollars on interdiction. Greater interagency cooperation, combined with sophisticated intelligence-gathering and Defense Department technology, can help stop drugs at our borders.

And our message to the drug cartels is this: The rules have changed. We will help any government that wants our help. When requested, we will for the first time make available the appropriate resources of America's Armed Forces. We will intensify our efforts against drug smugglers on the high seas, in international airspace, and at our borders. We will stop the flow of chemicals from the United States used to process drugs. We will pursue and enforce international agreements to track drug money to the front men and financiers. And then we will handcuff these money launderers and jail them, just like any street dealer. And for the drug kingpins: the death penalty.

The third part of our strategy concerns drug treatment. Experts believe that there are 2 million American drug users who may be able to get off drugs with proper treatment, but right now only 40 percent of them are actually getting help. This is simply not good enough. Many people who need treatment won't seek it on their own, and some who do seek it are put on a waiting list. Most programs were set up to deal with heroin addicts, but today the major problem is cocaine users. It's time we expand our treatment systems and do a better job of providing services to those who need them.

And so, tonight I'm proposing an increase of 1 million in Federal spending on drug treatment. With this strategy, we will do more. We will work with the States. We will encourage employers to establish employee assistance programs to cope with drug use; and because addiction is such a cruel inheritance, we will intensify our search for ways to help expectant mothers who use drugs.

Fourth, we must stop illegal drug use before it starts. Unfortunately, it begins early—for many kids, before their teens. But it doesn't start the way you might think, from a dealer or an addict hanging around a school playground. More often, our kids first get their drugs free, from friends or even from older brothers or sisters. Peer pressure spreads drug use; peer pressure can help stop it. I am proposing a quarter-of-a-billion-dollar increase in Federal funds for school and community prevention programs that help young people and adults reject enticements to try drugs. And I'm proposing something else. Every school, college, and university, and every workplace must adopt tough but fair policies about drug use by students and employees. And those that will not adopt such policies will not get Federal funds—period!

The private sector also has an important role to play. I spoke with a businessman named Jim Burke who said he was haunted by the thought—a nightmare, really—that somewhere in America, at any given moment, there is a teenage girl who should be in school instead of giving birth to a child addicted to cocaine. So, Jim did something. He led an antidrug partnership, financed by private funds, to work with advertisers and media firms. Their partnership is now determined to work with our strategy by generating educational messages worth a million dollars a day every day for the next 3 years—a billion dollars worth of advertising, all to promote the antidrug message.

As President, one of my first missions is to keep the national focus on our offensive against drugs. And so, next week I will take the antidrug message to the classrooms of America in a special television address, one that I hope will reach every school, every young American. But drug education doesn't begin in class or on TV. It must begin at home and in the neighborhood. Parents and families must set the first example of a drug-free life. And when families are broken, caring friends and neighbors must step in.

These are the most important elements in our strategy to fight drugs. They are all designed to reinforce one another, to mesh into a powerful whole, to mount an aggressive attack on the problem from every angle. This is the first time in the history of our country that we truly have a comprehensive strategy. As you can tell, such an approach will not come cheaply. Last February I asked for a $700 million increase in the drug budget for the coming year.

And now, over the past 6 months of careful study, we have found an immediate need for another billion and a half dollars. With this added .2 billion, our 1990 drug budget totals almost billion, the largest increase in history. We need this program fully implemented—right away. The next fiscal year begins just 26 days from now. So, tonight I'm asking the Congress, which has helped us formulate this strategy, to help us move it forward immediately. We can pay for this fight against drugs without raising taxes or adding to the budget deficit. We have submitted our plan to Congress that shows just how to fund it within the limits of our bipartisan budget agreement.

Now, I know some will still say that we're not spending enough money, but those who judge our strategy only by its pricetag simply don't understand the problem. Let's face it, we've all seen in the past that money alone won't solve our toughest problems. To be strong and efficient, our strategy needs these funds. But there is no match for a united America, a determined America, an angry America. Our outrage against drugs unites us, brings us together behind this one plan of action—an assault on every front.

This is the toughest domestic challenge we've faced in decades. And it's a challenge we must face not as Democrats or Republicans, liberals or conservatives, but as Americans. The key is a coordinated, united effort. We've responded faithfully to the request of the Congress to produce our nation's first national drug strategy. I'll be looking to the Democratic majority and our Republicans in Congress for leadership and bipartisan support. And our citizens deserve cooperation, not competition; a national effort, not a partisan bidding war. To start, Congress needs not only to act on this national drug strategy but also to act on our crime package announced last May, a package to toughen sentences, beef up law enforcement, and build new prison space for 24,000 inmates.

You and I both know the Federal Government can't do it alone. The States need to match tougher Federal laws with tougher laws of their own: stiffer bail, probation, parole, and sentencing. And we need your help. If people you know are users, help them—help them get off drugs. If you're a parent, talk to your kids about drugs—tonight. Call your local drug prevention program; be a Big Brother or Sister to a child in need; pitch in with your local Neighborhood Watch program. Whether you give your time or talent, everyone counts: every employer who bans drugs from the workplace; every school that's tough on drug use; every neighborhood in which drugs are not welcome; and most important, every one of you who refuses to look the other way. Every one of you counts. Of course, victory will take hard work and time, but together we will win. Too many young lives are at stake.

Not long ago, I read a newspaper story about a little boy named Dooney who, until recently, lived in a crack house in a suburb of Washington, D.C. In Dooney's neighborhood, children don't flinch at the sound of gunfire. And when they play, they pretend to sell to each other small white rocks that they call crack. Life at home was so cruel that Dooney begged his teachers to let him sleep on the floor at school. And when asked about his future, 6-year-old Dooney answers, "I don't want to sell drugs, but I'll probably have to."

Well, Dooney does not have to sell drugs. No child in America should have to live like this. Together as a people we can save these kids. We've already transformed a national attitude of tolerance into one of condemnation. But the war on drugs will be hard-won, neighborhood by neighborhood, block by block, child by child.

If we fight this war as a divided nation, then the war is lost. But if we face this evil as a nation united, this will be nothing but a handful of useless chemicals. Victory—victory over drugs—is our cause, a just cause. And with your help, we are going to win.

Thank you, God bless you, and good night.

Note: The President spoke at 9 p.m. from the Oval Office at the White House. The address was broadcast live on nationwide radio and television.

10. Joint Statement on the Education Summit with the Nation's Governors in Charlottesville, Virginia
September 28, 1989

The President and the nation's Governors agree that a better educated citizenry is the key to the continued growth and prosperity of the United States. Education has historically been, and should remain, a state responsibility and a local function, which works best when there is also strong parental involvement in the schools. And, as [a] Nation we must have an educated workforce, second to none, in order to succeed in an increasingly competitive world economy.

Education has always been important, but never this important because the stakes have changed: Our competitors for opportunity are also working to educate their people. As they continue to improve, they make the future a moving target. We believe that the time has come, for the first time in U.S. history, to establish clear, national performance goals, goals that will make us internationally competitive.

The President and the nation's Governors have agreed at this summit to:

—establish a process for setting national educational goals;

—to seek greater flexibility and enhanced accountability in the use of Federal resources to meet the goals, through both regulatory and legislative changes;

—to undertake a major state-by-state effort to restructure our education system; and

—to report annually on progress in achieving our goals.

This agreement represents the first step in a long-term commitment to reorient the education system and to marshal widespread support for the needed reforms.

National Education Goals

The first step in restructuring our education system is to build a broad-based consensus around a defined set of national education goals. The National Governors' Association Task Force on Education will work with the President's designees to recommend goals to the President and the Nation's Governors. The process to develop the goals will involve teachers, parents, local school administrators, school board members, elected officials, business and labor communities, and the public at large. The overriding objective is to develop an ambitious, realistic set of performance goals that reflect the views of those with a stake in the performance of our education system. To succeed we need a common understanding and a common mission. National goals will allow us to plan effectively, to set priorities, and to establish clear lines of accountability and authority. These goals will lead to the development of detailed strategies that will allow us to meet these objectives.

The process for establishing these goals should be completed and the goals announced in early 1990.

By performance we mean goals that will, if achieved, guarantee that we are internationally competitive, such as goals related to:

—the readiness of children to start school;

—the performance of students on international achievement tests, especially in math and science;

—the reduction of the dropout rate and the improvement of academic performance, especially among at-risk students;

—the functional literacy of adult Americans;

—the level of training necessary to guarantee a competitive workforce;

—the supply of qualified teachers and up-to-date technology; and

—the establishment of safe, disciplined, and drug-free schools.

The Federal/State Partnership

Flexibility and Accountability

The President and the Governors are committed to achieving the maximum return possible from our investments in the Nation's education system. We define maximum return as the following: significant and sustained educational improvement for all children. Nothing less will meet the Nation's needs for a strong, competitive workforce; nothing less will meet our children's needs for successful citizenship and economic opportunity.

Federal funds, which represent only a small part of total education spending, are directed particularly toward services for young people most at risk. Federal laws and regulations control where and for whom states and localities spend this money. State and local laws and regulations control what is taught, and how, for all students.

At present, neither Federal nor State and local laws and regulations focus sufficiently on results, or on real educational improvement for all children. Federal and State executives need authority to waive statutory and regulatory provisions in return for greater accountability for results.

The President and the Governors have agreed:

—to examine Federal regulations under current law and to move in the direction of greater flexibility;

—to take parallel steps in each state with respect to State laws and administrative rules.

—to submit legislation to Congress early next year that would provide State and local recipients greater flexibility in the use of Federal funds, in return for firm commitments to improved levels of education and skill training.

The President and the Governors have agreed to establish a working group of Governors and the President's designees to begin work immediately to accomplish these tasks.

We know that other voices need to be heard in this discussion—voices of educators, parents, and those whose primary interest is the protection of the disadvantaged, minorities, and the handicapped. We need to work with the Congress. The processes we will set up immediately following this conference will involve all parties.

The urgent need for flexibility in using Federal funds can best be illustrated by a few examples.

First, the Federal Vocational Education Act, which mandates specific set-asides that often result in individual awards that are too small to be meaningful and that prohibit the money from being spent to achieve its purpose. One state reported being required to divide $300,000 in aid among far too many categories and set-asides.

Second, similarly, the Chapter 1 program requires that equipment purchased to provide remedial education services cannot be used for non-Chapter 1 institutions in areas such as adult education. Several States report that large numbers of computers purchased by Federal funds are idle at night, while adult education classes that need them either do without or use scarce tax dollars to buy other equipment.

Third, the requirements that children who benefit from Federal funds for compensatory and special education be taught separately often undermines their achievement. Waivers that permit these students to return to regular classes and receive extra help have produced large increases in their test scores. This option should be available for all school districts.

These commitments are historic steps toward ensuring that young people with the greatest needs receive the best our schools and training programs can give them, and that all children reach their highest educational potential.

In a phrase, we want to swap redtape for results.

The Federal Government's Financial Role

State and local Governments provide more than 90 percent of education funding. They should continue to bear that lion's share of the load. The Federal financial role is limited and has even declined, but it is still important. That role is:

—to promote National education equity by helping our poor children get off to a good start in school, giving disadvantaged and handicapped children extra help to assist them in their school years, ensuring accessibility to a college education, and preparing the workforce for jobs;

—and second, to provide research and development for programs that work, good information on the real performance of students, schools, and states, and assistance in replicating successful state and local initiatives all across the United States.

We understand the limits imposed on new spending by the Federal deficit and the budget process. However, we urge that priority for any further funding increases be given to prepare young children to succeed in school. This is consistent with the President's recommenda-tion for an increase in the number of children served by Head Start in this year's budget. If we are ever to develop a system that ensures that our children are healthy and succeed in school, the Federal Government will have to play a leading role.

Further, we urge that the Congress not impose new Federal mandates that are unre-lated to children, but that require States to spend state tax money that could otherwise go to education.

Commitment to Restructuring

Virtually every State has substantially increased its investment in education, increased stan-dards, and improved learning. Real gains have occurred. However, we still have a long way to go. We must make dramatic improvements in our education system. This cannot be done without a genuine, National, Bipartisan com-mitment to excellence and without a willing-ness to dramatically alter our system of education.

The President and the Nation's Governors agree that significant steps must be taken to restructure education in all states. We share the view that simply more of the same will not achieve the results we need. We must find ways to deploy the resources we commit to educa-tion more effectively.

A similar process has been going on in American manufacturing industry over the last decade with astonishing results: An increase in productivity of nearly 4 percent a year.

There are many promising new ideas and strategies for restructuring education. These include greater choice for parents and students, greater authority and accountability for teach-ers and principals, alternative certification pro-grams for teachers, and programs that systematically reward excellence and perfor-mance. Most successful restructuring efforts seem to have certain common characteristics:

—a system of accountability that focuses on results, rather than on compliance with rules and regulations;

—decentralization of authority and decision-making responsibility to the school site, so that educators are empowered to determine the means for achieving the goals and to be held accountable for accomplishing them;

—a rigorous program of instruction designed to ensure that every child can acquire the knowledge and skills required in an economy in which our citizens must be able to think for a living;

—an education system that develops first-rate teachers and creates a professional environment that provides real rewards for success with students, real consequences for failure, and the tools and flexibility required to get the job done; and

—active, sustained parental and business community involvement.

Restructuring efforts are now underway in many states. The Nation's Governors are committed to a major restructuring effort in every state. The Governors will give this task high priority and will report on their programs in one year.

Assuring Accountability

As elected chief executives, we expect to be held accountable for progress in meeting the new additional goals and we expect to hold others accountable as well.

When goals are set and strategies for achieving them are adopted, we must establish clear measures of performance and then issue annual Report Cards on the progress of students, schools, the states, and the Federal Government.

Over the last few days we have humbly walked in the footsteps of Thomas Jefferson. We have started down a promising path. We have entered into a compact—a Jeffersonian compact to enlighten our children and the children of generations to come.

The time for rhetoric is past; the time for performance is now.

Note: The statement was not released by the Office of the Press Secretary.

11. Statement on the Flag Protection Act of 1989
October 26, 1989

On June 21, 1989, the Supreme Court in *Texas v. Johnson* held unconstitutional a Texas statute prohibiting flag desecration. The Court reasoned that, under the principles of the First Amendment, a State could punish a person who desecrates the flag to communicate a message only if the State had a compelling reason to do so. The Court held that the Government's interest in preserving the symbolic value of the flag is not compelling.

After a careful study of the Court's opinion, the Department of Justice concluded that the only way to ensure protection of the flag is through a constitutional amendment. Pursuant to that advice, I urged the adoption of such an amendment.

After several months of debate about how best to protect the flag from desecration, the Congress has forwarded to me H.R. 2978. The bill provides for a prison term of up to 1 year for anyone who "knowingly mutilates, defaces, physically defiles, burns, maintains on the floor or ground, or tramples upon" any United States flag.

While I commend the intentions of those who voted for this bill, I have serious doubts that it can withstand Supreme Court review. The Supreme Court has held that the Government's interest in preserving the flag as a symbol can never be compelling enough to justify prohibiting flag desecration that is intended to express a message. Since that is precisely the target of this bill's prohibition, I suspect that any subsequent court challenge will reach a similar conclusion.

Nevertheless, because this bill is intended to achieve our mutual goal of protecting our Nation's greatest symbol, and its constitutionality must ultimately be decided by the courts, I have decided to allow it to become law without my signature. I remain convinced, however, that a constitutional amendment is the only way to ensure that our flag is protected from desecration.

George Bush
The White House,
October 26, 1989

12. Remarks of the President and Soviet Chairman Gorbachev and a Question-and-Answer Session with Reporters in Malta
December 3, 1989

The President. Ladies and gentlemen, President Gorbachev has graciously suggested I go first. And I don't think anyone can say that the saltwater get-together was anything other than adventure—at least out in the harbor here.

First, I want to thank Prime Minister Adami and the people of Malta and others for their warm and gracious hospitality. I want to thank the captain and crew of *Belknap* for the great support that they have given us. I think they were wondering if I was about to become a permanent guest. And a special thanks to the captain and crew of *Gorky* for their hospitality, and also thanks to the captain and crew of *Slava*, who have been so hospitable to many on the American side.

I first approached Chairman Gorbachev about an informal meeting of this kind after my trip to Europe last July. Amazing changes that I witnessed in Poland and in Hungary—hopeful changes—led me to believe that it was time to sit down with Chairman Gorbachev face to face to see what he and I could do to seize the opportunities before us to move this relationship forward. He agreed with that concept of a meeting, and so, we got rapid agreement. And I think that the extraordinary developments in Europe since the time that the meeting was proposed only reinforce the importance of our getting together.

And so, I'm especially glad we had this meeting. And we did gain a deeper understanding of each other's views. We set the stage for progress across a broad range of issues. And while it is not for the United States and the Soviet Union to design the future for Europeans or for any other people, I am convinced that a cooperative U.S.-Soviet relationship can, indeed, make the future safer and brighter. And there is virtually no problem in the world, and certainly no problem in Europe, that improvement in the U.S.-Soviet relationship will not help to ameliorate. A better U.S.-Soviet relationship is to be valued in and of itself, but it also should be an instrument of positive change for the world.

For 40 years, the Western alliance has stood together in the cause of freedom. And now, with reform underway in the Soviet Union, we stand at the threshold of a brand-new era of U.S.-Soviet relations. And it is within our grasp to contribute, each in our own way, to overcoming the division of Europe and ending the military confrontation there. We've got to do more to ameliorate the violence and suffering that afflicts so many regions in the world and to remove common threats to our future: the deterioration of the environment, the spread of nuclear and chemical weapons, ballistic missile technology, the narcotics trade. And our discussions here will give greater impetus to make real progress in these areas.

There's also a great potential to develop common opportunities. For example, the Soviet Union now seeks greater engagement with the international market economy, a step that certainly I'm prepared to encourage in every way I can.

As I leave Malta for Brussels and a meeting with our NATO allies, I am optimistic that as the West works patiently together and increasingly cooperates with the Soviet Union, we can realize a lasting peace and transform the East-West relationship to one of enduring cooperation. And that is a future that's worthy of our peoples. And that's the future that I want to help in creating. And that's the future that Chairman Gorbachev and I began right here in Malta.

Thank you, sir, for your hospitality.

The Chairman. Ladies and gentlemen, comrades, there are many symbolic things about this meeting, and one of them—it has never been in the history that the leaders of our two countries hold a joint press conference. This is also an important symbol. I share the view voiced by President Bush that we are satisfied, in general, with the results of the meeting.

We regard this informal meeting—the idea of it was an informal meeting, and the idea belongs to President Bush. And I supported it—that we would have this informal meeting without restricting it to any formal agenda, to have a free exchange of views—because the time makes great demands to our countries, and this increases the responsibility and the role of our two countries. And I can assure you that in all our discussions—and our discussions lasted for 8 hours, in general—this responsibility on both sides was present.

Our meeting was characterized by openness, by a full scope of the exchange of views.

Today it is even difficult, and perhaps there is no sense, to explain the entire range of issues that we have discussed. I wish to say right away, nevertheless, that on all the major issues we attempted in a frank manner, using each side's arguments, to explain our own positions, both with regard to the assessment of the situation and the current changes in the world and Europe and as it regards disarmament issues. We addressed the Geneva negotiating process, the Vienna process, and also negotiations on the elaboration of the convention on chemical weapons ban. All those questions were considered thoroughly.

The President and I myself also felt it necessary to exchange views on our perception, both from Moscow and Washington, of the hot points on our planet. And this exchange of views was very significant and thorough. We reaffirmed our former positions that all those acute issues must be resolved by political methods, and I consider that this was a very important statement of fact.

We not only discussed problems and explained our positions. I think that both sides had many elements which, if they are taken into account in our future activities—activities of both governments—then we can count on progress. This concerns the subject of the reduction of strategic offensive arms by 50 percent, and we have an optimistic assessment of the possibility to move even next year to the conclusion of the Vienna treaty. We both are in favor, and this is our position—naturally, we can be responsible only for our position—we are in favor of signing this document at the summit meeting.

This time we discussed much bilateral relations; and I, on my part, would like to note many positive elements and points which were contained in statements and words by President Bush. Thus, I would say that in all directions of the political dialog of our discussion, including bilateral relations, we not only confirmed the consistency of our political course, the continuity of our political course—and I should say it—although we had an informal meeting, we met only for the first time with President Bush in his capacity, and the confirmation of the continuity of the course is an important element. What is also important is that during this informal meeting, we have laid the foundation for increasing this capital. And I believe that, in the first place, it serves the interests of our both countries and also the interests of the entire world community.

Well, we have made our contact, a good contact. The atmosphere was friendly, straightforward, open; and this enabled us to make good work. In our position, the most dangerous thing is to exaggerate. And it is always that we should preserve elements of cautiousness, and I use the favorite word by President Bush. [Laughter] Our world and our relations are at a crucial juncture. We should be highly responsible to face up to the challenges of today's world. And the leaders of our two countries cannot act as a fire brigade, although fire brigades are very useful. We have to keep it in mind also. This element was also present.

I would like once again to thank the President for the idea of holding this meeting with which we are satisfied, I hope. And I would like to thank the people and the Government of Malta and to express the words of appreciation and gratitude for the hospitality. Thank you, Mr. President, for your cooperation.

The President. Thank you.

The Cold War

Q. Chairman Gorbachev, President Bush called on you to end the cold war once and for all. Do you think that has been done now?

The Chairman. In the first place, I assured the President of the United States that the Soviet Union would never start hot war against the United States of America, and we would like our relations to develop in such a way that they would open greater possibilities for cooperation. Naturally, the President and I had a wide discussion—rather, we sought the answer to the question where we stand now. We stated, both of us, that the world leaves one epoch of cold war and enters another epoch. This is just the beginning. We're just at the very beginning of our long road to a long-lasting peaceful period.

Thus, we were unanimous in concluding about the special responsibility of such countries as the United States and the Soviet Union. Naturally, we had a rather long discussion, but this is not for the press conference; that is, we shouldn't explain that discussion regarding the fact that the new era calls for a new approach. And thus, many things that were characteristic of the cold war should be abandoned, both the—[inaudible]—in force, the arms race, mistrust, psychological and ideological struggle, and all that. All that should be things of the past.

Central America

Q. President Gorbachev. What are the hot spots, President Gorbachev, that you spoke about? There's El Salvador. Were you able to assure President Bush that the Soviet Union would use its influence on either Cuba or Nicaragua to stop the arms shipments? And, President Bush, were you satisfied with President Gorbachev's response?

The Chairman. This question is addressed to me? This subject has been thoroughly discussed. We have reaffirmed once again to the President that we have ceased arms shipment to Central America. We also reaffirmed our position that we're sympathetic with the political process that is going on there regarding the settlement of the situation. We are in favor of free elections, with the representatives of the United Nations and other Latin American countries, to determine the fate of Nicaragua. We understand the concerns of the United States. We listened carefully to the arguments by President Bush, in this respect, and we assured him that our position of principle is that we are in favor of a political settlement of the situation in Central America.

I believe—and now I wouldn't like to explain everything that we discussed on the subject—but to sum up, I would say that there are possibilities to have peace in that area, tranquillity in the interests above all of the peoples of that region, which does not run counter to the interests of the people of the United States.

The President. Please ask the question.

Q. The question was: Were you, Mr. President, satisfied with—[inaudible]—

The President. My answer is that we had an in-depth discussion on these questions, as President Gorbachev said. I will not be satisfied until total self-determination takes place through verifiably free elections in Nicaragua. And the Chairman gave me every opportunity to express in detail the concerns I feel about that region. He, indeed, has cited his concerns. So, I can't say there are no differences between us. But we had a chance to talk about them. And if there are remaining differences, I like to think they have been narrowed. But you know—all you from the United States— the concerns we feel that the Nicaraguans go through with certifiably free elections and that they not export revolution into El Salvador. So, we had a big, wide-ranging discussion, and I would simply say that I feel we have much more understanding between the parties as a result of that discussion.

East-West Economic Cooperation

Q. The *Izvestia* newspaper to President Bush, and if there are comments from Comrade Gorbachev, we would welcome it. There has been a longstanding issue of expanding economic [co]operation between the United States and the Soviet Union. It is a very acute problem, taking into account our economic reforms and our economic difficulties. To what degree that issue has been discussed during your meeting, and what is the position of your administration, Mr. President, regarding the expanding of your economic [co]operation and whether the U.S. business would like to promote contacts with the Soviet Union?

The President. We had a long discussion on economic matters. We made some specific representations about how we can work more closely on the economic front with the Soviet Union, and we've made certain representations that I will now follow through with, in terms of observer status. And I think one of the most fruitful parts of our discussions related to the economy. And I would like to have a climate in which American businessmen can help in what Chairman Gorbachev is trying to do with reform and, obviously, with *glasnost*. But I think the climate, as a result of these talks, for investment inside the Soviet Union and for certain things we can do to help the Soviet Union and, indeed, other countries seek common ground with these multilateral organizations related to finance: All of that is a big plus. It was an extraordinarily big plus as far as I'm concerned.

Q. President Gorbachev?

The Chairman. I would like to comment, the answer. First of all, I confirm what I've said, what the President said. And the second point: The things that have taken place at the meeting could be regarded as a political impetus which we were lacking for our economic cooperation to gain momentum and to acquire forms and methods which would be adequate to our contemporary life.

Well, as to the future course of this process, this will depend on the Soviet actions, whether legal or economic. You understand that today we tried to turn drastically our economy towards cooperation with other countries so that it will be part and parcel of the world economic system. Therefore, we think and hope that that which has happened during the meeting on this subject of the agenda—well, let's call it the agenda—these are of principal importance.

Lebanon

Q. With the tense situation in Lebanon—how did you discuss the military option in Lebanon? And what have you decided on the Middle East in general? How did you discuss it? The question is for both President Bush and President Gorbachev.

The Chairman. We couldn't address this Lebanese conflict because both the U.S. and the Soviet people are sympathetic with the grave situation and sufferings of that people. We shared our views and assessments in this respect and agreed to continue the exchange of views so that each, according to its possibilities—and I think that everyone has its own possibilities—well, President Bush thought that we had more possibilities and I thought that we had equal possibilities, in order to resolve positively this conflict.

The President. And our aspirations, shared in by President Gorbachev, is to see a peaceful resolution to the question regarding Lebanon. We support the tripartite agreement. He has supported it very actively. We do not want to see any more killing in Lebanon. The Chair-

man agrees with us. We're in total agreement on that. And so, Lebanon was discussed in detail, and we would like to see a return to a peaceful, democratic Lebanon. And everybody in the United States, I think, shares the agony that I feel about the turmoil in Lebanon. But we're going to try to help. We're trying any way we can to help.

Soviet-U.S. Relations

Q. My question is to President Bush. You, as President of the United States, participate for the first time at the summit meeting, but you were the Vice President of the previous administration that took part in forming foreign policies. So, what is your assessment of the course that our two countries have passed since Geneva to Malta?

The President. That's what we call a "slow ball" in the trade. [Laughter] It's an easy question because I really think they are improving dramatically. There is enormous support in our country for what Chairman Gorbachev is doing inside the Soviet Union. There is enormous respect and support for the way he has advocated peaceful change in Europe. And so, this meeting accomplished everything that I had hoped it would. It was a no-agenda meeting, and yet it was a meeting where we discussed, as the Chairman said, many, many subjects. So, I think if a meeting can improve relations, I think this one has.

Arms Control

Q. Did you reach any actual understandings on instructions or timetables or deadlines to negotiators on chemical weapons, nuclear weapons, conventional arms?

The Chairman. Well, we devoted much time to the discussion of concrete issues related to disarmament negotiations on different types of arms. And just as an example, to show you that this was a substantive discussion, I'll tell you that in the near future our foreign ministers will meet, which have been instructed to do some specific work to move the positions closer.

In connection with new interesting proposals by President Bush regarding chemicals weapons, which have the goal of a global ban and provides for certain phases and movement toward this global ban, then we have the possibility of a rapid movement towards it.

As to strategic offensive arms, the analysis of the situation and the instructions that have been given regarding the preparation of that treaty demonstrate that we may be able by the second half of June—and we agreed on the formal meeting at that time—to do the necessary work to agree on the basic provisions of this treaty, which there later in the coming months would be ready for signature.

Therefore, I highly assess and evaluate what we have done here. Well, of course, there are questions which would require detailed discussion so that there will be no concerns on both sides. As to our concerns, as regards to strategic offensive arms and the preparation of the treaty on the 50-percent cuts of such weapons, they concern SLCM's [sea-launched cruise missiles]. Well, and in general, we raised a question with the President that when we have events along different directions on the reduction of nuclear arms and conventional forces, when we move towards defensive doctrines—that is, we, the Soviet Union—we are interested in having new elements in the military doctrines of the NATO countries. And therefore, the time has come when we should begin discussing naval forces. We should discuss this problem also.

Thus, I would also like to confirm—and I think that the President would confirm it—

that our discussions were very thorough, which encourages; and therefore, we can count on success. This was a salute.

Malta Meeting Results

Q. Can I ask you a question, Mr. President? Will you tell us, President Gorbachev—will you tell me why you were so cautious at the beginning of the negotiations? The Soviet side was very optimistic, and now you voice certain optimistic elements. What is the reason for it? Maybe that optimism was not justified. This is Portuguese television to President Gorbachev.

The President. This is for you. Go ahead.

The Chairman. Well, I would say that there were elements of optimism and pessimism here, and I wouldn't dwell into the details.

Q. Could you just—

The Chairman. Well, the core of the question is that—if I read you correctly—is that to what degree we can speak of optimism or pessimism regarding the results of this meeting. Or perhaps, I didn't understand you correctly. Did I get you right? Yes. Well, you know, on the eve of the meeting, both sides were restrained and had a well-balanced position, a cautious one. I would say it again. This did not mean, however, that we were pessimists. That meant that we were highly responsible. Today, now that the meeting has taken place and we have summed up the results together with the President, I can tell you that I am optimistic about the results and the prospects that are open now. This is dialectics.

Naval Arms Control

Q. President Bush, may I refer to the question of naval forces, please, that President

Gorbachev raised just a moment ago? Can you respond to your feeling and exactly what you've told President Gorbachev about your disposition toward reducing naval forces, NATO's disposition, on that regard? And if in fact the Soviets are prepared to move to a defensive posture, is not it time to consider some cuts in this regard?

The President. The answer is that this is not an arms control meeting in the sense of trying to hammer out details. We still have differences with the Soviet Union—he knows it, and I know it—as it relates to naval forces. But the point is we could discuss these things in a very constructive environment, and the Chairman knows that I could not come here and make deals in arms control. And I'm disinclined to think that that is an area where we will have immediate progress.

But we talked about a wide array of these issues, but we have no agreement at all on that particular question of naval arms control. But the point is he knows that, and I know that. The point is he had an opportunity to let me know how important it is. And I can, as a part of an alliance, have an opportunity to discuss a wide array of disarmament questions with our allies. So, it's exactly the kind of climate for a meeting that I had envisioned and that he had envisioned. We can sit there and talk about issues of which we've had divisions over the years, try to find ways to narrow them. And we did narrow them in some important areas. And there are still some differences that exist. There's no point covering that over.

European Security

Q. Did you discuss the Soviet proposal on Helsinki II? And an adjoining question: Are you prepared to take a joint initiative with Soviet Union about the Middle East crisis?

The Chairman. The first question is regarding Helsinki II. I think that we have found during this meeting, we have come to a common understanding of the extreme importance of the CSCE process and have noted the positive results of the CSCE process, the results that have made it possible to proceed with deep changes in Europe and in the world as well, as Europe has a great influence on the world due to certain reasons. Both the President and myself are in favor of developing the CSCE process in accordance with the new requirements that are required by our times so that we would think of and build a new Europe on the basis of common elements among the European countries. We reaffirmed that this is a common affair for all the European countries that signed the Helsinki Act, including the whole EC [European Community]. And this element was present everywhere whenever we discussed Europe and other parts of the world with the active and constructive participation of the United States and Canada. Thus, we are in favor of the process gaining in strength and in force.

The transformation of the CSCE-Helsinki institutions at this stage should be such that their nature would change, or rather would be adequate to the current changes. Take, for example, NATO and the Warsaw Pact. They should not remain military alliances, but rather military-political alliances, and later on just political alliances, so that their nature would change in accordance with the changes on the continent.

We are also entitled to expect that when the Common Market and the CMEC would also change in respect of greater openness, with the active participation in economic processes of the United States. Thus, we think that the time has come for us to act, step by step, in a thorough manner, in accordance with the requirements of the times, taking full responsibility, without damaging the balance and security. We should act in a way that we would improve the situation, stability, and security. We will strengthen security in this way.

This was the manner of our discussion. And I believe that the President can only nod and say that we have coincidence of views of this. [Laughter]

Q. President Gorbachev, did you assure President Bush that you will not—

Q. Mr. Gorbachev—a question to Chairman Gorbachev.

Military Forces in the Mediterranean

Q. The meeting took place at the center of the Mediterranean. How did you discuss the problem of the reduction of the military presence in the Mediterranean?

The President. Is this to me? Well, first on the reduction, we did not have specific figures in mind. The Chairman raised the questions of naval arms control, and I was not particularly positive in responding on naval arms control. But we agree that we want to move forward and bring to completion the CFE that does affect Italy and other countries, in a sense—they're a strong part of our NATO alliance. So, we didn't get agreements, crossing the "t's," dotting the "i's" on some of these issues, but that's not what we were trying to do.

May I respond to this gentleman's last half. The question was Soviet and U.S.——

Middle East Peace Process

Q. Joint initiative.

The President. It doesn't require joint initiatives to solve the Middle East question. But we have found that the Soviet Union is playing a constructive role in Lebanon and trying throughout the Middle East to give their support for the tripartite agreement, which clearly the U.S. has supported. And so, there's common ground there. That may not always have been the case in history. And that may not always have been the way the United States looked at it as to how constructive the role the Soviets might play. But I can tell you that after these discussions and after the discussions between [Secretary of State] Jim Baker and [Soviet Foreign Minister] Shevardnadze there is a constructive role that the Soviets are implementing. And again, I cite the tripartite agreement. I'm sure that they share our view after these talks, in terms of peaceful resolution to these questions in the Middle East, be it Lebanon or in West Bank questions. So, I don't think we're very far apart on this.

Q. President Gorbachev, did you assure President Bush that the Soviet Union will——

The Chairman. Well, my opinion on the Middle East, in terms of discussions at the meeting, I can only add to what President Bush has said—that we have just discussed very thoroughly, rather thoroughly, this subject. And I believe that we have come to an understanding that we should use our possibilities and interact in order to promote solution to this protracted conflict, which affects negatively the entire world situation.

As it seemed to me, we also agreed that, as a result of the side's progress, we have approached the point when we have a realistic chance to start the settlement process. Therefore, it is important not to lose this chance because the situation is changing very rapidly. Therefore, we think we will contribute to this.

Eastern European Reforms

Q. I'm from the group of Czechoslovak journalists. President Gorbachev, did you assure President Bush that the changes in Eastern Europe are irreversible and that the Soviet Union has forsaken the right to intervene there militarily? And President Bush, similarly, as a result of this meeting, are you now more trusting that the Soviets have indeed renounced the Brezhnev doctrine?

The Chairman. I wouldn't like you to consider me here or to regard me as a full-fledged representative of all European countries. This wouldn't be true. We are a part of Eastern Europe, of Europe. We interact with our allies in all areas, and our ties are deep. However, every nation is an independent entity in world politics, and every people has the right to choose its own destiny, the destiny of its own state. And I can only explain my own attitude.

I believe that those changes, both in the Soviet Union and in the countries of Eastern Europe, have been prepared by the course of the historic evolution itself. No one can avoid this evolutionary process; and those problems should be resolved on a new basis, taking into account the experience and the potential of those countries, opening up possibilities for utilizing anything positive that has been accumulated by mankind. And I believe that we should welcome the thrust of those processes because they are related to the desire of the people to make those societies more democratic, more humane, and to face the world. Therefore, I'm encouraged by the thrust of those processes, and I believe that this is highly assisted by other countries.

I also see deep, profound changes in other countries, including Western European countries, and this is also very important because this is a reciprocal movement so that the people will become more close around the continent, and preserving at the same time the identity of one's own people. This is very important for us to understand.

Q. I ask a question on the part of the Czechoslovak journalists. We are discussing the future of Europe?

The President. May I just respond briefly? There is no question that there is dramatic change. Nobody can question it. And as President Gorbachev talks about democratic change and peaceful—that certainly lays to rest previous doctrines that may have had a different approach. And so, he knows that not just the President but all the people in the United States would like to see this peaceful, democratic evolution continue. And so, I think that's the best way to answer the question because the change is so dramatic and so obvious to people.

But I will say we had a very good chance to discuss it in considerably more detail than I think would be appropriate to discuss it here.

Central America

Q. President Bush, you have accused the Soviet Union for sending arms to Central America, and, President Gorbachev, you have denied those charges. Now both of you sit here together. Who is right? [Laughter]

The President. Maybe I ought to take the first shot at that one. I don't think we accused the Soviet Union of that. What we did say is arms were going in there in an unsatisfactory way. My view is that not only did the Nicaraguans acquiesce in it but they encouraged that to happen. And the evidence is demonstrable. But I'm not challenging the word of the Foreign Minister. He and Jim Baker talked about that, and President Gorbachev and I talked about it.

All I know is that—and he said it earlier—elections, free elections, should be the mode. And I also reported to him what Mr. Oscar Arias [President of Costa Rica] called me about, blaming Castro and the Sandinistas for exporting revolution and for tearing things up there in Central America.

So, we may have a difference on that one, but I want to be careful when you say I accused them of sending these weapons. I did not, because Mr. Shevardnadze made a direct representation to Mr. Baker. And everyone knows that there's a wide international arms flow out there. But whatever it is, however it comes, it is unsatisfactory for countries in the region that want to see the evolution toward democracy continue.

The Chairman. The President explained correctly the discussion on the subject. We were never accused, and we didn't have to accept or reject anything. We informed the President that we had firm assurances from Nicaragua that no arms, including those aircraft, are being used. And the President took our arguments and agreed to them. As regard the fact of principle—I have mentioned it—is that we are for free elections so that this conflict would be resolved by political means and the situation was kept normal.

The President. Well, that's what we agreed on. I agree that that's the assessment. I still feel that arms are going into El Salvador. We've seen clear evidence of it. But I can't argue with the factual presentation made here.

But we have a difference—I don't believe that the Sandinistas have told the truth to our Soviet friends. And why? Because we know for fact-certain that arms have gone in there. I'm not saying they're Soviet arms. They've said they aren't shipping arms, and I'm accepting that. But they're going in there. And I am saying that they have misled

Mr. Shevardnadze when they gave a specific representation that no arms were going from Nicaragua into El Salvador. So, we have some differences in how we look at this key question. And the best way to have those differences ameliorated is to have these certifiably free elections in Nicaragua. And Castro: I have no influence with him whatsoever, and maybe somebody is yelling that question at President Gorbachev. But look, we've got some differences in different places around the world.

Q. What about Cuba?

Q. Question to both Presidents.

The Chairman. What do you mean?

Q. Oscar Arias apparently called President Bush and told him that Cuba was really creating the situation in the region by commenting—

The Chairman. We discussed the situation in Latin America and Central America, and explained our assessments. On the basis of our analysis, on our own analysis, and our assessment, I told the President that there were conditions emerging for improving the situation for the better, as different countries had the desire to change the situation and normalize the situation—both in the United States and in other countries.

Q. Will you give, Mr. President, an answer?

The President. I'd be glad to. Somebody better tell me what the question was then if I'm going to answer. The question of Germany?

German Reunification

Q. Whether the German question was discussed and your attitude toward the Kohl [Chancellor of the Federal Republic of Germany] plan.

The President. The United States, as part of NATO, has had a longstanding position. Helsinki spells out a concept of permanent borders. I made clear to President Gorbachev that we, for our part, do not want to do anything that is unrealistic and causes any country to end up going backwards or end up having its own people in military conflict, one with the other. And so, I think we have tried to act with the word that President Gorbachev has used to—and that is, with caution—not to go demonstrating on top of the Berlin Wall to show how happy we are about the change. We are happy about the change.

I've heard many leaders speak about the German question. And I don't think it is a role of the United States to dictate the rapidity of change in any country. It's a matter for the people to determine themselves. So, that's our position, and the last word goes to the Chairman on this.

The Chairman. Yes, and the President wrote a note to me in English. I don't read English, but I answered in Russian—he doesn't read Russian—but we agreed on it anyway. [Laughter]

I'll be brief. In the past few days, I already answered a few times on the question. I can only confirm what I said before. But as we have discussed with the President this question, I can say that we approach this subject on the basis of the Helsinki process, which summed up the results of the Second World War and consolidated the results of the war. And those are realities. And the reality is such that we have today's Europe with two German states, the Federal Republic of Germany and the German Democratic Republic, which are both members of the United Nations and sovereign states.

This was the decision of history. And I always revert to this subject, or thesis, which

saves me. Indeed, in order to remain realists, we should say that history itself decides the processes and fates on the European continent and also the fates of those two states. I think this is a common understanding shared by anyone. And any artificial acceleration of the process would only exacerbate and make it more difficult to change in many European countries those changes that are now taking place now in Europe. Thus, we wouldn't serve that process by an artificial acceleration or prompting of the processes that are going on in those two countries.

I think we can thank the media for their cooperation. We are not yet aware of what they will write about us.

The President. Right to thank them afterward you mean? [Laughter] After they've written?

The Chairman. We should thank them in advance, and therefore, they will do better in the future. I would like to thank you, Mr. President, for your cooperation.

The President. We're going to have to leave at 1:20 p.m. Should we each take one more question or not? Last one to me, right here. No rebuttal. No backup questions. Last one.

Soviet-U.S. Relations

Q. What's your personal relationship now between you two leaders? And would regular contacts that would perhaps no longer be called summits be helpful?

The President. I had known President Gorbachev before, and I'd let him speak for himself. But I think we have a good personal relationship, and I believe that helps each side be frank, point out the differences, as well as the areas we agree on. And that is a very, very important ingredient, I think, because of the standing of the two powers and because of the dramatic change that is taking place.

And I am not saying that if he likes me, he is going to change long-held policies, and I am going to say that if I like him, we're not going to change long-held policies. But what we've been able to do here is to get together and talk about the difference without rancor, and frankly as possible. And I think it's been very constructive. So, I couldn't have asked for a better result out of this nonsummit summit. [Laughter]

The question is regular meetings. I'm open to see him as much as it requires to keep things moving forward. We've already set a summit meeting. That summit meeting will drive the arms control agenda. And that's a good thing because I represented to him that we wanted to see a START agreement, a CFE agreement, and hopefully, a chemical agreement. That's a very ambitious agenda, but I think if we hadn't sat here and talked we might not have understood how each other feels on these important questions.

The Chairman. I would like to confirm what President Bush has said: that we have known each other for a long time. But I would also add—and I have not agreed on it with the President in advance, but this is no secret—that we have had considerable exchanges of views in previous contacts, and we had an understanding of the positions of each other. And we would only mention the Governors Island or our discussion in the car, and then we would understand what we are talking about. Then we exchanged letters.

And today's meeting boosts our contacts to a higher level. I'm satisfied with the discussions and meetings we had, including our two private discussions. I share the view of the President that personal contacts are a very important element in the relations between leaders of state, the more so we are talking about the leaders of such countries as the United States and the Soviet Union. And I welcome those personal relations.

And the President was quite correct in saying that this didn't mean that we would sacrifice our long-held positions at the expense of our personal ties or that we forget our responsibility. I think our personal contacts help us implement our responsibilities and help us better interact in the interests of our two nations and in the interests of the entire world community. And I, myself, would like to thank the President for cooperation for this meeting, for the cooperation in a very important joint Soviet-U.S. endeavor. And our share is 50-50.

The President. Well, I guess we're going to fly away to Brussels.

13. Address to the Nation Announcing United States Military Action in Panama December 20, 1989

My fellow citizens, last night I ordered U.S. military forces to Panama. No President takes such action lightly. This morning I want to tell you what I did and why I did it.

For nearly 2 years, the United States, nations of Latin America and the Caribbean have worked together to resolve the crisis in Panama. The goals of the United States have been to safeguard the lives of Americans, to defend democracy in Panama, to combat drug trafficking, and to protect the integrity of the Panama Canal treaty. Many attempts have been made to resolve this crisis through diplomacy and negotiations. All were rejected by the dictator of Panama, General Manuel Noriega, an indicted drug trafficker.

Last Friday, Noriega declared his military dictatorship to be in a state of war with the United States and publicly threatened the lives of Americans in Panama. The very next day, forces under his command shot and killed an unarmed American serviceman; wounded another; arrested and brutally beat a third American serviceman; and then brutally interrogated his wife, threatening her with sexual abuse. That was enough.

General Noriega's reckless threats and attacks upon Americans in Panama created an imminent danger to the 35,000 American citizens in Panama. As President, I have no higher obligation than to safeguard the lives of American citizens. And that is why I directed our Armed Forces to protect the lives of American citizens in Panama and to bring General Noriega to justice in the United States. I contacted the bipartisan leadership of Congress last night and informed them of this decision, and after taking this action, I also talked with leaders in Latin America, the Caribbean, and those of other U.S. allies.

At this moment, U.S. forces, including forces deployed from the United States last night, are engaged in action in Panama. The United States intends to withdraw the forces newly deployed to Panama as quickly as possible. Our forces have conducted themselves courageously and selflessly. And as Commander in Chief, I salute every one of them and thank them on behalf of our country.

Tragically, some Americans have lost their lives in defense of their fellow citizens, in defense of democracy. And my heart goes out to their families. We also regret and mourn the loss of innocent Panamanians.

The brave Panamanians elected by the people of Panama in the elections last May, President Guillermo Endara and Vice Presidents Calderón and Ford, have assumed the rightful leadership of their country. You remember those horrible pictures of newly elected Vice President Ford, covered head to toe with blood, beaten mercilessly by so-called "dignity battalions." Well, the United States today recognizes the democratically elected government of President Endara. I will send our Ambassador back to Panama immediately.

Key military objectives have been achieved. Most organized resistance has been eliminated, but the operation is not over yet: General Noriega is in hiding. And nevertheless, yesterday a dictator ruled Panama, and today constitutionally elected leaders govern.

I have today directed the Secretary of the Treasury and the Secretary of State to lift the economic sanctions with respect to the democratically elected government of Panama and, in cooperation with that government, to take steps to effect an orderly unblocking of Panamanian Government assets in the United States. I'm fully committed to implement the Panama Canal treaties and turn over the Canal to Panama in the year 2000. The actions we have taken and the cooperation of a new, democratic government in Panama will permit us to honor these commitments. As soon as the new government recommends a qualified candidate—Panamanian—to be Administrator of the Canal, as called for in the treaties, I will submit this nominee to the Senate for expedited consideration.

I am committed to strengthening our relationship with the democratic nations in this hemisphere. I will continue to seek solutions to the problems of this region through dialog and multilateral diplomacy. I took this action only after reaching the conclusion that every other avenue was closed and the lives of American citizens were in grave danger. I hope that the people of Panama will put this dark chapter of dictatorship behind them and move forward together as citizens of a democratic Panama with this government that they themselves have elected.

The United States is eager to work with the Panamanian people in partnership and friendship to rebuild their economy. The Panamanian people want democracy, peace, and the chance for a better life in dignity and freedom. The people of the United States seek only to support them in pursuit of these noble goals. Thank you very much.

14. The President's News Conference December 21, 1989

The President. I have a brief statement to be followed by a brief press conference—because I have a pain in the neck—seriously. [Laughter]

Q. Why?

The President. Is that your first question?

Q. No. [Laughter]

The President. Our efforts to support the democratic processes in Panama and to ensure continued safety of American citizens is now moving into its second day. I'm gratified by the precision and the effectiveness of the military forces in achieving their objectives. I'm pleased that the Endara government is taking charge, and they've made several appointments today—starting to govern the country.

The young men and women involved in the exercise have demonstrated the highest standards of courage and excellence in defending America's interests and protecting American life. They have been outstanding.

In carrying out the mission of our nation, there has been, and they have sustained, a tragic loss of life. Military casualties are a burden which a nation must endure and all Presidents have to face up to, but which we can never accept. Maybe it's just this time of

year, but I don't think so. Put it this way: Particularly at this time of year, my heart goes out to the families of those who have died in Panama, those who have been wounded.

This operation is not over, but it's pretty well wrapped up. We've moved aggressively to neutralize the PDF [Panamanian Defense Forces], to provide a stable environment for the freely elected Endara government. And I mentioned that it helps to ensure the integrity of the Panama Canal and to create an environment that is safe for American citizens.

General Noriega is no longer in power. He no longer commands the instruments of government or the forces of repression that he's used for so long to brutalize the Panamanian people. And we're continuing the efforts to apprehend him, see that he's brought to justice.

I appreciate the support that we've received—strong support—from the United States Congress, from our Latin American neighbors, from our allies, from the American people. And it's always difficult to order forces into battle, but that difficulty is mitigated by the moral and personal support that is granted by our friends and allies.

You've received detailed briefings from the Pentagon on the logistical aspects, and I might say that I think [Secretary of Defense] Dick Cheney and [Chairman of the Joint Chiefs of Staff] Colin Powell—and ably assisted by others—have done an outstanding job of keeping the American people informed.

I wanted you to know that as we move into the days ahead, we will continue to support the Endara government, to help establish stability in the country, to allow those desires for freedom and democracy to flourish.

And I'll be glad to take some questions.

U.S. Military Action in Panama

Q. Mr. President, one of your major objectives was to get Noriega. Are you frustrated that he got away? How long will you keep on chasing him? And are you confident that you'll get him?

The President. I've been frustrated that he's been in power this long—extraordinarily frustrated. The good news: He's out of power. The bad news: He has not yet been brought to justice. So, I'd have to say, Terry [Terence Hunt, Associated Press], there is a certain level of frustration on that account. The good news, though, is that the government's beginning to function. And the man controls no forces and he's out, but yes, I won't be satisfied until we see him come to justice.

Q. How long will you keep up this full-scale pursuit?

The President. As long as it takes.

Q. Mr. President, you did mention the casualties. Did you expect them to be so high on both sides? I mean—

The President. We had some very—

Q.—and also, is it really worth it to send people to their death for this, to get Noriega?

The President. We had some estimates, Helen [Helen Thomas, United Press International], on the casualties ahead of time, but not in numbers. I mean, it was more general: Look, Mr. President, no way can you do an operation this large and not have American casualties. So, the Defense Department was very up front with us about that, and every human life is precious. And yet I have to answer: Yes, it has been worth it.

Q. Mr. President, a few months ago you said your complaint was not with the PDF, not with the Panamanian people, but with Noriega only. You also said only a month ago that you didn't think it would be prudent to launch a large-scale military operation. What changed your mind? And particularly, why did you opt for the maximum use of force in this situation?

The President. I think what changed my mind was the events that I cited in briefing the American people on this yesterday: the death of the marine; the brutalizing, really obscene torture of the Navy lieutenant; and the threat of sexual abuse and the terror inflicted on that Navy lieutenant's wife; the declaration of war by Noriega; the fact that our people down there felt that they didn't know where this was going—they weren't sure what all that meant and whether that meant we could guarantee the safety of Americans there. And so, I made a decision to move and to move with enough force—this was a recommendation of the Pentagon—to be sure that we minimize the loss of life on both sides and that we took out the PDF—which we did—took it out promptly.

And so, I would like to think that what I said some time ago still stands. I'm not sure what's left on the ground in terms of people. But what David Hoffman [Washington Post] is referring to is that I said our argument was not with the PDF but with Noriega. And if they would get rid of him and recognize a democratically elected government, we could go back to more normalized relations. We've done that, but we have to see who emerges in the PDF. But I would like to repeat here that we have no continuing axe to grind with the institution of the PDF. Endara's going to need loyal troops who recognize the constitution and the fairness and the legitimacy of his election.

Q. Mr. President, in light of what you've said about the Endara government getting started—the need for stability, the need for some kind of police action down there—we really are in a kind of open-ended military occupation there, aren't we, sir?

The President. Well, I wouldn't say it's open-ended, except it's open-ended as far as going after Noriega; open-ended in terms of the restoration of order in Panama, cleaning up a few ragtag elements of this so-called "dignity battalion." You ever talk about a misnomer, that's it: "dignity battalion"—going after them. PDF units have been rolled up, but we will keep the number of forces as necessary there until our military are satisfied and recommend to the President that they be withdrawn. I want them out of there as soon as possible.

Q. Mr. President, just to follow up, if I could, sir. In the planning of this operation, surely you must have recognized that these actions would be needed and some force would have to be on the ground there for a while. What estimate did you have as you undertook this operation as to how long it would take?

The President. Brit [Brit Hume, ABC News], no number-of-day estimate was given to me. I think everyone recognized some of that would depend on when Noriega was brought to justice, some of that depended on how a restructured PDF behaved.

Q. Mr. President, what do you know about Americans held against their will? And what are you doing now to free them?

The President. I'm looking for help on that because we don't have a count. And if there are a lot of them, we don't know about it, but I just had a briefing—I don't know whether Cheney is still here.

Q. The Pentagon said, sir, there were 12 open cases.

The President. Well, I'll tell you, that included, probably, those Smithsonian people who have now been released. And I think there may have been 9 or 10 of those, but I just have to get Marlin to get back to you.

Q. Well, does that indicate that that's not a priority in the reporting to you that people are held against their will?

The President. No, it indicates to me that it's very hard to know what's going on when there's a firefight and a battle because we heard all kinds of rumors. We had calls from your network, your chairman of the board, urging us to go in and take the—[laughter]. No, he did, and I understand it. He had a producer that he felt was held. We've gone there; that place is secure, I'm told, but I don't know that we can tell him this minute about the life of that individual. But we will keep on going until we can tell him about the life of that individual. There's been an awful lot of interest in the Marriott Hotel, but I'm very pleased to say that it's secure. And we've had heads of corporations, we've had news organizations other than his, concerned about their people. And we must be as responsive as we can.

Q. We're hearing that American troops have surrounded the Cuban and Nicaraguan Embassies in Panama City and that in Managua the Nicaraguans have retaliated by surrounding our Embassy there with their own tanks. Are you hearing the same thing? And what message—

The President. We were told that is not true.

Q. That is not true?

The President. Yeah. As of the briefing I just had.

Q. Mr. President, you've referred to the elected government of Mr. Endara. As you know, there was never an accurate final count that confirmed that, even though most polls suggested he had probably won by a 3-to-1 margin. In talking with him, or in the future, have you encouraged or would you encourage him to seek again elections that would verify that he, indeed, or whoever, would be a legally elected President?

The President. I would encourage as much as their constitution calls for. But the election of Endara was, as you point out, so overwhelming, the vote count so high, that I don't think anybody can suggest somebody else might well have won that election.

Q. But, Mr. President, what I pointed out was that it was never final and it was never verified. It was stolen, as you point out.

The President. Well, because it was aborted by this dictator Noriega—Maximum Leader, so decreed 3 days ago, but he was acting like Maximum Leader before that—thwarting, frustrating the will of the Panamanian people. So, I think the international community that oversaw those elections, including a former President of the United States, felt that it went pretty well.

Q. If I could go back to the question of hostages, aides say that you anticipated Noriega might escape the initial assault, and so, there were plans to go after him. Where are your priorities, sir? In getting Manuel Noriega or in dealing with the Americans who might be held? Because if you get Noriega, the Americans may still be held.

The President. And if we get Noriega—pretty much likelihood they'll be released unless somebody wants to use a held American as a ticket to get out of town. So, we're doing

both. We are concentrating every way we possibly can to find Noriega. And that is not drawing down— here's my answer—it is not drawing down on the assets that we have available to safeguard the lives of Americans. They're not mutually exclusive.

Q. Sir, why is it that tens of thousands of American fighting men, and with all of our intelligence, were still unable to snatch one bad guy from Panama?

The President. Because intelligence is imperfect, Ellen [Ellen Warren, Knight Ridder].

Q. And, sir, did we make an effort—

The President. It's good. Sometimes it's counting numbers—very sure. The intention of a person to be someplace or move—very difficult, but it's still sophisticated. I'm convinced we've got the best, but that's why it is imperfect.

Q. A follow-up, sir. Have you made an effort prior to the invasion to go down and capture General Noriega?

The President. Have I? No, I've been right here on the job. And I—[laughter]—

Q. Has the administration, sir? Had Americans made an effort to do so?

The President. Was there some operation, you mean? Not that I know of.

Q. What led you to approve of the decision to have a bounty on Noriega? And is this the type of thing that we will be doing in the future?

The President. His picture will be in every post office in town. That's the way it works. He's a fugitive drug dealer, and we want to see him brought to justice. And if that helps, if there's some incentive for some Panamanian to turn him in, that's a million bucks that I would be very happy to sign the check for.

Q. I was going to ask you about Panama and the Panamanians who have suffered mightily as a result of all this, not only because of the sanctions that we've imposed for a long time but the military actions, the homes destroyed, the lives lost, and so forth. Are you willing to make, now, a major commitment in terms of aid to Panama to help rebuild what has been destroyed down there?

The President. Yes, I'm willing to help the Panamanian people. We've already ordered the lifting of sanctions. I'm convinced that as we open up economic channels they'll do much better. The standard of living will increase for all as we go forward with investment. We have permitted now the reflagging—or put it this way, don't have to unflag—there are Panamanian vessels, and there are other things that we can do. We've released escrowed funds, but we are trying to help Mr. Endara already with operating funds to pay the workers and the people. And beyond that, though, I think we will feel obligated to try to help in every way possible.

Q. Mr. President, what can you tell us about civilian casualties, specifically Panamanian civilian casualties down there? And was there any estimate given in the preplanning of this invasion of civilian casualties?

The President. Our numbers are almost nonexistent. And I heard some reports from a hospital—and we've not been able to confirm those numbers—that some civilians were killed. And I just asked that of our defense chief who had the latest information when he came over here. And so, I just can't help you on the total numbers.

Q. The other question was—the second part—was there an estimate in the preplanning of this invasion?

The President. I don't think an estimate of numbers, but a great concern about that. And one of the reasons we went in with the force we did to take down the PDF and do it as quickly was to minimize civilian casualties. And the way we went after some of these targets was to minimize civilian casualties.

A lot of kids risked their lives going in at night. Parachuting in someplace at night is not a piece of cake. And some of that was to stay away from the fact that civilians would be out and about in the morning.

Q. Mr. President, how do you rate the chances now that Noriega might—

The President. Come on, Marlin [Marlin Fitzwater, Press Secretary to the President], a little help here. [Laughter]

Q.—that Noriega might be able to mount some kind of a hit-and-run guerrilla operation from hiding? What are the chances of that?

The President. I don't think so. The military doesn't seem to think that he has the communications or a PDF continued loyalty that would make him go into the woods. I like the way Colin Powell put it: He hasn't been in a jungle in a long time. And it's tough living. And he's been living high off the hog off the Panamanian people. And so, we don't expect kind of a Sierra Madre approach to this.

Sarah [Sarah McClendon, McClendon News Service], you've been very good and kind all year long. This is my last press conference here.

Mr. Fitzwater. How about a final question.

The President. And this is the second-to-last question. I hope it's a gentle one.

Q. Your last press conference? What do you mean, your last press conference here, sir?

The President. Is that your question? [Laughter] Well, here's the thing. How many have we had this year?

Mr. Fitzwater. Thirty.

The President. We've had 30 press conferences this year, Helen. And some in your midst here have come to me and said, Please, Sarah, lighten up, don't do this quite so much. Thank you very much.

Q. Who said that?

Q. Actually, this is a very mild question. Are you sending a letter today to the Senate to coordinate with the War Powers Act? They understood—

The President. I don't know whether it goes today, but we will do what—

Q. You will do that?

The President. Well, in fact, there's certain technical language on this that—but notification of the Congress will be done in accordance with our policy.

Q. Tell us about your—

The President. This is the last one.

Q. Romania.

Q. The Soviets have criticized very sharply the decision of yours to the point of saying they're going forwards and the United States is going backwards. What is your reaction to this?

The President. My reaction is: I need to get on a wire there—in a telegram or something—explain this to Mr. Gorbachev. It's not altogether surprising that he doesn't understand some of the special arrangements that the United States has in Panama. It's not surprising that he doesn't fully understand that

this freely elected man had been deprived of the democracy.

And I also need to let him know: Look, if they kill an American marine, that's real bad. And if they threaten and brutalize the wife of an American citizen, sexually threatening the lieutenant's wife while kicking him in the groin over and over again, then, Mr. Gorbachev, please understand this President is going to do something about it. So, we'll have to explain it very—last one, Maureen [Maureen Dowd, *New York Times*], and then I really do have to go.

Q. Are you going to bring any troops home by Christmas?

Covert Diplomacy

Q. Mr. President, we now find out that last summer, when we thought that your policy was no contacts with the Chinese Government, that you've sent a high-level delegation there to talk to them. Don't you feel that American people deserve to know that when you say something's not happening, it's really not happening?

The President. Yes, I do think they do. But I didn't say that. I said no high-level exchanges. So, please look at it carefully.

Q. But you didn't tell us that this was happening. Don't people—

The President. No, I feel no obligation to do that. I feel an obligation to keep you informed, but I have an obligation as President to conduct the foreign policy of this country the way I see fit, reporting under the law to the United States Congress. You could say, How come you didn't tell me that you were going to send in those troops down into Panama? Because I didn't want to take a chance the information would get out. That is the responsibility of a President. And

I will continue to exercise it while having 37 press conferences next year.

Q. Romania, sir?

The President. She's got a follow-up.

Q. Does that mean there are all kinds of other secret diplomatic missions going on around that we have no idea of?

The President. Maybe not of that magnitude. But there's a lot going on that in the conduct of the foreign policy or a debate within the U.S. Government has to be sorted out without the spotlight of the news. There has to be that way. The whole opening to China never would have happened if Kissinger hadn't undertaken that mission. It would have fallen apart. So, you have to use your own judgment. And you've got your job, and that is to find out absolutely everything you can, careful—I'm sure most of you are—about legitimate national security concerns. But I have mine, and that is to conduct the foreign policy of this country the way I think best.

If the American people don't like it, I expect they'll get somebody else to take my job, but I'm going to keep doing it. And we've had a very open administration—very—but once in a while, if I go to try to set up a meeting with Mr. Gorbachev, we've got people here screaming, saying, You should have told us that the day you wrote the letter to him. I don't agree with that. And I was elected, so I'm going to keep on trying to do this with an openness—I hope a new openness—but also the right of a President to conduct his business—in this case of Panama, to safeguard the lives of American kids and the other one, to go and see what happens—I know how China works—see what we can do, make a representation of how strongly we feel against the human

rights abuse, but see what it's going to take to go forward.

Q. Mr. President, Romania, sir?

Q. One question on Romania, sir?

The President. You already had one.

Q. What about Romania?

The President. I'd like the spokesman to tell you about it.

Q. What about Romania, sir?

Mr. Fitzwater. The President's in excellent health. [Laughter]

Q. Mr. President, what about the violence in Romania?

The President. The longer you stay under the lights, the worse it gets.

Mr. Fitzwater. We have a brief interlude here. But we have Christmas presents from the President for each of you, and we'll bring those in in a moment if you want to pick those up as you leave. [Laughter] We will bribe and try anything possible. [Laughter] We know no shame at all.

15. Address before a Joint Session of the Congress on the State of the Union January 31, 1990

Mr. President, Mr. Speaker, Members of the United States Congress:

I return as a former President of the Senate and a former Member of this great House. And now, as President, it is my privilege to report to you on the state of the Union.

Tonight I come not to speak about the state of the Government, not to detail every new initiative we plan for the coming year nor to describe every line in the budget. I'm here to speak to you and to the American people about the state of the Union, about our world—the changes we've seen, the challenges we face—and what that means for America.

There are singular moments in history, dates that divide all that goes before from all that comes after. And many of us in this Chamber have lived much of our lives in a world whose fundamental features were defined in 1945; and the events of that year decreed the shape of nations, the pace of progress, freedom or oppression for millions of people around the world.

Nineteen forty-five provided the common frame of reference, the compass points of the postwar era we've relied upon to understand ourselves. And that was our world, until now. The events of the year just ended, the Revolution of '89, have been a chain reaction, changes so striking that it marks the beginning of a new era in the world's affairs.

Think back—think back just 12 short months ago to the world we knew as 1989 began.

One year—one year ago, the people of Panama lived in fear, under the thumb of a dictator. Today democracy is restored; Panama is free. Operation Just Cause has achieved its objective. The number of military personnel in Panama is now very close to what it was before the operation began. And tonight I am announcing that well before the end of February, the additional numbers of American troops, the brave men and women of our Armed Forces who made this mission a success, will be back home.

A year ago in Poland, Lech Walesa declared that he was ready to open a dialog with the Communist rulers of that country; and today, with the future of a free Poland in their own hands, members of Solidarity lead the Polish Government.

A year ago, freedom's playwright, Vaclav Havel, languished as a prisoner in Prague. And today it's Vaclav Havel, President of Czechoslovakia.

And 1 year ago, Erich Honecker of East Germany claimed history as his guide, and he predicted the Berlin Wall would last another hundred years. And today, less than 1 year later, it's the Wall that's history.

Remarkable events—events that fulfill the long-held hopes of the American people; events that validate the longstanding goals of American policy, a policy based on a single, shining principle: the cause of freedom.

America, not just the nation but an idea, alive in the minds of people everywhere. As this new world takes shape, America stands at the center of a widening circle of freedom—today, tomorrow, and into the next century. Our nation is the enduring dream of every immigrant who ever set foot on these shores, and the millions still struggling to be free. This nation, this idea called America, was and always will be a new world—our new world.

At a workers' rally, in a place called Branik on the outskirts of Prague, the idea called America is alive. A worker, dressed in grimy overalls, rises to speak at the factory gates. He begins his speech to his fellow citizens with these words, words of a distant revolution: "We hold these truths to be self-evident, that all men are created equal, that they are endowed by their Creator with certain unalienable Rights, and that among these are Life, Liberty and the pursuit of Happiness."

It's no secret that here at home freedom's door opened long ago. The cornerstones of this free society have already been set in place: democracy, competition, opportunity, private investment, stewardship, and of course leadership. And our challenge today is to take this democratic system of ours, a system second to none, and make it better: a better America, where there's a job for everyone who wants one; where women working outside the home can be confident their children are in safe and loving care and where government works to expand child-care alternatives for parents; where we reconcile the needs of a clean environment and a strong economy; where "Made in the USA" is recognized around the world as the symbol of quality and progress; where every one of us enjoys the same opportunities to live, to work, and to contribute to society and where, for the first time, the American mainstream includes all of our disabled citizens; where everyone has a roof over his head and where the homeless get the help they need to live in dignity; where our schools challenge and support our kids and our teachers and where all of them make the grade; where every street, every city, every school, and every child is drug-free; and finally, where no American is forgotten—our hearts go out to our hostages who are ceaselessly on our minds and in our efforts.

That's part of the future we want to see, the future we can make for ourselves, but dreams alone won't get us there. We need to extend our horizon, commit to the long view. And our mission for the future starts today.

In the tough competitive markets around the world, America faces the great challenges and great opportunities. And we know that we can succeed in the global economic arena of the nineties, but to meet that challenge, we must make some fundamental changes—some crucial investment in ourselves.

Yes, we are going to invest in America. This administration is determined to encourage the creation of capital, capital of all kinds: physical capital—everything from our farms and factories to our workshops and production lines, all that is needed to produce and deliver quality goods and quality services; intellectual capital—the source of ideas that spark tomorrow's products; and of course our human capital—the talented work force that we'll need to compete in the global market.

Let me tell you, if we ignore human capital, if we lose the spirit of American ingenuity, the spirit that is the hallmark of the American worker, that would be bad. The American worker is the most productive worker in the world.

We need to save more. We need to expand the pool of capital for new investments that need more jobs and more growth. And that's the idea behind a new initiative I call the Family Savings Plan, which I will send to Congress tomorrow.

We need to cut the tax on capital gains, encourage risktakers, especially those in our small businesses, to take those steps that translate into economic reward, jobs, and a better life for all of us.

We'll do what it takes to invest in America's future. The budget commitment is there. The money is there. It's there for research and development, R&D—a record high. It's there for our housing initiative—HOPE—to help everyone from first-time homebuyers to the homeless. The money's there to keep our kids drug-free—70 percent more than when I took office in 1989. It's there for space exploration. And it's there for education—another record high.

And one more thing: Last fall at the education summit, the Governors and I agreed to look for ways to help make sure that our kids are ready to learn the very first day they walk into the classroom. And I've made good on that commitment by proposing a record increase in funds—an extra half-a-billion dollars—for something near and dear to all of us: Head Start.

Education is the one investment that means more for our future because it means the most for our children. Real improvement in our schools is not simply a matter of spending more: It's a matter of asking more—expecting more—of our schools, our teachers, of our kids, of our parents, and ourselves. And that's why tonight I am announcing America's education goals, goals developed with enormous cooperation from the Nation's Governors. And if I might, I'd like to say I'm very pleased that Governor Gardner [Washington] and Governor Clinton [Arkansas], Governor Branstad [Iowa], Governor Campbell [South Carolina], all of whom were very key in these discussions, these deliberations, are with us here tonight.

By the year 2000, every child must start school ready to learn.

The United States must increase the high school graduation rate to no less than 90 percent.

And we are going to make sure our schools' diplomas mean something. In critical subjects—at the 4th, 8th, and 12th grades—we must assess our students' performance.

By the year 2000, U.S. students must be first in the world in math and science achievement.

Every American adult must be a skilled, literate worker and citizen.

Every school must offer the kind of disciplined environment that makes it possible for our kids to learn. And every school in America must be drug-free.

Ambitious aims? Of course. Easy to do? Far from it. But the future's at stake. The Nation will not accept anything less than excellence in education.

These investments will keep America competitive. And I know this about the American people: We welcome competition. We'll match our ingenuity, our energy, our experience and technology, our spirit and enterprise against anyone. But let the competition be free, but let it also be fair. America is ready.

Since we really mean it and since we're serious about being ready to meet that challenge, we're getting our own house in order. We have made real progress. Seven years ago, the Federal deficit was 6 percent of our gross national product—6 percent. In the new budget I sent up 2 days ago, the deficit is down to 1 percent of gross national product.

That budget brings Federal spending under control. It meets the Gramm-Rudman target. It brings that deficit down further and balances the budget by 1993 with no new taxes. And let me tell you, there's still more than enough Federal spending. For most of us, $2 trillion is still a lot of money.

And once the budget is balanced, we can operate the way every family must when it has bills to pay. We won't leave it to our children and our grandchildren. Once it's balanced, we will start paying off the national debt.

And there's something more we owe the generations of the future: stewardship, the safe-keeping of America's precious environmental inheritance. It's just one sign of how serious we are. We will elevate the Environmental Protection Agency to Cabinet rank—not more bureaucracy, not more redtape, but the certainty that here at home, and especially in our dealings with other nations, environmental issues have the status they deserve.

This year's budget provides over $2 billion in new spending to protect our environment, with over $1 billion for global change research, and a new initiative I call America the Beautiful to expand our national parks and wildlife preserves that improve recreational facilities on public lands, and something else, something that will help keep this country clean from our forestland to the inner cities and keep America beautiful for generations to come: the money to plant a billion trees a year.

And tonight let me say again to all the Members of the Congress: The American people did not send us here to bicker. There is work to do, and they sent us here to get it done. And once again, in the spirit of cooperation, I offer my hand to all of you. Let's work together to do the will of the people: clean air, child care, the Educational Excellence Act, crime, and drugs. It's time to act. The farm bill, transportation policy, product-liability reform, enterprise zones—it's time to act together.

And there's one thing I hope we will be able to agree on. It's about our commitments. I'm talking about Social Security. To every American out there on Social Security, to every American supporting that system today, and to everyone counting on it when they retire, we made a promise to you, and we are going to keep it.

We rescued the system in 1983, and it's sound again—bipartisan arrangement. Our budget fully funds today's benefits, and it assures that future benefits will be funded as well. The last thing we need to do is mess around with Social Security.

There's one more problem we need to address. We must give careful consideration to the recommendations of the health-care studies underway now. That's why tonight I'm asking Dr. Sullivan, Lou Sullivan, Secretary of Health and Human Services, to lead a Domestic Policy Council review of recommendations on the quality, accessibility, and cost of our nation's health-care system. I am committed to bring the staggering costs of health care under control.

The state of the Government does indeed depend on many of us in this very chamber. But the state of the Union depends on all Americans. We must maintain the democratic decency that makes a nation out of millions of individuals. I've been appalled at the recent mail bombings across this country. Every one of us must confront and condemn racism, anti-Semitism, bigotry, and hate, not next week, not tomorrow, but right now—every single one of us.

The state of the Union depends on whether we help our neighbor—claim the problems of our community as our own. We've got to step forward when there's trouble, lend a hand, be what I call a point of light to a stranger in need. We've got to take the time after a busy day to sit down and read with our kids, help them with their homework, pass along the values we learned as children. That's how we sustain the state of the Union. Every effort is important. It all adds up. It's doing the things that give democracy meaning. It all adds up to who we are and who we will be.

Let me say that so long as we remember the American idea, so long as we live up to the American ideal, the state of the Union will remain sound and strong.

And to those who worry that we've lost our way—well, I want you to listen to parts of a letter written by Private First Class James Markwell, a 20-year-old Army medic of the 1st Battalion, 75th Rangers. It's dated December 18th, the night before our armed forces went into action in Panama. It's a letter servicemen write and hope will never be sent. And sadly, Private Markwell's mother did receive this letter. She passed it along to me out there in Cincinnati.

And here is some of what he wrote: "I've never been afraid of death, but I know he is waiting at the corner. I've been trained to kill and to save, and so has everyone else. I am frightened of what lays beyond the fog, and yet do not mourn for me. Revel in the life that I have died to give you. But most of all, don't forget the Army was my choice. Something that I wanted to do. Remember I joined the Army to serve my country and ensure that you are free to do what you want and live your lives freely."

Let me add that Private Markwell was among the first to see battle in Panama, and one of the first to fall. But he knew what he believed in. He carried the idea we call America in his heart.

I began tonight speaking about the changes we've seen this past year. There is a new world of challenges and opportunities before us, and there's a need for leadership that only America can provide. Nearly 40 years ago, in his last address to the Congress, President Harry Truman predicted such a time would come. He said: "As our world grows stronger, more united, more attractive to men on both sides of the Iron Curtain, then inevitably there will come a time of change within the Communist world." Today, that change is taking place.

For more than 40 years, America and its allies held communism in check and ensured that democracy would continue to exist. And today, with communism crumbling, our aim must be to ensure democracy's advance, to take the lead in forging peace and freedom's best hope: a great and growing commonwealth of free nations. And to the Congress and to all Americans, I say it is time to acclaim a new consensus at home and abroad, a common vision of the peaceful world we want to see.

Here in our own hemisphere, it is time for all the peoples of the Americas, North and South, to live in freedom. In the Far East and Africa, it's time for the full flowering of free governments and free markets that have served as the engine of progress. It's time to offer our hand to the emerging democracies of Eastern Europe so that continent—for too long a continent divided—can see a future whole and free. It's time to build on our new relationship with the Soviet Union, to endorse and encourage a peaceful process of internal change toward democracy and economic opportunity.

We are in a period of great transition, great hope, and yet great uncertainty. We recognize that the Soviet military threat in Europe is diminishing, but we see little change in Soviet strategic modernization. Therefore, we must sustain our own strategic offense modernization and the Strategic Defense Initiative.

But the time is right to move forward on a conventional arms control agreement to move us to more appropriate levels of military forces in Europe, a coherent defense program that ensures the U.S. will continue to be a catalyst for peaceful change in Europe. And I've consulted with leaders of NATO. In fact, I spoke by phone with President Gorbachev just today.

I agree with our European allies that an American military presence in Europe is essential and that it should not be tied solely to the Soviet military presence in Eastern Europe. But our troop levels can still be lower. And so, tonight I am announcing a major new step for a further reduction in U.S. and Soviet manpower in Central and Eastern Europe to 195,000 on each side. This level reflects the advice of our senior military advisers. It's designed to protect American and European interests and sustain NATO's defense strategy. A swift conclusion to our arms control talks—conventional, chemical, and strategic—must now be our goal. And that time has come.

Still, we must recognize an unfortunate fact: In many regions of the world tonight, the reality is conflict, not peace. Enduring animosities and opposing interests remain. And thus, the cause of peace must be served by an America strong enough and sure enough to defend our interests and our ideals. It's this American idea that for the past four decades helped inspire this Revolution of '89.

Here at home and in the world, there's history in the making, history to be made. Six months ago, early in this season of change, I stood at the gates of the Gdansk shipyard in Poland at the monument to the fallen workers of Solidarity. It's a monument of simple majesty. Three tall crosses rise up from the stones, and atop each cross, an anchor—an ancient symbol of hope.

The anchor in our world today is freedom, holding us steady in times of change, a symbol of hope to all the world. And freedom is at the very heart of the idea that is America. Giving life to that idea depends on every one of us. Our anchor has always been faith and family.

In the last few days of this past momentous year, our family was blessed once more, celebrating the joy of life when a little boy became our 12th grandchild. When I held the little guy for the first time, the troubles at home and abroad seemed manageable and totally in perspective.

Now, I know you're probably thinking, well, that's just a grandfather talking. Well, maybe you're right. But I've met a lot of children this past year across this country, as all of you have, everywhere from the Far East to Eastern Europe. And all kids are unique, and yet all kids are alike—the budding young environmentalists I met this month who joined me in exploring the Florida Everglades; the little leaguers I played catch with in Poland, ready to go from Warsaw to the World Series; and even the kids who are ill or alone—and God bless those boarder babies, born addicted to drugs and AIDS and coping with problems no child should have to face. But you know, when it comes to hope and the future, every kid is the same—full of dreams, ready to take on the world—all special, because they are the very future of freedom. And to them belongs this new world I've been speaking about.

And so, tonight I'm going to ask something of every one of you. Now, let me start with my generation, with the grandparents out there. You are our living link to the past. Tell your grandchildren the story of struggles waged at home and abroad, of sacrifices freely made for freedom's sake. And tell them your own story as well, because every American has a story to tell.

And, parents, your children look to you for direction and guidance. Tell them of faith and family. Tell them we are one nation under God. Teach them that of all the many gifts they can receive liberty is their most precious legacy, and of all the gifts they can give the greatest is helping others.

And to the children and young people out there tonight: With you rests our hope, all that America will mean in the years and decades ahead. Fix your vision on a new century—your century, on dreams we cannot see, on the destiny that is yours and yours alone.

And finally, let all Americans—all of us together here in this Chamber, the symbolic center of democracy—affirm our allegiance to this idea we call America. And let us remember that the state of the Union depends on each and every one of us.

God bless all of you, and may God bless this great nation, the United States of America.

16. Remarks at a White House Briefing for Conservative Leaders
April 26, 1990

Did I interrupt Porter? And if so—well, to Roger, my thanks if I did, and may I say hello to Doug Weed and, of course, the people that herded this outstanding group together: Jerry Falwell, Ed Prince, Mike Valerio. But in any event, I'm delighted to see you all. With all the traveling that I'm doing, it's a little different for me to be making an appearance so close to the White House. I was just talking to Barbara. She says, "You spend more time on the road than Charles Kuralt." [Laughter]

This morning, I was talking about this, and I said, I'm looking forward this afternoon to going over and spending some time with friends, and indeed with people who were very instrumental in helping me get to be President at perhaps the most fascinating time in history, or among the most fascinating, certainly, I think, since World War II.

I'm delighted to be with a group for whom "conservatism" is not a catchword. As the past two decades show, it's a philosophy to which most Americans subscribe, and I think that's still very true across the country. Conservatives believe in Yankee ingenuity. I recall how a mother once told her son, "I have a pretty good idea that you skipped your piano lesson and played baseball." The son said he hadn't, and the mother said, "Are you sure?" And the son said, "Yes, I have a fish to prove it." [Laughter]

Conservatives also believe in science and technology. The more I know about the Hubble telescope, the more impressed I am. So powerful that it'll help us, I'm told, understand the black holes. What I don't understand is why anyone would want to know more about the liberal philosophy.

Conservatives share a vision. I know some reporters say I don't have a vision—sorry, I don't see it. [Laughter] Instead, I see a vision—I really do see a vision—as sweeping as our heritage: an America of prosperity, a world of real peace. And the question is how do we ensure that vision for our generation? As you get a little older, you think even more about the kids.

For an answer, recall how 150 years ago de Tocqueville envisioned a future that would open before us. Its possibilities were infinite, he wrote, because of America's new model, this paradigm of government. A democracy based on a free market unleashing the full energy of the human heart and mind. And that government arose from perhaps the ultimate exercise in returning power to people: the American Revolution.

Now, two centuries later, when old centralized bureaucratic systems are crumbling, the time has come for yet another paradigm; a form of government which, like the spirit of '76, gives power back to localities and States and, most important, to the people; a model which rejects the view that progress is measured in money spent and bureaucracies built.

The first principle in our new paradigm is that as market forces grow stronger our world becomes smaller. Put another way, we must be competitive to ensure economic growth. So, I'd like to take this opportunity to urge the Congress once again—and I'm going to keep on urging this—that they pass our capital gains tax cut, spurring investment and thus creating jobs. We don't want government to spend more: we want private enterprise to thrive so that people will have more money to save, to invest, and to spend. To most Americans, I feel, that's a good idea.

As a second principle of our new paradigm—the freedom to choose. We want to reduce what government should do and increase what people can do. And so, I support a constitutional amendment, will continue to support it, restoring voluntary prayer. We need the faith of our fathers back in our schools. I haven't been Pres-

ident very long, but the longer I am in this job, the more strongly I feel about that.

A choice also means that parents should decide which public school is best for their kids. So, we have proposed—what many of you have been helpful to us on this—the Education Excellence Act of 1990 to provide incentives for these magnet school programs. Many States are trying out policies based on choice and finding out they work.

In this one, I want to give credit. It isn't just my party, the Republicans; it's some of the Democratic Governors are out front, way out front, on this particular theory—choice. Some only think that Big Brother can revive education, but I believe that excellence comes from higher standards, a greater accountability, and more freedom to move within a school system. And if you agree—I don't want this many influential people to go untapped or arms untwisted—if you agree with me, I would strongly solicit your help in convincing Congress that the time for this is now.

That leads me to the third principle in the new paradigm—that means the means to choose. We must empower disadvantaged Americans. So, we've unveiled a program to help the poor run or, better yet, own their public housing units. And we support a child-care tax credit for low-income working parents that enable them to care for their kids in the manner they choose. I will not see the option of religious-based child care restricted or eliminated. We're going to fight against that.

I know many liberals disagree with what I've just said and the philosophy behind it. But that's why last month the House Democratic leadership passed a bill that would cost nearly $30 billion, three times our original proposal, and force, compel, many States to change their rules. In effect, it would produce national child-care standards intended to replace local standards that meet local needs and put in place a lot more unnecessary paperwork.

Conservatives know that we don't need this bureaucracy. It would merely prove what Will Rogers once said: "Half of America does nothing but prepare propaganda for the other half to read." [Laughter] So, let's expand the horizons of our kids, not the budget of the bureaucracy, and through tax incentives give families the help that they need to solve their child-care problems themselves.

Next comes the fourth principle of this new paradigm: decentralization. In America, this means dispersing authority to the level closest to the source of authority—the people. Places such as Peru, for example—Hernando deSoto, the brilliant Peruvian economist, found that without any centralized bureaucratic direction the ordinary streetside entrepreneurs of Lima are producing wealth on a scale that rivals the economy officially approved by the state bureaucracy. Elsewhere in the world, decentralization has come about through nothing less than the triumph of democracy over bureaucracy.

Conservatives know that a strong defense has and will continue to help all people secure the right to think and dream and worship as they please. In Lithuania—as in Czechoslovakia and Nicaragua, Budapest, Berlin—the words of Thomas Dewey ring true: You can't beat down ideas with a club. Today freedom is on the march and will not be denied.

The fifth and final principle of the new paradigm is what I referred to earlier: We want what works. Our principles, conservative principles, were always right. And now the whole world can see that what's right is also what works. As I've said many times before, and I don't say it with arrogance, we know what works—freedom works. We are not going to let discredited ideologies block the progress of our principles. You can ask anyone in Poland or Panama: Tyranny doesn't work; freedom does.

At home, we also want what works. So, we've reached agreement with the Senate in the first rewrite of the Clean Air Act in over a decade. I call on the House to respond soon and respond responsibly. This one is difficult because I think we are all committed to leaving the Earth a little better than we found it, and yet we've got to do it in a balanced way—forward-looking, forward-leaning. But I will not accept legislation that needlessly throws a lot of Americans out of work because of lack of scientific data. I'm going to hold that line, and I would appeal for your help in urging the Congress to keep reality in mind as we go about getting ourselves out front on the cutting edge of environmental protection. I'm determined to be both a person who protects the environment and one who protects the rights of Americans to have jobs. It isn't easy, but I'm convinced that it can be done.

We've unveiled a comprehensive strategy to free America of crime and drugs. A lot of people in this room have given our planners and Roger and his able team—because of respects, you've worked very closely with Bill Bennett—to help us with this comprehensive strategy to free America of crime and drugs. We're asking Congress to expand the death penalty for drug kingpins. We need to toughen the crime laws at the State level, just as we are in Washington. My vision for the nineties is an America where punishment is at least as tough as the crime.

Just yesterday, we sent up to the Congress a three-part budget reform package that proposes an amendment to the Constitution—and I campaigned on this, so there's no surprise—to provide a line-item veto. We endorsed the Legislative Line-Item Veto Act to strengthen the President's rescission authority and endorse a balanced budget amendment.

The time has come to enact into law these important changes. I sent up to the Congress a special piece of legislation to help Nicaragua and to help Panama. I think we have a real commitment to seeing the success of these fragile new democracies. Before it leaves the House of Representatives, billions—literally billions, plural—of spending is added to this very special legislation. I think I need the authority to make the tough decision on spending. Nobody likes to have to say no to constituents or to interests around the country, but if the Congress continues to demonstrate that they can't do it, only the President can.

So, I'd love to have your support on this package on the line-item veto, the legislative line-item veto that will strengthen the President's rescission authority; and then, of course, our commitment to this balanced budget concept. This vision, if you will, is one that I think most conservatives support. It's a vision of limited government, but unlimited opportunity—a vision to protect the family, empower the poor, and reward creativity.

I like bass fishing. There's a young bass fisherman who is a national champion, a guy named Ricky Clune. Texans will know his name. He's from Montgomery, Texas. One time I was down in Arkansas and saw him win—or, at the weigh-in—they did it—4,000 or 5,000 people, as these bass boats were driven into the coliseum there. I couldn't believe this—4,000 or 5,000 watching people weigh fish there in the middle—but Ricky Clune, when he got up to speak, said this: "I learned to fish following my dad down the creeks in my underpants," he said, "down the creeks of Oklahoma." And then he said this: "Isn't it great to live in a country with no limits?"

I've thought about that a great deal. What we're talking about here in this conservative philosophy is unlimited opportunity—a vision to protect the family, empower the poor, and reward creativity. This new paradigm can fulfill it. I really would ask for your support to achieve promise, not empty promises: lifting people up, helping keep the government bureaucracies at all levels under control and, as conservatives,

reject the hand of big government in favor of a Thousand Points of Light, joining hands and linking hearts.

You know, when we started talking about a Thousand Points of Light, there was a few snickers out there. I had to keep defining what I meant. But I think people understand this. I think Americans—well, since de Tocqueville took a look at America—understand it. It's real, one American wanting to help another. So, I am going to continue to say that any definition of a successful life must be the involvement in the lives of others, one American helping another. That, I think, is a fundamental part of my concept of how we can do an awful lot more to help people who are desperately in need of help in our country.

So, this is my vision—yours, I think. What a dream: to enrich America and help us to continue to lead, help us to enrich the world. I am really pleased you were here. Thanks for the privilege of addressing you. And might I say, God bless the United States of America. Thank you all very much.

17. Remarks and an Exchange with Reporters on the Soviet–United States Summit
May 31, 1990

The President. Well, I'll just say, at the end of a very interesting day, that the talks have gone reasonably well. The mood is very positive in the sense that I had a very good, and I mean genuinely—not in a diplomatic sense—very good, exchange for a couple hours this morning with President Gorbachev. I'm very well pleased with the ground we've covered. This afternoon's meeting—the tone was positive. Differences remain.

We talked about the German question there. I believe President Gorbachev indicated after the meeting that he didn't think the whole question of Germany would be resolved.

Certainly, we're not in any position to resolve that entire question, but when he said that the differences had been narrowed somewhat—I'm taking some heart from that. And we'll continue these discussions tomorrow.

But I think, given the difficulties of some of the problems we face, the talks have gone, certainly, as well as I could have expected up to now. We still have a lot of discussion.

We've touched on almost every contentious issue, as well as spelling out the areas of which we have common interest, where things are going very well between us.

So, that's the report for tonight; and tomorrow, why, we'll be able to say a little bit more. But I won't go into details because we've agreed we're going to talk about them.

Trade Agreement

Q. None of us understand why you can't sign a trade agreement if it's all wrapped up.

The President. We haven't said whether we can sign a trade agreement or not yet.

Q. Why?

The President. We haven't discussed that yet.

German Reunification

Q. Mr. Gorbachev said you've instructed the Foreign Ministers to discuss something that emerged today about Germany, sir. Could you tell us about that?

The President. No, because we agreed we wouldn't. We agreed we'd let them discuss it. I think when I heard what President Gorbachev said—that's exactly what we had

agreed he would talk about. So, we're just going to stay with that guidance.

Q. When will they meet again?

The President. I don't know. Probably tomorrow.

Q. Was there some narrowing of differences that made you decide the Foreign Ministers should get together or some specific details you have them working on?

The President. That was a proposal that President Gorbachev made, and I think the Foreign Ministers need to discuss in great detail the subjects we discussed to see. But I must say, Michael [Michael Gelb, Reuters], I took some heart from that. I was encouraged by that. Our position has been stated and restated, and we'll see where we go. But I think the important point is, we've talked very frankly—no rancor there. And let's hope some of the differences have been narrowed. But when he says this whole German question will not be solved in a meeting of this nature, I would agree with that. We consult our allies, and he knows that. He knows we have a lot of consultation. But basically, my position is the same as it was when I went into the meetings, but I'm listening very carefully—listening to their views and trying to understand their position.

Q. Did he offer something specific for the Foreign Ministers to discuss on Germany?

The President. I think they do have some specifics to discuss, but that can be discussed after they get through talking—

Q. Mr. President, did you offer any concessions? Did you give him anything in return?

The President. No. I want to stay with the guidance that we agreed on. But our position is well-known, and—

Q. You gave nothing?

The President.—the fundamentals have not changed.

Q. You gave nothing at all?

The President. The fundamentals have not changed.

Soviet-U.S. Differences

Q. Has he taken offense to your stand on Lithuania or your remarks today in the arrival ceremony?

The President. He didn't seem to take offense to anything. He knows that we have differences. I've been very up front with him, and he's been very, very direct and up front with me. So, that's one of the good things about the meeting. Great powers have differences. Sometimes they haven't been able to talk about them in a civil way. We are talking about them in a very civil way. I commend him for that approach. It's one I like, it's one I understand, and it's one I think benefits not just the United States and the Soviet Union but a lot of other countries as well.

Trade Agreement

Q. Would a trade bill be contingent on what you hear on Lithuania?

The President. We're going to discuss the details of that—probably get into some of that tomorrow.

German Reunification

Q. Does he feel that he has a proposal to talk about on Germany—means that he is more ready to come your way than you are to his, sir?

The President. We're not dealing on that. Look, we agreed to some guidance, he and I, and I'm going to stick with it. And he did, and I think that's a good sign. We're in the middle of some discussions about where it stands.

Summit Tone

Q. Why do you think it is going so well? Both of you have talked about a really good relationship that—the two of you have talked about the hours he's spent here. Why do you think this time there has been such—is it a good chemistry?

The President. Well, I don't know. That's a good question. I feel very comfortable with him. I feel very free to bring up positions that I know he doesn't agree with. And as I've said, that hasn't always been the case. There have been times when people banged their shoes when they didn't agree. That's not the mood or the tone of this meeting. And we both realize we're engaged in very, very historic and important work here. I think when these meetings are over people in this country are going to be pleased with some of the positions he takes concerning U.S. interests. And hopefully, I can be reassuring to people in the Soviet Union about the kind of relationship we want. But the tone of it is important so that we can try to "narrow differences."

Lithuanian Independence

Q. Mr. President, does either side have a better understanding of the other's position on Lithuania now? Have you narrowed any differences?

The President. That subject has been discussed, but not in the plenary meetings and not in great detail yet. It will certainly be discussed in more detail.

Q. You said you were heartened by the discussion on Germany. Was there any reason for similar encouragement on Lithuania?

The President. As I say, that matter has not been discussed. And I can't quantify for you my hopes on each important question, and that is an important question.

German Membership in NATO

Q. Mr. President, has he backed off anything since his comment yesterday about dictating to the Soviets?

The President. I don't recall. You mean, something he said in Canada?

Q. Yes, sir.

The President. I think when I said out there that we're dealing from positions of unique responsibility, I think he understood that I have certain respect for the standing of the Soviet Union and I'm not attempting to dictate. But I clearly am entitled to and will put forward the views of the American side as forcefully as I can. But you don't get any progress if you give the impression that you're in a situation of dictation. The age of the dictator is over. Remember my speech a while back?

Q. Mulroney [Prime Minister of Canada] seems to think that most of the West is insensitive to what the Soviets suffered in World War II.

The President. I think Mulroney, with whom I've talked twice in the last 2 days, knows very well the United States is not insensitive to the fact that the Soviets lost 27 million lives in the war. And I know Mr. Gorbachev understands that I'm quite sensitive to that. I think he's also sensitive to the fact that a lot of American kids lost their lives. It might have been that I was only one of the two of

us who was old enough to remember from being there.

Q. That's why he doesn't want Germany in NATO as a military—

The President. You're putting words into his mouth.

Q. Mr. President, is there any change in his ability to negotiate—

Length of the Summit

Q. Will you have enough time in 3 days, or is that too short a period of time?

The President. Well, I don't know. I think the Camp David meeting, where we have a lot of one-on-one time, is going to be fruitful. I think we've got to do better on—simultaneous, as opposed to consecutive, translation speeds things up. And today in the Oval Office we had the longer version, so I'd like to move that up a little bit. But I guess there's never enough time when you're dealing with an agenda that is this important. We've got regional questions that we haven't touched on yet. We have more refinement on—each side to refine its views on the European questions. We have arms control that's still being talked about behind the scenes, but that he and I have not gone into. So, we've got a big agenda. Whether we'll have enough time to do everything that he wants and that I want, I don't know.

I am convinced that, out of this meeting, we will narrow differences and the two ships are less apt to pass in the night based on simple misunderstanding. And I'm convinced of that because I can talk very frankly with him. And when he talks, I listen, and when I talk, he listens. We're not shouting at each other. There's not a rancor in there. And once in a while, both of us, if we feel strongly about something, we might get a little more passionate than the rest of the time in presenting our views. But I'm very pleased with that mood of his wanting to understand the United States position, my having the opportunity to express it. And I hope he understands the receptivity on my part.

German Reunification

Q. Mr. President, may I try once more on the question of Germany, sir?

The President. You can try, but I'm not going to give you any more because we agreed with the President of the Soviet Union on the guidance—if you want me to read it to you again, I'll get my notes. I can't help you on it. Nice try. Another question, though, maybe.

President Gorbachev and Soviet Domestic Problems

Q. Mr. President, have you noticed a change in the Soviet President since Malta? Have his domestic problems constrained him at all in your talks?

The President. He's 6 months older. No, I don't really—I don't—

Q. Has he brought up his own domestic problems and offered that as a stumbling block in these solutions?

The President. No. He's not done that. He's not trying to hide anything, nor is he wringing his hands. To me, there is a certain—I don't know whether Brent [Brent Scowcroft, assistant to the president for national security affairs] felt this way—but a certain strength and confidence that was there in Malta and certainly is still there now. And

you can feel that. I mean, this wasn't just a casual observation. I felt strongly about that. So, I don't feel a weakened presence or anything of that nature. I feel a man determined to do his job.

Q. Do you think there is anything you can or should do to help him in the short term?

The President. I'm going to do what's in the national interest of the United States—our security interests, our global interests. And working closely with the Soviet Union—a lot of questions—is in our interest. So, with that approach in mind, I think maybe he can go away feeling that he's got people here that are not just dealing with some innate animosity towards the Soviet Union. We're in a fantastic era of change. We focus on the problems at meetings like this; but we ought not to neglect the fact that we're sitting here, talking to the head of the Soviet Union at a time when Eastern Europe, for the most part, enjoys the democratic process and enjoys a freedom that none of us would have predicted possible. A lot of that is because of the way in which Mr. Gorbachev has conducted himself.

So, there's some problems out there. But we ought not to overlook the fact that we've come a long, long way, and there is less tension in terms of world catastrophe. But there are still some big problems. So, it's that kind of an approach that I'm bringing to these meetings.

Arms Reduction Negotiations

Q. Sir, was there any progress today on START or CFE?

Q. Conventional weapons? What about conventional? You haven't talked about that. Any problems on—

The President. That's going on, but didn't come up—the arms control agenda was not discussed today.

Q. Do you think he'll invite you to Moscow?

President Gorbachev's Meeting with American People

Q. Did you watch him when he got out of the car down there at 15th Street?

The President. No, I didn't see that.

Q. A big crowd.

The President. Was it?

Q. A big crowd. Yes. I hear he's taken your advice about parades.

The President. How was it received?

Summit Discussions

Q. When did he last indicate that he was hoping there would be more in-depth discussions? Weren't there in-depth discussions today?

The President. I thought they were in depth.

Q. He didn't seem to feel that way.

The President. I think he thinks they were in depth.

President Gorbachev's Meeting with American People

Q. Did you talk with him about the handshaking out on the street, pressing the flesh, working—

The President. No, we didn't discuss that.

Q. You didn't really settle anything today, did you?

President Bush's Exchange with Reporters

Q. Did you come out here because you felt you weren't in the game, and he was getting all the publicity by talking to us?

The President. Michael, I knew you'd want a debriefing. You know how I'm jealous about air time. [Laughter] It's one of my driving factors is to be sure you're on for 30 seconds. You know how I am. [Laughter]

Good seeing you guys. You've got to stop laughing. [Laughter]

18. Statement on Signing the Americans with Disabilities Act of 1990
July 26, 1990

Today, I am signing S. 933, the "Americans with Disabilities Act of 1990." In this extraordinary year, we have seen our own Declaration of Independence inspire the march of freedom throughout Eastern Europe. It is altogether fitting that the American people have once again given clear expression to our most basic ideals of freedom and equality. The Americans with Disabilities Act represents the full flowering of our democratic principles, and it gives me great pleasure to sign it into law today.

In 1986, on behalf of President Reagan, I personally accepted a report from the National Council on Disability entitled "Toward Independence." In that report, the National Council recommended the enactment of comprehensive legislation to ban discrimination against persons with disabilities. The Americans with Disabilities Act (ADA) is such legislation. It promises to open up all aspects of American life to individuals with disabilities—employment opportunities, government services, public accommodations, transportation, and telecommunications.

This legislation is comprehensive because the barriers faced by individuals with disabilities are wide-ranging. Existing laws and regulations under the Rehabilitation Act of 1973 have been effective with respect to the Federal Government, its contractors, and the recipients of Federal funds. However, they have left broad areas of American life untouched or inadequately addressed. Many of our young people, who have benefited from the equal educational opportunity guaranteed under the Rehabilitation Act and the Education of the Handicapped Act, have found themselves on graduation day still shut out of the mainstream of American life. They have faced persistent discrimination in the workplace and barriers posed by inaccessible public transportation, public accommodations, and telecommunications.

Fears that the ADA is too vague or too costly and will lead to an explosion of litigation are misplaced. The Administration worked closely with the Congress to ensure that, wherever possible, existing language and standards from the Rehabilitation Act were incorporated into the ADA. The Rehabilitation Act standards are already familiar to large segments of the private sector that are either Federal contractors or recipients of Federal funds. Because the Rehabilitation Act was enacted 17 years ago, there is already an extensive body of law interpreting the requirements of that Act. Employers can turn to these interpretations for guidance on how to meet their obligations under the ADA.

The Administration and the Congress have carefully crafted the ADA to give the business community the flexibility to meet the requirements of the Act without incurring undue costs. Cost may be taken into account in determining how an employee is "reasonably accommodated," whether the removal of a barrier is "readily achievable," or whether the provision of a particular auxiliary aid would result in an "undue burden." The ADA's most rigorous access requirements are reserved for new construction where the added costs of accessible features are minimal in relation to overall construction costs. An elevator exemption is provided for many buildings.

The careful balance struck between the rights of individuals with disabilities and the legitimate interests of business is shown in the various phase-in provisions in the ADA. For example, the employment provisions take effect 2 years from today for employers of 25 or more employees. Four years from today that coverage will be extended to employers with 15–24 employees. These phase-in periods and effective dates will permit adequate time for businesses to become acquainted with the ADA's requirements and to take the necessary steps to achieve compliance.

The ADA recognizes the necessity of educating the public about its rights and responsibilities under the Act. Under the ADA, the Attorney General will oversee Government-wide technical assistance activities. The Department of Justice will consult with the Architectural and Transportation Barriers Compliance Board, the Equal Employment Opportunity Commission, the Department of Transportation, the Federal Communications Commission, the National Council on Disability, and the President's Committee on Employment of People with Disabilities, among others, in the effort. We will involve trade associations, advocacy groups, and other similar organizations that have existing lines of communications with covered entities and persons with disabilities. The participation of these organizations is a key element in assuring the success of the technical assistance effort.

In signing this landmark bill, I pledge the full support of my Administration for the Americans with Disabilities Act. It is a great honor to preside over the implementation of the responsibilities conferred on the executive branch by this Act. I pledge that we will fulfill those responsibilities efficiently and vigorously.

The Americans with Disabilities Act presents us all with an historic opportunity. It signals the end to the unjustified segregation and exclusion of persons with disabilities from the mainstream of American life. As the Declaration of Independence has been a beacon for people all over the world seeking freedom, it is my hope that the Americans with Disabilities Act will likewise come to be a model for the choices and opportunities of future generations around the world.

George Bush
The White House,
July 26, 1990.

19. Remarks and an Exchange with Reporters on the Iraqi Invasion of Kuwait
August 2, 1990

The President. Let me make a brief statement here about recent events. The United States strongly condemns the Iraqi military invasion of Kuwait. We call for the immediate and unconditional withdrawal of all the Iraqi forces. There is no place for this sort of naked aggression in today's world, and I've taken a number of steps to indicate the deep concern that I feel over the events that have taken place.

Last night I instructed our Ambassador at the United Nations, Tom Pickering, to work with Kuwait in convening an emergency meeting of the Security Council. It was convened, and I am grateful for that quick, overwhelming vote condemning the Iraqi action and calling for immediate and unconditional withdrawal. Tom Pickering will be here in a bit, and we are contemplating with him further United Nations action.

Second, consistent with my authority under the International Emergency Economic Powers Act, I've signed an Executive order early this morning freezing Iraqi assets in this country and prohibiting transactions with Iraq. I've also signed an Executive order freezing Kuwaiti assets. That's to ensure that those assets are not interfered with by the illegitimate authority that is now occupying Kuwait. We call upon other governments to take similar action.

Third, the Department of State has been in touch with governments around the world urging that they, too, condemn the Iraqi aggression and consult to determine what measures should be taken to bring an end to this totally unjustified act. It is important that the international community act together to ensure that Iraqi forces depart Kuwait immediately.

Needless to say, we view the situation with the utmost gravity. We remain committed to take whatever steps are necessary to defend our longstanding, vital interests in the Gulf, and I'm meeting this morning with my senior advisers here to consider all possible options available to us. I've talked to Secretary Baker just now; General Scowcroft and I were on the phone with him. And after this meeting, I will proceed to deliver a longstanding speech. I will have consultations—short ones—there in Aspen with Prime Minister Thatcher, and I will be returning home this evening, and I'll be here in Washington tomorrow.

I might say on a much more pleasant note, I just hung up from talking to Mr. and Mrs. Swanson, the parents of Tim Swanson, the Peace Corps volunteer who has been held against his will—held hostage or kidnaped—there in the Philippines. And I want to thank everybody in the U.S. Government that was so instrumental in working for his release. And, Bob, I hope you'll convey that to the Ambassador and others in our Philippines country team.

Q. Mr. President?

The President. Yes, Helen [Helen Thomas, United Press International]?

Q. Do you contemplate intervention as one of your options?

The President. We're not discussing intervention. I would not discuss any military options even if we'd agreed upon them. But one of the things I want to do at this meeting is hear from our Secretary of Defense, our Chairman, and others. But I'm not contemplating such action.

Q. You're not contemplating any intervention or sending troops?

The President. I'm not contemplating such action, and I again would not discuss it if I were.

Q. What is the likely impact on U.S. oil supplies and prices?

The President. This is a matter that concerns us, and I don't know yet. Again, I'm going to hear from our experts now. Our Secretary of Energy is here, if you'll note, and others who understand this situation very well indeed—our Secretary of Defense. And we'll be discussing that. But this is a matter of considerable concern, and not just to the United States, I might add.

Q. Are you planning to break relations?

The President. You've heard me say over and over again, however, that we are dependent for close to 50 percent of our energy requirements on the Middle East. And this is one of the reasons I felt that we have to not let our guard down around the world.

Q. Are you contemplating breaking diplomatic relations?

The President. I'm discussing this matter with our top advisers here in just a minute.

Q. Is this action in your view limited to Kuwait?

The President. There's no evidence to the contrary. But what I want to do is have it limited back to Iraq and have this invasion be reversed and have them get out of Kuwait.

Q. Do you think Saudi Arabia is threatened or any of the other Emirates?

The President. I think Saudi Arabia is very concerned; and I want to hear from our top officials here, our Director of Intelligence and others, as to the worldwide implications of this illegal action that has been condemned by the United Nations.

Q. And you were taken by surprise?

The President. Not totally by surprise because we have good intelligence, and our intelligence has had me concerned for some time here about what action might be taken.

Thank you all very much. And I expect I will say something further because I'm having a joint press meeting with Margaret Thatcher and, at that time, I might be able to take a few more questions on this subject. But the main thing I want to do now is hear from our advisers, and then we will go forth from this meeting all on the same wavelength. I'm sure there will be a lot of frenzied diplomatic activity. I plan to participate in some of that myself, because at this time, it is important to stay in touch with our many friends around the world, and it's important that we work in concert with our friends around the world.

Q. Gorbachev?

The President. Thank you very much.

Obviously—Helen, you might be interested—this matter has been discussed at very high level between Secretary Baker and the Foreign Minister of the Soviet Union. And so far I've been pleased with the Soviet reaction.

Q. Well, do you expect to make decisions?

The President. That's all I've got to say right now. We've got to go on with this meeting.

20. Remarks and an Exchange with Reporters on the Iraqi Invasion of Kuwait
August 5, 1990

The President. Hello, everybody. I just wanted to fill you all in on the diplomatic activity that is taking place—intensive diplomatic activity around the world. I've got to go in now. I'm getting another call from President Ozal of Turkey, with whom I have been in previous conversation. Yesterday I talked to him.

I talked this morning to Prime Minister Kaifu, and I applaud Japan's stance: cracking down on the imports from Iraq. I just hung up, up there in Camp David, talking with Prime Minister Mulroney. We're all in the same accord—he and President Mitterrand, with whom I've spoken, Chancellor Kohl, Margaret Thatcher. I think the alliance, the NATO alliance, is thinking exactly the same way on this. I also talked yesterday to Kuwait's Amir and gave him certain assurances.

What's emerging is nobody seems to be showing up as willing to accept anything less than total withdrawal from Kuwait of the Iraqi forces, and no puppet regime. We've been down that road, and there will be no puppet regime that will be accepted by any countries that I'm familiar with. And there

seems to be a united front out there that says Iraq, having committed brutal, naked aggression, ought to get out, and that this concept of their installing some puppet—leaving behind—will not be acceptable.

So, we're pushing forward on diplomacy. Tomorrow I'll meet here in Washington with the Secretary General of NATO. And Margaret Thatcher will be coming in here tomorrow, and I will be continuing this diplomatic effort. And I'm sure you know of the meeting I had in Camp David with some of our top military people, and I will continue that kind of consultation as well.

Q. How are you going to keep the puppet government from being accepted and installed? And are you going to move militarily?

The President. There is no intention on the part of any of these countries to accept a puppet government, and that signal is going out loud and clear to Iraq. I will not discuss with you what my options are or might be, but they're wide open, I can assure you of that.

Q. Have you talked to Saudi Arabia and the Turks about turning off the oil pipeline to their countries to—

The President. All options are open. There is a strong feeling on the part of the NATO countries to whom I've talked, Turkey being one of them, that we must have concerted and, I'd say—well, concerted action to isolate Iraq economically. And you can just assume from there that those matters are being considered.

Q. Are the Saudis inclined to cut off the pipeline, Mr. President?

The President. I can't tell you the state of play. I've discussed this with King Fahd and I—whether I'll be talking to him again today, I don't know. But I'm not going to characterize their position on this. Let them speak for themselves.

Q. Mr. President, what is the situation on the ground? Do the Iraqis appear to be dug in, or are they readying for—

The President. Iraqi lied once again. They said they were going to start moving out today, and we have no evidence of their moving out.

Q. Do we have evidence that there's 18 new divisions coming in as—

The President. I'm not going to discuss the intelligence situation on the ground right now, but I've not heard a figure of 18 new divisions going in.

Q. Have you given any time of ultimatum—

Q. Are Americans in danger in Kuwait or other areas down there? And you said—

The President. I wouldn't want to say they're in danger, but you know how I feel about the protection of American life and willingness to do whatever is necessary to protect it. But I don't have the feeling that they're in imminent danger right now.

Q. And the people who are now in control in Kuwait are saying they may close some of the Embassies in Kuwait City, that they will regard any reaction against them as, "You should take care if you have your nationals in our country." Isn't that a threat?

The President. I'm not trying to characterize threats. The threat is a vicious aggression against Kuwait, and that speaks for itself. And anything collaterally is just simply more indication that these are outlaws, international outlaws and renegades. And I want to see the United Nations move soon with chapter VII sanctions; and I want to see the rest of the world join us, as they are

in overwhelming numbers, to isolate Saddam Hussein.

Q. Mr. President, how can you and other world leaders prevent the installation of what you term a puppet government?

The President. Just wait. Watch and learn.

Q. Mr. President, have you, in fact, tried to reach Saddam Hussein to tell him all these other things?

The President. No. No, I have not.

Q. But King Hussein has embraced him.

Q. Mr. President, have we asked the Saudi Arabians for the use of their military bases?

The President. I'm not going to discuss what I'm talking to the Saudis about. I'm not going to discuss anything to do about military options at all.

Q. Mr. President, have you talked to King Hussein of Jordan, because he indicated his support for—

The President. I talked to him once, and that's all.

Q. Are you disappointed in what he said?

Q. But he's embraced Saddam Hussein. He went to Baghdad and embraced him.

The President. What's your question? I can read.

Q. Are you disappointed in what King Hussein has said?

The President. I want to see the Arab States join the rest of the world in condemning this outrage, in doing what they can to get Saddam Hussein out. Now, he was talking— King Hussein—about an Arab solution. But I am disappointed to find any comment by anyone that apologizes or appears to condone what's taken place.

Q. Is Secretary Cheney going to Saudi Arabia, sir?

The President. I'm not going to comment on anything that we're doing of that nature.

Q. Mr. President, are you disappointed in the failure of the Arab nations—

The President. Well, I was told by one leader that I respect enormously—I believe this was back on Friday—that they needed 48 hours to find what was called an Arab solution. That obviously has failed. And of course, I'm disappointed that the matter hasn't been resolved before now. It's a very serious matter.

I'll take one more, and then I've got to go to work over here.

Q. Have you already taken steps to protect Americans over there? Have you—

The President. I'm not going to discuss what we're doing in terms of moving of forces, anything of that nature. But I view it very seriously, not just that but any threat to any other countries, as well as I view very seriously our determination to reverse out this aggression. And please believe me, there are an awful lot of countries that are in total accord with what I've just said, and I salute them. They are staunch friends and allies, and we will be working with them all for collective action. This will not stand. This will not stand, this aggression against Kuwait.

I've got to go. I have to go to work. I've got to go to work.

21. Address to the Nation Announcing the Deployment of U.S. Armed Forces to Saudi Arabia
August 8, 1990

In the life of a nation, we're called upon to define who we are and what we believe. Some-

times these choices are not easy. But today as President, I ask for your support in a decision I've made to stand up for what's right and condemn what's wrong, all in the cause of peace.

At my direction, elements of the 82d Airborne Division as well as key units of the United States Air Force are arriving today to take up defensive positions in Saudi Arabia. I took this action to assist the Saudi Arabian Government in the defense of its homeland. No one commits America's Armed Forces to a dangerous mission lightly, but after perhaps unparalleled international consultation and exhausting every alternative, it became necessary to take this action. Let me tell you why.

Less than a week ago, in the early morning hours of August 2d, Iraqi Armed Forces, without provocation or warning, invaded a peaceful Kuwait. Facing negligible resistance from its much smaller neighbor, Iraq's tanks stormed in blitzkrieg fashion through Kuwait in a few short hours. With more than 100,000 troops, along with tanks, artillery, and surface-to-surface missiles, Iraq now occupies Kuwait. This aggression came just hours after Saddam Hussein specifically assured numerous countries in the area that there would be no invasion. There is no justification whatsoever for this outrageous and brutal act of aggression.

A puppet regime imposed from the outside is unacceptable. The acquisition of territory by force is unacceptable. No one, friend or foe, should doubt our desire for peace; and no one should underestimate our determination to confront aggression.

Four simple principles guide our policy. First, we seek the immediate, unconditional, and complete withdrawal of all Iraqi forces from Kuwait. Second, Kuwait's legitimate government must be restored to replace the puppet regime. And third, my administration, as has been the case with every President from President Roosevelt to President Reagan, is committed to the security and stability of the Persian Gulf. And fourth, I am determined to protect the lives of American citizens abroad.

Immediately after the Iraqi invasion, I ordered an embargo of all trade with Iraq and, together with many other nations, announced sanctions that both freeze all Iraqi assets in this country and protected Kuwait's assets. The stakes are high. Iraq is already a rich and powerful country that possesses the world's second largest reserves of oil and over a million men under arms. It's the fourth largest military in the world. Our country now imports nearly half the oil it consumes and could face a major threat to its economic independence. Much of the world is even more dependent upon imported oil and is even more vulnerable to Iraqi threats.

We succeeded in the struggle for freedom in Europe because we and our allies remain stalwart. Keeping the peace in the Middle East will require no less. We're beginning a new era. This new era can be full of promise, an age of freedom, a time of peace for all peoples. But if history teaches us anything, it is that we must resist aggression or it will destroy our freedoms. Appeasement does not work. As was the case in the 1930's, we see in Saddam Hussein an aggressive dictator threatening his neighbors. Only 14 days ago, Saddam Hussein promised his friends he would not invade Kuwait. And 4 days ago, he promised the world he would withdraw. And twice we have seen what his promises mean: His promises mean nothing.

In the last few days, I've spoken with political leaders from the Middle East, Europe, Asia, and the Americas; and I've met with Prime Minister Thatcher, Prime Minister Mulroney, and NATO Secretary General Woerner. And all agree that Iraq cannot be allowed to benefit from its invasion of Kuwait.

We agree that this is not an American problem or a European problem or a Middle East problem: It is the world's problem. And that's why, soon after the Iraqi invasion, the United Nations Security Council, without dissent, condemned Iraq, calling for the immediate and unconditional withdrawal of its troops from Kuwait. The Arab world, through both the Arab League and the Gulf Cooperation Council, courageously announced its opposition to Iraqi aggression. Japan, the United Kingdom, and France, and other governments around the world have imposed severe sanctions. The Soviet Union and China ended all arms sales to Iraq.

And this past Monday, the United Nations Security Council approved for the first time in 23 years mandatory sanctions under chapter VII of the United Nations Charter. These sanctions, now enshrined in international law, have the potential to deny Iraq the fruits of aggression while sharply limiting its ability to either import or export anything of value, especially oil.

I pledge here today that the United States will do its part to see that these sanctions are effective and to induce Iraq to withdraw without delay from Kuwait.

But we must recognize that Iraq may not stop using force to advance its ambitions. Iraq has massed an enormous war machine on the Saudi border capable of initiating hostilities with little or no additional preparation. Given the Iraqi government's history of aggression against its own citizens as well as its neighbors, to assume Iraq will not attack again would be unwise and unrealistic.

And therefore, after consulting with King Fahd, I sent Secretary of Defense Dick Cheney to discuss cooperative measures we could take. Following those meetings, the Saudi Government requested our help, and I responded to that request by ordering U.S. air and ground forces to deploy to the Kingdom of Saudi Arabia.

Let me be clear: The sovereign independence of Saudi Arabia is of vital interest to the

United States. This decision, which I shared with the congressional leadership, grows out of the longstanding friendship and security relationship between the United States and Saudi Arabia. U.S. forces will work together with those of Saudi Arabia and other nations to preserve the integrity of Saudi Arabia and to deter further Iraqi aggression. Through their presence, as well as through training and exercises, these multinational forces will enhance the overall capability of Saudi Armed Forces to defend the Kingdom.

I want to be clear about what we are doing and why. America does not seek conflict, nor do we seek to chart the destiny of other nations. But America will stand by her friends. The mission of our troops is wholly defensive. Hopefully, they will not be needed long. They will not initiate hostilities, but they will defend themselves, the Kingdom of Saudi Arabia, and other friends in the Persian Gulf.

We are working around the clock to deter Iraqi aggression and to enforce U.N. sanctions. I'm continuing my conversations with world leaders. Secretary of Defense Cheney has just returned from valuable consultations with President Mubarak of Egypt and King Hassan of Morocco. Secretary of State Baker has consulted with his counterparts in many nations, including the Soviet Union, and today he heads for Europe to consult with President Ozal of Turkey, a staunch friend of the United States. And he'll then consult with the NATO Foreign Ministers.

I will ask oil-producing nations to do what they can to increase production in order to minimize any impact that oil flow reductions will have on the world economy. And I will explore whether we and our allies should draw down our strategic petroleum reserves. Conservation measures can also help; Americans everywhere must do their part. And one more thing: I'm asking the oil companies to do their fair share. They should show restraint and not abuse today's uncertainties to raise prices.

Standing up for our principles will not come easy. It may take time and possibly cost a great deal. But we are asking no more of anyone than of the brave young men and women of our Armed Forces and their families. And I ask that in the churches around the country prayers be said for those who are committed to protect and defend America's interests.

Standing up for our principles is an American tradition. As it has so many times before, it may take time and tremendous effort, but most of all, it will take unity of purpose. As I've witnessed throughout my life in both war and peace, America has never wavered when her purpose is driven by principle. And on this August day, at home and abroad, I know she will do no less.

Thank you, and God bless the United States of America.

22. Order for Emergency Deficit Control Measures for Fiscal Year 1991 August 25, 1990

By the authority vested in me as President by the laws of the United States of America, including section 252 of the Balanced Budget and Emergency Deficit Control Act of 1985 (Public Law No. 99–177), as amended by the Balanced Budget and Emergency Deficit Control Reaffirmation Act of 1987 (Public Law 100–119) (hereafter referred to as "the Act"), and in accordance with the report of the Director of the Office of Management and Budget issued August 25, 1990, pursuant to section 251(a)(2) of the Act, I hereby order, pursuant to section 252(a), that the following actions be taken effective October 1, 1990, to implement the sequestrations and reductions determined by the Director in that report:

(1) Each automatic spending increase that would, but for the provisions of the Act, take effect during fiscal year 1991 is suspended as provided in section 252. The programs with such automatic spending increases subject to reduction in this manner, specified by account title, are National Wool Act, Special Milk Program, and Vocational Rehabilitation.

(2) The following are sequestered as provided in section 252: new budget authority; unobligated balances; new loan guarantee commitments or limitations; new direct loan obligations, commitments, or limitations; spending authority as defined in section 401(c)(2) of the Congressional Budget Act of 1974, as amended; and obligation limitations.

(3) For accounts making payments otherwise required by substantive law, the head of each Department or agency is directed to modify the calculation of each such payment to the extent necessary to reduce the estimate of total required payments for the fiscal year by the amount specified in the Director's report.

(4) For accounts making commitments for guaranteed loans and obligations for direct loans as authorized by substantive law, the head of each Department or agency is directed to reduce the level of such commitments or obligations to the extent necessary to conform to the limitations established by the Act and specified in the Director's determination of August 25, 1990.

In accordance with section 252(a)(4)(A), amounts suspended or sequestered under this order shall be withheld from obligation or expenditure pending the issuance of a final order under section 252(b).

This order shall be reported to the Congress and shall be published in the Federal Register.

George Bush
The White House,
August 25, 1990.

23. Soviet Union–United States Joint Statement on the Persian Gulf Crisis September 9, 1990

With regard to Iraq's invasion and continued military occupation of Kuwait, President Bush and President Gorbachev issue the following joint statement:

We are united in the belief that Iraq's aggression must not be tolerated. No peaceful international order is possible if larger states can devour their smaller neighbors.

We reaffirm the joint statement of our Foreign Ministers of August 3, 1990 and our support for United Nations Security Council Resolutions 660, 661, 662, 664 and 665. Today, we once again call upon the Government of Iraq to withdraw unconditionally from Kuwait, to allow the restoration of Kuwait's legitimate government, and to free all hostages now held in Iraq and Kuwait.

Nothing short of the complete implementation of the United Nations Security Council Resolutions is acceptable.

Nothing short of a return to the pre-August 2 status of Kuwait can end Iraq's isolation.

We call upon the entire world community to adhere to the sanctions mandated by the United Nations, and we pledge to work, individually and in concert, to ensure full compliance with the sanctions. At the same time, the United States and the Soviet Union recognize that UN Security Council Resolution 661 permits, in humanitarian circumstances, the importation into Iraq and Kuwait of food. The Sanctions Committee will make recommendations to the Security Council on what would constitute humanitarian circumstances. The United States and the Soviet Union further agree that any such imports must be strictly monitored by the appropriate international agencies to ensure that food reaches only those for whom it is intended, with special priority being given to meeting the needs of children.

Our preference is to resolve the crisis peacefully, and we will be united against Iraq's aggression as long as the crisis exists. However, we are determined to see this aggression end, and if the current steps fail to end it, we are prepared to consider additional ones consistent with the UN Charter. We must demonstrate beyond any doubt that aggression cannot and will not pay.

As soon as the objectives mandated by the UN Security Council resolutions mentioned above have been achieved, and we have demonstrated that aggression does not pay, the Presidents direct their Foreign Ministers to work with countries in the region and outside it to develop regional security structures and measures to promote peace and stability. It is essential to work actively to resolve all remaining conflicts in the Middle East and Persian Gulf. Both sides will continue to consult each other and initiate measures to pursue these broader objectives at the proper time.

24. Address before a Joint Session of the Congress on the Persian Gulf Crisis and the Federal Budget Deficit
September 11, 1990

Mr. President and Mr. Speaker and Members of the United States Congress, distinguished guests, fellow Americans, thank you very much for that warm welcome. We gather tonight, witness to events in the Persian Gulf as significant as they are tragic. In the early morning hours of August 2d, following negotiations and promises by Iraq's dictator Saddam Hussein not to use force, a powerful Iraqi army invaded its trusting and much weaker neighbor, Kuwait. Within 3 days, 120,000 Iraqi troops with 850 tanks had poured into Kuwait and moved south to threaten Saudi Arabia. It was then that I decided to act to check that aggression.

At this moment, our brave servicemen and women stand watch in that distant desert and on distant seas, side by side with the forces of more than 20 other nations. They are some of the finest men and women of the United States of America. And they're doing one terrific job. These valiant Americans were ready at a moment's notice to leave their spouses and their children, to serve on the front line halfway around the world. They remind us who keeps America strong: they do. In the trying circumstances of the Gulf, the morale of our service men and women is excellent. In the face of danger, they're brave, they're well-trained, and dedicated.

A soldier, Private First Class Wade Merritt of Knoxville, Tennessee, now stationed in Saudi Arabia, wrote his parents of his worries, his love of family, and his hope for peace. But Wade also wrote, "I am proud of my country and its firm stance against inhumane aggression. I am proud of my army and its men. I am proud to serve my country." Well, let me just say, Wade, America is proud of you and is grateful to every soldier, sailor, marine, and airman serving the cause of peace in the Persian Gulf. I also want to thank the Chairman of the Joint Chiefs of Staff, General Powell; the Chiefs here tonight; our commander in the Persian Gulf, General Schwarzkopf; and the men and women of the Department of Defense. What a magnificent job you all are doing. And thank you very, very much from a grateful people. I wish I could say that their work is done. But we all know it's not.

So, if there ever was a time to put country before self and patriotism before party, the time is now. And let me thank all Americans, especially those here in this Chamber tonight, for your support for our armed forces and for their mission. That support will be even more important in the days to come. So, tonight I want to talk to you about what's at stake—what we must do together to defend civilized values around the world and maintain our economic strength at home.

Our objectives in the Persian Gulf are clear, our goals defined and familiar: Iraq must withdraw from Kuwait completely, immediately, and without condition. Kuwait's legitimate government must be restored. The security and stability of the Persian Gulf must be assured. And American citizens abroad must be protected. These goals are not ours alone. They've been endorsed by the United Nations Security Council five times in as many weeks. Most countries share our concern for principle. And many have a stake in the stability of the Persian Gulf. This is not, as Saddam Hussein would have it, the United States against Iraq. It is Iraq against the world.

As you know, I've just returned from a very productive meeting with Soviet President Gorbachev. And I am pleased that we are working together to build a new relationship. In Helsinki, our joint statement affirmed to the world our shared resolve to counter Iraq's threat to peace. Let me quote: "We are united in the belief that Iraq's aggression must not be tolerated. No peaceful international order is possible if larger states can devour their smaller neighbors." Clearly, no longer can a dictator count on East-West confrontation to stymie concerted United Nations action against aggression. A new partnership of nations has begun.

We stand today at a unique and extraordinary moment. The crisis in the Persian Gulf, as grave as it is, also offers a rare opportunity to move toward an historic period of cooperation. Out of these troubled times, our fifth objective—a new world order—can emerge: a new

era—freer from the threat of terror, stronger in the pursuit of justice, and more secure in the quest for peace. An era in which the nations of the world, East and West, North and South, can prosper and live in harmony. A hundred generations have searched for this elusive path to peace, while a thousand wars raged across the span of human endeavor. Today that new world is struggling to be born, a world quite different from the one we've known. A world where the rule of law supplants the rule of the jungle. A world in which nations recognize the shared responsibility for freedom and justice. A world where the strong respect the rights of the weak. This is the vision that I shared with President Gorbachev in Helsinki. He and other leaders from Europe, the Gulf, and around the world understand that how we manage this crisis today could shape the future for generations to come.

The test we face is great, and so are the stakes. This is the first assault on the new world that we seek, the first test of our mettle. Had we not responded to this first provocation with clarity of purpose, if we do not continue to demonstrate our determination, it would be a signal to actual and potential despots around the world. America and the world must defend common vital interests—and we will. America and the world must support the rule of law—and we will. America and the world must stand up to aggression—and we will. And one thing more: In the pursuit of these goals America will not be intimidated.

Vital issues of principle are at stake. Saddam Hussein is literally trying to wipe a country off the face of the Earth. We do not exaggerate. Nor do we exaggerate when we say Saddam Hussein will fail. Vital economic interests are at risk as well. Iraq itself controls some 10 percent of the world's proven oil reserves. Iraq plus Kuwait controls twice that. An Iraq permitted to swallow Kuwait would have the economic and military power, as well as the arrogance, to intimidate and coerce its neighbors—neighbors who control the lion's share of the world's remaining oil reserves. We cannot permit a resource so vital to be dominated by one so ruthless. And we won't.

Recent events have surely proven that there is no substitute for American leadership. In the face of tyranny, let no one doubt American credibility and reliability. Let no one doubt our staying power. We will stand by our friends. One way or another, the leader of Iraq must learn this fundamental truth. From the outset, acting hand in hand with others, we've sought to fashion the broadest possible international response to Iraq's aggression.

The level of world cooperation and condemnation of Iraq is unprecedented. Armed forces from countries spanning four continents are there at the request of King Fahd of Saudi Arabia to deter and, if need be, to defend against attack. Moslems and non-Moslems, Arabs and non-Arabs, soldiers from many nations stand shoulder to shoulder, resolute against Saddam Hussein's ambitions.

We can now point to five United Nations Security Council resolutions that condemn Iraq's aggression. They call for Iraq's immediate and unconditional withdrawal, the restoration of Kuwait's legitimate government, and categorically reject Iraq's cynical and self-serving attempt to annex Kuwait. Finally, the United Nations has demanded the release of all foreign nationals held hostage against their will and in contravention of international law. It is a mockery of human decency to call these people "guests." They are hostages, and the whole world knows it.

Prime Minister Margaret Thatcher, a dependable ally, said it all: "We do not bargain over hostages. We will not stoop to the level of using human beings as bargaining chips ever." Of course, of course, our hearts go out to the hostages and to their families. But our policy cannot change, and it will not change. America

and the world will not be blackmailed by this ruthless policy.

We're now in sight of a United Nations that performs as envisioned by its founders. We owe much to the outstanding leadership of Secretary-General Javier Pérez de Cuéllar. The United Nations is backing up its words with action. The Security Council has imposed mandatory economic sanctions on Iraq, designed to force Iraq to relinquish the spoils of its illegal conquest. The Security Council has also taken the decisive step of authorizing the use of all means necessary to ensure compliance with these sanctions. Together with our friends and allies, ships of the United States Navy are today patrolling Mideast waters. They've already intercepted more than 700 ships to enforce the sanctions. Three regional leaders I spoke with just yesterday told me that these sanctions are working. Iraq is feeling the heat. We continue to hope that Iraq's leaders will recalculate just what their aggression has cost them. They are cut off from world trade, unable to sell their oil. And only a tiny fraction of goods gets through.

The communique with President Gorbachev made mention of what happens when the embargo is so effective that children of Iraq literally need milk or the sick truly need medicine. Then, under strict international supervision that guarantees the proper destination, then food will be permitted.

At home, the material cost of our leadership can be steep. That's why Secretary of State Baker and Treasury Secretary Brady have met with many world leaders to underscore that the burden of this collective effort must be shared. We are prepared to do our share and more to help carry that load; we insist that others do their share as well.

The response of most of our friends and allies has been good. To help defray costs, the leaders of Saudi Arabia, Kuwait, and the UAE—the United Arab Emirates—have pledged to provide our deployed troops with all the food and fuel they need. Generous assistance will also be provided to stalwart front-line nations, such as Turkey and Egypt. I am also heartened to report that this international response extends to the neediest victims of this conflict—those refugees. For our part, we've contributed millions for relief efforts. This is but a portion of what is needed. I commend, in particular, Saudi Arabia, Japan, and several European nations who have joined us in this purely humanitarian effort.

There's an energy-related cost to be borne as well. Oil-producing nations are already replacing lost Iraqi and Kuwaiti output. More than half of what was lost has been made up. And we're getting superb cooperation. If producers, including the United States, continue steps to expand oil and gas production, we can stabilize prices and guarantee against hardship. Additionally, we and several of our allies always have the option to extract oil from our strategic petroleum reserves if conditions warrant. As I've pointed out before, conservation efforts are essential to keep our energy needs as low as possible. And we must then take advantage of our energy sources across the board: coal, natural gas, hydro, and nuclear. Our failure to do these things has made us more dependent on foreign oil than ever before. Finally, let no one even contemplate profiteering from this crisis. We will not have it.

I cannot predict just how long it will take to convince Iraq to withdraw from Kuwait. Sanctions will take time to have their full intended effect. We will continue to review all options with our allies, but let it be clear: we will not let this aggression stand.

Our interest, our involvement in the Gulf is not transitory. It predated Saddam Hussein's aggression and will survive it. Long after all our troops come home—and we all hope it's soon, very soon—there will be a lasting role for the United States in assisting the nations of the Persian Gulf. Our role then: to deter future aggression. Our role is to help our friends in their own self-defense. And something else: to curb the proliferation of chemical, biological, ballistic missiles and, above all, nuclear technologies.

Let me also make clear that the United States has no quarrel with the Iraqi people. Our quarrel is with Iraq's dictator and with his aggression. Iraq will not be permitted to annex Kuwait. That's not a threat, that's not a boast, that's just the way it's going to be.

Our ability to function effectively as a great power abroad depends on how we conduct ourselves at home. Our economy, our Armed Forces, our energy dependence, and our cohesion all determine whether we can help our friends and stand up to our foes. For America to lead, America must remain strong and vital. Our world leadership and domestic strength are mutual and reinforcing; a woven piece, strongly bound as Old Glory. To revitalize our leadership, our leadership capacity, we must address our budget deficit—not after election day, or next year, but now.

Higher oil prices slow our growth, and higher defense costs would only make our fiscal deficit problem worse. That deficit was already greater than it should have been—a projected $2 billion for the coming year. It must—it will—be reduced.

To my friends in Congress, together we must act this very month—before the next fiscal year begins on October 1st—to get America's economic house in order. The Gulf situation helps us realize we are more economically vulnerable than we ever should be. Americans must never again enter any crisis, economic or military, with an excessive dependence on foreign oil and an excessive burden of Federal debt.

Most Americans are sick and tired of endless battles in the Congress and between the branches over budget matters. It is high time we pulled together and get the job done right. It's up to us to straighten this out. This job has four basic parts. First, the Congress should, this month, within a budget agreement, enact growth-oriented tax measures—to help avoid recession in the short term and to increase savings, investment, productivity, and competitiveness for the longer term. These measures include extending incentives for research and experimentation; expanding the use of IRA's for new homeowners; establishing tax-deferred family savings accounts; creating incentives for the creation of enterprise zones and initiatives to encourage more domestic drilling; and, yes, reducing the tax rate on capital gains.

And second, the Congress should, this month, enact a prudent multiyear defense program, one that reflects not only the improvement in East-West relations but our broader responsibilities to deal with the continuing risks of outlaw action and regional conflict. Even with our obligations in the Gulf, a sound defense budget can have some reduction in real terms; and we're prepared to accept that. But to go beyond such levels, where cutting defense would threaten our vital margin of safety, is something I will never accept. The world is still dangerous. And surely, that is now clear. Stability's not secure. American interests are far reaching. Interdependence has increased. The consequences of regional instability can be global. This is no time to risk America's capacity to protect her vital interests.

And third, the Congress should, this month, enact measures to increase domestic energy production and energy conservation in order to reduce dependence on foreign oil. These measures should include my proposals to increase incentives for domestic oil and gas exploration, fuel-switching, and to accelerate the development of the Alaskan energy resources without damage to wildlife. As you know, when the oil embargo was imposed in the early 1970's, the United States imported almost 6 million barrels of oil a day. This year, before the Iraqi invasion, U.S. imports had risen to nearly 8 million barrels per day. And we'd moved in the wrong direction. And now we must act to correct that trend.

And fourth, the Congress should, this month, enact a 5-year program to reduce the projected debt and deficits by $500 billion— that's by half a trillion dollars. And if, with the Congress, we can develop a satisfactory program by the end of the month, we can avoid the ax of sequester—deep across-the-board cuts that would threaten our military capacity and risk substantial domestic disruption. I want to be able to tell the American people that we have truly solved the deficit problem. And for me to do that, a budget agreement must meet these tests: It must include the measures I've recommended to increase economic growth and reduce dependence on foreign oil. It must be fair. All should contribute, but the burden should not be excessive for any one group of programs or people. It must address the growth of government's hidden liabilities. It must reform the budget process and, further, it must be real.

I urge Congress to provide a comprehensive 5-year deficit reduction program to me as a complete legislative package, with measures to assure that it can be fully enforced. America is tired of phony deficit reduction or promise-now, save-later plans. It is time for a program that is credible and real. And finally, to the extent that the deficit reduction program includes new revenue measures, it must avoid any measure that would threaten economic growth or turn us back toward the days of punishing income tax rates. That is one path we should not head down again.

I have been pleased with recent progress, although it has not always seemed so smooth. But now it's time to produce. I hope we can work out a responsible plan. But with or without agreement from the budget summit, I ask both

Houses of the Congress to allow a straight up-or-down vote on a complete $500-billion deficit reduction package not later than September 28. If the Congress cannot get me a budget, then Americans will have to face a tough, mandated sequester. I'm hopeful, in fact, I'm confident that the Congress will do what it should. And I can assure you that we in the executive branch will do our part.

In the final analysis, our ability to meet our responsibilities abroad depends upon political will and consensus at home. This is never easy in democracies, for we govern only with the consent of the governed. And although free people in a free society are bound to have their differences, Americans traditionally come together in times of adversity and challenge.

Once again, Americans have stepped forward to share a tearful goodbye with their families before leaving for a strange and distant shore. At this very moment, they serve together with Arabs, Europeans, Asians, and Africans in defense of principle and the dream of a new world order. That's why they sweat and toil in the sand and the heat and the sun. If they can come together under such adversity, if old adversaries like the Soviet Union and the United States can work in common cause, then surely we who are so fortunate to be in this great Chamber—Democrats, Republicans, liberals, conservatives—can come together to fulfill our responsibilities here. Thank you. Good night. And God bless the United States of America.

25. Address to the People of Iraq on the Persian Gulf Crisis
September 16, 1990

I'm here today to explain to the people of Iraq why the United States and the world community has responded the way it has to Iraq's occupation of Kuwait. My purpose is not to trade accusations, not to escalate the war of words, but to speak with candor about what has caused this crisis that confronts us. Let there be no misunderstanding: We have no quarrel with the people of Iraq. I've said many times, and I will repeat right now, our only object is to oppose the invasion ordered by Saddam Hussein.

On August 2d, your leadership made its decision to invade, an unprovoked attack on a small nation that posed no threat to your own. Kuwait was the victim; Iraq, the aggressor.

And the world met Iraq's invasion with a chorus of condemnation: unanimous resolutions in the United Nations. Twenty-seven States—rich and poor, Arab, Moslem, Asian, and African—have answered the call of Saudi Arabia and free Kuwait and sent forces to the Gulf region to defend against Iraq. For the first time in history, 13 States of the Arab League, representing 80 percent of the Arab nation, have condemned a brother Arab State. Today, opposed by world opinion, Iraq stands isolated and alone.

I do not believe that you, the people of Iraq, want war. You've borne untold suffering and hardship during 8 long years of war with Iran—a war that touched the life of every single Iraqi citizen; a war that took the lives of hundreds of thousands of young men, the bright promise of an entire generation. No one knows better than you the incalculable costs of war, the ultimate cost when a nation's vast potential and vital energies are consumed by conflict. No one knows what Iraq might be today, what prosperity and peace you might now enjoy, had your leaders not plunged you into war. Now, once again, Iraq finds itself on the brink of war. Once again, the same Iraqi leadership has miscalculated. Once again, the Iraqi people face tragedy.

Saddam Hussein has told you that Iraqi troops were invited into Kuwait. That's not true. In fact, in the face of far superior force, the people of Kuwait are bravely resisting this occupation. Your own returning soldiers will tell you the Kuwaitis are fighting valiantly in any way they can.

Saddam Hussein tells you that this crisis is a struggle between Iraq and America. In fact, it is Iraq against the world. When President Gorbachev and I met at Helsinki [September 9], we agreed that no peaceful international order is possible if larger states can devour their neighbors. Never before has world opinion been so solidly united against aggression.

Nor, until the invasion of Kuwait, has the United States been opposed to Iraq. In the past, the United States has helped Iraq import billions of dollars worth of food and other commodities. And the war with Iran would not have ended 2 years ago without U.S. support and sponsorship in the United Nations.

Saddam Hussein tells you the occupation of Kuwait will benefit the poorer nations of the world. In fact, the occupation of Kuwait is helping no one and is now hurting you, the Iraqi people, and countless others of the world's poor. Instead of acquiring new oil wealth by annexing Kuwait, this misguided act of aggression will cost Iraq over $20 billion a year in lost oil revenues. Because of Iraq's aggression, hundreds of thousands of innocent foreign workers are fleeing Kuwait and Iraq. They are stranded on Iraq's borders, without shelter, without food, without medicine, with no way home. These refugees are suffering, and this is shameful.

But even worse, others are being held hostage in Iraq and Kuwait. Hostage-taking punishes the innocent and separates families. It is barbaric. It will not work, and it will not affect my ability to make tough decisions.

I do not want to add to the suffering of the people of Iraq. The United Nations has put binding sanctions in place not to punish the Iraqi people but as a peaceful means to convince your leadership to withdraw from Kuwait. That decision is in the hands of Saddam Hussein.

The pain you now experience is a direct result of the path your leadership has chosen. When Iraq returns to the path of peace, when Iraqi troops withdraw from Kuwait, when that country's rightful government is restored, when all foreigners held against their will are released, then, and then alone, will the world end the sanctions.

Perhaps your leaders do not appreciate the strength of the forces united against them. Let me say clearly: There is no way Iraq can win. Ultimately, Iraq must withdraw from Kuwait.

No one—not the American people, not this President—wants war. But there are times when a country—when all countries who value the principles of sovereignty and independence—must stand against aggression. As Americans, we're slow to raise our hand in anger and eager to explore every peaceful means of settling our disputes; but when we have exhausted every alternative, when conflict is thrust upon us, there is no nation on Earth with greater resolve or stronger steadiness of purpose.

The actions of your leadership have put Iraq at odds with the world community. But while those actions have brought us to the brink of conflict, war is not inevitable. It is still possible to bring this crisis to a peaceful end.

When we stand with Kuwait against aggression, we stand for a principle well understood in the Arab world. Let me quote the words of one Arab leader, Saddam Hussein himself: "An Arab country does not have the right to occupy another Arab country. God forbid, if Iraq should deviate from the right path, we would want Arabs to send their armies to put things right. If Iraq should become intoxicated by its power and move to overwhelm another Arab State, the Arabs would be right to deploy their armies to check it."

Those are the words of your leader, Saddam Hussein, spoken on November 28, 1988, in a speech to Arab lawyers. Today, 2 years later, Saddam has invaded and occupied a member of the United Nations and the Arab League. The world will not allow this aggression to stand. Iraq must get out of Kuwait for the sake of principle, for the sake of peace, and for the sake of the Iraqi people.

26. Remarks Announcing a Federal Budget Agreement September 30, 1990

The President. I am joined here today by the bipartisan leadership of the Congress—the Speaker of the House, the Senate majority leader, the Senate Republican leader, the President pro tem of the Senate, the House majority leader, and the House Republican leader—and other members of the budget summit negotiating group. The bipartisan leaders and I have reached agreement on the Federal budget. Over 5 years, it would reduce the projected deficit by $500 billion; that is half a trillion dollars.

The agreement has five basic parts. First, it would save $9 billion in entitlement and mandatory programs.

Second, it would produce $182 billion in discretionary program savings. These savings would come principally from defense. In the next 3 years, defense outlays would be reduced by $67 billion, relative to the projected baseline. All other discretionary programs would be firmly capped at the projected baseline levels; that is, for the next 3 years they would in total be allowed to grow at no more than the inflation rate.

Third, the agreement would increase tax revenues by $4 billion. The largest single increase, single contributor, would be a phased-in increase in the gasoline tax of 5 cents per gallon in the first year and another 5 cents in the following years. I do not welcome any such tax measure, nor do I expect anybody up here does. However, this one does have the virtue not only of contributing to deficit reduction but also, over time, of decreasing America's dependence on foreign oil, an objective whose importance has become increasingly evident in the face of the Iraqi invasion of Kuwait. I am pleased to be able to note that the budget agreement also includes several new incentives to increase domestic exploration and development of oil and gas resources. The combination of these measures should help reduce America's vulnerability to the interruption of supplies of foreign oil imports.

Fourth, the agreement extends the Gramm-Rudman budget discipline for 5 years. In addition, it improves the budget process and substantially strengthens the enforceability of the 5-year budget plan to which we have agreed.

Fifth, this agreement includes important new initiatives to stimulate economic growth: it authorizes new tax incentives for the development of enterprise zones; extends the R&D tax credit; it provides powerful new incentives for productive investment in the kinds of companies that account for most of America's job growth. These incentives include: a new 30-percent credit for R&D; 25-percent deduction for the purchase of new equity; indexing of the basis of new stock in such companies; expansion of expensing of investment in tangible equipment and scientific equipment; a minimum basis rule that encourages investment in new ventures and in companies with high growth potential; and other such incentives.

In addition to these targeted growth incentives I would note that prompt enactment of this entire 5-year deficit reduction package would itself help stimulate long-term economic growth with a half a trillion dollars in real deficit reduction. And let me repeat: The leaders here and I think that these are real deficit reduction figures. Long-term interest rates should be able to come down.

This package should be a strong component of a positive, responsible fiscal and monetary policy. I heartily thank the negotiators who have worked so long and so hard to develop this package. The bipartisan congressional leadership and I have pledged our very best to get this entire package signed into law by October 19th. As any such plan would have to, ours requires that virtually everyone contribute in some way. It is balanced, it is fair, and in my view it is what the United States of America needs at this point in its history. And we are united in our firm determination to see this program enacted.

I do not want to imply that some who have not been in the final negotiations are for every part of this. But I can only speak for my part, and then the top leadership here will speak. But I will simply say: This is priority. This is priority for our nation. This is something that the country is calling out for and world markets are looking for. And so, there will be some tough fights ahead; but I have pledged to the Speaker, to Congressman Gephardt, to Bob Michel on our side, to George Mitchell and Bob Dole and the Senate pro tem leader, Senator Byrd, that I will do everything I can to lay aside partisanship here and to take the case for this deal to the American people in every way I can. Sometimes you don't get it just the way you want, and this is such a time for me, and I expect it's such a time for everybody standing here. But it's time we put the interest of the United States of America first and get this deficit under control.

Mr. Speaker, I am grateful to you, the Democrats, and the Republicans that have seen that the interest of this country come first. Thank you for what you've been doing, and I'd appreciate it if you want to say a few words.

Speaker Foley. Thank you very much, Mr. President. I'll be brief in just echoing what you, yourself, just said, sir, that this is a package that your negotiators and the bipartisan participating negotiators from the House and the Senate—ranking Republican Members, chairmen, and the leadership on both sides—have sought to achieve. It's not going to be easy or simple to obtain the votes that are necessary in both the House and the Senate, the majority of both parties and both bodies, that will have to be found to enact this package—and within the next 3 weeks. But we pledge our efforts with yours to convince our colleagues in the country that this is a strong undergirding of our economic future, our national prosperity, and joint national interest. And in that spirit, we are going to begin today to present to you legislation which will allow the orderly functioning of the Federal Government for the continuation of this next week, in preparing to take the first step to implement this program.

I want to pay a word, if I can, of special thanks to all of my colleagues who have participated in this, and especially to Dick Gephardt, the chairman of these budget negotiations, who, all sides—Republicans and Democrats, Senators and House Members, and you, yourself—have spoken eloquently to his patience and leadership. Thank you, sir, for your involvement and your determination to aid in the process of bringing this package and the interests of the country to final achievement.

The President. Now if I might ask Senator Mitchell and then Senator Dole, Congressman Gephardt, and Congressman Michel to speak.

Senator Mitchell. Thank you, Mr. President. Now comes the hard part. It's one thing to get a budget agreement among ourselves for which all involved should be commended. It's another thing to get the votes to pass it through the House and the Senate. That is a task to which we must now commit ourselves.

This agreement is a compromise. Both sides can accurately say that the agreement includes provisions they don't like. Both sides can also accurately say the agreement doesn't include some provisions they think should be included. Cutting the deficit requires difficult choices. But our nation's economic future requires that we make those choices. We have already debated too long. Now we must act decisively.

Senator Dole. Mr. President, thank you very much. And I want to thank my colleagues and again, particularly Dick Gephardt. The nay-sayers and the nitpickers may have a field day because the easy vote in this case is to find something you don't like and vote no. But in my view, we owe more to the American people than finding fault with what I consider to be a good, positive, solid agreement that, in my view, will help the American economy and demonstrate to the American people, who are sometimes somewhat cynical, that the Congress and the President of the United States can work together, and we can look ahead and we can do the right thing for our country. And so, I would hope that my colleagues—and I speak now to my colleagues—certainly will study this document very carefully, will give it their best effort, and when the roll is called that we'll have a majority of Republicans and Democrats for this outstanding package.

Thank you, Mr. President.

The President. Thank you. Dick?

Representative Gephardt. Thank you, Mr. President. Forty years ago a mountaineer who joined in the first successful climb of Mount Everest explained the success by saying no expedition enjoyed better teamwork. To the Speaker of the House, Congressman Foley; the Senate majority leader, George Mitchell; to the Members of Congress who are here with us on the stage; to the administration and their representatives and the great staffs of all sides who worked so long and so hard with us: You have been heroic as we've made this climb together.

The American people are today asking: Why was this summit necessary, why did it take so long, and what did it achieve? If we are to enact this agreement—and I think we must—these questions must be answered persuasively and honestly. For 10 years we have chosen a course together that has created large deficits and limited our capacity to meet the needs of our people and the demands of a very challenging age. Today, we face a weakened economy and high rates of interest and inflation. Tomorrow, in absence of an agreement, massive across-the-board budget cuts would occur.

The alternative to this agreement is fiscal chaos. To meet our responsibility to America's working families, this summit simply had to succeed. What delayed us for months is what has divided us for a decade. The parties to these talks had—and continue to have—deep disagreements over values, the role of government, and the fairness of our taxes. But we all made compromises in the national interest.

To bring this process to a successful conclusion, all of us—the American people and our national leaders—must accept the responsibilities of the day. And as this debate unfolds I hope this will be said: that we achieved the largest deficit reduction package in our history, that we focused the national debate on whether the tax code will be based on everybody's individual ability to pay. The vital issues—investing in our people, making our nation competitive, and realizing social justice—will rise again on the national agenda, and then enactment of this measure will enable us to confront these important issues successfully in the years to come.

I thank you, Mr. President, and I thank all the members of the summit.

The President. Bob?

Representative Michel. Well, thank you, Mr. President, and my colleagues. I support the package wholeheartedly because I was one of the narrower group that, within the last 10 days or so, made some of the final decisions.

There may be some reservations with respect to some of our other summiteers on the platform. I think probably rightly so because we're making decisions that will reach far out, to 5 years. Everyone is entitled to know exactly what we have wrought in the printed word. As a matter of fact, I wasn't privy to the last few lines that were written early this morning.

But, on balance, when I look at what we were originally faced with—and here we are refraining from increasing marginal rates and not touching the unmentionable out there, Social Security—and then to have the incentives for growth that I see here and the expenditure caps over the next several years that are real and enforceable, it seems to me that in the alternative so much better that we've done what we've done, and hopefully that in the ensuing days we'll be able to sell a majority of the Members on both sides of the aisle in both Houses to give us the affirmative vote that I think is so imperative that we have before we adjourn.

Thank you, Mr. President.

The President. Well, thank you all very much. And let me conclude by singling out the White House team by name: Secretary Brady and Dick Darman, John Sununu, who stayed in there day in and day out with the Members of Congress. In my view they did an outstanding job, too.

You know, Senator Bentsen said in this meeting—I hope it's not betraying a confidence—that he hoped that I would do my level-best to take this case to the American people. And I told him inside what I want to repeat here: I will do everything I can to generate support from the American people for this compromise.

I am convinced that the American people do not want to see us continue to mortgage the futures of their children and their grandchildren. And as I say, compromise is the word here. All of us have had to do that. But to Senator Bentsen I said in there, and I would say it here publicly: I want the American people to understand how important we feel this is. I want them to understand this is real. It is not a phony smoke-and-mirrors deficit-cutting program. And I will do everything in my power to help the leadership, Republican and Democrat, get this passed in the United States Congress.

Thank you all very much for coming.

27. The President's News Conference on the Federal Budget Crisis October 6, 1990

The President. I just wanted to comment. I know the leaders have been speaking. And I have not yet signed but, within the next couple of minutes, will veto the continuing resolution. We've had good cooperation from the Democrat and Republican leaders. The Congress has got to get on with the people's business. I'd like them to do that business—get a budget resolution—and get it done in the next 24 hours or 48 hours.

But as President, I cannot let the people's business be postponed over and over again. I've jotted down the numbers. There have been three dozen in the last decade—three dozen continuing resolutions—business as usual. And we can't have it. The President can only do this one thing: send that message back and say this is not a time for business as usual. The deficit is too important to the American people.

So, I expressed my appreciation to the Speaker, the majority leader in the Senate, the majority leader in the House, two Republican leaders—thanked them for coming together in a spirit of compromise to get an agreement that I strongly supported. It didn't have everything I wanted in there, but now I'm calling on those who did not vote for it on the Republican side and on the Democratic side to get up with the leadership and send down something that will take care of the people's business once and for all.

I am sorry that I have to do this, but I made very clear that I am not going to be a part of business as usual when we have one deficit after another piling up. Had enough of it, and I think the American people have had enough of it.

Q. What changed your mind, sir?

Q. Mr. Mitchell [House majority leader] came out here a minute ago and said that this served no useful purpose. What useful purpose?

The President. We have a disagreement with him. I think it disciplines the United States Congress, Democrats and Republicans. They're the ones that have to pass this budget, and they ought to get on with it. And the leaders, to their credit, tried. But a lot of

Members think they can get a free shot, right and left. What this message says is: No more business as usual. So, we did have a difference on that particular point. I think both the Speaker and the majority leader did not want me to do this.

But look, let me take you guys back a while. In August I wanted to keep the Congress in. That story was written. And I've listened to the leadership, both Republicans and Democrats; said no, we'll acquiesce—because they said that to keep the Congress here in August will be counterproductive: "Everybody will be angry with you. But the way to get it done is with the discipline of the calendar running after the summer recess."

And so, I acquiesced. I compromised. I gave. I'm not going to do it anymore. I'm very sorry if people are inconvenienced, but I am not going to be a part of business as usual by the United States Congress.

Q. Mr. President, Senator Dole [Republican leader] said that you had agreed to send up a new short-term spending bill that would include spending cuts—a sequester. Could you tell us something about that?

The President. I'm going to stay out of exactly what we're going to do and let the leaders handle the details of this now. It's in the Congress, and I still strongly support the agreement that both Democrat leaders and Republican leaders came down on. And I'll say this: I do think that there's a lot of agreement and good will still existing for that. It's not going to be passed exactly that way. It was defeated. But let's leave the details of negotiation on that to the Congress—starting back in right now. They're going to have to contend with this veto I sent up—and obviously, I want to see that veto sustained.

Q. You say no more business as usual—in one breath you say no more CR's [continuing resolutions], and in the next breath, Dole says there's some CR which is—

The President. Well, if it has some discipline—what I'm saying is, I want to see the system disciplined. If what Bob Dole said is correct—I'll sign one if it puts some discipline on the system. And if it doesn't discipline the system, then I stay with my current position. No, excuse me, I'm glad you brought that up, because I would strongly support that.

Q. Mr. President, the leadership made a strong point in saying that it's the average Americans who are going to be hurt, the Federal workers and so forth. It's not Congressmen but average Americans who are going to be strongly hurt by this.

The President. The average American is smart. The average American knows what's going on, I think. And I think they know that the Congress will continue to kick this can down the road and that they've got to act. I am very sorry for people that are inconvenienced by this or hurt by this. But this is the only device one has for making something happen, and that is to get the Congress to act, to do its business.

Q. Mr. President, you seem to be blaming Congress, but in fact, a lot of their constituents are the ones that urged them to vote against this. They say it's unfair—the burden is unfairly divided, that the poor and the middle class are paying too much. Is it possible that maybe this program that you proposed with the leaders just was not acceptable to the American public?

The President. Well, certain aspects of it might well not have been acceptable to the American public on both the right or the left. But when you're trying to do the country's business, I've discovered you have to compromise from time to time, and that's exactly what I did. Took a few shots in the process,

but it doesn't matter. What matters is, let's move this process ahead now.

But, yes, you're right—some people didn't like one aspect or another. We had Republicans jumping up on our side of the aisle and saying, "I'll vote for it if you change this," or "I don't like this part of it, but if you change that—" And similarly, you've got people that you were quoting that were on the other side.

But at times, one has to come together to do the country's business for the overall good. And these outrageous deficits cannot be permitted to go on and on and on and on. I'm worried about international markets. I'm worried about this country—the opinion that it can't take care of its fiscal business.

And to their leaders' credit, Democrat and Republican, they tried very hard. They failed to get a majority on the Democratic side. And Republican leaders, with the help from this President and all I could bring to bear on it—we failed, because we had people—were looking at one narrow part of the package and not at the overall good. And I am hopeful now that with the urgency this veto brings to bear on the situation, that reasonable people, men and women in the Congress, can come together.

Q. Mr. President, what kind of progress is being made on a new budget resolution? And sources on the Hill are saying that there is growing support for raising the tax rates of the wealthy in exchange, perhaps, for the cuts on premiums for Medicare. But you have opposed that in the past. Are you willing to give on tax rates for the wealthy?

The President. I don't know the answer to your question. They're just going back up now to try. I like the parameters of the other deal wherein I compromise. We've got people—your question reflects the views on the more liberal or left side of the political spectrum—

who raised those questions. We have some on the right side of the political spectrum coming at the process from another way.

Now, I say: Let them go up and negotiate it. This is the business of the Congress. And our people will stay in touch. I won't mislead them. If there's something that's so outrageous I can't accept it, I'll let them know at the beginning so they don't waste their time. But we're flexible. I've already compromised. And I'm not saying that I can't take a look at new proposals. But you've got to put together a majority in the Congress, and that's where the leaders are having great difficulty.

Q. Following up on that, members of your own party dislike the deal so much, how could you and your advisers have misjudged the sentiments of members of your own party?

The President. Because it's easy when you don't have to be responsible for something. It's easy to just get up and say, hey, I've got an election in 3 weeks, and I'm going to stand up against this particular package— Medicare, the taxes, the home heating oil, or the fact there's not enough growth or not enough incentive. Any individual Member can do that. Maybe it plays well at home. The President and the leadership of both Houses have to be responsible for the overall good of the country, have to make something happen. I can't get it done just my way. I don't control both Houses of Congress. I'd love to think that that luxury would come my way someday, but it hasn't. Therefore, we've had to compromise. So, I will keep trying in that spirit—that cooperative, positive spirit.

But when it comes to the discipline that comes from saying, "I'm sorry, no more business as usual," that's where I can stand up. I don't need a consultation to do that. I've got plenty of advice on one side of that

question and the other. But I am absolutely convinced this is right.

Even those who are inconvenienced by this are going to say, thank God, we'll get the American people's business of getting this deficit under control done. That's my objective. I think every parent out there who sees his kid's future being mortgaged by the outrageous deficit, sees a shaky economy that's being affected by prolonging these deliberations, will be grateful in the long run. In the meantime, we've got to take a little heat.

Q. Mr. President, the budget resolution that failed is one that you worked hard for. Despite the fact that you gave a national televised speech, despite the fact that your popularity is very high—and you failed to sway even a majority of votes in your own party. Does that concern you, and do you think this is a major setback for your Presidency?

The President. No, I don't think that at all. But I do think—yes, it concerns me. I'd like everybody to do it exactly the way I want, but it doesn't work that way. So, now we have to use a little discipline—

Q. Mr. President—

The President.—nice guy stuff, and we'll try. It's a tough decision, it's not an easy decision I've made, but it is the right decision. So, I'm disappointed they didn't do it my way. But I'm in here to do what is best for the country; and what is best for the country is to get this deficit under control, to get this economy moving again, and to see people at jobs, not out on some welfare line. And that's what's at stake here—economic soundness of the United States.

We've got a lot of things going on in the world, and a strong economy is vital to what I want to see achieved in this country. So, you have to take some hits. I mean, you don't get it done exactly your own way.

But I read these speculative stories. Tomorrow, there's going to be another vote. Tomorrow, somebody else will move the previous question or second the motion, or some committee chairman will jump up and say, hey, what about me—my little empire is being invaded here. And I'll say, hey, the President's the guy that has to look at the overall picture.

I can understand Congressmen doing that. But we came together on a deal. We worked for it. Everybody had a chance to posture that didn't like it. They have no responsibility. But I feel a certain responsibility to the American people to move something forward here—want a compromise. Now we're going to say: We'll try it this way. No more business as usual. Do not just keep putting off the day of reckoning. And I don't want to be a part of that, and that's why I've had to veto this resolution.

Q. Mr. President, you've talked a lot about discipline today. Do you think the American people on average are willing to accept the discipline of a tough budget?

The President. That's a very good question. And if you look at the vote in the House of Representatives, you might say no. But I think in the final analysis the answer will be yes, because I think we sometimes underestimate the intelligence of the American people. I can see where a Congressman can jump up on a specific spending program that'll help him in his district. I can see when somebody will give you the broad tax speech or help him in his district.

But in the final analysis, what the American people look at is: Do we have an economy in which I can feed my family, where I can have opportunity to work for a living, and where I can put a little aside to educate my kids? And therein lies the problem, because that's what we're working for—is we're trying to get this Federal deficit down.

But I think you raise a good point. I think a lot of these Congressmen can jump up without any responsibility for running the country, or even cooperating with their leaders, and make a point that's very happy for the home folks. But I think that view underestimates the overall intelligence of the American people, whether conservative, whether a guy's working on a factory line someplace, whether he's an investor someplace.

That's why I think this is very important that the Congress now finally come to grips with this.

Q. There's some talk about this special challenge to Civiletti.

Q. Mr. President, it sounds like you're now saying: Hands off. It's up to the congressional leaders to do the negotiating.

The President. They've already started up the road there to go to Congress and start negotiating. But, no, we've made very clear that we're continuing to help. I don't want to mislead them. There are certain things I can accept. There are certain things I can't. So, I think it's very important that our able team, in whom I have total confidence, stay in touch with them.

Q. But not sit at the negotiating table with them?

The President. Oh, I think they'll be there. I think it all depends on what forum. I think there is some feeling, Ann [Ann Devroy, *Washington Post*], that on the part of Members, both Democrats and Republicans—hey, you summiteers handed us a deal. Well, what the heck? I mean, how do you expect to get as far along toward an agreement as we did get? But what I want to do is facilitate it.

And if they want to know where the White House is, fine. If they want the ideas that largely led to an agreement, fine, and I think they will. But we're not going to force our way in. This is the business of the Congress. The American people know that. They know that the President doesn't pass the budget and doesn't vote on all this stuff. It's the Congress who does it.

So, I'm not trying to assign blame. I'm simply saying, we're available. We want to talk—fine. I think both leaders have indicated they wanted to stay in fairly close touch with the White House.

Q. Mr. President, there is some talk of a constitutional challenge to Civiletti on the bill that the Attorney General's opinion is not sufficient to run the Government, and that violates section 7 of the Constitution.

The President. I haven't heard anything about that.

Q. Mr. President, are you going to cancel your campaign schedule next week if this impasse is not resolved?

The President. I don't know. I've got to cancel everything that has to do with government, I guess. Maybe that's a good chance to get out there in the political process.

Q. How long can you hold out? How long can you let the Government stay shut down before you decide to toss—

The President. Watch and learn.

Q. How long do you think the Government can stay shut before—

The President. It's not a question of how long I can take it; it's how long the Congress can take it. But Congress is where the action is. It's the Congress that has to pass this in the House and in the Senate. That's where the action is. They've postponed this tough

decision as I've mentioned—how many— 30-some times. And we just can't have it. The American people are saying, "I want something done about this." That's where the focus will be.

So, I don't think it's a question of taking heat here or these guys marching out here about honking their horns on taxes. They know I don't like taxes. You get some other guy in Washington out here with a little placard, demonstrating—something about the government employees—we've been supporters of the government employees. But we cannot have business as usual.

The American people—I don't know about inside the beltway, but outside they are fed up with business as usual, and so am I. I wish I had total control so we could do it exactly my way, but we don't. So, I've compromised. Now we're prepared to say, I'm not going to accept a resolution that just postpones it. I've told you I tried that approach.

I tried it in August. Let everybody go home on vacation when I had some good, sound advice I probably should have taken: Make the Congress stay in August. And I listened to the leaders, and they said: "Oh, please don't do that. It will be counterproductive." Now they're saying to me: "Please don't veto this. It will be counterproductive." When do the American people have a say? They want to see this deficit under control. And I don't have many weapons here as President, but one is the veto. When I do it, cast it on principle, I hope it is supported.

Q. What's happened to the prestige—

Q. If Dole sends up another CR, if the Congress sends up a CR with sequestration, when could that happen? Do you have some timeframe?

The President. I don't know.

Q. Could it happen the next couple of days, sir?

The President. Oh, yes, absolutely. It could happen this afternoon.

Q. It could happen this afternoon?

The President. Sure. Whether we—together? I'm not that certain. Perhaps it's a little over-simplification because they're telling me there are some difficult problems right and left, both sides. But, no, they're going right back to negotiating. Let's hope it does. That's the way to serve the constituents.

Q. If it came up this afternoon, sir, would you sign it this afternoon?

The President. It depends what it is. I'll be around.

Q. You have vetoed the CR?

The President. Yes—well, I haven't actually signed it, but I've got to rush right in there now and do that and send it up to the Hill. They know that they've——
    Last question.

Q. Why did you change your mind?

Q. What's all this done to the prestige and influence of you and your office?

The President. Well, I think it will demonstrate that there is some power in the Presidency to compel the Congress to do something, and I think that's good.

Q. You are vetoing, though?

The President. Oh, yes. It hasn't been vetoed yet, but I need a typewriter in there to get it done. By the time we finish this press conference that has gone longer than I thought, it'll—probably all typed up.

Q. Might you trade the bubble for capital gains now? Do you foresee that as a compromise?

The President. The negotiators in the Congress have a lot of flexibility. I remain in

a flexible frame of mind. Certain things I can accept and can't. But I'd like to think that now those who postured on one side or another with no responsibility will join the leaders, Republican and Democrat, and say: Hey, we've got a responsibility to the overall good here. We can no longer just give a speech. We've got to pitch in and come together. And that's what my pitch is.

    And that's why I'm doing it and doing this veto—saying, hey, no more business as usual. And I think people understand that sometimes a President has to make a difficult decision. So, I don't worry about the prestige. I was elected to do what—in a case like this—what I think is best and in the national interest. And that's exactly what I'm doing.

    Thank you all very much.

28. Message to the Senate Returning without Approval the Civil Rights Act of 1990
October 22, 1990

To the Senate of the United States:
    I am today returning without my approval S. 2104, the "Civil Rights Act of 1990." I deeply regret having to take this action with respect to a bill bearing such a title, especially since it contains certain provisions that I strongly endorse.

    Discrimination, whether on the basis of race, national origin, sex, religion, or disability, is worse than wrong. It is a fundamental evil that tears at the fabric of our society, and one that all Americans should and must oppose. That requires rigorous enforcement of existing antidiscrimination laws. It also requires vigorously promoting new measures such as this year's Americans with Disabilities Act, which for the first time adequately protects persons with disabilities against invidious discrimination.

One step that the Congress can take to fight discrimination right now is to act promptly on the civil rights bill that I transmitted on October 20, 1990. This accomplishes the stated purpose of S. 2104 in strengthening our Nation's laws against employment discrimination. Indeed, this bill contains several important provisions that are similar to provisions in S. 2104:

Both shift the burden of proof to the employer on the issue of "business necessity" in disparate impact cases.

Both create expanded protections against on-the-job racial discrimination by extending 42 U.S.C. 1981 to the performance as well as the making of contracts.

Both expand the right to challenge discriminatory seniority systems by providing that suit may be brought when they cause harm to plaintiffs.

Both have provisions creating new monetary remedies for the victims of practices such as sexual harassment. (The Administration bill allows equitable awards up to $150,000 under this new monetary provision, in addition to existing remedies under Title VII.)

Both have provisions ensuring that employers can be held liable if invidious discrimination was a motivating factor in an employment decision.

Both provide for plaintiffs in civil rights cases to receive expert witness fees under the same standards that apply to attorneys' fees.

Both provide that the Federal Government, when it is a defendant under Title VII, will have the same obligation to pay interest to compensate for delay in payment as a nonpublic party. The filing period in such actions is also lengthened.

Both contain a provision encouraging the use of alternative dispute resolution mechanisms.

The congressional majority and I are on common ground regarding these important provisions. Disputes about other, controversial provisions in S. 2104 should not be allowed to impede the enactment of these proposals.

Along with the significant similarities between my Administration's bill and S. 2104, however, there are crucial differences. Despite the use of the term "civil rights" in the title of S. 2104, the bill actually employs a maze of highly legalistic language to introduce the destructive force of quotas into our Nation's employment system. Primarily through provisions governing cases in which employment practices are alleged to have unintentionally caused the disproportionate exclusion of members of certain groups, S. 2104 creates powerful incentives for employers to adopt hiring and promotion quotas. These incentives are created by the bill's new and very technical rules of litigation, which will make it difficult for employers to defend legitimate employment practices. In many cases, a defense against unfounded allegations will be impossible. Among other problems, the plaintiff often need not even show that any of the employer's practices caused a significant statistical disparity. In other cases, the employer's defense is confined to an unduly narrow definition of "business necessity" that is significantly more restrictive than that established by the Supreme Court in Griggs and in two decades of subsequent decisions. Thus, unable to defend legitimate practices in court, employers will be driven to adopt quotas in order to avoid liability.

Proponents of S. 2104 assert that it is needed to overturn the Supreme Court's Wards Cove decision and restore the law that had existed since the Griggs case in 1971. S. 2104, however, does not in fact codify Griggs or the Court's subsequent decisions prior to Wards Cove. Instead, S. 2104 engages in a sweeping rewrite of two decades of Supreme Court jurisprudence, using language that appears in no decision of the Court and that is contrary to principles acknowledged even by Justice Stevens' dissent in Wards Cove: "The opinion in Griggs made it clear that a neutral practice that operates to exclude minorities is nevertheless lawful if it serves a valid business purpose."

I am aware of the dispute among lawyers about the proper interpretation of certain critical language used in this portion of S. 2104. The very fact of this dispute suggests that the bill is not codifying the law developed by the Supreme Court in Griggs and subsequent cases. This debate, moreover, is a sure sign that S. 2104 will lead to years—perhaps decades—of uncertainty and expensive litigation. It is neither fair nor sensible to give the employers of our country a difficult choice between using quotas and seeking a clarification of the law through costly and very risky litigation.

S. 2104 contains several other unacceptable provisions as well. One section unfairly closes the courts, in many instances, to individuals victimized by agreements, to which they were not a party, involving the use of quotas. Another section radically alters the remedial provisions in Title VII of the Civil Rights Act of 1964, replacing measures designed to foster conciliation and settlement with a new scheme modeled on a tort system widely acknowledged to be in a state of crisis. The bill also contains a number of provisions that will create unnecessary and inappropriate incentives for litigation. These include unfair retroactivity rules; attorney's fee provisions that will discourage settlements; unreasonable new statutes of limitation; and a "rule of construction" that will make it extremely difficult to know how courts can be expected to apply the law. In order to assist the Congress regarding legislation in this area, I enclose herewith a memorandum from the Attorney General explaining in detail the defects that make S. 2104 unacceptable.

Our goal and our promise has been equal opportunity and equal protection under the law. That is a bedrock principle from which we cannot retreat. The temptation to support a bill—any bill—simply because its title includes the words "civil rights" is very strong. This impulse is not entirely bad. Presumptions have too often run the other way, and our Nation's history on racial questions cautions against complacency. But when our efforts, however well intentioned, result in quotas, equal opportunity is not advanced but thwarted. The very commitment to justice and equality that is offered as the reason why this bill should be signed requires me to veto it.

Again, I urge the Congress to act on my legislation before adjournment. In order truly to enhance equal opportunity, however, the Congress must also take action in several related areas. The elimination of employment discrimination is a vital element in achieving the American dream, but it is not enough. The absence of discrimination will have little concrete meaning unless jobs are available and the members of all groups have the skills and education needed to qualify for those jobs. Nor can we expect that our young people will work hard to prepare for the future if they grow up in a climate of violence, drugs, and hopelessness.

In order to address these problems, attention must be given to measures that promote accountability and parental choice in the schools; that strengthen the fight against violent criminals and drug dealers in our inner cities; and that help to combat poverty and inadequate housing. We need initiatives that will empower individual Americans and enable them to reclaim control of their lives, thus helping to make our country's promise of opportunity a reality for all. Enactment of such initiatives, along with my Administration's civil rights bill, will achieve real advances for the cause of equal opportunity.

29. Statement on Signing the Omnibus Budget Reconciliation Act of 1990 November 5, 1990

Today I am signing H.R. 5835, the "Omnibus Budget Reconciliation Act of 1990," the center-piece of the largest deficit reduction package in history and an important measure for ensuring America's long-term economic growth. This Act is the result of long, hard work by the Administration and the Congress. No one got everything he or she wanted, but the end product is a compromise that merits enactment.

H.R. 5835, and the discretionary spending caps associated with it, will achieve nearly $500 billion—almost half a trillion dollars—in deficit reduction over the next 5 years. Over 70 percent of that deficit reduction derives from outlay reductions; less than 30 percent from revenue increases. In addition, the Act enacts significant budget process reforms to ensure that the agreement is fulfilled and that budgetary discipline is extended and strengthened.

Entitlement Reforms. The Act provides for the most comprehensive and substantial reform of mandatory "entitlement" programs ever—about $100 billion in savings from restructuring and reforms in the following major programs:

Farm programs;

Federal housing programs;

Student loan programs;

Veterans programs;

Postal subsidies;

Federal employee benefits; and Medicare.

Discretionary Program Caps. The Act establishes 5-year caps on overall discretionary spending that will result in savings of over $180 billion. To keep domestic and international spending from growing any faster than infla-

tion, the Act creates new automatic "mini-sequesters." The Act also provides for an orderly defense reduction without threatening national security.

Energy Security. The Act provides incentives for energy conservation and for exploration and development of domestic energy resources.

Social Security. Social Security is fully protected and taken off-budget.

Enforcement and Process Reform. The Act contains the toughest enforcement system ever. The Gramm-Rudman-Hollings sequester process is extended and strengthened with caps, mini-sequesters, and a new "pay-as-you-go" system.

Credit Reform. The Act implements a new Federal accounting and budgeting system to expose and limit previously hidden (and rapidly growing) liabilities.

Tax Changes. The Act includes a tax rate cut from 33 percent to 31 percent for about 3.5 million middle and upper-middle income taxpayers and an overall decrease in taxes paid by those with incomes under $20,000. There are higher excise taxes on luxury items and limitations on itemized deductions and the personal exemption for higher income taxpayers. The total net tax changes comprise 28 percent of the deficit reduction package.

This Act creates the conditions that should allow future interest rates to be lower than they would be otherwise. Lower interest rates can benefit the entire economy. They can mean more housing starts; more Americans driving new cars; reductions in mortgage payments for homeowners; more long-term investment; greater productivity; and increased numbers of jobs.

In signing this landmark Act, I pledge the continuing best efforts of my Administration to maintain not only the letter, but the spirit of the new fiscal order for the Federal Government that is embodied in this agreement.

H.R. 5835 also contains child care provisions, strongly supported by this Administration, that will enlarge the opportunities of parents to obtain the child care they desire, including care that is provided by sectarian institutions if the parents so choose. The largest portion of this new child care program will come from tax credits to people—as requested by the Administration. In addition, a Child Care and Development Block Grant program includes provisions for the issuance of child care certificates or vouchers that would enable parents to exercise their own judgment as to what type of child care best suits the particular needs of their own child.

I note my understanding of these child care provisions and sign the bill based on that understanding, as follows:

First, I understand that the definition of child care certificates in section 658P(2) ensures that States may not restrict parental choice by limiting the range of providers from whom parents may seek child care, using certificates as payment, and that such certificates shall not be considered to be grants or contracts.

Second, section 658N(a)(1)(B) specifically permits sectarian organizations that are child care providers to require that all of their employees adhere to the religious tenets and teachings of the organization and comply with rules forbidding the use of drugs or alcohol. As I understand it, the term "sectarian organization" in this provision includes religious organizations generally.

Third, as used in sections 658N(a)(2)(B) and 658N(a)(3)(B), the term "organization" means not only the particular provider but also a broader association with which that provider may be identified.

Finally, all of the provisions of the Child Care and Development Block Grant program will be interpreted in light of the requirements of the establishment and free exercise clauses of the First Amendment.

I would also note certain constitutional difficulties in other titles of the Omnibus Budget Reconciliation Act. In particular, section 4117 of the Act requires the Secretary of Health and Human Services, in certain conditions, to treat the States of Nebraska and Oklahoma as single fee schedule areas for purposes of determining the adjusted historical payment basis and the fee schedule amount for physicians' services furnished on or after January 1, 1992. Such treatment is made to depend on the Secretary's receiving written expressions of support for treatment of the State as a single fee schedule area from each member of the congressional delegation from the State and from organizations representing urban and rural physicians in the State. This provision requires the Secretary to base a substantive decision on the allocation of Federal benefits on the statements of members of congressional delegations and other persons who are not appointed by the President. Therefore, it must be understood either (1) as an attempt to vest significant authority to execute Federal law in those persons, in which case it violates the Appointments Clause, Article II, section 2; see *Buckley v. Valeo*, 424 U.S. 1 (1975); or (2) as an attempt to confer lawmaking power on individual members of the Congress and others, in which case it violates Article I, section 7; see *INS v. Chadha*, 462 U.S. 919 (1983). Accordingly, this requirement is without legal force, and I am so instructing the Secretary of Health and Human Services. I am also instructing the Attorney General and the Secretary of Health and Human Services to prepare remedial legislation to amend this section for submission to the next session of the Congress, so that the Act can be brought into compliance with the Constitution's requirements.

Further, the Constitution empowers the President to "recommend to [Congress] such Measures as he shall judge necessary and expedient." U.S. Const. Art. II, Sec. 3. Several sections of the Act raise constitutional difficulties by appearing or purporting to impose requirements that the executive branch submit legislative proposals of a predetermined kind. The executive branch has consistently treated provisions of this type as advisory rather than as mandatory, and to avoid a constitutional question will so construe the provisions at issue here.

30. The President's News Conference on the Persian Gulf Crisis
November 8, 1990

The President. I have a brief statement, and I'd be glad to take a couple of questions and then turn to Secretary Cheney, who will take some questions. And then he will go over to the Pentagon for more of an indepth briefing.

On August 6th, in response to the unprovoked Iraqi invasion of Kuwait, I ordered the deployment of U.S. military forces to Saudi Arabia and the Persian Gulf to deter further Iraqi aggression and to protect our interests in the region. What we've done is right, and I'm happy to say that most Members of Congress and the majority of Americans agree.

Before the invasion in August, we had succeeded in the struggle for freedom in Eastern Europe, and we'd hopefully begun a new era that offered the promise of peace. Following the invasion, I stated that if history had taught us any lesson it was that we must resist aggression or it would destroy our freedom. Just ask the people of Kuwait and the foreign nationals in hiding there and the staffs of the remaining Embassies who have experienced the horrors of Iraq's illegal occupation, its systematic dismantling of Kuwait, and its abuse of Kuwaitis and other citizens.

The world community also must prevent an individual clearly bent on regional domination from establishing a chokehold on the world's economic lifeline. We're seeing global economic stability and growth already at risk as, each day, countries around the world pay dearly for Saddam Hussein's [President of Iraq] aggression.

From the very beginning, we and our coalition partners have shared common political goals: the immediate, complete, and unconditional withdrawal of Iraqi forces from Kuwait; restoration of Kuwait's legitimate government; protection of the lives of citizens held hostage by Iraq both in Kuwait and Iraq; and restoration of security and stability in the Persian Gulf region.

To achieve these goals, we and our allies have forged a strong diplomatic, economic, and military strategy to force Iraq to comply with these objectives. The framework of this strategy is laid out in 10 United Nations resolutions, overwhelmingly supported by the United Nations Security Council. In 3 months, the U.S. troop contribution to the multinational force in Saudi Arabia has gone from 10,000 to 230,000 as part of Operation Desert Shield. General Schwarzkopf [commander of the U.S. forces in the Persian Gulf] reports that our forces, in conjunction with other coalition forces, now have the capability to defend successfully against any further Iraqi aggression.

After consultation with King Fahd [of Saudi Arabia] and our other allies, I have today directed the Secretary of Defense to increase the size of U.S. forces committed to Desert Shield to ensure that the coalition has an adequate offensive military option should that be necessary to achieve our common goals. Toward this end, we will continue to discuss the possibility of both additional allied force contributions and appropriate United Nation actions.

Iraq's brutality, aggression, and violations of international law cannot be allowed to succeed. Secretary Baker has been consulting with our key partners in the coalition. He's met with the Amirs of Bahrain ['Isa bin Salman Al Khalifa] and Kuwait [Jabir al-Ahmad al-Jabir al-Sabah], King Fahd, President Mubarak [of Egypt], as well as the Chinese Foreign Minister [Qian Qichen], President Ozal [of Turkey], [Soviet] Foreign Minister Shevardnadze, President Gorbachev. He also will be meeting with Prime Minister Thatcher [of the United Kingdom] and President Mitterrand [of France]. I've been heartened by Jim's appraisal of the strong international solidarity and determination to ensure that Iraq's aggression does not stand and is not rewarded.

But right now, Kuwait is struggling for survival. And along with many other nations, we've been called upon to help. The consequences of our not doing so would be incalculable because Iraq's aggression is not just a challenge to the security of Kuwait and other Gulf nations but to the better world that we all have hoped to build in the wake of the Cold War. And therefore, we and our allies cannot and will not shirk our responsibilities. The state of Kuwait must be restored, or no nation will be safe and the promising future we anticipate will indeed be jeopardized.

Let me conclude with a word to the young American GI's deployed in the Gulf. We are proud of each and every one of you. I know you miss your loved ones and want to know when you'll be coming home. We won't leave you there any longer than necessary. I want every single soldier out of there as soon as possible. And we're all grateful for your continued sacrifice and your commitment.

Now, with no further ado, I'd be glad to take a couple of questions. And when I leave, Dick, take some questions and then go over to the Pentagon.

Q. Mr. President, it sounds like you're going to war. You have moved from a defensive position to an offensive position, and you have not said how many more troops you are sending or, really, why.

The President. Well, I've said why right now. And I hope it's been very clear to the American people.

Q. Are there new reasons that have moved this posture?

The President. No, it's just continuing to do what we feel is necessary to complete our objectives, to fulfill our objectives, that have been clearly stated.

Q. Well, are you going to war?

The President. I would love to see a peaceful resolution to this question, and that's what I wanted.

Q. What made the change from the defense to offense?

The President. I would like to see a peaceful solution to this question. I think Saddam Hussein should fully, without condition, comply to the U.N. resolutions. And if this movement of force is what convinces him, so much the better.

Q. You said last week that the sanctions haven't had the impact that you wanted. Some members of the coalition are urging a go-slow approach. The President of Egypt says you've got to wait 2 or 3 months before you judge whether the sanctions have worked. Are you willing to wait that long?

The President. Wait for what?

Q. To see if the sanctions have worked?

The President. I think from talking to Jim Baker and recently to President Mubarak that we are in total sync with him. But I hope that the sanctions will work within a 2-month period. But I don't think we've got a difference with Egypt on this at all, Terry [Terence Hunt, Associated Press].

Q. The question is how long are you willing to give the sanctions?

The President. Well, I can't tell you how long. If I knew, I certainly wouldn't want to signal that to Saddam Hussein.

Q. Prime Minister Thatcher said yesterday that if, indeed, Saddam doesn't withdraw from Kuwait that you and the allies will use force. I haven't heard you say that before. You've talked about wanting to retain the option of war, but would you use force?

The President. Well, I don't want to say what I will or will not do. But certainly, I noted what Prime Minister Thatcher said—one of the strongest members of this coalition. And she's an eloquent spokesman for her views and speaks in a way that shows that we're all together. So, I have not ruled out the use of force at all, and I think that's evident by what we're doing here today.

Q. Sir, can I just follow that up by going back to the speech you gave at the Pentagon back in August, when you talked about oil, protecting Middle East oil reserves, and you talked about American jobs, in fact the American way of life being endangered. Yet when you went out on the campaign trail, you seemed to shy away from oil. You said demonstrators don't seem to understand that we're not going to go to war for oil. But that was one of the things you talked about. And in fact, isn't oil part of the American national interest? Isn't that a main reason we're there?

The President. It is a part of it, but it is not the main reason—or I'd say, a main reason. The main reason we're there is to set back aggression, to see that aggression is unrewarded. My argument with some of the protesters is that they seem to suggest that oil is the sole reason that we are involved in this enormous commitment. And that is simply not correct. There's a lot of other interests, and the restoration of the security and stability in the Persian Gulf region clearly relates to the world's economic interest. I'm not denying that, and I'm not backing away from the fact that all the Western world has real interest in that. But my argument with those people is that they are missing the point. The point is: It is the aggression against Kuwait that has caused this coalition to come together as it has.

Q. Do you feel that you are free to take offensive action without any kind of U.N. resolution authorizing it?

The President. Yes, we have authority. But we've been great believers in going to the United Nations. I think one of the major successes has been the ability to have world opinion totally on our side because of U.N. action. The peacekeeping function of the United Nations has indeed been rejuvenated by the actions of the Security Council.

Way in the back, because I've been accused by a distinguished senior reporter of not getting into the back of the room, so I'd like to rectify that.

Q. Mr. President, do you yet have the support you need in order to secure an additional resolution from the U.N. Security Council to explicitly authorize the use of force? Do you now have sufficient support on the Security Council to get that?

The President. I would say that the Baker mission is—what it is about is consultation.

That subject will be discussed in some ways, I'm sure, but that's not why he's there. We're talking about a wide array of issues, and so I'd say we have not tried to specifically poll the other 14 members of the Security Council along those lines. So, I can't answer whether we would or not.

Q. If I may follow: Has any country told you they would block such a resolution?

The President. Some may have said such a thing, but it's not been brought to my attention at all. And again, I think I'd know if that were the case. But I don't think so.

Q. Mr. President, it would seem that the situation at the U.S. Embassy in Kuwait is crucial to the future of the overall situation in the Gulf. What is the latest there? What is the situation with their food and water supplies? And do you have any plan in the works to resupply them?

The President. I think it's unconscionable to try to starve people out and to isolate them from food and supplies of all kinds, and that's exactly what's going on. In terms of how long they can survive, I'm not sure I could give you a specific answer, but I believe the answer would be a few weeks, something of that nature.

Q. Are there plans to resupply them when they run out or—

The President. Well, if there were, given the hostile environment in which these people are living, it would be unproductive to discuss it.

Q. Mr. President, what has happened in the last 2 weeks that has led you to put now an offensive force into Saudi Arabia?

The President. Well, we have not only offensive but defensive forces there already. And what leads me to do this is just because I believe, upon the advice of our able Secre-

tary of Defense and others, that this is in the best security interests of our people that are there and of the coalition. I think it is just a guarantee of the safety of all, and I think it sends a very strong signal—another strong signal—to Saddam Hussein that we are very, very serious about seeing the United Nations resolutions complied to in their entirety, without any kind of watering down.

Q. Would you say that we're in a critical phase now between a peaceful solution and a possible armed conflict?

The President. I wouldn't phrase it that way.

Q. Mr. President, the longer that you wait and the longer that no action is taken in Kuwait, the less and less there seems to be of Kuwait. What's the point of waiting if there's not going to be anything left of that country when you finally decide to go in?

The President. Well, I've told you that I would like to feel that Saddam Hussein would come to his senses and comply under economic pressure with the sanctions that have been taken in the United Nations and with the objectives. I would like to think the economic sanctions would compel him to do that which he has been unwilling to do. Regrettably, he keeps reiterating his view that this is not Kuwait but Province 19, and that is unacceptable to the United States and to our partners. So, I think we're giving these sanctions time to work. We're giving world opinion time to mobilize and impress on him that we're all serious. But now we're moving up our forces for the reasons I've given you.

Q. But there might not be much left of Kuwait.

The President. Well, that worries me. It worries me very much, as do the lives of those who have been forced into hiding by his brutality and his violation of international law. Of course, it concerns me deeply. And I've spoken about that, the dismantling of Kuwait and the systematic brutality that is exercised against the citizens of Kuwait. And as each day goes by it's worse. So, I take your point that it's—I guess it's your point—that it's a very bad situation. But I just keep reiterating my determination to see our objectives fulfilled here.

Q. Sir, on your consultation that your Secretary of State's doing now in Moscow, could you just spell out for us what your understanding is as of today with Mikhail Gorbachev on the use of force?

The President. Well, I talked to Jim Baker—it's a very timely question because I talked to him, just before coming in here, from Moscow; and he had a long series of consultations and discussions there with the Foreign Minister and with Mr. Gorbachev. I am convinced, from what the Secretary has told me, that we are on the same wavelength in terms of the objectives that I spelled out here. But I can't go in with you into what the Soviet position will be on the use of force. I don't think they've been asked to send forces. Is that—maybe I missed the question.

Q. Mr. Shevardnadze on the record today said that they, too, would not rule out the use of force, while they still wanted a peaceful solution. Does that at least help you send the kind of signal to Saddam Hussein that you're also trying to send here?

The President. I think it is very helpful. But I think the signal of solidarity between the United States and the Soviet Union and the rest of the Security Council has already gone out. But, no, I think that it is very helpful to have a position like that stated and restated, because that's the way the whole world feels. And it is good to have this solid front

between ourselves and the Soviet Union. And I think Jim felt that he had a constructive visit with the Chinese Foreign Minister. And he's looking forward to his meetings with President Mitterrand and Prime Minister Thatcher in the next couple of days. But his trip has been extraordinarily helpful in sending that signal of solidarity and determination on the part of those that are involved here, strong determination.

I'm going to take a couple more, and then let Dick take some questions.

Q. I understand that we're going to be getting that briefing and General Powell [Chairman of the Joint Chiefs of Staff] will speak later, but can you please give us some sense of the numbers and types of reinforcements that you're sending to the Gulf? And do you believe that this will be the final deployment? We keep seeing the numbers ratcheting up and hearing that this should be sufficient to do the job.

The President. Let me simply say we're talking about substantial numbers. I will defer, with your permission, of course, to the Secretary of Defense and the Chairman of the Joint Chiefs, who will be able to help more than I will on the details of this move. But I can't say whether—after this is completed—whether there will be anything else done or not. I mean, I am still hopeful that Saddam Hussein will get the message that he is not going to prevail and that he has to get out of Kuwait without condition, and that the rulers have to come back and that the stability of the Gulf must be guaranteed. So, I would simply leave it there and, if you would, let the defense experts take the rest of it.

Q. As you have consulted—if I may follow up—on this deployment and, in fact, on the military situation overall with the other countries involved in the multinational forces, there have been complaints, observations out of Israel that, were there to be offensive action, there needs to be coordination or some sort of chain of command involving the Israelis, too, where they may end up being involved. To what extent are you communicating with the Israelis, and to what extent do you envision any role or possible role for the Israelis should this come to war?

The President. I think the whole world knows that the United States has a very special relationship with Israel—a strong relationship. I think we are in close touch with the key players there in terms of our objectives, and I think they have conducted themselves regarding all of this very well, indeed. But I am not going to discuss any more details than that. But I feel that we're on a good wavelength there. We had some differences, obviously.

One and one, and then I've got to go.

Q. Mr. President, to follow up on Wyatt's [Wyatt Andrews, CBS News] question: After Foreign Minister Shevardnadze made his comments today, President Gorbachev seemed to say that it was too early to talk about the use of force. Are the Soviets sending us mixed signals—

The President. No—

Q.—or is this just an indication that—like President Mubarak made earlier in the week—that some of our allies want more time to try to find a diplomatic solution before use of force?

The President. I don't get the feeling we're getting any mixed signals at all from the Soviets, particularly after I've talked to Jim Baker. I know there was some feeling there were mixed signals because of Mr. Primakov's [Soviet Presidential Council mem-

ber] mission, but upon the completion of that, I think people recognize that we are still very much in agreement with the Soviet on matters as it relates to the Gulf. It's good, Ann [Ann Devroy, *Washington Post*], and it's strong. And I just can't worry about that point at all, after talking to Jim Baker.

Q. Does Jim Baker have an explanation for the difference between Mr. Shevardnadze's remarks and Mr. Gorbachev's remarks today?

The President. No. He made the point that we were together with them, and that was not discussed—any differences.

Last one, on the aisle.

Q. Mr. President, I have a very important question to ask you.

The President. Only if he'll yield. You know, in the Congress, they say, "I yield to the distinguished lady from Texas." But if he don't want to yield, I'm sorry; I've recognized the gentleman.

Q. Some members of your administration—

Q. I don't expect him to yield, but I would expect you to. [Laughter]

The President. Sarah [Sarah McClendon, McClendon News], I've disappointed you so much.

Please go ahead.

Q. Some members of your administration are convinced that Saddam Hussein will not move until the 11th hour, or 11:59, when he is totally convinced that you are about to use military force. Why is he not convinced now, do you think? How do you expect that you will be able to get to that 11:59 minute?

The President. Well, I'm not sure I accept the 11:59 analogy. But if there has ever been any doubt in his mind about the seriousness of the West and of the other Arab countries and of the coalition—put it that way—I think that those doubts are rapidly being dispelled. You see, I do believe that when he moved into Kuwait I think he felt he was going to have just an easy time of it and that the world would not rise up in arms against the aggression. I think he miscalculated there. I believe he thought he could just take over Kuwait and then there would be a lot of talk and discussion and he would be able to turn Kuwait, a sovereign nation, a member of the Arab League, a member of the United Nations, into Province 19.

And the United States, along with other countries, said no, we're not going to permit this aggression to stand, because an unchecked aggression today could lead to some horrible world conflagration tomorrow. And so, I think there's where the miscalculation originally was. I find it hard to believe that today, November 8th, he does not understand that he's up against a determined, unprecedented alliance.

And so, I hope that he is rethinking his position of unyielding opposition to the will of the rest of the world. And I would think that when he surveys the force that's there, the force that's going, what other countries are doing in this regard, he will recognize that he is up against just a foe that he can't possibly manage militarily. Margaret Thatcher touched on that yesterday, and I thought she did it very well, indeed. And so, if nothing else happens, I'm convinced that this move will show him how serious we are as a significant partner in this coalition. I think it's a good thing, and it will have strong support from others around the world. Let's hope he comes to his senses and does tomorrow that which he should have done weeks ago, because this aggression simply will not stand.

Now, Dick, it's all yours.

31. Radio Address to the Nation on the Persian Gulf Crisis January 5, 1991

As the new year begins, new challenges unfold—challenges to America and the future of our world. Simply put: 1990 saw Iraq invade and occupy Kuwait. Nineteen ninety-one will see Iraq withdraw—preferably by choice; by force, if need be. It is my most sincere hope 1991 is a year of peace. I've seen the hideous face of war and counted the costs of conflict in friends lost. I remember this all too well, and have no greater concern than the well-being of our men and women stationed in the Persian Gulf. True, their morale is sky-high. True, if they are called upon to fight the aggressors, they will do their job courageously, professionally and, in the end, decisively. There will be no more Vietnams.

But we should go the extra mile before asking our service men and women to stand in harm's way. We should, and we have. The United Nations, with the full support of the United States, has already tried to peacefully pressure Iraq out of Kuwait, implementing economic sanctions and securing the condemnation of the world in the form of no less than 12 resolutions of the U.N. Security Council.

This week, we've taken one more step. I have offered to have Secretary of State James Baker meet with Iraqi Foreign Minister Tariq 'Aziz in Switzerland. Yesterday, we received word that Iraq has accepted our offer to meet in Geneva. This will not be secret diplomacy at work. Secretary Baker will restate, in person, a message for Saddam Hussein: Withdraw from Kuwait unconditionally and immediately, or face the terrible consequences.

Eleven days from today, Saddam Hussein will either have met the United Nations deadline for a full and unconditional withdrawal, or he will have once again defied the civilized world. This is a deadline for Saddam Hussein to comply with the United Nations resolution, not a deadline for our own Armed Forces. Still, time is running out. It's running out because each day that passes brings real costs.

Saddam already poses a strategic threat to the capital cities of Egypt, Saudi Arabia, Turkey, Israel, and Syria, as well as our own men and women in the Gulf region. In fact, Saddam has used chemical weapons of mass destruction against innocent villagers, his own people. Each day that passes brings Saddam Hussein further on the path to developing biological and nuclear weapons and the missiles to deliver them. If Saddam corners the world energy market, he can then finance further aggression, terror, and blackmail. Each day that passes increases Saddam's worldwide threat to democracy.

The struggling newborn democracies of Eastern Europe and Latin America already face a staggering challenge in making the transition to a free market. But the added weight of higher oil prices is a crushing burden they cannot afford. And our own economy is suffering, suffering the effects of higher oil prices and lower growth stemming from Saddam's aggression.

Each day that passes, Saddam's forces also fortify and dig in deeper into Kuwait. We risk paying a higher price in the most precious currency of all—human life—if we give Saddam more time to prepare for war. And each day that passes is another day of fear, suffering, and terror for the people of Kuwait, many who risked their lives to shelter and hide Americans from Iraqi soldiers. As the Amir of Kuwait said to our Vice President just last week, those who advocate waiting longer for sanctions to work do not have to live under such brutal occupation.

As I have discussed with Members of Congress just 2 days ago and in our many other consultations, economic sanctions are taking a toll, but they are still not forcing Saddam out of Kuwait. Nor do we know when or even if they will be successful. As a result, America and her partners in this unprecedented coalition are sharing the burden of this important mission, and we are ready to use force to defend a new order emerging among the nations of the world—a world of sovereign nations living in peace.

We have seen too often in this century how quickly any threat to one becomes a threat to all. At this critical moment in history, at a time the cold war is fading into the past, we cannot fail. At stake is not simply some distant country called Kuwait. At stake is the kind of world we will inhabit.

Last Thanksgiving, I broke bread with some of our men and women on the front lines. They understand why we are in Saudi Arabia, and what we may have to do. I witnessed courage unfazed by the closeness of danger and determination undiminished by the harsh desert sun. These men and women are America's finest. We owe each of them our gratitude and full support. That is why we must all stand together, not as Republicans or Democrats, conservatives or liberals, but as Americans.

32. Address to the Nation Announcing Allied Military Action in the Persian Gulf January 16, 1991

Just 2 hours ago, allied air forces began an attack on military targets in Iraq and Kuwait. These attacks continue as I speak. Ground forces are not engaged.

This conflict started August 2d when the dictator of Iraq invaded a small and helpless neighbor. Kuwait—a member of the Arab League and a member of the United Nations—

was crushed; its people, brutalized. Five months ago, Saddam Hussein started this cruel war against Kuwait. Tonight, the battle has been joined.

This military action, taken in accord with United Nations resolutions and with the consent of the United States Congress, follows months of constant and virtually endless diplomatic activity on the part of the United Nations, the United States, and many, many other countries. Arab leaders sought what became known as an Arab solution, only to conclude that Saddam Hussein was unwilling to leave Kuwait. Others traveled to Baghdad in a variety of efforts to restore peace and justice. Our Secretary of State, James Baker, held an historic meeting in Geneva, only to be totally rebuffed. This past weekend, in a last-ditch effort, the Secretary-General of the United Nations went to the Middle East with peace in his heart—his second such mission. And he came back from Baghdad with no progress at all in getting Saddam Hussein to withdraw from Kuwait.

Now the 28 countries with forces in the Gulf area have exhausted all reasonable efforts to reach a peaceful resolution—have no choice but to drive Saddam from Kuwait by force. We will not fail.

As I report to you, air attacks are underway against military targets in Iraq. We are determined to knock out Saddam Hussein's nuclear bomb potential. We will also destroy his chemical weapons facilities. Much of Saddam's artillery and tanks will be destroyed. Our operations are designed to best protect the lives of all the coalition forces by targeting Saddam's vast military arsenal. Initial reports from General Schwarzkopf are that our operations are proceeding according to plan.

Our objectives are clear: Saddam Hussein's forces will leave Kuwait. The legitimate government of Kuwait will be restored to its rightful place, and Kuwait will once again be free.

Iraq will eventually comply with all relevant United Nations resolutions, and then, when peace is restored, it is our hope that Iraq will live as a peaceful and cooperative member of the family of nations, thus enhancing the security and stability of the Gulf.

Some may ask: Why act now? Why not wait? The answer is clear: The world could wait no longer. Sanctions, though having some effect, showed no signs of accomplishing their objective. Sanctions were tried for well over 5 months, and we and our allies concluded that sanctions alone would not force Saddam from Kuwait.

While the world waited, Saddam Hussein systematically raped, pillaged, and plundered a tiny nation, no threat to his own. He subjected the people of Kuwait to unspeakable atrocities—and among those maimed and murdered, innocent children.

While the world waited, Saddam sought to add to the chemical weapons arsenal he now possesses, an infinitely more dangerous weapon of mass destruction—a nuclear weapon. And while the world waited, while the world talked peace and withdrawal, Saddam Hussein dug in and moved massive forces into Kuwait.

While the world waited, while Saddam stalled, more damage was being done to the fragile economies of the Third World, emerging democracies of Eastern Europe, to the entire world, including to our own economy.

The United States, together with the United Nations, exhausted every means at our disposal to bring this crisis to a peaceful end. However, Saddam clearly felt that by stalling and threatening and defying the United Nations, he could weaken the forces arrayed against him.

While the world waited, Saddam Hussein met every overture of peace with open contempt. While the world prayed for peace, Saddam prepared for war.

I had hoped that when the United States Congress, in historic debate, took its resolute action, Saddam would realize he could not prevail and would move out of Kuwait in accord with the United Nation resolutions. He did not do that. Instead, he remained intransigent, certain that time was on his side.

Saddam was warned over and over again to comply with the will of the United Nations: Leave Kuwait, or be driven out. Saddam has arrogantly rejected all warnings. Instead, he tried to make this a dispute between Iraq and the United States of America.

Well, he failed. Tonight, 28 nations—countries from 5 continents, Europe and Asia, Africa, and the Arab League—have forces in the Gulf area standing shoulder to shoulder against Saddam Hussein. These countries had hoped the use of force could be avoided. Regrettably, we now believe that only force will make him leave.

Prior to ordering our forces into battle, I instructed our military commanders to take every necessary step to prevail as quickly as possible, and with the greatest degree of protection possible for American and allied service men and women. I've told the American people before that this will not be another Vietnam, and I repeat this here tonight. Our troops will have the best possible support in the entire world, and they will not be asked to fight with one hand tied behind their back. I'm hopeful that this fighting will not go on for long and that casualties will be held to an absolute minimum.

This is an historic moment. We have in this past year made great progress in ending the long era of conflict and cold war. We have before us the opportunity to forge for ourselves and for future generations a new world order—a world where the rule of law, not the law of the jungle, governs the conduct of nations. When we are successful—and we will be—we have a real chance at this new world order, an order in which a credible United Nations can use its peacekeeping role to fulfill the promise and vision of the U.N.'s founders.

We have no argument with the people of Iraq. Indeed, for the innocents caught in this conflict, I pray for their safety. Our goal is not the conquest of Iraq. It is the liberation of Kuwait. It is my hope that somehow the Iraqi people can, even now, convince their dictator that he must lay down his arms, leave Kuwait, and let Iraq itself rejoin the family of peace-loving nations.

Thomas Paine wrote many years ago: "These are the times that try men's souls." Those well-known words are so very true today. But even as planes of the multinational forces attack Iraq, I prefer to think of peace, not war. I am convinced not only that we will prevail but that out of the horror of combat will come the recognition that no nation can stand against a world united, no nation will be permitted to brutally assault its neighbor.

No President can easily commit our sons and daughters to war. They are the Nation's finest. Ours is an all-volunteer force, magnificently trained, highly motivated. The troops know why they're there. And listen to what they say, for they've said it better than any President or Prime Minister ever could.

Listen to Hollywood Huddleston, Marine lance corporal. He says, "Let's free these people, so we can go home and be free again." And he's right. The terrible crimes and tortures committed by Saddam's henchmen against the innocent people of Kuwait are an affront to mankind and a challenge to the freedom of all.

Listen to one of our great officers out there, Marine Lieutenant General Walter Boomer. He said: "There are things worth fighting for. A world in which brutality and lawlessness are allowed to go unchecked isn't the kind of world we're going to want to live in."

Listen to Master Sergeant J. P. Kendall of the 82d Airborne: "We're here for more than just the price of a gallon of gas. What we're doing is going to chart the future of the world for the next 100 years. It's better to deal with this guy now than 5 years from now."

And finally, we should all sit up and listen to Jackie Jones, an Army lieutenant, when she says, "If we let him get away with this, who knows what's going to be next?"

I have called upon Hollywood and Walter and J. P. and Jackie and all their courageous comrades-in-arms to do what must be done. Tonight, America and the world are deeply grateful to them and to their families. And let me say to everyone listening or watching tonight: When the troops we've sent in finish their work, I am determined to bring them home as soon as possible.

Tonight, as our forces fight, they and their families are in our prayers. May God bless each and every one of them, and the coalition forces at our side in the Gulf, and may He continue to bless our nation, the United States of America.

33. Address before a Joint Session of the Congress on the State of the Union January 29, 1991

Mr. President and Mr. Speaker and Members of the United States Congress:

I come to this House of the people to speak to you and all Americans, certain that we stand at a defining hour. Halfway around the world, we are engaged in a great struggle in the skies and on the seas and sands. We know why we're there: We are Americans, part of something larger than ourselves. For two centuries, we've done the hard work of freedom. And tonight, we lead the world in facing down a threat to decency and humanity.

What is at stake is more than one small country; it is a big idea: a new world order, where diverse nations are drawn together in common cause to achieve the universal aspirations of mankind—peace and security, freedom, and the rule of law. Such is a world worthy of our struggle and worthy of our children's future.

The community of nations has resolutely gathered to condemn and repel lawless aggression. Saddam Hussein's unprovoked invasion—his ruthless, systematic rape of a peaceful neighbor—violated everything the community of nations holds dear. The world has said this aggression would not stand, and it will not stand. Together, we have resisted the trap of appeasement, cynicism, and isolation that gives temptation to tyrants. The world has answered Saddam's invasion with 12 United Nations resolutions, starting with a demand for Iraq's immediate and unconditional withdrawal, and backed up by forces from 28 countries of 6 continents. With few exceptions, the world now stands as one.

The end of the cold war has been a victory for all humanity. A year and a half ago, in Germany, I said that our goal was a Europe whole and free. Tonight, Germany is united. Europe has become whole and free, and America's leadership was instrumental in making it possible.

Our relationship to the Soviet Union is important, not only to us but to the world. That relationship has helped to shape these and other historic changes. But like many other nations, we have been deeply concerned by the violence in the Baltics, and we have communicated that concern to the Soviet leadership. The principle that has guided us is simple: Our objective is to help the Baltic peoples achieve their aspirations, not to punish the Soviet Union. In our recent discussions with the Soviet leadership we have been given representations which, if fulfilled, would result in the withdrawal of some Soviet forces, a reopening of dialog with the Republics, and a move away from violence.

We will watch carefully as the situation develops. And we will maintain our contact with the Soviet leadership to encourage continued commitment to democratization and reform. If it is possible, I want to continue to build a lasting basis for U.S.-Soviet cooperation—for a more peaceful future for all mankind.

The triumph of democratic ideas in Eastern Europe and Latin America and the continuing struggle for freedom elsewhere all around the world all confirm the wisdom of our nation's founders. Tonight, we work to achieve another victory, a victory over tyranny and savage aggression.

We in this Union enter the last decade of the 20th century thankful for our blessings, steadfast in our purpose, aware of our difficulties, and responsive to our duties at home and around the world. For two centuries, America has served the world as an inspiring example of freedom and democracy. For generations, America has led the struggle to preserve and extend the blessings of liberty. And today, in a rapidly changing world, American leadership is indispensable. Americans know that leadership brings burdens and sacrifices. But we also know why the hopes of humanity turn to us. We are Americans; we have a unique responsibility to do the hard work of freedom. And when we do, freedom works.

The conviction and courage we see in the Persian Gulf today is simply the American character in action. The indomitable spirit that is contributing to this victory for world peace and justice is the same spirit that gives us the power and the potential to meet our toughest challenges at home. We are resolute and resourceful. If we can selflessly confront the evil for the sake of good in a land so far away, then surely we can make this land all that it should be. If anyone tells you that America's best days are behind her, they're looking the wrong way.

Tonight I come before this House and the American people with an appeal for renewal. This is not merely a call for new government initiatives; it is a call for new initiatives in government, in our communities, and from every American to prepare for the next American century.

America has always led by example. So, who among us will set the example? Which of our citizens will lead us in this next American century? Everyone who steps forward today—to get one addict off drugs, to convince one troubled teenager not to give up on life, to comfort one AIDS patient, to help one hungry child.

We have within our reach the promise of a renewed America. We can find meaning and reward by serving some higher purpose than ourselves, a shining purpose, the illumination of a Thousand Points of Light. And it is expressed by all who know the irresistible force of a child's hand, of a friend who stands by you and stays there, a volunteer's generous gesture, an idea that is simply right.

The problems before us may be different, but the key to solving them remains the same. It is the individual—the individual who steps forward. And the state of our Union is the union of each of us, one to the other—the sum of our friendships, marriages, families, and communities.

We all have something to give. So, if you know how to read, find someone who can't. If you've got a hammer, find a nail. If you're not hungry, not lonely, not in trouble, seek out someone who is. Join the community of conscience. Do the hard work of freedom. And that will define the state of our Union.

Since the birth of our nation, "We the People" has been the source of our strength. What government can do alone is limited, but the potential of the American people knows no limits.

We are a nation of rock-solid realism and clear-eyed idealism. We are Americans. We are the Nation that believes in the future. We are the Nation that can shape the future. And we've begun to do just that, by strengthening the power and choice of individuals and families.

Together, these last 2 years, we've put dollars for child care directly in the hands of parents instead of bureaucracies; unshackled the potential of Americans with disabilities; applied the creativity of the marketplace in the service of the environment, for clean air; and made home ownership possible for more Americans.

The strength of a democracy is not in bureaucracy. It is in the people and their communities. In everything we do, let us unleash the potential of our most precious resource—our citizens, our citizens themselves. We must return to families, communities, counties, cities, States, and institutions of every kind the power to chart their own destiny and the freedom and opportunity provided by strong economic growth. And that's what America is all about.

I know that tonight, in some regions of our country, people are in genuine economic distress. And I hear them. Earlier this month, Kathy Blackwell, of Massachusetts, wrote me about what can happen when the economy slows down, saying, "My heart is aching, and I think that you should know your people out here are hurting badly."

I understand, and I'm not unrealistic about the future. But there are reasons to be optimistic about our economy. First, we don't have to fight double-digit inflation. Second, most industries won't have to make big cuts in production because they don't have big inventories piled up. And third, our exports are running solid and strong. In fact, American businesses are exporting at a record rate.

So, let's put these times in perspective. Together, since 1981, we've created almost 20 million jobs, cut inflation in half, and cut interest rates in half. And yes, the largest peacetime economic expansion in history has been temporarily interrupted. But our economy is still over twice as large as our closest competitor.

We will get this recession behind us and return to growth soon. We will get on our way to a new record of expansion and achieve the competitive strength that will carry us into the next American century. We should focus our efforts today on encouraging economic growth, investing in the future, and giving power and opportunity to the individual.

We must begin with control of Federal spending. That's why I'm submitting a budget that holds the growth in spending to less than the rate of inflation. And that's why, amid all the sound and fury of last year's budget debate, we put into law new, enforceable spending caps, so that future spending debates will mean a battle of ideas, not a bidding war.

Though controversial, the budget agreement finally put the Federal Government on a pay-as-you-go plan and cut the growth of debt by nearly $500 billion. And that frees funds for saving and job-creating investment.

Now, let's do more. My budget again includes tax-free family savings accounts; penalty-free withdrawals from IRA's for first-time home buyers; and to increase jobs and growth, a reduced tax for long-term capital gains.

I know there are differences among us—[laughter]—about the impact and the effects of a capital gains incentive. So tonight, I'm asking the congressional leaders and the Federal Reserve to cooperate with us in a study, led by Chairman Alan Greenspan, to sort out our technical differences so that we can avoid a return to unproductive partisan bickering.

But just as our efforts will bring economic growth now and in the future, they must also be matched by long-term investments for the next American century. That requires a forward-looking plan of action, and that's exactly what we will be sending to the Congress. We've prepared a detailed series of proposals that include: a budget that promotes investment in America's future—in children, education, infrastructure, space, and high technology; legislation to achieve excellence in education, building on the partnership forged with the 50 Governors at the education summit, enabling parents to choose their children's schools and helping to make America number one in math and science; a blueprint for a new national highway system, a critical investment in our transportation infrastructure; a research and development agenda that includes record levels of Federal investment, and a permanent tax credit to strengthen private R&D and to create jobs; a comprehensive national energy strategy that calls for energy conservation and efficiency, increased development, and greater use of alternative fuels; a banking reform plan to bring America's financial system into the 21st century so that our banks remain safe and secure and can continue to make job-creating loans for our factories, our businesses, and home buyers.

You know, I do think there has been too much pessimism. Sound banks should be making sound loans now, and interest rates should be lower, now.

In addition to these proposals, we must recognize that our economic strength depends on being competitive in world markets. We must continue to expand American exports. A successful Uruguay round of world trade negotiations will create more real jobs and more real growth for all nations. You and I know that if the playing field is level, America's workers and farmers can out-work, out-produce anyone, anytime, anywhere.

And with a Mexican free trade agreement and our Enterprise for the Americas Initiative, we can help our partners strengthen their economies and move toward a free trade zone throughout this entire hemisphere.

The budget also includes a plan of action right here at home to put more power and opportunity in the hands of the individual. And that means new incentives to create jobs in our inner cities by encouraging investment through enterprise zones. It also means tenant control and ownership of public housing. Freedom and the power to choose should not be the privilege of wealth. They are the birthright of every American.

Civil rights are also crucial to protecting equal opportunity. Every one of us has a responsibility to speak out against racism, big-otry, and hate. We will continue our vigorous enforcement of existing statutes, and I will once again press the Congress to strengthen the laws against employment discrimination without resorting to the use of unfair preferences.

We're determined to protect another fundamental civil right: freedom from crime and the fear that stalks our cities. The Attorney General will soon convene a crime summit of our nation's law enforcement officials. And to help us support them, we need tough crime control legislation, and we need it now.

And as we fight crime, we will fully implement our national strategy for combating drug abuse. Recent data show that we are making progress, but much remains to be done. We will not rest until the day of the dealer is over, forever.

Good health care is every American's right and every American's responsibility. And so, we are proposing an aggressive program of new prevention initiatives—for infants, for children, for adults, and for the elderly—to promote a healthier America and to help keep costs from spiraling.

It's time to give people more choice in government by reviving the ideal of the citizen politician who comes not to stay but to serve. And one of the reasons that there is so much support across this country for term limitations is that the American people are increasingly concerned about big-money influence in politics. So, we must look beyond the next election to the next generation. And the time has come to put the national interest above the special interest and to totally eliminate political action committees. And that would truly put more competition in elections and more power in the hands of individuals.

And where power cannot be put directly in the hands of the individual, it should be moved closer to the people, away from Washington. The Federal Government too often treats government programs as if they are of Washington, by Washington, and for Washington.

Once established, Federal programs seem to become immortal. It's time for a more dynamic program life cycle. Some programs should increase. Some should decrease. Some should be terminated. And some should be consolidated and turned over to the States.

My budget includes a list of programs for potential turnover totaling more than $20 billion. Working with Congress and the Governors, I propose we select at least $15 billion in such programs and turn them over to the States in a single consolidated grant, fully funded, for flexible management by the States.

The value, the value of this turnover approach is straightforward. It allows the Federal Government to reduce overhead. It allows States to manage more flexibly and more efficiently. It moves power and decisionmaking closer to the people. And it reinforces a theme of this administration: appreciation and encouragement of the innovative powers of States as laboratories.

This nation was founded by leaders who understood that power belongs in the hands of people. And they planned for the future. And so must we, here and all around the world.

As Americans, we know that there are times when we must step forward and accept our responsibility to lead the world away from the dark chaos of dictators, toward the brighter promise of a better day. Almost 50 years ago we began a long struggle against aggressive totalitarianism. Now we face another defining hour for America and the world.

There is no one more devoted, more committed to the hard work of freedom than every soldier and sailor, every marine, airman, and coastguardsman, every man and woman now serving in the Persian Gulf. Oh, how they deserve—[applause]—and what a fitting tribute to them.

You see—what a wonderful, fitting tribute to them. Each of them has volunteered, volunteered to provide for this nation's defense, and now they bravely struggle to earn for America,

for the world, and for future generations a just and lasting peace. Our commitment to them must be equal to their commitment to their country. They are truly America's finest.

The war in the Gulf is not a war we wanted. We worked hard to avoid war. For more than 5 months we—along with the Arab League, the European Community, the United Nations—tried every diplomatic avenue. U.N. Secretary-General Pérez de Cuellar; Presidents Gorbachev, Mitterrand, Ozal, Mubarak, and Bendjedid; Kings Fahd and Hassan; Prime Ministers Major and Andreotti—just to name a few—all worked for a solution. But time and again, Saddam Hussein flatly rejected the path of diplomacy and peace.

The world well knows how this conflict began and when: It began on August 2d, when Saddam invaded and sacked a small, defenseless neighbor. And I am certain of how it will end. So that peace can prevail, we will prevail. [Applause] Thank you.

Tonight I am pleased to report that we are on course. Iraq's capacity to sustain war is being destroyed. Our investment, our training, our planning—all are paying off. Time will not be Saddam's salvation.

Our purpose in the Persian Gulf remains constant: to drive Iraq out of Kuwait, to restore Kuwait's legitimate government, and to ensure the stability and security of this critical region.

Let me make clear what I mean by the region's stability and security. We do not seek the destruction of Iraq, its culture, or its people. Rather, we seek an Iraq that uses its great resources not to destroy, not to serve the ambitions of a tyrant, but to build a better life for itself and its neighbors. We seek a Persian Gulf where conflict is no longer the rule, where the strong are neither tempted nor able to intimidate the weak.

Most Americans know instinctively why we are in the Gulf. They know we had to stop Saddam now, not later. They know that this brutal dictator will do anything, will use any weapon, will commit any outrage, no matter how many innocents suffer.

They know we must make sure that control of the world's oil resources does not fall into his hands, only to finance further aggression. They know that we need to build a new, enduring peace, based not on arms races and confrontation but on shared principles and the rule of law.

And we all realize that our responsibility to be the catalyst for peace in the region does not end with the successful conclusion of this war.

Democracy brings the undeniable value of thoughtful dissent, and we've heard some dissenting voices here at home—some, a handful, reckless; most responsible. But the fact that all voices have the right to speak out is one of the reasons we've been united in purpose and principle for 200 years.

Our progress in this great struggle is the result of years of vigilance and a steadfast commitment to a strong defense. Now, with remarkable technological advances like the Patriot missile, we can defend against ballistic missile attacks aimed at innocent civilians.

Looking forward, I have directed that the SDI program be refocused on providing protection from limited ballistic missile strikes, whatever their source. Let us pursue an SDI program that can deal with any future threat to the United States, to our forces overseas, and to our friends and allies.

The quality of American technology, thanks to the American worker, has enabled us to successfully deal with difficult military conditions and help minimize precious loss of life. We have given our men and women the very best. And they deserve it.

We all have a special place in our hearts for the families of our men and women serving in the Gulf. They are represented here tonight by Mrs. Norman Schwarzkopf. We are all very grateful to General Schwarzkopf and to all those serving with him. And I might also rec-

ognize one who came with Mrs. Schwarzkopf: Alma Powell, the wife of the distinguished Chairman of the Joint Chiefs. And to the families, let me say our forces in the Gulf will not stay there one day longer than is necessary to complete their mission.

The courage and success of the RAF pilots, of the Kuwaiti, Saudi, French, the Canadians, the Italians, the pilots of Qatar and Bahrain— all are proof that for the first time since World War II, the international community is united. The leadership of the United Nations, once only a hoped-for ideal, is now confirming its founders' vision.

I am heartened that we are not being asked to bear alone the financial burdens of this struggle. Last year, our friends and allies provided the bulk of the economic costs of Desert Shield. And now, having received commitments of over $40 billion for the first 3 months of 1991, I am confident they will do no less as we move through Desert Storm.

But the world has to wonder what the dictator of Iraq is thinking. If he thinks that by targeting innocent civilians in Israel and Saudi Arabia, that he will gain advantage, he is dead wrong. If he thinks that he will advance his cause through tragic and despicable environmental terrorism, he is dead wrong. And if he thinks that by abusing the coalition prisoners of war he will benefit, he is dead wrong.

We will succeed in the Gulf. And when we do, the world community will have sent an enduring warning to any dictator or despot, present or future, who contemplates outlaw aggression.

The world can, therefore, seize this opportunity to fulfill the long-held promise of a new world order, where brutality will go unrewarded and aggression will meet collective resistance.

Yes, the United States bears a major share of leadership in this effort. Among the nations of the world, only the United States of America has both the moral standing and the means to back it up. We're the only nation on this Earth that could assemble the forces of peace. This is the burden of leadership and the strength that has made America the beacon of freedom in a searching world.

This nation has never found glory in war. Our people have never wanted to abandon the blessings of home and work for distant lands and deadly conflict. If we fight in anger, it is only because we have to fight at all. And all of us yearn for a world where we will never have to fight again.

Each of us will measure within ourselves the value of this great struggle. Any cost in lives—any cost—is beyond our power to measure. But the cost of closing our eyes to aggression is beyond mankind's power to imagine. This we do know: Our cause is just; our cause is moral; our cause is right.

Let future generations understand the burden and the blessings of freedom. Let them say we stood where duty required us to stand. Let them know that, together, we affirmed America and the world as a community of conscience.

The winds of change are with us now. The forces of freedom are together, united. We move toward the next century more confident than ever that we have the will at home and abroad to do what must be done—the hard work of freedom.

34. Address to the Nation Announcing Allied Military Ground Action in the Persian Gulf
February 23, 1991

Good evening. Yesterday, after conferring with my senior national security advisers, and following extensive consultations with our coalition partners, Saddam Hussein was given one last chance—set forth in very explicit terms—to do what he should have done more than 6 months ago: withdraw from Kuwait without

condition or further delay, and comply fully with the resolutions passed by the United Nations Security Council.

Regrettably, the noon deadline passed without the agreement of the Government of Iraq to meet demands of United Nations Security Council Resolution 660, as set forth in the specific terms spelled out by the coalition to withdraw unconditionally from Kuwait. To the contrary, what we have seen is a redoubling of Saddam Hussein's efforts to destroy completely Kuwait and its people.

I have therefore directed General Norman Schwarzkopf, in conjunction with coalition forces, to use all forces available including ground forces to eject the Iraqi army from Kuwait. Once again, this was a decision made only after extensive consultations within our coalition partnership.

The liberation of Kuwait has now entered a final phase. I have complete confidence in the ability of the coalition forces swiftly and decisively to accomplish their mission.

Tonight, as this coalition of countries seeks to do that which is right and just, I ask only that all of you stop what you are doing and say a prayer for all the coalition forces, and especially for our men and women in uniform who this very moment are risking their lives for their country and for all of us.

May God bless and protect each and every one of them. And may God bless the United States of America. Thank you very much.

35. Address to the Nation on the Suspension of Allied Offensive Combat Operations in the Persian Gulf
February 27, 1991

Kuwait is liberated. Iraq's army is defeated. Our military objectives are met. Kuwait is once more in the hands of Kuwaitis, in control of their own destiny. We share in their joy, a joy tempered only by our compassion for their ordeal.

Tonight the Kuwaiti flag once again flies above the capital of a free and sovereign nation. And the American flag flies above our Embassy.

Seven months ago, America and the world drew a line in the sand. We declared that the aggression against Kuwait would not stand. And tonight, America and the world have kept their word.

This is not a time of euphoria, certainly not a time to gloat. But it is a time of pride: pride in our troops; pride in the friends who stood with us in the crisis; pride in our nation and the people whose strength and resolve made victory quick, decisive, and just. And soon we will open wide our arms to welcome back home to America our magnificent fighting forces.

No one country can claim this victory as its own. It was not only a victory for Kuwait but a victory for all the coalition partners. This is a victory for the United Nations, for all mankind, for the rule of law, and for what is right.

After consulting with Secretary of Defense Cheney, the Chairman of the Joint Chiefs of Staff, General Powell, and our coalition partners, I am pleased to announce that at midnight tonight eastern standard time, exactly 100 hours since ground operations commenced and 6 weeks since the start of Desert Storm, all United States and coalition forces will suspend offensive combat operations. It is up to Iraq whether this suspension on the part of the coalition becomes a permanent cease-fire.

Coalition political and military terms for a formal cease-fire include the following requirements:

Iraq must release immediately all coalition prisoners of war, third country nationals, and the remains of all who have fallen. Iraq must release all Kuwaiti detainees. Iraq also must inform Kuwait authorities of the location and nature of all land and sea mines. Iraq must comply fully with all relevant United Nations Security Council resolutions. This includes a rescinding of Iraq's August decision to annex Kuwait and acceptance in principle of Iraq's responsibility to pay compensation for the loss, damage, and injury its aggression has caused.

The coalition calls upon the Iraqi Government to designate military commanders to meet within 48 hours with their coalition counterparts at a place in the theater of operations to be specified to arrange for military aspects of the cease-fire. Further, I have asked Secretary of State Baker to request that the United Nations Security Council meet to formulate the necessary arrangements for this war to be ended.

This suspension of offensive combat operations is contingent upon Iraq's not firing upon any coalition forces and not launching Scud missiles against any other country. If Iraq violates these terms, coalition forces will be free to resume military operations.

At every opportunity, I have said to the people of Iraq that our quarrel was not with them but instead with their leadership and, above all, with Saddam Hussein. This remains the case. You, the people of Iraq, are not our enemy. We do not seek your destruction. We have treated your POW's with kindness. Coalition forces fought this war only as a last resort and look forward to the day when Iraq is led by people prepared to live in peace with their neighbors.

We must now begin to look beyond victory and war. We must meet the challenge of securing the peace. In the future, as before, we will consult with our coalition partners. We've already done a good deal of thinking and planning for the postwar period, and Secretary Baker has already begun to consult with our coalition partners on the region's challenges. There can be, and will be, no solely American answer to all these challenges. But we can assist and support the countries of the region and be a catalyst for peace. In this spirit, Secretary Baker will go to the region next week to begin a new round of consultations.

This war is now behind us. Ahead of us is the difficult task of securing a potentially historic peace. Tonight though, let us be proud of what we have accomplished. Let us give thanks to those who risked their lives. Let us never forget those who gave their lives. May God bless our valiant military forces and their families, and let us all remember them in our prayers.

Good night, and may God bless the United States of America.

36. Address before a Joint Session of the Congress on the Cessation of the Persian Gulf Conflict
March 6, 1991

Speaker Foley. Mr. President, it is customary at joint sessions for the Chair to present the President to the Members of Congress directly and without further comment. But I wish to depart from tradition tonight and express to you on behalf of the Congress and the country, and through you to the members of our Armed Forces, our warmest congratulations on the brilliant victory of the Desert Storm Operation.

Members of the Congress, I now have the high privilege and distinct honor of presenting to you the President of the United States.

The President. Mr. President. And Mr. Speaker, thank you, sir, for those very generous words spoken from the heart about the wonderful performance of our military.

Members of Congress, 5 short weeks ago I came to this House to speak to you about the state of the Union. We met then in time

of war. Tonight, we meet in a world blessed by the promise of peace.

From the moment Operation Desert Storm commenced on January 16th until the time the guns fell silent at midnight 1 week ago, this nation has watched its sons and daughters with pride, watched over them with prayer. As Commander in Chief, I can report to you our armed forces fought with honor and valor. And as President, I can report to the Nation aggression is defeated. The war is over.

This is a victory for every country in the coalition, for the United Nations. A victory for unprecedented international cooperation and diplomacy, so well led by our Secretary of State, James Baker. It is a victory for the rule of law and for what is right.

Desert Storm's success belongs to the team that so ably leads our Armed Forces: our Secretary of Defense and our Chairman of the Joint Chiefs, Dick Cheney and Colin Powell. And while you're standing—[laughter]— this military victory also belongs to the one the British call the "Man of the Match"—the tower of calm at the eye of Desert Storm— General Norman Schwarzkopf.

And recognizing this was a coalition effort, let us not forget Saudi General Khalid, Britain's General de la Billiere, or General Roquejeoffre of France, and all the others whose leadership played such a vital role. And most importantly, most importantly of all, all those who served in the field.

I thank the Members of this Congress— support here for our troops in battle was overwhelming. And above all, I thank those whose unfailing love and support sustained our courageous men and women: I thank the American people.

Tonight, I come to this House to speak about the world—the world after war. The recent challenge could not have been clearer. Saddam Hussein was the villain; Kuwait, the victim. To the aid of this small country came nations from North America and Europe, from Asia and South America, from Africa and the Arab world, all united against aggression. Our uncommon coalition must now work in common purpose: to forge a future that should never again be held hostage to the darker side of human nature.

Tonight in Iraq, Saddam walks amidst ruin. His war machine is crushed. His ability to threaten mass destruction is itself destroyed. His people have been lied to, denied the truth. And when his defeated legions come home, all Iraqis will see and feel the havoc he has wrought. And this I promise you: For all that Saddam has done to his own people, to the Kuwaitis, and to the entire world, Saddam and those around him are accountable.

All of us grieve for the victims of war, for the people of Kuwait and the suffering that scars the soul of that proud nation. We grieve for all our fallen soldiers and their families, for all the innocents caught up in this conflict. And, yes, we grieve for the people of Iraq, a people who have never been our enemy. My hope is that one day we will once again welcome them as friends into the community of nations. Our commitment to peace in the Middle East does not end with the liberation of Kuwait. So, tonight let me outline four key challenges to be met.

First, we must work together to create shared security arrangements in the region. Our friends and allies in the Middle East recognize that they will bear the bulk of the responsibility for regional security. But we want them to know that just as we stood with them to repel aggression, so now America stands ready to work with them to secure the peace. This does not mean stationing U.S. ground forces in the Arabian Peninsula, but it does mean American participation in joint exercises involving both air and ground forces. It means maintaining a capable U.S. naval presence in the region, just as we have for over 40 years. Let it be clear: Our vital national interests depend on a stable and secure Gulf.

Second, we must act to control the proliferation of weapons of mass destruction and the missiles used to deliver them. It would be tragic if the nations of the Middle East and Persian Gulf were now, in the wake of war, to embark on a new arms race. Iraq requires special vigilance. Until Iraq convinces the world of its peaceful intentions—that its leaders will not use new revenues to rearm and rebuild its menacing war machine—Iraq must not have access to the instruments of war.

And third, we must work to create new opportunities for peace and stability in the Middle East. On the night I announced Operation Desert Storm, I expressed my hope that out of the horrors of war might come new momentum for peace. We've learned in the modern age geography cannot guarantee security, and security does not come from military power alone.

All of us know the depth of bitterness that has made the dispute between Israel and its neighbors so painful and intractable. Yet, in the conflict just concluded, Israel and many of the Arab States have for the first time found themselves confronting the same aggressor. By now, it should be plain to all parties that peacemaking in the Middle East requires compromise. At the same time, peace brings real benefits to everyone. We must do all that we can to close the gap between Israel and the Arab States—and between Israelis and Palestinians. The tactics of terror lead absolutely nowhere. There can be no substitute for diplomacy.

A comprehensive peace must be grounded in United Nations Security Council Resolutions 242 and 338 and the principle of territory for peace. This principle must be elaborated to provide for Israel's security and recognition and at the same time for legitimate Palestinian political rights. Anything else would fail the twin test of fairness and security. The time has come to put an end to Arab-Israeli conflict.

The war with Iraq is over. The quest for solutions to the problems in Lebanon, in the Arab-Israeli dispute, and in the Gulf must go forward with new vigor and determination. And I guarantee you: No one will work harder for a stable peace in the region than we will.

Fourth, we must foster economic development for the sake of peace and progress. The Persian Gulf and Middle East form a region rich in natural resources with a wealth of untapped human potential. Resources once squandered on military might must be redirected to more peaceful ends. We are already addressing the immediate economic consequences of Iraq's aggression. Now, the challenge is to reach higher, to foster economic freedom and prosperity for all the people of the region.

By meeting these four challenges we can build a framework for peace. I've asked Secretary of State Baker to go to the Middle East to begin the process. He will go to listen, to probe, to offer suggestions—to advance the search for peace and stability. I've also asked him to raise the plight of the hostages held in Lebanon. We have not forgotten them, and we will not forget them.

To all the challenges that confront this region of the world there is no single solution, no solely American answer. But we can make a difference. America will work tirelessly as a catalyst for positive change.

But we cannot lead a new world abroad if, at home, it's politics as usual on American defense and diplomacy. It's time to turn away from the temptation to protect unneeded weapons systems and obsolete bases. It's time to put an end to micromanagement of foreign and security assistance programs— micromanagement that humiliates our friends and allies and hamstrings our diplomacy. It's time to rise above the parochial and the pork barrel, to do what is necessary, what's right, and what will enable this nation to play the leadership role required of us.

The consequences of the conflict in the Gulf reach far beyond the confines of the Middle East. Twice before in this century, an entire world was convulsed by war. Twice this century, out of the horrors of war hope emerged for enduring peace. Twice before, those hopes proved to be a distant dream, beyond the grasp of man. Until now, the world we've known has been a world divided—a world of barbed wire and concrete block, conflict, and cold war.

Now, we can see a new world coming into view. A world in which there is the very real prospect of a new world order. In the words of Winston Churchill, a world order in which "the principles of justice and fair play protect the weak against the strong. . . ." A world where the United Nations, freed from cold war stalemate, is poised to fulfill the historic vision of its founders. A world in which freedom and respect for human rights find a home among all nations. The Gulf war put this new world to its first test. And my fellow Americans, we passed that test.

For the sake of our principles, for the sake of the Kuwaiti people, we stood our ground. Because the world would not look the other way, Ambassador al-Sabah, tonight Kuwait is free. And we're very happy about that.

Tonight, as our troops begin to come home, let us recognize that the hard work of freedom still calls us forward. We've learned the hard lessons of history. The victory over Iraq was not waged as "a war to end all wars." Even the new world order cannot guarantee an era of perpetual peace. But enduring peace must be our mission. Our success in the Gulf will shape not only the new world order we seek but our mission here at home.

In the war just ended, there were clear-cut objectives—timetables—and, above all, an overriding imperative to achieve results. We must bring that same sense of self-discipline, that same sense of urgency, to the way we meet challenges here at home. In my State of the Union Address and in my budget, I defined a comprehensive agenda to prepare for the next American century.

Our first priority is to get this economy rolling again. The fear and uncertainty caused by the Gulf crisis were understandable. But now that the war is over, oil prices are down, interest rates are down, and confidence is rightly coming back. Americans can move forward to lend, spend, and invest in this, the strongest economy on Earth.

We must also enact the legislation that is key to building a better America. For example, in 1990, we enacted an historic Clean Air Act. And now we've proposed a national energy strategy. We passed a child-care bill that put power in the hands of parents. And today, we're ready to do the same thing with our schools and expand choice in education. We passed a crime bill that made a useful start in fighting crime and drugs. This year, we're sending to Congress our comprehensive crime package to finish the job. We passed the landmark Americans with Disabilities Act. And now we've sent forward our civil rights bill. We also passed the aviation bill. This year, we've sent up our new highway bill. And these are just a few of our pending proposals for reform and renewal.

So, tonight I call on the Congress to move forward aggressively on our domestic front. Let's begin with two initiatives we should be able to agree on quickly: trans-portation and crime. And then, let's build on success with those and enact the rest of our agenda. If our forces could win the ground war in 100 hours, then surely the Congress can pass this legislation in 100 days. Let that be a promise we make tonight to the American people.

When I spoke in this House about the state of our Union, I asked all of you: If we can selflessly confront evil for the sake of good in a land so far away, then surely we can make this land all that it should be. In the time since then, the brave men and women of Desert Storm accomplished more than even they may realize. They set out to confront an enemy abroad, and in the process, they transformed a nation at home. Think of the way they went about their mission—with confidence and quiet pride. Think about their sense of duty, about all they taught us about our values, about ourselves.

We hear so often about our young people in turmoil—how our children fall short, how our schools fail us, how American products and American workers are second-class. Well, don't you believe it. The America we saw in Desert Storm was first-class talent. And they did it using America's state-of-the-art technology. We saw the excellence embodied in the Patriot missile and the patriots who made it work. And we saw soldiers who know about honor and bravery and duty and country and the world-shaking power of these simple words. There is something noble and majestic about the pride, about the patriotism that we feel tonight.

So, to everyone here and everyone watching at home, think about the men and women of Desert Storm. Let us honor them with our gratitude. Let us comfort the families of the fallen and remember each precious life lost.

Let us learn from them as well. Let us honor those who have served us by serving others. Let us honor them as individuals—men and women of every race, all creeds and colors—by setting the face of this nation against discrimination, bigotry, and hate. Eliminate them.

I'm sure that many of you saw on the television the unforgettable scene of four terrified Iraqi soldiers surrendering. They emerged from their bunker broken, tears streaming from their eyes, fearing the worst. And then there was an American soldier. Remember what he said? He said: "It's okay. You're all right now. You're all right now." That scene says a lot about America, a lot about who we are. Americans are a caring people. We are a good people, a generous people. Let us always be caring and good and generous in all we do.

Soon, very soon, our troops will begin the march we've all been waiting for—their march home. And I have directed Secretary Cheney to begin the immediate return of American combat units from the Gulf. Less than 2 hours from now, the first planeload of American soldiers will lift off from Saudi Arabia, headed for the U.S.A. That plane will carry the men and women of the 24th Mechanized Infantry Division bound for Fort Stewart, Georgia. This is just the beginning of a steady flow of American troops coming home. Let their return remind us that all those who have gone before are linked with us in the long line of freedom's march.

Americans have always tried to serve, to sacrifice nobly for what we believe to be right. Tonight, I ask every community in this country to make this coming Fourth of July a day of special celebration for our returning troops. They may have missed Thanksgiving and Christmas, but I can tell you this: For them and for their families, we can make this a holiday they'll never forget.

In a very real sense, this victory belongs to them—to the privates and the pilots, to the sergeants and the supply officers, to the men and women in the machines and the men and women who made them work. It belongs to the regulars, to the reserves, to the National Guard. This victory belongs to the finest fighting force this nation has ever known in its history.

We went halfway around the world to do what is moral and just and right. We fought hard and, with others, we won the war. We lifted the yoke of aggression and tyranny from a small country that many Americans had never even heard of, and we ask nothing in return.

We're coming home now—proud, confident, heads high. There is much that we must do, at home and abroad. And we will do it. We are Americans.

May God bless this great nation, the United States of America. Thank you all very, very much.

37. White House Statement on Weapons of Mass Destruction
March 7, 1991

The United States has taken a major step in its continuing efforts to halt the spread of weapons of mass destruction with the issuance of regulations extending export controls over chemicals, equipment, and other assistance that can contribute to the spread of missiles and chemical and biological weapons.

Saddam Hussein's use of chemical weapons against his own citizens, his use of Scud missiles to terrorize civilian populations, and the chilling specter of germ warfare and nuclear weapons have brought home the dangers proliferation poses to American interests and global peace and stability.

Our continuing efforts to stem the spread of weapons of mass destruction will contribute to the construction of a new world order. The new regulations will enhance our ability to head off these dangers so that in the future we will not be forced to confront them militarily as we have in Iraq. At the same time, the new regulations are sensitive to the importance of U.S. exports to our economic vitality and will not unfairly restrict legitimate commerce.

The expanded U.S. export controls apply to equipment, chemicals, and whole plants that can be used to manufacture chemical or biological weapons, as well as to activities of U.S. exporters or citizens when they know or are informed that their efforts will assist in a foreign missile or chemical or biological weapon program.

But the United States cannot do the job alone. Our experience in the Gulf has reinforced the lesson that the most effective export controls are those imposed multilaterally. The administration has therefore initiated vigorous efforts to obtain allied support for chemical and biological weapon export controls in the Australia Group, missile export controls in the Missile Technology Control Regime, and nuclear export controls through consultations with all major nuclear suppliers. These efforts will take advantage of the growing international consensus to redouble our efforts to stem the spread of weapons of mass destruction.

The proliferation of weapons of mass destruction may profoundly challenge our national security in the 1990's. The new regulations issued today and our multilateral initiatives will enhance our ability to meet that challenge squarely.

38. Remarks at Maxwell Air Force Base War College in Montgomery, Alabama April 13, 1991

Thank you all very, very much for that warm welcome. General Boyd and General McPeak, the distinguished Members of the Congress with us—Senators Heflin, Shelby, and Bill Dickinson. Mayor Folmar—a nonpartisan event, but I'm glad to see some friends of long standing over here—[laughter]—who were enormously helpful to me in getting to be President of the United States.

It is my great pleasure to look out across what essentially is a sea of blue, to meet this morning with the men and women of the Air University—the Air War College, the Air Command and Staff School, the Squadron Officers School, and of course, the NCO Academy. And I'm glad to see democracy in action—I see a Navy guy here or there, or maybe a coastguardsman—[laughter]—maybe the Marines, maybe the Army over here. And I think I recognize some friends from overseas, members of our coalition who helped us so much in achieving our objectives halfway around the world. They're more than welcome.

The history of aviation has been shaped here since the Wright brothers brought their strange new mechanical bird to Montgomery and housed it in a hangar not far from where we stand. This institution, from its early days as the Air Corps Tactical School, has defined the Nation's air strategy and tactics that have guided our operations over the fields of Europe and the seas of the Pacific, from the First World War to the 1,000 hours of Desert Storm.

It falls to all of you to derive the lessons learned from this war. Desert Storm demonstrated the true strength of joint operations: not the notion that each service must participate in equal parts in every operation in every war but that we use the proper tools at the proper time. In Desert Storm, a critical tool was certainly air power. And every one of you can take pride in that fact. Our technology and training ensured minimal losses, and our precision—your precision—spared the lives of innocent civilians.

But our victory also showed that technology alone is insufficient. A warrior's heart must burn with the will to fight. And if he fights but does not believe, no technology in the world can save him. We and our allies had more than superior weapons; we had the will to win.

I might say parenthetically, this will is personified by the man who leads you. I know that General Boyd often speaks about what he calls the unlimited liability of the military profession. He knows because he's put it all on the line. As a veteran of Vietnam, he flew 105 combat missions before being shot down over Hanoi. And he spent almost 7 years—2,500 cruel days—in captivity. And yet he emerged brave, unbroken. He kept the faith to himself and to his nation.

And let me just say a word about this man over here on my left, General McPeak. I remember early on a meeting up at Camp David with Tony McPeak. Secretary Cheney was there; General Powell was there; Brent Scowcroft; other chiefs—the other chiefs, I believe, were with us, Tony. And in a very laid-back way—typical of him with his modesty—but with total confidence, he told me exactly what he felt air power could do. And after he left—I don't mean to show my native skepticism—but I turned to my trusted national security adviser who's standing over here, General Brent Scowcroft, and I said, "Brent, does this guy really know what he's talking about?" [Laughter] And Lieutenant General Scowcroft—Air Force Lieutenant General—said, "Yes." And General McPeak did.

And to be doubly sure then—and he'll remember this—just before the war started, I invited General McPeak and Secretary Cheney to join me and General Scowcroft upstairs at the Residence in the White House—quiet lunch there. And I asked Tony—I think he'd just come back then from the theater, the other theater—[laughter]. And I put the question to him—I think this is exactly what I said: "Are you as certain now as you were up at Camp

David?" And he said, "Even more so." And the war started just a few days later, and history will record that General McPeak was 100 percent right, right on target.

Here at Air University it's your business to read the lessons of the past with an eye on the far horizon. And that's why I wanted to speak to you today about the new world taking shape around us, about the prospects for a new world order now within our reach.

For more than four decades we've lived in a world divided East from West, a world locked in a conflict of arms and ideas called the cold war. Two systems, two superpowers separated by mistrust and unremitting hostility. For more than four decades, America's energies were focused on containing the threat to the free world from the forces of communism. That war is over. East Germany has vanished from the map as a separate entity. Today in Berlin, the wall that once divided a continent, divided a world in two, has been pulverized, turned into souvenirs. And the sections that remain standing are but museum pieces. The Warsaw Pact passed into the pages of history last week, not with a bang but with a whimper—its demise reported in a story reported on page A16 of the *Washington Post.*

In the coming weeks I'll be talking in some detail about the possibility of a new world order emerging after the cold war. And in recent weeks I've been focusing not only on the Gulf but on free trade: on the North American Free Trade Agreement, the Uruguay round trade negotiations, and the essentiality of obtaining from the United States Congress a renewal of Fast Track authority to achieve our goals. But today I want to discuss another aspect of that order: our relations with Europe and the Soviet Union.

Twice this century, a dream born on the battlefields of Europe died after the shooting stopped—the dream of a world in which major powers worked together to ensure peace, to settle their disputes through cooperation, not confrontation. Today a transformed Europe stands closer than ever before to its free and democratic destiny. At long last, Europe is moving forward, moving toward a new world of hope.

At the same time, we and our European allies have moved beyond containment to a policy of active engagement in a world no longer driven by cold war tensions and animosities. You see, as the cold war drew to an end we saw the possibilities of a new order in which nations worked together to promote peace and prosperity.

I'm not talking here of a blueprint that will govern the conduct of nations or some supernatural structure or institution. The new world order does not mean surrendering our national sovereignty or forfeiting our interests. It really describes a responsibility imposed by our successes. It refers to new ways of working with other nations to deter aggression and to achieve stability, to achieve prosperity and, above all, to achieve peace.

It springs from hopes for a world based on a shared commitment among nations large and small to a set of principles that undergird our relations: peaceful settlements of disputes, solidarity against aggression, reduced and controlled arsenals, and just treatment of all peoples.

This order, this ability to work together, got its first real test in the Gulf war. For the first time, a regional conflict—the aggression against Kuwait—did not serve as a proxy for superpower confrontation. For the first time, the United Nations Security Council, free from the clash of cold war ideologies, functioned as its designers intended—a force for conflict resolution in collective security.

In the Gulf, nations from Europe and North America, Asia and Africa and the Arab world joined together to stop aggression, and sent a signal to would-be tyrants everywhere in the world. By joining forces to defend one small nation, we showed that we can work together against aggressors in defense of principle.

We also recognized that the cold war's end didn't deliver us into an era of perpetual peace. As old threats recede, new threats emerge. The quest for the new world order is, in part, a challenge to keep the dangers of disorder at bay.

Today, thank God, Kuwait is free. But turmoil in that tormented region of the world continues. Saddam's continued savagery has placed his regime outside the international order. We will not interfere in Iraq's civil war. Iraqi people must decide their own political future.

Looking out here at you and thinking of your families, let me comment a little further. We set our objectives. These objectives, sanctioned by international law, have been achieved. I made very clear that when our objectives were obtained that our troops would be coming home. And yes, we want the suffering of those refugees to stop, and in keeping with our nation's compassion and concern, we are massively helping. But yes, I want our troops out of Iraq and back home as soon as possible.

Internal conflicts have been raging in Iraq for many years. And we're helping out, and we're going to continue to help these refugees. But I do not want one single soldier or airman shoved into a civil war in Iraq that's been going on for ages. And I'm not going to have that.

I know the coalition's historic effort destroyed Saddam's ability to undertake aggression against any neighbor. You did that job. But now the international community will further guarantee that Saddam's ability to threaten his neighbors is completely eliminated by destroying Iraq's weapons of mass destruction.

And as I just mentioned, we will continue to help the Iraqi refugees, the hundreds and thousands of victims of this man's—Saddam Hussein's—brutality. See food and shelter and safety and the opportunity to return unharmed to their homes. We will not tolerate any interference in this massive international relief effort. Iraq can return to the community of nations only when its leaders abandon the brutality and repression that is destroying their country. With Saddam in power, Iraq will remain a pariah nation, its people denied moral contacts with most of the outside world.

We must build on the successes of Desert Storm to give new shape and momentum to this new world order, to use force wisely and extend the hand of compassion wherever we can. Today we welcome Europe's willingness to shoulder a large share of this responsibility. This new sense of responsibility on the part of our European allies is most evident and most critical in Europe's eastern half.

The nations of Eastern Europe, for so long the other Europe, must take their place now alongside their neighbors to the west. Just as we've overcome Europe's political division, we must help to ease crossover from poverty into prosperity.

The United States will do its part—we always have—as we have already in reducing Poland's official debt burden to the United States by 70 percent, increasing our assistance this year to Eastern Europe by 50 percent. But the key to helping these new democracies develop is trade and investment.

The new entrepreneurs of Czechoslovakia and Poland and Hungary aren't looking to government, their own or others, to shower them with riches. They're looking for new opportunities, a new freedom for the productive genius strangled by 40 years of state control.

Yesterday, my esteemed friend, a man we all honor and salute, President Vaclav Havel of Czechoslovakia called me up. He wanted to request advice and help from the West. He faces enormous problems. You see, Czechoslovakia wants to be democratic. This man is leading them towards perfecting their fledgling democracy. Its economy is moving from a failed socialist model to a market economy. We all must help. It's not easy to convert state owned and operated weapons plants into market-driven plants to produce consumer goods. But these new democracies can do just exactly that with the proper advice and help from the West. It is in our interest, it is in the interest of the United States of America, that Czechoslovakia, Poland, and Hungary strengthen those fledgling democracies and strengthen their fledgling market economies.

We recognize that new roles and even new institutions are natural outgrowths of the new Europe. Whether it's the European Community or a broadened mandate for the CSCE, the U.S. supports all efforts to forge a European approach to common challenges on the Continent and in the world beyond, with the understanding that Europe's long-term security is intertwined with America's and that NATO—NATO remains the best means to assure it.

And we look to Europe to act as a force for stability outside its own borders. In a world as interdependent as ours, no industrialized nation can maintain membership in good standing in the global community without assuming its fair share of responsibility for peace and security.

But even in the face of such welcome change, Americans will remain in Europe in support of history's most successful alliance, NATO. America's commitment is the best guarantee of a secure Europe, and a secure Europe is vital to American interests and vital to world peace. This is the essential logic of the Atlantic alliance which anchors America in Europe.

This century's history shows that America's destiny and interests cannot be separate from Europe's. Through the long years of cold war and conflict, the United States stood fast for freedom in Europe. And now, as Eastern Europe is opening up to democratic ideals, true progress becomes possible.

The Soviet Union is engaged in its own dramatic transformation. The policies of confrontation abroad, like the discredited dogma of communism from which those policies sprang, lies dormant, if not mortally wounded. Much has changed. The path of international cooperation fostered by President Gorbachev and manifested most clearly in the Persian Gulf marks a radical change in Soviet behavior. And yet, the course of change within the Soviet Union is far less clear.

Economic and political reform there is under severe challenge. Soviet citizens, facing the collapse of the old order while the new still struggles to be born, confront desperate economic conditions—their hard-won freedoms in peril. Ancient ethnic enmities, conflict between Republics and between Republics and the central Government add to these monumental challenges that they face.

America's policy toward the Soviet Union in these troubled times is, first and foremost, to continue our efforts to build the cooperative relationship that has allowed our nations and so many others to strengthen international peace and stability. At the same time, we will continue to support a reform process within the Soviet Union aimed at political and economic freedom—a process we believe must be built on peaceful dialog and negotiation. This is a policy that we will advocate steadfastly, both in our discussions with the central Soviet Government and with all elements active in Soviet political life.

Let there be no misunderstanding, the path ahead for the Soviet Union will be difficult and, at times, extraordinarily painful. History weighs heavily on all the peoples of the U.S.S.R.—liberation from 70 years of communism, from 1,000 years of autocracy. It's going to be slow. There will be setbacks. But this process of reform, this transformation from within, must proceed. If external cooperation and our progress toward true international peace is to endure, it must succeed. Only when this transformation is complete will we be able to take full measure of the opportunities presented by this new and evolving world order.

The new world order really is a tool for addressing a new world of possibilities. This order gains its mission and shape not just from shared interests but from shared ideals. And the ideals that have spawned new freedoms throughout the world have received their boldest and clearest expression in our great country, the United States. Never before has the world looked more to the American example. Never before have so many millions drawn hope from the American idea. And the reason is simple: Unlike any other nation in the world, as Americans we enjoy profound and mysterious bonds of affection and idealism. We feel our deep connections to community, to families, to our faiths.

But what defines this nation? What makes us America is not our ties to a piece of territory or bonds of blood; what makes us American is our allegiance to an idea that all people everywhere must be free. This idea is as old and enduring as this nation itself—as deeply rooted, and what we are as a promise implicit to all the world in the words of our own Declaration of Independence.

The new world facing us—and I wish I were your age—it's a wonderful world of discovery, a world devoted to unlocking the promise of freedom. It's no more structured than a dream, no more regimented than an innovator's burst of inspiration. If we trust ourselves and our values, if we retain the pioneer's enthusiasm for exploring the world beyond our shores, if we strive to engage in the world that beckons us, then and only then will America be true to all that is best in us.

May God bless our great nation, the United States of America. And thank you all for what you have done for freedom and for our fundamental values. Thank you very much.

39. Address to the Nation on the National Education Strategy
April 18, 1991

Thank you all for joining us here in the White House today. Let me thank the Speaker for being with us, and the majority leader; other distinguished Members, committee heads and ranking members, and very important education committees here with us today. I want to salute the Governors, the educators, the business and the labor leaders, and especially want to single out the National Teachers of the Year. I believe we have 10 of the previous 11 Teachers of the Year with us here today, and that's most appropriate and most fitting.

But together, all of us, we will underscore the importance of a challenge destined to define the America that we'll know in the next century.

For those of you close to my age, the 21st century has always been a kind of shorthand for the distant future—the place we put our most far-off hopes and dreams. And today, that 21st century is racing towards us—and anyone who wonders what the century will look like can find the answer in America's classrooms.

Nothing better defines what we are and what we will become than the education of our children. To quote the landmark case *Brown versus Board of Education*, "It is doubtful that any child may reasonably be expected to succeed in life if he is denied the opportunity of an education."

Education has always meant opportunity. Today, education determines not just which students will succeed but also which nations will thrive in a world united in pursuit of freedom in enterprise. Think about the changes transforming our world: the collapse of communism and the cold war, the advent and acceleration of the Information Age. Down through history, we've defined resources as soil and stones, land and the riches buried beneath. No more. Our greatest national resource lies within ourselves: our intelligence, ingenuity, the capacity of the human mind.

Nations that nurture ideas will move forward in years to come. Nations that stick to stale old notions and ideologies will falter and fail. So I'm here today to say America will move forward. The time for all the reports and rankings, for all the studies and the surveys about what's wrong in our schools is past. If we want to keep America competitive in the coming century, we must stop convening panels to report on ourselves. We must stop convening panels that report the obvious. And we must accept responsibility for educating everyone among us, regardless of background or disability.

If we want America to remain a leader, a force for good in the world, we must lead the way in educational innovation. And if we want to combat crime and drug abuse, if we want to create hope and opportunity in the bleak corners of this country where there is now nothing but defeat and despair, we must dispel the darkness with the enlightenment that a sound and well-rounded education provides.

Think about every problem, every challenge we face. The solution to each starts with education. For the sake of the future of our children, and of the Nation's, we must transform America's schools. The days of the status quo are over.

Across this country, people have started to transform the American school. They know that the time for talk is over. Their slogan is: Don't dither, just do it. Let's push the reform effort forward. Use each experiment, each advance to build for the next American century—new schools for a new world.

As a first step in this strategy, we must challenge not only the methods and the means that we've used in the past but also the yardsticks that we've used to measure our progress. Let's stop trying to measure progress in terms of money spent. We spend 33 percent more per pupil in 1991 than we did in 1981—33 percent more in real, constant dollars. And I don't think there's a person anywhere, anywhere in the country, who would say that we've seen a 33-percent improvement in our schools' performance.

Dollar bills don't educate students. Education depends on committed communities, determined to be places where learning will flourish; committed teachers, free from the noneducational burdens; committed parents, determined to support excellence; committed students, excited about school and learning. To those who want to see real improvement in American education, I say: There will be no renaissance without revolution.

We who would be revolutionaries must accept responsibilities for our schools. For too long, we've adopted a no-fault approach to education. Someone else is always to blame. And while we point fingers out there, trying to assign blame, the students suffer. There's no place for a no-fault attitude in our schools. It's time we held our schools—and ourselves—accountable for results.

Until now, we've treated education like a manufacturing process, assuming that if the gauges seemed right—if we had good pay scales, the right pupil-teacher ratios—good students would just pop out of our schools. It's time to turn things around—to focus on students, to set standards for our schools and let teachers and principals figure out how best to meet them.

We've made a good beginning by setting the Nation's sights on six ambitious national education goals—and setting for our target the year 2000. Our goals have been forged in partnership with the Nation's Governors, several of whom are with us here today in the East Room. And those who have taken a leadership are well-known to everyone in this room. And for those who need a refresher course—there may be a quiz later on—let me list those goals right now.

By 2000, we've got to, first, ensure that every child starts school ready to learn; second one, raise the high school graduation rate to 90 percent; the third one, ensure that each American student leaving the 4th, 8th, and 12th grades can demonstrate competence in core subjects; four, make our students first in the world in math and science achievements; fifth, ensure that every American adult is literate and has the skills necessary to compete in a global economy and exercise the rights and responsibilities of citizenship; and sixth, liberate every American school from drugs and violence so that schools encourage learning.

Our strategy to meet these noble national goals is founded in common sense and common values. It's ambitious and yet, with hard work, it's within our reach. And I can outline our strategy in one paragraph, and here it is: For today's students, we must make existing schools better and more accountable. For tomorrow's students, the next generation, we must create a new generation of American schools. For all of us, for the adults who think our school days are over, we've got to become a nation of students—recognize learning is a lifelong process. Finally, outside our schools we must cultivate communities where learning can happen. That's our strategy.

People who want Washington to solve our educational problems are missing the point. We can lend appropriate help through such programs as Head Start. But what happens here in Washington won't matter half as much as what happens in each school, each local community, and yes, in each home. Still, the Federal Government will serve as a catalyst for change in several important ways.

Working closely with the Governors, we will define new world-class standards for schools, teachers, and students in the five core subjects: math and science, English, history and geography. We will develop voluntary—let me repeat it—we will develop voluntary national tests for 4th, 8th, and 12th graders in the five core subjects. These American Achievement Tests will tell parents and educators, politicians, and employers just how well our schools are doing. I'm determined to have the first of these tests for fourth graders in place by the time that school starts in September of 1993. And for high school seniors, let's add another incentive—a distinction sure to attract attention of colleges and companies in every community across the country—a Presidential Citation to students who excel on the 12th-grade test.

We can encourage educational excellence by encouraging parental choice. The concept of choice draws its fundamental strength from the principle at the very heart of the democratic idea. Every adult American has the right to vote, the right to decide where to work, where to live. It's time parents were free to choose the schools that their children attend. This approach will create the competitive climate that stimulates excellence in our private and parochial schools as well.

But the centerpiece of our national education strategy is not a program, it's not a test. It's a new challenge: To reinvent American education—to design new American schools for the year 2000 and beyond. The idea is simple but powerful: Put America's special genius for invention to work for America's schools. I will challenge communities to become what we will call America 2000 communities. Governors will honor communities with this designation if the communities embrace the national education goals, create local strategies for reaching these goals, devise report cards for measuring progress, and agree to encourage and support one of the new generation of America's schools.

We must also foster educational innovation. I'm delighted to announce today that America's business leaders, under the chairmanship of Paul O'Neill, will create the New American Schools Development Corporation, a private

sector research and development fund of at least $150 million to generate innovation in education.

This fund offers an open-end challenge to the dreamers and the doers eager to reinvent, eager to reinvigorate our schools. With the results of this R&D in hand, I will urge Congress to provide $1 million in startup funds for each of the 535 New American Schools—at least one in every congressional district—and have them up and running by 1996.

The New American Schools must be more than rooms full of children seated at computers. If we mean to prepare our children for life, classrooms also must cultivate values and good character—give real meaning to right and wrong.

We ask only two things of these architects of our New American Schools: that their students meet the new national standards for the five core subjects, and that outside of the costs of the initial research and development, the schools operate on a budget comparable to conventional schools. The architects of the New American Schools should break the mold. Build for the next century. Reinvent—literally start from scratch and reinvent the American school. No question should be off limits, no answers automatically assumed. We're not after one single solution for every school. We're interested in finding every way to make schools better.

There's a special place in inventing the New American School for the corporate community, for business and labor. And I invite you to work with us not simply to transform our schools but to transform every American adult into a student.

Fortunately, we have a secret weapon in America's system of colleges and universities—the finest in the entire world. The corporate community can take the lead by creating a voluntary private system of world-class standards for the workplace. Employers should set up skill centers where workers can seek advice and learn new skills. But most importantly, every company and every labor union must bring the worker into the classroom and bring the classroom into the workplace.

We'll encourage every Federal agency to do the same. And to prove no one's ever too old to learn, Lamar, with his indefatigable determination and leadership, has convinced me to become a student again myself. Starting next week, I'll begin studying. And I want to know how to operate a computer. [Laughter] Very candidly—I don't expect this new tutorial to teach me how to set the clock on the VCR or anything complicated. [Laughter] But I want to be computer literate, and I'm not. There's a lot of kids, thank God, that are. And I want to learn, and I will.

The workplace isn't the only place we must improve opportunities for education. Across this nation, we must cultivate communities where children can learn—communities where the school is more than a refuge, more than a solitary island of calm amid chaos. Where the school is the living center of a community where people care—people care for each other and their futures—not just in the school but in the neighborhood, not just in the classroom but in the home.

Our challenge amounts to nothing less than a revolution in American education—a battle for our future. And now, I ask all Americans to be Points of Light in the crusade that counts the most: the crusade to prepare our children and ourselves for the exciting future that looms ahead.

What I've spoken about this afternoon are the broad strokes of this national education strategy: accountable schools for today, a new generation of schools for tomorrow, a nation of students committed to a lifetime of learning, and communities where all our children can learn.

There are four people here today who symbolize each element of this strategy and point the way forward for our reforms. Esteban Pagan—Steve—an award-winning eighth-grade student in science and history at East Harlem Tech, a choice school. Steve? Right here, I think. Stand up, now.

Mike Hopkins, lead teacher in the Saturn School in St. Paul, Minnesota, where teachers have already helped reinvent the American school. Mike, where are you? Right here, sir. Thank you.

David Kelley, a high-tech troubleshooter at the Michelin Tire plant in Greenville, South Carolina. David has spent the equivalent of 1 full year of his 4 years at Michelin back at his college expanding his skills. David? There he is.

Finally, Michelle Moore, of Missouri, a single mother active in Missouri's Parents as Teachers program. She wants her year-old son, Alston, to arrive for his first day of school ready to learn. Michelle?

So, to sum it up, for these four people and for all the others like them, the revolution in American education has already begun. Now I ask all Americans to be Points of Light in the crusade that counts the most: the crusade to prepare our children and ourselves for the exciting future that looms ahead. At any moment in every mind, the miracle of learning beckons us all. Between now and the year 2000, there is not one moment or one miracle to waste.

Thank you all. Thank you for your interest, for your dedication. And may God bless the United States of America. Thank you very much.

40. Remarks at the University of Michigan Commencement Ceremony in Ann Arbor
May 4, 1991

President Duderstadt, thank you all very much. Thank you for that warm welcome. I want to salute the president, salute Governor and Mrs. John Engler, Representatives of the Congress—

Pursell, Upton, and Vander Jagt, and distinguished Regents, and especially I want to pay my respects to our fellow honorary degree recipients. Barbara and I are very grateful for this high honor. Before this, there wasn't one lawyer in the family, and now we have two.

The last time I was in Ann Arbor, we commemorated John Kennedy's unveiling of the Peace Corps. And as your commencement program indicates, Lyndon Johnson introduced the Great Society in a University of Michigan commencement address.

Today, I want to talk to you about this historic moment. Your commencement—your journey into the "real world"—coincides with this nation's commencement into a world freed from cold war conflict and thrust into an era of cooperation and economic competition.

The United States plays a defining role in the world. Our economic strength, our military power, and most of all, our national character brought us to this special moment. When our policies unleashed the economic expansion of the 1980's, we exposed forever the failures of socialism and reaffirmed our status as the world's greatest economic power. When we sent troops to the Gulf, we showed that we take principles seriously enough to risk dying for them.

But there's another message. There's another message. We also take them seriously enough to help others in need. Today, men and women of Operation Provide Comfort toil on behalf of suffering Kurds. And today, our thoughts and prayers also go to the hundreds of thousands of people victimized by a vicious cyclone in Bangladesh. Our Government has sent aid to that stricken land. Dozens of private agencies have sprung into action as well, sending food, water, supplies, and donations. The humanitarian instinct runs deep in our people, always has. It is an essential element of our American character.

Our successes have banished the Vietnam-era phantoms of doubt and distrust. In my recent travels around the country I have felt an idealism that we Americans supposedly had lost. People have faith in the future. And they ask: What next? And they ask: How can I help?

We have rediscovered the power of the idea that toppled the Berlin Wall and led a world to strike back at Saddam Hussein. Like generations before us, we have begun to define for ourselves the promise of freedom.

I'd like to talk today about the nature of freedom and how its demands will shape our future as a nation.

Let me start with the freedom to create. From its inception, the United States has been a laboratory for creation, invention, and exploration. Here, merit conquers circumstance. Here, people of vision—Abraham Lincoln, Henry Ford, Martin Luther King, Jr.—outgrow rough origins and transform a world. These achievements testify to the greatness of our free enterprise system. In past ages, and in other economic orders, people could acquire wealth only seizing goods from others. Free enterprise liberates us from this Hobbesian quagmire. It lets one person's fortune become everyone's gain.

This system, built upon the foundation of private property, harnesses our powerful instincts for creativity. It gives everyone an interest in shared prosperity, in freedom, and in respect. No system of development ever has nurtured virtue as completely and rigorously as ours. We've become the most egalitarian system in history—and one of the most harmonious—because we let people work freely toward their destinies.

When governments try to improve on freedom—say, by picking winners and losers in the economic market—they fail. No conclave of experts, no matter how brilliant, can match the sheer ingenuity of a market that collects and distributes the wisdoms of millions of people, all pursuing their destinies in different ways.

Our administration appreciates the power of free enterprise, and our economic and domestic programs try to apply the genius of the market to the needs of the Nation. For example, we want to eliminate rules and redtape that bind the hands and the minds of entrepreneurs and innovators.

Our America 2000 educational strategy challenges the Nation to reinvent the American school, to compete in the race to unleash our national genius.

We've incorporated market incentives into our legislative proposals, so taxpayers will get a fair return on their dollars. Just look at last year's child-care legislation and the Clean Air Act, or this year's transportation bill.

We've proposed a comprehensive banking reform package that strengthens the financial system upon which economic growth depends. We repeatedly have tried to slash the capital gains, so people with dreams have a chance of achieving them.

And we want to extend this dignity of home ownership to people who live now in government-owned apartments. Home ownership gives people dignity.

And although we have tried to transfer power into the hands of the people, we haven't done enough. In a world transformed by freedom, we must look for other ways to help people build good lives for themselves and their families. The average worker in the United States now spends more than 4 months of each year working just to pay the tax man, and increasing numbers of citizens see that burden as a barrier to achieving their dreams. We've tried to put on a lid on the spending that drives taxes and to concentrate government efforts on truly national purposes. It's only common sense. And if we want to build faith in government, we must demand public services that serve the people. We must insist upon compassion that works.

But the power to create also rests on other freedoms, especially the freedom—and I think about that right now—to think and speak one's mind. [Applause] You see—thank you. The freedom—I had this written into the speech, and I didn't even know these guys were going to be here.

No, but seriously, the freedom to speak one's mind—that may be the most fundamental and deeply revered of all our liberties. Americans, to debate, to say what we think—because, you see, it separates good ideas from bad. It defines and cultivates the diversity upon which our national greatness rests. It tears off the blinders of ignorance and prejudice and lets us move on to greater things.

Ironically, on the 200th anniversary of our Bill of Rights, we find free speech under assault throughout the United States, including on some college campuses. The notion of political correctness has ignited controversy across the land. And although the movement arises from the laudable desire to sweep away the debris of racism and sexism and hatred, it replaces old prejudice with new ones. It declares certain topics off-limits, certain expression off-limits, even certain gestures off-limits.

What began as a crusade for civility has soured into a cause of conflict and even censorship. Disputants treat sheer force—getting their foes punished or expelled, for instance—as a substitute for the power of ideas.

Throughout history, attempts to micromanage casual conversation have only incited distrust. They have invited people to look for an insult in every word, gesture, action. And in their own Orwellian way, crusades that demand correct behavior crush diversity in the name of diversity.

We all should be alarmed at the rise of intolerance in our land and by the growing tendency to use intimidation rather than reason in settling disputes. Neighbors who disagree no longer settle matters over a cup of coffee. They hire lawyers, and they go to court. And political extremists roam the land, abusing the privilege of free speech, setting citizens against one another on the basis of their class or race.

But, you see, such bullying is outrageous. It's not worthy of a great nation grounded in the values of tolerance and respect. So, let us fight back against the boring politics of division and derision. Let's trust our friends and colleagues to respond to reason. As Americans we must use our persuasive powers to conquer bigotry once and for all. And I remind myself a lot of this: We must conquer the temptation to assign bad motives to people who disagree with us.

If we hope to make full use of the optimism I discussed earlier, men and women must feel free to speak their hearts and minds. We must build a society in which people can join in common cause without having to surrender their identities.

You can lead the way. Share your thoughts and your experiences and your hopes and your frustrations. Defend others' rights to speak. And if harmony be our goal, let's pursue harmony, not inquisition.

The virtue of free speech leads naturally to another equally important dimension of freedom, and that is the freedom of spirit. In recent times, often with noble intentions, we as a nation have discouraged good works. Nowadays, many respond to misfortune by asking: "Whom can I sue?" Even worse, many would-be Samaritans wonder: "Will someone sue me?" Talented, concerned men and women avoid such noble professions as medicine for fear that unreasonable and undefined liability claims will force them to spend more time in court than in the office or in the hospital.

And at the same time, government programs have tried to assume roles once reserved for families and schools and churches. This is understandable, but dangerous. When government tries to serve as a parent or a teacher or a moral guide, individuals may be tempted to discard their own sense of responsibility, to argue that only government must help people in need.

If we've learned anything in the past quarter century, it is that we cannot federalize virtue. Indeed, as we pile law upon law, program upon program, rule upon rule, we actually can weaken people's moral sensitivity. The rule of law gives way to the rule of the loophole, the notion that whatever is not illegal must be acceptable. In this way, great goals go unmet.

When Lyndon Johnson—President Johnson—spoke here in 1964, he addressed issues that remain with us. He proposed revitalizing cities, rejuvenating schools, trampling down the hoary harvest of racism, and protecting our environment—back in 1964. He applied the wisdom of his time to these challenges. He believed that cadres of experts really could care for the millions. And they would calculate ideal tax rates, ideal rates of expenditures on social programs, ideal distributions of wealth and privilege. And in many ways, theirs was an America by the numbers: If the numbers were right, America was right.

And gradually, we got to the point of equating dollars with commitment. And when programs failed to produce progress, we demanded more money. And in time, this crusade backfired. Programs designed to ensure racial harmony generated animosity. Programs intended to help people out of poverty invited dependency.

We should have learned that while the ideals behind the Great Society were noble—and indeed they were—the programs weren't always up to the task. We need to rethink our approach. Let's tell our people: We don't want an America by the numbers. We don't want a land of loopholes. We want a community of commitment and trust.

When I talked of a kinder, gentler nation, I wasn't trying to just create a slogan. I was issuing a challenge. An effective government must know its limitations and respect its people's capabilities. In return, people must assume the final burden of freedom, and that's responsibility.

An introductory course in political philosophy teaches that freedom entails responsibility. Most of our greatest responsibilities confront us not in the government hearing rooms but around dinner tables, on the streets, at the office. If you teach your children and others how to hate, they will learn. And if you encourage them not to trust others, they'll follow your lead. And if you talk about compassion but refuse to help those in need, your children will learn to look the other way.

Once your commencement ends, you'll have to rely on the sternest stuff of all: yourself. And in the end, government will not make you good or evil. The quality of your life—and of our nation's future—depends as much on how you treat your fellow women and men as it does on the way in which we in Washington conduct our affairs of state. After all, the opposite of greed is not taxation. It is service.

My vision for America depends heavily on you. You must protect the freedoms of enterprise, speech, and spirit. You must strengthen the family. You must build a peaceful and prosperous future. We don't need another Great Society with huge and ambitious programs administered by the incumbent few. We need a Good Society built upon the deeds of the many, a society that promotes service, selflessness, action.

The Good Society poses a challenge: It dares you to explore the full promise of citizenship, to join in partnership with family, friends, government to make our world better. The Good Society does not demand agonizing sacrifice. It requires something within everyone's reach: common decency—common decency and commitment. Know your neighbors. Build bonds of trust at home, at work, wherever you go. Don't just talk about principles—live them.

Let me leave you today with an exhortation: Make the most of your abilities. Question authority, but examine yourself. Demand good government, but strive to do what is good. Take risks. Muster the courage to be what I call a Point of Light. Also, define your missions positively. Don't seek out villains. Don't fall prey to obsessions about "freedom from" various ills. Focus on freedom's promise, on your promise.

When John Kennedy talked of sending a man to the Moon, he didn't say, we want to avoid getting stranded on this planet. He said, we'll send a man to the Moon. We must be equally determined to achieve our common goals.

We live in the most exciting period of my lifetime, quite possibly of yours. The old ways of doing things have run their course. Find new ones. Dare to serve others, and future generations will never forget the example you set.

This is your day. Barbara and I are very proud to share it with you. Congratulations to each and every one of you. And thank you for the honor.

And God bless the United States of America.

41. The President's News Conference with Soviet President Mikhail Gorbachev in Moscow July 31, 1991

President Gorbachev. Good evening, ladies and gentlemen. The basic part of the visit, the official visit of the President of the United States of America to the Soviet Union, is behind us. And there are many things that are important which are still ahead within the framework of this big political international event.

These days were full of very substantial dialog over a wide spectrum of issues. And I must say that it's kind of difficult for me—

[At this point, President Bush's earphones for translation failed.]

I guess I'll have to repeat from the very beginning what I said in that case. [Laughter]

Q. Number two, Mr. President. [Laughter]

President Gorbachev. Now—do you hear me now? Is everything okay? It's tolerable?

I already said, addressing the international press, that we see the official visit of the President of the United States to the Soviet Union as a big event in our relations—really a global event. And I want to say that these days we have done a great deal of work which I think will create difficulties for me and the President in order to present it in condensed form. And nevertheless, this visit, to some extent, sums up the last stage of our cooperation at a very fundamental, dramatic time of development, of events in the world, when both the President of the United States of America and the Soviet Union were placed in very difficult circumstances, unusual ones, which demanded from them a great feeling of responsibility in taking very important decisions which have had consequences, and will have consequences in the further development of our cooperation and events in the world.

And so, with the President, he and I did not lose time, and immediately at our first meeting we summarized the overall situation in a fast-changing world and tried from these positions to look upon our cooperation, evaluate our joint efforts, and trying to map out some contours, directions of development of this cooperation which would correspond to these changing conditions within which we have to act.

The President showed great interest in the events taking place in our country, our domestic processes. I tried to satisfy his interest and did this on my part with a great deal of satisfaction, since in his interest, I felt a desire to understand even more what is going on in our country, and moreover, I felt also a feeling of solidarity in this.

We had an interesting, substantive discussion, and perhaps for the first time it covered the following in our bilateral cooperation. For the first time over the past period, we probably accented rather strongly what our economic relationship should be like, how we have to work together in this importance here so that—or so that relationship in this area would be appropriate to the international dialog which we have reached in other areas.

And here we have noted on the basis of mutual understanding—if not, President Bush will say so—that there must be movements in accommodation as well. Obviously, one can do a lot in the area of reform so that we can include ourselves in international economic ties. To play by the rules of the game—I like this expression. I haven't invented any other one for the time being. That's why I use the term I'm familiar with. We have to do a great deal, and we have made our choice to continue reforms, democratic changes, and especially now, to move decisively forward towards a market relationship, a relationship of property, and so on.

It's clear that our success in these internal affairs is tied to a great extent to the process of reform in the Federation. And I hope that I have satisfied the interest of the President about the state of this as of today. We both understand that this is very important for the success of our work, and thus, we must change, we must understand, and will understand here in the Soviet Union, that the basic responsibility for the fate of this country for reforms, for the making of decisions which are very important: is our prerogative, our responsibility.

And obviously, we are very interested in the more fruitful cooperation with the countries of the West. And in the light of continuing the discussion which we had in London, within the framework of my meeting at the G - 7, we spoke also about this subject as well. And I tried to develop a thesis, which I expressed in London, that we hope to see accommodating movement of the Western countries because they, too, in their approaches in the sphere of economic cooperation, must accommodate us.

We are talking about removing barriers which are connected with decisions taken during the cold war, during the arms race. This is a different time; different winds are blowing. And we must reevaluate all these decisions. I don't think they need to be preserved when our relationship is different now, and we want them not only to be preserved but to be more dynamic, to be based more firmly on trust.

Obviously, the question arose about the participation of the Soviet Union in international economic organizations, and I must say, for the first time we talked substantially about specific spheres of cooperation in implementing certain projects on the basis of bilateral cooperation. To speak about this briefly, we spoke about cooperating in the field of energy, especially in the area of conversion. We have great possibilities here, and specifically in the sphere in which we are very interested: that is the agricultural sphere, especially food distribution.

In this regard, I transmitted certain materials to the President as in a memoir; the same was done by the Foreign Minister Bessmertnykh—gave it to the Secretary of State, Mr. Baker, in a memoir about those projects in which we could cooperate fruitfully. This is a very interesting and substantive project. We would want to act in such a way that in implementing these projects—all of them—to give a possibility to each other to earn money. In other words, the process goes forward, and there's benefit from it.

But there are spheres of cooperation where movement forward will not give us a chance because of additional production to make these calculations, like in the area of food production, for example. In the food area, here there could be interesting accomplishments, an interesting project, but what we get as the result we need—we have problems in the food area, very acute ones. But we can't offer this to the United States. They have no interest now in buying food from us. So, we must implement other projects where we could earn hard currency and use this. And I've named such spheres, many such spheres.

We talked in general about continuing such works. Soon we will have competent groups of specialists, headed by important representatives of business circles, to realize these projects. And thus, I expanded this part, and the other parts will be shorter. For the first time, we discussed very substantially the sphere of bilateral relations, and not only with regard to disarmament, political dialog, and a resolution of world problems but had such a businesslike discussion and I greet this, I welcome it, and I hope that it will have positive consequences.

Then the President and I thought about the following, and what do we do next? We've signed the treaty and what's next? We've congratulated each other and our peoples and the world with the fact that such great progress has been accomplished as a result of almost a decade of work. And what's next?

And we did not want simply to be pragmatists here. We wanted to look at the problem of security, stability from the point of view of the present-day realities. Or should we simply continue the negotiations which already are taking place? And there are many problems which still need to be discussed. Or should we also look at the world from a somewhat different position from today's heights with the new reality which exists?

And I think that was the main item of our exchange because without understanding each other in this, it's hard to find the keys to resolution of specific issues. We agreed to continue discussion on this issue and even set up the mechanisms which must be implemented in order to do this.

Nevertheless, we also examined very many specific issues of disarmament without our—we did not leave unattended problems of the Middle East. And I must say, and if the President considers it appropriate, he could name certain things. And if you have questions, we could discuss this. We have worked out a joint document on this. I have in mind our common position with regard to the Middle East. I think that this is a very important result of our joint work, and I think that the fact that this position will be publicly announced will have serious influence on this process. And we consider that it is in a decisive stage and we should not—and here I want to use what our ministers use—to have a window of opportunity in order to really achieve progress in this very sensitive area of international politics.

The President and I talked about the situation in Europe in the context of implementing the agreement—the Helsinki Agreement, the Paris Charter, and especially with regard to the processes taking place in that region, and specifically noted the situation in Yugoslavia, and expressed our position, our understanding, our approach to the resolution of this issue—a very serious one which worries many of us. Also in a joint statement we expressed this.

I must say that we also moved forward and discussed other things. We tried to also look at many global processes, and in this regard, did not pass by many issues of international politics—compared our points of view. In some issues we reserved the opportunity to come back to this. We put off discussing this. In some cases, we required consultations on the U.S. side. In other cases, we needed time to study the issue. But that means that the process will continue. And in this case as well, we noted the necessity of cooperation and interaction in resolving those many international issues which exist and which must be resolved.

The atmosphere was a very warm one—sincere, frank, open. And today we sense the representatives of the press—said that the press didn't want to interfere with us somewhere out in a village to talk one-on-one and in an uninhibited manner. We did all of this. This is also important. It's very good.

One of the members of the delegation—I asked the question: How do you feel?—a very important person. And the answer was: Like at home. And that's the kind of atmosphere which we worked in.

I am satisfied with the fact that political dialog is developing in this way once in this hall. And there are many witnesses here; I want to repeat this—I talked about this to the President, he knows this as well—that I am convinced that without what we have today in our relationship, such a character of Soviet-American relations, we could hardly count on everything that has happened in the past year. And we could hardly have interacted in such a way when the world placed before us very serious problems.

If this had been in another time, if we had faced such problems in another time, it would be difficult to say what would have happened. But today we even understand better the value of our cooperation, the fact that this is necessary. So, perhaps this is not a question of a platonic love but a deep understanding of the fact that, as countries and states, we need each other today and tomorrow. And I feel and I know that our peoples welcome this direction of development of our relations between our countries.

And from this point of view, it moves ahead—far ahead—our cooperation. And thus, I want to ask the pardon of the President and the press. I am the host and I maybe, misused it, but perhaps I could listen to your comments as well that I'm speaking so much.

I understood that you almost agree with everything I have said. [Laughter]

President Bush. What I heard I liked. [Laughter]

Once again, this might be an appropriate time for Barbara and me to thank the President and Mrs. Gorbachev for this fantastic hospitality. And yes, I couldn't agree more about the productive nature of the talks, the enhancement of mutual understanding. This is not diplomatic language, in my view, this is fact.

You know my views on the START agreement. Indeed, it's the culmination of a long and historic negotiation. And I happen to believe that the winners on this are the young people, not just in the Soviet Union, not just in the United States but all around the world. And we are taking major steps in transforming our economic relations. President Gorbachev touched on some of this.

But we're going to send up the trade agreement to the U.S. Congress. We're going to grant most-favored-nation status now that the technicalities have been worked out. We have fulfilled thus our Malta goal, Mr. President, of normalizing our economic relationship. We agreed here to tackle the next challenge—President Gorbachev talked about that—furthering economic reform in the U.S.S.R., and seeking to integrate the Soviet economy into the international system. We're going forward

with space cooperation, cooperation in the environment. And we have several joint projects in mind there.

Building on our historic cooperation during the Gulf crisis, we discussed—the President and I discussed our partnership in resolving longstanding regional problems. As you mentioned, we're putting out statements on Yugoslavia, Central America. And, indeed, I want to comment now just briefly on the Middle East before taking your questions.

We did reaffirm our mutual commitment to promote peace and genuine reconciliation between the Arab States, Israel, and the Palestinians. And we believe there is an historic opportunity right now to launch a process that can lead to a just and enduring peace and to a comprehensive settlement in the Middle East. We share the strong conviction that this historic opportunity must not be lost. And while recognizing that peace cannot be imposed, it can only result from direct negotiations between the parties, the United States and the Soviet Union pledge to do their utmost to promote and sustain the peacemaking process.

And to that end, the United States and the Soviet Union, acting as cosponsors, are going to work to convene an October peace conference designed to launch bilateral and multilateral negotiations. Invitations to the conference will be issued at least 10 days prior to the date the conference is to convene. And in the interim, Secretary Baker and Foreign Minister Bessmertnykh will continue to work with the parties to prepare for this conference. And I am today asking Secretary of State Jim Baker to return to the Middle East to obtain Israel's answer to our proposal for peace.

And again, my thanks to you, and I'd be prepared to take questions along with you, sir.

Yugoslavia

Q. One question to Comrade Gorbachev. You said that you talked with Mr. Bush about Yugoslavia. What is the essence of that conversation about Yugoslavia?

And, Mr. Bush, when you received me several years ago in the White House in your capacity at that time as Vice President of the United States of America, you said to me that the relations between our two countries—there's a special relationship between Yugoslavia and the United States. Is that definition still valid? And whether the United States is still supporting Yugoslavian territorial integrity? Thank you.

President Gorbachev. You asked about the essence of the conversation. I will then make use of the fact that I will relate the content of the U.S.-Soviet statement on Yugoslavia. This is the result of our conversation on this subject. We, both countries, with a deep concern, have noted the dramatic development of events in Yugoslavia. And we have been against the use of force and call upon all sides to abide by the agreements on the cease-fire. We, the Soviet Union and the U.S., proceed from the premise that the resolution of issues must be found by the peoples of Yugoslavia, themselves, on the basis of democratic principles through peaceful negotiations and a constructive approach.

We emphasized the necessity of having all sides respect the basic principles indicated in the Helsinki Act and the Paris Charter. The U.S. and the U.S.S.R. support the efforts undertaken by the CSCE countries—specifically the European Community steps to resolve the problem. This is the essence of the statement.

President Bush. I would only add, sir, that inasmuch as that was a joint statement, that expresses our continued position as well.

Middle East Peace Talks

Q. Mr. President, can I ask you, the fact that you're going ahead with this peace conference, does that mean that you have Israel's acceptance of the outlines of your conditions for a peace conference, or is there still a hangup, or have you got a commitment from Mr. Shamir?

President Bush. Well, I would wait and let Secretary Baker answer that question after this next meeting. And if I had to express a degree of optimism or pessimism, I'd say I'm a little more optimistic today. But the visit of Jim Baker now is for what we said here, to obtain Israel's answer to our proposal for peace. And if I had the answer in my pocket—or he did—I'd expect that we would say so.

Soviet-U.S. Relations

Q. I have a question to both Presidents: You discussed many questions of international issues, bilateral issues. You signed a unique agreement today. What did you leave for the next meeting? And can we say when you're planning to have it?

President Gorbachev. I think that what we discussed today and what we have set in motion, both with regard to a political dialog and a continuation of the disarmament process and new subjects in the area of economic cooperation and trade, interaction in the resolution of important issues including regional conflicts, which, unfortunately, still take place, and especially since we have begun a significant discussion about the concept of future strategic stability, that means that we have many issues to discuss and many meetings ahead. So, I think that our contacts will continue.

But I would express myself in favor of the following: Perhaps not always can we go—

and this makes the positions of Presidents very specific—but it's harder for them than for the Ministers of Foreign Affairs to travel and discuss issues of foreign affairs. But nevertheless, the President and I have developed a method of conversation. We exchange opinions by telephone. As soon as we have a need, concerns, or simply to exchange opinions about something important, we do this by telephone, and this takes place on a regular basis.

And secondly, we regularly exchange letters. And this exchange of opinions has not ceased even in recent days when we have already reached agreement with the President. We were expecting him here. So, we have many channels in order to support this very high level of cooperation which we have. And I think a great role will be given to our Departments—the Ministries of Foreign Affairs, but other Departments as well because we have new areas of cooperation.

President Bush. I would only add to that, that though no date is set, it is my view—and I haven't always held this view—that a meeting without an agenda is a good idea from time to time between the Soviet President and the President of the United States. And with this—President Gorbachev talked about arms control and regional problems and other problems—but as this dynamic autonomy begins to move, a chance for a dynamic economy here, there's going to be much more to talk about on the economic side than we've ever had before—cooperation, partnerships, joint ventures. The whole approach to economics that he has endorsed that is going to benefit, I believe, the Soviet Union, and I think there's enormous potential for the United States.

So, it is my view that we've got plenty to talk about. And I, for one, would be prepared to, as I've stated before, to have a

meeting where there's not a crisis out there to be managed; rather we can be sure that we're not two ships passing in the night—the analogy I used, I believe, in Malta—appropriately. [Laughter] And I look forward to future meetings because you get a lot done where you can't put out—sign a 3-point program or a 20-point protocol. But a lot is done just by the kinds of conversations we've had today.

Lithuania

Q. President Gorbachev, there was an ugly border incident in Lithuania last night in which a number of Lithuanian border guards were killed. I wonder if we could have your reaction and any explanation you might have of it?

Also, President Bush, any reaction from you, in light particularly of your call yesterday afternoon for freedom for the Baltic States?

President Gorbachev. You know, we received this information when we were talking outside the city. The first information was such that the incident was on the border between Lithuania and Byelorussia, and when one of the citizens of Byelorussia went in the direction of Lithuania and at the customs point where he was approaching, he saw two wounded people and four that died. He quickly related this information, and now the state security agency of Lithuania and Byelorussia—the chairman of the state committee on security offered also to help in the cooperation. So, now we are investigating this.

I must say that, in addition to regret, we must simply sympathize with the families of the people that died. And I myself must say that we are doing everything in order not only to take actions but also to avoid such excesses, such conflicts on the basis of resolution of basic issues. And we have taken such basic mutual decisions with regard to issues—concerning Armenia and Azerbaijan there's a dialog. And the faster and more productive the dialog is, the more efforts there are to break it down. Not everyone likes this process that is developed in such a direction. And it's hard for us to say what happened. We heard versions, the President and I, but these are versions. This is not important at any rate. I will be monitoring this, and we will tell you what it was that happened in reality.

Q. I just wanted to get your reaction, sir, to the incident in light of your call yesterday afternoon for freedom for the Baltic States.

President Bush. Well, I don't think there's a connection, but I do regret the violence. I listened to what President Gorbachev said about the discussion. We clearly favor negotiation—he knows that—that would lead to a reduction of cross-border violence from both sides. And obviously, I'd like to join in expressing my regrets to those families whose loved ones are lost.

But the President immediately got on this and said they're conducting an investigation. I think there's hope that the investigation will be cooperative between the Lithuanian side and Byelorussia's side. And so, we can't prejudge the incident, but I had an opportunity to express my views to President Gorbachev on the whole question of the Baltic States. I don't think it's fair to link a border incident before you know what happened to that question, however.

Soviet Economic Integration

Q. Mr. President, how far did you go after London in moving ahead in the integration of the U.S.S.R. into the international econ-omy? Was there progress reached in this area? To both Presidents.

President Gorbachev. Perhaps you can begin.

President Bush. Well, let me say that's a serious objective to start with. Secondly, I believe that active participation in these international financial institutions and the status that was deemed best by the G - 7 is the most important thing that the Soviets can do right now. I have freed up, as you heard today, certain trade benefits or normalizing the trade procedures that, in my view, will help. And we've done that since the meeting in London.

But the answer is, full participation—full benefit of these international institutions requires full knowledge and steps towards the privatization and toward convertability, all the things that I believe the Soviet Union wants.

So, work with the international organizations and then bilaterally do what we've done and other countries will be doing, too, I'm sure, to remove the underbrush, remove the barriers to bilateral economic cooperation. So, quite a bit has happened between us since Paris. And we look forward with our representatives in these international organizations to working very cooperatively with the Soviet leaders.

President Gorbachev. I understand that I'm supposed to comment on this as well since the question was to both Presidents. I will be brief since I have already expressed my opinion about this. London was the beginning of a very important process. This was the meaning of the London meeting, and one must judge about this in that light.

It's very important that after London there's a desire on both parts to work out a mechanism which would permit the shifting of this cooperation, given the political will of the leadership of the Western countries. In the Soviet Union, we think that we should have special structures which would keep tab of the cooperation between the Soviet Union and the G - 7 countries, and first of all, in the area of investment, so the process would be easier in the taking of decisions of mutual interest.

And it's good that the mechanism has started to be implemented, which we discussed in London, and the Minister of Finances of England is already here. We first talked about the fact that there would be visits of the Minister of Finance, the Secretary of the Treasury of the U.S., and the representative of the FRG. So, in other words, there would be the mechanism of implementing specific areas of cooperation. And this is very important that there be a mechanism for real interaction.

And finally, the President mentioned that, on the part of the U.S., an important decision will be taken to make trade between our countries easier. I would say that I mention this in passing, but we often discussed this with the President. I asked, and we agreed, to study the question of COCOM restrictions today because many billion-dollar projects which are ready to go and even signed are not being implemented because of the fact that they have elements that come under COCOM restrictions.

And therefore, a very serious process has started and I think that this will continue and grow stronger, be more specific. It will give results. There is a will and a desire to do this. It's very important.

Nuclear Weapons

Q. I would ask both of you to think back to the 1986 Reykjavik summit when Ronald Reagan horrified quite a few American nuclear experts and almost all of the European leaders by giving serious consideration to your proposal, President Gorbachev, for a ban on all nuclear weapons. In the end, Reagan said no because of the belief that nuclear deterrence has, in fact, kept the peace. At that time, you had a massive conventional edge in Europe, though. Since then, we've had the CFE treaty. Why now are the two of you not saying we will now work towards a total nuclear ban? Do you still believe in the efficacy of nuclear deterrence in keeping the peace? Particularly, sir, I ask you, President Bush, given the fact that some of these breakaway Republics, they have nuclear weapons in there and who knows what would happen if they declare independence.

President Bush. The very fact that—I wouldn't suggest that a breakaway Republic is going to use a nuclear weapon against the United States, but I would suggest that we have every reason in the world to be concerned about renegades—not in these areas, perhaps; I hope not—getting hold of nuclear weapons. And that's one of the reasons I strongly support our GPALS program that is being debated in the Senate right now.

But in my view, other countries do possess nuclear weapons. It's not just the Soviet Union and the United States. And I do believe that we are on the right path by the path that President Gorbachev has outlined today on following on existing agreements. So, rather than try to have a ethereal or a utopian answer, let's follow through practically, as he suggested. And then as far as the U.S. is concerned, I'd like us to go forward with a system that puts nobody at threat, nobody at risk. The only thing at risk is an errant nuclear missile aiming at a country. And that's why I support the defensive approach, and that's why I think one of the lessons out of the Iraq war—and maybe President Gorbachev reads this differently—is that defenses work. And though we're talking about a different concept now, an expanded concept, a more high-tech concept, I think a lot of lives were saved by defense. So, that's my reply.

President Gorbachev. I will say a few words. I think that the argument which you want to ascribe to me, that in my policy I looked upon nuclear weapons as an element of deterrence, is not true. I have not said this. Yes, we got involved in the arms race in a very serious way. Thank God, as we say in Russian, that we stopped this and turned it back. And this is a great accomplishment since we understood where we were headed.

But it's hard to resolve all these issues which have piled up, and all these weapons that have piled up. And I think that there is still a lot that we have to do. We have mapped out a few things for the future, and then there will probably also be questions put to all members of the nuclear club, and they also have to think about what to do with nuclear weapons in the future.

And finally, we must very carefully act about having the mechanism which we have created and which seems has worked—but apparently not effectively enough—about nonproliferation of nuclear weapons. This was one of the important topics of our conversation with the President during these days. For if certain countries will lower their arms and disarm and head in the direction of a nonnuclear world, and at the same time, others will find ways to develop the process in order to have their own nuclear weapons, then we will have a situation which is absurd.

So, in continuing to support nuclear disarmament and within the framework of the negotiation process, which we have, we have agreed to continue this. We have the question of truly improving the mechanism of nonproliferation nuclear technology in order—missile technology—in order to create an unsurmountable barrier in this area. I think this is one of the most important things we have to do today.

Q. What significance does the process of European integration have in your conversations with the President, for example, the postwar unification of Europe? What image of this is the most acceptable to you from the point of view of the Soviet Union? For example, the image of a General de Gaulle Europe of fatherlands, countries with decisions being made on a national level, or a united states of Europe, with common decision being made among them? Thank you.

Europe

President Gorbachev. First of all, you can probably guess that everything that happens in Europe—in the world—we have always looked towards Europe for everything that happens in Europe, in our areas—I don't want to list them—has a great importance for the developments in the world. So, undoubtedly, the President and I noted the positive developments which are taking place in Europe and we noted support of the documents aimed at creating a new Europe. And we see that the Soviet Union and the U.S. must participate very actively in building a new Europe. All of this has existed and continues to exist. And we feel a responsibility to do this.

But you asked the question about how. I think perhaps you are a little hasty because when we are creating a certain schematic and then try to impose it, then we get one result. When a process is being developed in a logical way within the Helsinki process, a political process of choice, then we find that new forms of cooperation and new institutes come into being.

Now I would say the following: We must, within the framework of the documents, the general path mapped out in the Helsinki and the Paris agreements, act in such a way that the old institutions be transformed in the interest of a new Europe so that they serve the interest of a single economic territory, a single security of Europe, a legal aspect. And so, this is what we must aim for. That means when the old institutions, when they change, we have to bear this in mind. But apparently, we will also have new institutions which will arise, which will serve this process.

And now if we have, for example, a common energy approach, there will be mechanisms of administering this and will have a great significance in the fate of Europe and the process to realize this. Thus, in going along this path without destroying the old institutions in creating new ones, we probably will find the forms gradually to resolve these issues. But if we declare a specific course, but will keep the old structures, institutions without changing them at all, then again, there can be a process of simply regrouping of forces in Europe. And there can be new confrontations which would come into being with a different distribution of forces.

I am not in favor of this, so I would more quickly go through the process of creation of new institutions and would stimulate those tendencies which would move us towards a united Europe.

I don't think that here we need to have languages vanish; cultures, traditions vanish. I think this would be a mistake if we set ourselves such a goal. I think we should take into consideration those specific characteristics and traditions—the histories of the people—but also aim for their unification. I think this is compatible, although we see that there is also an explosion of nationalism, separatism, efforts to unravel everything. This is a dangerous process. I think that if we follow a path of chaotic develop-

ment of such processes, then we'll get into a bad situation.

So, I am for the transformation of all institutions. I am for new institutions which would act in the interest of unification processes in Europe.

Mr. Fitzwater. We used our allotted time. Thank you very much.

42. The President's News Conference in Kennebunkport, Maine, on the Attempted Coup in the Soviet Union August 20, 1991

The President. The events in the Soviet Union continue to deeply concern the whole world. The unconstitutional seizure of power is an affront to the goals and aspirations that the Soviet peoples have been nurturing over the past years. This action also puts the Soviet Union at odds with the world community and undermines the positive steps that have been undertaken to make the Soviet Union an integral and positive force in the world affairs.

I have this morning spoken with Boris Yeltsin, the freely elected leader of the Russian Republic, and I assured Mr. Yeltsin of continued U.S. support for his goal of the restoration of Mr. Gorbachev as the constitutionally chosen leader. And I also shared with him the support that other world leaders voiced in my several conversations yesterday, conversations I had with those leaders in Eastern Europe and leaders in Western Europe as well, Prime Minister Kaifu, and I gave him that reassurance. Mr. Yeltsin is encouraged by the support of the Soviet people and their determination in the face of these trying circumstances. He expressed his gratitude for our support of him and President Gorbachev.

The situation concerning President Gorbachev's status is still unclear. And I've twice tried to reach him by phone, including within the last hour, but have so far been unsuccessful.

We continue to closely monitor this situation. Our new, and I might add, very able Ambassador to the Soviet Union, Robert Strauss, just sworn in, will be departing immediately for Moscow to take charge of our Embassy and to report to me on the situation that he finds in the Soviet Union. So, I'm asking him to go over there, get the lay of the land, establish what will be strong leadership—the Embassy, we've got a good team in place, but this man is in charge of this important mission—and then to return within the next several days to give me a full, personal report on what he sees there.

He will not be presenting his credentials on this trip. It's going to be a short trip. And I've said that this group assumed power extra-constitutionally.

In conclusion, I want to emphasize that we are going to monitor the situation closely and consider its ramifications throughout the entire world. And I've emphasized in my conversation with the Eastern European leaders that the democratic processes in their country cannot be reversed. Eastern Europe is important. And I've called three of the leaders, and I want to take this opportunity to assure them of our continued interest and the need to retain calm in those countries. And indeed, they were very grateful for the contact by the United States.

The United States will continue to support the economic and political reforms in their countries. And I will continue to seek the advice and counsel of Eastern European leaders in the days ahead. And of course, the Secretary and I will be in close touch with the Western European leaders and others around the globe.

Because this is an ongoing process of consultations, we intend to maintain a more formal work schedule during the remainder of my stay in Maine. There will be a number of meetings with Government officials and private sector experts related to the events in the Soviet Union. There will be daily briefings on a formalized basis by my national security advisers, and I will be keeping in touch with Secretary Baker.

As you know, I will be receiving Prime Minister Mulroney and also Prime Minister Major and, of course, receiving Ambassador Strauss when he returns.

Secretary Baker will be leaving today for the NATO ministerial [meeting] that will be held in Brussels.

These difficult events in the Soviet Union I believe demonstrate the wisdom of our strong and continuous support for the process of reform and restructuring. We'll continue to support the democratic processes that have been set in motion in the Soviet Union. And most importantly, I know that the American people stand behind the people of the Soviet Union who are seeking more freedom and more opportunity in their society.

So, I'd like now to turn this podium over to Ambassador Strauss for a comment, and then Secretary Baker, and I will be glad to take questions, or the Ambassador. And I have here, of course, our top national security team and Secretary Cheney, and the Chairman of the Joint Chiefs is here, the Vice President. And if you want to direct questions to any of them, why, that would be fine, too. We're following all, the situations on all fronts there, economic, military, whatever it is, very, very closely.

Bob.

Ambassador Strauss. Thank you, Mr. President. Let me just very briefly say that circumstances have changed rather dramatically since I accepted this assignment. It's a different world. Nevertheless, although circumstances have changed, as I've said, it seems to me that my mission remains basically the same. And that is to go to Moscow to speak very clearly, speak very plainly, and if necessary with undiplomatic candor from time to time—to speak for you, Mr. President, and you, Mr. Secretary, and for the American people, and to speak for the principles of freedom and democracy and rule of law. And that I intend to do.

I thank you for this, I express my appreciation to you for the confidence you've shown in me, and I'll do my best to fulfill the job. Thank you, sir.

The President. Well, I'd be glad to entertain a few questions.

Q. Mr. President, is there any evidence, do you have any evidence that this coup might be on shaky ground, what you mentioned yesterday about sometimes coups fail and that possibly the opposition that's rallying around Yeltsin has any possibilities to turn it around? And what kind of support are you able, or will you give them other than verbal?

The President. Well, I said yesterday that some coups fail. The likelihood of this, it's hard to evaluate in this circumstance. However, there appears to be very strong support from the people in the Soviet Union for constitutional government, for democratic reform. And when you see the numbers turn out— President Yeltsin told me that he anticipated there were, he thought there were 100,000 people near his building when I talked to him a few minutes ago. He thinks that there will be strong support from the labor to his request that labor go out and don't produce until this matter is resolved. So, you don't take freedom away from people very easily.

You don't set back democracy very easily. And I'd say that it is in the best interest of the Soviet Union in its relations with other countries if a constitutional government is promptly put back into operation there.

Q. Mr. President, what kind of support, though, are you going to give Yeltsin, or are you—just have to stay on the sidelines and offer verbal encouragement?

The President. Well, we're certainly going to offer encouragement in every way we can. And we're making very clear to the coup plotters and the coup people that there will not be normal relations with the United States as long as this illegal coup remains in effect.

The Western Europeans have met, and they have come out with a statement along those lines. And I think, with the exception of a few renegade regimes around the world, we're seeing universal condemnation. So let's hope that that will bring these people to their senses.

I was just looking here at the statement from the EC decisions, and they have concluded that the CSCE human rights conference in Moscow should not go forward, and we will certainly back them in that. Technical assistance, they're following what I mentioned yesterday in holding back all of that. And they have some serious economic problems, and they need the help of the West, and they need the cooperation of Eastern Europe, and they're not going to get it under existing conditions.

Q. What happens now to the cosponsorship of the Middle East conference—will we do it alone—and other front-burner issues with the Soviet Union? And what was the gist of the letter from Yanayev?

The President. It's far too early to say what will happen to the Middle East conference. The whole world wants to see that succeed. The hopes for peace in the Middle East—and again, I credit Secretary Baker for his indefatigable efforts in putting together this peace process—the whole world wants to see it succeed. I hope that there will be no frustration to that on the part of the Soviet Union who have heretofore played a very constructive role in all of that.

But again, we are not in contact with Foreign Minister Bessmertnykh. We simply don't know what's going to happen.

What was the other part of your question?

Q.—go it alone?

The President. We will continue to fight for, continue to use our best efforts to bring peace to the Middle East, no matter what happens; of course we will. But let's face it, the Soviet Union heretofore has been constructive. They're important in the United Nations concept, and they're important on their own with the relations they have with some other countries.

It is ironic that only a handful of countries, predictably extreme countries, have supported what's happening in Moscow. I think of Libya, I think of Iraq, and I think of Cuba. These are renegades. These are people that have been swimming against the tide of democracy. The rest of the world appears to be very upset with this usurpation of power.

Q. Mr. President, in the past you've had differences with Chancellor Kohl over monetary aid to the Soviet Union. In your telephone conversation with him yesterday, did you say that it was imperative that they not give any money to the new regime?

The President. No. We worked out at the G - 7 meeting an agreement with Chancellor Kohl that he fully supported. Germany has some special problems. Germany wants

those Russian troops out of a unified Germany. We want the troops out of a unified Germany, but that was not discussed.

Q. Aside from Secretary Baker's trip to Brussels, is this situation such that you might want to see the European leaders meet together in a summit?

The President. Well, I'm not sure that that's the next step. We're in close contact with them. I talked to the G - 7 leaders yesterday, including Ruud Lubbers, the Prime Minister of The Netherlands who is head of the EC now. And I'm not sure that a face-to-face meeting of the European leaders and the United States and Japan would be productive at this point. But I think the process of Jim going to NATO, his doing that, is a very important step.

Yes, these two over here.

Q. Mr. President, when you say that economic relations with the Soviet Union are now on hold, does that mean that you're actively going after suspending grain credits, for example, or delaying most-favored-nation status?

The President. We're just sitting here for a while leaving everything on hold, as I've said. We're reviewing all these matters, and it's way too early to say how each individual category is going to work out. It's simply— we've got to just take our time. We've got to be prudent, a word I think is applicable here. And I think we've got to be strong. I think the world is turning to the United States for leadership here, many countries. And I think the best thing to do now is to put these matters on hold. We did this yesterday. As you've seen, the Europeans, Western Europeans, have followed suit. We don't want to hurt people anywhere in terms of starvation, things of that nature. But that's not the question right now. So, it's premature for me to say what agreements will go forward and what won't. I will always have in mind what is in the national interest of the United States, however.

Q. Mr. President, in light of your statement of yesterday, late yesterday afternoon, and in light of the fact that you're now denouncing the new regime in Moscow as illegitimate and unconstitutional, might you now or soon be considering granting to Lithuania and the other Baltic Republics that are, after all, elected governments the full recognition they have long demanded?

The President. Our position on the Baltic States has not changed. And if there's ever a change in the position, we'll let you know. As you all know, we have not ever recognized the forceable incorporation of the Baltic States into the Soviet Union. And that's where that matter is right now. But we are not giving up on the restoration of constitutional government in the Soviet Union itself. And so we'll leave that matter right there.

Q.—if that fails, sir, what—

The President. I'm not going to go into any hypothesis. I don't want to give hope to the coup plotters by suggesting that it is going to fail.

Let's see who we have over here.

Q. Are you saying that if the coup succeeds and the Soviet government, this new Soviet government is in power a long time, that the U.S. still would not recognize the Soviet Union?

The President. You must have missed what I said to Brit [Brit Hume, ABC News]. I'm not going to go into anything that hypothetical. There's no point in trying to spell out way in advance of events what we might or might not do. And the main thing I want

to do is see the restoration of constitutional government.

So, I'm sorry, I'm not going to take hypothetical questions or respond to questions of a hypothetical nature. I simply can't do that.

Q. You're very definite in the short term about not recognizing them?

The President. I'm very definite in what I said in this statement, yes.

Q. Mr. President, have you heard from Mr. Yeltsin on the whereabouts or the well-being of Mr. Gorbachev? Or from anyone else, for that matter?

The President. Mr. Yeltsin told me that he tried to send emissaries to see Mr. Gorbachev, that those emissaries were unsuccessful because Mr. Gorbachev is being prevented from seeing people. As I say, I've tried to call him yesterday. I think Prime Minister Major tried the same thing. I tried again today. Mr. Gorbachev is the duly constituted leader of the Soviet Union. And we will continue to try.

The other thing that Yeltsin told me is, and I think he's said this publicly, that he feels that if this medical answer has any validity to it that the World Health Organization should be permitted to see and examine Mr. Gorbachev. I can tell you that Yeltsin doesn't believe that, and I must tell you I don't believe it. But that is one of the canards being thrown out. It's really old-fashioned. But nevertheless, we will continue to try to stand with Mr. Gorbachev as Yeltsin is trying to do.

Q. Are you going to have to increase our stores of ammunition now, or are you going to leave more troops in Europe than you would have taken out?

The President. I'm not crossing any of those bridges now at all. I've mentioned the matter is where it stands. We're not moving any forces. Secretary Cheney and General Powell can respond to that when I finish if anyone wants to go further, but there's no—I'm not trying to elevate any chance of military confrontation. Nobody wants that, and I expect, I hope, that that's true of the coup plotters. It's certainly true of Eastern Europe, of Western Europe, and of the United States of America. And it's darn sure true of the people that elected Mr. Yeltsin, and it's true of the people that have supported constitutional reform in the Soviet Union which are vast majorities. So I'll leave it right there.

Q. Should the new Soviet regime be that concerned about American threats, considering it so far has been a bloodless coup and considering our response to the Tiananmen Square massacre?

The President. Who is threatening? Who is threatening?

Q. Well, you're not going to give them any diplomatic recognition at this point.

The President. I don't view that as a threat. I view that as a factual statement. That's not threatening at all. We are committed, nobody should be surprised that we remain committed to democratic reform and to constitutional government there. That means that Gorbachev, who was constitutionally installed, is in our view in power.

You know, it's interesting that Yanayev is saying he looks forward to working with Gorbachev. It seems to me that gives a certain credibility to what I'm just saying. I've raised the question, I hope not in a testy manner, about military confrontation because I think we want to cool that. This isn't a time to threaten militarily or to move forces around just to show machoism. That's not what's called for here. What's called for is diplomacy. What's called for is commit-

ment to principle, backing those people who are committed to reform, backing the people in the Soviet Union and in the Republics.

Q. Mr. President, you said that there are other democratic forces in the Soviet Union, that they may help. It seems that you wouldn't settle for anything but Gorbachev. But do you see other democratic forces emerging there that could play a very big role? Who are they? And also, do you trust them?

The President. There are plenty of people that are committed. Look at the mayor of Leningrad, for example. There are plenty of people who are committed to democracy and to reform there and in the Republics. I think one of the things that triggered this coup, the timing of the coup, was the fact that a union treaty was about to be signed which gave certain rights to these Republics.

So, believe me, there's thousands and millions of people that are committed to democratic reform. But why should I go into that question that might imply that we are turning our backs on the duly constituted leader? We're not going to do that.

Q. The present group seems to be trying to appeal to the people because they feel that they are hungry and they want food. Do you think that the London [economic] summit could have done something more financially?

The President. What they're trying to do is to say: "Look, we've got energy problems. We've got food problems. We've got health problems, and we, the unelected coup, are going to solve those problems." They can't do it without outside support. Mr. Yeltsin knows that. Mr. Gorbachev knows that. And these people will understand that. But what they're doing is trying to cloak their illegal move in the usurping power by saying to the people, "We're going to help you in these areas where you've been short-changed." That will not succeed. They're going to need to go forward with these reforms if the Soviet Union is going to fulfill its potential. So, that is a clear, obvious tactic they're using, but I don't think that people are going to buy into it.

I'm going to take two more after this, and then we've got to run.

Q. Mr. President, when you spoke with Yeltsin, did he give you any indication that he feared for his personal safety or that the Gorbachev family, Mrs. Gorbachev was in any way— was with her husband, away or—

The President. Yes. Nothing on the Gorbachev matter. Here was a man who was standing, Yeltsin, standing courageously against military force. And I told him that "We respect you. You've been duly elected here. We pray for you, and we hope that you're successful." And what he wants to see is the restoration of constitutional government. He wants to see the rights of the Republics, and he wants to see President Gorbachev restored to power. He didn't say he's afraid; he's a very courageous man. He says he's convinced that the people will stand with him, and well they should.

Q. Mr. President, for you or for Ambassador Strauss: When he gets there, with just whom will he be meeting?

The President. I'll leave that up to his good judgment, Charles [Charles Bierbauer, Cable News Network], because you know Moscow so well, and it's very hard to say with whom he will be meeting. The one thing I want him to do is establish his leadership in our Embassy, to consult with a highly professional staff there—one of whom is Mr. Collins who's the DCM [Deputy Chief of Mission] to whom I talked yesterday—get

the lay of the land from the ground. So, it's less reaching out to individual leaders, but I'll leave that to his good judgment and the judgment of the Secretary of State.

Last one. Owen [Owen Ullman, Knight-Ridder], and then we're going. I haven't seen you in a long time over here.

Q. A follow-up, sir. I'm trying to establish whether it's quicker for him to meet with Mr. Yanayev, for example?

The President. Well, we have no plans on that. And what we don't want to do is do anything that legitimizes this current regime or legitimizes what is clearly an illegal coup. And at this juncture, there are no plans for that. But again, this is a fast moving situation, and we'll have to wait and see what his judgment is when he gets there and what he and the Secretary decide.

Owen, and this is the last one.

Q.—Gorbachev over the past month, did either of you in your conversations talk about the possibility of something like this happening or the possibility of even civil war in the Soviet Union?

The President. No. What was talked about on his part was the irreversibility of this change, the fact that constitutional government is there, elections are over the horizon and have taken place in the Republics, some of the Republics, and his conviction that the people are committed to reform and certainly to openness, *glasnost*, as well. And I've seen nothing in the last day or two that would compel him or me to alter that.

Now, that isn't to say that there's a formidable obstacle right now in the way, and that is eight people that have usurped unto themselves all the power and are trying to take over by force, although Yanayev has said he looks forward to working with Mr. Gorbachev in the future.

So, there wasn't discussion of that. As you know, I think I have referred to—I know I have in our meetings—concerns that we conduct ourselves in such a way to minimize the chance of military takeovers. And that military takeover has taken place. But I believe that the policy that we've had into effect of supporting Gorbachev, as Yeltsin has been doing over the last few months, is the correct policy. I think it is the best hope for democracy, was the best hope for democracy and reform, and remains the best hope for democracy and reform.

You get hit from the left saying if you'd written out a better check this wouldn't have happened, and I don't believe that for one single minute. And you get hit on the other side by people that are suggesting that if we hadn't been supportive of the duly constituted President of the Soviet Union that things would have gone more swimmingly for democracy. I reject that. I don't believe there's any fact in that. And if there were, why was Boris Yeltsin, who was elected overwhelmingly, supportive as he was and continues to be of Mr. Gorbachev?

So, there it is. And as I say, we will be departing. I'm going to continue this vacation. I'm going to encourage our people to, but I don't want to be under any false color. It's going to be different now than it's been, maybe a little more like last year. What is it about August? [Laughter] But I will closely monitor this. We have extremely good communications up there, not only with our own key leaders, the Secretary of State, ambassadors, Secretary of Defense, Chairman of the Joint Chiefs, our Chief of Staff, our national security team, the Vice President. Communications are excellent.

But I don't want to again mislead people. I'm going to be spending a little more time, maybe quite a bit more time, in various formal ways that you will see unveiled in staying on top of this situation. But I don't want to panic. I don't want to send a signal, by sitting around the Oval Office here looking busy, that the American people should expect an instant satisfactory answer to this problem. I don't want to elevate hopes by succumbing to the whims of a few political critics that suggest that the matter can be better done in another way.

It happened, same thing, last year, and I did it the way I thought was best. And I hope I will have the full support of the American people as we follow this very, very closely. But I want to redefine it because I said that this vacation was going to be all rest and no work. And now it's going to be changed somewhat even though I have been getting briefed.

We have tremendous press coverage up there, get our message out. We have excellent communications and contacts. And rather than elevate the hopes by churning around in here, I'm going to finish what I started out to do. And I will receive various visitors, and you'll be fascinated, I am sure, by who they are. And it will show you my commitment to staying right on top of this situation because people are looking to the United States for the leadership in this, disproportionately.

I might add this point. Neither the Ambassador here or the Secretary of State or the Secretary of Defense or the Vice President or the Chairman of the Joint Chiefs or my White House advisers want to see this turn into an East-West confrontation. And we're going to get pushed. If I answer some of these hypothetical questions, I could inadvertently move things into an East-West confrontation. And that's not what this is about.

Many changes, constructive changes, have taken place in the world as a result of Mr. Gorbachev's leadership, as a result of Mr. Yeltsin's election. Adherence to democracy, for example, in the latter case. And clearly all you have to do is look at Eastern Europe, you have to look at a united Germany, you have to look at cooperation in various areas around the world to know what I'm talking about.

So, what we don't want to do is inadvertently set back any of those changes that are very, very important to the United States and to the rest of the world, particularly to Eastern Europe. And so we will conduct ourselves less flamboyantly than some would have us do our business, but I think with the proper mixture of strength and conviction to these democratic principles.

Thank you all very much.

43. The President's News Conference in Kennebunkport, Maine, on the Attempted Coup in the Soviet Union August 21, 1991

The President. I wanted to report to the American people on some of the latest developments related to the situation in the Soviet Union.

I spoke at length this morning to President Boris Yeltsin. The call began at about 8:30 a.m. And I also talked to Ambassador Strauss, who is now in our Embassy in Moscow, in position. And I also talked, in the last 20 hours, to President Menem in Argentina, to Prime Minister Mulroney, Prime Minister Major, and I will continue these kinds of consultative calls.

President Yeltsin was clearly encouraged by the fact that he had survived another night in the Russian Parliament building without a major assault by the forces supporting this coup. He told me that tens of thousands of Muscovites had turned out to help guard the building from attack.

Yeltsin said he was encouraged by indications that more and more military units and their commanders were abandoning support of the coup. His building is still surrounded, however, and special troops, the Spetznaz, are remaining loyal to the coup plotters. It is those troops who are moving to occupy additional sites in the Baltic States.

President Yeltsin said that the Russian Supreme Soviet had met and declared unanimously that the coup was illegal and without effect. And he also mentioned the importance of the next meeting of the Union Supreme Soviet, which will be held on August 26th. And they are, this is the way he put it, they are vigorously trying to line up support for that Supreme Soviet to declare this coup illegal.

President Yeltsin said he told the Supreme Soviet of the strong support being given by the United States to those resisting the illegal emergency committee activities and that the Supreme Soviet received the news very, very warmly.

There are at present, according to Yeltsin, flights of aircraft carrying his representatives, and also others with members of the emergency committee on their way to the Crimea to meet with President Gorbachev. Obviously he doesn't have all the details on that, and I won't be able to fill you in on any details on that, either.

President Yeltsin said he was prepared for all contingencies. He thanked the United States profusely for its support, which was making an important difference, and asked that we continue to stay in touch with him, which we will do.

Ambassador Bob Strauss, who had just arrived, gave me a rundown on developments in Moscow which paralleled those of President Yeltsin, the reports he was getting there.

Overall, while the situation remains highly fluid and uncertain, I think it is safe to say that the situation appears somewhat more positive than in the earliest hours of this coup. So, I will stay in touch with President Yeltsin, hopefully at some point be able to contact President Gorbachev, which we still are unable to do. But I guess I would say to the American people these developments are positive.

Q. Mr. President, this hardly sounds like a declaration the coup is over. What can you tell us, based on your conversations with Yeltsin and any other information you've got about the status of the coup plotters, whether the emergency committee is still in control there and the whereabouts and the condition on President Gorbachev?

The President. We don't know. We have all kinds of rumors. We have all kinds of raw intelligence coming in. But, Norm [Norman Sandler, United Press International], I think it would be a big mistake to add to the rumor mill. We simply don't know. Yeltsin tells me that he thinks five of the coup leaders have left Moscow; but he, I think, would be the first to tell you that he is not totally certain on this. He also feels that Pavlov is in the hospital. But we can't confirm it, and therefore it just—there's so much rumor and speculation. I want to try here now to avoid that as best I can.

Q. Do you know who is in control of the Soviet military right now, and were there any Western diplomats on these planes that are supposedly headed for the Crimea to meet with Gorbachev?

The President. Well, there were rumors about a flight that was taking some Western diplomats from the Embassies there. I talked to John Major about that, but there's no evidence that—when I talked to him, which was 15 minutes ago, there was no—in fact, he had confirmed that the plane had not left.

And yet, rumors had it that they were on their way. So, he had just talked to his emissary, who was going to be on the airplane.

Q. Mr. President, have you tried to reach President Gorbachev since yesterday?

The President. I haven't tried a direct phone call to him personally, but I'll keep trying.

Q. If the Soviets survive this constitutional crisis, would you be more inclined to provide direct economic aid to their economy which will be in no better shape?

The President. We will look at it. The G - 7 took action on that. We will continue to do what both Gorbachev and Yeltsin want, and that is to provide the kind of aid that the G - 7 said they would provide. And we will certainly, if things work out in a satisfactory fashion, get back into the business of furthering the economic recovery, certainly.

Q. Mr. President, could you elaborate a little bit on what you said about these special forces troops? The impression seems to have been that these were troops that were leaving the city, that that was a positive sign. Is it your understanding—

The President. There are two different groups of them. One of them is the airborne forces, and I believe that the airborne commander has come over to the Yeltsin side and pulled his forces back. The other are Spetznaz forces, which are the highly disciplined forces who answer to Defense Minister Yazov, and apparently they are still under command of Yazov, and they have not come over to the side of democracy and freedom.

Q. Is Yazov still there?

Q. So, Yazov is in charge, is still controlling the military?

The President. Well, it's very hard to tell. But according to Mr. Yeltsin, I've told you just exactly how it is working as of right now.

Q. As far as you know, though, Yazov is still—

The President. I would say that, as far as what Mr. Yeltsin knows, which is what I know, that the defense is not over on the side of Mr. Yeltsin at this point.

Q. Mr. President?

The President. Yes, we're going to work our way right down here.

Q. Mr. President, with Boris Yeltsin anchoring democratic opposition to this coup, where does that leave him if things do in fact resolve themselves satisfactorily?

The President. It leaves the world looking at him as a very courageous individual, duly elected by the people, standing firmly and courageously for democracy and freedom, with enormous stature as a result of that.

Q. Would that change the U.S. approach toward Mr. Yeltsin in any way?

The President. The U.S. approach towards Mr. Yeltsin, as you know, is to be supportive of those who are elected. Ever since he's been elected he has received total support. And before he was elected he was received properly. But I must say in terms of the respect level, I will join others all around the world, not just politicians or elected leaders of countries, in saying that he has shown tremendous courage, and the people appear to be rallying behind him.

And as I said earlier on, to some skepticism, 48 hours ago or more, that: Look, all these coups don't succeed and democracy, once unleashed, is a pretty powerful force. So, I think he will have a well-earned stature around the world that he might not have had—that he was on his way to having, but

might not have fully achieved before all this happened, provided it works out the way certainly the United States wants it to work out. But it is too early to declare these matters over. I don't want to be a part of that.

Q. How about Mr. Gorbachev's position, sir?

The President. Well, who knows? I mean, we can't even get in touch with Mr. Gorbachev, but Yeltsin is strongly supporting him, and so are we. He was constitutionally empowered. And that's the point here. Every time I talk to Yeltsin, or both times I've talked to Yeltsin, he makes this point of strong support for Gorbachev.

Q. Mr. President, are you planning any additional steps today, and have you given any additional instructions to Ambassador Strauss about what he should do?

The President. No, he will be in touch with me probably later today, and in touch with the Secretary of State. I missed a call, I think, from Jim Baker a few minutes ago. But he's over in Brussels. He will have met with the NATO leaders. I expect we may see him up here tomorrow, and we can get a little more detail out of that one. But I don't know the exact details of the Strauss plans yet. He just got there, he's surveying the situation as I asked him to do, and developments are happening so fast that I'll just have to wait and see how the clock runs and what he has to say.

Q. Did President Yeltsin's reports on the activities of the special forces and other military units—are they mirrored by U.S. intelligence on the subject, or do we have any U.S. intelligence on those subjects?

The President. Well, we have the best intelligence in the world, and sometimes it can accurately predict things, and sometimes it can actually count the beans and tell us the things you're asking about. We have some evidence of force movements in the Baltic area, but I don't want to go beyond that.

Q. Mr. Bush, when you say that Yeltsin says there's a delegation from the Russian Republic en route to the Crimea hoping to see Gorbachev, what is your understanding of what they hope will happen? Do they want to bring him back to Moscow?

The President. Absolutely. They want him back in power.

Q. Do they think he'll be able to?

The President. He was constitutionally put into office, and they want to have the law fully observed. So, they would like to see that, and they would like to see him in there unhampered by the illegality of the coup.

Q. Can you give us any sense of whether they think that will be possible today, tomorrow? Any timeframe?

The President. No, I can't because he was understandably vague as to whether they would get to see Gorbachev. He gave me the names of the people that were on the flight, which I'm not going to give because I think that should come from over there.

Q. Mr. President, given the way the world, if you will, is wired for sound and pictures, it's conceivable that Gorbachev is hearing you right now—

The President. I hope so.

Q.—or will. Since you can't get through to him on the phone, what would your message publicly be to him?

The President. I would say: Stay with your principles. Stay with your reforms. Stay with your commitment to democratic process and constitutional law. Stand shoulder-to-shoulder with Yeltsin, as you have been, in

seeing the evolution of democracy and *perestroika* and *glasnost* in the Soviet Union. And knowing Gorbachev, I'm convinced he will. Knowing what the objectives of the coup plotters must be, I would expect they would be trying to get him to do something else.

Q. Sir, in your communications with the Soviet Union, have there been any assurances to the U.S. at any level that the Soviet nuclear arsenal is safeguarded, that someone can't get their finger on the button?

The President. We see no reason to be concerned about that. Our people are taking a hard look at that all the time.

Q. Sir, I know you were glad to hear Boris Yeltsin say that American support has been very helpful to him. But in fact, you've talked about the limited impact the U.S. can have, your aides talked even more starkly about how little impact the limited economic aid we have, cutting off cultural exchanges. Is that the sort of thing that would have any impact on people, for these conservatives who are desperate to stay in power? Do you think you've any impact?

The President. Yes, I think—well, I would simply go by what Mr. Yeltsin says. And the statement I made yesterday—he was profuse in his gratitude for that. And it's not just the United States, but we are the United States of America and, thus, the disproportionately loud voice in matters of this nature.

But, John [John Mashek, *Boston Globe*], all I can tell you is what the man says. I'll tell you what I said to him. I said, "Now, would it be helpful to have another statement along the lines of the ones I made yesterday?" And he said, he repeated, "Yes, yes, yes, it is very important." And so, you know, there's some people in this country from one side or another of the spectrum that we have that say you ought to be able to wave a wand and solve a problem of this nature in the city of Moscow instantly. That's not what you can do. But what you can do if you're President is put the full force of the American people behind, emotionally, morally, behind the democratic forces. And that's what I'm trying to do. And apparently according to Mr. Yeltsin at least, and I think others, that's what we should be trying to do.

Q. But sir, these are pretty hard-boiled characters—

The President. Yes, they are.

Q.—who plotted this coup, and moral pleas to them probably have very little impact. Do you think the fact that they fear this economic aid being cut off, not only by you but by the EC countries, do you think that's the sort of thing that has an impact possibly on—

The President. Well, I would think it would have, or I wouldn't have—you know, I would have done it anyway. But I think it would have. Yes, John, they've got economic problems. As you know, some of their first decrees where they were going to put food on the shelves and do something about medicine and do something about energy, but as they see the reality of the world, they are going to need the help of the outside world. And when they see the United States and they see the European foreign ministers coming together, all saying they're not going to have business as usual, I think it does make an impact. And so, that is one thing that can be done.

Q. Could it have caused the apparent split within the coup plotters?

The President. No, I think what caused the current split in the coup plotters, and this is pure conjecture, is some of them realizing sooner than others that they may have bitten off more than they can chew here. But time

will tell on that one, and again, I don't want to be proclaiming this matter solved. I will say, once again, that I am pleased it is moving in the direction that it appears to be moving.

But they've got a lot of troops. They've got a lot of force. They've got a lot of people that look at these matters in a very hardline way. The one thing I don't want to do is inadvertently contribute to their will and their resolve. But I think some are flaking off because they think that they've gone about it wrong.

Q. Assuming that President Gorbachev does recover his authority, how will this affect his ability to keep the Soviet Union on a stable path? Will he be strengthened by it or weakened?

The President. I would say that, again, a little hypothetical for me to get into: Given Yeltsin's support for him and given the respect with which he's held by leaders all around the world, and that has certainly not been diminished by this at all, he will still be a force to be reckoned with.

Again, they can sort out inside their own matters. But what will be filtered away, should Gorbachev be reinstated, as we hope he will be, what will be filtered out will be the fear of a right-wing military takeover because the people will see that the power of the people to stand up against this illegality is pretty good, pretty strong.

Q. So, in effect, that might indeed strengthen his hand to move in a—

The President. It's possible, but again it's too hypothetical yet. We've got a big problem out there, and I'd want to try to keep it as factual as possible.

Q. Mr. President, when you were considering aid before the economic summit and other times, you had said you didn't want to give any serious aid until you saw credible reforms in place and the idea that it wouldn't go to waste. Does this delineation, the support of the people for Yeltsin and Gorbachev and the delineation of the progressives enhance their credibility? Do you now feel differently that you believe the reforms?

The President. I don't feel differently about their credibility. I never doubted the commitment to democracy or the commitment to *perestroika*, the commitment to reform. What has to happen, and what all of us addressed that problem in the G - 7 summit was, what had to happen was certain things had to take place before you send money.

But when you talk about economic support, we had put into effect in London, agreed on a program in London that was very acceptable to both Gorbachev and Yeltsin.

Q. Sir, you talked about the possibility of Mr. Gorbachev being reinstated. In this case, would you like to see popular Presidential elections in the Soviet Union?

The President. I think there will be, and I think those who are committed to democracy, as we are, strongly believe in that.

Q. Mr. President, given the "character" of the coup leaders, are you surprised they sort of went halfway with the coup and the incredible apparent disorganization of it?

The President. I think it's too early to decree how disorganized it is, but I think they underestimated the power of the people. They underestimated what a taste of democracy and freedom brings. Everyone recognizes that there were serious economic problems, and I think they felt, well, we'll come in there, promise food on the shelves and to solve these problems. And then they saw that, overriding all of that was a com-

mitment by many, many people in Russia and in the Soviet Union entirely, to democracy, for democracy. So, I think there, if this coup fails, that will be the serious miscalculation.

Q. Mr. President, if Gorbachev returns or some other, what you view as a constitutional figure returns, would you urge them to deal more forthrightly and decisively with the KGB, the interior forces and the military—

The President. It is too early to sort that out, and I wouldn't be bold enough to give advice to Mr. Yeltsin and Mr. Gorbachev to how to treat with those matters.

Q. Mr. President, you mentioned that we have the best intelligence in the world. Since there was a degree of surprise in the coup, do we have a better idea now as to when this coup was organized or who was the ringleader? Do you have any one person that you're now saying—

The President. Not yet. And, you know, I know a lot is expected of intelligence. But Mr. Gorbachev had pretty good intelligence. Mr. Yeltsin had pretty good intelligence. And all the intelligence services around the world think they've got good intelligence, and I know we've got the best, and I would simply say, based on this experience, that there are some things you cannot accurately predict.

That wasn't your question. We don't yet know the genesis of all of this, and it'll be a while before anybody does.

Q. Mr. President, you are reluctant to declare the coup over, but some are suggesting if this coup does fail, it will actually mean an end to the hard-liners and help to jump start democracy in the Soviet Union. What's your own feeling?

The President. It is so clear to me that if this coup fails, democracy will take a gigantic leap forward because we will have seen its underpinnings. We will have seen its inherent strength. We will have seen that a courageous leader, standing up for a principle, can rally an enormous number of people behind him.

Obviously, some of the determination will be based on the view of Mr. Gorbachev, but it would surprise me very much if he didn't stay totally committed to this path of democratic change.

Q. But in your view, is this the last hurrah for the hard-liners?

The President. Well, we'd have to wait and see. If I said that, I'd be declaring this over, and it's not the role of the President of the United States. Let's let these matters develop there.

One, two, three, and four, and then I'm out of here. [Laughter] That's the last question.

Q. Mr. President, you said that Yeltsin has prepared for all contingencies. Does he think, and do you think that there's still a possibility of a last-ditch military confrontation, and what does Yeltsin have at his disposal to hold up his end of such a confrontation?

The President. He made clear to me he doesn't think that the military threat is over. I think I stated that in the statement. But he was pleased, obviously, that the airborne troops had pulled back. But he made clear to me that he was not about to say that the threat is finished.

Q. What kind of forces does he have on his side, and is he prepared to fight?

The President. Well, they have some Russian forces, and he's got people on his side. He said, "tens of thousands" was the way he phrased it today.

Q. I'm wondering if you see any parallels between this situation and what we were going through last year at this time where the world unites to condemn an action in

hopes of reversing it through sort of moral suasion. It seems to be going a little better this time than last year. But if perhaps you talk about this force as a democracy, is it really just the fact that the people inside the Soviet Union weren't going to accept this?

The President. Well, I don't see a parallel on the democratic question. I do see a moral parallel: The world rising up against aggression last year, the world supporting the forces of democracy. This time there's a little difference. But there's a similarity if you want to put in terms of good-versus-evil which some philosophers might think is a little oversimplistic, and I don't. I think here we have a question of what's good and what's bad. What's good is the commitment to constitutional law and democracy, and what is bad is use of muscle to try to overthrow it.

Last year, what was good was the fact that the world stood up against aggression: democratic countries, nondemocratic countries. And what was bad is you had a handful of aggressors who had thought they could bully and the bludgeon a neighbor.

So, there are some parallels, Karen [Karen Hosler, Baltimore Sun], but I think there are also some distinct differences.

Q. Is the major difference, though, the forces of democracy that are being unleashed in the Soviet Union?

The President. I think it's a very important distinction here because the battle last year was not over democratic rule in Kuwait, for example; it was over aggression. Do you reward aggression or not? Do you let aggression stand or not? So that it was a different question, a different moral question. Both issues have strong moral underpinnings.

Q. Mr. President, the American relationship with Mr. Yeltsin has been fairly awkward at times over the last couple of years. No matter what happens precisely now, would you guess that the development in the last 3 days have changed that relationship forever, one way or another?

The President. In the first place, I think they were proper before the elections. Secondly, I think they properly improved dramatically after he was overwhelmingly elected by the people. That is a significant turning point for the way regimes all around the world, countries all around the world look at Mr. Yeltsin. And they have taken a quantum leap forward now by this man's displayed courage and by his commitment to democracy.

A follow-up?

Q. I was just going to say, have you found that in your personal relationship with him over the last couple of days that you've had an easier time talking with him? There has been some concern that he was somewhat erratic, somewhat flamboyant previously. Has that been a problem at any point in the last couple of days?

The President. I don't detect any less flamboyance. And in this instance, the flamboyance—[laughter]—the flamboyance is a very positive quality as you climb up there and encourage your people. But I don't see a turning point as a result of this. I mean, we had very cordial discussions as I think he, himself, confirmed in Moscow; I think he was accorded when he came to Washington as an elected leader. I think he felt, at least he said so, and I believe him, he felt that visit had gone very, very well.

So, I can't say to you, Jerry [Gerald Seib, *Wall Street Journal*], that there's been, in the personal contact way, been a dramatic change because I think as I have watched him in action as an elected leader his performance has been superb. And some were trying to make this long ago into a Gorbachev-versus-

Yeltsin battle, for example. I think that the way Yeltsin has conducted himself shows you that is not a Yeltsin-versus-Gorbachev battle. I don't think that Boris Yeltsin is sitting around thinking how do we dump Gorbachev. I think he is properly and with feeling expressing himself in total support of Mr. Gorbachev.

Last one.

Q. Yes, Mr. President, oil prices shoot up, and the markets have been unstable. Do you think that if the crisis should be very long, there could be a threat to the U.S. recovery?

The President. It's too hypothetical, but I think the answer is no. But you have to define "long" in something like that. But any time you have a conflagration of this magnitude, there are going to be some speculative losses. But the underpinning of the American economy is still pretty good, and so I wouldn't predict the kind of deleterious effect that the question, at least to me, implies.

I'm in trouble here. No, I'm out of here.

Q. Any hurricane damage at Walker's Point?

Q. Are you going to try to reach Gorbachev?

The President. We might give that another shot.

Q. Will you try to send anyone to see him?

The President. Come back tomorrow. I never knew what luxury you all were living in over here. [Laughter]

44. Remarks at the Swearing-In Ceremony for Supreme Court Designate Clarence Thomas
October 18, 1991

President Bush. Welcome all to the White House. Mr. Vice President and Mrs. Quayle, a warm welcome. And, of course, to the members of the Supreme Court. And may I simply say that Barbara and I join with you and with all the Nation in mourning the loss of Nan Rehnquist, the wife of the Chief Justice.

Let me also welcome the many Members of the United States Congress that are with us today. Single out but a few: Minority Leader Dole and Chairman Biden and ranking member Thurmond of the committee, and so many others; members of our Cabinet over here and so many friends of Clarence Thomas, who have worked with him here in Washington. And, of course, I should especially single out Senator Jack Danforth, a man every American would be proud to call friend.

And of course, those special guests, the many members of Clarence Thomas' family here today: his wife, Ginnie, son Jamal here in the front row, and Clarence's mother, Mrs. Leola Williams; his sister, Emma Mae Martin; his brother, Myers. His cousins, it reminds me of Pinafore, his cousins, sisters, aunts. [Laughter] But that's the way it ought to be. And all of you, some of whom drove all the way up, I see a little advertisement over here from Pin Point, Georgia, to be here this afternoon. That's 600 long miles, but I've got a feeling they might have driven 6,000 miles to be here today.

People from far and wide, from all walks of life, all levels of education and income, have come here today in testament to the character of Clarence Thomas. But what brought you here is also something more: the power of the American ideal; the values of faith and family, of hard work and opportunity. These are the values that unite us all, that give America meaning.

America is the first nation in history founded on an idea: On the unshakable certainty that all men are created equal. When we ask our Justices to uphold the Constitution, we entrust to them the laws that give life to our principles. Clarence Thomas now joins the distinguished ranks of jurists to whom we entrust this sacred task, who, in the stark and simple phrase of Chief Justice Marshall tells us "what the law is."

I said when I nominated Clarence Thomas that this man is a fiercely independent thinker, with an excellent legal mind, who believes passionately in equal opportunity for all Americans. Since then, the whole Nation has learned that the passion and the intellect and the independence of mind all spring from a single source: An inner strength stamped on his character long ago, when he walked the dirt roads of Pin Point.

Clarence Thomas comes to the Supreme Court having worked in the private sector, having served in State government and in every branch of Federal Government. Each position will serve him well on the Court, sharpening his vantage point on the many questions that come before him.

These are the man's qualifications. They are not the same as his experience.

Clarence Thomas knows firsthand the searing hate and sting of segregation. He knows the cold face of indifference, the unthinking cruelty that tells some men and women that society expects little of them and offers even less.

But Clarence Thomas would not be here today if there were not more to his story. He's known his share of the joys of life: the love of family, the devotion of friends, the kind gestures from people committed to decency and fairness, to justice and to the American dream.

Clarence Thomas has endured America at its worst, and he's answered with America at its best. He brings that hard-won experience to the High Court, and America will be better for it.

So, let me say to everyone here: Don't be overawed by the solemnity of this moment. Celebrate this day. See what this son of Pin Point has made of himself. See how he makes us proud of America, proud of all that is best in us.

In just a few moments, we will bear witness as the oath of office is administered to our Nation's newest Supreme Court Justice. Before we do, let me say on a personal level, America is blessed to have a man of this character serve on its Highest Court.

Clarence Thomas, Mr. Justice Thomas, congratulations. And now I'd like to ask Justice Byron White to administer the oath.

[At this point, Associate Justice Byron White administered the oath of Government service, and Judge Thomas then spoke.]

45. Remarks at the Welcoming Ceremony for President Vaclav Havel of Czechoslovakia
October 22, 1991

President Bush. Today we welcome a man whose moral authority makes him a hero not simply in his own land but everywhere that people cherish freedom: President Vaclav Havel.

I suspect the life of Vaclav Havel, President, would tax even the imagination of Vaclav Havel, playwright. Yet your life inspires us precisely because it shows that greatness begins with small acts of conscience and personal decency, acts that each one of us can perform.

Confronted with a wall of lies, you summoned the courage to "live in truth," to shun the silence that allows the lie to live, to speak out and risk the consequences. That courage sustained you through 5 long years in prison, as an outcast in your own country, to the chill autumn night 2 years ago when the people of Czechoslovakia came to Wenceslas Square. At first, a few candles flickered in the night sky. In time, the square was ablaze with light. The Velvet Revolution had begun.

Long before that night, you had written about "the power of the powerless." In the Revolution of '89, the world saw the Czech and Slovak people break their chains; the world witnessed once more the awesome power of the democratic idea.

Today, the electricity of revolution has given way to the sober business of democracy building. Your Federal Republic faces the challenge of three revolutions: First, an economic revolution, to replace the failed command system with the free market. Second, a political revolution, to replace the totalitarian travesty with democratic government and the tyranny of men with the rule of law, so that Czechs and Slovaks, working together, can build a secure future. And third and most important, you face a moral revolution, the need to build public trust and tolerance, to trade the cynicism that helped people survive the old regime for the idealism that will help you build a new one.

For 40 years, the ruling regime fed your people nothing but lies: a steady diet of quotas fulfilled, record harvests, unanimous votes, and unending progress; an elaborate fantasy that fooled no one. Today, Mr. President, you lead a people who know that being free means facing the truth, preferring fact to fiction, no matter how harsh the truth may be.

Your struggle is far from over. Everywhere across your country you feel the strains, the dislocations, and depressed standard of living. And I know the transition has hit particularly hard in Slovakia.

Yet your country has made impressive progress. You've taken decisive steps to privatize State enterprises, to liberalize trade and investment, to lift restrictions on private enterprise.

Each barrier you sweep away unleashes the energies of free enterprise, liberates the Czech and Slovak people to pursue their ideas and ideals.

America stands with you in this effort. Our trade enhancement initiative aims at opening American markets to your products. We seek through a special review to expand your benefits under our Generalized System of Preferences. Our enterprise fund will channel capital to Czech and Slovak entrepreneurs ready to put it to work. OPIC—the U.S. Government's Overseas Private Investment Corporation—has just completed a mission to Czechoslovakia, the largest mission OPIC has ever led to any country.

During your visit, our governments will sign the new Bilateral Investment Treaty, assuring an attractive investment climate for American firms that do business in your country.

A few days ago, I signed a document exempting the Czech and Slovak Federal Republic from the requirement of an annual Jackson-Vanik review. I hope for early congressional action to grant your country permanent most-favored-nation status. And to aid Czechoslovakia in its efforts to join the global economy, I call on the World Bank and the European Bank for Reconstruction and Development to provide assistance to pipeline projects already under consideration.

As your Federal Republic transforms itself within, it also has claimed its place in the councils of Europe. Mr. President, as a founder of Charter 77, you lived through the days when the secret police ransacked homes for papers related to the Helsinki accords. You must marvel that Prague now serves as home to the permanent Secretariat of the CSCE.

Nearly 1 year ago when I addressed your Federal Assembly, sir, I spoke of America's enduring role in Europe and of our vision of a new commonwealth of freedom. I know you share that vision, and I value your strong conviction that the U.S. should remain in Europe as a guarantor of security.

Together, on both sides of the Atlantic, we can work as partners in a growing community of free nations to extend the values of democracy, free enterprise, and the rule of law.

Your country knows better than most the harsh lessons of history, what happens when aggression goes unchecked. When Iraq invaded Kuwait, the Czech and Slovak people stepped forward to take their place in the coalition against the aggressor. Even as it struggled to secure its own fragile independence, your country came to the defense of a nation in need.

You led the way in showing a new Europe that the security of one State is inseparable from the security of all. I welcome the opportunity to reaffirm today my country's commitment to your success, to the promise of democracy and independence.

Once again, Mr. President, welcome to the White House. And may God bless the Czech and Slovak people.

President Havel. Mr. President, ladies and gentlemen. Let me, on behalf of the whole Czechoslovak delegation, thank you for your warm welcome. I have a good feeling that we are coming to friends with whom we share the same attitude toward the principal values of life, and who, therefore, understand our problems and needs.

Our friendship has deep roots and has gone through a difficult test of time. In the hearts and minds of our people, it survived the adversity of the long decades of the totalitarian era to be given a new dimension by the freedom reborn in my country 2 years ago. The legacy of the fathers of Czechoslovak-American cooperation—the founder of our State, Tomas Garrigue Masaryk, and President Woodrow Wilson—has thus been fulfilled.

It makes me happy to feel that I can regard you, Mr. President, as a friend of Czechoslovakia and as my personal friend. This is not the first time when I have an opportunity to step on the soil of your country. I shall never forget the reception accorded to me during my last year's visit when I came here for the first time in the capacity of head of state. Today, I am starting my first official State visit to your country, and I am looking forward to seeing it unfold no less successfully.

It will certainly be a breakthrough in our relations as significant documents are to be signed on this occasion. A permanent place among them will be held by the declaration on the relations between our countries in which we shall express our resolve to work together for the advancement of our cooperation. In so doing, we shall make a contribution, even if a limited one, to the strengthening of the traditional partnership between the United States and Europe.

We do see in this partnership a guarantee of our own stability and security. It is my conviction that our visit to your country, for which we prepared with utmost care, will achieve its purpose and confirm what I have said with much pleasure a number of times already, namely, that relations between Czechoslovakia and the United States have never been as good as they are now.

Thank you.

46. The President's News Conference with President Gorbachev of the Soviet Union in Madrid, Spain
October 29, 1991

President Bush. Well, just very briefly, I want to thank President Gorbachev. We've had yet another very constructive meeting. We're here, of course, for this international conference on the Middle East, and I can express my gratitude to President Gorbachev for the very constructive role that the Soviet Union has played in the actions leading up to this conference. We're grateful to him for that.

We also discussed some of the matters of mutual interests involving the situation inside the Soviet Union, the dynamic change there, the commitment to reform that is still very strong. And all in all, as far as I'm concerned, it was yet one more very good meeting with the President.

President Gorbachev. I join what Mr. President just said and wanted only to say a couple of words for myself. We agreed on holding this meeting since it was a very convenient opportunity in order to coordinate our watches, synchronize our watches, to talk a little about what is of mutual interest to the Soviet Union and to the United States.

Yes, it's true that we began by—we talked about all the many years of effort that we made. Especially our joint efforts in the very recent past, both of the United States and the Soviet Union, has brought us to the point now where, today, tomorrow, this long-awaited forum, this long-awaited conference is opening. And let's hope that given everything that we might encounter along the way during these negotiations within the confines of this conference, let's hope that it all turns out for the best and positively.

In any case, President Bush and I have agreed that having opened this conference and having left Madrid, we not at all expect to be somewhere on the side. On the contrary, we're going to facilitate as much as possible, use all the remedies that we have at our disposal. I think that all the participants of the conference and we, too, wanted to—both today and tomorrow we'll talk about it some more, maybe to appeal to everybody that they act responsibly with great understanding that what is beginning within the framework of this Madrid conference—how meaningful it is, and that everybody be very constructive as much as possible.

Further, we said a lot and talked a lot about—since I had the intention to pose before President Bush several questions, several issues vis-á-vis what's happening internally in the Soviet Union, and also because he and Mr. Secretary of State also had a whole series of questions in order to ask, for the benefit of their own understanding, to try to find out where we now are in the Soviet Union and to get a better grasp of what kind of issues and problems we're trying to solve.

This took quite a large percentage of our time, probably the majority of our meeting. I'm very satisfied by the position which was held, by the position of the President of the United States, and hope that—have all the basis to believe and feel that this is yet another step in strengthening the mutual understanding and cooperation between our two countries, right at the stage of all the great and momentous changes that are taking place.

And finally, we had an exchange of information and views as to what each of the sides is doing in the context of disarmament and all the initiatives that have been undertaken.

The President and I gave a very high mark to the way we are solving a lot of these very burning issues which for many years have plagued us. But now basing ourselves on all the experiences that have happened over the last few years, especially how well we're getting along now with our two countries, between the Soviet Union and the United States, also among the members of the two governments of the two countries, that we're finding very good solutions.

In any event, we wanted to have a very short meeting to chat and maybe not overload ourselves too much because the subject of this meeting, in fact, is the opening of the conference. But in fact, we had a very substantive discussion; I think it will be very useful for both parties, for both sides. Thank you.

Nuclear Arms Reduction

Q. This is a question to President Bush and President Gorbachev. You are now talking about disarmament or arms control. How much of the two schedules of both the Soviet Union and the United States, schedules of disarmament and arms control, how much are they similar, the two schedules of the two countries?

President Bush. We made some sweeping proposals a while back. President Gorbachev immediately responded positively to our proposals. Then he came forward with some additional proposals. And I would say, after analyzing his, and his analyzing our proposals, that our schedules are very close to in line. And what we've agreed to do today is to talk further on the practical steps involved.

We had good discussions on the whole question of nuclear arms reduction and nuclear safety, but I can assert from the U.S. side that our schedules, as you refer to them, talk to them, are very close. And now what we've got to do is iron out more detail, have more discussion. And we've agreed to send our top people, including Mr. Bartholomew, to discuss with the Soviet side what additional steps we can agree on, additional to those that have already been agreed. I think we both want to go forward with CFE and START ratification very promptly.

President Gorbachev. I would have to merely confirm what President Bush said. There's no reason to worry or have any concern from either one or the other side. In view of the thing that people say, "Well, maybe this was found or that was found," certain initiatives, some people have concerns on schedule. No, there's nothing to worry about, I think. That's very important to say. And this is also a sign of responsibility and determination.

Secondly, I want to confirm what was said. We did, in fact, agree how this mechanism will work, the mechanism which will give us, or provide the opportunity for us to continue discussing these issues, to keep each other informed, and to clarify issues for each other as they arrive.

In addition, we've also agreed that there be created two groups which will discuss issues having to do with strategic stability. Included among that is strategic stability for the future. I think we'll also be handling these kinds of issues and looking far into the future.

Aid to the Soviet Union

Q. Mr. President, did you tell Mr. Gorbachev that you would provide any additional aid to the Soviet Union? And further, do you think the Western nations should withhold aid from breakaway Republics, such as the Ukraine, who refuse to cooperate on military and economic matters?

President Bush. On the latter point, we discussed a lot that relates to the Republics, but we still are very respectful of the changes that are taking place. I asked for certain clarification from President Gorbachev on this.

What was your point on the Ukraine?

Q. I was wondering whether or not the Ukraine, which says that it won't cooperate on the economic union, and it's also insisting on joint control with Moscow of nuclear missiles—if you think that Western countries should provide aid to—

President Bush. I think that what we ought to do, and we did have a long discussion with President Gorbachev, is figure out the best package that we can do that will come as close to meeting his requirements as possible for economic aid. And clearly, some will go to the Republics. So, that all requires negotiation. There is no agreement on specific amounts or anything of that nature, but we did have a strong—we had a good discussion of the requirements.

And again, I think the American people, when it comes to food aid and medicines, clearly want to be of assistance to the Soviet Union. And secondly, we are very interested in trying to do our part to see the reforms continue. And so we had a wide discussion about that. But no specifics have been agreed on. We will go back and talk to our representative that attended the G - 7; David Mulford attended the G - 7 finance meetings in Moscow. And then we'll have more negotiation and discussion with President Gorbachev on that.

Q. But it's not a barrier if the Ukraine refuses to cooperate on the economic and military matters?

President Bush. Well, I think it's President Gorbachev's feeling that they will cooperate on economic matters, but I defer to him on that.

President Gorbachev. I'm used to answering tough questions, so I agree. I agree to answer this part of your question as well. Yes, we for a long time now, President Bush and I have been discussing the cooperation at this very, very difficult phase of our reform process where the Soviet Union now finds itself. And I must say that, inevitably, given the very substantive nature and the principal nature and sometimes even sharpness of our discussions, nonetheless, we and the President, and the administration, we know that the President and the administration in Washington has shown great understanding and cooperation towards our plight.

We today, as well, discussed this within the context of saying that today in the Soviet Union—today people from the G - 7, the deputy finance ministers of the G - 7 are meeting there to discuss this issue in particular. The very specific answer is that the result of the meeting—there have participated 12 Soviet Republics and every one of them signed a memorandum by which they confirm the unified responsibility that they bear for paying the debts of the Soviet Union. They have empowered, all the 12 Republics have empowered their representatives to delegate their powers over to Vneshekonom Bank and have it be the central juridical face, also to decide who bears what responsibility in the Republics, who to have dealings with, who's going to have the authority.

So, I think that when you look at it at first glance, it might be a technical issue, but in very fact, it points out that if you have solidarity among all the Republics today on this, let's hope that in the future that is contin-

ued. So, let's say now today that all 12 have signed.

Now, how about the Ukraine? Two days ago, I think it was Friday morning, I spoke with the Prime Minister of the Ukraine, Mr. Volkin, who said to me in this talk, he told me that the Ukraine, after the decision by the Supreme Soviet, when he put forth his own program, among a whole series of other things that was said in that program, one of those issues was to enter the circle of Republics and sign the economic treaty. The Supreme Soviet voted, I think it was 283 or 284 in favor of the position of the Prime Minister of the Ukraine and only 39 against. This gave him the opportunity, now based upon the decision of the Supreme Soviet, to tell us and report to us that, in fact, he will sign. Maybe he's already signed it since I left Moscow, but in these last several days he will have signed this. So, I hope this takes care of your concern.

And finally, returning to today's conversation, I told President Bush I felt it necessary to report to him the most important thought, that now we have come up through this stage and now are actually beginning to make realistic, concrete steps toward the marketplace, stabilizing finances, taking steps to liberalize prices, taking steps aimed at quickening, speeding up the process of regularizing the financial order in the country. To really take a hard look and get our hands around the debts. In other words, that very specific process that has to move us to the marketplace, that is now beginning.

And in fact, all of our society is now faced with a rather complex set of decisions. This precise moment when we are especially sensitive to what we are doing in our country, and we feel sensitively what the attitude is of all of our partners abroad. We have to take a look at what's been going on. I've reported to all the people—I just told the President what all the G - 7 partners were talking about in Moscow, and we will get back once again to this issue and help them find a specific solution. Thank you.

Leadership in the Soviet Union

Q. Since your departure from Moscow, who is taking your place in Moscow? Who is fulfilling your duties?

President Gorbachev. Okay, I'll try to answer quickly because I know that nobody is. I'm still the President. Nobody is taking my place. Everybody else is doing what they're supposed to be doing and carrying out their functions. Whether I am more calm and confident now than I was before, I didn't lose my balance then, and I haven't lost it now. I'm fully confident that what we're doing is ultimately necessary, and I will do everything that's in my power to do everything necessary. Nobody is going to take me out of the action. The choice has been made.

President Bush. Let me respond to this, what I understand was the second part of the question. I have had a history of very satisfactory negotiations with President Gorbachev. You're correct in that. Secondly, when the coup attempt took place, we stood up against that. And thirdly, I sense no difference in how we talk and the frankness with which we exchange views, no difference, certainly from my standpoint, in the respect level for President Gorbachev. We in the United States watch with fascination and keen interest the developments inside the Soviet Union, the dramatic movements towards the reforms that he, himself, committed himself to years ago.

So, it is not for me to fine-tune every detail of change inside the Soviet Union. It is for

me to continue to negotiate with President Gorbachev, with his total understanding, I'm sure. We've had many contacts with the Republics as well. And so, we will deal with what's there. And I'm very happy to see my friend again and to have had very fruitful discussions that have not in any way been altered by the tragic coup attempt last summer.

Middle East Peace Conference

Q. Mr. President, both of you, in terms of the Madrid conference, can there be a lasting, a just settlement in the Middle East unless there is a tradeoff of conquered land for peace? And also, with your hands-off policy, aren't you really—you've brought them to the table. Does it mean "you guys fight it out" and there will be no involvement of the sponsors?

President Bush. Did you have an order in which you'd like that replied to?

Q. No, you can answer it any way you like.

President Bush. Thank you, Helen [Helen Thomas, United Press International].

Do you want to go first?

Look, the invitation went out. In the invitation it talked about Resolution 242 and 338. The American position is well-known. The Soviet position is well-known. But what is important here is getting the parties together. And one way you don't do that is for either the Soviet Union or the United States to try to impose a settlement. So, let them sort it out. We're available. We're there, the Soviet side, the U.S. side. Secretary Baker will remain on our side after I leave tomorrow.

But, we're not here to impose a settlement. We are here to be a catalyst. I think the worst thing we could do is reiterate our own positions to such a degree that one side or the other became disenchanted before they even talk to each other. This is historic because people are sitting down to talk to each other for the first time. So, at least from the U.S. side, it is not my intention to try to impose a settlement or to go back to years of differences and reiterate strongly held convictions.

On the U.S. side, what we're interested in is getting Israel and its neighbors to sit down and talk, talk in a multilateral facet and then go forward bilaterally.

Q. But you didn't answer my question.

President Bush. What was it? I thought I gave a good answer to it. [Laughter]

Q. Can there be peace if there is not a tradeoff?

President Bush. I told you, let the parties work all this out, Helen. Who is it for you and me to sit here in this lovely Soviet Embassy to try to say what the requirements are going to be? I told you what the invitation said, based on 242 and 338. Everybody knows what that means. So, there's no point in me going beyond that. Please don't try me again today, as you did yesterday. [Laughter]

You know Helen?

President Gorbachev. Yes. I've got to say that President Bush really vocalized what our approach is, what we decided to follow and to keep to. So, I think that this is the proper way, the proper approach. Respect also to the participants of the negotiating process. This is very tough for them, very difficult meetings where they're going to have to maybe do quite a bit of work, all of them, so that they all come out to a final, positive conclusion.

Because it doesn't mean, like I said before, I want to reiterate again: This does not mean that we are simply going to stand on the side and that it doesn't really make any

difference to us what happens. No, that's not at all. Our role of playing our good offices, using our good offices, we will perform. But everything else, what is decided upon, what is agreed to, must use what we have today, all of us, at our disposal.

We need a new climate of international relations, a new situation has to be developed, new relations among leading countries in the world, first of all, the Soviet Union and the United States. And then included in that also, reestablishment of diplomatic relations with Israel. Use everything that we have to find the keys, to find all the right chords, to get rid of all those old, outdated issues and problems. Find a solution which would satisfy the interests of everybody. Without a balance, without taking into account everybody's needs, we will not succeed.

Therefore, President Bush has just informed you about the process that we have agreed to and the kinds of approaches we will be dedicated to. Thank you.

Q. Given Syria's position regarding the regional negotiations, is it—and of course, its refusal so far to enter these negotiations—is it your position, sir, that the parties to the regional negotiations should go on and conclude agreements regardless and independent of the element of withdrawal that is apparently most important to the Syrian position? And secondly, should settlements and negotiations for peace go on hand-in-hand, independently?

President Bush. These are both very important questions and they're very substantive questions, but once again, I think it would be counterproductive for me—let President Gorbachev decide on his own—but it would be counterproductive for me to give definitive answers to how I feel those two important questions should be resolved. The U.S.

has historic positions; the Soviet side has historic positions.

We brought these parties together now in something that most people thought could never happen. And once again, it would be counterproductive for me to set conditions or to say from the U.S. side how these two questions that you properly asked about be resolved. I'm simply not going to do that. This is too sensitive a time. We're trying to get in here to have people start discussions on their own. And I don't want to give anybody any reason whatsoever to walk away or to make additional demands because of something I have said.

So, I simply, respectfully, will not answer your question in the detail that I know you'd like me to do.

President Gorbachev. During the preliminary stages where we were preparing this conference, there was quite a number of very sharp issues that were raised, even in the press a lot, quite a bit is being written, publicized, people's points of view, opinions. But tomorrow the conference starts. And so, this preliminary, preparatory phase, in spite of all the difficulties that we've encountered, all the discussions that have been had, all the things said in the press—nonetheless, we are here at the opening. Let's just open the conference, and let's start working.

It seems to me that the sides themselves can only win if they maintain a position of principle but are constructive. Everybody's concerns are real. But let's really say we're not going to substitute by our actions that which happens at the negotiations at the conference.

Aid to the Soviet Union

Q. The issue of economic assistance that the United States said for all the time that first

they have to deal with the center when it comes to foreign aid, and now in many of the enterprises we're moving hard currency—in what position the United States found itself. In other words, is the United States more actively working with the Republics, and namely Russia itself, or still going to deal only through the center?

President Bush. Well, I thought I addressed myself to that. Clearly, we're here today, and we're dealing with President Gorbachev. I have kept contacts with President Yeltsin. You asked specifically about the Russian Republic. But on a matter of this nature where we're talking about credit, and we're talking about hopefully humanitarian assistance, it is important that Americans get the view that the center and the Republics are together on these matters. But we don't plan to change our dealings with President Gorbachev or, indeed, with President Yeltsin or leaders of the other Republics. And I think, I have the feeling they both understand that. It's a little vague, but I don't believe I can be more specific on your question than that.

I think under the economic agreement, President Gorbachev was explaining to me today, the Republics are indeed together with the center, closer together with the center on these economic matters than ever before, which makes it much easier for the United States or the G - 7 or the other countries that clearly want to assist in the reform process, in helping this go forward.

Q. President Gorbachev and President Bush as well, despite what you've said about the economic situation, it's not entirely clear to me. Did you, sir, President Gorbachev, make any specific, any new requests for assistance? And did you, Mr. Bush—you've indicated in talking about a package, is this something over and beyond what we have heard before? If you could be more specific, it would help us.

President Gorbachev. Well, in general, if you would bear in mind the fact that recently, between myself and the leaders of the G - 7, there is a regular exchange of views and information, then many of the issues directed to President Bush. Well, he knew about a lot of these issues anyway. He already was informed of it.

At the same time, based upon our requests, the President of the United States and other leaders of the European Community were working on these kinds of questions. Now, in this connection for them to decide, a couple of days ago they decided to have this meeting of the deputy ministers of finance who came to Moscow to discuss this cooperation, the assistance, and they, I think very substantively, went through and made assessments of what is the real situation and came to one, single, unified understanding. And that's very important if you're going to make decisions.

They had a unified, single opinion of what is going on. They established a series of positions, opinions that they came up with, and the governments and these countries will then be told about this.

So now, when the President goes back to Washington and I go back to Moscow, we will listen to what these recommendations of the specialists are, talk about it, think about it. Then we will then be able to be in a position to finally make a determination on this question.

I don't think that everything is solved by this. Maybe it will be several times in the future we may have to come back and ask other assistance, because life casts up a whole variety of surprises. But the very fact that we have fruitful, constructive, specific, businesslike, and very promising work going

on, and it also bodes well for future results. Thank you.

President Bush. That's essentially the way I would have answered the question.

Q. That there is nothing specific?

President Bush. You heard President Gorbachev use the word "specific," but I'd say we're in a phase of discussing details, which obviously means specificity. But I endorse what he said about needing further work and consultation on this, each with our own economic side, and then follow through with more discussion.

So, there were some specifics discussed, but we will go forward as he indicated.

Q. What is the magnitude of what you're discussing now in contrast to what it was—

President Bush. We've agreed, we're not going to go into magnitudes of it right now.
Thank you.

47. Remarks on the Civil Rights Act of 1991
November 21, 1991

Welcome to the White House. And may I salute the members of the Cabinet who are here today, Members of the Congress, many Members of Congress, distinguished guests.

Today we celebrate a law that will fight the evil of discrimination while also building bridges of harmony between Americans of all races, sexes, creeds, and backgrounds.

For the past few years, the issue of civil rights legislation has divided Americans. No more. From day one, I told the American people that I wanted a civil rights bill that advances the cause of equal opportunity. And I wanted a bill that advances the cause of racial harmony. And I wanted a bill that encourages people to work together. And today I am signing that bill, the Civil Rights Act of 1991.

Discrimination, whether on the basis of race, national origin, sex, religion, or disability, is worse than wrong. It's an evil that strikes at the very heart of the American ideal. This bill, building on current law, will help ensure that no American will discriminate against another.

For these reasons, this is a very good bill. Let me repeat: This is a very good bill. Last year, back in May of 1990 in the Rose Garden, right here with some of you present, I appealed for a bill I could sign. And I said that day that I cannot and will not sign a quota bill. Instead, I said that the American people deserved a civil rights bill that number one, insisted that employers focus on equal opportunity, not on developing strategies to avoid litigation. Number two, they deserved a bill that was based upon fundamental principles of fairness, that anyone who believes their rights have been violated is entitled to their day in court, and that the accused are innocent until proved guilty. And number three, they deserved a bill that provided adequate deterrent against harassment based upon race, sex, religion, or disability.

I also said that day back in 1990 that this administration is committed to action that is truly affirmative, positive action in every sense, to strike down all barriers to advancement of every kind for all people. And in that same spirit, I say again today, "I support affirmative action. Nothing in this bill overturns the Government's affirmative action programs."

And unlike last year's bill, a bill I was forced to veto, this bill will not encourage quotas or racial preferences because this bill will not create lawsuits on the basis of numbers alone. I oppose quotas because they incite tensions between the races, between the sexes, between people who get trapped in a numbers game.

This bill contains several important innovations. For example, it contains strong new remedies for the victims of discrimination and harassment, along with provisions capping damages that are an important model to be followed in tort reform. And it encourages mediation and arbitration between parties before the last resort of litigation. Our goal and our promise is harmony, a return to civility and brotherhood, as we build a better America for ourselves and our children.

We had to work hard for this agreement. This bill passed both Houses of Congress overwhelmingly with broad support on both sides of the aisle. A tip of the hat goes to Senator Kennedy and former Congressman Hawkins, who, way back in February of 1990, got the ball rolling. And I congratulate and thank particularly Senators Dole, Danforth, and Hatch, Congressmen Michel, Goodling, and Hyde for ensuring that today's legislation fulfills those principles that I outlined in the Rose Garden last year.

No one likes to oppose a bill containing the words "civil rights," especially me. And no one in Congress likes to vote against one, either. I owe a debt of gratitude to those who stood with us against counterproductive legislation last year and again earlier this year, as well as to those who led the way toward the important agreement we've reached today. I'm talking about Democrats, I'm talking about Republicans, and those outside the Congress who played a constructive role. And to all of you, I am very, very grateful, because I believe this is in the best interest of the United States.

But to the Congress I also say this: The 1991 civil rights bill is only the first step. If we seek—and I believe that every one of us does—to build a new era of harmony and shared purpose, we must make it possible for all Americans to scale the ladder of opportunity. If we seek to ease racial tensions in America, civil rights legislation is, by itself, not enough. The elimination of discrimination in the workplace is a vital element of the American dream, but it is simply not enough.

I believe in an America free from racism, free from bigotry.

I believe in an America where anyone who wants to work has a job.

I believe in an America where every child receives a first-rate education, a place where our children have the same chance to achieve their goals as everyone else's kids do.

I believe in an America where all people enjoy equal protection under the law, where everyone can live and work in a climate free from fear and despair, where drugs and crime have been banished from our neighborhoods and from our schools.

And I believe in an America where everyone has a place to call his own, a stake in the community, the comfort of a home.

I believe in an America where we measure success not in dollars and lawsuits but in opportunity, prosperity, and harmony. I believe in the ideals we all share, ideals that made America great: Decency, fairness, faith, hard work, generosity, vigor, and vision.

The American dream rests on the vision of life, liberty, and the pursuit of happiness. In our workplaces, in our schools, or on our streets, this dream begins with equality and opportunity. Our agenda for the next American century, whether it be guaranteeing equal protection under the law, promoting excellence in education, or creating jobs, will ensure for generations to come that America remains the beacon of opportunity in the world. Now, with great pride—and thanks to so many people here in the Rose Garden today, especially the Members of Congress with us—with great pride I will sign this good, sound legislation into law. Thank you very much.

48. Letter Accepting the Resignation of John H. Sununu as Chief of Staff to the President
December 3, 1991

Dear John,

I now have your letter resigning as Chief of Staff effective December 15th. It is with reluctance, regret and a sense of personal loss that I accept your resignation as Chief of Staff.

I am very pleased, however, that you have agreed to remain as a Counsellor to the President, with Cabinet rank, through March 1, 1992.

During the period, December 15th to March 1, you will be an official member of my administration and I will continue to seek your counsel on the important issues facing our country.

John, I find it very difficult to write this letter both for professional reasons and for personal reasons.

On the professional side, thanks to your leadership we have made significant accomplishments for which you deserve great credit.

Working with others here in the White House, throughout the administration, and on Capitol Hill, you have played a major role in achieving some of our significant goals.

I will not attempt to list each legislative achievement for which you deserve an awful lot of personal credit. Having said that, your adherence to principle and your endless hours at the negotiating table were clearly instrumental in achieving good Clean Air Legislation; the ADA Bill and the Civil Rights Act of 91, both of which moved this country forward in a sensible way; groundbreaking Child Care legislation that strengthened the principle of family choice; and a budget agreement that for the first time in history put real enforceable caps on discretionary government spending. For all of this and much, much more, I am very grateful to you.

In your letter, you generously mention my family and our personal relationship. The longer I serve as President the more importance I place on true friendships—friendships tested by fire and time. Ours is such a friendship. Barbara feels this way. Our four sons feel this way and so of course does Dorothy.

You have never wavered in your loyalty to us and more importantly, your loyalty to the principles and goals of this administration. You have indeed helped with the issues and you have intercepted many of the "arrows" aimed my way.

Thank you from the bottom of my grateful heart for your distinguished service. I look forward to working with you in the future, first as Counsellor inside government and then as a trusted advisor outside government.

And, yes, from my vantage point and our families as well, the friendship we treasure is stronger than ever.

I hope you and Nancy, free of the enormous pressures of the office you have served so well, will enjoy life to its fullest. You deserve the best.

Most sincerely from this grateful President,
George Bush

Dear Mr. President,

A little over three years ago you asked me to be your Chief of Staff. I eagerly and appreciatively accepted.

Over these years it has been one of the most gratifying and satisfying experiences of my life to serve a President whom I admire, respect and will always consider a dear friend.

These have been amazing times for the world and the nation; they have been exciting and thrilling times for me. I am truly grateful for the opportunity to have been a part of it.

But most of all, from a purely personal perspective, I want to thank you for the fun we have had these last three years. In a way that will be very difficult for historians to capture, this White House was an unbelievably "fun place"

to work. You, the Vice President, Scowcroft, Gates and I proved we could do very serious things well without taking the process or ourselves too seriously. I believe that chemistry, friendship, caring and irreverence was a singularly unique period for the Oval office, probably impossible ever to replicate. You were just great to let us do it that way.

I must also take this opportunity to tell you again how proud I am of the White House staff you allowed me to put together. They will eventually be recognized as the most talented, mutually supportive, cooperative team ever to serve a President. In fact, one of the challenges ahead of us will be to make very clear the significance of all you and they have accomplished in the domestic area as well as in foreign policy.

I have always said I wanted to serve as Chief of Staff as long as I could contribute to your success and help deal effectively with both the issues and the arrows. Until recently I was convinced that even with the distorted perceptions being created, I could be a strong contributor to your efforts and success.

But in politics, especially during the seasons of a political campaign, perceptions that can be effectively dealt with at other times, can be—and will be—converted into real political negatives. And I would never want to not be contributing positively, much less be a drag on your success. Therefore, as we enter the contentious climate of a political campaign, I believe it is in your best interest for me to resign as Chief of Staff to the President of the United States effective December 15, 1991.

As much as I will truly miss the opportunity to continue to work in the West Wing with you and my other friends there, I want you to know how strong and positive and upbeat I feel about doing this. I think you know that the responsibility and authority (contrary to the legends out there) never meant as much to me as the chance to assist you to be (and to be recognized) a great President. I intend to continue that effort as an ordinary citizen, with all the benefits that accrue to man and family in the private sector of our magnificent system.

I assure you that in pit bull mode or pussy cat mode (your choice, as always) I am ready to help.

I also want to thank Barbara and all the Bush clan for being such wonderful friends and strong supporters even during the toughest of days. Nancy and I and our family will always remember and cherish that kindness and friendship. I hope we will all have a chance to share a few laughs over the holidays.

Thanks again for the privilege of serving you and this wonderful country. It really has been great!!!

Sincerely and respectfully,

John H. Sununu

49. Statement on the Resignation of Mikhail Gorbachev as President of the Soviet Union
December 25, 1991

Mikhail Gorbachev's resignation as President of the Soviet Union culminates a remarkable era in the history of his country and in its long and often difficult relationship with the United States. As he leaves office, I would like to express publicly and on behalf of the American people my gratitude to him for years of sustained commitment to world peace, and my personal respect for his intellect, vision, and courage.

President Gorbachev is responsible for one of the most important developments of this century, the revolutionary transformation of a totalitarian dictatorship and the liberation of his people from its smothering embrace. His personal commitment to democratic and economic reform through *perestroika* and *glasnost*, a commitment which demanded the highest degree of political and personal ingenuity and courage, permitted the peoples of Russia and other Republics to cast aside decades of dark oppression and put in place the foundations of freedom.

Working with President Reagan, myself, and other allied leaders, President Gorbachev acted boldly and decisively to end the bitter divisions of the cold war and contributed to the remaking of a Europe whole and free. His and Foreign Minister Eduard Shevardnadze's "New Thinking" in foreign affairs permitted the United States and the Soviet Union to move from confrontation to partnership in the search for peace across the globe. Together we negotiated historic reductions in chemical, nuclear, and conventional forces and reduced the risk of a nuclear conflict.

Working together, we helped the people of Eastern Europe win their liberty and the German people their goal of unity in peace and freedom. Our partnership led to unprecedented cooperation in repelling Iraqi aggression in Kuwait, in bringing peace to Nicaragua and Cambodia, and independence to Namibia. And our work continues as we seek a lasting and just peace between Israelis and Arabs in the Middle East and an end to the conflict in Afghanistan.

President Gorbachev's participation in these historic events is his legacy to his country and to the world. This record assures him an honored place in history and, most importantly for the future, establishes a solid basis from which the United States and the West can work in equally constructive ways with his successors.

50. Remarks at the Annual Convention of the National Religious Broadcasters
January 27, 1992

Thank you for that wonderfully warm welcome. And to President Dave Clark, may I thank you, sir; Brandt Gustavson, the executive director. And let me salute your leadership of the NRB. I understand that former Secretary Dole was to be here; I don't know that she is. I know FCC Chairman Sykes is. And I see, of course, two good, respected friends, Jim Dobson and Billy Graham.

Ladies and gentlemen, this marks the fifth time that I've had the honor of addressing the annual convention of the National Religious Broadcasters. A year ago we met in the first week of a struggle to protect what is right and true. And I came before you to talk of what was not a Christian or Jewish war, not a Moslem war. It was a just war. And in the Persian Gulf we fought for good versus evil. It was that clear to me: right versus wrong, dignity against oppression. And America stood fast so that liberty could stand tall.

Today I want to thank you for helping America, as Christ ordained, to be "a light unto the world." Your support honored the finest soldiers, the finest sailors, marines, airmen, and coastguardsmen that any nation has ever known. And what they did in war, let us now do in peace. Just as our forces fought to defend all of what is best about America, we need you to help instill the traditional values that make life and liberty worth defending.

Let me begin with some good news for modern man. According to Gallup, the Gallup surveys, no society is more religious than the United States of America. Seven in ten Americans believe in life after death; 8 in 10, that God works miracles. Nine in ten Americans pray. And more than 90 percent believe in God, to which I say, thank God. I wish it were 100 percent.

Now, I know this is an election year. And I don't know about Damascus, but this primary season we're seeing a lot of conversions on the road to New Hampshire. [Laughter] But I don't want this to be a partisan speech, and I appreciated so much what David Clark said about values. I want to speak of the values that

I know you all believe in, values which sustain America, values that are always in fashion.

The first value is not simply American but universal. And I refer to the sanctity of life. I will stand on the side of choosing life.

Next comes a value which gives each life meaning: the self-reliance central to the dignity of work. Go to the barrios of San Antonio or the suburbs of St. Paul, and there you will find people who ask for only what our forefathers had, the same opportunity which helped us brave independence, push back the wilderness, win two World Wars, and create the highest standard of living in the history of man. The Bible reminds us, "By thy works shall ye know them." What we must do is give working Americans that level playing field to keep us as rich in goods as we have been blessed in spirit.

Tomorrow I'm giving a speech. [Laughter] The State of the Union Address will detail how we can nurture creativity as old as 1776, harness it to the needs of a new American century. Remember, to this day the only footsteps on the Moon are American footsteps. The only flag on the Moon is the Stars and Stripes. The knowledge that put it there is stamped "Made in the U.S.A." Yes, the world looks to us to lead, and lead we will. Americans can outwork, outproduce, outcompete any nation in the world. And we must do all we can to further that end. And I will do my level-best. And I need your help.

The next value I speak of must be forever cast in stone. I speak of decency, the moral courage to say what is right and condemn what is wrong. And we need a Nation closer to "The Waltons" than "The Simpsons"—[laughter]—an America that rejects the incivility, the tide of incivility, and the tide of intolerance. We see this tide in the naked epithet and in the code words that play to our worst prejudices. We see it when people ridicule religion and religious leaders, like the group which desecrated communion hosts on the steps of St. Patrick's

Cathedral. We see this tide of incivility and intolerance in bigotry, in discrimination, and anti-Semitism.

Have they no decency? Have they no honor? Have they no respect for the rights of others? I will continue to speak out against these apostles of hate who poison our kids' minds and debase their souls. There is no place, whatever our views, there is no place in America for religious prejudice, for anti-Semitism, or racial prejudice.

This, then, brings me to a fourth value crucial to America: the belief in the family, the foundation of our strength. Take my kids, for example. Having helped put them through college, I remember receiving letters from them. Barbara does, too. And there would always be a P.S. at the bottom. It was those three words that said so much about the bond between parents at home and kids at school, "Please send money." [Laughter]

But this one is true. The other day I was visited by the leaders of the National League of Cities, mayors from big cities and small, liberal and conservative, Republican and Democrat. And they were unanimous in their view that the major underlying problem in our cities is the decline of the American family. And they are right; too often, family is under siege. Each one of us, parents, preachers, politicians, and teachers, must do our part to defend it. I do not want one single action that I take as President to weaken the American family. And I want to strengthen it in every way that I can. Every law that is passed should guard against weakening the family.

And that is why I insisted that the child care bill that I signed in 1990 allow parents, not bureaucrats, to decide how to care for their children. I refused to see the option of a religious-based child care restricted or eliminated.

Our national education strategy—we call it America 2000, and it is an exciting program—helps the family by enhancing parental involvement in education, insisting that choice include both private and public schools. I do not believe it is unconstitutional for schoolkids to have the same choice that I got under the GI bill or that college kids now get under the Pell grant or that ex-servicemen now get under the Montgomery bill.

Last week, I announced another policy to strengthen the family, expanding the preschool program to serve all those 4-year-olds who are eligible, the largest funding increase in the history of project Head Start. And when this is enacted, we will be much closer to achieving one of our six national educational goals, that every schoolchild should start school ready to learn.

And finally, families will stay together only if drugs do not drive them apart. Winning the war on drugs means waging war on crime. Now, we've made the commitment. And altogether, the new Federal budget that I'll introduce 2 days from now will increase spending to combat crime by $1.2 billion, to a total of almost $16 billion. Now that's nearly 60 percent higher than when I took office in 1989.

My new budget will provide a half a billion dollars for an initiative that we call "Weed and Seed." Not enthralled with the name, but listen to what it does. [Laughter] Today our very able Attorney General, Bill Barr, point man in this new operation, is spelling out all its details. But let me say this much right now. "Weed and Seed" works this way. First, we join Federal, State, and local forces to weed out the gang leaders, the violent criminals, the drug dealers who plague our neighborhoods. And when we break their deadly grip, we follow up with part two: We seed those neighborhoods with expanded educational opportunities, job training, health care, and other social services. But the key to the "seed" concept will be jobs-generating initiatives such as enterprise zones to give people who call these neighborhoods home something to hope for.

There is more to do to win the final victory in our war on drugs. We are making progress. We are winning. Over the past 4 years, marijuana, crack, and cocaine use has definitively declined. And what's more, today kids aged 9 to 12 are the most antidrug group in America. The highest at-risk group remains 13- to 17-year-olds. But last year, for the first time, 13-year-olds mirrored the behavior of preteenagers.

Drugs affect a multitude of issues. They contribute to AIDS; they contribute to homelessness, shattering families and futures, hopes and dreams. And that's why, literally, we should thank God for the drug use decline. The drop in use doesn't just prove we were right in our assault on substance use, it shows how we can achieve drugs' unconditional surrender. We will triumph through tough enforcement and through education, increasing awareness of the damage drugs do.

And in that spirit, let us resolve to treat the victims of AIDS and drug abuse with compassion and caring. Let us redouble our efforts to help with treatment and with education. That will help eliminate the risks involved.

Over the last 4 years, more kids talked about drugs with their parents and teachers. Another reason for drug use decline has been America's print and electronic media, the major source of drug information and the primary influencer on drug use, especially among the young. Together, they have helped reawaken America's conscience which, in turn, inspires America's greatness.

Later today I will unveil our fourth national drug control strategy to build on these beginnings. It will say no to drugs. It will say yes to life. But it cannot just be done by the Government. To stop drug use will require caring and community, above all, abundant love.

Let me tell you, remind you, for some of you, tell you others a story. Once, a great First Lady, Pat Nixon, toured a medical center. And she stopped to embrace a little girl that was blinded by rubella. And for a few minutes, she talked to the girl and held her close. And then later, someone told her that the child was deaf as well as blind. And Pat answered that she had known that. "But she knows what love is," Mrs. Nixon said. "She can feel love."

America's love is conveyed in many ways: in what we oppose, injustice and tyranny; in what we support, the inalienable rights that include the freedom to think and dream and worship and, yes, vote as we please. To preserve our liberty, America once deposed a king, fought a great Civil War, and five times in this century sent Americans into major battle.

And yet, freedom is not ours alone; it is our most treasured export. If you doubt freedom's victory, look to the Persian Gulf. Look to the former Soviet Union, where those once oppressed crowd reopened churches and synagogues. Look to Eastern Europe, where Christmas carols warm the bright winter chill. It is written, "In the beginning was the Word." Here is the word for 1992: Today, the times are on the side of peace because the world, increasingly, is on the side of God.

I remember an early trip to the Soviet Union by our friend Billy Graham. He came back, and he reported that faith in God was very much alive in Russia. And some hard-liners ridiculed him. Some even thought he shouldn't go. Today, we see that he clearly was right.

This brings me, then, to the ultimate value that sustains America and the values I have already cited: a belief in prayer. Obviously, no country can claim a special place in God's heart. Yet we are better as a people because He has a special place in ours.

I once asked one of my grandkids how he felt about prayer. And he said, "Just try getting through a math test without it." [Laughter] In Sunday school children learn that God is everywhere, but in public school they find that He's absent from class. And I continue to believe, as do the overwhelming majority of Americans, in the right to nondenominational voluntary school prayer.

The values I have spoken of remind us of the truth that comes on one's knees. And I believe with all my heart that one cannot have this job, cannot be America's President, without a belief in God, without a belief in prayer.

The poet Walt Whitman once asked what made America America, and he replied simply, "Its religion. Otherwise there is no real and permanent grandeur." Let that be our essence as a people and our message as a Nation.

Thank you for this occasion. And may God bless this most wondrous land on Earth, the United States of America. Thank you very, very much.

51. Address before a Joint Session of the Congress on the State of the Union January 28, 1992

Mr. Speaker and Mr. President, distinguished Members of Congress, honored guests, and fellow citizens:

Thank you very much for that warm reception. You know, with the big buildup this address has had, I wanted to make sure it would be a big hit, but I couldn't convince Barbara to deliver it for me. [Laughter]

I see the Speaker and the Vice President are laughing. They saw what I did in Japan, and they're just happy they're sitting behind me. [Laughter]

I mean to speak tonight of big things, of big changes and the promises they hold, and of some big problems and how, together, we can solve them and move our country forward as the undisputed leader of the age.

We gather tonight at a dramatic and deeply promising time in our history and in the history of man on Earth. For in the past 12 months, the world has known changes of almost biblical proportions. And even now, months after the failed coup that doomed a failed system, I'm not sure we've absorbed the full impact, the full import of what happened. But communism died this year.

Even as President, with the most fascinating possible vantage point, there were times when I was so busy managing progress and helping to lead change that I didn't always show the joy that was in my heart. But the biggest thing that has happened in the world in my life, in our lives, is this: By the grace of God, America won the cold war.

I mean to speak this evening of the changes that can take place in our country, now that we can stop making the sacrifices we had to make when we had an avowed enemy that was a superpower. Now we can look homeward even more and move to set right what needs to be set right.

I will speak of those things. But let me tell you something I've been thinking these past few months. It's a kind of rollcall of honor. For the cold war didn't end; it was won. And I think of those who won it, in places like Korea and Vietnam. And some of them didn't come back. Back then they were heroes, but this year they were victors.

The long rollcall, all the G.I. Joes and Janes, all the ones who fought faithfully for freedom, who hit the ground and sucked the dust and knew their share of horror. This may seem frivolous, and I don't mean it so, but it's moving to me how the world saw them. The world saw not only their special valor but their special style: their rambunctious, optimistic bravery, their do-or-die unity unhampered by class or race or region. What a group we've put forth, for generations now, from the ones who wrote "Kilroy was here" on the walls of the German stalags to those who left signs in the Iraqi desert that said, "I saw Elvis." What a group of kids we've sent out into the world.

And there's another to be singled out, though it may seem inelegant, and I mean a mass of people called the American taxpayer. No one ever thinks to thank the people who pay a country's bill or an alliance's bill. But for half a century now, the American people have shouldered the burden and paid taxes that were higher than they would have been to support a defense that was bigger than it would have been if imperial communism had never existed. But it did; doesn't anymore. And here's a fact I wouldn't mind the world acknowledging: The American taxpayer bore the brunt of the burden and deserves a hunk of the glory.

So now, for the first time in 35 years, our strategic bombers stand down. No longer are they on 'round-the-clock alert. Tomorrow our children will go to school and study history and how plants grow. And they won't have, as my children did, air raid drills in which they crawl under their desks and cover their heads in case of nuclear war. My grandchildren don't have to do that and won't have the bad dreams children had once, in decades past. There are still threats. But the long, drawn-out dread is over.

A year ago tonight, I spoke to you at a moment of high peril. American forces had just unleashed Operation Desert Storm. And after 40 days in the desert skies and 4 days on the ground, the men and women of America's Armed Forces and our allies accomplished the goals that I declared and that you endorsed: We liberated Kuwait. Soon after, the Arab world and Israel sat down to talk seriously and comprehensively about peace, an historic first. And soon after that, at Christmas, the last American hostages came home. Our policies were vindicated.

Much good can come from the prudent use of power. And much good can come of this: A world once divided into two armed camps now recognizes one sole and preeminent power, the United States of America. And they regard this with no dread. For the world trusts us with power, and the world is right. They trust us to be fair and restrained. They trust us to be on the side of decency. They trust us to do what's right.

I use those words advisedly. A few days after the war began, I received a telegram from Joanne Speicher, the wife of the first pilot killed in the Gulf, Lieutenant Commander Scott Speicher. Even in her grief, she wanted me to know that some day when her children were old enough, she would tell them "that their father went away to war because it was the right thing to do." And she said it all: It was the right thing to do.

And we did it together. There were honest differences right here in this Chamber. But when the war began, you put partisanship aside, and we supported our troops. This is still a time for pride, but this is no time to boast. For problems face us, and we must stand together once again and solve them and not let our country down.

Two years ago, I began planning cuts in military spending that reflected the changes of the new era. But now, this year, with imperial communism gone, that process can be accelerated. Tonight I can tell you of dramatic changes in our strategic nuclear force. These are actions we are taking on our own because they are the right thing to do. After completing 20 planes for which we have begun procurement, we will shut down further production of the B-2 bombers. We will cancel the small ICBM program. We will cease production of new warheads for our sea-based ballistic missiles. We will stop all new production of the Peacekeeper missile. And we will not purchase any more advanced cruise missiles.

This weekend I will meet at Camp David with Boris Yeltsin of the Russian Federation. I've informed President Yeltsin that if the Commonwealth, the former Soviet Union, will eliminate all land-based multiple-warhead ballistic missiles, I will do the following: We will eliminate all Peacekeeper missiles. We will reduce the number of warheads on Minuteman missiles to one and reduce the number of warheads on our sea-based missiles by about one-third. And we will convert a substantial portion of our strategic bombers to primarily conventional use. President Yeltsin's early response has been very positive, and I expect our talks at Camp David to be fruitful.

I want you to know that for half a century, American Presidents have longed to make such decisions and say such words. But even in the midst of celebration, we must keep caution as a friend. For the world is still a dangerous place. Only the dead have seen the end of conflict. And though yesterday's challenges are behind us, tomorrow's are being born.

The Secretary of Defense recommended these cuts after consultation with the Joint Chiefs of Staff. And I make them with confidence. But do not misunderstand me. The reductions I have approved will save us an additional billion over the next 5 years. By 1997, we will have cut defense by 30 percent since I took office. These cuts are deep, and you must know my resolve: This deep, and no deeper. To do less would be insensible to progress, but to do more would be ignorant of history. We must not go back to the days of "the hollow army." We cannot repeat the mistakes made twice in this century when armistice was followed by recklessness and defense was purged as if the world were permanently safe.

I remind you this evening that I have asked for your support in funding a program to protect our country from limited nuclear missile attack. We must have this protection because too many people in too many countries have access to nuclear arms. And I urge you again to pass the Strategic Defense Initiative, SDI.

There are those who say that now we can turn away from the world, that we have no special role, no special place. But we are the United States of America, the leader of the West that has become the leader of the world. And as long as I am President, I will continue to lead in support of freedom everywhere, not out of arrogance, not out of altruism, but for the safety and security of our children. This is a fact: Strength in the pursuit of peace is no vice; isolationism in the pursuit of security is no virtue.

And now to our troubles at home. They're not all economic; the primary problem is our economy. There are some good signs. Inflation, that thief, is down. And interest rates are down. But unemployment is too high, some industries are in trouble, and growth is not what it should be. Let me tell you right from the start and right from the heart, I know we're in hard times. But I know something else: This will not stand.

In this Chamber, in this Chamber we can bring the same courage and sense of common purpose to the economy that we brought to Desert Storm. And we can defeat hard times together. I believe you'll help. One reason is that you're patriots, and you want the best for your country. And I believe that in your hearts you want to put partisanship aside and get the job done because it's the right thing to do.

The power of America rests in a stirring but simple idea, that people will do great things if only you set them free. Well, we're going to set the economy free. For if this age of miracles and wonders has taught us anything, it's that if we can change the world we can change America. We must encourage investment. We must make it easier for people to invest money and create new products, new industries, and new jobs. We must clear away the obstacles to growth: high taxes, high regulation, redtape, and yes, wasteful Government spending.

None of this will happen with a snap of the fingers, but it will happen. And the test of a plan isn't whether it's called new or dazzling. The American people aren't impressed by gimmicks; they're smarter on this score than all of us in this room. The only test of a plan is: Is it sound, and will it work?

We must have a short-term plan to address our immediate needs and heat up the economy. And then we need a longer term plan to keep combustion going and to guarantee our place in the world economy. There are certain things that a President can do without Congress, and I'm going to do them.

I have, this evening, asked major Cabinet departments and Federal agencies to institute a 90-day moratorium on any new Federal regulations that could hinder growth. In those 90 days, major departments and agencies will carry out a top-to-bottom review of all regulations, old and new, to stop the ones that will hurt growth and speed up those that will help growth.

Further, for the untold number of hard-working, responsible American workers and business men and women who've been forced to go without needed bank loans, the banking credit crunch must end. I won't neglect my responsibility for sound regulations that serve the public good, but regulatory overkill must be stopped. And I've instructed our Government regulators to stop it.

I have directed Cabinet departments and Federal agencies to speed up progrowth expenditures as quickly as possible. This should put an extra $10 billion into the economy in the next 6 months. And our new transportation bill provides more than $150 billion for construction and maintenance projects that are vital to our growth and well-being. And that means jobs building roads, jobs building bridges, and jobs building railways.

And I have, this evening, directed the Secretary of the Treasury to change the Federal tax withholding tables. With this change, millions of Americans from whom the Government withholds more than necessary can now choose to have the Government withhold less from their paychecks. Something tells me a number of taxpayers may take us up on this one. This initiative could return about $25 billion back into our economy over the next 12 months, money people can use to help pay for clothing, college, or to get a new car.

Finally, working with the Federal Reserve, we will continue to support monetary policy that keeps both interest rates and inflation down.

Now, these are the things I can do. And now, Members of Congress, let me tell you what you can do for your country. You must pass the other elements of my plan to meet our economic needs. Everyone knows that investment spurs recovery. I am proposing this evening a change in the alternative minimum tax and the creation of a new 15-percent investment tax allowance. This will encourage businesses to accelerate investment and bring people back to work.

Real estate has led our economy out of almost all the tough times we've ever had. Once building starts, carpenters and plumbers work; people buy homes and take out mortgages. My plan would modify the passive loss rule for active real estate developers. And it would make it easier for pension plans to purchase real estate. For those Americans who dream of buying a first home but who can't quite afford it, my plan would allow first-time homebuyers to withdraw savings from IRA's without penalty and provide a $5,000 tax credit for the first purchase of that home.

And finally, my immediate plan calls on Congress to give crucial help to people who own a home, to everyone who has a business or a farm or a single investment. This time, at this hour, I cannot take no for an answer. You must cut the capital gains tax on the people of our country. Never has an issue been more demagogued by its opponents. But the demagogs are wrong. They are wrong, and they know it. Sixty percent of the people who benefit from lower capital gains have incomes under $50,000. A cut in the capital gains tax increases jobs and helps just about everyone in our country. And so, I'm asking you to cut the capital gains tax to a maximum of 15.4 percent.

I'll tell you, those of you who say, "Oh, no, someone who's comfortable may benefit from that," you kind of remind me of the old definition of the Puritan who couldn't sleep at night, worrying that somehow, someone somewhere was out having a good time. [Laughter] The opponents of this measure and those who have authored various so-called soak-the-rich bills that are floating around this Chamber should be reminded of something: When they aim at the big guy, they usually hit the little guy. And maybe it's time that stopped.

This, then, is my short-term plan. Your part, Members of Congress, requires enactment of these commonsense proposals that will have a strong effect on the economy without breaking the budget agreement and without raising tax rates.

While my plan is being passed and kicking in, we've got to care for those in trouble today. I have provided for up to .4 billion in my budget to extend Federal unemployment benefits. And I ask for congressional action right away. And I thank the committee. [Applause] Well, at last.

Let's be frank. Let's be frank. Let me level with you. I know and you know that my plan is unveiled in a political season. [Laughter] I know and you know that everything I propose will be viewed by some in merely partisan terms. But I ask you to know what is in my heart. And my aim is to increase our Nation's good. I'm doing what I think is right, and I am proposing what I know will help.

I pride myself that I'm a prudent man, and I believe that patience is a virtue. But I understand that politics is, for some, a game and that sometimes the game is to stop all progress and then decry the lack of improvement. [Laughter] But let me tell you: Far more important than my political future and far more important than yours is the well-being of our coun-

try. Members of this Chamber are practical people, and I know you won't resent some practical advice. When people put their party's fortunes, whatever the party, whatever side of this aisle, before the public good, they court defeat not only for their country but for themselves. And they will certainly deserve it.

I submit my plan tomorrow, and I'm asking you to pass it by March 20th. And I ask the American people to let you know they want this action by March 20th. From the day after that, if it must be, the battle is joined. And you know, when principle is at stake I relish a good, fair fight.

I said my plan has two parts, and it does. And it's the second part that is the heart of the matter. For it's not enough to get an immediate burst. We need long-term improvement in our economic position. We all know that the key to our economic future is to ensure that America continues as an economic leader of the world. We have that in our power. Here, then, is my long-term plan to guarantee our future.

First, trade: We will work to break down the walls that stop world trade. We will work to open markets everywhere. And in our major trade negotiations, I will continue pushing to eliminate tariffs and subsidies that damage America's farmers and workers. And we'll get more good American jobs within our own hemisphere through the North American free trade agreement and through the Enterprise for the Americas Initiative.

But changes are here, and more are coming. The workplace of the future will demand more highly skilled workers than ever, more people who are computer-literate, highly educated. We must be the world's leader in education. And we must revolutionize America's schools. My America 2000 strategy will help us reach that goal. My plan will give parents more choice, give teachers more flexibility, and help communities create new American schools. Thirty States across the Nation have established America 2000 programs. Hundreds of cities and towns have joined in. Now Congress must join this great movement: Pass my proposals for new American schools.

That was my second long-term proposal, and here's my third: We must make common-sense investments that will help us compete, long-term, in the marketplace. We must encourage research and development. My plan is to make the R&D tax credit permanent and to provide record levels of support, over $76 billion this year alone, for people who will explore the promise of emerging technologies.

Fourth, we must do something about crime and drugs. It is time for a major, renewed investment in fighting violent street crime. It saps our strength and hurts our faith in our society and in our future together. Surely a tired woman on her way to work at 6 in the morning on a subway deserves the right to get there safely. And surely it's true that everyone who changes his or her life because of crime, from those afraid to go out at night to those afraid to walk in the parks they pay for, surely these people have been denied a basic civil right. It is time to restore it. Congress, pass my comprehensive crime bill. It is tough on criminals and supportive of police, and it has been languishing in these hallowed halls for years now. Pass it. Help your country.

Fifth, I ask you tonight to fund our HOPE housing proposal and to pass my enterprise zone legislation which will get businesses into the inner city. We must empower the poor with the pride that comes from owning a home, getting a job, becoming a part of things. My plan would encourage real estate construction by extending tax incentives for mortgage revenue bonds and low-income housing. And I ask tonight for record expenditures for the program that helps children born into want move into excellence, Head Start.

Step six, we must reform our health care system. For this, too, bears on whether or not we can compete in the world. American health costs have been exploding. This year America will spend over $800 billion on health, and that is expected to grow to 1.6 trillion by the end of the decade. We simply cannot afford this. The cost of health care shows up not only in your family budget but in the price of everything we buy and everything we sell. When health coverage for a fellow on an assembly line costs thousands of dollars, the cost goes into the products he makes, and you pay the bill.

We must make a choice. Now, some pretend we can have it both ways. They call it "play or pay," but that expensive approach is unstable. It will mean higher taxes, fewer jobs, and eventually a system under complete Government control.

Really, there are only two options. And we can move toward a nationalized system, a system which will restrict patient choice in picking a doctor and force the Government to ration services arbitrarily. And what we'll get is patients in long lines, indifferent service, and a huge new tax burden. Or we can reform our own private health care system, which still gives us, for all its flaws, the best quality health care in the world.

Well, let's build on our strengths. My plan provides insurance security for all Americans while preserving and increasing the idea of choice. We make basic health insurance affordable for all low-income people not now covered, and we do it by providing a health insurance tax credit of up to $3,750 for each low-income family. And the middle class gets help, too. And by reforming the health insurance market, my plan assures that Americans will have access to basic health insurance even if they change jobs or develop serious health problems. We must bring costs under control, preserve quality, preserve choice, and reduce the people's nagging daily worry about health insurance. My plan, the details of which I'll announce very shortly, does just that.

Seventh, we must get the Federal deficit under control. We now have, in law, enforceable spending caps and a requirement that we pay for the programs we create. There are those in Congress who would ease that discipline now. But I cannot let them do it, and I won't.

My plan would freeze all domestic discretionary budget authority, which means no more next year than this year. I will not tamper with Social Security, but I would put real caps on the growth of uncontrolled spending. And I would also freeze Federal domestic Government employment. And with the help of Congress, my plan will get rid of 246 programs that don't deserve Federal funding. Some of them have noble titles, but none of them is indispensable. We can get rid of each and every one of them.

You know, it's time we rediscovered a home truth the American people have never forgotten: This Government is too big and spends too much. And I call upon Congress to adopt a measure that will help put an end to the annual ritual of filling the budget with pork barrel appropriations. Every year, the press has a field day making fun of outrageous examples: a Lawrence Welk museum, research grants for Belgian endive. We all know how these things get into the budget, and maybe you need someone to help you say no. I know how to say it, and I know what I need to make it stick. Give me the same thing 43 Governors have, the line-item veto, and let me help you control spending.

We must put an end to unfinanced Federal Government mandates. These are the requirements Congress puts on our cities, counties, and States without supplying the money. If Congress passes a mandate, it should be forced to pay for it and balance the cost with savings elsewhere. After all, a mandate just increases someone else's burden, and that means higher taxes at the State and local level.

Step eight, Congress should enact the bold reform proposals that are still awaiting congressional action: bank reform, civil justice reform, tort reform, and my national energy strategy.

And finally, we must strengthen the family because it is the family that has the greatest bearing on our future. When Barbara holds an AIDS baby in her arms and reads to children, she's saying to every person in this country: Family matters.

And I am announcing tonight a new Commission on America's Urban Families. I've asked Missouri's Governor John Ashcroft to be Chairman, former Dallas Mayor Annette Strauss to be Cochair. You know, I had mayors, the leading mayors from the League of Cities, in the other day at the White House, and they told me something striking. They said that every one of them, Republican or Democrat, agreed on one thing, that the major cause of the problems of the cities is the dissolution of the family. They asked for this Commission, and they were right to ask because it's time to determine what we can do to keep families together, strong and sound.

There's one thing we can do right away: Ease the burden of rearing a child. I ask you tonight to raise the personal exemption by $500 per child for every family. For a family with four kids, that's an increase of $2,000. This is a good start in the right direction, and it's what we can afford.

It's time to allow families to deduct the interest they pay on student loans. I am asking you to do just that. And I'm asking you to allow people to use money from their IRA's to pay medical and education expenses, all without penalties.

And I'm asking for more. Ask American parents what they dislike about how things are going in our country, and chances are good that pretty soon they'll get to welfare. Americans are the most generous people on Earth. But we have to go back to the insight of Franklin Roosevelt who, when he spoke of what became the welfare program, warned that it must not become "a narcotic" and a "subtle destroyer" of the spirit. Welfare was never meant to be a lifestyle. It was never meant to be a habit. It was never supposed to be passed from generation to generation like a legacy. It's time to replace the assumptions of the welfare state and help reform the welfare system.

States throughout the country are beginning to operate with new assumptions that when able-bodied people receive Government assistance, they have responsibilities to the taxpayer: A responsibility to seek work, education, or job training; a responsibility to get their lives in order; a responsibility to hold their families together and refrain from having children out of wedlock; and a responsibility to obey the law. We are going to help this movement. Often, State reform requires waiving certain Federal regulations. I will act to make that process easier and quicker for every State that asks for our help.

I want to add, as we make these changes, we work together to improve this system, that our intention is not scapegoating or finger-pointing. If you read the papers and watch TV, you know there's been a rise these days in a certain kind of ugliness: racist comments, anti-Semitism, an increased sense of division. Really, this is not us. This is not who we are. And this is not acceptable.

And so, you have my plan for America. And I'm asking for big things, but I believe in my heart you'll do what's right.

You know, it's kind of an American tradition to show a certain skepticism toward our democratic institutions. I myself have sometimes thought the aging process could be delayed if it had to make its way through Congress. [Laughter] You will deliberate, and you will discuss, and that is fine. But, my friends, the people cannot wait. They need help now.

There's a mood among us. People are worried. There's been talk of decline. Someone even said our workers are lazy and uninspired.

And I thought: Really? You go tell Neil Armstrong standing on the moon. Tell the men and women who put him there. Tell the American farmer who feeds his country and the world. Tell the men and women of Desert Storm.

Moods come and go, but greatness endures. Ours does. And maybe for a moment it's good to remember what, in the dailiness of our lives, we forget: We are still and ever the freest nation on Earth, the kindest nation on Earth, the strongest nation on Earth. And we have always risen to the occasion. And we are going to lift this Nation out of hard times inch by inch and day by day, and those who would stop us had better step aside. Because I look at hard times, and I make this vow: This will not stand.

And so, we move on together, a rising nation, the once and future miracle that is still, this night, the hope of the world. Thank you. God bless you, and God bless our beloved country. Thank you very, very much.

52. Remarks to the United Nations Security Council in New York City
January 31, 1992

Thank you, Mr. President, for your key role in convening this first-ever summit of the United Nations Security Council.

Fellow members and Mr. Secretary-General, congratulations to you, sir, as you take office at this time of tremendous challenge and opportunity. And for the United States, it's a high honor to participate, to speak at this history-making event.

We meet at a moment of new beginnings for this institution and, really, for every member nation. And for most of its history, the United Nations was caught in a cold-war crossfire. And I think back to my days here in the early seventies as a Permanent Representative, of the way then polemics displaced peacekeeping. And long before I came on the scene and long after I left, the U.N. was all too often paralyzed by cruel ideological divisions and the struggle to contain Soviet expansion. And today, all that's changed. And the collapse of imperial communism and the end of the cold war breathe new life into the United Nations.

It was just one year ago that the world saw this new, invigorated United Nations in action as this Council stood fast against aggression and stood for the sacred principles enshrined in the U.N. Charter. And now it's time to step forward again, make the internal reforms, accelerate the revitalization, accept the responsibilities necessary for a vigorous and effective United Nations. I want to assure the members of this Council and the Secretary-General, the United Nations can count on our full support in this task.

Today, for these brief remarks, I'll talk not on the economic and social agenda so eloquently addressed by President Borja, but rather I'll mention the proliferation of mass destruction, regional conflicts, destabilizing renegade regimes that are on the horizon, terrorism, human rights. They all require our immediate attention.

The world also challenges us to strengthen and sustain positive change. And we must advance the momentous movement toward democracy and freedom—democratization, I believe Boutros-Ghali called this, our distinguished Secretary-General—and expand the circle of nations committed to human rights and the rule of law. It's an exciting opportunity for our United Nations, and we must not allow it to slip away.

Right now, across the globe, the U.N. is working night and day in the cause of peace. And never before in its four decades has the U.N.'s Blue Helmets and Blue Berets been so engaged in the noble work of peacekeeping, even to the extent of building the foundation for free elections. And never before has the United Nations been so ready and so com-

pelled to step up to the task of peacemaking, both to resolve hot wars and to conduct that forward-looking mission known as preventive diplomacy.

We must be practical as well as principled as we seek to free people from the specter of conflict. We recognize every nation's obligation to invest in peace. As conflicts are resolved and violence subsides, then the institutions of free societies can take hold. And as they do, they become our strongest safeguards against aggression and tyranny.

Democracy, human rights, the rule of law, these are the building blocks of peace and freedom. And in the lives of millions of men and women around the world its import is simple. It can mean the difference between war and peace, healing and hatred, and where there is fear and despair, it really can mean hope.

We look to the Secretary-General to present to this Council his recommendations to ensure effective and efficient peacekeeping, peacemaking, and preventive diplomacy. And we look forward to exploring these ideas together.

We have witnessed change of enormous breadth and scope, all in but a few short years. A remarkable revolution has swept away the old regimes from Managua to Moscow. But everywhere, free government and the institutions that give it form will take time to flourish and mature.

Free elections give democracy a foothold, but true democracy means more than simply the rule of the majority. It means an irrevocable commitment to democratic principles. It means equal rights for minorities. And above all, it means the sanctity of even a single individual against the unjust power of the state.

The will of the majority must never degenerate into the whim of majority. This fundamental principle transcends all borders. Human dignity, the inalienable rights of man, these are not the possessions of the state. They're universal. In Asia, in Africa, in Europe, in the Americas, the United Nations must stand with those who seek greater freedom and democracy. And that is my deep belief; that is the belief of the American people. And it's the belief that breathes life into the great principle of the universal declaration of human rights.

Our changed world is a more hopeful world, indeed, but it is not absent those who would turn back the clock to the darker days of threats and bullying. And our world is still a dangerous world, rife with far too many terrible weapons.

In my first address here to the United Nations as President, I challenged the Soviet Union to eliminate chemical weapons and called on every nation to join us in this crusade, His Majesty King Hassan of Morocco making this point so well right here today. What greater cause for this great body: to make certain the world has seen the last of these terrible weapons. And so, let us vow to make this year the year all nations at long last join to ban this scourge.

There is much more to do regarding weapons of mass destruction. Just 3 days ago, in my State of the Union Message here, I announced the steps, far-reaching, unilateral steps, that we will take to reduce our nuclear arsenal. And these steps affect each element in our strategic triad, the land, the sea, and the air.

In addition to these unilateral steps, we are prepared to move forward on mutual arms reduction. I noted his constructive comments here today, and tomorrow, in my meeting with President Yeltsin, we will continue the search for common ground on this vitally important issue. He responded with some very serious proposals just the other day.

We welcome, the world welcomes statements by several of the new States that won independence after the collapse of the U.S.S.R. that they will abide by the Nuclear Non-Proliferation Treaty. And yet, realism requires us to remain vigilant in this time of transition.

The danger of proliferation remains. And again, let me single out the earlier remarks by the President of the French Republic, President Mitterrand, on this subject, the clarion call to do something about it. We must act together so that from this time forward, people involved in sophisticated weapons programs redirect their energies to peaceful endeavors.

We'll do more in cooperation with our allies to ensure that dangerous materials and technology don't fall into the hands of terrorists or others. And we will continue to work with these new States to ensure a strong commitment in word and deed to all global nonproliferation standards.

Today, the threat of global nuclear war is more distant than at any time in the nuclear era. Drawing down the old cold war arsenals will further ease that dread. But the specter of mass destruction remains all too real, especially as some nations continue to push to acquire weapons of mass destruction and the means to deliver them.

Our triumph in the Gulf is testament to the U.N.'s mission. Its security is a shared responsibility. Today, this institution spearheads a quarantine against the outlaw regime of Saddam Hussein. It is the strong belief of my country that we must keep sanctions in place and take the following steps to preserve our common security: We must continue to focus on Iraq's capability to build or maintain weapons of mass destruction. And we must make clear to the world and, most important, to the people of Iraq that no normalization is possible so long as Saddam Hussein remains there, remains in power.

As on all of the urgent issues I've mentioned today, progress comes from acting in concert, and we must deal resolutely with these renegade regimes, if necessary, by sanctions or stronger measures, to compel them to observe international standards of behavior. We will not be blind to the dangers we still face. Terrorists and their state sponsors must know there will be serious consequences if they violate international law.

Two weeks ago, this Council, in unity, sent a very strong message to Libya. And let me repeat today Resolution 731, passed unanimously by this body, by the Security Council, calls on Libya to comply fully with the requests of three states on this Council. And I would just like to use this meeting today to call on Libya to heed the call of the Security Council of the United Nations.

Last year in the Gulf, in concert, we responded to an attack on the sovereignty of one nation as an assault on the security of all. So, let us make it our mission to give this principle the greatest practical meaning in the conduct of nations.

Today, we stand at another crossroads. Perhaps the first time since that hopeful moment in San Francisco, we can look at our Charter as a living, breathing document. And yes, after so many years, it still may be in its infancy, requiring a careful and vigilant nurturing of its parents, but I believe in my heart that it is alive and well.

Our mission is to make it strong and sturdy through increased dedication and cooperation, and I know that we are up to the challenge. The nations represented here, like the larger community of the U.N. represented by so many Perm Reps here today, have it in their power to act for peace and freedom.

So, may God bless the United Nations as it pursues its noble goal. Thank you, Mr. President.

53. Remarks Announcing the Bush-Quayle Candidacies for Reelection February 12, 1992

The President. Thank you all very much. And Barbara, thank you for those kind remarks.

And may I salute our Vice President, Dan Quayle, just back from overseas, and Marilyn. And my respects to the members of our great Cabinet, and friends all. Thanks to all of you for this wonderful, warm reception.

I have an announcement to make. [Laughter] I want to continue serving as your President, 4 more years. So from this moment on, I'm a candidate for President of the United States, officially.

Let me tell you why I'm running. I came here to do important work, and I finish what I start. In 1980 I came to Washington as a part of a team. We started a revolution to free America from, you remember, the politics of malaise and to set sail toward America's destiny. Then in 1988, Dan Quayle and I began our own partnership built on the same principles.

My message then and my message now is simple: I believe Government is too big, and it costs too much. I believe in a strong defense for this country and good schools, safe streets, a Government really worthy of the people. I believe that parents, not Government, should make the important decisions about health, child care, and education. I believe in personal responsibility. I believe in opportunity for all. We should throw open wide the doors of possibility to anyone who has been locked out. And I believe in a piece of wisdom passed on by my favorite political philosopher, Barbara Bush: What happens in your house is more important than what happens in the White House.

You see, America's future doesn't take shape in small rooms with heavy, polished wooden desks. It takes place in homes, where parents read to their children, talk about responsibility, teach them values, show them how to love one another, respect one another, and work hard, and live good lives. We must encourage families to remain strong and whole. We must extend our hearts and hands to children who have no one to hold them or call them by their names. Our future rides on the important things, the big things: Family, home, school, church, community, and country.

We're gathered here because the American people wanted leadership, and we answered the call. We didn't do the easy things. We did the right things. From day one, I fought for strong and effective national defense. I stuck to my principles, and we kept strong, and we won the cold war. And we stayed strong, and that enabled us to win a battle called Desert Storm.

But we did far more than that. We liberated the entire world from old fears, fears of tense, endless confrontation, fears of nuclear holocaust. Now our children grow up freed from the looming specter of nuclear war.

But having won the cold war, we did more. We led nations away from ancient hatreds and toward a table of peace. And we did still more than that. We forged a new world order, an order shaped by the sweat and sacrifice of our families, the sweat and sacrifice of generation upon generation of American men and women.

Think of it: Two years ago, the Berlin Wall came tumbling down. And last year, the Soviet Union collapsed. Imperial communism became a four-letter word: D-E-A-D, dead. And today, because we stood firm, because we did the right things, America stands alone, the undisputed leader of the world. We put an end to the decades of cold war and reaped a springtime harvest of peace. The American people should be proud of what together we have achieved. Now, together, we will transform the arsenal of democracy into the engine of growth.

I understand the world. That's crucial. But that's not enough. I understand America. And I know that American workers are the most productive in the world, bar none.

And I know, to succeed economically at home, we need to lead economically abroad. If you want to lead in the world, you've got to know the neighborhood. Economic leadership means markets for American products, jobs for American workers, and growing room for the American dream. The American people do not believe in isolationism because they believe in themselves. We Americans don't hide from a good test of our abilities. We rise to the challenge. And after all, our national bird is the eagle, not the ostrich.

In 1992, the American people will decide what kind of leadership they want. They'll decide which team has the character, the experience, and the toughness to make the important decisions. They could cast their lot with a lot of fresh faces who tout stale ideas. But they won't. Voters know the difference between a sound bite and sound policy.

Let's not kid ourselves. We're in a tough fight. But you know me: I don't seek unnecessary conflict, but when principle is at stake, I fight to win. And I am determined to win. And I will win. This will be a long campaign. That's all right. Our campaign will focus on the future, the only subject that counts. We'll fight hard. We'll fight fair. And we will win.

Abraham Lincoln, whose birth we celebrate today, once told fellow Republicans, "We will make converts day by day, and unless truth be a mockery and justice a hollow lie, we will be in the majority after a while. The battle of freedom is to be fought out on principle."

And so be it. That's the way it will be. For 3 years an entrenched opposition in Washington has clung to the old failed ways, not out of principle but out of sheer politics. They blocked our comprehensive efforts to fight crime and drugs. They refused to join the revolution in American education. They stalled our efforts to cut taxes and slash regulation and encourage economic growth. And then they complained that nothing got done.

This year we say: No more. To those who want to obstruct progress, we say: Get moving, or get out of the way. We've got an agenda.

Audience members. Four more years! Four more years! Four more years!

The President. We've got an agenda, and here's what we will do: Together, we'll get our economy up and running at full speed. We'll restore decency to the American way of life. We will silence the voices of hatred and gloom. And we will attack programs that lock people in bleak dependency as we work to reform our dismal welfare program. And we will, in the process, provide the best kind of a welfare system imaginable, good jobs for Americans able to work. And we will build the America of our dreams.

In my life, I've seen miracles, and I've learned that no dream is too big for the American heart. When I was a little boy, the world moved at an easy pace. Then came the Depression; then came a World War. And in the fires of battle, I learned freedom's painful price. And I've seen wondrous changes, new ideas and new technologies, tempered by the humanity that makes us what we are. Amid the swells of change, gentle fundamentals anchor us still. Decency, honor, hard work, caring: That's the America I know.

And I have been blessed in my life, blessed by Barbara and by a family that fills me with wonder and joy and love. And I'm blessed with so many friends, friends like you. And I have been especially blessed because I have been given the opportunity to serve as your President, the President of the United States.

The glory of this century is America. And history will call this the American century because we fought the battle of freedom, and we won. And history will tell of a second American century when we led the world to new heights of achievement and liberty. This is our legacy. This is our challenge. And this is our destiny. And together, we will win. I am certain of that.

Thank you very, very much. And may God bless you. May God bless each and every one of you and our great country, the United States of America. Thank you very, very much.

54. Declaration of San Antonio [Following International Drug Summit] February 27, 1992

San Antonio Drug Summit 1992

We, the Presidents of Bolivia, Colombia, Ecuador, Mexico, Peru, and the United States of America, and the Minister of Foreign Relations of Venezuela, met in San Antonio, Texas, on the 26th and 27th of February, one thousand nine hundred and ninety-two and issued the following.

Declaration of San Antonio

We recognize that the Cartagena Declaration, issued on February 15, 1990, by the Presidents of Bolivia, Colombia, Peru, and the United States of America, laid the foundation for the development of a comprehensive and multilateral strategy to address the problem of illegal drugs. Those of us who represent the countries that met in Cartagena strongly reaffirm the commitments assumed at that time. Meeting now as representatives of seven governments, we express our determination to move beyond the achievements of Cartagena, build upon the progress attained, and adapt international cooperation to the new challenges arising from worldwide changes in the drug problem.

We recognize that the overall problem of illegal drugs and related crimes represents a direct threat to the health and well-being of our peoples, to their economies, the national security of our countries, and to harmony in international relations. Drugs lead to violence and addiction, threaten democratic institutions, and waste economic and human resources that could be used for the benefit of our societies.

We applaud the progress achieved over the past two years in reducing cocaine production, in lowering demand, in reducing cultivation for illicit purposes, in carrying out alternative development programs, and in dismantling and disrupting transnational drug trafficking organizations and their financial support networks. The close cooperation among our governments and their political will have led to an encouraging increasing in drug seizures and in the effectiveness of law enforcement actions. Also as a result of this cooperation and political will, a number of the principal drug lords who were actively engaged in the drug trade two years ago are in prison in several countries. Alternative development programs have proven to be an effective strategy for replacing coca cultivation in producer countries.

Although we are encouraged by these achievements, we recognize that mutual cooperative efforts must be expanded and strengthened in all areas. We call on all sectors of society, notably the media, to increase their efforts in the anti-drug struggle. The role of the media is very important, and we urge them to intensify their valuable efforts. We undertake to promote, through the media, the values essential to a healthy society.

In addition to the cocaine problem, we recognize the need to remain alert to the expansion of the production, trafficking, and consumption of heroin, marijuana, and other drugs. We emphasize the need to exert greater control over substances used in the production of these drugs, and to broaden consultations on the eradication of these illegal crops.

We are convinced that our anti-drug efforts must be conducted on the basis of the principle of shared responsibility and in a balanced manner. It is essential to confront the drug problem through an integrated approach, addressing demand, cultivation for illicit purposes, production, trafficking, and illegal distribution networks, as well as related crimes, such as traffic in firearms and in essential and precursor chemicals, and money laundering. In addition, our governments will continue to perfect strategies that include alternative development, eradication, control and interdiction, the strengthening of judicial systems, and the prevention of illicit drug use.

We recognize the fundamental importance of strengthening judicial systems to ensure that effective institutions exist to bring criminals to justice. We assume responsibility for strengthening judicial cooperation among our countries to attain these objectives. We reaffirm our intention to carry out these efforts in full compliance with the international legal framework for the protection of human rights.

We reaffirm that cooperation among us must be carried out in accordance with our national laws, with full respect for the sovereignty and territorial integrity of our nations, and in strict observance of international law.

We recognize that the problem of illicit drugs is international. All countries directly or indirectly affected by the drug problem should take upon themselves clear responsibilities and actions in the anti-drug effort. We call on the countries of the region to strengthen national and international cooperative efforts and to participate actively in regional programs. We recognize that in the case of Peru, complicity between narco-trafficking and terrorism greatly complicates the anti-drug effort, threatens democratic institutions, and undermines the viability of the Peruvian economy.

We express our support for the anti-drug struggle being carried out by our sister nations of the Western Hemisphere, we call on them to increase their efforts, and we offer to strengthen our governments' cooperation with them through specific agreements they may wish to sign. We value and encourage regional unity in this effort.

We note with concern the opening and expansion of markets for illicit drugs, particularly cocaine, in Europe and Asia. We call upon the nations of those continents and on other member countries of the international community to strengthen, through bilateral or multilateral agreements, cooperation in the anti-drug effort in which the nations of the Western Hemisphere are engaged. To this end, we have agreed to form a high-level group with representatives designated by the signatory countries of this Declaration, to visit other countries of this Hemisphere, Europe, and Japan, with the purpose of inviting them to participate actively in the efforts and cooperative strategies described in this Declaration.

We reaffirm our solid commitment to the anti-drug efforts of international organizations, notably the United Nations and the Organization of American States. Inspired by the mandate of the Inter-American Commission on the Control of Drug Abuse, we express our full support for its programs.

We recognize the fundamental importance of strong economies and innovative economic initiatives to the successful conduct of the anti-drug effort. Further progress in the areas of trade and investment will be essential. We support the Enterprise for the Americas Initiative as a means of improving economic conditions in the Hemisphere, and we are encouraged by the progress the countries of the region have made in restructuring their economies.

We reaffirm the importance of alternative development in the anti-drug effort. We note that the victims of narco-trafficking in the region include those sectors of society that live in extreme poverty and that are attracted to illicit drug production and trafficking as a means of livelihood. We consider that if our efforts to reduce illegal drug trafficking are to be successful, it will be essential to offer legitimate options that generate employment and income.

We propose to achieve the objectives and goals defined above in this Declaration and in its attached Strategies for Action.

Recognizing the need to ensure cohesion and progress in our anti-drug efforts, our governments intend to hold a high-level meeting on an annual basis.

In order to broaden international anti-drug efforts still further, we invite additional countries or representatives of groups of countries to associate themselves with this Declaration.

Done at San Antonio, Texas, on this, the 27th day of February, 1992, in the English and Spanish languages.

Strategies for Drug Control and the Strengthening of the Administration of Justice

The Countries intend to strengthen unilateral, bilateral, and multilateral enforcement efforts and strengthen judicial systems to attack illicit trafficking in narcotic drugs, psychotropic substances, and precursor and essential chemicals. The Countries are determined to combat drug trafficking organizations through the arrest, prosecution, sentencing, and imprisonment of their leaders, lieutenants, members, accomplices, and accessories through the seizure and forfeiture of their assets, pursuant to the Countries' respective domestic legal systems and laws in force. To attain these objectives, the Countries intend to carry out coordinated cooperative actions through their national institutions.

Enforcement efforts cannot be carried out without economic programs such as alternative development.

The Countries request financial support from the international community in order to obtain funds for alternative development programs in nations that require assistance.

1. Training Centers

The Countries intend to provide training for the personnel who are responsible for or support the counter-drug battle in the signatory Countries at national training centers already in existence in the region. Emphasis will be given to the specialties of each of these centers in which personnel from governments of the other Countries may be enrolled as appropriate, in accordance with their respective legal systems. The signatory Countries, other governments, and international organizations are encouraged to provide financial and technical support for this training.

2. Regional Information Sharing

The Countries intend to expand reciprocal information sharing concerning the activities of organizations, groups, and persons engaged in illicit drug trafficking. The Countries will establish channels of communication to ensure the rapid dissemination of information for purposes of effective enforcement. This information sharing will be consistent with the security procedures, laws, and regulations of each country.

3. Control of Sovereign Air Space

The Countries recognize that drug traffickers move illicit drugs via identified air corridors and without regard to international borders or national airspace. The Countries also recognize that monitoring of airspace is an impor-

tant factor in the apprehension of aircraft and crews involved in illicit drug traffic.

The Countries recognize that there is a need to exchange timely information on potential drug traffickers in and around each country's sovereign air space.

The Countries also agree to exchange information on their experiences and to provide one another with technical assistance in detecting, monitoring, and controlling aerial drug trafficking, when such assistance is requested in accordance with the domestic laws of each country and international laws in force.

4. Aircraft, Airfield and Landing Strip Control

The Countries, recognizing that private and commercial aircraft are being utilized with increasing frequency in illicit trafficking of narcotic drugs and psychotropic substances, intend to establish and increase the necessary enforcement actions to prevent the utilization of such aircraft, pursuant to the domestic laws of each country and international regulations in force.

The Countries also intend, if necessary, to examine their domestic regulations pertaining to civil aviation in order to prevent the illicit use of aircraft and airports. They will also take the enforcement measures necessary to prevent the establishment of clandestine landing strips and eliminate those already in existence.

The Countries will cooperate closely with each other in providing mutual assistance when requested in order to investigate aircraft suspected of illicit drug trafficking. The Countries, pursuant to their domestic legal systems, also intend to seize and confiscate private aircraft when it has been proven that they have been used in the illicit traffic of narcotic drugs and psychotropic substances.

5. Maritime Control Actions

As called for in Article 17 of the 1988 United Nations Convention against Illicit Traffic in

Narcotic Drugs and Psychotropic Substances, the Countries intend to strengthen cooperation to eliminate to the extent possible illicit trafficking by sea. To this end, they will endeavor to establish mechanisms to determine the most expeditious means to verify the registry and ownership of vessels suspected of illicit trafficking that are operating seaward of the territorial sea of any nation. The Countries further intend to punish illicit traffic in narcotic drugs and psychotropic substances by sea under their national laws.

6. Chemical Control Regimes

The Countries recognize that progress has been made in international efforts to eliminate the diversion of chemicals used in the illicit production of narcotic drugs and psychotropic substances. They specifically support the "Model Regulations to Control Chemical Precursors and Chemical Substances, Machines and Materials" of the Organization of American States, the chemical control measures adopted at the April 1991 International Drug Enforcement Conference (IDEC) meeting, and the recommendations in the Final Report of the Group of Seven Chemical Action Task Force, published in June 1991. The Countries call on all nations, and in particular, chemical exporting countries, to adopt the recommendations of the Group of Seven Chemical Action Task Force. They welcome the work of the above-mentioned Task Force and await with interest its report to the 1992 Economic Summit, in which it will make recommendations for the proper organization of worldwide control of those chemical products.

The Countries express their support for including ten additional chemicals in the United Nations Convention Against Illicit Traffic in Narcotic Drugs and Psychotropic Substances, as proposed by the United States on behalf of the Chemical Action Task Force in the U.S. notification to the Secretary General.

The Countries call on the International Narcotics Control Board to strengthen its actions aimed at controlling essential and precursor chemicals.

The Countries intend to investigate, in their respective countries, the legitimacy of significant commercial transactions in controlled chemical products. The Countries call on the chemical producing nations to establish an effective system for certification of end uses and end users.

The Countries will take appropriate legal action against companies violating chemical control regulations.

Studies will be conducted in the countries where narcotic drugs and psychotropic substances are produced in order to quantify the demand for chemicals for legitimate purposes in order to assist in the control of these products. The United States intends to provide financial and technical assistance for conducting the aforementioned studies and for setting up national data banks.

The Countries urge all nations and international organizations to cooperate effectively with programs aimed at strengthening border control in order to prevent the illegal entry of chemicals.

7. Port and Free Trade Zone Control

The Countries intend to implement measures to suppress illicit drug trafficking in free trade zones and ports, as called for in Article 18 of the 1988 United Nations Convention Against Illicit Traffic in Narcotic Drugs and Psychotropic Substances and in accordance with the recommendations of the Ninth International Drug Enforcement Conference. A group of experts may be required to conduct a specialized study in order to identify the ports and free trade zones and identify the vulnerable points in the ports and free trade zones in the region that could be utilized for illicit traffic in drugs and chemicals. This study and subsequent reviews will serve as the basis for adopting measures to prevent illicit traffic in drugs and controlled substances in ports and free trade zones.

8. Carrier Cooperation Agreement

The Countries are concerned about the difficulties inherent in the identification of suspicious shipments included in the great volume of legitimate commerce. In order to improve the effectiveness of border controls and also facilitate the transit of legitimate merchandise, the Countries intend to enlist the cooperation of air, land, and maritime transport companies. The Countries agree, in principle, to implement common standards and practices in order to include carriers in measure to improve anti-drug security.

9. Money Laundering

The 1988 United Nations Convention Against Illicit Traffic in Narcotic Drugs and Psychotropic Substances establishes a series of measures related to the control of financial assets to which the Countries intend to conform their domestic laws. The Countries support full implementation of this Convention, which requires, inter alia, the criminalization of all money laundering operations related to illicit drug traffic.

The Countries recognize and support the efforts of the Group of Seven Financial Action Task Force. The Countries call upon the Eleventh Meeting of senior-level OAS/CICAD officials to approve the Model Regulations on Money Laundering related to illicit drug traffic.

The Countries intend to make recommendations regarding the following:

—The elements of a comprehensive financial enforcement and money laundering control program.

—Exchange of financial information among governments in accordance with bilateral understandings.

10. Strengthening the Administration of Justice

The Countries recognize and support efforts designed to improve their judicial systems, in those cases in which this may be necessary, in order to ensure the effectiveness of those systems in establishing the culpability and penalties applicable to traffickers in illicit drugs. They recognize the need for adequate protection for the persons responsible for administering justice in this area inasmuch as effective legal systems are essential for democracy and economic progress.

The Countries call on all nations to strengthen the United Nations Drug Control Program.

11. Strengthening Judicial Cooperation

The Countries support the provisions of the 1988 United Nations Convention Against Illicit Traffic in Narcotic Drugs and Psychotropic Substances related to increased cooperation and mutual legal assistance in the battle against illicit drug trafficking, money laundering, and investigations and proceedings involving seizure and forfeiture. The Countries must consider approval of the projects of the OAS Inter-American Judicial Committee on mutual legal assistance in criminal matters and on precautionary measures.

The Countries will encourage the expeditious exchange of information and evidence needed for legal proceedings involving illicit drug trafficking, pursuant to their domestic laws and bilateral and multilateral agreements.

12. Sharing of Assets and Property

The Countries shall seek to conclude bilateral or multilateral agreements on the sharing of property seized and forfeited in the struggle against drug trafficking in accordance with the laws in force and the practices in each country. The Countries also consider that asset sharing would encourage international cooperation among law enforcement officials, and that confiscated property would be a valuable source of funds and equipment for combatting drug production and trafficking and for preventing drug consumption and treating addicts.

13. Firearms Control

The Countries recommend that measures to control firearms, ammunition, and explosives be strengthened in order to avoid their diversion to drug traffickers. The Countries also call for an enhanced exchange of detailed and complete information regarding seized weapons in order to facilitate the identification and determination of origin of such weapons, as well as the prosecution of those responsible for their illegal export.

To this end, the United States intends to tighten its export controls and to cooperate with the Governments of the other Countries to verify the legitimacy of end users.

The Countries consider that close cooperation with the OAS/CICAD is essential in such firearms, ammunition, and explosives control efforts.

14. Other Cooperative Arrangements

The Countries recognize that cooperative operations have been a useful tool in the war against drug traffickers in the past. The Countries intend to continue and expand such cooperative measures through their national organizations responsible for the struggle against illegal drug trafficking.

Strategies in the Economic and Financial Areas

The Countries propose to strengthen unilateral, bilateral, and multilateral efforts aimed at improving economic conditions in the countries involved in the cycle of illegal drug production and trafficking. Extreme poverty and the growth of the drug problem are the main reasons that peasants become involved in illegal coca leaf production. The Countries reaffirm the principles in the Declaration of Cartagena, which accept that alternative economic development is an essential part of the comprehensive plan to reduce illegal trade in narcotic drugs and psychotropic substances. Alternative development cannot succeed in the absence of enforcement and interdiction efforts that effectively reduce this illegal drug trafficking.

The Countries recognize and approve of the structural changes that have taken place in the economies of the Andean countries and Mexico. These changes strengthen stability and increase prospects for economic growth. The Countries recognize that these reforms merit full support. Efforts to attract an increased flow of private investment will provide opportunities for sustained economic growth.

1. Economic Issues

The Countries recognize that the Enterprise for the Americas Initiative (EAI) with its three pillars—investment, trade, and debt—offers important means of improving economic conditions in the Hemisphere.

All of the Countries have signed bilateral trade and investment framework agreements with the United States. The Countries recognize that these agreements are important to encourage investment and trade liberalization, and they intend to move ahead with the three pillars of the EAI as follows:

a. Investment

The Countries recognize the critical importance of enacting laws and taking steps that encourage private investment and economic development. In this regard, the Countries have expressed their willingness to negotiate parallel bilateral agreements to protect intellectual property rights, as well as bilateral investment agreements, and others that promote trade liberalization. For this purpose, the Enterprise for the Americas Initiative includes trade and investment framework agreements.

The Countries express their satisfaction with the establishment of the Multilateral Investment Fund under the aegis of the Inter-American Development Bank. The Countries consider this Fund important to provide technical assistance and to encourage private investment.

The Countries note that the move towards a market economy in Latin America is a good vehicle for generating sustained economic growth, with benefits throughout society. They therefore view with interest experiences in privatizing services and industries that can serve to attract a significant flow of direct foreign investment. The initiation of operations by the Multilateral Investment Fund and technical assistance in support of privatization efforts will aid in the development of market economies. Some Andean countries plan to proceed with privatization programs and reforms of financial systems to the degree and depth possible in each country.

The Andean countries state that facilitating access to the 936 funds would have a catalytic effect in attracting private investment to that subregion.

The profound structural changes in the region make the active participation of financial entities in funding private projects more important than ever before. The Countries urge entities such as the International Finance Corporation (IFC) and the Inter-American Investment Corporation (IIC) to continue working with the Andean region. The countries of the Andean region are pleased by Mexico's participation as a stockholder in the Andean Development Corporation (ADC), which is a suitable channel for development activity in the subregion, particularly for the private sector, within a framework of productive integration. These countries express their interest in also being able to count on active participation by the United States Government in the ADC. The United States takes note of that interest.

b. Trade

The Countries express their satisfaction regarding enactment of the Andean Trade Preference Act which allows the countries of the Andean region to export a wide variety of products to the United States for a ten-year period without paying duties. Those eligible countries that wish to benefit from this law will take the required steps. The United States, furthermore, plans to implement the provisions of this law as rapidly as possible in order to extend its benefits to the countries determined to fulfill the criteria in the Law. The Andean countries also express their interest in having these preferences extended to Venezuela.

The Countries recognize that the proposed North American Free Trade Agreement will be an important step in the process of creating a hemispheric free trade agreement in accordance with the Enterprise for the Americas Initiative. The Countries stress the importance of continued economic integration and trade liberalization efforts.

c. Debt

The Countries express their satisfaction with the progress achieved by some Andean countries and Mexico in renegotiating their debt with the private international banking system and intend, when appropriate, to continue to support reduction of this debt. The Countries point out that the economic reforms implemented by Bolivia have already made it possible for that country to benefit from the reduction of a large part of its bilateral debt with the United States under the auspices and in the spirit of the Enterprise for the Americas Initiative, which will make it possible to implement environmental projects in Bolivia. The Government of the United States will continue to take the necessary steps to obtain the legislative approval required for the debt categories that still do not have this authorization.

2. Alternative Development

The Countries acknowledge that the goals of the Cartagena Declaration regarding the substitution of other agricultural products for coca and other plants that feed the drug cycle, and the creation of new sources of licit income, have not yet been fully achieved. The Countries note that in a major new initiative, the United States—in consultation with Bolivia, Colombia, Ecuador and Peru—is engaged in a program to provide training and technical assistance in agricultural marketing that will stress participation by the private sector as well as assistance for animal and plant health. The Countries applaud this program and intend to facilitate its implementation to the maximum extent possible.

Notwithstanding assistance already pledged by the United States and the United Nations, the Countries recognize the need to establish a broad basis of funding for alternative development. For this reason, and given the worldwide range of illicit narcotics, the Countries intend to strive for increased participation of countries such as Japan and others as well as international financial agencies and institutions such as the World Bank, the Inter-American Development Bank, the European Community, the OAS, the OECD and others. The Andean nations believe, and the United States takes note, that such actions should also include the establishment of a facility for alternative development in an international financial institution. The Countries are determined to enlist the support of the international community in their fight against drugs.

The Countries support the work of the OAS/CICAD Group of Experts charged with reviewing the alternative development approach and recommending ways to enhance it.

Under the alternative development program, the Countries recognize the importance of implementing short-term projects such as emergency food programs, food for work, and income and employment generation. The Countries recognize that these efforts must simultaneously accompany eradication efforts in order to reduce the economic impact on coca leaf producers. These short-term actions must be aimed at producing jobs and temporary income until such time as the alternative development projects are fully developed.

The Countries underscore the need for alternative development programs to be strengthened in coca leaf producing countries, or in those countries with areas that have potential for producing plants from which elements utilizable in the production of narcotics and psychotropic drugs can be extracted, so as to reduce the supply of raw material that feeds the narco-trafficking cycle. These programs will help farmers have different economic alternatives, which will allow them to move away from illegal coca production.

The Countries acknowledge the progress achieved in alternative development in Bolivia and the beginning of alternative development activities in Peru. In this context, the Countries note the bilateral agreements with the United States signed by Peru and by Bolivia to implement alternative economic development and drug control programs, as useful experiences applicable to other countries. These two most salient examples are summarized as follows:

Bolivia

In Bolivia, with the firm support of the United States, efforts undertaken to develop other crops in coca producing zones, as well as in those areas from which people have been expelled, are having some success, starting with the production of genetic material with a proven biological viability, acceptable rate of return and a potential for export. Technical assistance and credit, as well as continued training of farmers, permits the achievement of a good level of technology transfer.

Actions taken in the infrastructure area have made it possible to improve the means of transporting agricultural products to consumer markets and processing them.

Aggressive marketing is slowly allowing the opening of internal markets to the first items of this production, in accordance with phytosanitary and quality control requirements. The support being given to the social dimension by providing infrastructure in the health and education sectors is making it possible to improve the quality of life of the rural population.

A new five-year project, which will start in early June of 1992, will provide continuity and strengthen key activities, such as marketing and private investment.

Multilateral cooperation through the United Nations Drug Control Program (UNDCP) has also assisted in the alternative development process, especially in basic sanitation, roads, energy and agroindustry.

Nevertheless, based on the above-mentioned Bolivian experiences it is recommended that:

1. Recognition be given to the fact that implementation of coca reduction policy has to be adapted to the pace of alternative development in order to reduce the gap between the loss of income and its replacement. It is evident that the success in alternative development will discourage farmers from growing coca.

2. Recognition be given to the importance of full and active participation by the farmers in alternative development processes.

3. Bilateral and multilateral cooperation in alternative development be considered with regard to its specificity. It should include comprehensive, multisectoral and long-term program guidance and should also be sufficiently flexible, broad and timely to be able to promote qualitative changes beyond the short term.

Peru

In the case of Peru, progress can be summarized by the following points:

—The participation of the United States Government and Japan in the support group for the reentry of Peru into the international financial community. This allows the IDB and other bilateral donors to provide funds.

—The carrying out of massive food aid programs, promotion of a favorable economic policy framework for the development of the private sector and the liberalization of two-way trade.

—The existence of projects, especially in the Upper Huallaga Valley where 14,000 farmers have received technical assistance in seed research, production, and marketing. The project provided credit and land titles and made it possible to resurface 1,200 kilometers of roads and to set up potable water systems, health posts and latrines.

—The massive support received by President Fujimori from the rural population in coca producing areas.

—Plans for 1992 that call for the resurfacing of the road linking the Upper Huallaga Valley to the coast, a program for recognizing and awarding property rights, and the participation of multinational firms interested in investing in alternative development projects.

—All this has been achieved in spite of insidious narco-trafficking, terrorism and the alliance between the two. Under the Agreement on Narcotics Control and Alternative Development signed on May 14, 1991, which includes aspects relating to interdiction and security, an autonomous Peruvian institution will be responsible for distributing the necessary resources. This institution and its U.S. counterpart will hold meetings to implement the shared strategy, immediately after the Presidential Summit in San Antonio.

—With respect to human rights, the importance of conducting the anti-drug struggle within the framework of international standards is stressed.

—With respect to the citizens' commitment to the anti-drug effort, emphasis is placed on the need for them to have access to information and for efficient legal and administrative systems to exist.

—In order to have adequate farmer participation, consideration should be given, among other requirements, to:

(a) Creating the democratic tools that make it possible to involve the people directly in the decision-making process;

(b) Recognizing, awarding, and registering property rights;

(c) Concluding crop substitution agreements with farmers;

(d) Ensuring that eradication programs take into account the safeguarding of human health and preservation of the ecosystem;

(e) Fostering new economic opportunities, such as alternative development and crop substitution programs, that will help to dissuade growers from initiating or expanding illegal cultivation;

(f) Implementing reforestation programs in those areas where coca has been eradicated but where the land is not suitable for farming;

(g) Substantially facilitating access to business activity and to credit;

(h) Abolishing bureaucratic obstacles and mechanisms, particularly those that limit the production, marketing, and exportation of alternative goods;

(i) Promoting the participation of all countries interested in providing technical solutions and conducting specific alternative development projects with the peasants and/or their organizations.

3. The Environment

The Countries express their concern regarding the severe damage that coca cultivation and illegal processing of coca derivatives are causing to the environment of the Andean region. The slash-and-burn method employed by coca and opium poppy growers causes severe erosion of the soil, and indiscriminate disposal of the toxic chemicals used to produce coca derivatives is poisoning the rivers and the water table. These activities enrich a small group of traffickers and cause harm to thousands of people.

The United States Government notes that it is helping the Andean governments address the serious environmental problems caused by illegal coca and opium production. The United States is providing technical assistance and training under comprehensive environmental management programs that are important components of alternative development projects. The United States is providing assistance for watershed management, farm-level and community forestry, reforestation and environmental restoration, education on environmental problems, and environmental monitoring programs. These efforts are designed to prevent damage to—and to restore—the soil, water, and forest resources, thereby improving the quality of life and expanding opportunities for those who abandon, or never initiate, coca production in favor of alternative crops. The Countries agree that such technical assistance and training services must be designed to strengthen the capacity of Andean governments to protect their countries' natural environment.

The Countries agree to design and implement suitable programs to reduce the negative ecological impact of coca production and ensure that security, interdiction, and substitution activities take the protection of the ecosystem into account.

Strategies for Prevention and Demand Reduction

The Countries recognize that consumption of, and illicit traffic in, drugs and psychotropic substances are a comprehensive problem, and that it can therefore be resolved only if control, interdiction, and supply reduction measures are accompanied by vigorous and effective action in demand reduction.

It is also necessary for society, including its members who consume illegal drugs and those who are involved in illicit drug traffic or the cultivation of plants intended for conversion into illicit drugs, to be made aware of the harmful consequences of the production, traffic, and consumption of illicit drugs. It is imperative to provide warnings about the dangers of violence, crime, corruption, environmental damage, addiction, and the dissolution of society and the family resulting from the drug problem.

The Countries are convinced that raising awareness regarding the harmful impact of drug-related offenses will motivate society to develop a culture that rejects drug use and to support vigorously efforts to combat supply and demand. In order to support this awareness campaign, the Countries agree to assume the responsibility, either individually or jointly, to conduct long-term programs to inform the public through the appropriate mass media and other information resources.

The Countries also call on their respective private sectors to combine efforts to create a culture that rejects drugs.

In this regard, the Countries are aware that demand can be controlled and reduced and that the basis can be laid for increasing awareness by means of continuous, systematic actions that include:

1. Prevention

The Countries consider that prevention must be a priority aspect of national strategies to reduce the demand for drugs.

In order to prevent consumption of drugs and dissuade occasional users, the Countries must include in their national and drug control strategies comprehensive prevention programs that include, among other things:

a. Education

The Countries recognize that education is fundamental in the upbringing of the individual and the creation of positive values and attitudes toward life, and that the educational system at all levels and in all its forms is a suitable tool to reach most of the people. Consequently, the Countries undertake to engage in additional educational efforts for comprehensive prevention of drug use from pre-school through higher education, by means of scientific research, in order to create an attitude and a culture that rejects drugs and in which the family and the community play a fundamental role.

b. Community Mobilization

The Countries wish to emphasize the importance of mobilizing all sectors of society against drugs as a fundamental part of national prevention efforts. This mobilization includes carrying out actions at the individual, family, and social levels by means of activities that include recreation, sports, and cultural events that make it possible to achieve a total rejection of drug consumption.

2. Treatment and Rehabilitation

In order for drug addicts to receive suitable assistance, the Countries consider that it is necessary to increase their capacity with regard to treatment and rehabilitation, in addition to improving the quality of services. The Countries consider that these programs must be designed not only to rehabilitate drug addicts but also to help them reenter society.

The Countries believe that treatment and rehabilitation are basic in reducing the consequences arising from drug use, including AIDS transmission, societal violence, and the destruction of the family and social structure.

3. Scientific Research

The Countries recognize that it is necessary to establish programs for basic and social research, including epidemiology, in their national strategies. Epidemiological programs must be conducted using a methodology that makes it possible to compare findings at the regional and international levels. These findings will also be useful in evaluating prevention programs. The Countries undertake to exchange information on drug abuse through a regional information network and to support initiatives to establish a data bank on this subject, especially within the framework of CICAD.

4. Training

The Countries undertake to cooperate by providing appropriate technical assistance for the education and training of human resources in these areas.

The Countries will also endeavor to consult with one another and exchange information on the prevention of illicit drug use, treatment, rehabilitation, and scientific research. In this regard, they agree to cooperate in order to determine the most effective ways to utilize the research findings in implementing the various programs.

5. National Councils

The Countries are convinced that the creation of national councils to coordinate efforts to develop strategies against illicit drugs has made an important contribution to the development of prevention, treatment, and rehabilitation programs in all the countries.

6. Follow-Up

The Countries undertake to engage in ongoing follow-up of the actions described above. To that end, they will assign responsibility to their national councils in line with OAS/CICAD programs.

Note: The declaration was made available by the Office of the Press Secretary but was not issued as a White House press release.

55. Remarks to the American Society of Newspaper Editors
April 9, 1992

The President. Thank you, Dave. And may I start by thanking the members of the board and say to all the members of ASNE I'm grateful for this return engagement, glad to participate in an annual event that Washington looks forward to, this annual conference. Even in the age of VCR's and CNN, people who want to understand the times we live in still, as Dave indicated in that sweet and short introduction, turn to the printed word.

And today I want to share some serious observations with you on events around the world. Look around the world today. Think of the page-one stories of the past few years and our victory in the cold war, the collapse of imperial communism, the liberation of Kuwait. Think of the great revolutions of '89 that brought down the Berlin Wall and broke the chains of communism and brought a new world of freedom to Eastern Europe. And think of the role this Nation played in every one of these great triumphs, the sacrifices we made, the sense of mission that carried us through.

Each day brings new changes, new realities, new hopes, new horizons. In the past 6 months alone we've recognized 18, in 6 months, 18 brand-new nations. The bulk of those nations, of course, are born of one momentous event, the collapse of Soviet communism.

And today I want to talk to you all about the most important foreign policy opportunity of our time, an opportunity that will affect the security and the future of every American, young and old, throughout this entire decade. The democratic revolutions underway in Russia, in Armenia, Ukraine, and the other new nations of the old Soviet empire represent the best hope for real peace in my lifetime.

Shortly after taking office, I outlined a new American strategy in response to the changes underway in the Soviet Union and East and Central Europe. It was to move beyond containment, to encourage reform, to always support freedom for the captive nations of the East. And now, after dramatic revolutions in Poland and Hungary and Czechoslovakia, revolutions that spread then to Romania and Bulgaria and even Albania; after the unification of Germany in NATO; after the demise of the one power, the U.S.S.R., that threatened our way of life, that mission has been fulfilled. The cold war is over. The specter of nuclear armageddon has receded, and Soviet communism has collapsed. And in its wake we find ourselves on the threshold of a new world of opportunity and peace.

But with the passing of the cold war, a new order has yet to take its place. The opportunities, tremendous; they're great. But so, too, are the dangers. And so, we stand at history's hinge point. A new world beckons while the ghost of history stands in the shadows.

I want to outline today a new mission for American policy toward Russia and the other new nations of the old U.S.S.R. It's a mission that can advance our economic and security interests while upholding the primacy of American values, values which, as Lincoln said, are the "last, best hope of Earth."

Americans have always responded best when a new frontier beckoned. And I believe that the next frontier for us, and for the generation that follows, is to secure a democratic peace in Europe and the former U.S.S.R. that will ensure a lasting peace for the United States of America.

The democratic peace must be founded on twin pillars of political and economic freedom. The success of reform in Russia and Ukraine, Armenia and Kazakhstan, Byelarus and the Baltics will be the single best guarantee of our security, our prosperity, and our values. After the long cold war, this much is clear: Democrats in the Kremlin can assure our security in a way nuclear missiles never could. Much of my administration's foreign policy has been dedicated to winning the cold war peacefully. And the next 4 years must be dedicated to building a democratic peace, not simply for those of us who lived through the cold war and won it but for generations to come.

From the first moments of the cold war, our mission was containment, to use the combined resources of the West to check the expansion, the expansionist aims of the Soviet empire. It's been my policy as President to move beyond containment, to use the power of America and the West to end the cold war with freedom's victory. And today, we have reached a turning point. We have defeated imperial communism.

We've not yet won the victory for democracy, though. This democratic peace will not be easily won. The weight of history, 74 years of Communist misrule in the former U.S.S.R., tells us that democracy and economic freedom will be years in the building. America must, therefore, resolve that our commitment be equally firm and lasting. With this commitment, we have the chance to build a very different world, a world built on the common values of political and economic freedom between Russia and America, between East and West and at long last, a peace built on mutual trust, not on mutual terror.

And today, we find ourselves in an almost unimaginable world where democrats, not Communists, hold power in Moscow and Kiev and Yerevan; a new world where a new breed of leaders, Boris Yeltsin, Levon Ter-Petrosyan, Leonid Kravchuk, Askar Akayev, among others, are pushing forward to reform.

They seek to replace the rule of force with the rule of law. And they seek, for the first time in their countries' histories, not to impose rule in the name of the people but to build governments of, by, and for the people. And they seek a future of free and open markets where economic rights rest in the hands of individuals, not on the whims of the central planners. They seek partnerships. They seek alliances with us. And they also seek an end to competition and conflict. Our values are their values. And in this time of transition, they are reaching out to us. They seek our help. And if we're to act, we must see clearly what is at stake.

Forty years ago, Americans had the vision and the good sense to help defeated enemies back to their feet as democracies. Well, what a wise investment that proved to be. Those we helped became close allies and major trading partners. Our choice today, just as clear: With our help, Russia, Ukraine, other new States can become democratic friends and partners. And let me say here, they will have our help.

What difference can this make for America, you might ask. We can put behind us, for good, the nuclear confrontation that has held our very civilization hostage for over four decades. The threat of a major ground war in Western Europe has disappeared with the demise of the Warsaw Pact. A democratic Russia is the best guarantee against a renewed danger of competition and the threat of nuclear rivalry.

The failure of the democratic experiment could bring a dark future, a return to authori-tarianism or a descent into anarchy. In either case, the outcome would threaten our peace, our prosperity, and our security for years to come. But we should focus not on the dangers of failure but on the dividends of success.

First, we can reap a genuine peace dividend this year and then year after year, in the form of permanently reduced defense budgets. Already we've proposed $50 billion worth of defense spending reductions between now and 1997. Now, that cut comes on top of savings totaling $7 billion, more than a quarter of a trillion dollars in projected defense expenditures since the fall of the Berlin Wall. Make no mistake: I am not going to make reckless defense cuts that impair our own fundamental national security.

Second, working with our Russian partners and our allies, we can create a new international landscape, a landscape where emerging threats are contained and undone, where we work in concert to confront common threats to our environment, where terrorists find no safe haven, and where genuine coalitions of like-minded countries respond to dangers and opportunities together.

And finally, third, the triumph of free governments and free markets in the old Soviet Union will mean extensive opportunities for global trade and economic growth. A democratic Russia, one dedicated to free market economies, will provide an impetus for a major increase in global trade and investment. The people of the former Soviet Union are well-schooled and highly skilled. They seek for their families the same better future each of us wishes for our own. And together, they form a potentially vast market that crosses 11 time zones and comprises nearly 300 million people.

No economist can pinpoint the value of trade opportunities we hope to have. It's impossible to compute, but the potential for prosperity is great. Increased trade means vast new markets for American goods, new opportunities for American entrepreneurs, new jobs for American workers. And I'm committed to giving American business every possible opportunity to compete fairly and equally in these new markets.

For example, last week I asked the Congress to repeal the Stevenson and Byrd amendments that limit Export-Import Bank's ability to help promote American exports to the former U.S.S.R. And I'm pleased that Congress has acted. I'm also seeking to conclude trade, bilateral investment, and tax treaties with each of the new Commonwealth States. The first agreement between the U.S. and Armenia was signed last week, and we expect a lot more to follow.

Russian democracy is in America's interest. It's also in keeping with this Nation's guiding ideals. Across the boundaries of language and culture, across the cold war chasm of mistrust, we feel the pull of common values. And in the ordeal of long-suffering peoples of the Soviet empire, we see glimpses of this Nation's past. In their hopes and dreams, we see our own.

This is an article of the American creed: Freedom is not the special preserve of one nation; it is the birthright of men and women everywhere. And we have always dreamed of the day democracy and freedom will triumph in every corner of the world, in every captive nation and closed society. And this may never happen in our lifetime, but it can happen now for the millions of people who for so long suffered under that totalitarian Soviet rule.

Some may say this view of the future is a little unrealistic. Let me remind you that three of our leading partners in helping democracy succeed in Russia are none other than Germany, Japan, and Italy. And if we can now bring Russia into the community of free nations who share American ideals, we will have redeemed hope in a century that has known so much suffering. It is not inevitable, as de Tocqueville wrote, that America and Russia were destined

to struggle for global supremacy. De Tocqueville only knew a despotic Russia, but we see and can help secure a democratic Russia.

One of America's greatest achievements in this century has been our leadership of a remarkable community of nations, the free world. This community is democratic; it is stable; it's prosperous, cooperative; it is independent. In America all of us are the better for that. And we have strong allies. We have enormous trade, and we are safer as a result of our commitment to this free world. And now, we must expand this most successful of communities to include our former adversaries.

Now, this is good for America. A world that trades with us brings greater prosperity. A world that shares our values strengthens the peace. This is the world that lies out there before us. This is the world that can be achieved if we have the vision to reach for it. And this is the peace that we must not lose.

And this is what we're doing right now to win this peace. Strategically, we're moving with the Russians to reach historic nuclear reductions. We've urged speedy ratification of START and CFE. And we're working with all the new States to prevent the spread of weapons of mass destruction. We are offering our help in safety, in nuclear weapons safety, in security, and yes, in the dismantlement. And we're engaged in an intensive program of military-to-military exchanges to strengthen the ties between our two militaries, indeed, to build unprecedented defense cooperation, cooperation that would have simply been unthinkable a few short months ago.

Politically, we're reaching out so America and American values will be well represented in these new lands. We are the only country with embassies in all of the former republics. We're planning to bring American houses and American expertise to the former U.S.S.R., to send hundreds of Peace Corps volunteers to help create small businesses, to launch major exchanges of students, professionals, and scientists, so that our people can establish the bonds so important to permanent peace.

Economically, working with the European Community and many other countries, we organized a global coalition to provide urgently needed emergency food and medical supplies this past winter. And now we will send Americans to help promote improvements in food distribution, energy, defense conversion, and democratization.

I have sent Congress the "FREEDOM Support Act," a comprehensive and integrated legislative package that will provide new opportunities to support freedom and repeal all cold-war legislation. In its key features this bill asks Congress to meet my request for $12 million to fund technical assistance projects in the former U.S.S.R. It urges Congress to increase the U.S. quota in the IMF, International Monetary Fund, by $12 billion. And I pledge to work with the Congress on a bipartisan basis to pass this act. And I want to sign this bill into law before my June summit with President Yeltsin here in Washington, DC.

Just as the rewards of this new world will belong to no one nation, so too the burden does not fall to America alone. Together with our allies, we've developed a $24 billion package of financial assistance. Its aim: to provide urgently needed support for President Yeltsin's reforms.

And ours is a policy of collective engagement and shared responsibility. Working with the G - 7, the IMF, and the World Bank, we are seeking to help promote the economic transformation so central to an enduring democratic peace. Forty-five years after their founding, the Bretton Woods institutions we created after World War II are now serving their original purpose. By working with others we're sharing the burden responsibly and acting in the best interests of the American taxpayer.

I know that broad public support will be critical to our effort to get this program passed. And so, let me say something to those who say, "Yes, the people of Russia, and all across the old Soviet empire, are struggling; yes, we want to see them succeed, to join the democratic community. But what about us? What about the challenges and demands we must meet right here in America? Isn't it time we took care of our own?" And to them I would say this: Peace and prosperity are in the interest of every American, each one of us alive today and all the generations that will follow. As a Nation, we spent more than $4 trillion to wage and win the cold war. Compared to such monumental sacrifice, the costs of promoting democracy will be a fraction and the consequences for our peace and prosperity beyond measure. America must take the lead in creating this new world of peace.

Three times this century, America has been called on to help construct a lasting peace in Europe. Seventy-five years ago this month, the United States entered World War I to tip the balance against aggression. And yet, with the battle won, America withdrew across the ocean, and the "war to end all wars" produced a peace that did not last even a generation. Indeed, by the time I was born in 1924, the peace was already unraveling. Germany's economic chaos soon led to what, to Fascist dictatorship. The seeds of another, more terrible war were sown.

And still, the isolationist impulse remained strong. Years later, as the Nazis began their march across the Continent, I can still remember the editorials here in the United States talking about "Europe's war," as if America could close itself off, as if we could isolate ourselves from the world beyond our shores. As a consequence, you know the answer, we fought the most costly war in the history of man, a war that claimed the lives of countless millions. At war's end, once again we saw the prospect of a new world on the horizon. But the great victory over fascism quickly gave way to the grim reality of a new Communist threat.

We are fortunate that our postwar leaders, Democrats and Republicans alike, did not forget the lessons of the past in building the peace of the next four decades. They shaped a coalition that kept America engaged, that kept the peace through the long twilight struggle against Soviet communism. And they taught the lesson that we simply must heed today, that the noblest mission of the victor is to turn an enemy into a friend.

And now America faces a third opportunity to provide the kind of lasting peace that for so long eluded us. At this defining moment, I know where I stand. I stand for American engagement in support of a democratic peace, a peace that can secure for the next generation a world free from war, free from conflict.

After a half-century of fear and mistrust, America, Russia, and the new nations of the former U.S.S.R. must become partners in peace. After a half-century of cold war and harsh words, we must speak and act on common values. After a half-century of armed and uneasy peace, we must move forward toward a new world of freedom, cooperation, reconciliation, and hope.

Thank you all very much for inviting me here today. And may God bless the free peoples of the former Soviet empire, and may God bless the United States of America. Thank you very, very much.

Persian Gulf

Q. [Inaudible]

The President. [Inaudible]—of the Gulf area. At that time not only the United States but the United States and many of the Gulf countries, the GCC countries, felt that the major threat to stability in the Gulf was from Iran. We did not want an Iran that would take

over Iraq and then inexorably move south. So, there was a real logic for that.

Shelby [C. Shelby Coffey III, *Los Angeles Times*], I'm not going to, by my silence, acquiesce in all the charges that the question included, but some of this was true. We did some business with Iraq, but I just don't want to sign off on each one of the allegations that some of these stories have contained. But this was our policy.

And then we saw what Saddam Hussein did after this war ended. We tried to bring him into the family of nations through commerce, and we failed. And when he reached out to crush a neighboring country, we mobilized the best and most effective coalition, I think, that's been seen in modern times. And the objective was to set back aggression.

The U.N. resolutions never called for the elimination of Saddam Hussein. It never called for taking the battle into downtown Baghdad. And we have a lot of revisionists who opposed me on the war now saying, "How come you didn't go into downtown Baghdad and find Saddam Hussein and do him in?" We put together a coalition. We worked effectively with the coalition to fulfill the aims of the United Nations resolutions. And we fulfilled those aims. We set back aggression. And as any one of our respected military leaders will tell you, we have all but removed the threat of Saddam Hussein to his neighbors.

Now, we are still concerned about him. There's no question about that. And I am very much concerned, as he goes north of the 36th parallel the other day with airplanes, as to what that means to the safety of the Kurds. I am concerned about the Shiites in the south and to the southeast. I was also concerned when I saw an Iranian incursion of the Iraq borders to go after those Shiites. We can't condone that, as much as we detest the regime of Saddam Hussein.

So we will—do I have regrets, was your question? I guess if I had 90 - 90 hindsight and any action that we might have taken beforehand would guarantee that Saddam Hussein did not move down into Kuwait, which he did, I'd certainly rethink our position. But I can't certify that by not helping Iraq in the modest way we did, that that would have guaranteed that he would stay within his confines, the confines of his own border. And I can't say to you what would have happened in terms of Iran's aggression.

We are dealing with the facts as they came down the pike. And one of them was that he committed an aggression that mobilized the whole world against him. And he is going to remain isolated as long as I am President. He is going to live by those U.N. resolutions, and we are going to see that he complies with each and every one of them, including the most dangerous area of all, the one where he is doing things he ought not to be doing in terms of missiles and in terms of a nuclear capability.

So we're not going to lighten up on it. I think—oh, there's one other point since you've given me such a wonderful opening, Shelby. I read that General Norm Schwarzkopf wanted to keep going after I stopped the war. I will tell you unequivocally that that is simply totally untrue.

I sat in the Oval Office that fateful day—when you remember the turkey shoot along the highway going north—and Colin Powell came to me, our respected Chairman of the Joint Chiefs, and said, "Mr. President, it's our considered opinion that the war is over. We have achieved our objectives, and we should stop." And I said, "Do our commanders in the field feel that way?" And he said, "Yes." And I said, "Well, let's doublecheck," something to that effect. He walked over to my desk—I was sitting on this end near the Stewart picture in the Oval Office—picked up the secure phone, dialed a number, and talked to Norm Schwarzkopf out in the desert and said, "What

do you think? The President has asked me to doublecheck. We have achieved our objectives. We ought to stop." We agreed that we would stop at, I think it was midnight that night, 100 hours after the battle began.

And now we're caught up in a real peculiar election year. And you hear all kinds of people, some of whom supported what I did, many of whom oppose it, now going after this administration and our military for stopping too soon. I don't think that's right. Am I happy Saddam Hussein is still there? Absolutely not. Am I determined he's going to live with these resolutions? Absolutely. But we did the right thing. We did the honorable thing. And I have absolutely no regrets about that part of it at all.

Presidential Campaign

Q. Mr. President, as you know, another Texan is thinking about running for President in 1992. He'll be joining us tomorrow morning. As a matter of fact—

The President. Are you speaking about Lloyd Bentsen? [Laughter]

Q. Let's say two other Texans.

The President. Oh, I see.

Q. Some might even think that Ross Perot sounds a little more Texan than you do. My question would be, why do you think he's been as successful as he has in the early going in gaining support? What impact do you think he might have in the general election, particularly his possible ability to carry the State of Texas? And finally, do you feel part of his appeal is based on his ability to connect with the average American who wants to lift himself economically? Is he better able to do that than you are?

The President. You know, I'm going to give you another question because I am not going to do something now I've assiduously avoided all during the primary, going after anybody else, or quantify it in any way, that might run or is running. And I'm going to stay with that ground rule right now. When the battle is joined and the conventions are over and the nominees are out there, I will happily answer your question for you. But let him, Ross, make his determination. Let him do what the rest of us do, take our case to the American people. Let him enjoy the same scrutiny that I've had for, what, 12 years at this relatively high level of Government, Vice President and President.

But there's no point in me trying to define his candidacy nor the candidacy of the Democrats that are left in the race on the other side. What I'm trying to do, having gone into some of these primaries and emerged, I think, as the nominee of our party, is to lead this country, to talk about these serious issues.

You know, they say to me, as they say, "How can you be the candidate of change? You've been in Washington all this time." I say we're the ones that are trying to change things, whether it's education, whether it's tort reform, whether it's in matters of this nature that have to do with life and death and peace and war.

And so I'm going to keep on doing that now. And then, when the battle is joined and we get past the convention stage, I'll have plenty of comment to help you along in assessing the opposition. But I really am going to stay out of it now. And this isn't a new position. Just because I'm standing before a lot of editors, I think these traveling White House press will tell you that's the way it's been.

So, if you want another one that I can answer, shoot.

Abortion

Q. Let me ask one other one then, Mr. President. Abortion certainly continues to be one of the hottest issues not only in the United States but in the Republican Party. Is it your preference that the GOP platform in 1992 stay silent on that issue, come out flatly against abortion, or support those abortion rights activists who are inside the GOP?

The President. My position has not changed. I am pro-life. And I'm going to stay with that position. In terms of the platform, we have a platform committee that's going to debate that. You mentioned inside the Republican Party, take a look at the State of Pennsylvania. This isn't an issue that divides just Republicans; this is an issue that divides Democrats as well, if you look at the laws in the books and the position of the Governor of that State and other States as well.

So each of us should say what we feel, fight for our views, and then we've got a party platform process that will resolve that.

Multilateral Trade Negotiations

Q. Mr. President, you have attended three economic summits since taking office in which a very high priority was assigned to a new world trade agreement under GATT. Each time these deadlines have been broken; on Easter I think we're going to have another deadline broken. And you just spoke about a world in which we would trade with the Soviet Union or the former Soviet Union. How can the Soviet Union really survive unless we get a world trade agreement?

The President. Well, I think they could survive, but they would survive much less well. And we are going to keep on working for a successful conclusion of this Uruguay round of GATT. The major stumbling block has been agriculture. And we cannot have a satisfactory conclusion to the GATT round unless agriculture is addressed. That has been a particularly difficult problem for France and a particularly difficult problem for Germany.

And we, as you know from following this, have said we will work with the Dunkel text. This is highly technical, but it spells out some broad ground rules on agriculture. And we still have some problems other than agriculture.

I am told that the EC leader, Delors, now feels that we are very, very close on agriculture. He's coming here soon with Cavaco Silva of Portugal, and we're going to be sitting down in one of each—we have meetings twice a year. I will then be talking to him—I won't be doing the negotiating—but with our top negotiators and try to hammer out that agreement.

We still have some other problems, property rights and, you know, trademarks and all this kind of thing. But I am more optimistic now. I asked Brent the other day, my trusted and able National Security Adviser, where do each of these deadlines that you referred to come from? They keep coming. Well, we'd have a deadline, and you're right, somebody throws up a deadline and says we've got to meet it by February, we've got to do it by June. I don't know where the deadline comes from. But I do know that it is in the interest of the free world, say nothing of the now-freeing world, the Soviet Union, the former Soviet Union, that we achieve this agreement.

And one last point on the trade agreement. Far better, far better than a foreign aid program for the emerging democracies of the Third World, Africa particularly, is a trade agreement. Far better than aid is trade. And so we will keep on playing, I think, a very constructive role to achieve a conclusion of this.

And parenthetically, we are going to work for the North American free trade agreement. You know, we're in a political year, some of you may know, and we're getting shot at by various predictable organizations on the Mexican agreement. The Mexican agreement, in my view, will create jobs in the United States, will help the environment. A country that's doing better economically can do a lot more for its environment than one that is kept down on the ropes because we don't have fair and free trade.

So we're going to work to that end to get a Mexican agreement along with the Uruguay round. And yes, all of that will benefit the emerging republics that I've been talking about here today. But I'm not despairing about it. The point is, if we come to some new deadline, we're going to keep on pushing. But right now, it looks like we may have a better chance than we've had in the last years of negotiation.

Q. Your office says one more question.

The President. Do they? Okay.

Foreign Aid and Trade

Q. Mr. President, oddly enough part of your reply there dealt with my question. You've given a good vision of our obligations to help redeem the emergent nations of the former Soviet empire. But I wonder if anyone's paying much attention to our obligations to the truly hungry, starving nations of the world. Patrick Buchanan wants to do away with all foreign aid as part of his, I guess, Judeo-Christian tradition platform, forgetting the admonition that we bear one another's burdens. Our foreign aid appropriation has been about $18 billion a year.

Almost half went to Middle East countries. And our spending seems to me to be a disgraceful pittance in relation to the hunger and the deprivation of the really deprived nations of the Third World. I wonder if you think we should spend more to help the countries that have no influence, like Somalia and Ethiopia and even Haiti, closer, where there are millions of children with swollen stomachs crying for aid still. Do you think we are spending enough for actual food and aid for the hungry countries of the Earth?

The President. Not included in the figures you gave are other activities, such as the Peace Corps, such as some agricultural programs; and such is clearly the most important—the benefit of trade that you referred to in the first part.

Let me tell you something, it is going to be impossible to get anything through the Congress this year, in terms of foreign aid, beyond what we have suggested. We would be unrealistic to think that there might be more. I'm not suggesting, though, that the answer is to spend more money on it. I think the trade initiative is important. I think the position that our administration has taken in debt forgiveness has been tremendously important to many of these emerging democracies in Africa and, indeed, in this hemisphere.

Look at the basket case that was Argentina just a while back. And working with us, they are now on the move. They've come in, they've taken a very constructive approach to their economy. They are in the debt forgiveness. We've worked out a deal, they have, with the private financial institutions just very recently to lower their debt burden. The Enterprise for the Americas Initiative and the Brady plan are meaningful. And the impoverished people in that country and in other countries in our hemisphere are beginning to get a little break here.

So we're in a realistic time. I will continue to push for the trade agreements. I will continue to do what I can in these debt-reduction initiatives. And we'll continue to support foreign aid. And I think everybody here who writes, understands that that is not necessarily a popular position in an election year or any other time.

But we are dealing also with a time when we must address ourselves, and are trying so to do, to our own problems at home. And we are operating at enormous deficits in a sluggish economy, it isn't easy. And yet I want to not end here because we can take a couple more.

But I'm a little more optimistic on the economy. And I was very pleased today when the Fed lowered its rates by another quarter. That was instantly pretty well received in the market. Far be it for me to mention what levels markets should be at; I learned that long ago by mistake, saying something that triggered—I don't remember how it worked—triggered a market reaction. But I think the lowering of the rate by the Fed is a good thing, and I hope that it will guarantee that this fledgling recovery that we're seeing will now be a little more robust.

Q. Mr. President, over here, sir.

The President. Got you.

Federal Budget

Q. The Government's going in the hole about a billion dollars a day right now. And what reason can you give the American people for voting for 4 more years of the same kind of deficit spending?

The President. I certainly don't want them to vote for 4 more years of deficit spending. And I would like to get some changes in the United States Congress to guarantee against that. I would like to see them enact our budget that takes a major step towards the containment of an area that is the main area that's causing the deficit, and that is the entitlement area. And what are we proposing? We're proposing that the entitlements not grow beyond inflation and population growth. That in itself will save literally billions, billions, many billions of dollars.

So we've got to go forward with a sensible budget approach. Right now I'm battling against a Congress that wants to knock off the one guarantee that the American taxpayer has on spending, and that is the caps out of the nefarious 1990 budget agreement, the caps on discretionary spending. We're getting into an election year so we're trying to hold the line on those caps. And I'm determined to do it, and I think we will prevail.

But what I'll be doing is taking my case to the American people and say, yes, we've had some tough things. We've had banking problems that have cost the taxpayer enormously. We've had savings and loan problems that have cost the taxpayers enormously as we protect every single depositor. But we've got to try to exert some fiscal discipline on the system. And I'll be ready for the debate that will follow come fall because I think we're on the right track with what I've just told you here.

Dave says I'm out of here. We'll do one more, and then I'm gone.

Q. It's your staff, Mr. President, who says you're out of here. You can stay as long as you want.

The President. I don't want to be in trouble with them. [Laughter] Let's see what we've got here.

Presidential Campaign

Q. Mr. President, as you've astutely noted for us today, we are in an election year.

The President. Thank you. [Laughter]

Q. And in 7 months, much to the chagrin of this group, many Americans will be deciding their vote on the basis of television advertising. In 1988, many voters, most of us, were bombarded with what we would probably consider very negative television advertising that attacked the reputation of your opponent and seemed to pander to some of the fears of our society. I guess my question to you as you look into this election year, do you plan to direct, encourage, or discourage your consultants from pursuing a similar negative ad campaign in 1992?

The President. Well, you asked me at a time when this is in the heightened attention of the American people, isn't it? I look across at the Democratic primary, and anything that happened in 1988 is pale in comparison to what's going on there. We've tried to have most of ours positive.

You may recall an ad we ran in Michigan that triggered the famous line I used at the Gridiron Club, "Ich bin ein Mercedes owner." [Laughter] But that is a negative ad. Now, I don't know whether you consider that a turnoff or not, but just by the genesis of that ad came about that the opponent in this case was talking about protection and jobs and American jobs and American workers and all of this, and he was driving a Mercedes. Nobody was pointing it out. A lot of editors here—and I don't remember a brutal revelation of this terribly important fact. So we brought it out.

Now, I don't know if you consider that—I don't want to get into a debate since you might clearly win it—[laughter]—but is that a negative ad or is that fair in the way—everybody now that puts on the television at least have a thing—and the newspapers, too—here's why the ad was fair or unfair. I can't remember what they said about that one. I think when you define a person on issues, that's very, very important. I think some would consider it negative. But just seriously on that one. Then I can maybe answer your question a little better.

Q. I think what it does is set the tone. I guess people maybe care whether the opponent drives a Mercedes. But I guess we get into discussions of other character issues. I think that's really where the—

The President. Well, as I've said, I would like to see it on the issues and not on some of the sleaze questions. I've said that before, and I'll keep repeating that. I know that we will try hard, but I also know that this is about the ugliest political year I've ever seen already. And I don't know what it's going to hold, but I will try to keep my head up and try to do my job as President, and try to do it with a certain sense of decency and honor.

But we've seen it start off that way in the early primaries, and then something else evolved for reasons I'm not quite sure I fully understand. But I don't want to make you a firm statement because I don't know what's negative and what's not these days. If it's just ripping down somebody's character or tearing them apart, I don't want to do that. If it's factual and brings out something that hasn't been brought out, I think that's fair. And so we have to just use your judgment, I guess is the answer to that one.

Well, I guess I really do have to go. but thank you all very, very much. I appreciate it.

56. Address to the Nation on the Civil Disturbances in Los Angeles, California May 1, 1992

Tonight I want to talk to you about violence in our cities and justice for our citizens, two big issues that have collided on the streets of Los Angeles. First, an update on where matters stand in Los Angeles.

Fifteen minutes ago I talked to California's Governor Pete Wilson and Los Angeles Mayor Tom Bradley. They told me that last night was better than the night before; today, calmer than yesterday. But there were still incidents of random terror and lawlessness this afternoon.

In the wake of the first night's violence, I spoke directly to both Governor Wilson and Mayor Bradley to assess the situation and to offer assistance. There are two very different issues at hand. One is the urgent need to restore order. What followed Wednesday's jury verdict in the Rodney King case was a tragic series of events for the city of Los Angeles: Nearly 4,000 fires, staggering property damage, hundreds of injuries, and the senseless deaths of over 30 people.

To restore order right now, there are 3,000 National Guardsmen on duty in the city of Los Angeles. Another 2,200 stand ready to provide immediate support. To supplement this effort I've taken several additional actions. First, this morning I've ordered the Justice Department to dispatch 1,000 Federal riot-trained law enforcement officials to help restore order in Los Angeles beginning tonight. These officials include FBI SWAT teams, special riot control units of the U.S. Marshals Service, the Border Patrol, and other Federal law enforcement agencies. Second, another 1,000 Federal law enforcement officials are on standby alert, should they be needed. Third, early today I directed 3,000 members of the 7th Infantry and 1,500 marines to stand by at El Toro Air Station, California. Tonight, at the request of the Governor and the Mayor, I have committed these troops to help restore order. I'm also federalizing the National Guard, and I'm instructing General Colin Powell to place all those troops under a central command.

What we saw last night and the night before in Los Angeles is not about civil rights. It's not about the great cause of equality that all Americans must uphold. It's not a message of protest. It's been the brutality of a mob, pure and simple. And let me assure you: I will use whatever force is necessary to restore order. What is going on in L.A. must and will stop. As your President I guarantee you this violence will end.

Now let's talk about the beating of Rodney King, because beyond the urgent need to restore order is the second issue, the question of justice: Whether Rodney King's Federal civil rights were violated. What you saw and what I saw on the TV video was revolting. I felt anger. I felt pain. I thought: How can I explain this to my grandchildren?

Civil rights leaders and just plain citizens fearful of and sometimes victimized by police brutality were deeply hurt. And I know good and decent policemen who were equally appalled.

I spoke this morning to many leaders of the civil rights community. And they saw the video, as we all did. For 14 months they waited patiently, hopefully. They waited for the system to work. And when the verdict came in, they felt betrayed. Viewed from outside the trial, it was hard to understand how the verdict could possibly square with the video. Those civil rights leaders with whom I met were stunned. And so was I, and so was Barbara, and so were my kids.

But the verdict Wednesday was not the end of the process. The Department of Justice had started its own investigation immediately after the Rodney King incident and was monitoring the State investigation and trial. And so let me tell you what actions we are taking on the Federal level to ensure that justice is served.

Within one hour of the verdict, I directed the Justice Department to move into high gear on its own independent criminal investigation into the case. And next, on Thursday, five Federal prosecutors were on their way to Los Angeles. Our Justice Department has consistently demonstrated its ability to investigate fully a matter like this.

Since 1988, the Justice Department has successfully prosecuted over 100 law enforcement officials for excessive violence. I am confident that in this case, the Department of Justice will act as it should. Federal grand jury action is underway today in Los Angeles. Subpoenas are being issued. Evidence is being reviewed. The Federal effort in this case will be expeditious, and it will be fair. It will not be driven by mob violence but by respect for due process and the rule of law.

We owe it to all Americans who put their faith in the law to see that justice is served. But as we move forward on this or any other case, we must remember the fundamental tenet of our legal system. Every American, whether accused or accuser, is entitled to protection of his or her rights.

In this highly controversial court case, a verdict was handed down by a California jury. To Americans of all races who were shocked by the verdict, let me say this: You must understand that our system of justice provides for the peaceful, orderly means of addressing this frustration. We must respect the process of law whether or not we agree with the outcome. There's a difference between frustration with the law and direct assaults upon our legal system.

In a civilized society, there can be no excuse, no excuse for the murder, arson, theft, and vandalism that have terrorized the law-abiding citizens of Los Angeles. Mayor Bradley, just a few minutes ago, mentioned to me his particular concern, among others, regarding the safety of the Korean community. My heart goes out to them and all others who have suffered losses.

The wanton destruction of life and property is not a legitimate expression of outrage with injustice. It is itself injustice. And no rationalization, no matter how heartfelt, no matter how eloquent, can make it otherwise.

Television has become a medium that often brings us together. But its vivid display of Rodney King's beating shocked us. The America it has shown us on our screens these last 48 hours has appalled us. None of this is what we wish to think of as American. It's as if we were looking in a mirror that distorted our better selves and turned us ugly. We cannot let that happen. We cannot do that to ourselves.

We've seen images in the last 48 hours that we will never forget. Some were horrifying almost beyond belief. But there were other acts, small but significant acts in all this ugliness that give us hope. I'm one who respects our police. They keep the peace. They face danger every day. They help kids. They don't make a lot of money, but they care about their communities and their country. Thousands of police officers and firefighters are risking their lives right now on the streets of L.A., and they deserve our support. Then there are the people who have spent each night not in the streets but in the churches of Los Angeles, praying that man's gentler instincts be revealed in the hearts of people driven by hate. And finally, there were the citizens who showed great personal responsibility, who ignored the mob, who at great personal danger helped the victims of violence, regardless of race.

Among the many stories I've seen and heard about these past few days, one sticks in my mind, the story of one savagely beaten white truck driver, alive tonight because four strangers, four black strangers, came to his aid. Two were men who had been watching television and saw the beating as it was happening, and came out into the street to help; another was a woman on her way home from work; and the fourth, a young man whose name we may never know. The injured driver was able to get behind the wheel of his truck and tried to drive away. But his eyes were swollen shut. The woman asked him if he could see. He answered, "No." She said, "Well, then I will be your eyes." Together, those four people braved the mob and drove that truck driver to the hospital. He's alive today only because they stepped in to help.

It is for every one of them that we must rebuild the community of Los Angeles, for these four people and the others like them who in the midst of this nightmare acted with simple human decency.

We must understand that no one in Los Angeles or any other city has rendered a verdict on America. If we are to remain the most vibrant and hopeful Nation on Earth we must allow our diversity to bring us together, not drive us apart. This must be the rallying cry of good and decent people.

For their sake, for all our sakes, we must build a future where, in every city across this country, empty rage gives way to hope, where poverty and despair give way to opportunity. After peace is restored to Los Angeles, we must then turn again to the underlying causes of such tragic events. We must keep on working to create a climate of understanding and tolerance, a climate that refuses to accept racism, bigotry, anti-Semitism, and hate of any kind, anytime, anywhere.

Tonight, I ask all Americans to lend their hearts, their voices, and their prayers to the healing of hatred. As President, I took an oath to preserve, protect, and defend the Constitution, an oath that requires every President to establish justice and ensure domestic tranquility. That duty is foremost in my mind tonight.

Let me say to the people saddened by the spectacle of the past few days, to the good people of Los Angeles, caught at the center of this senseless suffering: The violence will end. Justice will be served. Hope will return.

Thank you, and may God bless the United States of America.

57. White House Fact Sheet: The North American Free Trade Agreement August 12, 1992

The President today announced that the United States, Mexico, and Canada have completed negotiation of a North American free trade agreement (NAFTA). The NAFTA will phase out barriers to trade in goods and services in North America, eliminate barriers to investment, and strengthen the protection of intellectual property rights. As tariffs and other trade barriers are eliminated, the NAFTA will create a massive open market, over 360 million people and over trillion in annual output.

Background

With sharp increases in global trade and investment flows, U.S. economic growth and job creation have become closely tied to our ability to compete internationally. Since 1986, U.S. exports have increased by almost 90 percent, reflecting our success in opening foreign markets and the competitiveness of American industry. In 1991, the U.S. exported over $422 billion of industrial and agricultural products and over $164 billion in services, making the United States the world's largest exporter, ahead of Germany and Japan. More than 7.5 million U.S. jobs are tied to merchandise exports, up from 5 million in 1986. Of these

jobs, 2.1 million are supported by exports to Canada and Mexico.

For many years, Mexico used high tariffs and licensing restrictions in an effort to encourage industrial development and import substitution. Under President Salinas and his predecessor, President de la Madrid, the Mexican Government has opened its market and implemented sweeping economic reforms. In 1986, Mexico joined the General Agreement on Tariffs and Trade (GATT) and began reducing its tariffs and trade barriers.

As a result, bilateral trade has increased dramatically. From 1986 to 1991, U.S. exports to Mexico increased from $12.4 billion to $33.3 billion, twice as fast as U.S. exports to the rest of the world. U.S. agricultural exports rose 173 percent to $3 billion, consumer goods tripled to $3.4 billion, and exports of capital goods surged to $11.3 billion from $5 billion. U.S. exports to Mexico now support approximately 600,000 American jobs, while exports to Canada support $1.5 million.

Economic reforms have also been good for Mexico. Its inflation rate has dropped from over 100 percent in 1986 to under 20 percent in 1991, and its economy has grown at an average annual rate of 3.1 percent over the last 4 years, after stagnating during the 1980's.

In June 1990, Presidents Bush and Salinas endorsed the idea of a comprehensive U.S.-Mexico free trade agreement and directed their trade ministers to begin preparatory work. Canada joined the talks in February 1991, leading to the three-way negotiation known as NAFTA. Formal negotiations began in June 1991 after Congress extended through May 1993 the Fast Track procedures originally enacted in the Trade Act of 1974, authorizing the administration to submit the agreement with implementing legislation for an up-or-down vote.

The President's trade strategy, which is a key part of his overall economic growth plan, is designed to create new markets for American products and provide new opportunities for American companies and workers.

The NAFTA Agreement

The NAFTA will create a free trade area (FTA) comprising the U.S., Canada, and Mexico. Consistent with GATT rules, all tariffs will be eliminated within the FTA over a transition period. The NAFTA involves an ambitious effort to eliminate barriers to agricultural, manufacturing, and services trade, to remove investment restrictions, and to protect effectively intellectual property rights. In addition, the NAFTA marks the first time in the history of U.S. trade policy that environmental concerns have been directly addressed in a comprehensive trade agreement. Highlights of the NAFTA include:

Tariff Elimination. Approximately 65 percent of U.S. industrial and agricultural exports to Mexico will be eligible for duty-free treatment either immediately or within 5 years. Mexico's tariffs currently average 10 percent, which is $2^1/_2$ times the average U.S. tariff.

Reduction of Motor Vehicle and Parts Tariffs. U.S. autos and light trucks will enjoy greater access to Mexico, which has the fastest growing major auto market in the world. With NAFTA, Mexican tariffs on vehicles and light trucks will immediately be cut in half. Within 5 years, duties on three-quarters of U.S. parts exports to Mexico will be eliminated, and Mexican "trade balancing" and "local content requirements" will be phased out over 10 years.

Auto Rule of Origin. Only vehicles with substantial North American parts and labor content will benefit from tariff cuts under NAFTA's strict rule of origin. NAFTA will require that autos contain 62.5 percent North American content, considerably more than the 50 percent required by the U.S.-Canada Free Trade Agreement. NAFTA contains tracing requirements so that individual parts can be identified to determine the North American content of major components and sub-assemblies, e.g. engines. This strict rule of origin is important in ensuring that the benefits of the NAFTA flow to firms that produce in North America.

Expanded Telecommunications Trade. NAFTA opens Mexico's $6 billion market for telecommunications equipment and services. It gives U.S. providers of voice mail or packet-switched services nondiscriminatory access to the Mexican public telephone network and eliminates all investment restrictions by July 1995.

Reduced Textiles and Apparel Barriers. Barriers to trade on $250 million (over 20 percent) of U.S. exports of textiles and apparel to Mexico will be eliminated immediately, with another $700 million freed from restrictions within 6 years. All North American trade restrictions will be eliminated within 10 years and tough rules of origin will ensure that benefits of trade liberalization accrue to North American producers.

Increased Trade in Agriculture. Mexico imported $3 billion worth of U.S. agricultural goods last year, making it our third-largest market. NAFTA will immediately eliminate Mexican import licenses, which covered 25 percent of U.S. agricultural exports last year, and will phase out remaining Mexican tariffs within 10 to 15 years.

Expanded Trade in Financial Services. Mexico's closed financial services markets will be opened, and U.S. banks and securities firms will be allowed to establish wholly owned subsidiaries. Transitional restrictions will be phased out by January 1, 2000.

New Opportunities in Insurance. U.S. firms will gain major new opportunities in the Mexican market. Firms with existing joint ventures will be permitted to obtain 100 percent ownership by 1996, and new entrants to the market can obtain a majority stake in Mexican firms by 1998. By the year 2000, all equity and market share restrictions will be eliminated, opening up completely what is now a $.5 billion market.

Increased Investment. Mexican "domestic content" rules will be eliminated, permitting additional sourcing of U.S. inputs. And for the first time, U.S. firms operating in Mexico will receive the same treatment as Mexican-owned firms. Mexico has agreed to drop export performance requirements, which presently force companies to export as a condition of being allowed to invest.

Land Transportation. More than 90 percent of U.S. trade with Mexico is shipped by land, but U.S. truckers currently are denied the right to carry cargo or set up subsidiaries in Mexico, forcing them to "hand off" trailers to Mexican drivers and return home empty. NAFTA will permit U.S. trucking companies to carry international cargo to the Mexican States contiguous to the U.S. by 1995 and gives them cross-border access to all of Mexico by the end of 1999. U.S. railroads will be able to provide their services in Mexico, and U.S. companies can invest in and operate land-side port services. The combination of truck, rail, and port breakthroughs will help create an efficient intermodal North American transport system.

Protection of Intellectual Property Rights. NAFTA will provide a higher level of protection for intellectual property rights than any other bilateral or multilateral agreement. U.S. high technology, entertainment, and consumer goods producers that rely heavily on protection for their patents, copyrights, and trademarks will realize substantial gains under NAFTA. The agreement will also limit compulsory licensing, resolving an important concern with Canada.

The objective of NAFTA is to open markets. It is not designed to create a closed regional trading bloc and does not erect new barriers to non-participants. The NAFTA is fully consis-tent with GATT criteria for free trade agreements and with U.S. support for strengthening the multilateral trading system in the Uruguay round.

Economic Studies

At the request of the Office of the U.S. Trade Representative, the U.S. International Trade Commission surveyed and evaluated the various economic analyses of NAFTA. In May of this year, the USITC reported that:

[T]here is a surprising degree of unanimity in the results regarding the aggregate effects of NAFTA. All three countries are expected to gain from a NAFTA.

These independent studies found that NAFTA would increase U.S. growth, jobs, and wages. They found that NAFTA would increase U.S. real GDP by up to 0.5 percent per year once it is fully implemented. They projected aggregate U.S. employment increases ranging from under 0.1 percent to 2.5 percent. The studies further project aggregate increases in U.S. real wages of between 0.1 percent to 0.3 percent.

U.S. exports to Mexico currently support over 600,000 American jobs. The Institute for International Economics recently estimated this figure will rise to over 1 million U.S. jobs by 1995 under NAFTA.

Environment, Labor, and Adjustment Issues

In a May 1, 1991, letter to the Congress, the President described actions that the administration would implement to address concerns regarding the impact of free trade on the environment, labor rights, and worker adjustment programs.

Environment. The administration has moved forward with a comprehensive bilateral environmental agenda to allay concerns that free trade could undermine U.S. environmental and food safety regulations or lead to environmental degradation on the U.S.-Mexico border. During the last year, substantial progress has been made. Highlights include the following:

—Standards. The NAFTA allows the U.S. to maintain its stringent environmental, health, and safety standards. It allows States and localities to enact tougher standards based on sound science. It encourages "upward harmonization" of national standards and regulations, and prohibits the lowering of standards to attract investment.

—Integrated Border Plan. In February 1992, EPA and its Mexican counterpart (SEDU-SOL) completed a comprehensive plan for addressing air, soil, water, and hazardous waste problems in the border area. Agreement has been reached on measures to implement the first stage of the plan covering the period 1992 to 1994.

—Border Infrastructure. The President has proposed a 70-percent increase in the budget for border environmental projects to $241 million for FY 1993, including $75 million for the "colonias" (unincorporated communities on the U.S. side of the border that often lack effective sanitation services and running water) and over $120 million for border wastewater treatment plants.

—Border Plan/FY 1993 Appropriations. To date, in the FY 1993 appropriations process, the House of Representatives has refused to fund the $50 million EPA request for the colonias and cut the administration's $65 million request for a Tijuana–San Diego sewage treatment plant to $32 million. For its part, the Senate failed to fund $120 million of the requested funds for border wastewater treatment. The President has called upon Congress to reverse these cuts.

—Environmental Conference. On September 17, 1992, EPA Administrator Reilly will host a trilateral meeting with the Canadian and Mexican environmental ministers in Washington, DC, to discuss environmental aspects of NAFTA.

Worker Rights. Mexico has a comprehensive labor law that provides workers with extensive legal rights. The economic benefits of the NAFTA will provide Mexico with resources to move forward with vigorous enforcement initiatives launched by the Salinas administration.

—Labor Cooperation. The U.S. Department of Labor has negotiated a 5-year Memorandum of Understanding (MOU) to strengthen bilateral cooperation with respect to occupational health and safety standards, child labor, labor statistics, worker rights, labor-management relations, and workplace training. Several joint MOU initiatives are now underway.

Safeguards. President Bush committed that NAFTA would contain measures to ease the transition for import-sensitive U.S. industries. For our sensitive sectors, tariffs will be phased out in 10 years, with particularly sensitive sectors having a transition of up to 15 years. In addition, NAFTA contains "safeguard" procedures that will allow the U.S. to reimpose tariffs in the event of injurious import surges.

Worker Adjustment. Dislocations in the U.S. are likely to be minimal, since U.S. trade barriers are already quite low. Nonetheless, during the Fast Track debate, the President promised that dislocated U.S. workers will receive timely, comprehensive, and effective services and retraining, whether through improvement or expansion of an existing program or creation of a new program. The administration has already begun consulting with the relevant congressional committees regarding adjustment services for displaced workers.

Next Steps

The timing of congressional consideration is governed by the Fast Track procedures, which require the President to notify the Congress of his intent to enter into the agreement at least 90 days before it is signed. Although today's announcement reflects the completion of negotiations, the draft text probably will not be finished until September, since further legal drafting and review are required to implement the understandings reached by the negotiators.

After the agreement is signed, legislation must be prepared to implement it, including any necessary changes to U.S. law. Under the Fast Track, the NAFTA will not go into effect until the Congress has approved the implementing legislation on an up-or-down vote. The approval process must occur within a specified time: 90 "session" days of Congress.

58. Remarks Accepting the Presidential Nomination at the Republican National Convention in Houston
August 20, 1992

The President. Thank you all very much. Thank you, thank you very much. And I am proud to receive and I am honored to accept your nomination for President of the United States.

May I thank my dear friend and our great leader, Bob Dole, for that wonderful introduction.

Let me say this: This nomination's not for me alone. It is for the ideas, principles, and values that we stand for.

My job has been made easier by a leader who's taken a lot of unfair criticism with grace and humor, the Vice President of the United States, Dan Quayle. And I am very grateful to him.

I want to talk tonight about the sharp choice that I intend to offer Americans this fall, a choice between different agendas, different directions, and yes, a choice about the character of the man you want to lead this Nation. I know that Americans have many questions about our economy, about our country's future, even questions about me. I'll answer them tonight.

First, I feel great. And I am heartened by the polls, the ones that say that I look better in my jogging shorts than the Governor of Arkansas.

Four years ago, I spoke about missions for my life and for our country. I spoke of one urgent mission, defending our security and promoting the American ideal abroad.

Just pause for a moment to reflect on what we've done. Germany is united, and a slab of the Berlin Wall sits right outside this Astrodome. Arabs and Israelis now sit face to face and talk peace, and every hostage held in Lebanon is free. The conflict in El Salvador is over, and free elections brought democracy to Nicaragua. Black and white South Africans cheered each other at the Olympics. The Soviet Union can only be found in history books. The captive nations of Eastern Europe and the Baltics are captive no more. And today on the rural streets of Poland, merchants sell cans of air labeled "the last breath of communism."

If I had stood before you 4 years ago and described this as the world we would help to build, you would have said, "George Bush, you must have been smoking something, and you must have inhaled."

This convention is the first at which an American President can say the cold war is over, and freedom finished first.

Audience members. U.S.A.! U.S.A.! U.S.A.!

The President. We have a lot to be proud of, a lot. Some want to rewrite history, want to skip over the struggle, claim the outcome was inevitable. And while the U.S. postwar strategy was largely bipartisan, the fact remains that the liberal McGovern wing of the other party, including my opponent, consistently made the wrong choices. In the seventies, they wanted a hollow army. We wanted a strong fighting force. In the eighties—and you remember this one—in the eighties, they wanted a nuclear freeze, and we insisted on peace through strength. From Angola to Central America, they said, "Let's negotiate, deliberate, procrastinate." We said, "Just stand up for freedom." Now the cold war is over, and they claim, "Hey, we were with you all the way."

Audience members. Boo-o-o!

The President. You know, their behavior reminds me of the old con man's advice to the new kid. He said, "Son, if you're being run out of town, just get out in front and make it look like a parade."

Well, make no mistake: The demise of communism wasn't a sure thing. It took the strong leadership of Presidents from both parties, including Republicans like Richard Nixon and Gerald Ford and Ronald Reagan. Without their vision and the support of the American people, the Soviet Union would be a strong superpower today, and we'd be facing a nuclear threat tonight.

My opponents say I spend too much time on foreign policy, as if it didn't matter that schoolchildren once hid under their desks in drills to prepare for nuclear war. I saw the chance to rid our children's dreams of the nuclear nightmare, and I did. Over the past 4 years, more people have breathed the fresh air of freedom than in all of human history. I saw a chance to help, and I did. These were the two defining opportunities not of a year, not of a decade, but of an entire span of human history. I seized those opportunities for our kids and our grandkids, and I make no apologies for that.

Now, the Soviet bear may be gone, but there are still wolves in the woods. We saw that when Saddam Hussein invaded Kuwait. The Mideast might have become a nuclear powder keg, our energy supplies held hostage. So we did what was right and what was necessary. We destroyed a threat, freed a people, and locked a tyrant in the prison of his own country.

What about the leader of the Arkansas National Guard, the man who hopes to be Commander in Chief? Well, I bit the bullet, and he bit his nails. Listen to this now. Two days after Congress followed my lead, my opponent said this, and I quote directly: "I guess I would have voted with the majority if it was a close vote. But I agree with the arguments the minority made." Now, sounds to me like his policy can be summed up by a road sign he's probably seen on his bus tour, "Slippery When Wet."

Look, this is serious business. Think about the impact of our foreign policy failures the last time the Democrats controlled both ends of Pennsylvania Avenue: gas lines, grain embargoes, American hostages blindfolded.

There will be more foreign policy challenges like Kuwait in the next 4 years, terrorists and aggressors to stand up to, dangerous weapons to be controlled and destroyed. Freedom's fight is not finished. I look forward to being the first President to visit a free, democratic Cuba. Who will lead the world in the face of these challenges?

Not my opponent. In his acceptance speech he devoted just 65 seconds to telling us about the world.

Then he said that America was, and I quote again—I want to be fair and factual—I quote, being "ridiculed" everywhere. Well, tell that to the people around the world, for whom America is still a dream. Tell that to leaders around the world, from whom America commands respect. Ridiculed? Tell that to the men and women of Desert Storm.

Audience members. U.S.A.! U.S.A.! U.S.A.!

The President. Let me just make an aside comment here because of what you've been reading in the paper. This is a political year, but there's a lot of danger in the world. You can be sure I will never let politics interfere with a foreign policy decision. Forget the election; I will do right, what is right for the national security of the United States of America, and that is a pledge from my heart.

Fifty years ago this summer, I was 18 years of age. I see some young people in the audience tonight, and I remember how I felt in those days. I believed deeply in this country, and we were faced with a world war. So I made a decision to go off and fight a battle much different from political battles.

I was scared, but I was willing. I was young, but I was ready. I had barely lived when I began to watch men die. I began to see the special place of America in the world. I began to see, even then, that the world would become a much smaller place, and faraway places could become more and more like America.

Fifty years later, after change of almost Biblical proportions, we know that when freedom grows, America grows. Just as a strong America means a safer world, we have learned that a safer world means a stronger America.

This election is about change. But that's not unusual, because the American revolution is never ending. Today, the pace of change is accelerating. We face new opportunities and new challenges. The question is: Who do you trust to make change work for you?

Audience members. George Bush! George Bush! George Bush!

The President. My opponent says America is a nation in decline. Of our economy, he says we are somewhere on the list beneath Germany, heading south toward Sri Lanka. Well, don't let anyone tell you that America is second-rate, especially somebody running for President.

Maybe he hasn't heard that we are still the world's largest economy. No other nation sells more outside its borders. The Germans, the British, the Japanese can't touch the productivity of you, the American worker and the American farmer. My opponent won't mention that. He won't remind you that interest rates are the lowest they've been in 20 years, and millions of Americans have refinanced their homes. You just won't hear that inflation, the thief of the middle class, has been locked in a maximum security prison.

You don't hear much about this good news because the media also tends to focus only on the bad. When the Berlin Wall fell, I half expected to see a headline, "Wall Falls, Three Border Guards Lose Jobs." [Laughter] And underneath, it probably says, "Clinton Blames Bush." [Laughter]

You don't hear a lot about progress in America. So let me tell you about some good things we've done together.

Just two weeks ago, all three nations of North America agreed to trade freely from Manitoba to Mexico. This will bring good jobs to Main Street, U.S.A.

We passed the Americans with Disabilities Act, bringing 43 million people into the economic mainstream. I must say, it's about time.

Our children will breathe easier because of our new clean air pact.

We are rebuilding our roads, providing jobs for more than half a million Americans.

We passed a child care law, and we took a stand for family values by saying that when it comes to raising children, Government doesn't know best; parents know best.

I have fought against prejudice and anti-Semitism all my life. I am proud that we strengthened our civil rights laws, and we did it without resorting to quotas.

One more thing of vital importance to all: Today, cocaine use has fallen by 60 percent among young people. To the teenagers, the parents, and the volunteers who are helping us battle the scourge of drugs in America, we say, thank you; thank you from the bottom of our hearts.

Do I want to do more? You bet. Nothing hurts me more than to meet with soldiers home from the Persian Gulf who can't find a job or workers who have a job but worry that the next day will bring a pink slip. And what about parents who scrape and struggle to send their kids to college, only to find them back living at home because they can't get work.

The world is in transition, and we are feeling that transition in our homes. The defining challenge of the nineties is to win the economic competition, to win the peace. We must be a military superpower, an economic superpower, and an export superpower.

In this election, you'll hear two versions of how to do this. Theirs is to look inward and protect what we already have. Ours is to look forward, to open new markets, prepare our people to compete, to restore our social fabric, to save and invest so we can win.

We believe that now that the world looks more like America, it's time for America to look more like herself. And so we offer a philosophy that puts faith in the individual, not the bureaucracy; a philosophy that empowers people to do their best, so America can be at its best. In a world that is safer and freer, this is how we will build an America that is stronger, safer, and more secure.

We start with a simple fact: Government is too big and spends too much.

I have asked Congress to put a lid on mandatory spending, except Social Security. I've proposed doing away with over 200 programs and 4,000 wasteful projects and to freeze all other spending.

The gridlock Democrat Congress said no.

Audience members. Boo-o-o!

The President. So, beginning tonight, I will enforce the spending freeze on my own. If Congress sends me a bill spending more than I asked for in my budget, I will veto it fast, veto it fast, faster than copies of Millie's book sold.

Now, Congress won't cut spending, but refuses to give the President the power to eliminate pork-barrel projects that waste your money. Forty-three Governors have that power. So I ask you, the American people: Give me a Congress that will give me the line-item veto.

Let me tell you about a recent battle fought with the Congress, a battle in which I was aided by Bob Michel and his troops, and Bob Dole and his. This spring, I worked day and night to get two-thirds of the House Members to approve a balanced budget amendment to the Constitution. We almost had it, but we lost by just nine votes. Now, listen how. Just before the vote, the liberal leaders of the Congress convinced 12 Members who cosponsored the bill to switch sides and vote no. Keep in mind, they voted against a bill they had already put their names on. Something fishy is going on.

And look at my opponent on this issue. Look at my opponent. He says he's for balanced budgets. But he came out against the amendment. He's like that on a lot of issues, first on one side, then the other. He's been spotted in more places than Elvis Presley.

After all these years, Congress has become pretty creative at finding ways to waste your money. So we need to be just as creative at finding ways to stop them. I have a brand-new idea. Taxpayers should be given the right to check a box on their tax returns so that up to 10 percent of their payments can go for one purpose alone: to reduce the national debt.

But we also need to make sure that Congress doesn't just turn around and borrow more money to spend more money. So I will require that for every tax dollar set aside to cut the debt, the ceilings on spending will be cut by an equal amount. That way, we will cut both debt and spending and take a whack out of the budget deficit.

My feelings about big government come from my experience; I spent half my adult life in the private sector. My opponent has a different experience; he's been in government nearly all his life. His passion to expand government knows no bounds.

He's already proposed, and listen to this carefully, he has already proposed $220 billion in new spending, along with the biggest tax increase in history, $150 billion. And that's just to start.

Audience members. Boo-o-o!

The President. He says he wants to tax the rich. But folks, he defines rich as anyone who has a job. [Laughter]

You've heard of the separations of powers. Well, my opponent practices a different theory: the power of separations. Government has the power to separate you from your wallet. [Laughter]

Now let me say this: When it comes to taxes, I've learned the hard way. There's an old saying, "Good judgment comes from experience, and experience comes from bad judgment." Two years ago, I made a bad call on the Democrats tax increase. I underestimated Congress' addiction to taxes. With my back against the wall, I agreed to a hard bargain: One tax increase one time in return for the toughest spending limits ever.

Well, it was a mistake to go along with the Democratic tax increase, and I admit it. But here's the question for the American people. Who do you trust in this election? The candidate who's raised taxes one time and regrets it, or the other candidate who raised taxes and fees 128 times and enjoyed it every time?

Audience members. Viva Bush! Viva Bush! Viva Bush!

The President. Thank you very much.

Audience members. Hit 'em again! Hit 'em again, harder, harder! Hit 'em again! Hit 'em again, harder, harder!

The President. When the new Congress convenes next January, I will propose to further reduce taxes across the board, provided we pay for these cuts with specific spending reductions that I consider appropriate, so that we do not increase the deficit. I will also continue to fight to increase the personal exemption and to create jobs by winning a cut in capital gains taxes.

That will especially help small businesses. You know, they create—small businesses—they create two-thirds of the new jobs in America. But my opponent's plan for small business is clear, present, and dangerous. Beside new income taxes, his plan will lead to a new payroll tax to pay for a Government takeover of health care and another new tax to pay for training. That is just the beginning.

If he gets his way, hardware stores across America will have a new sign up, "Closed for despair." I guess you'd say his plan really is "Elvis economics." America will be checking into the "Heartbreak Hotel."

I believe that small business needs relief from taxation, regulation, and litigation. And thus, I will extend for one year the freeze on paperwork and unnecessary Federal regulation that I imposed last winter. There is no reason that Federal regulations should live longer than my friend George Burns. I will issue an order to get rid of any rule whose time has come and gone.

I see something happening in our towns and in our neighborhoods. Sharp lawyers are running wild. Doctors are afraid to practice medicine, and some moms and pops won't even coach Little League any more. We must sue each other less and care for each other more. I am fighting to reform our legal system, to put an end to crazy lawsuits. If that means climbing into the ring with the trial lawyers, well, let me just say, round one starts tonight.

After all, my opponent's campaign is being backed by practically every trial lawyer who ever wore a tasselled loafer. He's not in the ring with them; he's in the tank.

There are other things we need to do to get our economy up to speed, prepare our kids for the next century. We must have new incentives for research and new training for workers. Small businesses need capital and credit, and defense workers need new jobs. I have a plan to provide affordable health care for every American, controlling costs by cut-

ting paperwork and lawsuits and expanding coverage to the poorest of the poor.

We do not need my opponent's plan for a massive Government takeover of health care, which would ration care and deny you the right to choose a doctor. Who wants health care with a system with the efficiency of the House post office and the compassion of the KGB?

What about our schools? What about our schools? My opponent and I both want to change the way our kids learn. He wants to change our schools a little bit, and I want to change them a lot. Take the issue of whether parents should be able to choose the best school for their kids. My opponent says that's okay, as long as the school is run by government. And I say every parent and child should have a real choice of schools, public, private, or religious.

So we have a clear choice to fix our problems. Do we turn to the tattered blanket of bureaucracy that other nations are tossing away? Or do we give our people the freedom and incentives to build security for themselves?

Here's what I'm fighting for: Open markets for American products; lower Government spending; tax relief; opportunities for small business; legal and health reform; job training; and new schools built on competition, ready for the 21st century.

Now, okay, why are these proposals not in effect today? Only one reason: the gridlock Democratic Congress.

Audience members. Clean your House! Clean your House! Clean your House!

The President. A very good idea, a very good idea.

Now, I know Americans are tired of the blame game, tired of people in Washington acting like they're candidates for the next episode of "American Gladiators." I don't like it, either. Neither should you. But the truth is the truth. Our policies have not failed. They haven't even been tried.

Americans want jobs, and on January 28th, I put before Congress a plan to create jobs. If it'd been passed back then, 500,000 more Americans would be at work right now. But in a Nation that demands action, Congress has become the master of inaction.

It wasn't always this way. I heard President Ford tonight. I served in Congress 22 years ago, under him. And back then, we cooperated. We didn't get personal. We put the people above everything else. Heck, we didn't even own blow dryers back in those days.

At my first Inauguration, I said that people didn't send us to bicker. I extended my hand, and I think the American people know this, I extended my hand to the congressional leaders, the Democratic leaders, and they bit it.

The House leadership has not changed in 38 years. It is a body caught in a hopelessly tangled web of PAC's, perks, privileges, partnership, and paralysis. Every day, Congress puts politics ahead of principle and above progress.

Now, let me give you just one example: February 20th, 1991. It was at the height of the Gulf war. On that very same day, I asked American pilots to risk their lives to fly missions over Baghdad. I also wanted to strengthen our economic security for the future. So that very same day, I introduced a new domestic energy strategy which would cut our dependence on foreign oil by 7 million barrels a day.

How many days did it take to win the Gulf war? Forty-three. How many did it take Congress to pass a national energy strategy? Five hundred and thirty-two, and still counting. I have ridden stationary bikes that can move faster than the United States

House of Representatives and the United States Senate, controlled by the Democrat leadership.

Audience members. Hit 'em again! Hit 'em again, harder, harder! Hit 'em again! Hit 'em again, harder, harder!

The President. Okay. All right. You wait. I'm fixing to.

Where does my opponent stand with Congress? Well, up in New York at their convention, they kept the congressional leaders away from the podium, hid them away. They didn't want America to hear from the people who really make the decisions. They hid them for a very good reason, because the American people would recognize a dangerous combination: a rubber-check Congress and a rubber-stamp President.

Governor Clinton and Congress know that you've caught on to their lingo. They know when they say "spending," you say "uh-oh." So now they have a new word, "investment." They want to "invest" $220 billion more of your money, but I want you to keep it.

Governor Clinton and Congress want to put through the largest tax increase in history, but I will not let that happen. Governor Clinton and Congress don't want kids to have the option of praying in school, but I do. Clinton and Congress don't want to close legal loopholes and keep criminals behind bars, but I will. Clinton and Congress will stock the judiciary with liberal judges who write laws they can't get approved by the voters.

Governor Clinton even says that Mario Cuomo belongs on the Supreme Court. [Laughter] Wait a minute, though. No, wait. Maybe not a bad idea. If you believe in judicial restraint, you probably ought to be happy. After all, the good Governor of New

York can't make up his mind between chocolate and vanilla at Baskin Robbins. He's there, we won't have another court decision for 35 years, and maybe that's all right, too.

Are my opponent and Congress really in cahoots? Look at one important question: Should we limit the terms of Congress?

Audience members. Yes.

The President. Governor Clinton says no. Congress says no. I say yes.

We tried this—look, we tried this once before, combining the Democratic Governor of a small southern State with a very liberal Vice President and a Democratic Congress. America does not need Carter II. We do not want to take America back to those days of malaise. But Americans want to know: Where's proof that we will have better days in Washington?

I'll give you 150 reasons. That's how many Members of Congress are expected to leave Washington this year. Some are tainted by scandal; the voters have bounced them the way they bounced their own checks. But others are good Members, Republican and Democrat, and they agree with me. The place just doesn't work anymore.

One hundred-fifty new Members, from both parties, will be coming to Washington this fall. Every one will have a fresh view of America's future.

I pledge today to the American people, immediately after this election, I will meet with every one of these Members, before they get attacked by the PAC's, overwhelmed by their staffs, and cornered by some camera crew. I will lay out my case for change, change that matters, real change that makes a difference, change that is right for America.

You see, there is a yearning in America, a feeling that maybe it's time to get back to our roots. Sure we must change, but some

values are timeless. I believe in families that stick together, fathers who stick around. I happen to believe very deeply in the worth of each individual human being, born or unborn. I believe in teaching our kids the difference between what's wrong and what's right, teaching them respect for hard work and to love their neighbors. I believe that America will always have a special place in God's heart, as long as He has a special place in ours. Maybe that's why I've always believed that patriotism is not just another point of view.

There are times in every young person's life when God introduces you to yourself. I remember such a time. It was back many years ago, when I stood watch at 4 a.m. up on the bridge of a submarine, the United States *Finback*, U.S.S. *Finback*. And I would stand there and look out on the blackness of the sky, broken only by the sparkling stars above. And I would think about friends I lost, a country I loved, and about a girl named Barbara. I remember those nights as clearly as any in my life.

You know, you can see things from up there that other people don't see. You can see storm clouds rise and then disappear, the first hint of the sun over the horizon, and the first outline of the shore far away.

Now, I know that Americans are uneasy today. There is anxious talk around our kitchen tables. But from where I stand, I see not America's sunset but a sunrise.

The world changes for which we've sacrificed for a generation have finally come to pass, and with them a rare and unprecedented opportunity to pass the sweet cup of prosperity around our American table.

Are we up to it? I know we are. As I travel our land, I meet veterans who once worked the turrets of a tank and can now master the keyboards of high-tech economy. I see teachers blessed with the incredible American capacity for innovation who are teaching our children a new way to learn for a new century. I meet parents, some working two jobs with hectic schedules, who still find new ways to teach old values to steady their kids in a turbulent world.

I take heart from what is happening in America, not from those who profess a new passion for government but from those with an old and enduring faith in the human potential, those who understand that the genius of America is our capacity for rebirth and renewal. America is the land where the sun is always peeking over the horizon.

Tonight I appeal to that unyielding, undying, undeniable American spirit. I ask you to consider, now that the entire world is moving our way, why would we want to go back their way? I ask not just for your support for my agenda but for your commitment to renew and rebuild our Nation by shaking up the one institution that has withstood change for over four decades. Join me in rolling away the roadblock at the other end of Pennsylvania Avenue, so that in the next 4 years, we will match our accomplishments outside by building a stronger, safer, more secure America inside.

Forty-four years ago in another age of uncertainty a different President embarked on a similar mission. His name was Harry S Truman. As he stood before his party to accept their nomination, Harry Truman knew the freedom I know this evening, the freedom to talk about what's right for America, and let the chips fall where they may.

Harry Truman said this: This is more than a political call to arms. Give me your help, not to win votes alone, but to win this new crusade and keep America safe and secure for its own people.

Well, tonight I say to you: Join me in our new crusade, to reap the rewards of our global victory, to win the peace, so that we may make America safer and stronger for all our people.

May God bless you, and may God bless the United States of America. Thank you very much.

59. Address to the Nation on Hurricane Andrew Disaster Relief September 1, 1992

Good evening, everyone. Eight days ago the people of south Florida and Louisiana were confronted by perhaps the most destructive natural disaster in our history. Tonight I want to report to the Nation on the aftermath of Hurricane Andrew and the effort required to help Andrew's survivors back on their feet.

In the past week I've twice visited Louisiana and Florida. And in Florida, where the storm was strongest, up to a quarter million people have lost their homes, many huddled beneath the busted timbers of what was once a living room or a kitchen. There's no running water, no electricity. Little children are left without even a toy to play with.

In the aftermath of Hurricane Andrew, a relief effort has risen, unprecedented in size and impact. And tonight as we speak, almost 20,000 troops are on the ground assisting in everything from providing meals to erecting tent cities. Basic human needs, food, water, shelter, and medical assistance, are being provided.

In Florida, a curfew is in place, and the National Guard and local police patrol the streets. It's a tribute to these officers and to the people of this region that looting has been kept to a minimum. Social Security checks are being delivered on time. Financial help is being made available to families who have lost their homes and their jobs.

This relief effort has generated incredible cooperation. My thanks go to so many people who slept so little the past 8 days, to State and local government officials, Federal Agencies, private charities, and the heroic men and women of the United States military. Most especially, my appreciation goes out to the volunteers. When we arrived in Florida, some of the first people we met were from South Carolina, victims of Hurricane Hugo who had spent the night driving so they could help others through their ordeal. We met doctors and firefighters spending sleepless vacations lending a helping hand. Through the eloquence of their action, I've been reminded that America will always be a nation of neighbors.

Although the relief effort is well underway, urgent needs still exist. And so tonight I make a special appeal to the generous spirit of the American people. People in Florida and Louisiana want to stay in their homes. They're in desperate need of rolls of plastic to cover open roofs, lumber to board up walls, and cots to sleep on. They also need diapers, baby formula, and other infant supplies. And fresh volunteers are needed to staff medical facilities or help with the cleanup.

Right now, America's churches and charities are mobilizing to meet these needs. And I encourage all Americans to pitch in, in any way you can. If you don't know where to turn and you want to help right now, please call the American Red Cross at 1-800-842-2200. 1-800-842-2200.

Once our relief effort is complete, we will accelerate the process of recovery. Already today we announced plans to rebuild Homestead Air Force Base, the linchpin of the economy in devastated areas. And a distinguished Florida business leader, Alvah Chapman, has agreed to head a national private sector effort to help rebuild south Florida. It's called "We Will Rebuild." This effort has my strong support and the support of Florida Governor Chiles. All of us are in this for the long haul. If you want to be a part of this effort, please write

We Will Rebuild. And the address is Post Office Box 010790, Miami, Florida, and the ZIP Code is 33131.

In the past 8 days we've seen on our TV screens real tears, real sorrow, real hurt. Livelihoods have been destroyed. Lives, even young lives, have been tragically lost. But already in Florida and Louisiana, we're talking not just of relief but of recovery. This is a tribute to what is inside us. And yes, Andrew blew a whirlwind of devastation. But he could never extinguish the American spirit, a spirit of compassion and sacrifice and endurance. We have seen that spirit in action the past 8 days. And with this spirit and your enduring commitment, our neighbors in south Florida and Louisiana will recover.

Thank you for your generosity. And our prayers are with all who stood in Andrew's path. Good night.

60. Presidential Debate in St. Louis October 11, 1992

Jim Lehrer. Good evening, and welcome to the first of three debates among the major candidates for President of the United States, sponsored by the Commission on Presidential Debates. The candidates are independent candidate Ross Perot; Governor Bill Clinton, the Democratic nominee; and President George Bush, the Republican nominee.

I am Jim Lehrer of *The MacNeil/Lehrer NewsHour* on PBS, and I will be the moderator for this 90-minute event, which is taking place before an audience here in the Athletic Complex on the campus of Washington University in St. Louis, Missouri.

Three journalists will be asking questions tonight. They are John Mashek of the *Boston Globe*; Ann Compton of ABC News; and Sander Vanocur, a freelance journalist. We will follow a format agreed to by representatives of the Clinton and Bush campaigns. That agreement contains no restrictions on the content or subject matter of the questions.

Each candidate will have up to 2 minutes for a closing statement. The order of those as well as the questioning was determined by a drawing. The first question goes to Mr. Perot. He will have 2 minutes to answer, to be followed by rebuttals of one minute each from Governor Clinton and then President Bush.

Distinction Among Candidates

Gentlemen, good evening. The first topic tonight is what separates each of you from the other. Mr. Perot, what do you believe tonight is the single most important separating issue of this campaign?

Mr. Perot. I think the principal issue that separates me is that 5 1/2 million people came together on their own and put me on the ballot. I was not put on the ballot by either of the two parties. I was not put on the ballot by any PAC money, by any foreign lobbyist money, by any special interest money. This is a movement that came from the people.

This is the way the framers of the Constitution intended our Government to be, a Government that comes from the people. Over time we have developed a Government that comes at the people, that comes from the top down, where the people are more or less treated as objects to be programmed during the campaign, with commercials and media events and fear messages and personal attacks and things of that nature.

The thing that separates my candidacy and makes it unique is that this came from millions of people in 50 States all over this country who wanted a candidate that worked and belonged to nobody but them. I go into this race as their servant, and I belong to them. So this comes from the people.

Mr. Lehrer. Governor Clinton, one-minute response.

Governor Clinton. The most important distinction in this campaign is that I represent real hope for change: a departure from trickle-down economics, a departure from tax-and-spend economics, to invest and grow. But before I can do that I must challenge the American people to change, and they must decide.

Tonight I say to the President: Mr. Bush, for 12 years you've had it your way. You've had your chance, and it didn't work. It's time to change. I want to bring that change to the American people, but we must all decide first we have the courage to change for hope and a better tomorrow.

Mr. Lehrer. President Bush, one-minute response, sir.

President Bush. Well, I think one thing that distinguishes is experience. I think we've dramatically changed the world. I'll talk about that a little bit later, but the changes are mind-boggling for world peace. Kids go to bed at night without the same fear of nuclear war. And change for change's sake isn't enough. We saw that message in the late seventies when we heard a lot about change. And what happened? That "misery index" went right through the roof.

But my economic program, I think, is the kind of change we want. And the way we're going to get it done is we're going to have a brand-new Congress. A lot of them are thrown out because of all the scandals. I'll sit down with them, Democrats and Republicans alike, and work for my Agenda for American Renewal which represents real change.

But I'd say, if you had to separate out, I think it's experience at this level.

Experience

Mr. Lehrer. Governor Clinton, how do you respond to the President—you have 2 minutes—on the question of experience? He says that is what distinguishes him from the other two of you.

Governor Clinton. I believe experience counts, but it's not everything. Values, judgment, and the record that I have amassed in my State also should count for something. I've worked hard to create good jobs and to educate people. My State now ranks first in the country in job growth this year, fourth in income growth, fourth in the reduction of poverty, third in overall economic performance, according to a major news magazine. That's because we believe in investing in education and in jobs.

We have to change in this country. You know, my wife, Hillary, gave me a book about a year ago in which the author defined insanity as just doing the same old thing over and over again and expecting a different result. We have got to have the courage to change. Experience is important, yes. I've gotten a lot of good experience in dealing with ordinary people over the last year and a month. I've touched more people's lives and seen more heartbreak and hope, more pain and more promise than anybody else who's run for President this year. And I think the American people deserve better than they're getting. We have gone from first to 13th in the world in wages in the last 12 years since Mr. Bush and Mr. Reagan have been in. Personal income has dropped while people have worked harder in the last 4 years. There have been twice as many bankruptcies as new jobs created.

We need a new approach. The same old experience is not relevant. We're living in a new world after the cold war. And what works in this new world is not trickle-down, not Government for the benefit of the privileged few, not tax-and-spend but a commitment to invest in American jobs and American education. Controlling American health care costs and bringing the American people together, that is what works. And you can have the right kind of experience and the wrong kind of experience. Mine is rooted in the real lives of real people. And it will bring real results if we have the courage to change.

Mr. Lehrer. President Bush, one minute to respond.

President Bush. I just thought of another, another big difference here between me—I don't believe Mr. Perot feels this way, but I know Governor Clinton did, because I want to accurately quote him. He thinks, I think he said, that the country is coming apart at the seams. Now, I know that the only way he can win is to make everybody believe the economy is worse than it is. But this country's not coming apart at the seams, for heaven sakes. We're the United States of America. In spite of the economic problems, we are the most respected economy around the world. Many would trade for it. We've been caught up in a global slowdown. We can do much, much better. But we ought not to try to convince the American people that America is a country that's coming apart at the seams.

I would hate to be running for President and think that the only way I could win would be to convince everybody how horrible things are. Yes, there are big problems. And yes, people are hurting. But I believe that this Agenda for American Renewal I have is the answer to do it. And I believe we can get it done now, whereas we didn't in the past, because you're going to have a whole brand-new bunch of people in the Congress that are going to have to listen to the same American people I'm listening to.

Mr. Lehrer. Mr. Perot, a minute response, sir.

Mr. Perot. Well, they've got a point. I don't have any experience in running up a $4 trillion debt. [Laughter] I don't have any experience in gridlocked Government where nobody takes responsibility for anything and everybody blames everybody else. I don't have any experience in creating the worst public school system in the industrialized world, the most violent, crime-ridden society in the industrialized world.

But I do have a lot of experience in getting things done. So if we're at a point in history where we want to stop talking about it and do it, I've got a lot of experience in figuring out how to solve problems, making the solutions work, and then moving on to the next one. I've got a lot of experience in not taking 10 years to solve a 10-minute problem. So if it's time for action, I think I have experience that counts. If it's more time for gridlock and talk and finger-pointing, I'm the wrong man.

Character Issues

Mr. Lehrer. President Bush, the question goes to you. You have 2 minutes. And the question is this: Are there important issues of character separating you from these other two men?

President Bush. I think the American people should be the judge of that. I think character is a very important question. I said something the other day where I was accused of being like Joe McCarthy because I questioned—put it this way—I think it's wrong to demonstrate against your own country or

organize demonstrations against your own country in foreign soil. I just think it's wrong. Maybe, they say, well, it was a youthful indiscretion. I was 19 or 20, flying off an aircraft carrier, and that shaped me to be Commander in Chief of the Armed Forces. And I'm sorry, but demonstrating—it's not a question of patriotism. It's a question of character and judgment.

They get on me, Bill's gotten on me about "Read my lips." When I make a mistake, I'll admit it. But he has not admitted the mistake. And I just find it impossible to understand how an American can demonstrate against his own country in a foreign land, organizing demonstrations against it, when young men are held prisoner in Hanoi or kids out of the ghetto were drafted.

Some say, well, you're a little old-fashioned. Maybe I am, but I just don't think that's right. Now, whether it's character or judgment, whatever it is, I have a big difference here on this issue. And so we'll just have to see how it plays out. But I couldn't do that. And I don't think most Americans could do that.

And they all say, well, it was a long time ago. Well, let's admit it then, say, "I made a terrible mistake." How could you be Commander in Chief of the Armed Forces and have some kid say, when you have to make a tough decision, as I did in Panama or in Kuwait, and then have some kid jump up and say, "Well, I'm not going to go. The Commander in Chief was organizing demonstrations halfway around the world during another era"?

So there are differences. But that's about the main area where I think we have a difference. I don't know about—we'll talk about that a little with Ross here in a bit.

Mr. Lehrer. Mr. Perot, you have one minute.

Mr. Perot. I think the American people will make their own decisions on character. And at a time when we have work to do and we need action, I think they need to clearly understand the backgrounds of each person. I think the press can play a huge role in making sure that the backgrounds are clearly presented in an objective way. Then make a decision.

Certainly anyone in the White House should have the character to be there. But I think it's very important to measure when and where things occurred. Did they occur when you were a young person in your formative years, or did they occur while you were a senior official in the Federal Government? When you're a senior official in the Federal Government, spending billions of dollars in taxpayers' money, and you're a mature individual and you make a mistake, then that was on our ticket. If you make it as a young man, time passes.

So I would say just look at all three of us, decide who you think will do the job, pick that person in November, because, believe me, as I've said before, the party's over, and it's time for the cleanup crew. And we do have to have change. And people who never take responsibility for anything when it happens on their watch, and people who are in charge—

Mr. Lehrer. Your time is up.

Mr. Perot.—the time is up. [Laughter]

Mr. Lehrer. Time is up.

Mr. Perot. More later.

Mr. Lehrer. Governor Clinton, you have one minute.

Governor Clinton. Ross gave a good answer, but I've got to respond directly to Mr. Bush. You have questioned my patriotism. You even brought some rightwing Congressmen into the White House to plot how to attack me for going to Russia in 1969–1970, when over 50,000 other Americans did.

Now, I honor your service in World War II. I honor Mr. Perot's service in uniform and the service of every man and woman who ever served, including Admiral Crowe, who was your Chairman of the Joint Chiefs and who's supporting me. But when Joe McCarthy went around this country attacking people's patriotism, he was wrong. He was wrong. And a Senator from Connecticut stood up to him, named Prescott Bush. Your father was right to stand up to Joe McCarthy. You were wrong to attack my patriotism. I was opposed to the war, but I love my country. And we need a President who will bring this country together, not divide it. We've had enough division. I want to lead a unified country.

Mr. Lehrer. All right. We move now to the subject of taxes and spending. The question goes to Governor Clinton for a two-minute answer. It will be asked by Ann Compton.

Taxes

Ann Compton. Governor Clinton, can you lock in a level here tonight on where middle-income families can be guaranteed a tax cut or, at the very least, at what income level they can be guaranteed no tax increase?

Governor Clinton. The tax increase I have proposed triggers in at family incomes of $200,000 and above. Those are the people who, in the 1980's, had their incomes go up while their taxes went down. Middle-class people, defined as people with incomes of $52,000 and down, had their incomes go down while their taxes went up in the Reagan-Bush years because of six increases in the payroll taxes. So that is where my income limit would trigger.

Ms. Compton. So there will be no tax increases below $200,000?

Governor Clinton. My plan, notwithstanding my opponent's ad, my plan triggers in at gross incomes, family incomes of $200,000 and above. And then we want to give modest middle-class tax relief to restore some fairness, especially to middle-class people with families with incomes of under $60,000.

In addition to that, the money that I raise from upper-income people and from asking foreign corporations just to pay the same income on their income earned in America that American corporations do will be used to give incentives back to upper-income people. I want to give people permanent incentives on investment tax credit like President Kennedy and the Congress inaugurated in the early sixties to get industry moving again; a research and development tax credit; a low-income housing tax credit; a long-term capital gains proposal for new business and business expansions.

We've got to have no more trickle-down. We don't need across-the-board tax cuts for the wealthy for nothing; we need to say, here's your tax incentive if you create American jobs the old-fashioned way.

I'd like to create more millionaires than were created under Mr. Bush and Mr. Reagan, but I don't want to have 4 years where we have no growth in the private sector. And that's what's happened in the last 4 years. We're down 35,000 jobs in the private sector. We need to invest and grow, and that's what I want to do.

Mr. Lehrer. President Bush, one minute, sir.

President Bush. I have to correct one thing. I didn't question the man's patriotism; I questioned his judgment and his character. What he did in Moscow, that's fine. Let him explain it. He did. I accept that. What I don't accept is demonstrating and organizing demonstrations in a foreign country when your country's at war. I'm sorry, I cannot accept that.

This one on taxes spells out the biggest difference between us. I do not believe we need to go back to the Mondale proposals or the Dukakis proposals of tax-and-spend. Governor Clinton says $200,000, but he also says he wants to raise $150 billion. Taxing people over $200,000 will not get you $150 billion. And then when you add in his other spending proposals, regrettably, you end up socking it to the working man.

That old adage that they use, "We're going to soak the rich, we're going to soak the rich," it always ends up being the poor cab driver or the working man that ends up paying the bill. And so I just have a different approach. I believe the way to get the deficit down is to control the growth of mandatory spending programs and not raise taxes on the American people. We've got a big difference there.

Mr. Lehrer. Mr. Perot, one minute.

Mr. Perot. We've got to have a growing, expanding job base to give us a growing, expanding tax base. Right now, we have a flat-to-deteriorating job base, and where it appears to be growing is minimum-wage jobs. So we've got to really rebuild our job base. That's going to take money for infrastructure and investment to do that. Our foreign competitors are doing it; we're not.

We cannot pay off the trillion debt, balance the budget, and have the industries of the future and the high-paying jobs in this country without having the revenue. We're going to go through a period of shared sacrifice. There's one challenge: It's got to be fair.

We've created a mess and don't have much to show for it, and we have got to fix it. And that's about all I can say in a minute.

Mr. Lehrer. Okay. Next question goes to President Bush for a 2-minute answer, and it will be asked by Sandy Vanocur.

U.S. Troops in Europe

Sander Vanocur. Mr. President, this past week your Secretary of the Army, Michael Stone, said he had no plans to abide by a congressional mandate to cut U.S. forces in Europe from 150,000 to 100,000 by the end of September 1996. Now, why, almost 50 years after the end of World War II and with the total collapse of the Soviet Union, should American taxpayers be taxed, support armies in Europe, when the Europeans have plenty of money to do it for themselves?

President Bush. Well, Sander, that's a good question. And the answer is: For 40-some years, we kept the peace. If you look at the cost of not keeping the peace in Europe, it would be exorbitant. We have reduced the number of troops that are deployed and going to be deployed. I have cut defense spending. And the reason we could do that is because of our fantastic success in winning the cold war. We never would have got there if we'd gone for the nuclear-freeze crowd; never would have got there if we'd listened to those that wanted to cut defense spending. I think it is important that the United States stay in Europe and continue to guarantee the peace. We simply cannot pull back.

Now, when anybody has a spending program they want to spend money on at home, they say, well, let's cut money out of the Defense Department. I will accept and have accepted the recommendations of two proven leaders, General Colin Powell and Dick, Secretary Dick Cheney. They feel that the levels

we're operating at and the reductions that I have proposed are proper. And so I simply do not think we should go back to the isolation days and start blaming foreigners.

We are the sole remaining superpower. And we should be that. We have a certain disproportionate responsibility. But I would ask the American people to understand that if we make imprudent cuts, if we go too far, we risk the peace. And I don't want to do that. I've seen what it is like to see the burdens of a war, and I don't want to see us make reckless cuts.

Because of our programs, we have been able to significantly cut defense spending. But let's not cut into the muscle. And let's not cut down our insurance policy, which is participation of American forces in NATO, the greatest peacekeeping organization ever made. Today, you've got problems in Europe still bubbling along, even though Europe's going democracy's route. But we are there. And I think this insurance policy is necessary. I think it goes with world leadership. And I think the levels we've come up with are just about right.

Mr. Lehrer. Mr. Perot, one minute, sir.

Mr. Perot. If I'm poor and you're rich and I can get you to defend me, that's good. But when the tables get turned, I ought to do my share. Right now we spend about $300 billion a year on defense. The Japanese spend around $30 billion in Asia. The Germans spend around $30 billion in Europe.

For example, Germany will spend a trillion dollars building infrastructure over the next 10 years. It's kind of easy to do if you only have to pick up a $30 billion tab to defend your country. The European Community is in a position to pay a lot more than they have in the past. I agree with the President, when they couldn't, we should have; now that they can, they should.

We sort of seem to have a desire to try to stay over there and control it. They don't want us to control it, very candidly. So it I think is very important for us to let them assume more and more of the burden and for us to bring that money back here and rebuild our infrastructure. Because we can only be a superpower if we are an economic superpower, and we can only be an economic superpower if we have a growing, expanding job base.

Mr. Lehrer. Governor Clinton, one minute, sir.

Governor Clinton. I agree with the general statement Mr. Bush made. I disagree that we need 150,000 troops to fulfill our role in Europe. We certainly must maintain an engagement there. There are certainly dangers there. There are certainly other trouble spots in the world which are closer to Europe than to the United States. But two former Defense Secretaries recently issued reports saying that 100,000 or slightly fewer troops would be enough, including President Reagan's former Defense Secretary, Mr. Carlucci. Many of the military experts whom I consulted on this agreed.

We're going to have to spend more money in the future on military technology and on greater mobility, greater airlift, greater sealift, the B-22 airplane. We're going to have to do some things that are quite costly, and I simply don't believe we can afford, nor do we need to keep 150,000 troops in Europe, given how much the Red Army, now under the control of Russia, has been cut; the arms control agreement concluded between Mr. Bush and Mr. Yeltsin, something I have applauded. I don't think we need 150,000 troops.

Let me make one other point. Mr. Bush talked about taxes. He didn't tell you that he vetoed a middle-class tax cut because it would be paid for by raising taxes on the wealthy and vetoed an investment tax credit paid for by raising taxes on the wealthy.

Taxes

Mr. Lehrer. All right. We go now to Mr. Perot for a 2-minute question, and it will be asked by John Mashek.

John Mashek. Mr. Perot, you talked about fairness just a minute ago, on sharing the pain. As part of your plan to reduce the ballooning Federal deficit, you've suggested that we raise gasoline taxes 50 cents a gallon over 5 years. Why punish the middle-class consumer to such a degree?

Mr. Perot. It's 10 cents a year, cumulative. It finally gets to 50 cents at the end of the fifth year. I think "punish" is the wrong word. Again, you see, I didn't create this problem; we're trying to solve it.

Now, if you study our international competitors, some of our international competitors collect up to .50 a gallon in taxes. And they use that money to build infrastructure and create jobs. We collect 35 cents, and we don't have it to spend. I know it's not popular. And I understand the nature of your question. But the people who will be helped the most by it are the working people who will get the jobs created because of this tax. Why do we have to do it? Because we have so mismanaged our country over the years, and it is now time to pay the fiddler. And if we don't, we will be spending our children's money. We have spent $4 trillion worth. An incredible number of young people are active in supporting my effort because they're deeply concerned that we have taken the American dream from them.

I think it's fitting that we're on the campus of a university tonight. These young people, when they get out of this wonderful university, will have difficulty finding a job.

We've got to clean this mess up, leave this country in good shape, and pass on the American dream to them. We're got to collect the taxes to do it. If there's a fairer way, I'm all ears. Ah-h-h. [Laughter]

But see, let me make it very clear. People don't have the stomach to fix these problems, I think it's a good time to face it in November. If they do, then they will have heard the harsh reality of what we have to do. I'm not playing Lawrence Welk music tonight.

Mr. Lehrer. Governor Clinton, you have a minute, sir.

Governor Clinton. I think Mr. Perot has confronted this deficit issue, but I think it's important to point out that we really have two deficits in America, not one. We have a budget deficit in the Federal Government, but we also have an investment, a jobs, an income deficit.

People are working harder for less money than they were making 10 years ago: two-thirds of our people, a $1,600 drop in average income in just the last 2 years. The problem I have with the Perot prescription is that almost all economists who have looked at it say that if you cut the deficit this much this quick, it will increase unemployment, it will slow down the economy. That's why I think we shouldn't do it that quickly. We have a disciplined reduction in the deficit of 50 percent over the next 4 years. But first, get incentives to invest in this economy, put the American people back to work. We've got to invest in growth. Nine Nobel Prize-winning economists and 500 others, including numerous Republican and Democratic business executives, have endorsed this approach because it offers the best hope to put America back to work and get our incomes rising instead of falling.

Mr. Lehrer. President Bush, one minute, sir.

President Bush. The question was on fairness. I just disagree with Mr. Perot. I don't believe it is fair to slap a 50-cent-a-gallon tax over whatever many years on the people that have to drive for a living, people that go long distances. I don't think we need to do it.

You see, I have a fundamental difference. I agree with what he's talking about in trying to get the spending down and to discipline, although I think we ought to totally exempt Social Security. But he's talking tough medicine, and I think that's good. I disagree with the tax-and-spend philosophy. You see, I don't think we need to tax more and spend more and then say that's going to make the problem better. And I'm afraid that's what I think I'm hearing from Governor Clinton.

I believe what you need to do is some of what Ross is talking about: control the growth of mandatory spending and get taxes down. He's mentioned some ways to do it, and I agree with those. I've been talking about getting a capital gains cut forever. And his friends in Congress have been telling me that's a tax break for the rich. It would stimulate investment. I'm for an investment tax allowance. I am for a tax break for first-time homebuyers. And with this new Congress coming in, gridlock will be gone and I'll sit down with them and say, let's get this done. But I do not want to go the tax-and-spend route.

Mr. Lehrer. All right. Let's move on now to the subject of jobs. The first question goes to President Bush for 2 minutes, and John will ask that question. John?

The Defense Industry

Mr. Mashek. Mr. President, last month you came to St. Louis to announce a very lucrative contract for McDonnell Douglas to build F-15's for Saudi Arabia. In today's *Post-Dispatch*, a retired saleswoman, a 75-year-old woman named Marjorie Roberts, asked if she could ask a question of the candidates, said she wanted to register her concern about the lack of a plan to convert our defense-oriented industries into other purposes. How would you answer her?

President Bush. Well, I assume she was supportive of the decision on McDonnell Douglas. I assume she was supporting me on the decision to sell those airplanes. I think it's a good decision. I took a little heat for it, but I think it was the correct decision to do. And we've worked it out, and indeed, we're moving forward all around the world in a much more peaceful way. So that one we came away with which—in creating jobs for the American people.

I would simply say to her, look, take a look at what the President has proposed on job retraining. When you cut back on defense spending, some people are going to be thrown out of work. If you throw another 50,000 kids on the street because of cutting recklessly in troop levels, you're going to put a lot more out of work. I would say to them, look at the job retraining programs that we're proposing. Therein is the best answer to her.

And another one is, stimulate investment and savings. I mean, we've got big economic problems, but we are not coming apart at the seams. We're ready for a recovery with interest rates down and inflation down, the cruelest tax of all; caught up in a global slowdown right now, but that will change if you go with the programs I've talked about and if you help with job retraining and education.

I am a firm believer that our America 2000 education problem is the answer. A lit-

tle longer run; it's going to take a while to educate, but it is a good program. So her best hope for short term is job retraining if she was thrown out of work at a defense plant. But tell her it's not all that gloomy. We're the United States. We've faced tough problems before. Look at the "misery index" when the Democrats had both the White House and the Congress. It was just right through the roof.

Now, we can do better. And the way to do better is not to tax and spend but to retrain, get that control of the mandatory spending programs. I am much more optimistic about this country than some.

Mr. Lehrer. Mr. Perot, you have one minute, sir.

Mr. Perot. Your defense industries are going to have to convert to civilian industries, many of them are. And the sooner they start, the sooner they'll finish. And there will be a significant transition.

And it's very important that we not continue to let our industrial base deteriorate. We had someone who I'm sure regrets said it in the President's staff, said he didn't care whether we make potato chips or computer chips. Well, anybody that thinks about it cares a great deal. Number one, you make more making computer chips than you do potato chips. Number two, 19 out of 20 computer chips that we have in this country now come from Japan. We've given away whole industries.

So as we phase these industries over, there's a lot of intellectual talent in these industries. A lot of these people in industries can be converted to the industries of tomorrow. And that's where the high-paying jobs are. We need to have a very carefully thought through phaseover.

See, we practice 19th century capitalism. The rest of the world practices 21st century capitalism. I can't handle that in a minute, but I hope we can get back into it later. The rest of the world, the countries and the businesses would be working together to make this transition in an intelligent way.

Mr. Lehrer. Governor Clinton, you have one minute, sir.

Governor Clinton. We must have a transition plan, a plan to convert from a defense to a domestic economy. No other nation would have cut defense as much as we already have without that. There are 200,000 people unemployed in California alone because we have cut defense without planning to retrain them and to reinvest in the technologies of the future here at home. That is what I want to do.

This administration may say they have a plan, but the truth is they have not even released all the money, the paltry sum of money that Congress appropriated. I want to take every dollar by which we reduced defense and reinvest it in technologies for the 21st century: in new transportation, in communication, and environmental cleanup technologies. Let's put the American people to work. And let's build the kind of high-tech, high-wage, high-growth economy that the American people deserve.

Mr. Lehrer. All right. The next question goes to Mr. Perot for a 2-minute answer. It will be asked by Ann.

Ann?

Jobs Program

Ms. Compton. Mr. Perot, you talked a minute ago about rebuilding the job base. But is it true what Governor Clinton just said, that that means that unemployment will increase, that it will slow the economy? And how would you specifically use the powers of the Presidency to get more people back into good jobs immediately?

Mr. Perot. Step one: The American people send me up there, the day after election, I'll get with the—we won't even wait until inauguration—I'll ask the President to help me, and I'll ask his staff to help me. And we will start putting together teams to put together—to take all the plans that exist and do something with them.

Please understand, there are great plans lying all over Washington nobody ever executes. It's like having a blueprint for a house you never built. You don't have anywhere to sleep. Now, our challenge is to take these things, do something with them.

Step one: You want to put America back to work, clean up the small business problem. Have one task force at work on that. The second: You've got your big companies that are in trouble, including the defense industries, have another one on that. Have a third task force on new industries of the future to make sure we nail those for our country, and they don't wind up in Europe and Asia. Convert from 19th to 21st century capitalism. You see, we have an adversarial relationship between Government and business. Our international competitors that are cleaning our plate have an intelligent relationship between Government and business and a supportive relationship.

Then, have another task force on crime, because next to jobs, our people are concerned about their safety. Health care, schools, one on the debt and deficit. And finally, in that 90-day period before the inauguration, put together the framework for the town hall and give the American people a Christmas present, show them by Christmas the first cut at these plans. By the time Congress comes into session to go to work, have those plans ready to go in front of Congress. Then get off to a flying start in '93 to execute these plans.

Now, there are people in this room and people on this stage who have been in meetings when I would sit there and say, is this one we're going to talk about or do something about? Well, obviously, my orientation is let's go do it.

Now, put together your plans by Christmas. Be ready to go when Congress goes. Nail these things—small business, you've got to have capital; you've got to have credit; and many of them need mentors or coaches. And we can create more jobs there in a hurry than any other place.

Mr. Lehrer. Governor Clinton, one minute.

Governor Clinton. This country desperately needs a jobs program. And my first priority would be to pass a jobs program, to introduce it on the first day I was inaugurated. I would meet with the leaders of the Congress, with all the newly elected Members of the Congress, and as many others with whom I could meet between the time of the election and the inauguration. And we would present a jobs program.

Then we would present a plan to control health care costs and phase in health care coverage for all Americans. Until we control health care costs, we're not going to control the deficit. It is the number one culprit. But first we must have an aggressive jobs program.

I live in a State where manufacturing job growth has far outpaced the Nation in the last few years; where we have created more private sector jobs since Mr. Bush has been President than have been created in the entire rest of the country, where Mr. Bush's Labor Secretary said the job growth has been enormous. We've done it in Arkansas. Give me a chance to create these kinds of

jobs in America. We can do it. I know we can.

Mr. Lehrer. President Bush, one minute.

President Bush. Well, we've got a plan announced for what we can do for small business. I've already put forward things that will get this country working fast, some of which have been echoed here tonight: investment tax allowance, capital gains reduction, more on research and development, a tax credit for first-time homebuyers.

What I'm going to do is say to Jim Baker when this campaign is over, "All right, let's sit down now. You do in domestic affairs what you've done in foreign affairs. Be the kind of economic coordinator of all the domestic side of the house, and that includes all the economic side, all the training side, and bring this program together." We're going to have a new Congress. And we're going to say to them, "You've listened to the voters the way we have. Nobody wants gridlock anymore. And so let's get the program through."

And I believe it will work, because, as Ross said, we've got the plans. The plans are all over Washington. And I have put ours together in something called the Agenda for American Renewal. And it makes sense. It's sensible. It creates jobs. It gets to the base of the kind of jobs we need. And so I'll just be asking for support to get that put into effect.

Mr. Lehrer. The next question goes to Governor Clinton for 2 minutes. It will be asked by Sandy.

Federal Reserve Board Chairman

Mr. Vanocur. Governor Clinton, when a President running for the first time gets into the office and wants to do something about the economy, he finds in Washington there's a person who has much more power over the economy than he does: the Chairman of the Federal Reserve Board, accountable to no one. That being the case, would you go along with proposals made by Treasury Secretary James Brady and Congressman Lee Hamilton to make the Federal Reserve Board Chairman somehow more accountable to elected officials?

Governor Clinton. Well, let me say that I think that we might ought to review the terms and the way it works. But frankly, I don't think that's the problem today. We have low interest rates today. At least we have low interest rates that the Fed can control. Our long-term interest rates are still pretty high because of our deficit and because of our economic performance.

And there was a terrible reaction internationally to Mr. Bush saying he was going to give us 4 more years of trickle-down economics and other across-the-board tax cuts and most of it going to the wealthy with no real guarantee of investment. But I think the important thing is to use the powers the President does have on the assumption that given the condition of this economy, we're going to keep interest rates down if we have the discipline to increase investment and reduce the debt at the same time. That is my commitment.

I think the American people are hungry for action. I think Congress is hungry for someone who will work with them, instead of manipulate them; someone who will not veto a bill that has an investment credit, middle class tax relief, research and development tax credits, as Mr. Bush has done. Give me a chance to do that.

I don't have to worry, I don't think, in the near term, about the Federal Reserve. Their

policies so far, it seems to me, are pretty sound.

Mr. Lehrer. President Bush, you have one minute.

President Bush. I don't think the Fed ought to be put under the Executive Branch. There is separation there. I think that's fine. Alan Greenspan is respected. I've had some arguments with him about the speed in which we might have lowered rates.

But Governor Clinton, he talks about the reaction to the markets. There was a momentary fear that he might win, and the markets went "rrrfft"—down like that—[laughter]—so I don't—we can judge on—the stock market has been strong. It's been very strong since I've been President. And they recognize we've got great difficulties. But they're also much more optimistic than the pessimists we have up here tonight.

In terms of vetoing tax bills, you're darn right. I am going to protect the American taxpayer against the spend-and-tax Congress. And I'm going to keep on vetoing them because I don't think we are taxed too little. I think the Government's spending too much. So Governor Clinton can label it tax for the rich or anything he wants. I'm going to protect the working man by continuing to veto and to threaten veto until we get this new Congress, when then we're going to move forward on our plan. I've got to protect them.

Mr. Lehrer. Mr. Perot, one minute.

Mr. Perot. Keep the Federal Reserve independent, but let's live in a world of reality. We live in a global economy, not a national economy. These interest rates we have now don't make any sense. We have a trillion debt, and only in America would you finance 70 percent of it 5 years or less. So 70 percent of our debt is 5 years or less, it's very interest-sensitive.

We have a 4-percent gap between what we pay for treasuries and what Germany pays for 1- to 5-year treasuries. That gap is going to close because the Arabs, the Japanese, and folks in this country are going to start buying German treasuries because they can get more money.

Every time our interest rates go up 1 percent, that adds $28 billion to the deficit or to the debt, whichever place you want to put it. We are sitting on a ticking bomb, folks, because we have totally mismanaged our country. And we had better get it back under control.

Just think, in your own business, if you had all of your long-term problems financed short term, you'd go broke in a hurry.

Mr. Lehrer. We're going to move to foreign affairs. The first question goes to Mr. Perot for a 2-minute answer, and Sandy will ask it.

Foreign Affairs

Mr. Vanocur. Mr. Perot, in the post-cold-war environment, what should be the overriding U.S. national interest? And what can the United States do, and what can it afford to do to defend that national interest?

Mr. Perot. Again, if you're not rich, you're not a superpower, so we have two that I'd put as number one. I have a "1" and "1a." One is, we've got to have the money to be able to pay for defense. And we've got to manufacture here. Believe it or not, folks, you can't ship it all overseas. You've got to make it here. And you can't convert from potato chips to airplanes in an emergency. You see, Willow Run could be converted from cars to airplanes in World War II because it was here. We've got to make things here. You

just can't ship them overseas anymore. I hope we talk more about that.

Second thing, on priorities, we've got to help Russia succeed in its revolution and all of its republics. When we think of Russia, remember we're thinking of many countries now. We've got to help them. That's pennies on the dollar compared to renewing the cold war.

Third, we've got all kinds of agreements on paper and some that are being executed on getting rid of nuclear warheads. Russia and its republics are out of control or, at best, in weak control right now. It's a very unstable situation. You've got every rich Middle Eastern country over there trying to buy nuclear weapons, as you well know. And that will lead to another five-star migraine headache down the road. We really need to nail down the intercontinental ballistic missiles, the ones that can hit us from Russia. We've focused on the tactical; we've made real progress there. We've got some agreements on the nuclear, but we don't have those things put away yet. The sooner, the better.

So in terms of priorities, we've got to be financially strong. Number two, we've got to take care of this missile situation and try to get the nuclear war behind us and give that a very high priority. And number three, we need to help and support Russia and the republics in every possible way to become democratic, capitalistic societies and not just sit back and let those countries continue in turmoil, because they could go back worse than things used to be. And believe me, there are a lot of old boys in the KGB and the military that like it better the way it used to be. Thank you.

Mr. Lehrer. Governor Clinton, one minute.

Governor Clinton. In order to keep America the strongest nation in the world, we need some continuity and some change. There are three fundamental challenges. First of all, the world is still a dangerous and uncertain place. We need a new military and a new national security policy equal to the challenges of the post-cold-war era; a smaller permanent military force, but one that is more mobile, well-trained, with high-technology equipment. We need to continue the negotiations to reduce nuclear arsenals in the Soviet Union, the former Soviet Union, and the United States. We need to stop this proliferation of weapons of mass destruction.

Second, we have to face that in this world economic security is a whole lot of national security. Our dollar is at an all-time low against some foreign currencies. We're weak in the world. We must rebuild America's strength at home.

Finally, we ought to be promoting the democratic impulses around the world. Democracies are our partners. They don't go to war with each other. They're reliable friends in the future. National security, economic strength, democracy.

Mr. Lehrer. President Bush, one minute.

President Bush. We still are the envy of the world in terms of our military; there's no question about that. We're the envy of the world in terms of our economy, in spite of the difficulties we're having; there's no question about that. Our exports are dramatically up.

I might say to Mr. Perot, I can understand why you might have missed it because there's so much fascination by trivia, but I worked out a deal with Boris Yeltsin to eliminate, get rid of entirely, the most destabilizing weapons of all, the SS-18, the big intercontinental ballistic missile. I mean, that's been done. And thank God it has, because the parents of these young people

around here go to bed at night without the same fear of nuclear war. We've made dramatic progress.

So we've got a good military—the question that says get a new military, get the best in the world—we've got it, and they're keeping the peace. They're respected around the world, and we are more respected because of the way we have conducted ourselves.

We didn't listen to the nuclear freeze crowd. We said, peace through strength. It worked, and the cold war is over. America understands that. But we're turned so inward we don't understand the global picture. We are helping democracy. Ross, the FREEDOM Support Act is something that I got through the Congress, and it's a very good thing because it does exactly what you say, and I think you agree with that, to help Russian democracy. We're going to keep on doing that.

Mr. Lehrer. All right, Next question is for Governor Clinton, and John will ask it.

China-U.S. Relations

Mr. Mashek. Governor Clinton, you've accused the President of coddling tyrants, including those in Beijing. As President, how would you exert U.S. power to influence affairs in China?

Governor Clinton. I think our relationships with China are important, and I don't think we want to isolate China. But I think it is a mistake for us to do what this administration did when all those kids went out there carrying the Statue of Liberty in Tiananmen Square, and Mr. Bush sent two people in secret to toast the Chinese leaders and basically tell them not to worry about it. They rewarded him by opening negotiations with Iran to transfer nuclear technology. That was their response to that sort of action.

Now that voices in the Congress and throughout the country have insisted that we do something about China, look what has happened. China has finally agreed to stop sending us products made with prison labor not because we coddled them but because the administration was pushed into doing something about it. Recently the Chinese have announced that they're going to lower some barriers to our products, which they ought to do since they have a billion trade surplus with the United States under Mr. Bush, the second biggest surplus of all, second to Japan.

So I would be firm. I would say, if you want to continue most-favored-nation status for your government-owned industries as well as your private ones, observe human rights in the future. Open your society. Recognize the legitimacy of those kids that were carrying the Statue of Liberty. If we can stand up for our economic interests, we ought to be able to pursue the democratic interests of the people in China. And over the long run they'll be more reliable partners.

Mr. Lehrer. President Bush, you have one minute.

President Bush. Well, the administration was the first major country to stand up against the abuse in Tiananmen Square. We are the ones that worked out the prison labor deal. We are the ones that have lowered the barrier to products, the Carla Hills negotiation. I am the one that said, let's keep the MFN because you see China moving toward a free market economy. To do what the Congress and Governor Clinton are suggesting, you would isolate and ruin Hong Kong. They are making some progress, not enough for us. We were the first ones to put sanctions on. We still have them on some things.

But Governor Clinton's philosophy is isolate them. He says don't do it, but the policies he's expounding of putting conditions on MFN and kind of humiliating them is not the way you make the kind of progress we are getting. I have stood up with these people, and I understand what you have to do to be strong in this situation. It's moving, not as fast as we'd like. But you isolate China and turn them inward, and then we've made a tremendous mistake. I'm not going to do it. I've had to fight a lot of people that were saying "human rights." We are the ones that put the sanctions on and stood for it. And he can insult General Scowcroft if he wants to. He didn't go over to coddle. He went over to say—

Mr. Lehrer. Mr. President, you're over—

President Bush.—you must make the very changes they're making now.

Mr. Lehrer. One minute, Mr. Perot.

Mr. Perot. China's a huge country, broken into many provinces. It has some very elderly leaders that will not be around too much longer. Capitalism is growing and thriving across big portions of China. Asia will be our largest trading partner in the future. It will be a growing and a closer relationship. We have a delicate tightwire walk that we must go through at the present time to make sure that we do not cozy up to tyrants, to make sure that they don't get the impression that they can suppress their people. But time is our friend there because their leaders will change in not too many years, worst case. And their country is making great progress.

One last point on the missiles. I don't want the American people to be confused. We have written agreements, and we have some missiles that have been destroyed, but we have a huge number of intercontinental ballistic missiles that are still in place in Russia. The fact that you have an agreement is one thing. Until they're destroyed, some crazy person can either sell them or use them.

Mr. Lehrer. All right. The next question goes to President Bush for a 2-minute answer, and Ann will ask it.

Bosnia and Somalia

Ms. Compton. Mr. President, how can you watch the killing in Bosnia and the ethnic cleansing, or the starvation and anarchy in Somalia, and not want to use America's might, if not America's military, to try to end that kind of suffering?

President Bush. Ann, both of them are very complicated situations. I vowed something, because I learned something from Vietnam: I am not going to commit U.S. forces until I know what the mission is, until the military tell me that it can be completed, until I know how they can come out.

We are helping. American airplanes are helping today on humanitarian relief for Sarajevo. It is America that's in the lead in helping with humanitarian relief for Somalia. But when you go to put somebody else's son or daughter into war, I think you've got to be a little bit careful, and you have to be sure that there's a military plan that can do this.

You have ancient ethnic rivalries that have cropped up as Yugoslavia is dissolved or getting dissolved. It isn't going to be solved by sending in the 82d Airborne, and I'm not going to do that as Commander in Chief. I am going to stand by and use the moral persuasion of the United States to get satisfaction in terms of prison camps, and we're making some progress there, and in terms of getting humanitarian relief in there.

Right now, as you know, the United States took the lead in a no-fly operation up there, no-fly order up in the United Nations. We're working through the international organizations. That's one thing I learned by forging that tremendous and greatly, highly successful coalition against Saddam Hussein, the dictator: Work internationally to do it. I'm very concerned about it. I'm concerned about ethnic cleansing. I'm concerned about attacks on Muslims, for example, over there. But I must stop short of using American force until I know how those young men and women are going to get out of there as well as get in, know what the mission is and define it. I think I'm on the right track.

Ms. Compton. Are you designing a mission that would—

Mr. Lehrer. Ann, sorry, sorry. Time is up. We have to go to Mr. Perot for a one-minute response.

Mr. Perot. If we learned anything in Vietnam, it's you first commit this Nation before you commit the troops to the battlefield. We cannot send our people all over the world to solve every problem that comes up.

This is basically a problem that is a primary concern to the European Community. Certainly we care about the people. We care about the children. We care about the tragedy. But it is inappropriate for us, just because there's a problem somewhere around the world, to take the sons and daughters of working people—and make no mistake about it, our all-volunteer armed force is not made up of the sons and daughters of the beautiful people. It's the working folks that send their sons and daughters to war, with a few exceptions. Very unlike World War II when FDR's sons flew missions; everybody went. It's a different world now. It's very important that we not just, without thinking it through, just rush to every problem in the world and have our people torn to pieces.

Mr. Lehrer. Governor Clinton, one minute.

Governor Clinton. I agree that we cannot commit ground forces to become involved in the quagmire of Bosnia or in the tribal wars of Somalia. But I think that it's important to recognize that there are things that can be done short of that and that we do have interests there. There are, after all, two million refugees now because of the problems in what was Yugoslavia, the largest number since World War II, and there may be hundreds of thousands of people who will starve or freeze to death in this winter.

The United States should try to work with its allies and stop it. I urged the President to support this air cover, and he did, and I applaud that. I applaud the no-fly zone, and I know that he's going back to the United Nations to try to get authority to enforce it. I think we should stiffen the embargo on the Belgrade government. I think we have to consider whether or not we should lift the arms embargo now on the Bosnians, since they are in no way in a fair fight with a heavily armed opponent bent on ethnic cleansing. We can't get involved in the quagmire, but we must do what we can.

Mr. Lehrer. All right. Moving on now to divisions in our country. The first question goes to Governor Clinton for two minutes, and Ann will ask it.

Family Values

Ms. Compton. Governor Clinton, can you tell us what your definition of the word "family" is?

Governor Clinton. A family involves at least one parent, whether natural or adoptive or foster, and children. A good family is a place where love and discipline and good values are transmitted from the elders to the children, a place where people turn for refuge and where they know they're the most important people in the world.

America has a lot of families that are in trouble today. There's been a lot of talk about family values in this campaign. I know a lot about that. I was born to a widowed mother who gave me family values, and grandparents. I've seen the family values of my people in Arkansas. I've seen the family values of all these people in America who are out there killing themselves, working harder for less in a country that's had the worst economic years in 50 years and the first decline in industrial production ever.

I think the President owes it to family values to show that he values America's families. Whether they're people on welfare, you're trying to move from welfare to work; the working poor, whom I think deserve a tax break to lift them above poverty if they've got a child in the house and working 40 hours a week; working families, who deserve a fair tax system and the opportunity for constant retraining. They deserve a strong economy. I think they deserve a family and medical leave act. Seventy-two other nations have been able to do it. Mr. Bush vetoed it twice because he says we can't do something 72 other countries do, even though there was a small business exemption.

So with all the talk about family values, I know about family values. I wouldn't be here without them. The best expression of my family values is that tonight's my 17th wedding anniversary, and I'd like to close my question by just wishing my wife a happy anniversary and thanking my daughter for being here.

Mr. Lehrer. President Bush, one minute.

President Bush. Well, I would say that one meeting that made a profound impression on me was when the mayors of the big cities, including the Mayor of Los Angeles, a Democrat, came to see me, and they unanimously said the decline in urban America stems from the decline in the American family. So I do think we need to strengthen family. When Barbara holds an AIDS baby, she's showing a certain compassion for family. When she reads to children, the same thing.

I believe that discipline and respect for the law, all of these things, should be taught to children, not in our schools but families have to do that. I'm appalled at the high, outrageous numbers of divorces. It's happened in families; it's happened in ours. But it's gotten too much, and I just think that we ought to do everything we can to respect the American family. It can be a single-parent family. Those mothers need help. One way to do it is to get these deadbeat fathers to pay their obligations to these mothers. That will help strengthen the American family. And there's a whole bunch of other things that I can't click off in this short period of time.

Mr. Lehrer. Mr. Perot, you have one minute.

Mr. Perot. If I had to solve all the problems that face this country and I could be granted one wish as we started down the trail to rebuild the job base, the schools, and so on and so forth, I would say a strong family unit in every home, where every child is loved, nurtured, and encouraged. A little child, before they're 18 months, learns to think well of himself or herself, or poorly. They develop a positive or negative self-image. At a very early age, they learn how to learn. If we have children who are not surrounded with love and affection—see, I look at my grandchildren and wonder if they'll ever learn to walk because they're always in someone's arms. I think, my gosh, wouldn't it be wonderful if every child had that love and support, but they don't.

We will not be a great country unless we have a strong family unit in every home. And I think you can use the White House as a bully pulpit to stress the importance of these little children, particularly in their young and formative years, to mold these little precious pieces of clay so that they, too, can live rich, full lives when they're grown.

Mr. Lehrer. New question, 2-minute answer, goes to President Bush. Sandy will ask it.

Legalization of Drugs

Mr. Vanocur. Mr. President, there's been a lot of talk about Harry Truman in this campaign, so much so that I think tomorrow I'll wake up and see him named as the next commissioner of baseball. [Laughter]

President Bush. We could use one.

Mr. Vanocur. The thing that Mr. Truman didn't have to deal with is drugs. Americans are increasingly alarmed about drug-related crimes in cities and suburbs, and your administration is not the first to have grappled with this. Are you at all of a mind that maybe it ought to go to another level, if not to what's advocated by William F. Buckley, Jr., and Milton Friedman, legalization, somewhere between there and where we are now?

President Bush. No. I don't think that's the right answer. I don't believe legalizing narcotics is the answer. I just don't believe that's the answer. I do believe that there's some fairly good news out there. The use of cocaine, for example, by teenagers is dramatically down. But we've got to keep fighting on this war against drugs.

We're doing a little better in interdiction. Many of the countries that used to say, "Well, this is a United States problem. If you'd get the demand down, then we wouldn't have the problem," are working cooperatively with the DEA and other law—the military. We're using the military more now in terms of interdiction. Our funding for recovery is up, recovering the addicts.

Where we're not making the progress, Sander, is in—we're making it in teenagers. And thank God, because I thought what Ross said was most appropriate about these families and these children. But where we're not making it is with the confirmed addicts. I'll tell you one place that's working well, and that is the private sector, Jim Burke and this task force that he has. You may know about it. Tell the American people, but this man said, "I'll get you a million dollars a day in pro bono advertising," something that's very hard for the Government to do. He went out and he did it, and people are beginning to educate through this program, teaching these kids you shouldn't use drugs.

So we're still in the fight. But I must tell you, I think legalization of narcotics or something of that nature, in the face of the medical evidence, would be totally counterproductive. And I oppose it, and I'm going to stand up and continue to oppose it.

Mr. Lehrer. Mr. Perot, one minute.

Mr. Perot. Any time you think you want to legalize drugs, go to a neonatal unit, if you can get in. They are between 100 and 200 percent capacity up and down the East Coast, and the reason is crack babies being born. Baby's in the hospital 42 days; typical cost to you and me is $5,000. Again and again and again, the mother disappears in 3 days, and the child becomes a ward of the State because he's permanently and genetically damaged. Just look at those little children, and if anybody can even think about legalizing drugs, they've lost me.

Now, let's look at priorities. We went on the Libyan raid, you remember that one, because we were worried to death that Qadhafi might be building up chemical weapons. We've got chemical warfare being conducted against our children on the streets in this country all day, every day, and we don't have the will to stamp it out.

Again, if I get up there, if you send me, we're going to have some blunt talks about this. We're really going to get out in the trenches and say, "Is this one you want to talk about or fix?" Because talk won't do it, folks. There are guys that couldn't get a job third shift in a Dairy Queen, driving BMW's and Mercedes, selling drugs. These old boys are not going to quit easy.

Mr. Lehrer. Governor Clinton, one minute.

Governor Clinton. Like Mr. Perot, I have held crack babies in my arms. But I know more about this, I think, than anybody else up here because I have a brother who's a recovering drug addict. I'm very proud of him. But I can tell you this: If drugs were legal, I don't think he'd be alive today. I am adamantly opposed to legalizing drugs. He is alive today because of the criminal justice system.

That's a mistake. What should we do? First, we ought to prevent more of this on the street. Thirty years ago there were three policemen for every crime. Now there are three crimes for every policeman. We need 100,000 more police on the street. I have a plan for that. Secondly, we ought to have treatment on demand. Thirdly, we ought to have boot camps for first-time nonviolent offenders so they can get discipline and treatment and education and get reconnected to the community, before they are severed and sent to prison where they can learn how to be first-class criminals.

There is a crime bill that, lamentably, was blocked from passage once again, mostly by Republicans in the United States Senate, which would have addressed some of these problems. That crime bill is going to be one of my highest priorities next January if I become President.

Mr. Lehrer. Next question is to you, Mr. Perot. You have 2 minutes to answer it, and John will ask it.

Racial Harmony

Mr. Mashek. Mr. Perot, racial division continues to tear apart our great cities, the last episode being this spring in Los Angeles. Why is this still happening in America? And what would you do to end it?

Mr. Perot. This is a relevant question here tonight. First thing I'd do is during political campaigns, I would urge everybody to stop trying to split this country into fragments and appeal to the differences between us, and then wonder why the melting pot's all broken to pieces after November the 3d.

We are all in this together. We ought to love one another, because united teams win and divided teams lose. If we can't love one another, we ought to get along with one another. If you can't get there, just recognize we're all stuck with one another, because nobody's going anywhere. Right? [Laughter]

Now, that ought to get everybody back up to let's get along together and make it work. Our diversity is a strength. We've turned it into a weakness.

Now, again, the White House is a bully pulpit. I think whoever's in the White House should just make it absolutely unconscionable and inexcusable. And if anybody's in the middle of a speech at, you know, one of these conventions, I would expect the candidate to go out and lift him off the stage if he starts preaching hate, because we don't have time for it.

Our differences are our strengths. We have got to pull together. In athletics, we know it. You see, divided teams lose; united teams win. We have got to unite and pull together. And there's nothing we can't do. But if we sit around blowing all this energy out the window on racial strife and hatred, we are stuck with a sure loser, because we have been a melting pot. We're becoming more and more of a melting pot. Let's make it a strength, not a weakness.

Mr. Lehrer. Governor Clinton, one minute.

Governor Clinton. I grew up in the segregated south, thankfully raised by a grandfather with almost no formal education but with a heart of gold who taught me early that all people were equal in the eyes of God. I saw the winds of hatred divide people and keep the people of my State poorer than they would have been, spiritually and economically. I've done everything I could in my public life to overcome racial divisions. We don't have a person to waste in this country.

We are being murdered economically because we have too many dropouts. We have too many low-birth weight babies. We have too many drug addicts as kids. We have too much violence. We are too divided by race, by income, by region. I have devoted a major portion of this campaign to going across this country and looking for opportunities to go to white groups and African-American groups and Latino groups, Asian-American groups and say the same thing: If the American people cannot be brought together, we can't turn this country around. If we can come together, nothing, nothing can stop us.

Mr. Lehrer. Mr. President, one minute.

President Bush. Well, I think Governor Clinton is committed. I do think it's fair to note—he can rebut it—that Arkansas is one of the few States that doesn't have any civil rights legislation.

I've tried to use the White House as a bully pulpit, speaking out against discrimination. We passed two very forward-looking civil rights bills. It's not going to be all done by legislation, but I do think that you need to make an appeal every time you can to eliminate racial divisions and discrimination. And I'll keep on doing that and pointing to some legislative accomplishment to back it up.

I have to take 10 seconds here at the end—the red light isn't on yet—to say to Ross Perot, please don't say to the DEA agents on the street that we don't have the will to fight drugs. Please, I have watched these people. The same for our local law enforcement people; we're backing them in every way we possibly can. But maybe you meant that some in the country don't have the will to fight it. But those that are out there on the front line—as you know; you've been a strong backer of law enforcement; really, I just want to clear that up—have the will to fight it. And frankly, some of them are giving their lives.

Mr. Lehrer. Time, Mr. President. All right, let's go now to another subject, the subject of health. The first question for 2 minutes is to President Bush, and John will ask it.

AIDS

Mr. Mashek. Mr. President, yesterday tens of thousands of people paraded past the White House to demonstrate their concern about the disease AIDS. A celebrated member of your Commission, Magic Johnson, quit, saying that there was too much inaction. Where is this widespread feeling coming from that your administration is not doing enough about AIDS?

President Bush. Coming from the political process. We have increased funding for AIDS. We've doubled it, on research and on every other aspect of it. My request for this year was .9 billion for AIDS, 10 times as much for AIDS victim as per cancer victim. I think that we're showing the proper compassion and concern. So I can't tell you where it's coming from, but I am very much concerned about AIDS, and I believe that we've got the best researchers in the world out there at NIH working the problem. We're funding them. I wish there was more money, but we're funding them far more than any time in the past. We're going to keep on doing that.

I don't know, I was a little disappointed in Magic, because he came to me and I said, "Now, if you see something we're not doing, get ahold of me, call me, let me know." He went to one meeting, and then we heard that he was stepping down. So he's been replaced by Mary Fisher, who electrified the Republican Convention by talking about the compassion and the concern that we feel. It was a beautiful moment. And I think she'll do a first-class job on that Commission.

So I think the appeal is, yes, we care. The other thing is, part of AIDS, it's one of the few diseases where behavior matters. And I once called on somebody, "Well, change your behavior. If the behavior you're using is prone to cause AIDS, change the behavior." The next thing I know, one of these ACT-UP groups is out saying, "Bush ought to change his behavior." You can't talk about it rationally. The extremes are hurting the AIDS cause. To go into a Catholic mass in a beautiful cathedral in New York under the cause of helping in AIDS and start throwing condoms around in the mass, I'm sorry, I think it sets back the cause. We cannot move to the extreme.

We've got to care. We've got to continue everything we can at the Federal and the local level. Barbara, I think, is doing a superb job in destroying the myth about AIDS. All of us are in this fight together. All of us care. Do not go to the extreme.

Mr. Lehrer. One minute, Mr. Perot.

Mr. Perot. First, I think Mary Fisher was a great choice. We're lucky to have her heading the Commission. Secondly, I think one thing, that if I were sent to do the job, I would sit down with the FDA, look exactly where we are. Then I would really focus on let's get these things out. If you're going to die, you don't have to go through this 10-year cycle that FDA goes through on new drugs. Believe me, people with AIDS are more than willing to take that risk. We could be moving out to the human population a whole lot faster than we are on some of these new drugs. So I think we can expedite the problem there.

Let me go back a minute to racial divisiveness. All-time low in our country was the Judge Thomas–Anita Hill hearings, and those Senators ought to be hanging their heads in shame for what they did there.

Second thing, there are not many times in your life when you get to talk to a whole country, but let me just say this to all of America: If you hate people, I don't want your vote. That's how strongly I feel about it.

Mr. Lehrer. Governor Clinton, one minute.

Governor Clinton. Over 150,000 Americans have died of AIDS. Well over a million and a quarter Americans are HIV-positive. We need to put one person in charge of the battle against AIDS to cut across all the agencies that deal with it. We need to accelerate the drug approval process. We need to fully fund the act named for that wonderful boy, Ryan White, to make sure we're doing everything we can on research and treatment. The President should lead a national effort to change behavior to keep our children alive in the schools, responsible behavior to keep people alive. This is a matter of life and death.

I've worked in my State to reduce teen pregnancy and illness among children. And I know it's tough. The reason Magic Johnson resigned from the AIDS Commission is because the statement you heard tonight from Mr. Bush is the longest and best statement he's made about it in public. I'm proud of what we did at the Democratic Convention, putting two HIV-positive people on the platform, and I'm proud of the leadership that I'm going to bring to this country in dealing with the AIDS crisis.

Mr. Lehrer. New question for Mr. Perot. You have 2 minutes to answer, and Ann will ask it.

Entitlement Programs

Ms. Compton. Mr. Perot, even if you've got what people say are the guts to take on changes in the most popular and the most sacred of the entitlements, Medicare, people say you haven't a prayer of actually getting anything passed in Washington. Since the President isn't a Lone Ranger, how in the world can you make some of those unpopular changes?

Mr. Perot. Two ways. Number one, if I get there, it will be a very unusual and historical event because—[laughter]—because the people, not the special interests, put me there. I will have a unique mandate. I have said again and again, and this really upsets the establishment in Washington, that we're going to inform the people in detail on the issues through an electronic town hall so that they really know what's going on. They will want to do what's good for our country.

Now, all these fellows with thousand-dollar suits and alligator shoes running up and down the Halls of Congress that make policy now, the lobbyists, the PAC guys, the foreign lobbyists, what have you, they'll be over there in the Smithsonian—[laughter]— because we're going to get rid of them. The Congress will be listening to the people. And the American people are willing to have fair, shared sacrifice. They're not as stupid as Washington thinks they are. The American people are bright, intelligent, caring, loving people who want a great country for their children and grandchildren. They will make those sacrifices. So I welcome that challenge. And just watch, because if the American people send me there, we'll get it done.

Now, everybody will faint in Washington. They've never seen anything happen in that town. [Laughter] This is a town where the White House says, "Congress did it." Congress says, "The White House did it." And I'm sitting there and saying, "Well, who else could be around?" And then when they get off by themselves, they said, "Nobody did it." [Laughter] And yet, the cash register is empty. And it used to have our money, the taxpayers' money, in it, and we didn't get the results. We'll get it done.

Mr. Lehrer. Governor, one minute.

Governor Clinton. Ross, that's a great speech, but it's not quite that simple. [Laughter] I mean, look at the facts. Both parties in Washington, the President and the Congress, have cut Medicare. The average senior citizen is spending a higher percent-

age of income on health care today than they were in 1965 before Medicare came in. The President's got another proposal to require them to pay $400 a year more for the next 5 years.

But if you don't have the guts to control cost by changing the insurance system and taking on the bureaucracies and the regulation of health care in the private and public sector, you can't fix this problem. Costs will continue to spiral. Just remember this, folks: A lot of folks on Medicare are out there every day making the choice between food and medicine. Not poor enough for Medicare, Medicaid; not wealthy enough to buy their medicine. I've met them, people like Mary Annie and Edward Davis of Nashua, New Hampshire, all over this country. They cannot even buy medicine. So let's be careful. When we talk about cutting health care costs, let's start with the insurance companies and the people that are making a killing instead of making our people healthy.

Mr. Lehrer. One minute, President Bush.

President Bush. Well, first place I'd like to clear up something, because every 4 years the Democrats go around and say, "Hey, Republicans are going to cut Social Security and Medicare." They've started it again. I am the President that stood up and said, "Don't mess with Social Security." And I'm not going to, and we haven't. We are not going to go after the Social Security recipient. I have one difference with Mr. Perot on that because I don't think we need to touch Social Security.

What we do need to do, though, is control the growth of these mandatory programs. And Ross properly says, "Okay, there's some pain in that." But Governor Clinton refuses to touch that, simply refuses. So what we've got to do is control it, the growth. Let it grow for inflation; let it grow for the amount of new people added, population. And then hold the line. I believe that is the way you get the deficit down, not by the tax-and-spend program that we hear every 4 years, whether it's Mondale, Dukakis, whoever else it is. I just don't believe we ought to do that. So hold the line on Social Security, and put a cap on the growth of the mandatory program.

Mr. Lehrer. New question. It is for Governor Clinton, 2-minute answer. Sandy will ask it.

Health Care Costs

Mr. Vanocur. Governor Clinton, Ann Compton has brought up Medicare. I remember in 1965 when Wilbur Mills of Arkansas, the chairman of Ways and Means, was pushing it through the Congress. The charge against it was it's socialized medicine. One, you never—

Governor Clinton. Mr. Bush made that charge.

Mr. Vanocur. Well, he served with him 2 years later in 1967 where I first met him. The second point, though, is that it is now skyrocketing out of control. People want it; we say it's going bonkers. Is not the Oregon plan, applied to Medicaid rationing, the proper way to go, even though the Federal Government last August ruled that violated the Americans with Disabilities Act of 1990?

Governor Clinton. I thought the Oregon plan should at least have been allowed to be tried because at least the people in Oregon were trying to do something.

Let me go back to the main point, Sandy. Mr. Bush is trying to run against Lyndon Johnson and Jimmy Carter and everybody in the world but me in this race. I have proposed a managed competition plan for health care. I will say again: You cannot control health care costs simply by cutting Medicare. Look what's happened. The Federal Government has cut Medicare and Medicaid in the last few years. States have cut Medicaid; we've done it in Arkansas under budget pressures. But what happens? More and more people get on the rolls as poverty increases. If you don't control the health care costs of the entire system, you cannot get control of it.

Look at our program. We've set up a national ceiling on health care costs tied to inflation and population growth set by health care providers, not by the Government. We provide for managed competition, not Government models, in every State, and we control private and public health care costs.

Now, just a few days ago, a bipartisan commission of Republicans and Democrats, more Republicans than Democrats, said my plan will save the average family $1,200 a year more than the Bush plan will by the year 2000; $2.2 trillion in the next 12 years; $400 billion a year by the end of this decade. I've got a plan to control health care costs. But you can't just do it by cutting Medicare. You have to take on the insurance companies, the bureaucracies, and you have to have cost controls, yes. But keep in mind, we are spending 30 percent more on health care than any country in the world, any other country. Yet, we have 35 million people uninsured. We have no preventive and primary care. The Oregon plan is a good start if the Federal Government is going to continue to abandon its responsibilities.

I say if Germany can cover everybody and keep costs under inflation, if Hawaii can cover 98 percent of their people at lower health care costs than the rest of us, if Rochester, New York, can do it with two-thirds of the cost of the rest of us, America can do it, too. I'm tried of being told we can't. I say we can. We can do better, and we must.

Mr. Lehrer. President Bush, one minute.

President Bush. Well, I don't have time in 30 seconds or one minute to talk about our health care reform plan. The Oregon plan made some good sense, but it's easy to dismiss the concerns of the disabled. As President, I have to be sure that those waivers which we're approving all over the place are covered under the law. Maybe we can work it out. But the Americans for Disabilities Act, speaking about sound and sensible civil rights legislation, was the foremost piece of legislation passed in modern times. So we do have something more than a technical problem.

Governor Clinton clicked off the things: You've got to take on insurance companies and bureaucracies. He failed to take on somebody else, the malpractice suit people, those that bring these lawsuits against—these frivolous trial lawyers' lawsuits that are running costs of medical care up by billion to billion. He refuses to put anything—controls on these crazy lawsuits.

If you want to help somebody, don't run the costs up by making doctors have to have five or six tests where one would do for fear of being sued, or have somebody along the highway not stop to pick up a guy and help him because he's afraid a trial lawyer will come along and sue him. We're suing each other too much and caring for each other too little.

Mr. Lehrer. Mr. Perot, one minute.

Mr. Perot. We've got the most expensive health care system in the world. It ranks behind 15 other nations when we come to life expectancy and 22 other nations when we come to infant mortality. So we don't have the best. Pretty simple, folks, if you're pay-

ing more and you don't have the best, if all else fails go copy the people who have the best who spend less, right? But we can do better than that. Again, we've got plans lying all over the place in Washington. Nobody ever implements them.

Now I'm back to square one: If you want to stop talking about it and do it, then I'll be glad to go up there and we'll get it done. But if you just want to keep the music going, just stay traditional this next time around, and 4 years from now you'll have everybody blaming everybody else for a bad health care system. Talk is cheap. Words are plentiful. Deeds are precious. Let's get on with it.

Mr. Lehrer. And that's exactly what we're going to do. That was, in fact, the final question and answer. We're now going to move to closing statements. Each candidate will have up to 2 minutes. The order, remember, was determined by a drawing. And Mr. Perot, you were first.

Closing Statements

Mr. Perot. Well, it's been a privilege to be able to talk to the American people tonight. I make no bones about it: I love this country. I love the principle it's founded on. I love the people here. I don't like to see the country's principles violated. I don't like to see the people in a deteriorating economy and a deteriorating country because our Government has lost touch with the people. The people in Washington are good people; we just have a bad system. We've got to change the system. It's time to do it because we have run up so much debt that time is no longer our friend. We've got to put our house in order.

When you go to bed tonight, look at your children. Think of their dreams. Think of your dreams as a child. And ask yourself,

"Isn't it time to stop talking about it? Isn't it time to stop creating images? Isn't it time to do it?" Aren't you sick of being treated like an unprogrammed robot? Every 4 years they send you all kinds of messages to tell you how to vote and then go back to business as usual. They told you at the tax and budget summit that if you agreed to a tax increase, we could balance the budget. They didn't tell you that that same year they increased spending .83 for every dollar we increased taxes. That's Washington in a nutshell right there.

In the final analysis, I'm doing this for your children, when you look at them tonight. There's another group that I feel very close to, and these are the men and women who fought on the battlefield, the children, the families of the ones who died, the people who left parts of their bodies over there. I'd never ask you to do anything for me, but I owe you this, and I'm doing it for you. I can't tell you what it means to me at these rallies when I see you and you come up, and the look in your eyes. I know how you feel, and you know how I feel. And then I think of the older people who are retired. They grew up in the Depression. They fought and won World War II. We owe you a debt we can never repay you. And the greatest repayment I can ever give is to recreate the American dream for your children and grandchildren. I'll give it everything I have if you want me to do it.

Mr. Lehrer. Governor Clinton, your closing statement.

Governor Clinton. I'd like to thank the people of St. Louis and Washington University, the Presidential Debate Commission, and all those who made this night possible. And I'd like to thank those of you who are watching. Most of all, I'd like to thank all of you who have touched me in some way over this last year, all the thousands of you whom I've seen. I'd like to thank the computer executives and the electronics executives in Silicon Valley, two-thirds of whom are Republicans, who said they wanted to sign on to a change to create a new America. I'd like to thank the hundreds of executives who came to Chicago, a third of them Republicans, who said they wanted a change. I'd like to thank the people who started with Mr. Perot who have come on to help our campaign. I'd like to thank all the folks around America that no one ever knows about: the woman who was holding the AIDS baby she adopted in Cedar Rapids, Iowa, who asked me to do something more for adoption; the woman who stopped along the road in Wisconsin and wept because her husband had lost his job after 27 years; all the people who are having a tough time; and the people who are winning, but who know how desperately we need to change.

This debate tonight has made crystal clear a challenge that is as old as America: the choice between hope and fear, change or more of the same; the courage to move into a new tomorrow or to listen to the crowd who says, "Things could be worse."

Mr. Bush has said some very compelling things tonight that don't quite square with the record. He was President for 3 years before he proposed a health care plan that still hasn't been sent to Congress in total; 3 years before an economic plan; and he still didn't say tonight that that tax bill he vetoed raised taxes only on the rich and gave the rest of you a break, but he vetoed it anyway.

I offer a new direction: Invest in American jobs, American education, control health care costs, bring this country together again. I want the future of this country to be as bright and brilliant as its past, and it can be if we have the courage to change.

Mr. Lehrer. President Bush, your closing statement.

President Bush. Well, let me tell you a little what it's like to be President. In the Oval Office, you can't predict what kind of crisis is going to come up. You have to make tough calls. You can't be on one hand this way and one hand another. You can't take different positions on these difficult issues.

Then you need a philosophical—I'd call it a philosophical underpinning; mine for foreign affairs is democracy and freedom. Look at the dramatic changes around the world. The cold war is over. The Soviet Union is no more, and we're working with a democratic country. Poland, Hungary, Czechoslovakia, the Baltics are free. Take a look at the Middle East. We had to stand up against a tyrant. The United States came together as we haven't in many, many years. We kicked this man out of Kuwait. In the process, as a result of that will and that decision and that toughness, we now have ancient enemies talking peace in the Middle East. Nobody would have dreamed it possible.

I think the biggest dividend of making these tough calls is the fact that we are less afraid of nuclear war. Every parent out there has much less worry that their kids are going to be faced with nuclear holocaust. All this is good.

On the domestic side, what we must do is have change that empowers people, not change for the sake of change, tax and spend. We don't need to do that anymore. What we need to do is empower people. We need to invest and save. We need to do better in education. We need to do better in job retraining. We need to expand our exports, and they're going very, very well indeed. We need to strengthen the American family.

I hope as President that I've earned your trust. I've admitted it when I make a mis-take, but then I go on and help try to solve the problems. I hope I've earned your trust, because a lot of being President is about trust and character. And I ask for your support for 4 more years to finish this job.

Thank you very, very much.

Mr. Lehrer. Don't go away yet. I just want to thank the three panelists and thank the three candidates for participating, President Bush, Governor Clinton, and Mr. Perot. They will appear again together on October the 15th and again on October 19th. Next Tuesday there will be a debate among the three candidates for Vice President.

And for now, from Washington University in St. Louis, Missouri, I'm Jim Lehrer. Thank you, and good night.

61. Presidential Debate in Richmond, Virginia October 15, 1992

Carole Simpson. Good evening, and welcome to the second of three Presidential debates between the major candidates for President of the United States. The candidates are the Republican nominee, President George Bush; the independent, Ross Perot; and Governor Bill Clinton, the Democratic nominee.

My name is Carole Simpson, and I will be the moderator for tonight's 90-minute debate which is coming to you from the campus of the University of Richmond in Richmond, Virginia.

Now, tonight's program is unlike any other Presidential debate in history. We're making history now, and it's pretty exciting. An independent polling firm has selected an audience of 209 uncommitted voters from this area. The candidates will be asked questions by these voters on a topic of their choosing, anything they want to ask about. My job as moderator is to, you know, take care of the questioning, ask questions myself if I think there needs to be continuity and balance, and sometimes I might ask the candidates to respond to what another candidate may have said.

Now, the format has been agreed to by representatives of both the Republican and Democratic campaigns, and there is no subject matter that is restricted. Anything goes. We can ask anything. After the debate the candidates will have an opportunity to make a closing statement.

So, President Bush, I think you said it earlier, let's get it on.

President Bush. Let's go.

Ms. Simpson. And I think the first question is over here.

Foreign Trade and Domestic Jobs

Q. I'd like to direct my question to Mr. Perot. What will you do as President to open foreign markets to fair competition from American business and to stop unfair competition here at home from foreign countries so that we can bring jobs back to the United States?

Mr. Perot. That's right at the top of my agenda. We've shipped millions of jobs overseas, and we have a strange situation because we have a process in Washington where after you've served for a while, you cash in, become a foreign lobbyist, make $30,000 a month, then take a leave, work on Presidential campaigns, make sure you got good contacts, and then go back out.

Now, if you just want to get down to brass tacks, first thing you ought to do is get all these folks that have got these one-way trade agreements that we've negotiated over the years and say, "Fellas, we'll take the same deal we gave you." They'll gridlock right at that point, because, for example, we've got international competitors who simply could not unload their cars off the ships if they had to comply, you see, if it was a two-way street, just couldn't do it.

We have got to stop sending jobs overseas. To those of you in the audience who are business people, pretty simple: If you're paying $12, $13, $14, an hour for factory workers, and you can move your factory south of the border, pay $1 an hour for labor, hire young—let's assume you've been in business for a long time; you've got a mature work force—pay $1 an hour for your labor, have no health care—that's the most expensive single element in making a car—have no environmental controls, no pollution controls, and no retirement, and you don't care about anything but making money, there will be a giant sucking sound going south. So if the people send me to Washington, the first thing I'll do is study that 2,000-page agreement and make sure it's a two-way street.

I have one last part here. I decided I was dumb and didn't understand it, so I called the "Who's Who" of the folks that have been around it. And I said, "Why won't everybody go south?" They say, "It would be disruptive." I said, "For how long?" I finally got them up for 12 to 15 years. And I said, "Well, how does it stop being disruptive?" And that is, when their jobs come up from $1 an hour to $6 an hour, and ours go down to $6 an hour, then it's leveled again. But in the meantime, you've wrecked the country with these kinds of deals. We've got to cut it out.

Ms. Simpson. Thank you, Mr. Perot. I see that the President has stood up, so he must have something to say about this.

President Bush. Well, Carole, the thing that saved us in this global economic slowdown has been our exports, and what I'm trying to do is increase our exports. If, indeed, all the jobs were going to move south because of lower wages, there are lower wages now, and they haven't done that. So I have just negotiated with the President of Mexico the North American free trade agreement, and the Prime Minister of Canada, I might add. I want to have more of these free trade agreements because export jobs are increasing far faster than any jobs that may have moved overseas. That's a scare tactic, because it's not that many. But any one that's here, we want to have more jobs here, and the way to do that is to increase our exports.

Some believe in protection. I don't. I believe in free and fair trade. That's the thing that saved us. And so I will keep on, as President, trying to get a successful conclusion to the GATT round, the big Uruguay round of trade which will really open up markets for our agriculture, particularly. I want to continue to work after we get this NAFTA agreement ratified this coming year. I want to get one with Eastern Europe. I want to get one with Chile. Free and fair trade is the answer, not protection.

As I say, we've had tough economic times, and it's exports that have saved us, exports that have built—

Ms. Simpson. Governor Clinton.

Governor Clinton. I'd like to answer the question, because I've actually been a Governor for 12 years, so I've known a lot of people who have lost their jobs because of jobs moving overseas, and I know a lot of people whose plants have been strengthened by increasing exports.

The trick is to expand our export base and to expand trade on terms that are fair to us. It is true that our exports to Mexico, for example, have gone up, and our trade deficit's gone down. It's also true that just today a record-high trade deficit was announced with Japan.

So what is the answer? Let me just mention three things very quickly. Number one, make sure that other countries are as open to our markets as our markets are to them. If they're not, have measures on the books that don't take forever and a day to implement.

Number two, change the Tax Code. There are more deductions in the Tax Code for shutting plants down and moving overseas than there are for modernizing plants and equipment here. Our competitors don't do that. Emphasize and subsidize modernizing plants and equipment here, not moving plants overseas.

Number three, stop the Federal Government's program that now gives low interest loans and job training funds to companies that will actually shut down and move to other countries, but we won't do the same thing for plants that stay here. So more trade, but on fair terms, and favor investment in America.

Ms. Simpson. Thank you. I think we have a question over here.

Federal Deficit

Q. This is for Governor Clinton. In the real world, that is, outside of Washington, DC, compensation and achievement are based on goals defined and achieved. My question is about the deficit. Would you define in specific dollar goals how much you would reduce the deficit in each of the 4 years of a Clinton administration and then enter into a legally binding contract with the American people that if you did not achieve those goals that you would not seek a second term?

Answer yes or no, and then comment on your answer, please.

Governor Clinton. No, and here's why; I'll tell you exactly why, because the deficit now has been building up for 12 years. I'll tell you exactly what I think can be done. I think we can bring it down by 50 percent in 4 years and grow the economy.

Now, I could get rid of it in 4 years in theory on the books now, but to do it you'd have to raise taxes too much and cut benefits too much to people who need them, and it would even make the economy worse.

Mr. Perot will tell you, for example, that the expert he hired to analyze his plan says that it will bring the deficit down in 5 years, but it will make unemployment bad for 4 more years. So my view is, sir, you have to increase investment, grow the economy, and reduce the deficit by controlling health care costs, prudent reductions in defense, cuts in domestic programs, and asking the wealthiest Americans and foreign corporations to pay their fair share of taxes, and investing in growing this economy.

I ask everybody to look at my economic ideas. Nine Nobel Prize winners and over 500 economists and hundreds of business people, including a lot of Republicans, said this is the way you've got to go. If you don't grow the economy, you can't get it done. But I can't foresee all the things that will happen, and I don't think a President should be judged solely on the deficit.

Let me also say we're having an election today. You'll have a shot at me in 4 years, and you can vote me right out if you think I've done a lousy job. I would welcome you to do that.

Ms. Simpson. Mr. President?

President Bush. Well, I've got to—I'm a little confused here because I don't see how you can grow the deficit down by raising peo-

ple's taxes. You see, I don't think the American people are taxed too little. I think they're taxed too much. I went for one tax increase, and when I make a mistake, I admit it, say that wasn't the right thing to do. Governor Clinton's program wants to tax more and spend more: $150 billion in new taxes, spend another $220 billion. I don't believe that's the way to do it.

Here's some things that will help. Give us a balanced budget amendment. He always talks about Arkansas having a balanced budget, and they do. But he has a balanced budget amendment; have to do it. I'd like the Government to have that. I think it would discipline not only the Congress, which needs it, but also the executive branch.

I'd like to have what 43 Governors have, the line-item veto. So if the Congress can't cut, we've got a reckless spending Congress, let the President have a shot at it by wiping out things that are pork barrel or something of that nature.

I've proposed another one. Some sophisticates think it may be a little gimmicky. I think it's good. It's a check-off. It says to you as a taxpayer—say, you're going to pay a tax of $1,000 or something; you can check 10 percent of that if you want to in one box, and that 10 percent, $100, or if you're paying $10,000, whatever it is, $1,000, check it off, and make the Government, make it lower the deficit by that amount. If the Congress won't do it, if they can't get together and negotiate how to do that, then you'd have a sequester across the board. You'd exempt Social Security. I don't want to tax or touch Social Security. I'm the President that said, "Hey, don't mess with Social Security." And we haven't.

So I believe we need to control the growth of mandatory spending, back to this gentleman's question, that's the main growing thing in the budget. The program that the President—two-thirds of the budget, I, as President, never get to look at, never get to touch. We've got to control that growth to inflation and population increase, but not raise taxes on the American people now. I just don't believe that would stimulate any kind of growth at all.

Ms. Simpson. How about you, Mr. Perot?

Mr. Perot. Well, we're $4 trillion in debt, and we're going into debt an additional $1 billion, a little more than $1 billion, every working day of the year. Now, the thing I love about it—I'm just a businessman. I was down in Texas, taking care of business, tending to my family. This situation got so bad that I decided I had better get into it. The American people asked me to get into it. But I just find it fascinating that while we sit here tonight, we will go into debt an additional $50 million in an hour and a half.

Now, it's not the Republicans' fault, of course, and it's not the Democrats' fault. What I'm looking for is who did it? Now, they're the two folks involved; so maybe if you put them together, they did it. Now, the facts are we have to fix it.

I'm here tonight for these young people up here in the balcony from this college. When I was a young man, when I got out of the Navy, I had multiple job offers. Young people with high grades can't get a job. The 18- to 24-year-old high school graduates 10 years ago were making more than they are now. In other words, we were down to—18 percent of them were making—the 18- to 24-year-olds were making less than $12,000. Now that's up to 40 percent. And what's happening in the meantime? The dollar's gone through the floor.

Now, whose fault is that? Not the Democrats; not the Republicans. Somewhere out there there's an extraterrestrial that's doing this to us, I guess. [Laughter]

And everybody says they take responsibility. Somebody, somewhere has to take responsibility for this. Put it to you bluntly, the American people: If you want me to be your President, we're going to face our problems. We'll deal with the problems. We'll solve our problems. We'll pay down our debt. We'll pass on the American dream to our children. I will not leave our children a situation that they have today.

When I was a boy, it took two generations to double the standard of living. Today it will take 12 generations. Our children will not see the American dream because of this debt that somebody, somewhere dropped on us.

Ms. Simpson. You're all wonderful speakers, and I know you have lots more to add. But I have talked to this audience, and they have lots of questions on other topics. Can we move to another topic, please?

We have one up here, I think.

Presidential Campaign

Q. Yes, I'd like to address all the candidates with this question. The amount of time the candidates have spent in this campaign trashing their opponents' character and their programs is depressingly large. Why can't your discussions and proposals reflect the genuine complexity and the difficulty of the issues to try to build a consensus around the best aspects of all proposals?

Ms. Simpson. Who wants to take that one? Mr. Perot, you have an answer for everything, don't you? Go right ahead, sir. [Laughter]

Mr. Perot. No, I don't have an answer for everything. As you all know, I've been buying 30-minute segments to talk about issues. Tomorrow night on NBC from 10:30 to 11, eastern, we're going to talk about how you pay the debt down. So we're going to come right down to that one, see. We'll be on again Saturday night 8 to 9 o'clock on ABC. [Laughter]

Ms. Simpson. Okay, okay.

Mr. Perot. So the point is, finally, I couldn't agree with you more, couldn't agree with you more. And I have said again and again and again, let's get off mud wrestling. Let's get off personalities, and let's talk about jobs, health care, crime, the things that concern the American people. I'm spending my money, not PAC money, not foreign money, my money to take this message to the people.

Ms. Simpson. Thank you, Mr. Perot. So that seems directed. He would say it's you gentlemen that have been doing that. Mr. Clinton, Governor Clinton, how do you—President Bush, how would you like to respond?

President Bush. Well, first place, I believe that character is a part of being President. I think you have to look at it. I think that has to be a part of candidate for President or being President. In terms of programs, I've submitted, what, four different budgets to the United States Congress in great detail. They're so heavy they'd give you a broken back. Everything in there says what I am for. Now, I've come out with a new agenda for America's renewal, a plan that I believe really will help stimulate the growth of this economy.

My record on world affairs is pretty well-known because I've been President for 4 years. So I feel I've been talking issues. Nobody likes "who shot John," but I think the first negative campaign run in this election was by Governor Clinton. And I'm not going to sit there and be a punching bag. I'm going to stand up and say, "Hey, listen, here's my side of it." But character is an important part of the equation.

The other night, Governor Clinton raised—I don't know if you saw the debate the other night, suffered through that. [Laughter] Well, he raised a question of my father. It was a good line, well-rehearsed and well-delivered. But he raised a question of my father and said, "Well, your father, Prescott Bush, was against McCarthy. You should be ashamed of yourself—McCarthyism."

I remember something my dad told me. I was 18 years old, going to Penn Station to go into the Navy. He said, "Write your mother," which I faithfully did. He said, "Serve your country." My father was an honor, duty, and country man. And he said, "Tell the truth." And I've tried to do that in public life, all through it. That has said something about character.

My argument with Governor Clinton— you can call it mud wrestling, but I think it's fair to put it in focus—is I am deeply troubled by someone who demonstrates and organizes demonstration in a foreign land when his country's at war. Probably a lot of kids here disagree with me, but that's what I feel. That's what I feel passionately about. I'm thinking of Ross Perot's running mate sitting in the jail; how would he feel about it? But maybe that's generational. I don't know.

But the big argument I have with the Governor on this is this taking different positions on different issues, trying to be one thing to one person here that's opposing the NAFTA agreement and then for it; what we call waffling. And I do think that you can't turn the White House into the waffle house. You've got to say what you're for. And you have got to—

Ms. Simpson. Mr. President, I am getting time cues, and with all due respect, I'm sorry.

President Bush. Excuse me, I don't want to— no, go ahead, Carole.

Ms. Simpson. Governor Clinton.

President Bush. I get wound up because I feel strongly.

Ms. Simpson. Yes, you do. [Laughter]

Governor Clinton. Let me say first of all to you that I believe so strongly in the question you asked that I suggested this format tonight. I started doing these formats a year ago in New Hampshire, and I found that we had huge crowds because all I did was let people ask questions, and I tried to give very specific answers. I also had a program starting last year.

I've been disturbed by the tone and the tenor of this campaign. Thank goodness the networks have a fact check so I don't have to just go blue in the face anymore. Mr. Bush said once again tonight I was going to have a $150 billion tax increase. When Mr. Quayle said that, all the networks said: that's not true; he's got over $100 billion in tax cuts and incentives.

So I'm not going to take up your time tonight, but let me just say this. We'll have a debate in 4 days, and we can talk about this character thing again, but the *Washington Post* ran a long editorial today saying they couldn't believe Mr. Bush was making character an issue, and they said he was the greatest political chameleon, for changing his positions, of all time.

Now, I don't want to get into that—

President Bush. Please don't say anything by the *Washington Post*.

Governor Clinton. Wait a minute. Let's don't—you don't have to believe that. Here's my point. I'm not interested in his character. I want to change the character of the Presidency. And I'm interested in what we can trust him to do and what you can trust me to do and what you can trust Mr. Perot to do

for the next 4 years. So I think you're right, and I hope the rest of the night belongs to you.

Ms. Simpson. May I—I talked to this audience before you gentlemen came, and I asked them about how they felt about the tenor of the campaign. Would you like to let them know what you thought about that, when I said, "Are you pleased with how the campaign's been going?"

Audience members. No!

Ms. Simpson. Who wants to say why you don't like the way the campaign is going? We have a gentleman back here?

Focusing on Issues

Q. If I may, and forgive the notes here, but I'm shy on camera. The focus of my work as a domestic mediator is meeting the needs of the children that I work with by way of their parents, and not the wants of their parents. I ask the three of you, how can we as, symbolically, the children of the future President, expect the two of you, the three of you, to meet our needs, the needs in housing and in crime and you name it, as opposed to the wants of your political spin doctors and your political parties?

Ms. Simpson. So your question is—

Q. Can we focus on the issues and not the personalities and the mud? I think there is a need—if we could take a poll here with the folks from Gallup, perhaps—I think there is a real need here to focus at this point on the needs.

Ms. Simpson. How do you respond? How do you gentlemen respond to—

Governor Clinton. I agree with him.

Ms. Simpson. President Bush?

President Bush. Let's do it. Let's talk about programs for children.

Q. Could we cross our hearts, and it sounds silly here, but could we make a commitment? You know, we're not under oath at this point, but could you make a commitment to the citizens of the United States to meet our needs, and we have many, and not yours again? You know, I repeat that; that's a real need I think that we all have.

President Bush. I think it depends on how you define it. I mean, I think, in general, let's talk about these issues, let's talk about the programs. But in the Presidency, a lot goes into it. Caring goes into it; that's not particularly specific. Strength goes into it; that's not specific. Standing up against aggression; that's not specific in terms of a program. This is what a President has to do.

So, in principle, though, I'll take your point. I think we ought to discuss child care or whatever else it is.

Ms. Simpson. And you two?

Governor Clinton. Ross had his hand up.

Mr. Perot. No hedges, no ifs, ands, and buts, I'll take the pledge, because I know the American people want to talk about issues and not tabloid journalism. So I'll take the pledge, and we'll stay on the issues.

Now, just for the record, I don't have any spin doctors. I don't have any speechwriters. Probably shows. [Laughter] I make those charts you see on television even. [Laughter] But you don't have to wonder if it's me talking. Hey, what you see is what you get. If you don't like it, you've got two other choices, right?

Governor Clinton. Wait a minute. I want to say just one thing now, Ross, in fairness. The ideas I express are mine. I've worked on these things for 12 years, and I'm the only person up here who hasn't been part of Washington in any way for the last 20 years. So I don't want the implication to be that somehow everything we say is just cooked up and put in our head by somebody else. I worked 12 years very hard as a Governor on the real problems of real people. I'm just as sick as you are by having to wake up and figure out how to defend myself every day. I never thought I'd ever be involved in anything like this.

Mr. Perot. May I finish?

Ms. Simpson. Yes, you may finish.

Mr. Perot. Very briefly?

Ms. Simpson. Yes, very briefly.

Mr. Perot. I don't have any foreign money in my campaign. I don't have any foreign lobbyists on leave in my campaign. I don't have any PAC money in my campaign. I've got 5 1/2 million hard-working people who have put me on the ballot, and I belong to them.

Ms. Simpson. Okay.

Mr. Perot. And they are interested in what you're interested in. I'll take the pledge. I've already taken the pledge on cutting the deficit in half. I never got to say that. There's a great young group, Lead or Leave, college students, young people who don't want us to spend their money. I took the pledge we'd cut it out.

Ms. Simpson. Thank you. We have a question here.

Domestic Infrastructure

Q. Yes. I would like to get a response from all three gentlemen. And the question is, what are your plans to improve the physical infrastructure of this Nation, which includes the water system, the sewer system, our transportation systems, et cetera? Thank you.

Ms. Simpson. The cities. Who is going to fix the cities, and how?

President Bush. I'd be glad to take a shot at it.

Ms. Simpson. Please.

President Bush. I'm not sure that—and I can understand if you haven't seen this because there's been a lot of hue and cry. We passed this year the most farthest looking transportation bill in the history of this country since Eisenhower started the interstate highways, $150 billion for improving the infrastructure. That happened when I was President. So I am very proud of the way that came about, and I think it's a very, very good beginning.

Like Mr. Perot, I am concerned about the deficits. And $150 billion is a lot of money, but it's awful hard to say we're going to go out and spend more money when we're trying to get the deficit down. But I would cite that as a major accomplishment.

We hear all the negatives. When you're President, you expect this. Everybody's running against the incumbent. They can do better; everyone knows that. But here's something that we can take great pride in because it really does get to what you're talking about. Our home initiative, our home-ownership initiative, HOPE, that passed the Congress is a good start for having people own their own homes instead of living in these deadly tenements.

Our enterprise zones that we hear a lot of lip service about in Congress would bring jobs into the inner city. There's a good program. I need the help of everybody across this country to get it passed in a substantial way by the Congress.

When we went out to South Central in Los Angeles—some of you may remember the riots there. I went out there. I went to a boys club, and every one of them, the boys club leaders, the ministers, all of them were saying, pass enterprise zones. We go back to Washington, and very difficult to get it through the Congress.

But there's going to be a new Congress. No one likes gridlock. There's going to be a new Congress because the old one, I don't want to get this man mad at me, but there was a post office scandal and a bank scandal. You're going to have a lot of new Members of Congress. And then you can sit down and say, "Help me do what we should for the cities. Help me pass these programs."

Ms. Simpson. Mr. President, aren't you threatening to veto the bill, the urban aid bill, that included enterprise zones?

President Bush. Sure, but the problem is you get so many things included in a great big bill that you have to look at the overall good. That's the problem with our system. If you had a line-item veto, you could knock out the pork. You could knock out the tax increases, and you could do what the people want, and that is create enterprise zones.

Ms. Simpson. Governor Clinton, you're chomping at the bit.

Governor Clinton. That bill pays for these urban enterprise zones by asking the wealthiest Americans to pay a little more, and that's why he wants to veto it, just like he vetoed an earlier bill this year. This is not mud slinging. This is fact slinging.

President Bush. There you go.

Governor Clinton. A bill earlier this year—this is fact—that would have given investment tax credits and other incentives to reinvest in our cities and our country. But it asked the wealthiest Americans to pay a little more. Mr. Perot wants to do the same thing. I agree with him. I mean, we agree with that.

Let me tell you specifically what my plan does: My plan would dedicate $20 billion a year in each of the next 4 years for investments in new transportation, communications, environmental cleanup, and new technologies for the 21st century. We would target it especially in areas that have been either depressed or which have lost a lot of defense-related jobs.

There are 200,000 people in California, for example, who have lost their defense-related jobs. They ought to be engaged in making high-speed rail. They ought to be engaged in breaking ground in other technologies, doing waste recycling, clean water technology, and things of that kind. We can create millions of jobs in these new technologies, more than we're going to lose in defense if we target it. But we're investing a much smaller percentage of our income in the things you just asked about than all of our major competitors. Our wealth growth is going down as a result of it. It's making the country poorer, which is why I answered the gentleman the way I did before.

We have to both bring down the deficit and get our economy going through these kinds of investments in order to get the kind of wealth and jobs and incomes we need in America.

Ms. Simpson. Mr. Perot, what about your plans for the cities? You want to tackle the economy and the deficit first.

Mr. Perot. First, you've got to have money to pay for these things. So you've got to create jobs, and there are all kinds of ways to create jobs in the inner city. Now, I am not a politician, but I think I could go to Washington in a week and get everybody holding hands and get this bill signed, because I talked to the Democratic leaders, and they want it. I talked to the

Republican leaders, and they want it. But since they are bred from childhood to fight with one another rather than get results, I would be glad to drop in and spend a little time and see if we couldn't build some bridges.

Now, results is what counts. The President can't order Congress around. Congress can't order the President around. That's not bad for a guy that's never been there, right? But you have to work together. Now, I have talked to the chairmen of the committees that want this; they're Democrats. The President wants it. But we can't get it because we sit here in gridlock because it's a campaign year. We didn't fund a lot of other things this year, like the savings and loan mess. That's another story that we're going to pay a big price for right after the election.

The facts are, though, the facts are the American people are hurting. These people are hurting in the inner cities. We're shipping the low-paying, quote, "low-paying" jobs overseas. What are low-paying jobs? Textiles, shoes, things like that that we say are yesterday's industries. They're tomorrow's industries in the inner city.

Let me say in my case, if I'm out of work, I'll cut grass tomorrow to take care of my family. I'll be happy to make shoes. I'll be happy to make clothing. I'll make sausage. You just give me a job. Put those jobs in the inner cities, instead of doing diplomatic deals and shipping them to China, where prison labor does the work.

Washington Gridlock

Ms. Simpson. Mr. Perot, everybody thought you won the first debate because you were plain-speaking, and you make it sound, oh, so simple. "We'll just do it." What makes you think that you're going to be able to get the Democrats and Republicans together any better than these guys?

Mr. Perot. If you asked me if I could fly a fighter plane or be an astronaut, I can't. I've spent my life creating jobs. It's something I know how to do, and very simply in the inner city, they're starved. You see, small businesses is the way to jump-start the inner city.

Ms. Simpson. Are you answering my question? [Laughter]

Mr. Perot. You want jobs in the inner city? Do you want jobs in the inner city? Is that your question?

Ms. Simpson. No, I want you to tell me how you're going to be able to get the Republicans and Democrats in Congress—

Mr. Perot. Oh, I'm sorry.

Ms. Simpson.—to work together better than these two gentlemen.

Mr. Perot. I've listened to both sides. If they would talk to one another instead of throwing rocks, I think we could get a lot done. And among other things, I would say, okay, over here in this Senate committee, to the chairman who is anxious to get this bill passed, to the President who's anxious, I'd say, "Rather than just yelling at one another, why don't we find out where we're apart; try to get together. Get the bill passed, and give the people the benefits, and not play party politics right now."

I think the press would follow that so closely that probably they would get it done. That's the way I would do it. I doubt if they'll give me the chance, but I will drop everything and go work on it.

Ms. Simpson. Okay. I have a question here.

Gun Control and Crime

Q. My question was originally for Governor Clinton, but I think I would welcome a response from all three candidates. As you are aware, crime is rampant in our cities. In the Richmond area, and I'm sure it's happened elsewhere, 12-year-olds are carrying guns to school. And I'm sure when our Founding Fathers wrote the Constitution, they did not mean for the right to bear arms to apply to 12-year-olds. So I'm asking, where do you stand on gun control, and what do you plan to do about it?

Ms. Simpson. Governor Clinton?

Governor Clinton. I support the right to keep and bear arms. I live in a State where over half the adults have hunting or fishing licenses or both. But I believe we have to have some way of checking handguns before they're sold, to check the criminal history, the mental health history, and the age of people who are buying them. Therefore, I support the Brady bill, which would impose a national waiting period, unless and until a State did what only Virginia has done now, which is to automate its records. Once you automate your records, then you don't have to have a waiting period, but at least you can check.

I also think we should have, frankly, restrictions on assault weapons, whose only purpose is to kill. We need to give the police a fighting chance in our urban areas where the gangs are building up.

The third thing I would say doesn't bear directly on gun control, but it's very important. We need more police on the street. There is a crime bill which would put more police on the street, which was killed for this session by a filibuster in the Senate, mostly by Republican Senators. I think it's a shame it didn't pass. I think it should be made the law, but it had the Brady bill in it, the waiting period.

I also believe that we should offer college scholarships to people who will agree to work them off as police officers. I think as we reduce our military forces, we should let people earn military retirement by coming out and working as police officers.

Thirty years ago there were three police officers on the street for every crime. Today, there are three crimes for every police officer. In the communities which have had real success putting police officers near schools where kids carry weapons, to get the weapons out of the schools, or on the same blocks, you've seen crime go down. In Houston there's been a 15-percent drop in the crime rate in the last year because of the work the Mayor did there in increasing the police force. So I know it can work. I've seen it happen.

Ms. Simpson. Thank you.
President Bush?

President Bush. I think you put your finger on a major problem. I talk about strengthening the American family. It's very hard to strengthen the family if people are scared to walk down to the corner store and send their kid down to get a loaf of bread. It's very hard. I have been fighting for very strong anticrime legislation: habeas corpus reform, so you don't have these endless appeals; so when somebody gets sentenced, hey, this is for real. I've been fighting for changes in the exclusionary rule, so if an honest cop stops somebody and makes a technical mistake, the criminal doesn't go away. I'll probably get into a fight in this room with some, but I happen to think that we need stronger death penalties for those that kill police officers.

Virginia's in the lead in this, as Governor Clinton properly said, on this identification system for firearms. I am not for national registration of firearms. Some of the States that have the toughest antigun laws have the highest levels of crime. I am for the right—

as the Governor says, I'm a sportsman, and I don't think you ought to eliminate all kinds of weapons.

But I was not for the bill that he was talking about because it was not tough enough on the criminal. I'm very pleased that the Fraternal Order of Police in Little Rock, Arkansas, endorsed me, because I think they see I'm trying to strengthen the anticrime legislation. We've got more money going out for local police than any previous administration.

So we've got to get it under control. And as one last point I'd make: drugs. We have got to win our national strategy against drugs, the fight against drugs. We're making some progress, doing a little better on interdiction. We're not doing as well amongst the people that get to be habitual drug users. The good news is, and I think it's true in Richmond, teenage use of cocaine is down substantially, 60 percent in the last couple of years. So we're making progress. But until we get that one done, we're not going to solve the neighborhood crime problem.

Ms. Simpson. Mr. Perot, there are young black males in America dying at unprecedented—

Mr. Perot. I would just make a comment on this.

Ms. Simpson. Yes, I'm getting—

Mr. Perot. Oh, you're going to elaborate. Okay, excuse me.

Ms. Simpson.—to the fact that homicide is the leading cause of death among young black males, 15 to 24 years old. What are you going to do to get the guns off the street?

Mr. Perot. On any program, and this includes crime, you'll find we have all kinds of great plans lying around that never get enacted into law and implemented. I don't care what it is, competitiveness, health care, crime, you name it. The Brady bill, I agree that it's a timid step in the right direction, but it won't fix it. So why pass a law that won't fix it?

Now, what it really boils down to is can you live—we have become so preoccupied with the rights of the criminal that we have forgotten the rights of the innocent. In our country, we have evolved to a point where we've put millions of innocent people in jail, because you go to the poor neighborhoods and they've put bars on their windows and bars on their doors and put themselves in jail to protect the things that they acquired legitimately. Now, that's where we are.

We have got to become more concerned about people who play by the rules and get the balance we require. This is going to take, first, building a consensus in grassroots America. Right from the bottom up, the American people have got to say they want it. And at that point, we can pick from a variety of plans and develop new plans. And the way you get things done is bury yourselves in the room with one another, put together the best program, take it to the American people, use the electronic town hall, the kind of thing you're doing here tonight, build a consensus, and then do it and then go on to the next one. But don't just sit here slow dancing for 4 years doing nothing.

Ms. Simpson. Thank you. Thank you, Mr. Perot.

We have a question up here.

Term Limits

Q. Please state your position on term limits. And if you are in favor of them, how will you get them enacted?

President Bush. Any order? I'll be glad to respond. I strongly support term limits for Members of the United States Congress. I believe it would return the Government closer to the people, the way that Ross Perot is talking about. The President's terms are limited to two, a total of 8 years. What's wrong with limiting the terms of Members of Congress to 12? Congress has gotten kind of institutionalized. For 38 years, one party has controlled the House of Representatives. And the result? A sorry little post office that can't do anything right and a bank that has more overdrafts than all of Chase Bank and Citibank put together.

We've got to do something about it. I think you get a certain arrogance, bureaucratic arrogance if people stay there too long. So I favor, strongly favor term limits. And how to get them passed? Send us some people that will pass the idea, and I think you will. I think the American people want it now. Everyplace I go, I talk about it, and I think they want it done.

Actually, you'd have to have some amendments to the Constitution because of the way the Constitution reads.

Ms. Simpson. Thank you.
Governor Clinton?

Governor Clinton. I know they're popular, but I'm against them. I'll tell you why. I believe, number one, it would pose a real problem for a lot of smaller States in the Congress who would have enough trouble now making sure their interests are heard. Number two, I think it would increase the influence of unelected staff members in the Congress who have too much influence already. I want to cut the size of the congressional staffs, but I think you're going to have too much influence there with people who were never elected who have lots of expertise.

Number three, if the people really have a mind to change, they can. You're going to have 120 to 150 new Members of Congress. Now, let me tell you what I favor instead. I favor strict controls on how much you can spend running for Congress, strict limits on political action committees, requirements that people running for Congress appear in open public debates like we're doing now. If you did that, you could take away the incumbent's advantage, because challengers like me would have a chance to run against incumbents like him for the House races and Senate races, and then the voters could make up their own mind without being subject to an unfair fight. So that's how I feel about it, and I think if we had the right kind of campaign reform, we'd get the changes you want.

Ms. Simpson. Mr. Perot, would you like to address term limitations?

Mr. Perot. Yes. Let me do it first on a personal level. If the American people send me up to do this job, I intend to be there one term. I do not intend to spend one minute of one day thinking about reelection. It is a matter of principle. My situation is unique, and I understand it. I will take absolutely no compensation. I go as their servant.

Now, I have set as strong an example as I can. And at that point, when we sit down over at Capitol Hill—tomorrow night I'm going to be talking about Government reform. It is a long subject; you wouldn't let me finish tonight. If you want to hear it, you can get it tomorrow night. [Laughter] But the point is, you'll hear it tomorrow night. But we have got to reform Government.

If you put term limits in and don't reform Government, you won't get the benefit you thought. It takes both. So we need to do the reforms and the term limits. And after we reform it, it won't be a lifetime career opportunity. Good people will go serve and then go back to their homes, and not become for-

eign lobbyists and cash in at 30,000 bucks a month, and then take time off to run some President's campaign.

They're all nice people. They're just in a bad system. I don't think there are any villains, but boy, is the system rotten.

Ms. Simpson. Thank you very much.
We have a question over here.

Health Care Reform

Q. I'd like to ask Governor Clinton, do you attribute the rising costs of health care to the medical profession itself, or do you think the problem lies elsewhere? And what specific proposals do you have to tackle this problem?

Governor Clinton. I've had more people talk to me about their health care problems, I guess, than anything else. All across America, people who have lost their jobs, lost their businesses, had to give up their jobs because of sick children—so let me try to answer you in this way.

Let's start with the premise. We spend 30 percent more of our income than any nation on Earth on health care. And yet, we insure fewer people. We have 35 million people without any insurance at all, and I see them all the time. One hundred thousand Americans a month have lost their health insurance just in the last 4 years.

So if you analyze where we're out of line with other countries you come up with the following conclusions: Number one, we spend at least $60 billion a year on insurance, administrative costs, bureaucracy, and Government regulation that wouldn't be spent in any other nation. So we have to have, in my judgment, a drastic simplification of the basic health insurance policies of this country, be very comprehensive for everybody. Employers would cover their employees. Government would cover the unemployed.

Number two, I think you have to take on specifically the insurance companies and require them to make some significant change in the way they rate people in the big community pools. I think you have to tell the pharmaceutical companies they can't keep raising drug prices at 3 times the rate of inflation. I think you have to take on medical fraud. I think you have to help doctors stop practicing defensive medicine. I've recommended that our doctors be given a set of national practice guidelines and that if they follow those guidelines, that raises the presumption that they didn't do anything wrong. I think you have to have a system of primary preventive clinics in our inner cities and our rural areas so people can have access to health care.

But the key is to control the costs and maintain the quality. To do that, you need a system of managed competition where all of us are covered in big groups, and we can choose our doctors and our hospitals from a wide range, but there is an incentive to control costs. And I think there has to be—I think Mr. Perot and I agree on this—there has to be a national commission of health care providers and health care consumers that set ceilings to keep health costs in line with inflation plus population growth.

Now, let me say, some people say we can't do this, but Hawaii does it. They cover 98 percent of their people, and their insurance premiums are much cheaper than the rest of America. So does Rochester, New York. They now have a plan to cover everybody, and their premiums are two-thirds the rest of the country. This is very important. It's a big human problem and a devastating economic problem for America. I'm going to send a plan to do this within the first 100 days of my Presidency. It's terribly important.

Ms. Simpson. Thank you. Sorry to cut you short, but, President Bush, health care reform.

President Bush. I just have to say something. I don't want to stampede—Ross was very articulate. Across the country, I don't want anybody to stampede to cut the President's salary off altogether. Barbara is sitting over here, and I—[laughter]—but what I have proposed, 10 percent cut, downsize the Government, and we can get that done.

She asked the question, I think, is whether the health care profession was to blame. No. One thing to blame is these malpractice lawsuits. They are breaking the system. It costs $20 to $25 billion a year, and I want to see those outrageous claims capped. Doctors don't dare to deliver babies sometimes because they're afraid that somebody's going to sue them. People don't dare, medical practitioners, to help somebody along the highway that are hurt because they're afraid that some lawyer's going to come along and get a big lawsuit.

So you can't blame the practitioners or the health—and my program is this: Keep the Government as far out of it as possible, make insurance available to the poorest of the poor through vouchers, next range in the income bracket through tax credits, and get on about the business of pooling insurance. A great, big company can buy—Ross has got a good size company, been very successful. He can buy insurance cheaper than mom-and-pop stores on the corner. But if those mom-and-pop stores all get together and pool, they, too, can bring the cost of insurance down.

So I want to keep the quality of health care. That means keep Government out of it. I don't like this idea of these boards. It all sounds to me like you're going to have some Government setting price. I want competition, and I want to pool the insurance and take care of it that way.

Here's the other point. I think medical care should go with the person. If you leave a business, I think your insurance should go with you to some other business. You shouldn't be worrying if you get a new job as to whether that's going to—and part of our plan is to make it what they call portable, big word, but that means if you're working for the Jones Company and you go to the Smith Company, your insurance goes with you. I think it's a good program. I'm really excited about getting it done, too.

Ms. Simpson. Mr. Perot?

Mr. Perot. We have the most expensive health care system in the world. Twelve percent of our gross national product goes to health care. Our industrial competitors, who are beating us in competition, spend less and have better health care. Japan spends a little over 6 percent of its gross national product; Germany spends 8 percent.

It's fascinating. You bought a front-row box seat, and you're not happy with your health care. You're saying tonight we've got bad health care but very expensive health care. Folks, here's why. Go home and look in the mirror. You own this country, but you have no voice in it the way it's organized now. If you want to have a high-risk experience comparable to bungee jumping—[laughter]—go into Congress sometime when they're working on this kind of legislation, when the lobbyists are running up and down the halls. Wear your safety-toe shoes when you go. [Laughter] And as a private citizen, believe me, you are looked on as a major nuisance. The facts are, you now have a Government that comes at you. You're supposed to have a Government that comes from you.

Now, there are all kinds of good ideas, brilliant ideas, terrific ideas on health care. None of them ever get implemented because—let me give you an example. A Senator runs every 6 years. He's got to raise 20,000 bucks a week to have enough money to run. Who's he going to listen to, us or the folks running up and down the aisle with money, the lobbyists, the PAC money? He listens to them. Who do they represent? Health care industry. Not us.

Now, you've got to have a Government that comes from you again. You've got to reassert your ownership in this country, and you've got to completely reform our Government. And at that point, they'll just be like apples falling out of a tree. The programs will be good because the elected officials will be listening, too. I said the other night I was all ears and I would listen to any good idea. I think we ought to do plastic surgery on a lot of these guys so that they're all ears, too, and listen to you. Then you get what you want, and shouldn't you? You paid for it. Why shouldn't you get what you want as opposed to what some lobbyist cuts a deal, writes the little piece in the law, and it goes through. That's the way the game's played now. Until you change it, you're going to be unhappy.

Ms. Simpson. Thank you.

Governor Clinton, you wanted one brief point.

Governor Clinton. One brief point. We have elections so people can make decisions about this. The point I want to make to you is, a bipartisan commission reviewed my plan and the Bush plan and concluded—there were as many Republicans as Democratic health care experts on it—they concluded that my plan would cover everybody, and his would leave 27 million behind by the year 2000, and that my plan in the next 12 years would save $2.2 trillion in public and private money to reinvest in this economy. The average family would save $1,200 a year under the plan that I offered, without any erosion in the quality of health care. So I ask you to look at that.

You have to vote for somebody with a plan. That's what you have elections for. If people say, "Well, he got elected to do this," and then the Congress says, "Okay, I'm going to do it." That's what the election was about.

Ms. Simpson. Brief, Governor Clinton. Thank you.

We have a question right here.

Personal Impact of the Economy

Q. Yes, how has the national debt personally affected each of your lives? And if it hasn't, how can you honestly find a cure for the economic problems of the common people if you have no experience in what's ailing them?

Mr. Perot. May I answer it?

Ms. Simpson. Well, Mr. Perot, yes, of course.

Mr. Perot. Who do you want to start with?

Q. My question is for each of you, so—

Mr. Perot. Yes, it caused me to disrupt my private life and my business to get involved in this activity. That's how much I care about it. Believe me, if you knew my family and if you knew the private life I have, you would agree in a minute that that's a whole lot more fun than getting involved in politics.

I have lived the American dream. I came from a very modest background. Nobody's been luckier than I've been, all the way across the spectrum, and the greatest riches of all are my wife and children. It's true of any family. But I want all the children, I want these young people up here to be able to start with nothing but an idea like I did and build a business. But they've got to have a strong basic economy. And if you're in debt, it's like having a ball and chain around you.

I just figure as lucky as I've been, I owe it to them, and I owe it to the future genera-

tions. And on a very personal basis, I owe it to my children and grandchildren.

Ms. Simpson. Thank you, Mr. Perot.
Mr. President.

President Bush. Well, I think the national debt affects everybody. Obviously, it has a lot to do with interest rates—

Ms. Simpson. She's saying you personally.

Q. You, on a personal basis, how has it affected you?

Ms. Simpson. Has it affected you personally?

President Bush. Well, I'm sure it has. I love my grandchildren. I want to think that—

Q. How?

President Bush. I want to think that they're going to be able to afford an education. I think that that's an important part of being a parent. If the question—maybe I get it wrong. Are you suggesting that if somebody has means that the national debt doesn't affect them?

Q. What I'm saying—

President Bush. I'm not sure I get it. Help me with the question, and I'll try to answer it.

Q. Well, I've had friends that have been laid off in jobs—

President Bush. Yes.

Q. I know people who cannot afford to pay the mortgage on their homes, their car payment. I have personal problems with the national debt. But how has it affected you? And if you have no experience in it, how can you help us if you don't know what we're feeling?

Ms. Simpson. I think she means more the recession, the economic problems today the country faces rather than—

President Bush. Well, listen, you ought to be in the White House for a day and hear what I hear and see what I see and read the mail I read and touch the people that I touch from time to time.

I was in the Lomax AME Church. It's a black church just outside of Washington, DC, and I read in the bulletin about teenage pregnancies, about the difficulty that families are having to make ends meet. I talked to parents. I mean, you've got to care. Everybody cares if people aren't doing well. But I don't think it's fair to say you haven't had cancer, therefore you don't know what it's like. I don't think it's fair to say, whatever it is, if you haven't been hit by it personally. But everybody's affected by the debt, because of the tremendous interest that goes into paying on that debt, everything's more expensive. Everything comes out of your pocket and my pocket. So it's that. But I think in terms of the recession, of course, you feel it when you're President of the United States. That's why I'm trying to do something about it by stimulating the export, investing more, better education system.

Thank you. I'm glad you clarified it.

Governor Clinton. Tell me how it's affected you again? You know people who have lost their jobs and lost their homes?

Q. Yes.

Governor Clinton. Well, I've been Governor of a small State for 12 years. I'll tell you how it's affected me. Every year, Congress and the President sign laws that make us do more things; it gives us less money to do it with. I see people in my State, middle-class people, their taxes have gone up from Washington and their services have gone down, while the wealthy have gotten tax cuts.

I have seen what's happened in this last 4 years when, in my State, when people lose their jobs there's a good chance I'll know them by their names. When a factory closes, I know the people who ran it. When the businesses go bankrupt, I know them. And I've been out here for 13 months, meeting in meetings just like this ever since October with people like you all over America, people that have lost their jobs, lost their livelihood, lost their health insurance.

What I want you to understand is, the national debt is not the only cause of that. It is because America has not invested in its people. It is because we have not grown. It is because we've had 12 years of trickle-down economics. We've gone from 1st to 12th in the world in wages. We've had 4 years where we've produced no private sector jobs. Most people are working harder for less money than they were making 10 years ago. It is because we are in the grip of a failed economic theory. And this decision you're about to make better be about what kind of economic theory you want, not just people saying, "I want to go fix it," but what are we going to do.

What I think we have to do is invest in American jobs, in American education, control American health care costs, and bring the American people together again.

Ms. Simpson. Thank you, Governor Clinton. We are a little more than halfway through this program, and I'm glad that we're getting the diversity of questions that we are.

And I don't want to forget these folks on the wings over here, so let's go over here. Do you have a question?

Entitlement Programs

Q. Yes, I do. My name is Ben Smith. I work in the financial field, counseling retirees. And I'm personally concerned about three major areas. One is the Social Security Administration or trust fund is projected to be insolvent by the year 2036. We've funded the trust fund with IOU's in the form of Treasury bonds. The pension guaranty fund which backs up our private retirement plans for retirees is projected to be bankrupt by the year 2026, not to mention the cutbacks by private companies. And Medicare is projected to be bankrupt maybe as soon as 1997.

I would like from each of you a specific response as to what you intend to do for retirees relative to these issues, not generalities but specifics, because I think they're very disturbing issues.

Ms. Simpson. President Bush, may we start with you?

President Bush. Well, the Social Security— you're an expert and I could, I'm sure, learn from you the details of the pension guaranty fund and the Social Security fund. The Social Security system was fixed, about 5 years, and I think it's projected out to be sound beyond that. So at least we have time to work with it.

But on all of these things, a sound economy is the only way to get it going. Growth in the economy is going to add to the overall prosperity and wealth. I can't give you a specific answer on pension guaranty fund. All I know is that we have firm Government credit to guarantee the pensions, and that is very important.

But the full faith in credit of the United States, in spite of our difficulties, is still pretty good. It's still the most respected credit. So I would simply say, as these dates get close you're going to have to reorganize and refix as we did with the Social Security fund. I think that's the only answer. But the more immediate answer is to do what this lady was suggesting we do, and that is to get this deficit down and get on without adding to the woes, and then restructure.

One thing I've called for that has been stymied, and I'll keep on working for it, is a whole financial reform legislation. It is absolutely essential in terms of bringing our banking system and credit system into the new age instead of having it living back in the dark ages, and it's a big fight. I don't want to give my friend Ross another shot at me here, but I am fighting with the Congress to get this through.

You can't just go up and say, "I'm going to fix it." You've got some pretty strong-willed guys up there that argue with you. But that's what the election's about; I agree with the Governor. That's what the election is about. Sound fiscal policy is the best answer, I think, to all the three problems you mentioned.

Ms. Simpson. Thank you.
Mr. Perot?

Mr. Perot. Just on a broad issue here. When you're trying to solve a problem, you get the best plans. You have a raging debate about those plans. Then out of that debate, with leadership, comes consensus. And if the plans are huge and complex, like health care, I would urge you to implement pilot programs. Like the older carpenter says, measure twice, cut once. Let's make sure this thing's as good as we all think it is at the end of the meeting.

Then, finally, our Government passes laws and freezes the plan in concrete. Anybody that's ever built a successful business will tell you, you optimize, optimize, optimize after you put something into effect. The reason Medicare and Medicaid are a mess is we froze them. Everybody knows how to fix them. There are people all over the Federal Government if they could just touch it with a screwdriver could fix it.

Now, back over here. See, we've got a $4 trillion debt, and only in America would you have $2.8 trillion of it, or 70 percent of it, financed 5 years or less. Now, that's another thing for you to think about when you go home tonight. You don't finance long-term debt with short-term money. Why did our Government do it? To get the interest rates down. A one-percent increase in interest rates in that $2.8 trillion is $28 billion a year.

Now, when you look at what Germany pays for money and what we don't pay for money, you realize there's quite a spread, right? You realize this is a temporary thing and there's going to be another sucking sound that runs our deficit through the roof.

You know, and everybody's ducking it so I'm going to say it, that we are not letting that surplus stay in the bank. We are not investing that surplus like a pension fund. We are spending that surplus to make the deficit look smaller to you than it really is. Now, that puts you in jail in corporate America if you kept books that way, but in Government it's just kind of the way things are. That's because it comes at you, not from you.

Now then, that money needs to be—they don't even pay interest on it, they just write a note for the interest.

Ms. Simpson. Mr. Perot, can you wrap it up?

Mr. Perot. Sure. But the point, see, do you want to fix the problem or sound-bite it? I understand the importance of time, but see, here's how we get to this mess we're in. This is just 1 of 1,000.

Ms. Simpson. But we've got to be fair.

Mr. Perot. Now then, to nail it, there's one way out, a growing, expanding job base, a growing, expanding job base to generate the funds and the tax revenues to pay off the mess and rebuild America. We've got to double hit. If we're $4 trillion down, we should have everything perfect, but we don't. We've got to pay it off and build

money to renew it, spend money to renew it, and that's going to take a growing, expanding job base. That is priority one in this country. Put everybody that's breathing to work. I'd love to be out of workers and have to import them, like some of our international competitors.

Ms. Simpson. Mr. Perot, I'm sorry, I'm going to—

Mr. Perot. Sorry.

Ms. Simpson. And I don't want to sound-bite you, but we are trying to be fair to everyone.

Mr. Perot. No, absolutely. I apologize.

Ms. Simpson. All right, Governor Clinton.

Governor Clinton. I think I remember the question. [Laughter] Let me say first of all, I want to answer your specific question, but first of all, we all agree that there should be a growing economy. What you have to decide is who's got the best economic plan. We all have ideas out there, and Mr. Bush has a record. I don't want you to read my lips, and I sure don't want you to read his. [Laughter] I do hope you will read our plans. Now, specifically—

President Bush. [Inaudible]—first rule?

Governor Clinton.—one, on Medicare, it is not true that everyone knows how to fix it; there are different ideas. The Bush plan, the Perot plan, the Clinton—we have different ideas. I am convinced, having studied health care for a year, hard, and talking to hundreds and hundreds of people all across America, that you cannot control the costs of Medicare until you control the cost of private health care and public health care with managed competition, a ceiling on cost, and radical reorganization of the insurance markets. You've got to do that. We've got to get those costs down.

Number two, with regard to Social Security, that program, a lot of you may not know this: It produces a $70 billion surplus a year. Social Security is in surplus $70 billion. Six increases in the payroll tax—that means people with incomes of $51,000 a year or less pay a disproportionately high share of the Federal tax burden, which is why I want some middle-class tax relief.

What do we have to do? By the time the century turns, we have got to have our deficit under control, we have to work out of that so surplus is building up, so when the baby boomers like me retire, we're okay.

Number three, on the pension funds, I don't know as much about it, but I will say this: What I will do is to bring in the pension experts of the country, take a look at it, and strengthen the pension requirements further, because it's not just enough to have the guarantee. We had a guarantee on the S&L's, right? We had a guarantee, and what happened? You picked up a $500 billion bill because of the dumb way the Federal Government deregulated it. So I think we are going to have to change and strengthen the pension requirements on private retirement plans.

Ms. Simpson. Thank you. I think we have a question here on international affairs, hopefully.

Foreign Affairs

Q. We've come to a position where we're in the new world order. And I'd like to know what the candidates feel our position is in this new world order and what our responsibilities are as a superpower.

Ms. Simpson. Mr. President?

President Bush. We have come to that position. Since I became President, 43, 44 countries have gone democratic. No longer totalitarian, no longer living under dictatorship or communist rule. This is exciting. This new world order to me means freedom and democracy.

I think we will have a continuing responsibility, as the only remaining superpower, to stay involved. If we pull back in some isolation and say we don't have to do our share, or more than our share, anymore, I believe you're going to just ask for conflagration that we'll get involved in in the future. NATO, for example, has kept the peace for many, many years. I want to see us keep fully staffed in NATO so we'll continue to guarantee the peace in Europe.

But the exciting thing is the fear of nuclear war is down. You hear all the bad stuff that's happened on my watch. I hope people will recognize that this is something pretty good for mankind. I hope they'll think it's good that democracy and freedom is on the move. And we're going to stay engaged, as long as I am President, working to improve things.

You know, it's so easy now to say, hey, cut out foreign aid, we've got a problem at home. I think the United States has to still have the Statue of Liberty as a symbol of caring for others. We're right this very minute, we're sending supplies in to help these little starving kids in Somalia. It's the United States that's taken the lead in humanitarian aid into Bosnia. We're doing this all around the world.

And yes, we've got problems at home. I think I've got a good plan to help fix those problems at home. But because of our leadership, because we didn't listen to the freeze, the nuclear freeze group—do you remember: "Freeze it," back in about in the late seventies. "Freeze, don't touch it. We're going to lock it in now, or else we'll have war." President Reagan said, "No. Peace through strength." It worked. The Soviet Union is no more. Now we're working to help them become totally democratic through the FREEDOM Support Act that I led on. A great Democratic Ambassador, Bob Strauss over there, Jim Baker, all of us got this thing passed, through cooperation, Ross. It worked with cooperation. And you're for that, I'm sure, helping Russia become democratic.

So the new world order to me means freedom and democracy, keep engaged, do not pull back into isolation. We are the United States, and we have a responsibility to lead and to guarantee the security. If it hadn't been for us, Saddam Hussein would be sitting on top of three-fifths of the oil supply of the world, and he'd have nuclear weapons. Only the United States could do this.

Excuse me, Carole.

Ms. Simpson. Thank you.
Mr. Perot.

Mr. Perot. Well, it's cost-effective to help Russia succeed in its revolution. It's pennies on the dollar compared to going back to the cold war. Russia's still very unstable. They could go back to square one and worse. All the nuclear weapons are not dismantled. I'm particularly concerned about the intercontinental weapons, the ones that can hit us. We've got agreements, but they're still there. With all this instability and breaking into Republics and all the Middle Eastern countries going over there and shopping for weapons, we've got our work cut out for us. So we need to stay right on top of that and constructively help them move toward democracy and capitalism.

We have to have money to do that. We have to have our people at work. See, for 45 years, we were preoccupied with the Red Army. I suggest now that our number one preoccupation is red ink in our country. And we've got to put our people back to work so

that we can afford to do these things we want to do in Russia.

We cannot be the policeman for the world any longer. We spend $300 billion a year defending the world. Germany and Japan spend around $30 billion apiece. It's neat. If I can get you to defend me and I can spend all my money building industry, that's a home run for me. Coming out of World War II, it made sense. Now the other superpowers need to do their part.

I'll close on this point: You can't be a superpower unless you're an economic superpower. If we're not an economic superpower, we are a used-to-be, and we will no longer be a force for good throughout the world. If nothing else gets you excited about rebuilding our industrial base, maybe that will, because job one is to put our people back to work.

Ms. Simpson. Governor Clinton, the President mentioned Saddam Hussein. Your vice president and you have had some words about the President and Saddam Hussein. Would you care to comment?

Governor Clinton. I'd rather answer her question first, and then I'll be glad to, because the question you ask is important. The end of the cold war brings an incredible opportunity for change, the winds of freedom blowing around the world, Russia demilitarizing. It also requires us to maintain some continuity, some bipartisan American commitment to certain principles.

I would just say there are three things that I would like to say. Number one, we do have to maintain the world's strongest defense. We may differ about what the elements of that are. I think the defense needs to be with fewer people and permanent armed services, but with greater mobility on the land, in the air, and on the sea, with a real dedication to continuing development of high-technology weaponry and well-trained people. I think we're going to have to work to stop the proliferation of weapons of mass destruction. We've got to keep going until all those nuclear weapons in Russia are gone and the other Republics.

Number two, if you don't rebuild the economic strength of this country at home, we won't be a superpower. We can't have any more instances like what happened when Mr. Bush went to Japan and the Japanese Prime Minister said he felt sympathy for our country. We have to be the strongest economic power in the world. That's what got me into this race, so we could rebuild the American economy.

Number three, we need to be a force for freedom and democracy. We need to use our unique position to support freedom, whether it's in Haiti or in China or in any other place, wherever the seeds of freedom are sprouting. We can't impose it, but we need to nourish it. That's the kind of thing that I would do as President, follow those three commitments into the future.

Ms. Simpson. Okay, we have a question up there.

Education

Q. We've talked a lot tonight about creating jobs. But we have an awful lot of high school graduates who don't know how to read a ruler, who cannot fill out an application for a job. How can we create high-paying jobs with the education system we have? And what would you do to change it?

Ms. Simpson. Who would like to begin? The education President?

President Bush. I'd be delighted to, because you can't do it the old way. You can't do it with the school bureaucracy controlling everything. And that's why we have a new program that I hope people have heard about. It's being worked now in 1,700 communities—I bypassed Congress on this one, Ross—1,700 communities across the country. It's called America 2000. It literally says to the communities: Reinvent the schools, not just the bricks and mortar but the curriculum and everything else. Think anew. We have a concept called the New American School Corporation, where we're doing exactly that.

So I believe that we've got to get the power in the hands of the teachers, not the teachers union—what's happening up there? [Laughter] So our America 2000 program also says this: It says let's give parents the choice of a public, private, or religious school. And it works. It works in Milwaukee. A Democratic woman up there taking the lead in this, the Mayor up there on the program, and the schools that are not chosen are improved. Competition does that.

So we've got to innovate through school choice. We've got to innovate through this America 2000 program. But she is absolutely right. The programs that we've been trying where you control everything and mandate it from Washington don't work.

The Governors—and I believe Governor Clinton was in on this, but I don't want to invoke him here—but they come to me, and they say, please get the Congress to stop passing so many mandates telling us how to control things. We know better how to do it in California or Texas or wherever it is. So this is what our program is all about. I believe—you're right onto something—that if we don't change the education, we're not going to be able to compete.

Federal funding for education is up substantially. Pell Grants are up. But it isn't going to get the job done if we don't change K through 12.

Ms. Simpson. Governor Clinton?

Governor Clinton. First of all, let me say that I've spent more of my time in life on this in the last 12 years than any other issue. Seventy percent of my State's money goes to public schools. I was really honored when *Time* magazine said that our schools have shown more improvement than any other State in the country except one other. They named two States showing real strides forward in the eighties. So I care a lot about this, and I've spent countless hours in schools.

But let me start with what you've said. I agree with some of what Mr. Bush said, but it's nowhere near enough. We live in a world where what you earn depends on what you can learn, where the average 18-year-old will change jobs eight times in a lifetime, and where none of us can promise any of you that what you now do for a living is absolutely safe from now on. Nobody running can promise that. There's too much change in the world.

So what should we do? Let me reel some things off real quick, because you said you wanted specifics. Number one, under my program we would provide matching funds to States to teach everybody with a job to read in the next 5 years and give everybody with a job a chance to get a high school diploma, in big places, on the job.

Number two, we would provide 2-year apprenticeship programs to high school graduates who don't go to college, in community colleges or on the job.

Number three, we'd open the doors to college education to high school graduates without regard to income. They could borrow the money and pay it back as a percentage of their income over the couple of years of service to our Nation here at home.

Number four, we would fully fund the Head Start program to get little kids off to a good start.

Five, I would have an aggressive program of school reform. More choices in the—I favor public schools or these new charter schools. We can talk about that if you want. I don't think we should spend tax money on private schools, but I favor public school choice. I favor radical decentralization in giving more power to better trained principals and teachers with parent councils to control their schools. Those things would revolutionize American education and take us to the top economically.

Ms. Simpson. Thank you, Governor Clinton. What the question is—what is it going to cost?

Q. What is it going to cost?

Ms. Simpson. What is it going to cost?

Governor Clinton. In 6 years—I budget all this in my budget. In 6 years, the college program would cost $8 billion over and above what—the present student loan program costs 4. You pay $3 billion for busted loans, because we don't have an automatic recovery system, and a billion dollars in bank fees. So the net cost will be $8 billion 6 years from now, in a trillion-plus budget: not very much.

The other stuff, all the other stuff I mentioned costs much less than that. The Head Start program, full funding, would cost about $5 billion more. It's all covered in my budget from the plans that I've laid out, from raising taxes on families with incomes above $200,000, and asking foreign corporations to pay the same tax that American corporations do on the same income; from $140 billion in budget cuts, including what I think are very prudent cuts in the defense budget. It's all covered in the plan.

Ms. Simpson. Mr. Perot, you on education, please.

Mr. Perot. Yes. I've got scars to show from being around education reform. The first words you need to say in every city and State and just draw a line in the sand—public schools exist for the benefit of the children—you're going to see a lot of people fall over it, because any time you're spending $199 billion a year, somebody's getting it, and the children get lost in the process. So that's step one.

Keep in mind in 1960 when our schools were the envy of the world, we were spending $16 billion on them. Now we spend more than any other nation in the world, $199 billion a year, and rank at the bottom of the industrialized world in terms of educational achievement. One more time, you've bought a front-row box seat and got a third-rate performance. This is a Government that's not serving you.

By and large, it should be local. The more local, the better. Interesting phenomenon, small towns have good schools, big cities have terrible schools. The best people in a small town will serve on the school board. You get into big cities, it's political patronage, stepping stones. You get the job, give your relatives the janitor's job at $57,000 a year, more than the teachers make. And with luck, they clean the cafeteria once a week. [Laughter]

Now, you're paying for that. Those schools belong to you, and we put up with that. As long as you put up with that, that's what you're going to get. These folks are just dividing up 199 billion bucks, and the children get lost.

If I could wish for one thing for great public schools, it would be a strong family unit in every home. Nothing will ever replace that. You say, "Well, gee, what are you going to do about that?" Well, the White House is a bully pulpit, and I think we ought to be pounding on the table every day. There's nothing—the most efficient unit of Government we'll ever know is a strong, loving family unit.

Next thing. You need small schools, not big schools. A little school, everybody's somebody. Individualism is very important. These big factories, everybody told me they were cost-effective. I did a study on it. They're cost-ineffective. Five thousand students: why is a high school that big? One reason. Sooner or later, you get 11 more boys that can run like the devil, that weigh 250 pounds, and they might win district. Now, that has nothing to do with learning.

Secondly, across Texas, typically half the school day was nonacademic pursuits. In one place, it was 35 percent. In Texas, you could have unlimited absences to go to livestock shows. Found a boy—excuse me, but this gives the flavor—a boy in Houston kept a chicken in the bathtub in downtown Houston. Missed 65 days going to livestock shows. Finally had to come back to school, the chicken lost his feathers. That's the only way we got him back. [Laughter] Now, that's your tax money being wasted.

Now, neighborhood schools. It is terrible to bus tiny little children across town. It is particularly terrible to take poor, tiny little children and wait until the first grade and bus them across town to Mars where the children know their numbers, know their letters, have had every advantage; the end of the first day, that little child wants out.

I close on this: You've got to have world-class teachers, world-class books. If you ever got close to how textbooks were selected, you wouldn't want to go back the second day. I don't have time to tell you the stories. [Laughter]

Ms. Simpson. No, you don't. [Laughter]

Mr. Perot. Finally. If we don't fix this, you're right, we can't have the industries of tomorrow unless we have the best educated work force. And here, for the disadvantaged children, you've got to have early childhood development, the cheapest money you'll ever spend. The first contact should be with the mother when she's pregnant. That little child needs to be loved and hugged and nurtured and made to feel special, like you children were. They learn to think well or poorly of themselves in the first 18 months.

Ms. Simpson. Thank you, Mr. Perot.

Mr. Perot. Within the first few years, they either learn how to learn or don't learn how to learn. If they don't, they wind up in prison, and it costs more to keep them in prison than it does to send them to Harvard. I rest my case.

Ms. Simpson. Thank you. President Bush, you wanted to add something.

President Bush. I just had a word of clarification because of something Governor Clinton said. My school choice program, "GI bill" for kids, does not take public money and give it to private schools. It does what the GI bill itself did when I came out of World War II. It takes public money and gives it to families or individuals to choose the school they want. Where it's been done, those schools, like in Rochester, those schools that weren't chosen find that they then compete and do better. So I think it's worth a shot.

We've got a pilot program. It ought to be tried: school choice, public, private, or religious, not to the schools, but to—46 percent of the teachers in Chicago, public schoolteachers, send their kids to private school. Now, I think we ought to try to help families and see if it will do what I think, make all schools better.

Governor Clinton. I just want to mention if I could—

Ms. Simpson. Very briefly.

Governor Clinton. Very briefly. Involving the parents in the preschool education of their kids, even if they're poor and uneducated, can make a huge difference. We have a big program in my State that teaches mothers or fathers to teach their kids to get ready for school. It's the most successful thing we've ever done.

Just a fact clarification real quickly. We do not spend a higher percentage of our income on public education than every other country. There are nine countries that spend more than we do on public education. We spend more on education because we spend so much more on colleges. But if you look at public education alone, and you take into account that we have more racial diversity and more poverty, it makes a big difference. There are great public schools where there are public school choice, accountability, and brilliant principals. I'll just mention one, the Beasley Academic Center in Chicago. I commend it to anybody. It's as good as any private school in the country.

Ms. Simpson. We have very little time left, and it occurs to me that we have talked all this time and there has not been one question about some of the racial tensions and ethnic tensions in America. Is there anyone in this audience that would like to pose a question to the candidates on this? Yes?

Women or Minority Presidential Candidates

Q. What I'd like to know, and this is to any of the three of you, is aside from the recent accomplishments of your party, aside from those accomplishments in racial representation and without citing any of your current appointments or successful elections, when do you estimate your party will both nominate and elect an Afro-American and female ticket to the Presidency of the United States?

Ms. Simpson. Governor Clinton, why don't you answer that first.

Governor Clinton. Well, I don't have any idea, but I hope it will happen sometime in my lifetime.

Q. I do, too.

Governor Clinton. I believe that this country is electing more and more African-Americans and Latinos and Asian-Americans who are representing districts that are themselves not necessarily of a majority of their race. The American people are beginning to vote across racial lines, and I hope it will happen more and more. More and more women are being elected. Look at all these women Senate candidates we have here. You know, according to my mother and my wife and my daughter, this world would be a lot better place if women were running it most of the time.

I do think there are special experiences and judgments and backgrounds and understandings that women bring to this process, by the way. This lady said here, how have you been affected by the economy? I mean, women know what it's like to be paid an unequal amount for equal work; they know what's it like not to have flexible working hours; they know what it's like not to have family leave or child care. So I think it would be a good thing for America if it happened, and I think it will happen in my lifetime.

Ms. Simpson. Okay. I'm sorry we have just a little bit of time left. Let's try to get responses from each of them.
President Bush or Mr. Perot?

President Bush. I think if Barbara Bush were running this year she'd be elected. [Laughter] But it's too late.

You don't want us to mention appointees but when you see the quality of people in our administration, see how Colin Powell performed—I say administration, he's in the military.

Q. I said when's your guess?

President Bush. You weren't impressed with the fact that he performed—

Q. Excuse me, I'm extremely impressed with that.

President Bush. Yes, but wouldn't that suggest to the American people then here's a quality person, if he decided that he could automatically—

Q. Sure. I just wanted to know—

President Bush.—get the nomination of either party? Huh?

Q. I'm totally impressed with that. I just wanted to know is when is your guess of when.

President Bush. Oh, I see. You mean time?

Q. Yeah.

President Bush. I don't know. Starting after 4 years. [Laughter] No, I think you'll see—

Ms. Simpson. Mr. Perot?

President Bush. I think you'll see more minority candidates and women candidates coming forward.

Ms. Simpson. Thank you.

President Bush. This is supposed to be the year of the women in the Senate. Let's see how they do. I hope a lot of them lose.

Ms. Simpson. Mr. Perot, I don't want to cut you up any more, but we only have a minute left.

Mr. Perot. I have a fearless forecast. Unless he just won't do it, Colin Powell will be on somebody's ticket 4 years from now. Right? Right? You wanted—that's it. Four years.

Ms. Simpson. How about a woman?

Mr. Perot. Now, if he won't be, General Waller would be a—you say, why do you keep picking military people? These are people that I just happened to know and have a high regard for. I'm sure there are hundreds of others.

President Bush. How about Dr. Lou Sullivan?

Mr. Perot. Absolutely.

President Bush. Yeah, good man.

Mr. Perot. Absolutely.

Ms. Simpson. What about a woman?

Mr. Perot. Oh, oh.

President Bush. My candidate's right back there.

Mr. Perot. I can think of many.

Ms. Simpson. Many?

Mr. Perot. Absolutely.

Ms. Simpson. When?

Mr. Perot. How about Sandra Day O'Connor as an example? Dr. Bernadine Healy.

Ms. Simpson. Good.

Mr. Perot. National Institutes of Health. All right, I'll yield the floor. Name some more.

President Bush. Good Republicans. [Laughter]

Ms. Simpson. Thank you. I want to apologize to our audience because there were 209 people here, and there were 209 questions. We only got to a fraction of them, and I'm sorry to those of you that didn't get to ask your questions, but we must move to the conclusion of the program.

It is time now for the 2-minute closing statements. By prior agreement, President Bush will go first.

Closing Statements

President Bush. May I ask for an exception because I think we owe Carole Simpson a—anybody who can stand in between these three characters here and get the job done—we owe her a round of applause. [Applause] Just don't take it out of my time.

Ms. Simpson. That's right.

President Bush. I feel strongly about it, but I don't want it to come out of my time.

Ms. Simpson. That's right. [Laughter]

President Bush. No, but let me just say to the American people: In 2 1/2 weeks, we're going to choose who should sit in this Oval Office, who to lead the economic recovery, who to be the leader of the free world, who to get the deficit down. Three ways to do that: one is to raise taxes; one is to reduce spending, controlling that mandatory spending; another one is to invest and save and to stimulate growth.

I do not want to raise taxes. I differ with the two here on that. I'm just not going to do that. I do believe that we need to control mandatory spending. I think we need to invest and save more. I believe that we need to educate better and retrain better. I believe that we need to export more, so I'll keep working for export agreements where we can sell more abroad. And I believe that we must strengthen the family. We've got to strengthen the family.

Now, let me pose this question to America: If in the next 5 minutes a television announcer came on and said, there is a major international crisis, there is a major threat to the world, or in this country a major threat, my question is, if you were appointed to name one of the three of us, who would you choose? Who has the perseverance, the character, the integrity, the maturity to get the job done? I hope I'm that person.

Thank you very, very much.

Ms. Simpson. Thank you, Mr. President. And now a closing statement from Mr. Perot.

Mr. Perot. If the American people want to do it and not talk about it, then I'm one person they ought to consider. If they just want to keep slow dancing and talk about it and not do it, I'm not your man. I am results oriented. I am action oriented. I've built my businesses getting things done in 3 months that my competitors took 18 months to do.

Everybody says, you can't do that with Congress. Sure you can do that with Congress. Congress, they're all good people. They're all patriots. But you've got to link arms and work with them. Sure, you'll have arguments. Sure, you'll have fights. We have them all day, every day. But we get the job done.

Now, I have to come back in my close to one thing, because I am passionate about education. I was talking about early childhood education for disadvantaged little children. Let me tell you one specific pilot program where children who don't have a chance go to this program when they're 3. Now, we're going back to when the mother is pregnant, and they'll start right after they're born, starting when they're 3 and going to this school until they're 9, and then going into the public school in the fourth grade—90 percent are on the honor roll. Now, that will change America. Those children will all go to college. They will live the American dream.

I beg the American people, anytime they think about reforming education, to take this piece of society that doesn't have a chance, and take these little pieces of clay that can be shaped and molded and give them the same love and nurture and affec-

tion and support you give your children. Teach them that they're unique and that they're precious and there's only one person in the world like them, and you will see this Nation bloom. We will have so many people who are qualified for the top job that it will be terrific.

Now, finally, if you can't pay the bills, you're dead in the water. We have got to put our Nation back to work. Now, if you don't want to really do that, I'm not your man. I'd go crazy sitting up there slow dancing that one. In other words, unless we're going to do it, then pick somebody who likes to talk about it.

Now, just remember, when you think about me, I didn't create this mess. I've been paying taxes just like you. And Lord knows, I've paid my share, over $1 billion in taxes. And for a guy that started out with everything he owned in the trunk of his car, that ain't bad.

Ms. Simpson. I'm sorry, Mr. Perot. Once again—

Mr. Perot. But it's in your hands. I wish you well. I'll see you tomorrow night on NBC, 10:30 p.m., 11 p.m., eastern. [Laughter]

Ms. Simpson. And finally, last but not least, Governor Clinton.

Governor Clinton. Thank you, Carole, and thank you, ladies and gentleman. Since I suggested this format, I hope it's been good for all of you. I've really tried to be faithful to your request that we answer the questions specifically and pointedly. I thought I owed that to you. And I respect you for being here, and for the impact you've had on making this a more positive experience.

These problems are not easy. They're not going to be solved overnight. But I want you to think about just two or three things. First of all, the people of my State have let me be their Governor for 12 years because I made commitments to two things, more jobs and better schools.

Our schools are now better. Our children get off to a better start, from preschool programs and smaller classes in the early grades. We have one of the most aggressive adult education programs in the country. We talked about that.

This year, my State ranks first in the country in job growth, fourth in manufacturing job growth, fourth in income growth, fourth in the decline of poverty. I'm proud of that. It happened because I could work with people, Republicans and Democrats. That's why we've had 24 retired generals and admirals, hundreds of business people, many of them Republican, support this campaign.

You have to decide whether you want to change or not. We do not need 4 more years of an economic theory that doesn't work. We've had 12 years of trickle-down economics. It's time to put the American people first, to invest and grow this economy. I'm the only person here who's ever balanced a government budget, and I've presented 12 of them and cut spending repeatedly. But you cannot just get there by balancing the budget. We've got to grow the economy by putting people first, real people like you.

I got into this race because I did not want my child to grow up to be part of the first generation of Americans to do worse than their parents. We're better than that. We can do better than that. I want to make America as great as it can be, and I ask for your help in doing it.

Thank you very much.

Ms. Simpson. Thank you, Governor Clinton.

Ladies and gentlemen, this concludes the debate, sponsored by the Bipartisan Commission on Presidential Debates. I'd like to thank our audience of 209 uncommitted voters who may leave this evening maybe being committed. And hopefully, they'll go to the polls like everyone else on November 3d and vote.

We invite you to join us on the third and final Presidential debate next Monday, October 19th, from the campus of Michigan State University in East Lansing, Michigan.

I'm Carole Simpson. Good night.

62. Presidential Debate in East Lansing, Michigan October 19, 1992

Jim Lehrer. Good evening. Welcome to this third and final debate among the three major candidates for President of the United States: Governor Bill Clinton, the Democratic nominee; President George Bush, the Republican nominee; and independent candidate Ross Perot.

I am Jim Lehrer, of *The MacNeil/Lehrer NewsHour* on PBS. I will be the moderator for this debate, which is being sponsored by the Commission on Presidential Debates. It will be 90 minutes long. It is happening before an audience on the campus of Michigan State University in East Lansing.

The format was conceived by and agreed to by representatives of the Bush and Clinton campaigns. And it is somewhat different than those used in the earlier debates. I will ask questions for the first half under rules that permit follow-ups. A panel of three other journalists will ask questions in the second half under rules that do not. As always, each candidate will have 2 minutes, up to 2 minutes, to make a closing statement. The order of those as well as that for the formal questioning were all determined by a drawing.

Gentlemen, again, welcome. And again, good evening.

Credibility

Mr. Lehrer. It seems, from what some of those voters said at your Richmond debate and from polling and other data, that each of you, fairly or not, faces serious voter concerns about the underlying credibility and believability of what each of you says you would do as President in the next 4 years.

Governor Clinton, in accordance with the draw, those concerns about you are first. You are promising to create jobs, reduce the deficit, reform the health care system, rebuild the infrastructure, guarantee college education for everyone who is qualified, among many other things, all with financial pain only for the very rich. Some people are having trouble, apparently, believing that is possible. Should they have that concern?

Governor Clinton. No. There are many people who believe that the only way we can get this country turned around is to tax the middle class more and punish them more. But the truth is that middle-class Americans are basically the only group of Americans who have been taxed more in the 1980's and during the last 12 years even though their incomes have gone down. The wealthiest Americans have been taxed much less even though their incomes have gone up.

Middle-class people will have their fair share of changing to do and many challenges to face, including the challenge of becoming constantly reeducated. But my plan is a departure from trickle-down economics, just cutting taxes on the wealthiest Americans and getting out of the way. It's also a departure from tax-and-spend economics because you can't tax and divide an economy that isn't growing.

I propose an American version of what works in other countries. I think we can do it better: invest and grow. I believe we can increase investment and reduce the deficit at the same time if we not only ask the wealthiest Americans and foreign corporations to pay their fair share, we also provide over $100 billion in tax relief in terms of incentives for new plants, new small businesses, new technologies, new housing, and for middle class families, and we have $140 billion of spending cuts.

Invest and grow: raise some more money; spend the money on tax incentives to have growth in the private sector; take the money from the defense cuts and reinvest it in new transportation and communications and environmental cleanup systems. This will work.

On this, as on so many other issues, I have a fundamental difference from the present administration. I don't believe trickle-down economics will work. Unemployment is up. Most people are working harder for less money than they were making 10 years ago. I think we can do better if we have the courage to change.

Mr. Lehrer. Mr. President, a response.

President Bush. Do I have one minute? Just the ground rules here.

Mr. Lehrer. Well, you have roughly one minute. We can loosen that up a little bit. But go ahead.

President Bush. He doesn't like trickle-down Government, but hey, I think he's talking about the Reagan-Bush years where we created 15 million jobs. The rich are paying a bigger percent of the total tax burden. What I don't like is trickle-down Government. I think Governor Clinton keeps talking about trickle-down, trickle-down, and he's still talking about spending more and taxing more.

Government, he says, invest Government, grow Government. Government doesn't create jobs. If they do, they're make-work jobs. It's the private sector that creates jobs. And yes, we've got too many taxes on the American people, and we're spending too much. That's why I want to get the deficit down by controlling the growth of mandatory spending.

It won't be painless. I think Mr. Perot put his finger on something there. It won't be painless, but we've got to get the job done. But not by raising taxes.

Mr. and Mrs. America, when you hear him say we're going to tax only the rich, watch your wallet, because his figures don't add up, and he's going to sock it right to the middle class taxpayer and lower if he's going to pay for all the spending programs he's proposed. So we have a big difference on this trickle-down theory. I do not want any more trickle-down Government. It's gotten too big. I want to do something about that.

Mr. Lehrer. Mr. Perot, what do you think of the Governor's approach, what he just laid out?

Mr. Perot. Well, the basic problem with it is it doesn't balance the budget. If you forecast it out, you still will have a significant deficit under each of their plans, as I understand them. Our challenge is to stop the financial bleeding. If you take a patient into a hospital that's bleeding arterially, step one is to stop the bleeding. And we are bleeding arterially.

There's only one way out of this, and that is to stop the deterioration of our job base, to have a growing, expanding job base to give us the tax base. See, balancing the budget is not nearly as difficult as paying off the trillion debt and leaving our children the American dream intact. We have spent their money. We have got to pay it back. This is going to take fair-shared sacrifice.

My plan balances the budget within 6 years. We didn't do it faster than that because we didn't want to disrupt the economy. We got it off to a slow start and a fast finish to give the economy time to recover. But we faced it, and we did it. And we believe it's fair-shared sacrifice.

The one thing I have done is lay it squarely on the table in front of the American people. You've had a number of occasions to see in detail what the plan is and at least you'll understand it. I think that's fundamental in our country that you know what you're getting into.

Mr. Lehrer. Governor, the word "pain," one of the other leadership things that's put on you is that you don't speak of pain, that you speak of all things—nobody's going to really have to suffer under your plan. You've heard what Mr. Perot has said. He said to do the things you want to do, you can't do it by just taking the money from the rich. That's what the President says as well. How do you respond to that? The numbers don't add up.

Governor Clinton. I disagree with both of them. Let me just follow up here. I disagree with Mr. Perot that the answer is to put a 50-cent gas tax on the middle class and raise more taxes on the middle class and the working poor than on the wealthy. His own analysis says that unemployment will be slightly higher in 1995 under his plan than it is today. As far as what Mr. Bush says, he is the person who raised taxes on the middle class after saying he wouldn't. Just this year Mr. Bush vetoed a tax increase on the wealthy that gave middle class tax relief. He vetoed middle class tax relief this year.

Furthermore, under this administration, spending has increased more than it has in the last 20 years, and he asked Congress to spend more money than it actually spent.

Now, it's hard to outspend Congress, but he tried to for the last 3 years.

So my view is the middle class is the—they've been suffering, Jim. Now, should people pay more for Medicare if they can? Yes. Should they pay more for Social Security if they get more out of it than they've paid in and they're upper income people? Yes. But look what's happened to the middle class. Middle class Americans are working harder for less money than they were making 10 years ago, and they're paying higher taxes. The tax burden on them has not gone down; it has gone up.

I don't think the answer is to slow the economy down more, drive unemployment up more, and undermine the health of the private sector. The answer is to invest and grow this economy. That's what works in other countries, and that's what will work here.

Mr. Lehrer. As a practical matter, Mr. President, do you agree with the Governor when he says that the middle class—the taxes on the middle class—do your numbers agree that the taxes on the middle class have gone up during the last—

President Bush. I think everybody is paying too much taxes. He refers to one tax increase. Let me remind you it was a Democratic tax increase. I didn't want to do it, and I went along with it. I said I made a mistake. If I make a mistake, I admit it. That's quite different than some. But I think that's the American way.

I think everyone is paying too much. But I think this idea that you can go out and—then he hits me for vetoing a tax bill. Yes, I did, and the American taxpayer ought to be glad they have a President to stand up to a spending Congress. We remember what it was like when we had a spending President and a spending Congress and interest rates—who remembers that—they were 21.5 percent under Jimmy Carter, and inflation was 15. We don't want to go back to that. So yes, everybody's taxed too much, and I want to get the taxes down, but not by signing a tax bill that's going to raise taxes on people.

Mr. Lehrer. Mr. President, when you said just then that you admit your mistakes, and you looked at Governor Clinton and said—what mistake is it that you want him to admit to?

President Bush. Well, the record in Arkansas. I mean, look at it. And that's what we're asking America to have? Now, look, he says Arkansas's a poor State. They are. But in almost every category, they're lagging. I'll give you an example.

He talks about all the jobs he's created in 1 or 2 years. Over the last 10 years since he's been Governor, they're 30 percent behind. They're 30 percent of the national average. On pay for teachers, on all these categories, Arkansas is right near the very bottom.

You haven't heard me mention this before, but we're getting close now, and I think it's about time I start putting things in perspective. I'm going to do that. It's not dirty campaigning, because he's been talking about my record for half a year here, 11 months here, and so we've got to do that. I've got to get it in perspective.

What's his mistake? Admit it, that Arkansas is doing very, very badly against any standard: environment, support for police officers, whatever it is.

Mr. Lehrer. Governor, is that true?

Governor Clinton. Mr. Bush's Bureau of Labor Statistics says that Arkansas ranks first in the country in the growth of new jobs this year, first—

President Bush. This year.

Governor Clinton.—fourth in manufacturing jobs; fourth in the reduction of poverty; fourth in income increase. Over the last 10 years we've created manufacturing jobs much more rapidly than the national average. Over the last 5 years our income has grown more rapidly than the national average. We are second in tax burden, the second lowest tax burden in the country. We have the lowest per capita State and local spending in the country.

We are low-spending, low tax burden. We've dramatically increased investment and our jobs are growing. I wish America had that kind of record, and I think most people looking at us tonight would like it if we had more jobs and a lower spending burden on the Government.

Mr. Lehrer. Mr. Perot, if you were sitting at home now and just heard this exchange about Arkansas, who would you believe?

Mr. Perot. I grew up five blocks from Arkansas. [Laughter] Let's put it in perspective. It's a beautiful State. It's a fairly rural State. It has a population less than Chicago or Los Angeles, about the size of Dallas and Fort Worth combined. So I think probably we're making a mistake night after night after night to cast the Nation's future on a unit that small.

Mr. Lehrer. Why is that a mistake?

Mr. Perot. It's irrelevant. [Laughter]

Mr. Lehrer. What he did as Governor of Arkansas—

Mr. Perot. No, no, no. But you can't—I could say that I ran a small grocery store on the corner, therefore, I extrapolate that into the fact that I could run Wal-Mart. That's not true. I carefully picked an Arkansas company, you notice there, Governor.

Mr. Lehrer. Governor?

Governor Clinton. Mr. Perot, with all respect, I think it is highly relevant, and I think that a billion budget in State and Federal funds is not all that small. I think the fact that I took a State that was one of the poorest States in the country and had been for 153 years and tried my best to modernize its economy and to make the kind of changes that have generated support from people like the presidents of Apple Computer and Hewlett-Packard and some of the biggest companies in this country, 24 retired generals and admirals, and hundreds of business executives are highly relevant.

And you know, I'm frankly amazed that since you grew up five blocks from there you would think that what goes on in that State is irrelevant. I think it's been pretty impressive.

Mr. Perot. It's not—

Governor Clinton. And the people who have jobs and educations and opportunities that didn't have them 10 years ago don't think it's irrelevant at all. They think it's highly relevant and wish the rest of the country—

President Bush. I don't have a dog in this fight, but I'd like to get in on it.

Governor Clinton. You think it's relevant.

President Bush. Governor Clinton has to operate under a balanced budget amendment. He has to do it. That is the law. I'd like to see a balanced budget amendment for America, to protect the American taxpayers. Then that would discipline not only the executive branch but the spending Congress, the Congress that's been in control of one party, his party, for 38 years. We almost had it done. And that institution, the House of Representatives—everyone's yelling "Clean House!" One of the reasons is we almost had it done, and the Speaker, very able, decent fellow, I might add, but he twisted the arms of some of the sponsors of that legislation and had them change their vote.

What's relevant here is that tool, that discipline that he has to live by in Arkansas. And I'd like it for the American people. I want the line-item veto. I want a check-off so if the Congress can't do it, let people check off their income tax, 10 percent of it, to compel the Government to cut spending. If they can't do it, if the Congress can't do it, let them then have to do it across the board. That's what we call a sequester. That's the discipline we need. And I'm working for that to protect the American taxpayer against the big spenders.

Leadership

Mr. Lehrer. Mr. President, let's move to some of the leadership concerns that have been voiced about you. They relate to something you said in your closing statement in Richmond the other night about the President being the manager of crises, and that relates to an earlier criticism that you began to focus on the economy, on health care, on racial divisions in this country only after they became crises. Is that a fair criticism?

President Bush. Jim, I don't think that's a fair shot. I hear it. I hear it echoed by political opponents, but I don't think it's fair. I think we've been fighting from day one to do something about the inner cities. I'm for enterprise zones. I have had it in every single proposal I've sent to the Congress. Now we hear a lot of talk, "Oh, well, we all want enterprise zones." Yet the House and the Senate can't send it down without loading it up with a lot of these Christmas tree ornaments they put on the legislation.

I don't think in racial harmony that I'm a laggard on that. I've been speaking out since day one. We've gotten the Americans for Disabilities Act, which I think is one of the foremost pieces of civil rights legislation. And yes, it took me to veto two civil rights quota bills, because I don't believe in quotas, and I don't think the American people believe in quotas. I beat back the Congress on that, and then we passed a decent civil rights bill that offers guarantees against discrimination in employment, and that is good. I've spoken out over and over again against anti-Semitism and racism, and I think my record as a Member of Congress speaks for itself on that.

What was the other part of it?

Mr. Lehrer. Well, it's just that—you've spoken to it, I mean, but the idea—not so much in specifics—

President Bush. Yes.

Mr. Lehrer.—but that it has to be a crisis before it gets your attention.

President Bush. I don't think that's true at all. I don't think that's true. But, you know, let others fire away on it.

Mr. Lehrer. Do you think that's true, Mr. Perot?

Mr. Perot. I'd like to just talk about issues, and so—

Mr. Lehrer. You don't think this is an issue?

Mr. Perot. Well, no. But the point is that's a subjective thing. The subjective thing is when does President Bush react. It would be very difficult for me to answer that in any short period of time.

Mr. Lehrer. Well, then, I'll phrase it differently then. He said the other night in his closing words in Richmond that one of the key things that he believes the American people should decide among the three of you, is who they want in charge if this country gets to a crisis. Now, that's what he said. And the rap on the President is that it's only crisis time that he focuses on some of these things. So my question to you—we're going to talk about you in a minute.

Mr. Perot. I thought you'd forgotten I was here. [Laughter]

Mr. Lehrer. No, no, no. No, no. But my question to you is—so, if you have nothing to say about it, fine. I'll go to Governor Clinton. But—

Mr. Perot. I will let the American people decide that. I would rather not critique the two candidates.

Mr. Lehrer. All right.

Governor, what do you think?

Governor Clinton. The only thing I would say about that is I think that on the economy, Mr. Bush said for a long time there was no recession and then said it would be better to do nothing than to have a compromise effort with the Congress. He really didn't have a new economic program until over 1,300 days into his Presidency and not all of his health care initiative has been presented to the Congress even now.

I think it's important to elect a President who is committed to getting this economy going again and who realizes we have to abandon trickle-down economics and put the American people first again and who will send programs to the Congress in the first 100 days to deal with the critical issues that America's crying out for leadership on: jobs, incomes, the health care crisis, the need to control the economy. Those things deserve to be dealt with from day one. I will deal with them from day one. They will be my first priority, not my election year concerns.

Mr. Lehrer. Mr. President.

President Bush. Well, I think you're overlooking that we have had major accomplishments in the first term. But if you're talking about protecting the taxpayer against his friends in the United States Congress, go back to what it was like when you had a Democratic President and a Democratic Congress. You don't have to go back to Herbert Hoover. Go back to Jimmy Carter. Interest rates were 21 percent. Inflation was 15 percent. The "misery index," unemployment, inflation added together, it was invented by the Democrats, went right through the roof. We've cut it in half, and all you hear about is how bad things are.

You know, you remember the question, "Are you better off?" Well, is a homebuyer better off who can refinance the home because interest rates are down? Is a senior citizen better off because inflation is not wiping out their family savings? I think they are. Is the guy out of work better off? Of course he's not. But he's not going to be better off if we grow the Government, if we invest, as Governor Clinton says, invest in more Government.

You've got to free up the private sector. You've got to let small business have more incentives. For 3 months—three quarters I've been fighting, three quarters, been fighting to get the Congress to pass some incentives for small business, capital gains, investment tax allowance, credit for first-time homebuyers, and it's blocked by the Congress. Then if a little of it comes my way, they load it up with Christmas trees and tax increases. And I have to stand up in favor of the taxpayer.

Staying the Course

Mr. Lehrer. We have to talk about Ross Perot now, or he'll get me, I'm sure.

Mr. Perot, on this issue that I have raised at the very beginning and we've been talking about, which is leadership as President of the United States, the concerns—my reading of it, at least—my concerns about you, as expressed by folks in the polls and other places, it goes like this: You've got a problem with General Motors. You took over $750 million, and you left. You had a problem in the spring and summer about some personal hits that you took as a potential candidate for President of the United States, and you walked out. Does that say anything relevant to how you would function as President of the United States?

Mr. Perot. I think the General Motors thing is very relevant. I did everything I could to get General Motors to face its problems in the mid-eighties while it was still financially strong. They just wouldn't do it. Everybody now knows the terrible price they're paying by waiting until it's obvious to the brain dead that they have problems. [Laughter]

Now, hundreds, thousands of good, decent people, whole cities up here in this State are adversely impacted because they would not move in a timely way. Our Government is at that point now. The thing that I am in this race for is to tap the American people on the shoulder and to say to every single one of you: Fix it while we're still relatively strong. If you have a heart problem, you don't wait until the heart attack to address it.

So the General Motors experience is relevant. At the point when I could not get them to address those problems, I had created so much stress in the board, who wanted just to keep the Lawrence Welk music going, that they asked to buy my remaining shares. I sold them my remaining shares. They went their way; I went my way, because it was obvious we had a complete disagreement about what should be done with the company.

But let's take my life in perspective. Again and again on complex, difficult tasks, I have stayed the course. When I was asked by our Government to do the POW project, within a year the Vietnamese had sent people into Canada to make arrangements to have me and my family killed. And I had five small children. And my family and I decided we would stay the course, and we lived with that problem for 3 years.

Then I got into the Texans' war on drugs program, and the big-time drug dealers got all upset. Then when I had two people imprisoned in Iran, I could have left them there. I could have rationalized it. We went over, we got them out, and we brought them back home. And since then, for years, I have lived with the burden of the Middle East, where it's eye-for-an-eye and tooth-for-a-tooth country, in terms of their unhappiness with the fact that I was successful in that effort.

Again and again and again, in the middle of the night, 2 or 3 o'clock in the morning, my Government has called me to take extraordinary steps for Americans in distress. And again and again and again, I have responded. And I didn't wilt, and I didn't quit.

Now, what happened in July we've covered again and again and again. But I think in terms of the American people's concern about my commitment—and I'm here tonight, folks. I've never quit supporting you as you put me on the ballot in the other 26 States. When you asked me to come back in, I came back in. And talk about not quitting, I'm spending my money on this campaign. The two parties are spending your money, taxpayer money. I've put my wallet on the table for you and your children. Over $60 million at least will go into this campaign to leave the American dream to you and your children, to get this country straightened out, because if anybody owes it to you, I do. I've lived the American dream. I'd like for your children to be able to live it, too.

Mr. Lehrer. Governor, do you have a response to the staying the course question about Mr. Perot?

Governor Clinton. I don't have any criticism of Mr. Perot. I think what I'd like to talk about a minute is, since you asked him the question, was the General Motors issue. I don't think there's any question that the automobile executives made some errors in the 1980's, but I also think we should look at how much productivity has increased lately, how much labor has done to increase productivity, and how much management has done. We're still losing a lot of auto jobs, in my judgment, because we don't have a national economic strategy that would build the industrial base of this country.

Just today, I met with the presidents and the vice presidents of the Willow Run union near here. They both said they were Vietnam veterans supporting me because I had an economic program that put them back to work. We need an investment incentive to modernize plant and equipment. We've got to control the health care costs for those people. Otherwise we can't keep the manufacturing jobs here. We need a tough trade policy that is fair, that insists on open markets in return for open markets. We ought to have a strategy that will build the economic and industrial base.

So I think Mr. Perot was right in questioning the management practices. But they didn't have much of a partner in Government here as compared with the policies the Germans and the Japanese followed. I believe we can do better. That's one of the things I want to change. I know that we can grow manufacturing jobs. We did it in my State, and we can do it nationally.

CAFE Standards

Mr. Lehrer. Mr. President, do you have a response?

President Bush. To this?

Mr. Lehrer. Yes.

President Bush. Well, I wondered when Governor Clinton was talking to the autoworkers whether he talked about his and Senator Gore's favoring CAFE standards, those are fuel efficiency standards, of 40 miles per gallon. That would break the auto industry and throw a lot of people out of work.

As regarding Mr. Perot, I take back something I said about him. I once said in a frivolous moment when he got out of the race, if you can't stand the heat, buy an air conditioning company. I take it back because I think he said he made a mistake. The thing I find is if I make a mistake, I admit it. I've never heard Governor Clinton make a mistake.

But one mistake he's made is fuel efficiency standards at 40 to 45 miles per gallon will throw many autoworkers out of work, and you can't have it both ways. There's a pattern here of appealing to the autoworkers and then trying to appeal to the spotted owl crowd or the extremes in the environmental movement. You can't do it as President. You can't have a pattern of one side of the issue one day and another the next.

So my argument is not with Ross Perot; it is more with Governor Clinton.

Mr. Lehrer. Governor, what about that charge that you want it both ways on this issue?

Governor Clinton. Let's just talk about the CAFE standards.

Mr. Lehrer. All right.

Governor Clinton. That's the fuel efficiency standards. They're now 27.5 miles per gallon per automobile fleet. I never said, and I defy you to find where I said—I gave an extensive environment speech in April. I said that we ought to have a goal of raising the fuel efficiency standards to 40 miles a gallon. I think that should be a goal. I never said we should write it into law if there is evidence that that goal cannot be achieved. The National Science Foundation did a study which said it would be difficult for us to reach fuel efficiency standards in excess of 37 miles per gallon by the year 2000.

I think we should try to raise the fuel efficiency. And let me say this: I think we ought to have incentives to do it. I think we ought to push to do it. That doesn't mean we have to write it into the law.

Look, I am a job creator, not a job destroyer. It is the Bush administration that has had no new jobs in the private sector in the last 4 years. In my State we're leading the country in private sector job growth. But it is good for America to improve fuel efficiency.

We also ought to convert more vehicles to compressed natural gas. That's another way to improve the environment.

NAFTA

Mr. Lehrer. Mr. Perot, based on your experience at General Motors, where do you come down on this? This has been thrown about, back and forth during this campaign from the very beginning about jobs and CAFE standards.

Mr. Perot. Well, everybody's nibbling around the edges. Let's go to the center of the bull's eye to the core problem. Believe me, everybody on the factory floor all over this country knows it. You implement that NAFTA, the Mexican trade agreement, where they pay people $1 an hour, have no health care, no retirement, no pollution controls, et cetera, et cetera, et cetera, and you're going to hear a giant sucking sound of jobs being pulled out of this country right at a time when we need the tax base to pay the debt and pay down the interest on the debt and get our house back in order. We have got to proceed very carefully on that.

See, there's a lot I don't understand. I do understand business. I do understand creating jobs. I do understand how to make things work. And I've got a long history of doing that. Now, if you want to go to the core problem that faces everybody in manufacturing in this country, it's that agreement that's about to be put into practice.

But here, very simply, everybody says it will create jobs. Yes, it will create bubble jobs. Now, watch this. Listen very carefully to this: One-time surge while we build factories and ship machine tools and equipment down there. Then year after year for decades they will have jobs. And I finally thought I didn't understand it. I called all the experts, and they said, "Oh, it will be disruptive for 12 to 15 years." We haven't got 12 days, folks. We cannot lose those jobs. They were saying Mexican jobs will eventually come to .50 an hour and ours will eventually go down to .50 an hour. It makes you feel real good to hear that, right?

Let's think it through, here. Let's be careful. I'm for free trade philosophically, but I have studied these trade agreements until the world has gone flat, and we don't have good trade agreements across the world. I hope we'll have a chance to get into that tonight, because I can get right to the center of the bull's eye and tell you why we're losing whole industries in this country. Excuse me.

Mr. Lehrer. Just for the record, though, Mr. Perot, I take it then for your answer you do not have a position on whether or not enforcing the CAFE standards will cost jobs in the auto industry.

Mr. Perot. Oh, no. It will cost jobs. But that's not—let me say this: I'd rather, if you gave me two bad choices—

Mr. Lehrer. Okay.

Mr. Perot. I'd rather have some jobs left here than just see everything head south, see?

Mr. Lehrer. So that means no—[laughter]—in other words, you agree with President Bush, is that right?

Mr. Perot. No, I'm saying our principal need now is to stabilize the tax base, which is the job base, and create a growing, dynamic base. Now, please, folks, if you don't hear anything else I say, remember millions of people at work are our tax base. One quick point: If you confiscate the Forbes 400 wealth, take it all, you cannot balance the budget this year. Kind of gets your head straight about where the taxes year-in and year-out have got to come from. Millions and millions of people at work.

Mr. Lehrer. I wanted—yes, sir.

President Bush. Well, I'm caught in the middle of NAFTA. Ross says, with great conviction, he opposes the North American free trade agreement. I am for the North American free trade agreement. My problem with Governor Clinton, once again, is that one time he's going to make up his mind, he will see some merit in it. But then he sees a lot of things wrong with it. And then the other day, he says he's for it; however, then we've got to pass other legislation. When you're President of the United States, you cannot have this pattern of saying, "Well, I'm for it, but I'm on the other side of it." And it's true on this, and it's true on CAFE.

Look, if Ross were right and we get a free trade agreement with Mexico, why wouldn't they have gone down there now? You have a differential in wages right now. I just have an honest philosophical difference. I think free trade is going to expand our job opportunity. I think it is exports that have saved us when we're in a global slowdown, a connected, global slowdown, a recession in some countries. It's free trade, fair trade that needs to be our hallmark, and we need more free trade agreements, not fewer.

Mr. Lehrer. Governor, a quick answer on trade, and I want to go on to something else.

Governor Clinton. I'd like to respond to that. You know, Mr. Bush was very grateful when I was among the Democrats who said he ought to have the authority to negotiate an agreement with Mexico. Neither I nor anybody else, as far as I know, agreed to give him our proxy to say that whatever he did was fine for the workers of this country and for the interests of this country.

I am the one who is in the middle on this. Mr. Perot says it's a bad deal. Mr. Bush says it's a hunky-dory deal. I say, on balance, it does more good than harm if we could get some protection for the environment so that the Mexicans have to follow their own environmental standards, their own labor law standards, and if we have a genuine commitment to reeducate and retrain the American workers who lose their jobs and reinvest in this economy.

I have a realistic approach to trade. I want more trade. I know there are some good things in that agreement, but it can sure be made better.

Let me just point out, just today in the *Los Angeles Times*, Clyde Prestowitz, who was one of President Reagan's leading trade advisers, and a lifelong conservative Republican, endorsed my candidacy because he knows that I'll have a free and fair trade policy, a hard-headed realistic policy, and not get caught up in rubber-stamping everything the Bush administration did. If I wanted to do that, why would I run for President, Jim? Anybody else can run the middle class down and run the economy in a ditch. I want to change it.

President Bush. I think he made my case. On the one hand, it's a good deal, but on the other hand, I'd make it better. You can't do that as President. You can't do it on the war, where he says, "Well, I was with the minority, but I guess I would have voted with the majority."

This is my point tonight: We're talking about 2 weeks from now you've got to decide who is going to be President. And there is this pattern that has plagued him in the primaries and now about trying to have it both ways on all these issues. You can't do that. If you make a mistake, say you made a mistake and go on about your business, trying to serve the American people.

Right now we heard it. Ross is against it. I am for it. He says, "On the one hand, I'm for it, and on the other hand, I may be against it."

Mr. Lehrer. Governor—

Governor Clinton. That's what's wrong with Mr. Bush. His whole deal is, you've got to be for it or against it, and you can't make it better. I believe we can be better. I think the American people are sick and tired of either-or solutions, people being pushed in the corner, polarized to extremes. I think they want somebody with common sense, who can do what's best for the American people. I'd be happy to discuss these other issues, but I can't believe he is accusing me of getting on both sides.

He said trickle-down economics was voodoo economics. Now, he's its biggest practitioner. Let me just say—

President Bush. I've always said trickle-down Government is bad.

Governor Clinton. I could run this string out a long time, but remember this, Jim: Those 209 Americans last Thursday night in Richmond told us they wanted us to stop talking about each other and start talking about Americans and their problems and their promises. I think we ought to get back to that. I'll be glad to answer any question you have, but this election ought to be about the American people.

Mr. Lehrer. Mr. Perot?

Mr. Perot. Is there an equal time rule here tonight?

President Bush. Yes.

Mr. Perot. Or do you just keep lunging in at will? I thought we were going to have equal time, but maybe I just have to interrupt the other two. Is that the way it works this—

Mr. Lehrer. No. Mr. Perot, you're doing fine. Go ahead. Whatever you want to say, say it.

Foreign Lobbyists

Mr. Perot. Now that we've talked all around the problem about free trade, let's go again to the center of the bull's eye.

Mr. Lehrer. Wait a minute. I was going to ask—I thought you wanted to respond to what we were talking about.

Mr. Perot. I do. I do. I just want to make— these foreign lobbyists, this whole thing. Our country has sold out to foreign lobbyists. We don't have free trade. Both parties have foreign lobbyists on leave in key roles in their campaigns. If there's anything more unwise than that, I don't know what it is. Every debate, I bring this up, and nobody ever addresses it.

I would like for them to look you in the eye and tell you why they have people representing foreign countries working on their campaigns. And you know, you've seen the list; I've seen the list. We won't go into the names. But no wonder they—if I had those people around me all day every day telling me it was fair and free, I might believe it. But if I look at the facts as a businessman, it's so tilted. The first thing you ought to do is just say, "Guys, if you like these deals so well, we'll give you the deal you gave us." Now, the Japanese couldn't unload the cars in this country if they had the same restrictions we had, and on and on and on and on and on.

I suggest to you that the core problem—one country spent $400 million lobbying in 1988—our country. And it goes on and on. And you look at a Who's Who in these campaigns around the two candidates. They're foreign lobbyists taking leaves. What do you think they're going to do when the campaign's over? Go back to work at 30,000 bucks a month representing some other country. I don't believe that's in the American people's interest.

I don't have a one of them, and I haven't taken a penny of foreign money, and I never will.

Mr. Lehrer. Mr. President, how do you respond to that? Mr. Perot has made that charge several times, the fact that you have people working in your campaign who are paid foreign lobbyists.

President Bush. Most people that are lobbying are lobbying the Congress. I don't think there's anything wrong with an honest person who happens to represent an interest of another country for making his case. That's the American way. What you're assuming is that that makes the recipient of the lobbying corrupt or the lobbyists themselves corrupt. I don't agree with that.

But if I found somebody that had a conflict of interest that would try to illegally do something as a foreign registered lobby, the laws cover this. I don't know why—I've never understood quite why Mr. Perot was so upset about it, because one of the guys he used to have working for him, I believe, had foreign accounts. Could be wrong, but I think so.

Mr. Perot. Soon as I found it out, he went out the door, too.

President Bush. Well, I think you've got to look at the integrity and the honor of the people that are being lobbied and those that are lobbyists. The laws protect the American taxpayer in this regard. If the laws are violated so much—but to suggest if somebody represents a foreign country on anything, that makes him corrupt or against the taxpayer, I don't agree with it.

Mr. Perot. One quick relevant specific. We're getting ready to dismantle the airlines industry in our country, and none of you know it. I doubt, in all candor, if the President knows it. But this deal that we're doing with BAC and USAir and KLM and Northwest—now, guess who is on the President's campaign big time? A guy from Northwest. This deal is terribly destructive to the U.S. airline industry. One of the largest industries in the world is the travel and tourist business. We won't be making airplanes in this country 10 years from now if we let deals like this go through.

If the press has any interest tonight, I'll detail it to you. I won't take 10 minutes tonight; all these things take a few minutes. But that's happening as we sit here today. We hammerlock the American companies,

American Airlines, Delta, the last few great we have, because we're trying to do this deal with these two European companies. Never forget, they've got Airbus over there, and it's a government-owned, privately owned consortium across Europe. They're dying to get the commercial airline business. Japan is trying to get the commercial airline business. I don't think there are any villains inside Government on this issue, but there sure are a lot of people who don't understand business. And maybe you need somebody up there who understands when you're getting your pocket picked.

Mr. Lehrer. Governor, I'm sorry, but that concludes my time with—

Governor Clinton. Boy, I had a great response to that.

Mr. Lehrer. All right. Go ahead, quickly. Just very briefly.

Governor Clinton. I think Ross is right and that we do need some more restrictions on lobbyists. We ought to make them disclose the people they've given money to when they're testifying before congressional committees. We ought to close the lawyers' loophole; they ought to have to disclose when they're really lobbying. We ought to have a much longer period of time, about 5 years, between the time when people can leave executive branch offices and then go out and start lobbying for foreign interests. I agree with that.

We've wrecked the airline industry already because there's all these leveraged buyouts and all these terrible things that have happened to the airline industry. We're going to have a hard time rebuilding it. But the real thing we've got to have is a competitive economic strategy. Look what's happening to McDonnell Douglas. Even Boeing is losing market share because we let the

Europeans spend 25 to 40 billion dollars on Airbus without an appropriate competitive response.

What I want America to do is to trade more, but to compete and win by investing in competitive ways. And we're in real trouble on that.

Mr. Lehrer. I'm going to be in real trouble if I don't bring out—it's about time—

President Bush. I promise it's less than 10 seconds.

Mr. Lehrer. Okay.

President Bush. I heard Governor Clinton congratulate us on one thing. First time he said something pleasant about this administration. Productivity in this country is up. It is way up. Productivity is up, and that's a good thing. There are many other good ones, but I was glad he acknowledged that.

Mr. Perot. I've volunteered—now, look, I'm just kind of a, you know, cur dog here. I was put on the ballot by the people, not special interest, so I have to stand up for myself. Now, Jim, let me net it out. On the second debate, I offered, since both sides want the enterprise zones but can't get together, I said I'll take a few days off and go to Washington and hold hands with you, and we'll get it done. I'll take a few days off, hold hands with you, and get this airline thing straightened out, because that's important to this country.

That's kind of pathetic I have to do it, and nobody's called me yet to come up, I might mention—[laughter]—but if they do, if they do, it's easy to fix. If you all want the enterprise zones, why don't we pass the dang thing and do it? Right?

Mr. Lehrer. All right. Now we're going to bring in three other journalists to ask questions. They are Susan Rook of CNN, Gene

Gibbons of Reuters, and Helen Thomas of United Press International.

You thought you'd never get in here, didn't you?

President Bush. Uh-oh.

Mr. Lehrer. Okay, we are going to continue on the subject of leadership, and the first question goes to Governor Clinton for a 2-minute answer. It will be asked by Helen Thomas. Helen?

The Draft Issue

Helen Thomas. Governor Clinton, your credibility has come into question because of your different responses on the Vietnam draft. If you had to do it over again, would you put on the Nation's uniform? And, if elected, could you, in good conscience, send someone to war?

Governor Clinton. If I had to do it over again, I might answer the questions a little better. You know, I had been in public life a long time and no one had ever questioned my role, and so I was asked a lot of questions about the things that happened a long time ago. I don't think I answered them as well as I could have.

Going back 23 years, I don't know, Helen. I was opposed to the war. I couldn't help that. I felt very strongly about it, and I didn't want to go at the time. It's easy to say in retrospect I would have done something differently.

President Lincoln opposed the war, and there were people who said maybe he shouldn't be President. But I think he made us a pretty good President in wartime. We've got a lot of other Presidents who didn't wear their country's uniform and had to order our young soldiers into battle, including President Wilson and President Roosevelt. So

the answer is, I could do that. I wouldn't relish doing it, but I wouldn't shrink from it.

I think that the President has to be prepared to use the power of the Nation when our vital interests are threatened, when our treaty commitments are at stake, when we know that something has to be done that is in the national interest. And that is a part of being President. Could I do it? Yes, I could.

Mr. Lehrer. A reminder now, we're back on the St. Louis rules, which means that the Governor had his answer, and then each of you will have one minute to respond.

Mr. President.

President Bush. Well, I've expressed my heartfelt difference with Governor Clinton on organizing demonstrations while in a foreign land against your country when young ghetto kids have been drafted and are dying.

My argument with him on—the question was about the draft is that there is this same pattern. In New Hampshire, Senator Kerry said you ought to level, you ought to tell the truth about it. And April 17th, he said he'd bring out all the records on the draft. They have not been forthcoming. He got a deferment, or he didn't. He got a notice, or he didn't. I think it's this pattern that troubles me more than the draft. A lot of decent, honorable people felt as he did on the draft. But it is this pattern.

And again, you might be able to make amendments all the time, Governor, but as President, you can't be on all these different sides, and you can't have this pattern of saying, well, I did this, or I didn't. Then the facts come out, and you change it. That's my big difference with him on the draft. It wasn't failing to serve.

Mr. Lehrer. Your minute is up, sir.

Mr. Perot, one minute.

Mr. Perot. I've spent my whole adult life very close to the military; feel very strongly about the people who go into battle for our country; appreciate their idealism, their sacrifices; appreciate the sacrifices their families make. That's been displayed again and again in a very tangible way.

I look on this as history. I don't look on it, personally, as relevant. I consider it really a waste of time tonight when you consider the issues that face our country right now.

Mr. Lehrer. All right. The next question goes to President Bush, and Gene Gibbons will ask it.

1990 Budget Agreement

Gene Gibbons. Mr. President, you keep saying that you made a mistake in agreeing to a tax increase to get the 1990 budget deal with Congress. But if you hadn't gotten that deal you would have either had to get repeal of the Gramm-Rudman deficit control act or cut defense spending drastically at a time when the country was building up for the Gulf war and decimate domestic discretionary spending, including such things as air traffic control. If you had it to do all over again, sir, which of those alternatives would you choose?

President Bush. I wouldn't have taken any of the alternatives. I believe I made a mistake. I did it for the very reasons you say. There was one good thing that came out of that budget agreement, and that is we put a cap on discretionary spending. One-third of the President's budget is at the President's discretion, or really, the Congress', since they appropriate every dime and tell the President how to spend every dime. We've put a cap on the growth of all that spending, and that's good. And that's helped. But I was wrong because I thought the tax compro-

mise, going along with one Democratic tax increase, would help the economy. I see no evidence that it has done it.

So what would I have done, what should I have done? I should have held out for a better deal that would have protected the taxpayer and not ended up doing what we had to do or what I thought at the time would help.

So I made a mistake. You know, the difference, I think, is that I knew at the time I was going to take a lot of political flak. I knew we'd have somebody out there yelling, "Read my lips." And I did it because I thought it was right. And I made a mistake. That's quite different than taking a position where you know it's best for you. That wasn't best for me, and I knew it in the very beginning. I thought it would be better for the country than it was. So there we are.

Mr. Lehrer. Mr. Perot, one minute.

Mr. Perot. The 101 in leadership is be accountable for what you do. Let's go back to the tax and budget summit briefly. Nobody ever told the American people that we increased spending .83 for every dollar of taxes raised. That's absolutely unconscionable. Both parties carry a huge blame for that on their shoulders. This was not a way to pay on the deficit. This was a trick on the American people. That's not leadership.

Let's go back in terms of accepting responsibilities for your actions. To create Saddam Hussein over a 10-year period, using billions of dollars of U.S. taxpayer money, step up to the plate and say it was a mistake. To create Noriega using taxpayer money, step up to the plate and say it was a mistake. If you can't get your act together to pick him up one day when a Panamanian major has kidnaped him, a special forces team is 400 yards away and it's a stroll across the park to get him, and if you can't get your act together, at least pick up the Panamanian major who they then killed, step up to the plate and admit it was a mistake. That's leadership, folks.

Now, leaders will always make mistakes. And I'm not aiming at any one person here. I'm aiming at our Government. Nobody takes responsibility for anything. We've got to change that.

Mr. Lehrer. I'll take responsibility for saying your time is up.

Mr. Perot. I'm watching the light.

Mr. Lehrer. All right.

Governor Clinton, one minute, sir.

Governor Clinton. The mistake that was made was making the "read my lips" promise in the first place just to get elected, knowing what the size of the deficit was, knowing there was no plan to control health care costs, and knowing that we did not have a strategy to get real economic growth back into this economy. The choices were not good then.

I think at the time the mistake that was made was signing off on the deal late on Saturday night in the middle of the night. That's just what the President did when he vetoed the family leave act. I think what he should have done is gone before the American people on the front end and said, "Listen, I made a commitment, and it was wrong. I made a mistake because I couldn't have foreseen these circumstances. And this is the best deal we can work out at the time."

He said it was in the public interest at the time, and most everybody who was involved in it, I guess, thought it was. The real mistake was the "read my lips" promise in the first place. You just can't promise something like that just to get elected if you know

there's a good chance that circumstances may overtake you.

Mr. Lehrer. All right, Mr. Perot, the question is for you. You have a 2-minute answer, and it will be asked by Susan Rook.

Leadership

Susan Rook. Mr. Perot, you've talked about going to Washington to do what the people who run this country want you to do. But it is the President's duty to lead and often lead alone. How can you lead if you are forever seeking consensus before you act?

Mr. Perot. Let's talk about two different subjects. In order to lead, you first have to use the White House as a bully pulpit and lead. Then you have to develop consensus, or you can't get anything done. That's where we are now. We can't get anything done. How do you get anything done when you've got all of these political action committees, all of these thousands of registered lobbyists, 40,000 registered lobbyists, 23,000 special interest groups, and the list goes on and on and on, and the average citizen out here just working hard every day. You've got to go to the people. I just love the fact that everybody, particularly in the media, goes bonkers over the town hall. I guess it's because you will lose your right to tell them what to think. [Laughter] The point is, they'll get to decide what to think.

President Bush. Hey, you've got something there.

Mr. Perot. I love the fact that people will listen to a guy with a bad accent and a poor presentation manner talking about flip charts for 30 minutes, because they want the details. See, all the folks up there at the top said, people, "The attention span of the

American people is no more than 5 minutes. They won't watch it." They're thirsty for it.

You want to have a new program in this country? If you get grassroots America excited about it and if they tap Congress on the shoulder and say, "Do it, Charlie," it will happen. That's a whole lot different from these fellows running up and down the halls whispering in their ears now and promising campaign funds for the next election if they do it. Now, I think that's going back to where we started. That's having a Government from the people. I think that's the essence of leadership, rather than cutting deals in dark rooms in Washington.

Mr. Lehrer. Governor Clinton, one minute.

Governor Clinton. Well, I believe in the town hall meetings. They started with my campaign in New Hampshire. I think Ross Perot has done a good job in having them. And I, as you know, pushed for the debate to include 209 American citizens who were part of it in Richmond a few days ago. I've done a lot of them, and I'll continue to do them as President.

But I'd also like to point out that I haven't been part of what we're criticizing in Washington tonight. Of the three of us, I have balanced a government budget 12 times. I have offered and passed campaign finance reform; offered, pushed for, and passed in public referendum lobbyist restrictions; done the kinds of things you have to do to get legislators together, not only to establish consensus but to challenge them to change. In 12 years as Governor, I guess I've taken on every interest group there was in my State at one time or another to fight for change. It can be done. That's why I've tried to be so specific in this campaign: to have a mandate, if elected, so that Congress will know what the American people have voted for.

Mr. Lehrer. President Bush, one minute.

President Bush. I would like the record to show the panelists that Ross Perot took the first shot at the press. My favorite bumper sticker, though, is "Annoy the Media. Reelect President Bush." [Laughter] I just had to work that in. Sorry, Helen. I'm going to pay for this later on.

Look, you have to build a consensus, but in some things—Ross mentioned Saddam Hussein. Yes, we tried, and yes, we failed to bring him into the family of nations. He had the fourth largest army. But then when he moved against Kuwait I said, this will not stand. And it's hard to build a consensus. We went to the U.N. We made historic resolutions up there. The whole world was united. Our Congress was dragging its feet. Governor Clinton said, "Well, I might have been with the minority, let sanctions work. But I guess I would have voted with the majority."

A President can't do that. Sometimes he has to act. In this case, I'm glad we did, because if we'd have let sanctions work and had tried to build a consensus on that, Saddam Hussein today would be in Saudi Arabia controlling the world's oil supply, and he would be there maybe with a nuclear weapon. We busted the fourth largest army, and we did it through leadership.

Mr. Lehrer. All right, we're going to go on to another subject now, and the subject is priorities. And the first question goes to you, President Bush, and Susan will ask it.

Women Advisers

Ms. Rook. President Bush, gentlemen, I acknowledge that all of you have women and ethnic minorities working for you and working with you. But when we look at the circle of the key people closest to you, your inner circle of advisers, we see white men only. Why, and when will that change?

President Bush. You don't see Margaret Tutwiler sitting in there with me today?

Ms. Rook. The key people, President Bush.

President Bush. What?

Ms. Rook. The key people, the people beyond the glass ceiling.

President Bush. I happen to think she's a key person. I think our Cabinet members are key people. I think the woman that works with me, Rose Zamaria, is about as tough as a boot out there and makes some discipline and protects the taxpayer. Look at our Cabinet. You talk about somebody strong, look at Carla Hills. Look at Lynn Martin, who's fighting against this glass ceiling and doing a first-class job on it. Look at our Surgeon General, Dr. Novello. You can look all around and you'll see first-class, strong women.

Jim Baker's a man. Yes, I plead guilty to that. [Laughter] But look who's around with him there. I mean, this is a little defensive on your part, Susan, to be honest with you. We've got a very good record appointing women to high positions and positions of trust. And I'm not defensive at all about it.

What we've got to do is keep working, as the Labor Department is doing a first-class job on, to break down discrimination, to break down the glass ceiling. I am not apologetic at all about our record with women. You think about women in Government. I think about women in business. Why not try to help them with my small business program to build some incentives into the system?

I think we're making progress here. You've got a lot of women running for office. As I said the other night, I hope a lot of them lose, because they're liberal Democrats, and we don't need more of them in the Senate or more of them in the House. But nevertheless, they're out there. And we've got some very good Republican women running. So we're making dramatic progress.

Mr. Lehrer. Mr. Perot, one minute.

Mr. Perot. Well, I've come from the computer business, and everybody knows women are more talented than the men. So we have a long history of having a lot of talented women. One of our first officers was a woman, a chief financial officer. She was a director. And it was so far back, it was considered so odd. And even though we were a tiny little company at the time, it made all the national magazines.

But in terms of being influenced by women and being a minority, there they are right out there, my wife and my four beautiful daughters. And I just have one son. So he and I are surrounded by women telling us what to do all the time. [Laughter]

Iraq

Mr. Perot. For the rest of my minute, I want to make a very brief comment here in terms of Saddam Hussein. We told him that we wouldn't get involved with this border dispute, and we've never revealed those papers that were given to Ambassador Glaspie on July 25. I suggest, in the sense of taking responsibility for your actions, we lay those papers on the table. They're not the secrets to the nuclear bomb.

Secondly, we got upset when he took the whole thing, but to the ordinary American out there who doesn't know where the oilfields are in Kuwait, they're near the border. We told him he could take the northern part of Kuwait, and when he took the whole thing, we went nuts. And if we didn't tell him that, why won't we even let the Senate Foreign Relations Committee and the Senate Intelligence Committee see the written instructions for Ambassador Glaspie?

President Bush. I'd like to reply on that. That gets to the national honor. We did not say to Saddam Hussein, Ross, "You can take the northern part of Kuwait." That is absolutely absurd. Glaspie has testified—

Mr. Perot. Where are the papers?

President Bush.—and Glaspie's papers have been presented to the United States Senate. So please—

Mr. Perot. If you have time, go through NEXIS and LEXIS, pull all the old news articles. Look at what Ambassador Glaspie said all through the fall and what have you, and then look at what she and Kelly and all the others in State said at the end when they were trying to clean it up. And talk to any head of any of those key committees in the Senate. They will not let them see the written instructions given to Ambassador Glaspie. And I suggest that in a free society owned by the people, the American people ought to know what we told Ambassador Glaspie to tell Saddam Hussein. Because we spent a lot of money and risked lives and lost lives in that effort, and did not accomplish most of our objectives. We got Kuwait back to the Amir; but he still got his nuclear, his chemical, his bacteriological, and he's still over there, right? I'd like to see those written instructions. Sorry.

Mr. Lehrer. Mr. President, when you—just make sure that everybody knows what's going on here. When you responded directly to Mr. Perot then—

President Bush. Yes.

Mr. Lehrer.—you violated the rule, your rules. Now, I'm willing—

President Bush. I apologize. When I make a mistake, I say—[laughter].

Mr. Lehrer. No, no, no. I just want to make sure that everybody understands. If you all want to change the rules, we can do it.

President Bush. No, I don't. I apologize for it. But that one got right to the national honor.

Mr. Lehrer. All right. Okay.

President Bush. And I'm sorry.

Mr. Lehrer. Okay. But Governor Clinton, you have a minute.

Women Advisers

Governor Clinton. Susan, I don't agree that there are no women and minorities in important positions in my campaign. There are many. But I think even more relevant is my record at home. For most of my time as Governor, a woman was my chief of staff, an African American was my chief cabinet officer, an African American was my chief economic development officer.

It was interesting, there was a story either today or yesterday in the *Washington Post* about my economic programs. My chief budget officer and my chief economic officer were both African Americans, even though the *Post* didn't mention that, which I think is a sign of progress. The National Women's Political Caucus gave me an award, one of their good guy awards, for my involvement of women in high levels of government. I've appointed more minorities to positions of high levels in government than all the Governors in the history of my State combined before me.

So that's what I'll do as President. I don't think we've got a person to waste. I think I owe the American people a White House staff, a Cabinet, and appointments that look like America, but that meet high standards of excellence, and that's what I'll do.

Mr. Lehrer. All right. The next question goes to you, Mr. Perot, for 2 minutes. It's a 2-minute question, and Helen will ask it. Helen?

Investigations

Ms. Thomas. Mr. Perot, what proof do you have that Saddam Hussein was told that he could have—do you have any actual proof, or are you asking for the papers? And also, I really came in with another question. What is this penchant you have to investigate everyone? Are those accusations correct, investigating your staff, investigating the leaders of the grassroots movement, investigating associates of your family?

Mr. Perot. No, they're not correct. And if you look at my life for the first—until I got involved in this effort, I was one person. And then after the Republican dirty tricks group got through with me, I'm another person, which I consider an absolutely sick operation. And all of you in the press know exactly what I'm talking about. They investigated every single one of my children. They investigated my wife. They interviewed all my children's friends from childhood on. They went to extraordinary, sick lengths. And I just found it amusing that they would take two or three cases where I was involved in lawsuits and would engage an investigator, the lawyers would engage an investigator, which is common. And the only difference between me and any other businessman that has the range of businesses I have is I haven't had that many lawsuits.

So that's just another one of those little fruit-loopy things they make up to try to, instead of facing issues, to try to redefine a person that's running against them. This

goes on night and day. I will do everything I can, if I get up there, to make dirty tricks a thing of the past. One of the two groups has raised it to an art form. It's a sick art form.

Iraq

Now, let's go back to Saddam Hussein. We gave Ambassador Glaspie written instructions. That's a fact. We've never let the Congress and these Foreign Relations—Senate Intelligence Committee see them. That's a fact.

Ambassador Glaspie did a lot of talking, right after July the 25th, and that's a fact, and it saw the newspapers. You pull all of it at once and read it, and I did, and it's pretty clear what she and Kelly and the other key guys around that thing thought they were doing.

Then, at the end of the war when they had to go testify about it, their stories are a total disconnect from what they said in August, September, and October. So I say, this is very simple: Saddam Hussein released a tape, as you know, claiming it was a transcript of their meeting, where she said, "We will not become involved in your border dispute," and in effect, "You can take the northern part of the country."

We later said, "No, that's not true." I said, well, this is simple. What were her written instructions? We guard those like the secrets to the atomic bomb, literally. Now, I say: Whose country is this? This is ours. Who will get hurt if we lay those papers on the table? The worst thing is, again, it's a mistake. Nobody did any of this with evil intent. I just object to the fact that we cover up and hide things, whether it's Iran-contra, Iraq-gate, or you name it. It's a steady stream.

Mr. Lehrer. Governor Clinton, you have one minute.

Governor Clinton. Let's take Mr. Bush for the moment at his word. I mean, he's right, we don't have any evidence, at least, that our Government did tell Saddam Hussein he could have that part of Kuwait. And let's give him the credit he deserves for organizing Operation Desert Storm and Desert Shield. It was a remarkable event.

But let's look at where, I think, the real mistake was made. In 1988, when the war between Iraq and Iran ended, we knew Saddam Hussein was a tyrant. We had dealt with him because he was against Iran. The enemy of my enemy maybe is my friend.

All right, the war is over. We know he's dropping mustard gas on his own people. We know he's threatened to incinerate half of Israel. Several Government Departments, several, had information that he was converting our aid to military purposes and trying to develop weapons of mass destruction. But in late '89, the President signed a secret policy saying we were going to continue to try to improve relations with him, and we sent him some sort of communication on the eve of his invasion of Kuwait that we still wanted better relations.

So I think what was wrong—I give credit where credit is due, but the responsibility was in coddling Saddam Hussein when there was no reason to do it and when people at high levels in our Government knew he was trying to do things that were outrageous.

Mr. Lehrer. Mr. President, you have a moment—a minute, I'm sorry.

President Bush. It's awful easy when you're dealing with 90/90 hindsight. We did try to bring Saddam Hussein into the family of nations. He did have the fourth largest army. All our Arab allies out there thought we ought to do just exactly that. When he crossed the line, I stood up and looked into the camera and I said, "This aggression will not stand." We formed a historic coalition, and we brought him down. We destroyed the fourth largest army, and the battlefield was searched, and there wasn't one single iota of evidence that any U.S. weapons were on that battlefield. The nuclear capability has been searched by the United Nations, and there hasn't been one single scintilla of evidence that there's any U.S. technology involved in it.

What you're seeing on all this Iraqgate is a bunch of people who were wrong on the war trying to cover their necks here and try to do a little revisionism. I cannot let that stand, because it isn't true. Yes, we had grain credits for Iraq, and there isn't any evidence that those grain credits were diverted into weaponry, none, none whatsoever. And so I just have to say it's fine. You can't say there, Governor Clinton, and say, "Well, I think I have supported the minority"—let sanctions work or wish that it would go away—"but I would have voted with the majority." Come on, that's not leadership.

Mr. Lehrer. The next question goes to Governor Clinton, and Gene Gibbons will ask it. Gene?

Banking Situation

Mr. Gibbons. Governor, an important aspect of leadership is, of course, anticipating problems. During the 1988 campaign, there was little or no mention of the savings and loan crisis that has cost the American people billions and billions of dollars. Now there are rumblings that a commercial bank crisis is on the horizon. Is there such a problem, sir? If so, how bad is it, and what will it cost to clean it up?

Governor Clinton. Gene, there is a problem in the sense that there are some problem banks. And on December 19th, new regulations will go into effect which will, in effect, give the Government the responsibility to close some banks that are not technically insolvent but that are plainly in trouble.

On the other hand, I don't think that we have any reason to believe that the dimensions of this crisis are anywhere near as great as the savings and loan crisis. The mistake that both parties made in Washington with the S&L business was deregulating them without proper capital requirements, proper oversight and regulation, proper training of the executives. Many people predicted what happened, and it was a disaster.

The banking system in this country is fundamentally sound, with some weak banks. I think that our goal ought to be, first of all, not to politicize it, not to frighten people; secondly, to say that we have to enforce the law in two ways. We don't want to overreact as the Federal regulators have, in my judgment, on good banks so that they've created credit crunches that have made our recession worse in the last couple of years, but we do want to act prudently with the banks that are in trouble.

We also want to say that, insofar as is humanly possible, the banking industry itself should pay for the cost of any bank failures, the taxpayers should not, and that will be my policy. I believe we have a good, balanced approach. We can get the good banks loaning money again in the credit crunch, have proper regulation on the ones that are in trouble, and not overreact. It is a serious problem, but I don't see it as the kind of terrible, terrible problem that the S&L problem was.

Mr. Lehrer. President Bush, one minute.

President Bush. Well, I don't believe it would be appropriate for a President to suggest that the banking system is not sound; it is sound. There are some problem banks out there. But what we need is financial reform.

We need some real financial reform, banking reform legislation. I have proposed that, and when I am reelected I believe one of the first things ought to be to press a new Congress, not beholden to the old ways, to pass financial reform legislation that modernizes the banking system, doesn't put a lot of inhibitions on it, and protects the depositors through keeping the FDIC sound. I just was watching some of the proceedings of the American Bankers Association, and I think the general feeling is most of the banks are sound. Certainly there's no comparison here between what happened to the S&L's and where the banks stand right now, in my view.

Mr. Lehrer. Mr. Perot, one minute.

Mr. Perot. Well, nobody's gotten into the real issue yet on the savings and loan. Again, nobody's got a business background, I guess. The whole problem came up in 1984. The President of the United States was told officially it was a $20 billion problem.

These crooks—now, Willie Sutton would have gone to own a savings and loan rather than rob banks. He robbed banks because that's where the money is; owning a savings and loan is where the money was.

Now, in 1984 they were told. I believe the Vice President was in charge of deregulation. Nobody touched that tar baby until the day after election in 1988, because they were flooding both parties with crooked PAC money. And it was, in many cases, stolen PAC money. Now, you and I never got a ride on a lot of these yachts and fancy things it bought, but you and I are paying for it. And they buried it until right after the election.

Now, if you believe the *Washington Post* and you believe this extensive study that's been done, and I'm reading it, right after election day this year they're going to hit us with 100 banks. It'll be a $100 billion problem. Now, if that's true, just tell me now. I'm grown up. I can deal with it. I'll pay my share. But just tell me now. Don't bury it until after the election twice. I say that to both political parties. The people deserve that, since we have to pick up the tab. You've got the PAC money. We'll pay the tab. Just tell us.

Mr. Lehrer. All right, Mr. Perot. The next question, we're going into a new round here on a category just called "differences." And the question goes to you, Mr. Perot, and Gene will ask it. Gene?

Government Reform

Mr. Gibbons. Mr. Perot, aside from the deficit, what Government policy or policies do you really want to do something about? What really sticks in your craw about conditions in this country, beside the deficit, that you would want to fix as President?

Mr. Perot. The debt and the deficit. Well, if you watched my television show the other night, you saw it. If you watch it Thursday, Friday, Saturday this week, you'll get more. So, a shameless plug there, Mr. President. But in a nutshell, we've got to reform our Government or we won't get anything done. We have a Government that doesn't work. All these specific examples I'm giving tonight, if you had a business like that, they'd be leading you away and boarding up the doors. We have a Government that doesn't work. It's supposed to come from the people. It comes at the people. The people need to take their Government back.

You've got to reform Congress. They've got to be servants to the people again. You've got to reform the White House. We've got to turn this thing around. It's a long list of specific items, and I've covered it again and again in print and on television. But very specifically, the key thing is to turn the Government back to the people and take it away from the special interests and have people go to Washington to serve.

Who can give themselves a 23-percent pay raise anywhere in the world except Congress? Who would have 1,200 airplanes worth $2 billion a year just to fly around in? I don't have a free reserved parking place at National Airport. Why should my servants? I don't have an indoor gymnasium and an indoor tennis court, an indoor every other thing they can think of. I don't have a place where I can go make free TV to send to my constituents to try to brainwash them to elect me the next time. And I'm paying for all that for those guys.

I'm going to be running an ad pretty soon that shows—they promised us they were going to hold the line on spending, a tax and budget summit—and I'm going to show how much they've increased this little stuff they do for themselves. It is Silly Putty, folks, and the American people have had enough of it.

Step one, if I get up there, we're going to clean that up. You say, how can I get Congress to do that? I'll have millions of people shoulder-to-shoulder with me, and we will see it done warp speed, because it's wrong. We've turned the country upside down.

Mr. Lehrer. Governor Clinton, you have one minute. Governor.

Governor Clinton. I would just point out on the point Mr. Perot made, I agree that we need to cut spending in Congress. I've called for a 25-percent reduction in congressional staffs and expenditures. But the White House staff increased its expenditures by considerably more than Congress has in the last 4 years under the Bush administration, and Congress has actually spent $1 billion less than President Bush asked them to spend. Now, when you outspend Congress, you're really swinging.

That, however, is not my only passion. The real problem in this country is that most people are working hard and falling further behind. My passion is to pass a jobs program to get incomes up with an investment incentive program to grow jobs in the private sector, to waste less public money and invest more, to control health care costs and provide for affordable health care for all Americans, and to make sure we've got the best trained work force in the world. That is my passion.

We've got to get this country growing again and this economy strong again, or we can't bring down the deficit. Economic growth is the key to the future of this country.

Mr. Lehrer. President Bush, one minute.

President Bush. On Government reform?

Mr. Lehrer. Sir?

President Bush. Government reform?

Mr. Lehrer. Yes. Well, to respond to the subject that Mr. Perot mentioned.

President Bush. How about this for a Government reform policy? Reduce the White House staff by a third after or at the same time the Congress does the same thing for their staff; term limits for Members of the United States Congress. Give the Government back to the people. Let's do it that way. The President has term limits. Let's limit some of these guys sitting out here tonight. Term limits, and then how about a balanced budget amendment to the Constitution? Forty-three States, more than that, States have it, I believe. Let's try that.

You want to do something about all this extra spending that concerns Mr. Perot and me? Okay, how about a line-item veto? Forty-three Governors have that. Give it to the President. If the Congress isn't big enough to do it, let the President have a shot at this excess spending. A line-item veto, that means you can take a line and cut out some of the pork out of a meaningful bill. Governor Clinton keeps hitting me on vetoing legislation. Well, that's the only protection the taxpayer has against some of these reckless pork programs up there. I'd rather be able to just line it right out of there and get on about passing some good stuff, but leave out the garbage. Line-item veto, there's a good reform program for you.

Mr. Lehrer. The next question goes to Governor Clinton. You have two minutes, Governor, and Susan will ask it.

Taxes

Ms. Rook. Governor Clinton, you said that you will raise taxes on the rich, people with incomes of $200,000 a year or higher. A lot of people are saying that you will have to go lower than that, much lower. Will you make a pledge tonight below which—an income level that you will not go below? I am looking for numbers, sir, not just a concept.

Governor Clinton. You can read my plan. My plan says that we want to raise marginal incomes on family incomes above $200,000 from 31 to 36 percent; that we want to ask foreign corporations simply to pay the same percentage of taxes on their income that American corporations pay in America; that we want to use that money to provide over $100 billion in tax cuts for investment in new plants and equipment, for small business, for new technologies, and for middle class tax relief.

Now, I can tell you this: I will not raise taxes on the middle class to pay for these programs. If the money does not come in there to pay for these programs, we will cut other Government spending, or we will slow down the phase-in to the programs. I am not going to raise taxes on the middle class to pay for these programs.

Now, furthermore, I am not going to tell you "Read my lips" on anything because I cannot foresee what emergencies might develop in this country. And the President said never, never, never would he raise taxes, in New Jersey. Within a day, Marlin Fitzwater, his spokesman, said, now, that's not a promise. So I think even he has learned that you can't say "Read my lips" because you can't know what emergencies might come up.

But I can tell you this: I'm not going to raise taxes on middle class Americans to pay for the programs I've recommended. Read my plan. And you know how you can trust me about that? Because you know, in the first debate, Mr. Bush made some news. He had just said Jim Baker was going to be Secretary of State, but in the first debate he said no, now he's going to be responsible for domestic economic policy. Well, I'll tell you, I'll make some news in the third debate: The person responsible for domestic economic policy in my administration will be Bill Clinton. I'm going to make those decisions, and I won't raise taxes in the middle class to pay for my program.

Mr. Lehrer. President Bush, you have one minute.

President Bush. That's what worries me, that he's going to be responsible. He would do for the United States what he has done for Arkansas. He would do for the United States what he's done to Arkansas. We do not want to be the lowest of the low. We are not a nation in decline. We are a rising nation. My problem is, I heard what he said. He said, "I want to take it from the rich, raise $150 billion from the rich." To get it, to get $150 billion in new taxes, you've got to go down to the guy that's making $36,600. And if you want to pay for the rest of his plan, all the other spending programs, you're going to sock it to the working man.

So when you hear "tax the rich," Mr. and Mrs. America, watch your wallet. Lock your wallet, because he's coming right after you just like Jimmy Carter did, and just like you're going to get—you're going to end up with interest rates at 21 percent, and you're going to have inflation going through the roof. Yes, we're having tough times. But we do not need to go back to the failed policies of the past when you had a Democratic President and a spendthrift Democratic Congress.

Mr. Lehrer. Mr. Perot.

Governor Clinton. You permitted Mr. Bush to break the rules, he said to defend the honor of the country. What about the honor of my State? We rank first in the country in job growth. We've got the lowest spending, State and local, in the country and the second lowest tax burden. The difference between Arkansas and the United States is that we're going in the right direction, and this country's going in the wrong direction. And I have to defend the honor of my State.

Mr. Lehrer. We've got a wash, according to my calculations. We have a wash. And we'll go to Mr. Perot for one minute. In other words, the violation of the rule; that's what I meant.

Mr. Perot. I'm the only one that's untarnished at this point.

Mr. Lehrer. That's right, you're clean. [Laughter]

Mr. Perot. I'm sure I'll do it before it's over.

The key thing here, see, we all come up with images. Images don't fix anything. You know, I'm starting to understand it. You stay around this long enough, you think about—if you talk about it in Washington, you think you did it. If you've been on television about it, you think you did it. [Laughter] What we need is people to stop talking and start doing.

Now, our real problem here is they both have plans that will not work. The *Wall Street Journal* said your numbers don't add up. And you can take it out on charts; you look at all the studies that different groups have done; you go out 4, 5, 6 years: We're still drifting along with a huge deficit.

So let's come back to harsh reality. Everybody said, "Gee, Perot, you're tough." I say, well, this is not as tough as World War II; and it's not as tough as the Revolution. It's fair-shared sacrifice to do the right thing for our country and for our children. And it will be fun if we all work together to do it.

Mr. Lehrer. This is the last question, and it goes to President Bush for a 2-minute answer. And it will be asked by Helen.

Presidential Campaign

Ms. Thomas. Mr. President, why have you dropped so dramatically in the leadership polls, from the high eighties to the forties? And you have said you will do anything you have to do to get reelected. What can you do in 2 weeks to win reelection?

President Bush. Well, I think the answer to why the drop, I think, has been the economy in the doldrums. Why I'll win is I think I have the best plan of the three of us up here to do something about it. Mine does not grow the Government. It does not have Government invest. It says we need to do better in terms of stimulating private business. We've got a big philosophical difference here tonight between one who thinks the Government can do all these things through tax and spend, and one who thinks it ought to go the other way.

So I believe the answer is, I'm going to win it because I'm getting into focus my agenda for America's renewal, and also I think that Governor Clinton's had pretty much of a free ride on looking specifically at the Arkansas record. He keeps criticizing us, criticizing me; I'm the incumbent. Fine. But he's an incumbent. And we've got to look at all the facts. They're almost at the bottom on every single category. We can't do that to the American people.

Then, Helen, I really believe where people are going to ask this question about trust—because I do think there's a pattern by Governor Clinton of saying one thing to please one group and then trying to please another group. I think that pattern is a dangerous thing to suggest would work for the Oval Office. It doesn't work that way when you're President. Truman is right: The buck stops there. You have to make decisions, even when it's against your own interest. I've done that. It's against my political interests to say go ahead and go along with the tax increase. But I did what I thought was right at the time. So I think people are going to be looking for trust and experience.

Then, I mentioned it the other night, I think if there's a crisis, people are going to say, "Well, George Bush has taken us through some tough crises, and we trust him to do that." So I'll make the appeal on a wide array of issues.

Also I've got a philosophical difference—I've got to watch the clock here—I don't think we're a declining nation. The whole world has had economic problems. We're doing better than a lot of the countries in the world. And we're going to lead the way out of this economic recession across this world and economic slowdown here at home.

Mr. Lehrer. Mr. Perot, you have one minute.

President Bush. That's why I think I'll win.

Mr. Lehrer. Mr. Perot, you have—sorry. Excuse me, sir. Mr. Perot, you have one minute.

Mr. Perot. I'm the last one, right?

Mr. Lehrer. No. Governor Clinton has a minute after you. Then we have the closing statements.

Mr. Perot. One minute after you?

Mr. Lehrer. Right.

Mr. Perot. I'm totally focused on the fact that we may have bank failures, and nobody answered it. I'm totally focused on that fact that we are still evading the issue of the Glaspie papers. I'm totally focused on the fact that we still could have enterprise zones, according to both parties, but we don't. So I'm still focused on gridlock, I guess.

I'm also focused on the fact that isn't it a paradox that we have the highest productivity in our work force in the industrialized world and at the same time have the largest trade deficit, and at the same time rank behind nine other nations in what we pay our most productive people in the world. We're losing whole industries overseas. Now, can't somebody agree with me that the Government is breaking business' legs with these trade agreements? They're breaking business' legs in a number of different ways. We have an adversarial relationship that's destroying jobs and sending them overseas, while we have the finest workers in the world. Keep in mind the factory worker has nothing to do with anything except putting it together on the factory floor. It's our obligation to make sure that we give him the finest products in the world to put together, and we don't break his legs in the process.

Mr. Lehrer. Governor Clinton, one minute.

Governor Clinton. I really can't believe Mr. Bush is still trying to make trust an issue after "read my lips" and "15 billion new jobs" and embracing what he called "voodoo economics" and embracing an export enhancing program for farmers he threatened to veto and going all around the country giving out money and programs that he once opposed. But the main thing is he still didn't get it, from what he said the other night to that fine woman on our program, the 209 people in Richmond. They don't want us talking about each other. They want us to talk about the problems of this country.

I don't think he'll be reelected because trickle-down economics is a failure, and he's offering more of it. And what he's saying about my program is just not true. Look at the Republicans that have endorsed me, high-tech executives in northern California. Look at the 24 generals and admirals, retired, who have endorsed me, including the deputy commander of Desert Storm. Look at Sarah Brady, Jim Brady's wife, President Reagan's Press Secretary, who endorsed me because he knuckled under to the NRA and wouldn't fight for the Brady bill. We've got a broad-based coalition that goes beyond party, because I am going to change this country and make it better with the help of the American people.

Mr. Lehrer. All right. That was the final question and answer, and we now go to the closing statements. Each candidate will have up to 2 minutes. The order was determined by a drawing. Governor Clinton, you are first. Governor.

Closing Statements

Governor Clinton. First I'd like to thank the Commission and my opponents for participating in these debates and making them possible. I think the real winners of the debates were the American people. I was especially moved in Richmond a few days ago when 209 of our fellow citizens got to ask us questions. They went a long way toward reclaiming this election for the American people and taking their country back.

I want to say, since this is the last time I'll be on a platform with my opponents, that even though I disagree with Mr. Perot on how fast we can reduce the deficit and how much we can increase taxes on the middle class, I really respect what he's done in this campaign to bring the issue of deficit reduction to our attention. I'd like to say to Mr. Bush, even though I've got profound differences with him, I do honor his service to our country. I appreciate his efforts, and I wish him well. I just believe it's time to change.

I offer a new approach. It's not trickle-down economics; it's been tried for 12 years, and it's failed. More people are working harder for less, 100,000 people a month losing their health insurance, unemployment going up, our economy slowing down. We can do better. And it's not tax-and-spend economics. It's invest and grow, put our people first, control health care costs and provide basic health care to all Americans, have an education system second to none, and revitalize the private economy. That is my commitment to you. It is a kind of change that can open up a whole new world of opportunities to America as we enter the last decade of this century and move toward the 21st century. I want a country where people who work hard and play by the rules are rewarded, not punished. I want a country where people are coming together across the lines of race and region and income. I know we can do better.

It won't take miracles, and it won't happen overnight. But we can do much, much better if we have the courage to change. Thank you very much.

Mr. Lehrer. President Bush, your closing statement, sir.

President Bush. Three weeks from now—two weeks from tomorrow, America goes to the polls. You're going to have to decide who you want to lead this country to economic recovery. On jobs, that's the number one priority, and I believe my program for stimulating investment, encouraging small business, brand-new approach to education, strengthening the American family, and yes, creating more exports is the way to go. I don't believe in trickle-down Government. I don't believe in larger taxes and larger Government spending.

On foreign affairs, some think it's irrelevant. I believe it's not. We're living in an interconnected world. The whole world is having economic difficulties. The U.S. is doing better than a lot. But we've got to do even better. If a crisis comes up, I ask: Who has the judgment and the experience and, yes, the character to make the right decision?

Lastly, the other night on character, Governor Clinton said it's not the character of the President but "the character of the Presidency." I couldn't disagree more. Horace Greeley said, "The only thing that endures is character." And I think it was Justice Black who talked about "Great nations, like great men, must keep their word." And so the question is: Who will safeguard this Nation? Who will safeguard our people and our children?

I need your support. I ask for your vote. And may God bless the United States of America.

Mr. Lehrer. Mr. Perot, your closing statement, sir.

Mr. Perot. To the millions of fine, decent people who did the unthinkable and took their country back in their own hands and put me on the ballot, let me pledge to you that tonight is just the beginning. These next 2 weeks we will be going full steam ahead to make sure that you get a voice and that you get your country back.

This Thursday night on ABC from 8:30 to 9, Friday night on NBC from 8 to 8:30, and Saturday night on CBS from 8 to 8:30, we'll be down in the trenches, under the hood, working on fixing the old car to get it back on the road. [Laughter]

Now, the question is: Can we win? Absolutely we can win, because it's your country. The question really is: Who do you want in to the White House? It's that simple. Now, you've got to stop letting these people tell you who to vote for. You've got to stop letting these folks in the press tell you you're throwing your vote away. You've got to start using your own head.

Then the question is: Can we govern? I love that one. The "we" is you and me. You bet your hat we can govern, because we will be in there together, and we will figure out what to do. You won't tolerate gridlock. You won't tolerate endless meandering and wandering around. You won't tolerate nonperformance. And believe me, anybody who knows me understands I have a very low tolerance for nonperformance also. Together we can get anything done.

The President mentioned that you need the right person in a crisis. Well, folks, we've got one. And that crisis is a financial crisis. Pretty simply, who's the best qualified person up here on the stage to create jobs? Make your decision and vote on November the 3d. I suggest you might consider somebody who's created jobs.

Second, who's the best person to manage money? I suggest you pick a person who's successfully managed money. Who's the best person to get results and not talk? Look at the record; make your decision.

Finally, who would you give your pension fund and your savings account to to manage? And the last one, who would you ask to be the trustee of your estate and take care of your children if something happened to you?

Finally, to you students up there, God bless you. I'm doing this for you. I want you to have the American dream. And to the American people, to the American people, I'm doing this because I love you. That's it. Thank you very much.

Mr. Lehrer. Thank you, Mr. Perot. Thank you, Mr. President. Thank you, Governor Clinton, for being with us tonight and the previous debates. Thank you to the panel.

The only thing that is left to be said is, from Michigan State University in East Lansing, I'm Jim Lehrer. Thank you, and good night.

63. Remarks in Houston on the Results of the Presidential Election November 3, 1992

The President. Thank you. Thank you very, very much. Hey, listen, we've got to get going. Thank you. Thank you very much. Hey, listen, you guys.

Audience members. Thank you, George! Thank you, George! Thank you, George!

The President. Hey, thank you very much. Look, thank you so much. Well, here's the way I see it. Here's the way we see it and the country should see it, that the people have spoken. And we respect the majesty of the democratic system.

I just called Governor Clinton over in Little Rock and offered my congratulations. He did run a strong campaign. I wish him well in the White House. And I want the country to know that our entire administration will work closely with his team to ensure the smooth transition of power. There is important work to be done, and America must always come first. So we will get behind this new President and wish him well.

To all who voted for us, voted for me here, especially here, but all across the country, thank you for your support. We have fought the good fight, and we've kept the faith. And I believe I have upheld the honor of the Presidency of the United States. Now I ask that we stand behind our new President. Regardless of our differences, all Americans share the same purpose: to make this, the world's greatest nation, more safe and more secure and to guarantee every American a shot at the American dream.

I would like to thank so many of you who have worked beside me to improve America and to literally change the world. Let me thank our great Vice President, Dan Quayle. You know, in the face of a tremendous pounding, he stood for what he believes in. He will always have my profound gratitude and certainly my respect.

I would like to salute so many that did special work: Rich Bond up at the RNC; Bob Teeter, who ran the campaign; Bob Mosbacher; our entire campaign team. They've run a valiant effort in a very, very difficult year. I also want to salute the members of the Cabinet, all of whom who have served this Nation with honor, with integrity, and with great distinction. And I would like to single out two leaders who represent the ideal in public service. Together they've helped lead the world through a period of unprecedented transition. I'm talking, of course, about my National Security Advisor, Brent Scowcroft, and my good friend and fellow Texan, our Secretary of State, Jim Baker.

Finally, of course, I want to thank my entire family, with a special emphasis on a woman named Barbara. She's inspired this entire Nation, and I think the country will always be grateful.

But tonight is really not a night for speeches. But I want to share a special message with the young people of America. You see, I remain absolutely convinced that we are a rising nation. We have been in an extraordinarily difficult period. But do not be deterred, kept away from public service by the smoke and fire of a campaign year or the ugliness of politics. As for me, I'm going to serve and try to find ways to help people. But I plan to get very active in the grandchild business and in finding ways to help others. But I urge you, the young people of this country, to participate in the political process. It needs your idealism. It needs your drive. It needs your conviction.

And again, my thanks, my congratulations to Governor Clinton; to his running mate, Senator Gore. And a special thanks to each and every one of you, many of you who have been at my side in every single political battle.

May God bless the United States of America. Thank you very, very much. Thank you so much. Thank you.

64. Address to the Nation on the Situation in Somalia
December 4, 1992

I want to talk to you today about the tragedy in Somalia and about a mission that can ease suffering and save lives. Every American has seen the shocking images from Somalia. The scope of suffering there is hard to imagine. Already, over a quarter-million people, as many people as live in Buffalo, New York, have died in the Somali famine. In the months ahead 5 times that number, 1 1/2 million people, could starve to death.

For many months now, the United States has been actively engaged in the massive international relief effort to ease Somalia's suffering. All told, America has sent Somalia 200,000 tons of food, more than half the world total. This summer, the distribution system broke down. Truck convoys from Somalia's ports were blocked. Sufficient food failed to reach the starving in the interior of Somalia.

So in August, we took additional action. In concert with the United Nations, we sent in the U.S. Air Force to help fly food to the towns. To date, American pilots have flown over 1,400 flights, delivering over 17,000 tons of food aid. And when the U.N. authorized 3,500 U.N. guards to protect the relief operation, we flew in the first of them, 500 soldiers from Pakistan.

But in the months since then, the security situation has grown worse. The U.N. has been prevented from deploying its initial commitment of troops. In many cases, food from relief flights is being looted upon landing; food convoys have been hijacked; aid workers assaulted; ships with food have been subject to artillery attacks that prevented them from docking. There is no government in Somalia. Law and order have broken down. Anarchy prevails.

One image tells the story. Imagine 7,000 tons of food aid literally bursting out of a warehouse on a dock in Mogadishu, while Somalis starve less than a kilometer away because relief workers cannot run the gauntlet of armed gangs roving the city. Confronted with these conditions, relief groups called for outside troops to provide security so they could feed people. It's now clear that military support is necessary to ensure the safe delivery of the food Somalis need to survive.

It was this situation which led us to tell the United Nations that the United States would be willing to provide more help to enable relief to be delivered. Last night the United Nations Security Council, by unanimous vote and after the tireless efforts of Secretary-General Boutros-Ghali, welcomed the United States' offer to lead a coalition to get the food through.

After consulting with my advisers, with world leaders, and the congressional leadership, I have today told Secretary-General Boutros-Ghali that America will answer the call. I have given the order to Secretary Cheney to move a substantial American force into Somalia. As I speak, a Marine amphibious ready group, which we maintain at sea, is offshore Mogadishu. These troops will be joined by elements of the 1st Marine Expeditionary Force, based out of Camp Pendleton, California, and by the Army's 10th Mountain Division out of Fort Drum, New York. These and other American forces will assist in Operation Restore Hope. They are America's finest. They will perform this mission with courage and compassion, and they will succeed.

The people of Somalia, especially the children of Somalia, need our help. We're able to ease their suffering. We must help them live. We must give them hope. America must act.

In taking this action, I want to emphasize that I understand the United States alone cannot right the world's wrongs. But we also know that some crises in the world cannot be resolved without American involvement, that American action is often necessary as a catalyst for broader involvement of the community of nations. Only the United States has the global reach to place a large security force on the ground in such a distant place quickly and efficiently and thus save thousands of innocents from death.

We will not, however, be acting alone. I expect forces from about a dozen countries to join us in this mission. When we see Somalia's children starving, all of America hurts. We've tried to help in many ways. And make no mistake about it, now we and our allies will ensure that aid gets through. Here is what we and our coalition partners will do:

First, we will create a secure environment in the hardest hit parts of Somalia, so that food can move from ships over land to the people in the countryside now devastated by starvation.

Second, once we have created that secure environment, we will withdraw our troops, handing the security mission back to a regular U.N. peacekeeping force. Our mission has a limited objective: To open the supply routes, to get the food moving, and to prepare the way for a U.N. peacekeeping force to keep it moving. This operation is not open-ended. We will not stay one day longer than is absolutely necessary.

Let me be very clear: Our mission is humanitarian, but we will not tolerate armed gangs ripping off their own people, condemning them to death by starvation. General Hoar and his troops have the authority to take whatever military action is necessary to safeguard the lives of our troops and the lives of Somalia's people. The outlaw elements in Somalia must understand this is serious business. We will accomplish our mission. We have no intent to remain in Somalia with fighting forces, but we are determined to do it right, to secure an environment that will allow food to get to the starving people of Somalia.

To the people of Somalia I promise this: We do not plan to dictate political outcomes. We respect your sovereignty and independence. Based on my conversations with other coalition leaders, I can state with confidence: We come to your country for one reason only, to enable the starving to be fed.

Let me say to the men and women of our Armed Forces: We are asking you to do a difficult and dangerous job. As Commander in Chief I assure you, you will have our full support to get the job done, and we will bring you home as soon as possible.

Finally, let me close with a message to the families of the men and women who take part in this mission: I understand it is difficult to see your loved ones go, to send them off knowing they will not be home for the holidays, but the humanitarian mission they undertake is in the finest traditions of service. So, to every sailor, soldier, airman, and marine who is involved in this mission, let me say, you're doing God's work. We will not fail.

Thank you, and may God bless the United States of America.

SELECTED BIBLIOGRAPHY

Reference

Galub, Arthur L., and George J. Lankevich. *The Rehnquist Court: 1986–1994.* Danbury, Conn.: Grolier Educational Corporation, 1995.

Graff, Henry F., ed. *The Presidents: A Reference History.* 3rd ed. New York: Scribner's, 2002.

Levy, Peter B. *Encyclopedia of the Reagan-Bush Years.* Westport, Conn.: Greenwood Press, 1996.

Public Papers of the President: George Bush. Washington, D.C.: U.S. Government Printing Office, 1990–1993.

General

Barilleaux, Ryan J., and Mary E. Stuckey. *Leadership and the Bush Presidency: Prudence or Drift in an Era of Change?* Westport, Conn.: Greenwood Press, 1992.

Berman, William C. *America's Right Turn: From Nixon to Clinton.* Baltimore: Johns Hopkins University Press, 1998.

Campbell, Colin, and Bert Rockman, eds. *The Bush Presidency: First Appraisals.* Chatham, N.J.: Chatham House, 1991.

Duffy, Michael, and Dan Goodgame. *Marching in Place: The Status Quo Presidency of George Bush.* New York: Simon and Schuster, 1992.

Greene, John Robert. *The Presidency of George Bush.* Lawrence: University Press of Kansas, 2000.

Heagerty, Leo E., ed. *Eyes on the President—George Bush: History in Essays and Cartoons.* Occidental, Calif.: Chronos Publishing, 1993.

Hill, Dilys, and Phil Williams, eds. *The Bush Presidency: Triumphs and Adversities.* New York: St. Martin's Press, 1994.

Mervin, David. *George Bush and the Guardianship Presidency.* New York: St. Martin's Press, 1996.

Rose, Richard. *The Postmodern President: George Bush Meets the World.* Chatham, N.J.: Chatham House, 1990.

Thompson, Kenneth W., ed. *Portraits of American Presidents.* Vol. 10, *The Bush Presidency.* Lanham, Md.: University Press of America, 1997.

Tiefer, Charles. *The Semi-Sovereign Presidency: The Bush Administration's Strategy for Governing without Congress.* Boulder, Colo.: Westview Press, 1994.

By George Bush

Bush, George. *All the Best, George Bush: My Life in Letters and Other Writings.* New York: Simon and Schuster, 1999.

———. *Looking Forward: An Autobiography.* New York: Bantam Books, 1987.

Bush, George, and Brent Scowcroft. *A World Transformed: The Collapse of the Soviet Empire, the Unification of Germany, Tiananmen Square, and the Gulf War.* New York: Knopf, 1998.

Biographies and Photo Essays: Bush

Green, Fitzhugh. *George Bush: An Intimate Portrait.* New York: Hippocrene Books, 1989.

King, Nicholas. *George Bush: A Biography.* New York: Donald Mease and Company, 1980.

Parmet, Herbert S. *George Bush: The Life of a Lone Star Yankee.* New York: Scribner's, 1997.

Sufrin, Mark. *The Story of George Bush: The Forty-First President of the United States.* Milwaukee: Gareth Stevens Publishing, 1989.

Tarpley, Webster Griffin, and Anton Chaitkin. *George Bush: The Unauthorized Biography.* Washington, D.C.: Executive Intelligence Review, 1992.

Valdez, David. *George Herbert Walker Bush: A Photographic Profile.* College Station: Texas A&M University Press, 1997.

Wead, Doug. *Man of Integrity.* Eugene, Ore.: Harvest House Publishers, 1988.

Weinberg, Bill. *George Bush: The Super-Spy Drug-Smuggling President.* New York: Shadow Press, 1992.

Bush: The Pre-Presidency (World War II—1988)

Abrams, Herbert. *"The President's Been Shot": Confusion, Disability and the 25th Amendment in the Aftermath of the Attempted Assassination of Ronald Reagan.* New York: W. W. Norton, 1992.

Helgesen, Sally. *Wildcatters: A Story of Texas.* Garden City, N.Y.: Doubleday, 1981.

Hyams, Joe. *Flight of the Avenger: George Bush at War.* New York: Harcourt Brace Jovanovich, 1991.

Knaggs, John R. *Two-Party Texas: The John Tower Era, 1961–1984.* Austin: Eakins Press, 1986.

Messick, William Lee. *America's Fighting Presidents.* Boyne City, Mich.: Harbor House Publishing, 1993.

Ranelagh, John. *The Agency: The Rise and Decline of the CIA, from Wild Bill Donovan to William Casey.* New York: Simon and Schuster, 1986.

Cabinet Members, Staff, Family, and Advisers

Baker, James. *The Politics of Diplomacy: Revolution, War, and Peace, 1989–1992.* New York: G. P. Putnam's Sons, 1995.

Brady, John. *Bad Boy: The Life and Politics of Lee Atwater.* Reading, Mass.: Addison-Wesley, 1997.

Bromley, D. Alan. *The President's Scientists: Reminiscences of a White House Science Advisor.* New Haven, Conn.: Yale University Press, 1994.

Bush, Barbara. *A Memoir.* New York: St. Martin's Press, 1994.

———. *Millie's Book: As Dictated to Barbara Bush.* New York: William Morrow and Company, 1990.

Darman, Richard. *Who's in Control? Polar Politics and the Sensible Center.* New York: Simon and Schuster, 1996.

Fenno, Richard F., Jr. *The Making of a Senator: Dan Quayle.* Washington, D.C.: Congressional Quarterly Press, 1989.

Fitzwater, Marlin. *Call the Briefing! Bush and Reagan, Sam and Helen: A Decade with Presidents and the Press.* New York: Times Books, 1995.

Kilian, Pamela. *Barbara Bush: A Biography.* New York: St. Martin's Press, 1992.

Matalin, Mary, and James Carville. *All's Fair: Love, War, and Running for President.* New York: Random House, 1994.

Noonan, Peggy. *What I Saw at the Revolution: A Political Life in the Reagan Era.* New York: Ivy Books, 1990.

Pinkerton, James P. *What Comes Next: The End of Big Government—and the New Paradigm Ahead.* New York: Hyperion, 1995.

Podhoretz, John. *Hell of a Ride: Backstage at the White House Follies, 1989–1993.* New York: Simon and Schuster, 1993.

Powell, Colin. *My American Journey.* New York: Random House, 1995.

Quayle, Dan. *Standing Firm.* New York: Harper, 1994.

Radcliffe, Donnie. *Simply Barbara Bush: A Portrait of America's Candid First Lady.* New York: Warner Books, 1989.

Roth, David. *Sacred Honor: Colin Powell.* New York: HarperCollins, 1993.

Schwarzkopf, Norman H. *It Doesn't Take a Hero.* New York: Bantam Books, 1992.

Seidman, L. William. *Full Faith and Credit: The Great S&L Debacle and Other Washington Sagas.* New York: Times Books, 1993.

Tower, John G. *Consequences: A Personal and Political Memoir.* Boston: Little, Brown, 1991.

Witcover, Jules. *Crapshoot: Rolling the Dice on the Vice Presidency.* New York: Crown, 1992.

Woodward, Bob, and David S. Broder. *The Man Who Would Be President: Dan Quayle.* New York: Simon and Schuster, 1992.

Presidential Election of 1988 and Transition

Bennett, W. Lance. *The Governing Crisis: Media, Money, and Marketing in American Elections.* New York: St. Martin's Press, 1996.

Black, Christine M., and Thomas Oliphant. *All by Myself: The Unmaking of a Presidential Campaign.* Chester, Conn.: Globe Pequot Press, 1989.

Blumenthal, Sidney. *Pledging Allegiance: The Last Campaign of the Cold War.* New York: Harper-Collins, 1990.

Cramer, Richard Ben. *What It Takes: The Way to the White House.* New York: Random House, 1992.

Dukakis, Kitty. *Now You Know.* New York: Simon and Schuster, 1990.

Duncan, David. *Grass Roots: One Year in the Life of the New Hampshire Presidential Primary.* New York: Viking, 1990.

Dunkel, David R., ed. *Campaign for President: The Managers Look at '88.* Dover, Mass.: Auburn House Publishing, 1989.

Gaines, Richard, and Michael Segal. *Dukakis: The Man Who Would Be President.* New York: William Morrow and Company, 1987.

Germond, Jack W., and Jules Witcover. *Whose Broad Stripes and Bright Stars? The Trivial Pursuit of the Presidency, 1988.* New York: Warner Books, 1989.

Gilette, Michael. *Snapshots of the 1988 Presidential Campaign.* 3 vols. Austin: Lyndon B. Johnson School of Public Affairs, University of Texas, 1992.

Goldman, Peter, Tom Matthews, and the *Newsweek* Special Election Team. *The Quest for the Presidency, 1988.* New York: Touchstone Books/ Simon and Schuster, 1989.

Grimes, Ann. *Running Mates: The Making of a First Lady.* New York: William Morrow and Company, 1990.

Jamieson, Kathleen Hall. *Dirty Politics: Deception, Distraction, and Democracy.* New York: Oxford University Press, 1992.

Loevy, Robert D. *The Flawed Path to the Presidency, 1992.* Albany: State University of New York Press, 1995.

Morrison, Donald, ed. *The Winning of the White House, 1988.* New York: New American Library, 1989.

Pfiffner, James P. *The Bush Transition: A Friendly Takeover.* Richmond, Va.: Institute of Public Policy, George Mason University, 1995.

Pomper, Gerald M., ed. *The Election of 1988: Reports and Interpretations.* Seven Bridges Press, 1989.

Ridley, Matt. *Warts and All: The Men Who Would Be Bush.* New York: Viking, 1989.

Simon, Roger. *Road Show: In America, Anyone Can Become President—Its One of the Risks We Take.* New York: Farrar, Straus, and Giroux, 1990.

Stempel, Guido H., and John W. Windhauser. *The Media in the 1984 and 1988 Presidential Campaigns.* Westport, Conn.: Greenwood Publishing, 1991.

Turner, Robert, and Charles Kenney. *Dukakis: An American Odyssey.* New York: Houghton Mifflin, 1991.

Congress/Congressional Ethics

Barry, John M. *The Ambition and the Power: The Fall of Jim Wright: A True Story of Washington.* New York: Viking, 1989.

Davidson, Roger, ed. *The Postreform Congress.* New York: St. Martin's Press, 1992.

Tiefer, Charles. *The Semi-Sovereign Presidency: The Bush Administration's Strategy for Governing without Congress.* Boulder, Colo.: Westview Press, 1994.

The Savings and Loans Crisis

Bartholomew, Philip F. *Resolving the Thrift Crisis.* Collingdale, Pa.: Diane Publishing Company, 1993.

Long, Robert Emmet. *Banking Scandals: The S&L and BCCI.* New York: H. W. Wilson, 1993.

Mayer, Martin. *The Greatest Ever Bank Robbery: The Collapse of the Savings and Loan Industry.* New York: Scribner's, 1990.

Meigs, A. James, and John C. Goodman. *Federal Deposit Insurance Corporation: A Case for Radical Reform.* Washington, D.C.: National Center for Policy Analysis, 1990.

Pizzo, Stephen, Mary Fricker, and Paul Muolo. *Inside Job: The Looting of America's Savings and Loans.* New York: McGraw-Hill, 1989.

White, Laurence J. *The SL Debacle: Public Policy Lessons for Bank and Thrift Regulation.* New York: Oxford University Press, 1992.

Wilmsen, Steven K. *Silverado: Neil Bush and the Savings and Loan Scandal.* Washington, D.C.: National Press Books, 1991.

Supreme Court/Nomination of Clarence Thomas

Danforth, John C. *Ressurection: The Confirmation of Clarence Thomas.* New York: Viking Penguin, 1994.

Galub, Arthur L., and George J. Lankevich. *The Rehnquist Court: 1986–1994.* Danbury, Conn.: Grolier Educational Corporation, 1995.

Hill, Anita. *Speaking Truth to Power.* New York: Doubleday, 1997.

Mayer, Jane, and Jill Abramson. *Strange Justice: The Selling of Clarence Thomas.* Boston: Houghton Mifflin, 1994.

Miller, Anita, ed. *The Complete Transcripts of the Clarence Thomas/Anita Hill Hearings.* Chicago: Academy Chicago Publishers, 1994.

Phelps, Timothy M., and Helen Winternitz. *Capitol Games: The Inside Story of Clarence Thomas, Anita Hill, and a Supreme Court Nomination.* New York: HarperPerennial, 1992.

Domestic Policies: General

Cohen, Richard E. *Washington at Work: Back Rooms and Clean Air.* [The Clean Air Act Amendments of 1990] New York: Macmillan Publishing Company, 1992.

Davidson, Roger, ed. *The Postreform Congress.* New York: St. Martin's Press, 1992.

Fuss, Charles M., Jr. *Sea of Grass: The Maritime Drug War, 1970–1990.* Annapolis, Md.: Naval Institute Press, 1996.

Goldstein, Robert J. *Burning the Flag: The Great 1989–1990 American Flag Desecration Controversy.* Kent, Ohio: Kent State University Press, 1998.

Goldstein, Robert Justin. *Saving "Old Glory": The History of the American Flag Desecration Controversy.* Boulder, Colo.: Westview Press, 1994.

Griffen, Rodman D. *The Disabilities Act: Protecting the Rights of the Disabled Will Have Far-Reaching Effects.* Washington, D.C.: Congressional Quarterly, Inc., in conjunction with EBSCO Publishing, 1991.

Kolb, Charles. *White House Daze: The Unmaking of Domestic Policy in the Bush Years.* New York: The Free Press, 1993.

Logsdon, John M., ed. *Exploring the Unknown: Selected Documents in the History of the U.S. Civilian Space Program.* Vol. 3. *Using Space.* Washington, D.C.: U.S. Government Printing Office, 1998.

Mitchell, George. *World on Fire: Saving an Endangered Earth.* New York: Scribner's and Sons, 1991.

Owens, Major R. *Americans with Disabilities Act: Initial Accessibility Good but Important Barriers Remain.* Washington, D.C.: U.S. General Accounting Office, 1993.

Percy, Stephen. *Disability, Civil Rights and Public Policy.* Tuscaloosa: University of Alabama Press, 1992.

Phillips, Kevin. *Boiling Point: Democrats, Republicans, and the Decline of Middle-Class Prosperity.* New York: Random House, 1993.

———. *The Politics of Rich and Poor: Wealth and the American Electorate in the Reagan Aftermath.* New York: Random House, 1990.

Schull, Stephen. *A Kinder Gentler Racism? The Reagan-Bush Civil Rights Legacy.* New York: M. E. Sharpe, 1993.

Foreign Policies/Defense Policies/ Intelligence: General

Andrew, Christopher. *For the President's Eyes Only: Secret Intelligence and the American Presidency from Washington to Bush.* New York: Harper-Collins, 1995.

Baker, James. *The Politics of Diplomacy: Revolution, War, and Peace, 1989–1992.* New York: G. P. Putnam's Sons, 1995.

Kagan, Robert. *A Twilight Struggle: American Power and Nicaragua, 1977–1990.* New York: The Free Press, 1996.

Prados, John. *Keeper of the Keys: A History of the NSC from Truman to Bush.* New York: Morrow, 1991.

Reed, Terry, and John Commungs. *Compromise: Clinton, Bush, and the CIA.* Granite Bay, Calif.: Clandestine Publishing, 1995.

Said, Edward W. *The Politics of Dispossession: The Struggle for Palestinian Self-Determination, 1969–1994.* New York: Random House, 1994.

Simpson, Christopher. *National Security Directives of the Reagan and Bush Administrations: The Declassified History of U.S. Political and Military Policy, 1981–1991.* Boulder, Colo.: Westview Press, 1995.

Tucker, Robert W., and David C. Hendrickson. *The Imperial Temptation: The New World Order and America's Purpose.* New York: Council on Foreign Relations, 1992.

Von Bertrab, Hermann. *Negotiating NAFTA: A Mexican Envoy's Account.* Westport, Conn.: Praeger Publishing, 1997.

The "End of the Cold War"

Beschloss, Michael, and Strobe Talbott. *At the Highest Levels: The Inside Story of the End of the Cold War.* Boston: Little, Brown, 1993.

Doder, Dusko, and Louise Branson. *Gorbachev: Heretic in the Kremlin.* New York: Penguin, 1990.

Garthoff, Raymond L. *The Great Transition: American-Soviet Relations and the End of the Cold War.* Washington, D.C.: Brookings Institution Press, 1997.

Gorbachev, Mikhail. *Memoirs.* New York: Doubleday, 1996.

Haass, Richard. *Intervention: The Use of American Military Force in the Post–Cold War World.* Washington, D.C.: Carnegie Endowment for International Peace, 1998.

Lewin, Moshe. *The Gorbachev Phenomenon: A Historical Interpretation.* Berkeley: University of California Press, 1991.

Markusen, Ann, and Joel Yudken. *Dismantling the Cold War Economy.* New York: Basic Books, 1992.

Matlock, Jack F. *Autopsy of an Empire: The American Ambassador's Account of the Collapse of the Soviet Union.* New York: Random House, 1995.

Oksenberg, Michel, ed. *Beijing Spring, 1989: Confrontation and Conflict—The Basic Documents.* New York: M. E. Sharpe, 1990.

Pond, Elizabeth. *Beyond the Wall: Germany's Road to Unification.* Washington, D.C.: Brookings Institution Press, 1993.

Schweizer, Peter. *Victory: The Reagan Administration's Secret Strategy That Hastened the Collapse of the Soviet Union.* New York: Grove Atlantic, 1994.

Sheehy, Gail. *The Man Who Changed the World: The Lives of Mikhail S. Gorbachev.* New York: HarperCollins, 1990.

Tucker, Robert W., and David C. Hendrickson. *The Imperial Temptation: The New World Order and America's Purpose.* New York: Council on Foreign Relations, 1992.

Panama and Noriega

Buckley, Kevin. *Panama: The Whole Story.* New York: Simon and Schuster, 1991.

Dinges, John. *Our Man in Panama: How General Noriega Used the United States—and Made Millions in Drugs and Arms.* New York: Random House, 1990.

Kempe, Frederick. *Divorcing the Dictator: America's Bungled Affair with Noriega.* New York: G. P. Putnam's Sons, 1990.

Woodward, Bob. *The Commanders.* New York: Simon and Schuster, 1991.

The Gulf War

Allen, Thomas B., F. Clifton Berry, and Norman Polmar. *War in the Gulf*. Atlanta: Turner Publishing, 1991.

Aspin, Les. *The Aspin Papers: Sanctions, Diplomacy, and War in the Persian Gulf*. Washington, D.C.: Center for Strategic and International Studies, 1991.

Atkinson, Rick. *Crusade: The Untold Story of the Persian Gulf War*. Boston: Houghton Mifflin, 1993.

Bennett, W. Lance, and David L. Paletz, eds. *Taken by Storm: The Media, Public Opinion, and U.S. Foreign Policy in the Gulf War*. Chicago: University of Chicago Press, 1994.

Bennis, Phyllis, and Michael Moushabeck, eds. *Beyond the Storm: A Gulf Crisis Reader*. New York: Olive Branch Press, 1991.

Blair, Col. Arthur H. *At War in the Gulf: A Chronology*. College Station: Texas A&M University Press, 1992.

Blackwell, James. *Thunder in the Desert: The Strategy and Tactics of the Persian Gulf War*. New York: Bantam Books, 1991.

Bulloch, John, and Harvey Morris. *Saddam's War*. London: Faber and Faber, 1991.

Caraccilo, Dominic J. *The Ready Brigade of the 82nd Airborne in Desert Storm: A Combat Memoir by the Headquarters Company Commander*. Jefferson, N.C.: McFarland and Company, 1993.

Cohen, Roger, and Claudio Gatti. *In the Eye of the Storm: The Life of Norman Schwarzkopf*. New York: Farrar, Straus and Giroux, 1991.

Crowe, William J. *The Line of Fire: From Washington to the Gulf*. New York: Simon and Schuster, 2001.

Crystal, Jill. *Oil and Politics in the Gulf: Rulers and Merchants in Kuwait and Qatar*. New York: Cambridge University Press, 1990.

Dunnigan, James F., and Thomas A. Bay. *From Shield to Storm: High-Tech Weapons, Military Strategy, and Coalition Warfare in the Persian Gulf*. New York: W. Morrow, 1992.

Freedman, Lawrence, and Efraim Karsh. *The Gulf Conflict, 1990–1991: Diplomacy and War in the New World Order*. Princeton, N.J.: Princeton University Press, 1993.

Friedman, Alan. *Spider's Web: The Secret History of How the White House Illegally Armed Iraq*. New York: Bantam Books, 1994.

Friedman, Norman. *Desert Victory: The War for Kuwait*. Annapolis, Md.: Naval Institute Press, 1991.

Gordon, Michael R., and General Bernard E. Trainor. *The General's War: The Inside Story of the Conflict in the Gulf*. New York: Little, Brown, 1995.

Graubard, Stephen. *Mr. Bush's War: Adventures in the Politics of Illusion*. New York: I. B. Tauris, 1992.

Grossman, Mark. *Encyclopedia of the Persian Gulf War*. Santa Barbara, Calif.: ABC-CLIO, 1995.

The Gulf Crisis: A Chronology, July, 1990—July, 1991. London: U.S. Information Service, 1991.

Hallion, Richard. *Storm over Iraq: Air Power and the Gulf War*. Washington, D.C.: Smithsonian Institution Press, 1997.

Helms, Christine M. *Iraq: Eastern Flank of the Arab World*. Washington, D.C.: Brookings Institution Press, 1984.

Hilsman, Roger. *George Bush versus Saddam Hussein*. Novato, Calif.: Presidio Press, 1992.

Hiro, Dilop. *Desert Shield to Desert Storm: The Second Gulf War*. London: HarperCollins, 1992.

Human Rights Watch Staff. *Needless Deaths in the Gulf War: Civilian Casualties during the Air Campaign and Violations of the Laws of War*. Lanham, Md.: University Press of America, 1991.

Hiro, Dilip. *Desert Shield to Desert Storm: The Second Gulf War*. London: HarperCollins, 1992.

Hume, Cameron R. *The United Nations, Iran, and Iraq: How Peacemaking Changed*. Bloomington: Indiana University Press, 1994.

Ismael, Tareq Y., and Jacqueline S. Ismael. *The Gulf War and the New World Order: International Relations of the Middle East*. Gainesville: University Press of Florida, 1994.

Jentleson, Bruce W. *With Friends Like These: Reagan, Bush, and Saddam, 1982–1990*. New York: W. W. Norton, 1990.

Karsh, Efraim, and Inari Rautsi. *Saddam Hussein: A Political Biography.* New York: The Free Press, 1991.

Lauterpacht, E., et al. *The Kuwait Crisis: Basic Documents.* Cambridge: Grotius Publications, 1991.

Marr, Phebe. *The Modern History of Iraq.* Boulder, Colo.: Westview Press, 2003.

McNaugher, Thomas L. *Arms and Oil: U.S. Military Strategy and the Persian Gulf.* Washington, D.C.: Brookings Institution Press, 1985.

Miller, Judith, and Laurie Mylorie. *Saddam Hussein and the Crisis in the Gulf.* New York: Times Books/Random House, 1990.

Mueller, John. *Policy and Opinion in the Gulf War.* Chicago: University of Chicago Press, 1994.

Navias, Martin. *Saddam's Scud War and Ballistic Missile Proliferation.* London: Brassey's Centre for Defence Studies, University of London, August, 1991.

Nichol, Jim. *Iraq-Kuwait Crisis: Soviet Response.* Washington, D.C.: Congressional Research Service, 17 August 1990.

Powell, Colin. *My American Journey.* New York: Random House, 1995.

Renshon, Stanley A., ed. *The Political Psychology of the Gulf War: Leaders, Publics, and the Process of Conflict.* Pittsburgh: University of Pittsburgh Press, 1993.

Salinger, Pierre, with Eric Laurent. *Secret Dossier: The Hidden Agenda behind the Gulf War.* London: Penguin, 1991.

Sasson, Jean P. *The Rape of Kuwait: The True Story of Iraqi Atrocities against a Civilian Population.* Knightsbridge Publishing, 1991.

Scales, Brig. Gen. Robert H., Jr. *Certain Victory: The U.S. Army in the Gulf War.* New York: Brassey's, 1994.

Schubert, Frank N., and Theresa L. Kraus, eds. *The Whirlwind War: The United States Army in Operations Desert Shield and Desert Storm.* Washington, D.C.: Center of Military History, U.S. Army, 1995.

Schwarzkopf, Norman H. *It Doesn't Take a Hero.* New York: Bantam Books, 1992.

Sifry, Micah L., and Christopher Cerf. *The Gulf War Reader: History, Documents, Opinions.* New York: Times Books, 1991.

Smith, Jean Edward. *George Bush's War.* New York: Henry Holt, 1992.

Stewart, Gen. John. *Operation Desert Storm: The Military Intelligence Story: A View from the G-2.* Washington, D.C.: U.S. Army, 1991.

Swain, Richard M. *Lucky War: Third Army in Desert Storm.* Leavenworth, Kans.: U.S. Army Command and General Staff College Press, 1997.

Summers, Col. Harry G. *On Strategy II: A Critical Analysis of the Gulf War.* New York: Dell, 1992.

———. *Persian War Gulf Almanac.* New York: Facts On File, 1995.

Time. Desert Storm: The War in the Persian Gulf. Boston: Little, Brown, 1991.

Whicker, Marcia Lynn, James Pfiffner, and Raymond Moore. *The Presidency and the Persian Gulf War.* Westport, Conn.: Praeger, 1993.

Winnefeld, James A., Preston Niblack, and Dana J. Johnson. *A League of Airmen: U.S. Airpower in the Gulf War.* Washington, D.C.: Rand Corporation, 1994.

Woodward, Bob. *The Commanders.* New York: Simon and Schuster, 1991.

The Los Angeles Riots

Alan-Williams, Gregory. *Gathering of Heroes: Reflections on Rage and Responsibility, A Memoir of the Los Angeles Riots.* Chicago: Academy Chicago Publishers, 1994.

The Press/Public Relations/Bush as Communicator

Fitzwater, Marlin. *Call the Briefing! Bush and Reagan, Sam and Helen: A Decade with Presidents and the Press.* New York: Times Books, 1995.

Rozell, Mark J. *The Press and the Bush Presidency.* Westport, Conn.: Greenwood Press, 1996.

Scandals, etc.

Bainerman, Joel. *The Crimes of a President: New Revelations on Conspiracy and Cover-Up in the Bush and Reagan Administrations.* New York: S.P.I. Books, 1992.

Blanton, Tom, ed. *E-Mail: The Top Secret Messages the Reagan/Bush White House Thought They Had Destroyed.* New York: New Press, 1995.

Burnham, David. *Above the Law: Secret Deals, Political Fixes and Other Misadventures of the U.S. Department of Justice.* New York: Scribner, 1995.

Sick, Gary. *October Surprise: America's Hostages in Iran and the Election of Ronald Reagan.* New York: Times Books, 1991.

Presidential Election of 1992

Aldich, John H., and David W. Rohde. *Change and Continuity in the 1992 Elections.* Washington, D.C.: Congressional Quarterly Press, 1995.

Barta, Carolyn. *Perot and His People.* Irving, Tex.: Summit Publishing Group, 1994.

Bennett, W. Lance. *The Governing Crisis: Media, Money, and Marketing in American Elections.* New York: St. Martin's Press, 1996.

Black, Christine M. *The Pursuit of the Presidency: '92 and Beyond.* Westport, Conn.: Greenwood Press, 1993.

Brown, Peter. *Minority Party: Why Democrats Face Defeat in 1992 and Beyond.* Washington, D.C.: Regnery Gateway, 1991.

1-800-President: The Report of the Twentieth Century Fund Task Force on Television and the Campaign of 1992. Washington, D.C.: Brookings Institution Press, 1993.

Clinton, Bill, and Al Gore. *Putting People First.* New York: Random House, 1992.

Denton, Robert E., ed. *The 1992 Presidential Campaign: A Communication Perspective.* Westport, Conn.: Greenwood Press, 1994.

Germond, Jack W., and Jules Witcover. *Mad as Hell: Revolt at the Ballot Box, 1992.* New York: Warner Books, 1993.

King, Larry. *On the Line: The New Road to the White House.* New York: Harcourt-Brace Company, 1993.

Loevy, Robert D. *The Flawed Path to the Presidency, 1992: Unfairness and Inequality in the Presidential Selection Process.* Albany: State University of New York Press, 1995.

Nelson, Michael, ed. *The Elections of 1992.* Washington, D.C.: Congressional Quarterly Press, 1993.

Phillips, Kevin. *Boiling Point: Democrats, Republicans and the Decline of Middle-Class Prosperity.* New York: HarperPerennial, 1993.

Pomper, Gerald M., ed. *The Election of 1992.* Chatham, N.J.: Chatham House, 1993.

Posner, Gerald. *Citizen Perot: His Life and Times.* New York: Random House, 1996.

Rollins, Ed. *Bare Knuckles and Back Rooms: My Life in American Politics.* New York: Broadway Books, 1996.

Rosensteil, Tom. *Strange Bedfellows: How Television and the Presidential Candidates Changed American Politics, 1992.* New York: Hyperion Press, 1992.

Tsongas, Paul E. *A Call to Economic Arms: Forging a New American Mandate.* Boston: The Tsongas Committee, 1992.

———. *Journey of Purpose: Reflections on the Presidency, Multiculturalism, and Third Parties.* New Haven, Conn.: Yale University Press, 1995.

Wayne, Stephen J. *The Road to the White House, 1992: The Politics of Presidential Elections.* New York: St. Martin's Press, 1992.

INDEX

❧

Boldface page numbers indicate primary discussions and documents. *Italicized* page numbers indicate photographs. An italicized *c* following a page number indicates chronology; an italicized *m* indicates a map.

A

abortion 101*c*
  antiabortion march
    102c, 106c
  GHWB on xx–xxi
  in remarks to
    American Society
    of Newspaper
    Editors 376
  Louis W. Sullivan
    79
  Supreme Court
    rulings 71
  vetoed measures
    xxi, 101*c*
acid rain 189
acquired
  immunodeficiency
  syndrome (AIDS) 79,
  101c, 105c, 177, 344,
  417–418
ADA. *See* Americans
  with Disabilities Act
  of 1990
Address before a Joint
  Session of Congress
  on Administration
  Goals (February 9,
  1989) **174–181**
Address before a Joint
  Session of Congress
  on Cessation of the
  Persian Gulf Conflict
  (March 6, 1991)
  284–288
Address before a Joint
  Session of Congress
  on Persian Gulf Crisis
  and Federal Budget
  Deficit (September
  11, 1990) **245–250**

Address before a Joint
  Session of Congress
  on the State of the
  Union (January 28,
  1992) **345–352**
Address before a Joint
  Session of Congress
  on the State of the
  Union (January 29,
  1991) **276–282**
Address before a Joint
  Session of Congress
  on the State of the
  Union (January 31,
  1990) **221–227**
Address to People of
  Iraq on Persian Gulf
  Crisis (September 16,
  1990) **250–252**
Address to the Nation
  Announcing Allied
  Military Ground
  Action in the Persian
  Gulf (February 23,
  1991) **282**
Address to the Nation
  Announcing
  Deployment of U.S.
  Armed Forces to Saudi
  Arabia (August 8,
  1990) **241–243**
Address to the Nation
  Announcing U.S.
  Military Action in
  Panama (December
  20, 1989) **213–215**
Address to the Nation
  on Civil Disturbances
  in Los Angeles (May
  1, 1992) **380–383**

Address to the Nation
  on Hurricane Andrew
  Disaster Relief
  (September 1, 1992)
  395–360
Address to the Nation
  on National Drug
  Control Strategy
  (September 5, 1989)
  193–198
Address to the Nation
  on Situation in
  Somalia (December 4,
  1992) **482–484**
Address to the Nation
  on the National
  Education Strategy
  (April 18, 1991)
  294–297
Address to the Nation
  on the Suspension of
  Allied Offensive
  Combat Operations in
  the Persian Gulf
  (February 27, 1991)
  282–284
administration goals
  174–181, 246
adoption expenses 178
affirmative action 83,
  338
Afghanistan 19, 34,
  40–41
agriculture xxvi, 384
AIDS (acquired
  immunodeficiency
  syndrome) 79, 101*c*,
  105*c*, 177, 344,
  417–418
Ailes, Roger xiv, **1,** 4,
  29

air control, in war on
  drugs 360
air pollution 187–188
Akayev, Askar 371
Akihito (crown prince of
  Japan) 100*c*
Akin, Gump, Strauss,
  Hauer, and Feld 36
Alaska National Wildlife
  Refuge 177, 249
Albania 94*m*, 370
Alexander, Lamar xviii,
  2
Alternative Certification
  of Teachers and
  Principals Program
  186
alternative development
  programs, in war on
  drugs 359, 365
American Achievement
  Tests 296
American Bar
  Association (ABA)
  105*c*
American Cause, The
  13
American flag xix–xx,
  101*c*, **201–202**
American Red Cross
  28–29
Americans for Victory
  over Terrorism 9, 10
American Society of
  Newspaper Editors
  (ASNE), remarks to
  369–380
Americans with
  Disabilities Act of
  1990 xix, 45, 57,
  235–237, 390

American values 69,
343, 351, 372–373
America the Beautiful
initiative 224
America 2000 xviii, 2,
104c, 296, 299, 343,
349–350
Amtrak Board of
Directors 31
Andean Development
Corporation (ADC)
364
Andean region,
environmental
damage to 367–368
Andean Trade
Preference Act 364
Andrews, Wyatt 271
Andropov, Yuri 40
apartheid 104c
APCO Associates 32
apparel trade, under
NAFTA 384
approval ratings
xxix–xxx, 19, 26
Aqua International
Partners 72
Aquino, Benigno S.
"Ninoy," Jr. 2–3
Aquino, Maria Corazon
Cojuangco 2–3, 65
Arab-Israeli conflict
285–286
Arab League 59
Architectural and
Transportation
Barriers Compliance
Board 236
Arens, Moshe 3–4
Arias, Arnulfo 61
Arkansas 25
Armenia 370
arms control 42–43,
206–207, 226
arms race 40
arms reductions 102c,
234–235, 303,
331–332, 346–347,
354. See also Strategic
Arms Reduction
Treaty (START)
Ashcroft, John 351
Assad, Hafez al- 59
asset seizure, in war on
drugs 362–363
attack politics 4

Atwater, Harvey Leroy
"Lee" xiii–xiv, xvi,
xxx, **4–6,** 5, 30
Azerbaijan 94m
'Aziz, Tariq 272

B
Ba'ath Party 48
Bahrain 95m
Baker, Donelson,
Bearrnan, and
Caldwell 33
Baker, Howard xiii
Baker, James A. III **7–9**
Moshe Arens 4
Tariq 'Aziz 272,
274
William J. Bennett
10
Richard N. Bond
11
as campaign
manager for
GHWB 100c
as chief of staff xxx
Lawrence S.
Eagleburger 33
Robert Gates 38
GHWB and 8
C. Boyden Gray 44
in remarks on
results of
presidential
election 482
as secretary of state
xvi, 284
Margaret H.
Thatcher 82
Clayton K. Yeutter
90
Baker and Botts 9
Bakker, Jim 101c
Baltics 276, 370
Bangladesh 298
banking industry 12,
100c, 299, 473–475.
See also savings and
loan crisis
Barbara Bush
Foundation for
Family Literacy 14
Barbara Franklin
Enterprises 37
Barco, Virgilio 195
Barr, William P. **9**

base closures 24, 104c,
105c
Begala, Paul 26
Begin, Menachem 3,
76
Beijing, China
xxiii–xxiv, 76,
100c–101c, **181–185**
Belorussia 94m
Bennett, William J.
9–10
William P. Barr and
9
declares "war on
crime" in
Washington,
D.C. 100c
as drug czar xviii,
176
Empower America
10, 52
Office of National
Drug Control
Policy xvi
Republican
National
Committee 6
and war on drugs
194
Bentsen, Lloyd M., Jr.
10
at Democratic
National
Convention 100c
as Dukakis running
mate 17, 30
election as Senator
from Texas 98c
on federal budget
agreement 255
in vice presidential
debate 68
Berlin Wall xxiv, 18, 40,
102c, 222, 290
*Bethel School District v.
Fraser* 71
Biden, Joseph 30
Bierbauer, Charles 317
Bilateral Investment
Treaty with
Czechoslovakia 329
Blackwell, Kathy 277
Blythe, William 25
Bolivia 195, 363–366
Bond, Richard N.
10–11, 482

Boomer, Walter 275
border plan, under
NAFTA 386
Boskin, Michael J. **11**
Bosnia 412–413
Bosnia and Herzegovina
94m
"bounce polling" 5
Boutrous-Ghali,
Boutrous 483
Boyd (General) 290
Bradley, Tom 380–382
Brady, Nicholas F. xvi,
11–12, 12
"Brady Bonds" 12
Brennan, William xxi,
102c
Briscoe, Frank 98c
*Brown v. Board of
Education* 294
Buchanan, Patrick J.
xxxi, 11, **12–13,** 19, 64
Bulgaria 40, 94m, 370
Burg, Simpson,
Eldridge, and Hersh
77
Bush, Barbara Pierce
xiv, **13–14,** 15, 59,
97c, 355, 482
Bush, Dorothy ("Doro")
Walker 13, 15, 98c
Bush, George H. W.
xxv, **14–19**
Americans with
Disabilities Act
signing xx
in baseball uniform
16
and 1992 Cabinet
xxxii
campaign
whistlestop xxxi
at Celebration for
Young Americans
5
as congressman,
with family 16
electoral votes
96m
family chronology
97c–98c
at Helsinki Summit
41
and National
Security Council
xxviii

as naval aviator
cadet *16*
in oil fields *16*
at presidential
debates *31, 64*
Dan Qualye and *69*
Ronald Reagan and
17
at Reagan's
President's
Dinner *xiv*
at Royal Pavilion in
Saudi Arabia *35*
Norman
Schwarzkopf and
74
Margaret Thatcher
and *81*
at the White
House *23, 44,
59, 72, 80*
Boris Yeltsin and
88
Bush, George W. **19**
Lee Atwater and 4,
6
birth of *97c*
Michael J. Boskin
and 11
Robert C. Byrd on
motives of 20
Andrew Card and
21
Richard B. Cheney
and 25
family of 13, 14, 15
Frederic Malek and
56
transition team 6
Bush, John ("Jeb") Ellis
13, 14, 15, *98c*
Bush, Marvin 13, 15,
98c
Bush, Neil Mallon 13,
15, *98c*
Bush, Pauline Robinson
("Robin") 13, 15, *97c*,
98c
Bush, Prescott Sheldon
15
Bush Brigades 10
Bush team xv–xvii
Bush v. Gore 78
Byelarus 370
Byrd, Robert C.
19–20

C
cabinet, 1992 *xxxii*
CAFE standards
460–461
Campbell, Carroll 4
Canada 383–387
capital gains taxes *103c*,
176, 228, 278,
348–349
Card, Andrew **21**
Carlyle Group 28
Cartagena Declaration
357–358, 363, 365
Carter, Jimmy, and
administration of 33,
38, 65, 85, *99c*
Carville, James 26
Casey, William 85–86
Cavasos, Lauro F., Jr.
xvi, xviii, **21–22**, *103c*
Ceau\sc\escu, Nicolae
22, *102c*
Central America 180,
204–205, 210–211
Central Intelligence
Agency (CIA) 9, 35,
38–39, 61, 85
C. Fred's Story (Bush) 14
Chapman, Alvah 396
Chapter 1 program 199
Chechen rebellion
87–88
chemical control, in war
on drugs 361
Cheney, Richard
("Dick") B. **22–25**
announcement on
military base
closures *104c*
with GHWB in the
Oval Office *23*
as nominee for
Secretary of
Defense xvii
on offensive against
Iraq xxvii
position on
expulsion of
Saddam Hussein
8
Colin L. Powell
and 65
and Somalia relief
efforts 483
child care 178,
228–229, 343

Child Care and
Development Block
Grant program 265
China. *See* People's
Republic of China
(PRC)
chronology *97c–107c*
Churchill, Winston
181, 286
CICAD (Inter-American
Commission on the
Control of Drug
Abuse) 359, 362, 363,
365, 369
civil disturbances in
Los Angeles, address
to the nation on
380–383
civil rights xix–xxi, 50,
53, 71, 279. *See also*
King, Glen
("Rodney")
Civil Rights Act
of 1990 xxi, 19,
261–263
of 1991 xxi, 45,
106c, **337–339**
of 1964 263
Clean Air Act
amendments of
1990 57, 72,
177, **187–190**,
229
C. Boyden Gray
and 45
of 1970 xix, 20,
103c
Clinton, Hillary
Rodham 25, 26
Clinton, Virginia
Cassidy 25
Clinton, William
Jefferson **25–26**
Lloyd M. Bentsen,
Jr. 10
on Andrew Card
21
Michael Dukakis
appointment to
Amtrak Board of
Directors 31
election of 19,
107c
electoral votes *96m*
factors in defeat of
GHWB by 1

GHWB concession
to 481–482
in GHWB's
remarks
accepting
presidential
nomination 388,
393–394
Al Gore 43
inauguration of
xxxii
Jesse Jackson 51
marijuana
admission by
106c
Robert H. Michel
57
George Mitchell
58
Colin L. Powell 66
presidential
campaign of, in
1988 xiii–xv
presidential
campaign of, in
1992 xxxi–xxxii
at presidential
debate *64*
presidential debate,
East Lansing
452–481
presidential debate,
Richmond
423–452
presidential debate,
St. Louis
396–423
Boris Yeltsin and 88
Clune, Ricky 230
coal 189
cocaine xviii, 357–358
Coelho, Anthony **26,**
101c
cold war
break with Reagan
administration on
75–76
end of 18
in remarks
announcing
candidacy for
reelection 356
in remarks at
Maxwell Air
Force Base War
College 290, 291

cold war *(continued)*
in remarks to
American Society
of Newspaper
Editors 370, 373
in remarks to UN
Security Council
354
in remarks with
Gorbachev in
Malta 204
in statement on
resignation of
Gorbachev 341
in State of the
Union Address,
1991 276
in State of the
Union Address,
1992 345–346
College Republicans
National Committee
(CRNC) 4
Colombia 195, 357–369
Commission on
America's Urban
Families 351
Commonwealth of
Independent States
xxxi, 87, 106c
communism
Communist states
pre-1991 94m
GHWB's approach
toward xxiii–xxiv
in remarks accepting
presidential
nomination 388
in remarks to
American Society
of Newspaper
Editors 370–371
in State of the
Union Address,
1990 225–226
in State of the
Union Address,
1992 345
Communist Party
demise of xxiv, xxx,
42
Mikhail Gorbachev
and 40
in Romania 22
Boris Yeltsin and
87

community
mobilization, in war
on drugs 368
community service, in
Points of Light
initiative 190–191
Compton, Ann
presidential debate
in St. Louis
396–423
Conference of
Governors, 1989 xviii
Congress
address before a
joint session on
administration
goals **174–181**
address before a
joint session on
state of the
union, 1990
221–227
address before a
joint session on
state of the
union, 1991
276–282
address before a
joint session on
state of the
union, 1992
345–352
address before a
joint session on
cessation of
Persian Gulf
crisis **284–288**
address before a
joint session on
Persian Gulf
crisis and federal
budget deficit
245–250
authorization for use
of force in Persian
Gulf 104c
Congressional
Black Caucus
105c
debate on
president's
authority to send
troops into
combat xxvii
Democratic control
of xv

message
transmitting
proposed
legislation on
educational
excellence to
185–187. *See also*
House of
Representatives;
Senate
Congressional Black
Caucus 105c
congressional elections,
1990 xxi–xxiii
Congress of People's
Deputies 87
Consequences (Tower) 84
conservation 188, 243
conservatism 227–228,
230
conservative leaders
remarks at a White
House briefing
for **227–230**
Conservative Party,
Britain 81
Consortium for
Oceanographic
Research and
Education (CORE) 85
continuing resolutions
256–257, 260–261
Contract with America
39–40
Council of Economic
Advisors (CEA) 11,
45–46
covert diplomacy
220–221
Cox, Jack 98c
crack cocaine xviii
credibility, in
presidential debates
453–457
credit reform 264
crime
in presidential
debates 433–435
war on 100c, 287,
343, 350
criminal justice system
195
Croatia 94m, 105c
Crossfire 13, 80
Crowe, William
xxiv–xxv

Crown Heights riots
105c
Cuéllar, Javier Pérez de
247
Cuomo, Mario xv,
393–394
Czechoslovakia 94m,
102c, 222, 292,
329–330, 370
Czech Republic 94m,
328–329

D
Danforth, John 82
Darman, Richard G.
xvi, **27–28**, 79, 89
death penalty, in war on
drugs 176, 196
debt renegotiation, in
war on drugs 364
decentralization 228–229
Declaration of
Cartagena 357–358,
363, 365
Declaration of
Independence 235,
237
Declaration of San
Antonio (February 27,
1992) **357–369**
defense budget 23, 24,
179, 346–347
defense industry, in
presidential debates
404–406
defense program 226,
249
de Klerk, F. W.
(president of South
Africa) 104c
de la Billiere, Peter 284
democracy
in Inaugural
Address 171
in remarks
announcing
candidacy for
reelection
353–354
in Russia 372
and Soviet Union
reform 341
Democratic Leadership
Council 25
Democratic National
Convention 107c

Democratic Party xvii
democratic reform of
Soviet Union 341
Department of
Agriculture 55, 89
Department of
Commerce 37, 58
Department of Defense
arms reductions
347
budget for 179
national security
policy 23–24
nominations for
Secretary xvi–xvii
H. Ross Perot and
63
Colin Powell and
65
Brent Scowcroft
and 75
Tower nomination
failure 185
Department of
Education xviii, 2, 22,
82–83
Department of Energy
85
Department of Health
and Human Services
78–79, 265
Department of Housing
and Urban
Development 48, 52
Department of Justice
9, 201, 236, 379–380,
381–382
Department of Labor
28, 56–57
Department of State
7–8, 33, 67, 180, 237
Department of the
Interior 54
Department of
Transportation 21,
28, 77
Department of Treasury
11–12
Department of Veterans
Affairs 28, 100c
Derwinski, Edward J.
xvi, **28**
Desert Shield. *See*
Persian Gulf War
(Operation Desert
Storm)

Desert Storm. *See*
Persian Gulf War
(Operation Desert
Storm)
Devroy, Ann 259, 271
Dewey, Thomas 229
Dillon, Read and
Company 12
diplomacy
GHWB's talent for
18
in Panama crisis
213–214
in Persian Gulf crisis
239, 243,
247–248, 267, 280
disarmament 102c,
234–235, 303,
331–332, 346–347,
354. *See also* Strategic
Arms Reduction
Treaty (START)
discretionary program
caps, in Omnibus
Budget Reconciliation
Act 264
discrimination 235–236,
261–262, 338, 343
Dole, Elizabeth Hanford
xvi, **28–29**
Dole, Robert **29–30**
William J. Bennett
and 10
Michael J. Boskin
and 11
Elizabeth Dole and
28–29
and federal budget
crisis 256–257,
260–261
Jack Kemp and 52
in New Hampshire
primary 79, 99c
in 1988 presidential
race xiii, xiv–xv
in 1996 presidential
election 25
remarks on federal
budget
agreement 254
domestic agenda 17
domestic economy. *See
also* federal budget
in address before
joint session of
Congress 287

Council of
Economic
Advisors (CEA)
11, 45–46
Newt Gingrich on
policies of
GHWB 39
in presidential
debate 439–440
recession xxxi, 103c
recovery 27
in State of the
Union Address,
1992 347–349
domestic energy
production 249, 393
domestic infrastructure,
in presidential debates
430–432
domestic jobs, in
presidential debates
424–425
domestic policies
xvii–xix
Domestic Policy council
90
Dooney (child in crack
house) 197
Dowd, Maureen 220
Dow Jones Industrial
Average 101c, 104c
drug control. *See* war on
drugs
drug crisis 101c
Drug-Free Schools
Urban Emergency
Grants 186
drug summits 102c,
106c, 357–369. *See also*
Declaration of San
Antonio
drug treatment, in war
on drugs 196
Dubček, Alexander 102c
Dugan, Michael 24
Dukakis, Kitty 31
Dukakis, Michael **30–31**
announcement of
candidacy 99c
Lloyd M. Bentsen,
Jr., and 10
at Democratic
National
Convention 100c
electoral votes 9,
93m

portrayal of, by
Bush campaign
5–6
at presidential
debate *31*
presidential race xv,
17
Duke, David 100c
DuPont, Pierre xiii
Durenberger, David F.
31–32, 103c

E
Eagleburger, Lawrence
S. **33,** 76
Earth in the Balance
(Gore) 43
Eastern Europe 210,
292, 344. *See also
individual countries*
East Germany xxiv,
94m, 102c, 222
economic cooperation
34, 205–206
economic development,
for peace 286
economic growth, in
administration goals
175
economic issues, in war
on drugs 363–364
Economic Policy
Council 90
economic reforms, in
Mexico 383
economic sanctions
xxvii, 214
Economic Summit,
Houston 102c
Economic Summit of
Industrialized
Nations, Paris 55,
101 c
Ecuador 357–369
education
accountability in
200
in address before
joint session of
Congress on
administration
goals 176–177
in address to joint
session of
Congress xviii

education (*continued*)
  address to the
    nation on
    294–297
  AIDS 79
  Lamar Alexander **2**
  America 2000
    announcement
    104*c*
  commitment to
    restructuring
    200–201
  federal
    government's
    financial role
    200
  federal/state
    partnership
    199–200
  of GHWB 15
  national goals
    198–199
  national strategy
    343
  in presidential
    debates 445–448
  in remarks
    accepting
    presidential
    nomination 392
  in State of the
    Union Address,
    1990 223–224
  summit of nation's
    governors 101*c*
  in war on drugs
    368
Educational Excellence
  Act of 1990 xviii,
  185–187, 228
Education of the
  Handicapped Act 236
education summit
  198–201, 223–224
Egypt 58–59, 95*m*
electoral votes 93*m*,
  96*m*
Electronic Data Systems
  (EDS) 63
Emergency Deficit
  Control Measures for
  FY 1991, Order for
  243–244
emissions 187–190
employee rights in the
  workplace 71

Empower America 10,
  52
Endara, Guillermo, and
  government of 61,
  214–219
energy production,
  domestic 249, 393
energy security, in
  Omnibus Budget
  Reconciliation Act
  264
enforcement and process
  reform, in Omnibus
  Budget Reconciliation
  Act 264
Enterprise for the
  Americas Initiative
  (EAI) 279, 359,
  363–364
Enterprise Zones 52
entitlement programs,
  in presidential
  debates 418–420,
  440–443
environmental agenda,
  under NAFTA
  385–387
Environmental Defense
  Fund 188
environmental
  management
  programs, in war on
  drugs 367–368
environmental
  philosophy 188
Environmental
  Protection Agency
  (EPA) 72, 189–190,
  224, 386
Equal Employment
  Opportunity
  Commission (EEOC)
  82–83
Estonia 94*m*, 104*c*,
  105*c*
Europe 208–210,
  290–293, 310–311,
  402–403. *See also
  individual countries*
European Bank 329
European Community
  373
Executive Department
  108–109
Exemplary Grants
  program 187

export controls
  288–289
Exxon Valdez (oil tanker)
  xix, 100*c*

F
Fahd Bin Abdul Aziz
  (king of Saudi Arabia)
  24, **34–35,** *35,* 82,
  247, 266
faith and family 175,
  226
Family Savings Plan
  initiative 223
Family Support Act 25
family values, in
  presidential debate
  413–414
famine, in Somalia
  482–484
Fast Track procedures
  383, 387
federal air quality
  standards 189
federal budget. *See also*
  defense budget
  address before joint
    session of
    Congress on
    deficit **245–250**
  in address on
    administration
    goals 174–181
  in address to the
    nation on
    national drug
    control strategy
    195–197
  anger over
    xxii–xxiii
  deficits xxi–xxiii,
    17–18, 103*c,* 106*c,*
    183, 224, 391
  emergency deficit
    control measures
    243–244
  NAFTA and 386
  news conference on
    crisis **255–261**
  Office of
    Management and
    Budget 27
  Omnibus Budget
    Reconciliation
    Act of 1990 xxiii,

  12, 57–58, 79,
    264–266
  in presidential
    debates 425–427,
    467–468
  proposed
    constitutional
    amendment to
    balance 390–391
  and proposed
    Educational
    Excellence Act
    187
  in remarks
    accepting
    presidential
    nomination
    390–391
  remarks
    announcing
    agreement on
    252–255
  in remarks at
    annual
    convention of
    National
    Religious
    Broadcasters 343
  in remarks to
    American Society
    of Newspaper
    Editors 373,
    378–379
  in State of the
    Union Address,
    1990 224
  in State of the
    Union Address,
    1991 278–280
  in State of the
    Union Address,
    1992 351
Federal Bureau of
  Investigation (FBI)
  85
Federal Deposit
  Insurance
  Corporation (FDIC)
  100*c*
federal regulations,
  moratorium on 348
Federal Republic of
  Germany 94*m*
Federal Reserve Board
  xxii, 46, 103*c,* 348,
  407–409

federal tax withholding tables 348

federal unemployment benefits 349

Federal Vocational Education Act 199

financial services trade, under NAFTA 384

firearms control, in war on drugs 363

First Amendment issues 71

first-time home buyers 348

Fitzwater, Marlin xvi

flag protection xix–xx, 101c, **201–202**

Florida, and Hurricane Andrew 395–396

Flowers, Gennifer 26

Foley, Thomas S. xvii, xx, 6, **36**, 106c, 253

Follett, Ken 63

Ford, Gerald R., and administration of 7, 45, 98c
    Richard B. Cheney and 22–23
    Richard G. Darman and 27
    Robert Dole and 29
    Lawrence S. Eagleburger 33
    Robert Gates 38
    Carla Hills 48
    Frederic Malek 55
    Clayton K. Yeutter 89

foreign lobbyists, in presidential debates 463–466

foreign policy
    James Baker and **7–8**
    Panama xxiv–xxv
    People's Republic of China xxiii–xxiv
    in presidential debates 409–410, 443–445
    in remarks accepting presidential nomination 388–389

in remarks to American Society of Newspaper Editors 370–378
    Brent Scowcroft and xvi
    Soviet-U.S. relationship xxiii

Forum for International Policy 76

Founding Fathers, in address on administration goals 175

Fox Television News 1, 40

France, and GATT 377

Frank, Barney 103c

Franklin, Barbara Hackman **36–37**

freedom
    of expression 71, 299–300
    in Inaugural Address 171, 173
    in remarks at annual convention of National Religious Broadcasters 344
    in remarks to American Society of Newspaper Editors 372
    of spirit 300
    in State of the Union Address, 1990 222–223, 226
    in State of the Union Address, 1991 277

FREEDOM Support Act 373

free enterprise system 298–299

free society, cornerstones of 222–223

free trade area (FTA) 384

free trade zone, in war on drugs 361–362

Fuerth, Leon 43

Fuller, Craig xv

G

Gandhi, Rajiv 105c

Gang of Eight 38

gas exploration 249, 393

gasoline taxes xxii–xxiii, 252

gas production and reserves 177, 248

Gates, Daryl 105c

Gates, Robert **38–39**, 106c

Gelb, Michael 231

General Agreement on Tariffs and Trade (GATT) 89, 279, 377, 383, 384

General Motors 21, 63, 106c

Genscher, Hans Dietrich 102c

George Bush School of Government and Public Service 39

Georgia, Republic of 94m, 104c

Gephardt, Richard 254–255

Germany 94m. See also East Germany
    and democracy in Russia 372
    and GATT 377
    NATO membership 233
    reunification of 211–212, 231–232, 234, 370

Gheorghui-Dej, Gheorghe 22

Gibbons, Gene 467–475

Gingrich, Newton ("Newt") Leroy xxii–xxiii, **39–40**

glasnost 40, 341

God 344–345

"Good Friday" peace accord 58

Good Society 301

Gorbachev, Mikhail Sergeyevich **40–42**
    Richard B. Cheney on 24

condemnation of Iraqi invasion xxvi

coup attempts against 105c

and end to Communist Party dominance in East Germany xxiv

Robert Gates and 38

in GHWB's address to joint session of Congress on Persian Gulf crisis 246

in GHWB's remarks at Maxwell Air Force Base War College 293

Helsinki Summit 41, 103c

Malta Summit xxiv, xxv, 3, 41, 102c, 202–213

meeting with American people 235

Middle East peace conference, Madrid 7, 106c, 330–337

ouster of xxx–xxxi

in president's news conference 220

president's news conferences on attempted coup against **311–319**, **319–326**

president's news conference with, in Moscow **301–311**

resignation of 106c

in Soviet-U.S. joint statement on Persian Gulf crisis 244–245

and Soviet-U.S. relationship xxiii

and START 18

statement of GHWB on resignation of **341**

Gorbachev, Mikhail Sergeyevich (*continued*) summits with GHWB 102*c* summit with Reagan and Bush, New York 100*c* Margaret H. Thatcher and 82 on use of force against Iraq 270 Boris Yeltsin and 87

Gore, Albert A., Jr. xxxi–xxxii, 26, 30, **42–43**, 107*c*

government reform, in presidential debate 475–476

governors, U.S. 163–164, 165–167, **198–201**

Graham, Billy 344

Gramm-Rudman-Hollings sequester process 264

Gray, C. Boyden xvi, 9, **43–45**, *44*

Gray, Gordon 43

Great Society 300

Green Cross International 42

Greenspan, Alan **45–46**, 278

Grenada, U.S. invasion of 73

gridlock xvii–xviii, 356–357, 392, 432–433

Group of Eight (G-8) 88

Group of Seven (G-7) 55, 101*c*, 314, 361, 362, 373

Gulf Cooperation Council 34

Gulf War. *See* Persian Gulf War (Operation Desert Storm)

gun control, in presidential debates 433–435

H

Haig, Alexander xiii

Hart, Gary 30

Havel, Vaclav 102*c*, 222, 292, 329–330

Head Start 343

health care reform Newt Gingrich and 39 in presidential debates 420–421, 436–439 in remarks accepting presidential nomination 392 in State of the Union Address, 1990 225 in State of the Union Address, 1991 279 in State of the Union Address, 1992 350

health standards, under NAFTA 386

Heath, Edward 81

Heinz, John 104*c*

Helsinki Summit xxvi, *41*, 42, 103*c*, 246

Heritage Foundation 10

Hill, Anita F. xxx, **47**, 77, 82–83, 105*c*–106*c*

Hills, Carla **47–48**

Hirohito (emperor of Japan) 100*c*

Historically Black Colleges and Universities grants 186–187

HIV (human immunodeficiency virus) 105*c*. *See also* AIDS (acquired immunodeficiency syndrome)

Hoffman, David 216

Hogan and Hartson 57, 90

Holliday, George 53

homelessness 178

Homestead Air Force Base 396

Honecker, Erich 222

Hoover Institution 11

HOPE housing initiative 223, 350

Hopkins, Mike 297

Hopkins and Sutter 78

Horton, Willie xv, 6, 30

Hosler, Karen 325

House of Representatives Thomas S. Foley 36 Newt Gingrich 39–40 Manuel Lujan, Jr. 54 Lynn Morley Martin 56 Robert H. Michel 57 102nd Congress 120–121, 142–152, 152–162 101st Congress 120, 121–131, 131–142 overdrafts by members of 106*c*

Huddleston, Hollywood 275

human immunodeficiency virus (HIV) 105*c*. *See also* AIDS (acquired immunodeficiency syndrome)

humanitarian mission, in Somalia 482–484

Hume, Brit 217

Hungary 94*m*, 292, 370

Hunt, Terence 216, 268

Hurricane Andrew 21, 107*c*, 395–360

Hussein, Abdullah II ibn al- (king of Jordan) 103*c*, 240

Hussein, Saddam **48–49**. *See also* Iraqi invasion of Kuwait; Persian Gulf crisis; Persian Gulf War (Operation Desert Storm) assurances of 34–35 Richard B. Cheney and 24 demands of Israel regarding 35 Robert Gates on expulsion of 38

in GHWB's address before joint session of Congress on cessation of Persian Gulf conflict 284–285 in GHWB's address to people of Iraq 250–252 in GHWB's address to the nation announcing allied military action in Persian Gulf 273–275 in GHWB's radio address to the nation on Persian Gulf crisis 272–273 in GHWB's remarks announcing candidacy for reelection 354 in GHWB's remarks at Maxwell Air Force Base War College 291–292 in GHWB's remarks to American Society of Newspaper Editors 374–375 in GHWB's remarks to reporters on invasion of Kuwait 240 Hosni Mubarak 59 no-fly zone violation xxxii in president's news conference on Persian Gulf crisis 267, 269, 270 release of hostages 103*c* in Soviet-U.S. joint statement on Persian Gulf crisis 245 in State of the Union Address, 1991 276

Margaret H.
Thatcher 82
UN sanctions
41–42
in White House
statement on
weapons of mass
destruction 288

I

Iacocca, Lee xiii
illegal drugs, social cost
of 193–194
illness, on trip to Japan
106c
Inaugural Address
(January 20, 1989)
xvii, **171–174**
Indiana 68
information sharing, in
war on drugs 360
infrastructure, domestic,
in presidential debates
430–432
Institute of Politics,
John F. Kennedy
School of
Government 83
insurance opportunities,
under NAFTA
384–385
integrated border plan,
under NAFTA 386
intellectual property
rights protection,
under NAFTA 385
Inter-American
Commission on the
Control of Drug
Abuse (CICAD) 359,
362, 363, 365, 369
International
Commission on
Missing Persons 30
International Drug
Enforcement
Conference (IDEC)
361–362
International Drug
Summit 102c, 106c.
See also Declaration of
San Antonio
international drug trade
61. See also war on
drugs

International
Emergency Economic
Powers Act 237
International Monetary
Fund (IMF) 373
International Narcotics
Control Board 361
intervention programs,
in war on drugs 196
Interview with Chinese
Television Journalists
in Beijing (February
26, 1989) **181–185**
intolerance 343
investment
opportunities, under
NAFTA 385
investment tax allowance
348
Iran 49, 95m, 103c
Iran-contra affair 17,
38, 57, 99c, 107c
Iraq 95m. See also
Hussein, Saddam;
Persian Gulf crisis
in address before
joint session of
Congress on
cessation of
Persian Gulf
crisis **284–285**
address to people
of, on Persian
Gulf crisis
250–252
address to the
nation
announcing allied
military action
against **273–274**
agriculture credits
xxvi
attack on Iran 49,
103c
attack on Israel 104c
coalition against
xxvii
freezing of assets
xxvi, 242
"no-fly" zone 107c
and occupied
territory, 1991
95m
in presidential
debates 470–471,
472–473

in president's news
conference on
Persian Gulf
crisis 266–267
production of
enriched uranium
105c
sanctions imposed
on 103c
terms of surrender
xxix
U.S. military action
against xxix, 19,
49, 107c. See also
Persian Gulf War
(Operation
Desert Storm)
violation of no-fly
zone xxxii
warning by Arab
states 104c
Iraqi invasion of Kuwait
103c. See also Hussein,
Saddam; Persian Gulf
crisis; Persian Gulf
War (Operation
Desert Storm)
Richard Cheney's
response to 24
deployment of U.S.
Armed Forces to
Saudi Arabia
241–243
and GHWB's
diplomatic skill
18
Margaret
Thatcher's
response to 82
in remarks accepting
presidential
nomination 388
remarks and
exchange with
reporters on
237–239
remarks to reporters
on **239–241**
Norman
Schwarzkopf's
response to 73–74
Brent Scowcroft's
response to 76
summary xxvi
UN Security
Council on 247

isolationism 373–374
Israel 95m
in address before
joint session of
Congress on
cessation of
Persian Gulf
conflict 285–286
Moshe Arens 3–4
demands regarding
Saddam Hussein
35
Iraq attack on xxix,
104c
Persian Gulf
conflict xxvii
Yitzhak Shamir **76**
issues, focus on, in
presidential debates
429–430
Italy 372

J

Jackson, Henry "Scoop"
36
Jackson, Jesse 30, **50–51**,
99c
Jackson, Robert 70
Japan 36, 372
Jaruzelski, Wojciech xxiv
JHS Associates, Ltd. 80
jobs, in presidential
debates 406–407,
424–425
"Job Training 2000" 57
Johnson, Gregory Lee
xix–xx
Johnson, Lyndon B. 28,
33, 84, 298, 300
Joint Chiefs of Staff
(JCS) 65–66, 75, 347
Joint Commission on
Commerce and Trade
37
Joint Oceanographic
Institutions (JOI) 85
Joint Remarks with
Soviet Chairman
Gorbachev at Malta
Summit (December 3,
1989) **202–213**
Joint Statement with
Nation's Governors
on Education Summit
(September 28, 1989)
198–201

Joint Statement with
Soviet Union on
Persian Gulf Crisis
(September 9, 1990)
244–245
Jones, Jackie 276
Jordan 95*m*
justice, in war on drugs
359–363

K

Kazakhstan 94*m*, 370
Kelley, David 297
Kemp, Jack F. xiii, xvi,
52
Kendall, J. P. 275–276
Kennedy, Edward xv
Kennedy, John F. 65,
298, 301
Khalid (Saudi general)
284
King, Glen ("Rodney")
xxxi, **52–53**, 104*c*,
107*c*, 380–383
King, Martin Luther, Jr.
50
Kirkpatrick, Jeane 52
Kirkpatrick and
Lockhart 83
Kissinger, Henry 33,
34, 75
Kleindienst, Richard 70
Kohl, Helmut 103*c*
Koop, Everett 101*c*
Korea 106*c*
Kravchuk, Leonid 371
Kurdistan 104*c*, 298
Kuwait 95*m*, 266–267,
273, 284–285. *See also*
Iraqi invasion of
Kuwait
Kyrgyzstan 94*m*

L

labor rights, under
NAFTA 385–387
Land and Water
Conservation Fund
177
land transportation,
under NAFTA 385
Larry King Live 63–64
Latvia 94*m*, 104*c*, 105*c*
lawsuits 392

leadership, in
presidential debates
457–458, 468–469
Lebanon 95*m*, 206
Lehrer, Jim 396–423,
452–481
Letter Accepting
Resignation of John
H. Sununu as Chief of
Staff (December 3,
1991) **339–341**
Libya 100*c*, 106*c*, 355
Liedke, Hugh 15
Liedke, William 15
Likud Party 3–4, 76
Lincoln, Abraham 180,
356
line-item veto 229, 230,
351, 390
Lithuania 40, 94*m*,
102*c*, 104*c*, 105*c*,
232–233, 307–308
Lockerbie, Scotland
100*c*, 106*c*
Los Angeles, civil
disturbance in 52–53,
77–78, 380–383
Louisiana, and
Hurricane Andrew
395–396
Lujan, Manuel Jr. **54**

M

Maastricht Treaty 106*c*
Macedonia 94*m*
Madigan, Edward **55**
Madrid Conference of
1991 7, 106*c*,
330–337
Magnet Schools of
Excellence program
186
Major, John 103*c*
Malek, Frederic
55–56
Mallon, Neil 15
Malta Summit xxiv,
xxv, 3, 41, 102*c*,
202–213
Mandela, Nelson 102*c*
Manuel Lujan Associates
54
Marcos, Ferdinand 2–3
maritime control, in war
on drugs 360–361

Markwell, James 225
Marshall, Burke 77
Marshall, Thurgood
xxx, 105*c*
Martin, Lynn Morley
56–57
Martinez, Bob xviii
Masaryk, Tomas
Garrigue 330
Mashek, John 322,
396–423
Massachusetts 30
Maxwell Air Force Base
War College, remarks
at **289–293**
Mayaguez (merchant
ship) 75
McClendon, Sarah
219–220, 271
McPeak, Tony 290
Medicaid 178.
See also entitlement
programs
Mediterranean, military
forces in 209
Merit Schools xviii
Merritt, Wade 245
Message to Congress
Transmitting
Proposed Legislation
on Educational
Excellence (April 5,
1989) **185–187**
Message to Senate
Returning without
Approval the Civil
Rights Act of 1990
(October 22, 1990)
261–263
Metropolitan West
Financial 43
Mexico 279, 357–369,
377, 383–387
Michel, Robert H. **57**,
255, 256
Middle East peace
process
in address before
joint session of
Congress on
cessation of
Persian Gulf
conflict
285–287
Madrid conference
7, 106*c*, 330–337

in president's news
conference on
attempted coup
in Soviet Union
313–314
in president's news
conference with
Gorbachev,
Moscow 303–306
in remarks of
GHWB and
Gorbachev, Malta
209
Mike Douglas Show, The
1
Milbank, Tweed,
Hadley, and McCloy
86
military actions. *See also*
Persian Gulf War
(Operation Desert
Storm)
deployment of U.S.
armed forces to
Saudi Arabia
241–243
against Iraq xxix,
19, 107*c*,
273–274,
282–284
in Panama 102*c*,
213–215, 225
U.S. destruction of
Libyan fighter
planes 100*c*
U.S. invasion of
Grenada 73
military draft 466–467
military installation
consolidation 24,
104*c*, 105*c*
military service by gay
men and gay women
66
military service of
GHWB 15
military spending. *See*
defense budget
military troops in
Europe, in
presidential debates
402–403
Millie's Book (Bush) 14
Milošević, Slobodan 103*c*
minimum wage 19,
101*c*, 102*c*

minority presidential candidates, in presidential debates 448–450
Mitchell, Andrea 46
Mitchell, George xix, xxvii, **57–58,** 100c, 254
Mitterrand, François 354
Miyazawa, Kiichi 106c
Moldavia 94m
Mondale, Walter 99c
money laundering, as issue in war on drugs 362
Moore, Michelle 297
Morehouse School of Medicine 79
Morrill and Associates 28
Morris, Robert 98c
Mosbacher, Robert A. xvi, **58,** 482
Moscow Summit 105c, **301–311**
Mubarak, Muhammad Hosni **58–59,** 59
Mulroney, Brian 188, 242
Multilateral Investment Fund 364
multilateral trade negotiations 376–377
Muskie, Edmund xix

N

NAFTA. *See* North American Free Trade Agreement (NAFTA)
National Aeronautics and Space Administration (NASA) 176
National Council on Disability 235–236
national councils, in war on drugs 369
National Drug Control Strategy, Address to the Nation on **193–198**
national education strategy 294–297, 343. *See also* America 2000
National Guard 380–381

National League of Cities 343
National Rainbow Coalition 50
National Religious Broadcasters, remarks at annual convention **341–345**
National Science Foundation 176
National Science Scholars program 176, 186
National Security Council (NSC) *xxviii,* 38–39, 65, 79, 179
national security policy 23–24
National Summit on Education, 1989 22
NATO (North Atlantic Treaty Organization) 88, 226, 233, 239, 242, 292
naval arms control 207–208
Nebraska 265
New American Schools Development Corporation 296–297
New Hampshire 78, 79
New Mexico 54
new world order 76, 288–289, 290–293, 370–374
Nicaragua 229–230
nitrogen oxide emissions 189
Nixon, Pat 344
Nixon, Richard M., and administration of
    Patrick J. Buchanan and 13
    Nicolae Ceaușescu and 22
    Richard G. Darman and 27
    Elizabeth Hanford Dole 28
    Robert Dole and 29
    Lawrence S. Eagleburger 33
    Fahd ibn Abdul Aziz 34

Barbara Hackman Franklin 37
GHWB as appointee of 17
Alan Greenspan 45
Frederic Malek 55
presidential campaign 1
resignation of 98c
Brent Scowcroft 75
Supreme Court nomination of William Rehnquist 70
Clayton K. Yeutter 89
"no new taxes" xv, 1, 27, 102c
Noonan, Margaret "Peggy" xv, **60**
Noriega, Manuel Antonio **60–62**
    conviction on drug trafficking and money laundering 106c
    coup attempts 65, 86, 101c
    in GHWB's address to the nation announcing U.S. military action in Panama 213–219
    overthrow of 18, 102c
    U.S. foreign policy xxiv–xxv
    U.S. indictment of 99c
North, Oliver 100c, 101c, 105c
North American Free Trade Agreement (NAFTA)
    James Baker and 7–8
    Carla Hills 48
    Robert A. Mosbacher 58
    negotiations announcement 107c
    H. Ross Perot 64
    in presidential debate 461–463
    William K. Reilly 72

in remarks accepting presidential nomination 389
    signing of xxxii
    in war on drugs 364
    White House fact sheet on **383–387**
North Korea 106c
North Vietnam 22
nuclear arms reduction 102c, 178, 309–310, 331–332
Nuclear Non-Proliferation Treaty 354

O

Office of Consumer Affairs 28
Office of Management and Budget 27
Office of National Drug Control Policy 9–10
Office of the Council to the President 43–44
Office of Thrift Supervision xxii
oil
    dependence on foreign 252
    exploration 249, 393
    production and reserves 177, 238, 243, 246–247, 248
    protection of 268
    spills xix, 100c
oil fields *16, 95m,* 104c
Oklahoma 265
Omnibus Budget Reconciliation Act of 1990 xxiii, 12, 57–58, 79, 264–266
O'Neill, Paul 296
one-to-one problem solving, in Points of Light initiative 191–192
On Wings of Eagles (Follett) 63

Open Skies plan xxiii
Operation Blue Spoon
    66. *See also* Operation
    Just Cause
Operation Desert
    Shield. *See* Persian
    Gulf War (Operation
    Desert Storm)
Operation Desert Storm
    95*m*. *See also* Persian
    Gulf War (Operation
    Desert Storm)
Operation Just Cause
    xxv, 61, 102*c*, 222
Operation Provide
    Comfort 298
Operation PUSH
    (People United to
    Save Humanity) 50
Operation Red Dawn
    49
Operation Restore Hope
    482–484
Order for Emergency
    Deficit Control
    Measures for FY 1991
    (August 25, 1990)
    243–244
Organization of
    American States
    (OAS) 361–363, 369
Overby, John 15
overdrafts by House of
    Representatives
    members 106*c*
Overseas Private
    Investment
    Corporation (OPIC)
    329

P
Pagan, Esteban "Steve"
    297
Paine, Thomas 275
Panama. *See also*
    Noriega, Manuel
    Antonio
    address to the
        nation
        announcing U.S.
        military action in
        213–215
    failed coup
        xxiv–xxv

in president's news
    conference
    215–220
in remarks at White
    House briefing
    for conservative
    leaders 229–230
U.S. foreign policy
    toward xxiv–xxv
U.S. military action
    in 102*c*, 225
Panama Canal treaties
    214
Panamanian Defense
    Forces (PDF)
    215–217, 219
Pan Am flight 103 100*c*,
    106*c*
parks 177
passive loss rule 348
*Patterson v. McLean
    Credit Union* xxi, 71
Paz, Robert 61
peace building 285–286,
    373–374
Peace Corps volunteers
    372–373
peace dividend 371
peer-to-peer working
    groups, in Points of
    Light initiative 192
Pennsylvania 83
Pentagon. *See*
    Department of
    Defense
People's Republic of
    China (PRC)
    Nicolae Ceaușescu
        22
    covert diplomacy
        with 220–221
    end of martial law
        102*c*
    Barbara Franklin's
        visit to 37
    GHWB as
        ambassador to
        180
    interview with
        Chinese
        television
        journalists in
        181–185
    in presidential
        debate 410–412

statement on
    suppression of
    student
    demonstrations
    in 187
Tiananmen Square
    protest xxiii–xxiv,
    76, 100*c*, 101*c*
trade status
    xxiii–xxiv, 104*c*,
    183–184
perestroika 24, 40, 341
Perot, H. Ross **63–65**
    in GHWB's
        remarks to
        American Society
        of Newspaper
        Editors 375–376
    at presidential
        debate *64*
    presidential debate,
        East Lansing
        452–481
    presidential debate,
        Richmond
        423–452
    presidential debate,
        St. Louis
        396–423
    presidential race
        xxxi, xxxii, 25,
        107*c*
Persian Gulf 95*m*
Persian Gulf crisis
    in address before
        joint session of
        Congress
        245–250
    address to people
        of Iraq on
        250–252
    Robert C. Byrd and
        20
    in joint statement
        with Gorbachev
        244–245
    president's news
        conference on
        266–272
    radio address to the
        nation on
        272–273
    in remarks to UN
        Security Council
        354–355

Persian Gulf War
    (Operation Desert
    Storm) xxv–xxvi,
    95*m*. *See also* Hussein,
    Saddam
    in address before
        joint session of
        Congress on
        cessation
        284–288
    in address to the
        nation
        announcing allied
        military ground
        action **282**
    in address to the
        nation on
        suspension of
        allied offensive
        combat
        operations
        282–284
    James Baker and 8
    Richard B. Cheney
        and 24
    coalition allies in
        18, 247–248,
        273–274
    congressional
        authorization for
        use of force 104*c*
    Robert Dole and
        29
    Fahd ibn Abdul
        Aziz and 35
    GHWB's goal in
        xxvii
    and increased taxes
        xxii
    key issues of
        xxvi–xxvii
    Robert H. Michel
        57
    Hosni Mubarak 59
    Colin Powell's role
        in 66
    Dan Quayle 69
    in remarks at
        Maxwell Air
        Force Base War
        College 289–290
    in remarks to
        American Society
        of Newspaper
        Editors 374–375

Herbert Norman
    Schwarzkopf 74
Yitzhak Shamir 76
in State of the
    Union Address,
    1991 280–282
in State of the
    Union Address,
    1992 346
summary xxv–xxix
John H. Sununu 79
William H.
    Webster 86
personal exemption,
    federal income taxes
    351
Peru 195, 358–359,
    366–367
Pin Point, Georgia
    327–328
Points of Light initiative
    172, **190–193**, 230,
    277, 297, 301
Poland xxiv, 94*m*, 222,
    226, 292, 370
Policy Coordinating
    Group (PRG) 90
political correctness
    299–300
port control, in war on
    drugs 361–362
Powell, Colin L.
    xxiv–xxv, xxvii, 3, 8,
    65–67, *66*
prayer 344–345
prayer in schools 228
PRC. *See* People's
    Republic of China
    (PRC)
presidential awards for
    excellence in teaching
    176
presidential campaigns
    of GHWB. *See also*
    presidential debate
    entries
    Roger Ailes and 1
    Lee Atwater and
        4–6
    James Baker 7–8
    Frederic Malek 56
    mistakes in xxxi
    Robert A.
        Mosbacher 58
1988 election
    xiii–xv, 1

1992 election
    xxxi–xxxii
remarks announcing
    candidacy for
    reelection
    355–357
in remarks to
    American Society
    of Newspaper
    Editors 375–376,
    379–380
Presidential Citation for
    students 296
Presidential Debate in
    East Lansing,
    Michigan (October
    19, 1992) **452–481**
Presidential Debate in
    Richmond, Virginia
    (October 15, 1992)
    423–452
Presidential Debate in
    St. Louis, Missouri
    (October 11, 1992)
    396–423
presidential debates 31,
    107*c*
presidential elections
    1988 xiii–xv, 29,
        30, 93*m*
    1992 xxix–xxxii, 13,
        25, 96*m*, 107*c*,
        481–482
    1996 29
    2000 43
presidential library
    dedication xxxii
Presidential Medal of
    Freedom 9, 51, 57,
    58, 86
Presidential Merit
    Schools program 186
presidential pardons 107*c*
President's Awards for
    Excellence in
    Education 186
President's Build a
    Community Awards
    193
President's Committee
    on Employment of
    People with
    Disabilities 236
President's Foreign
    Intelligence Advisory
    Board (PFIAB) 84

President's News
    Conference
    (December 21, 1989)
    215–221
President's News
    Conference on
    Attempted Coup in
    Soviet Union
    (August 20, 1991)
    311–319
President's News
    Conference on
    Attempted Coup in
    Soviet Union (August
    21, 1991) **319–326**
President's News
    Conference on
    Federal Budget Crisis
    (October 6, 1990)
    255–261
President's News
    Conference on
    Persian Gulf Crisis
    (November 8, 1990)
    266–272
President's News
    Conference with
    President Gorbachev
    in Madrid, Spain
    (October 29, 1991)
    330–337
President's News
    Conference with
    Soviet President
    Mikhail Gorbachev
    in Moscow (July 31,
    1991) **301–311**
President's Special
    Review Board on Iran
    Contra 75
prevention, in war on
    drugs 368
primary "firewall" 5
Prince William Sound,
    Alaska xix, 100*c*
private investigations
    472
private sector, in war on
    drugs 196
Project 88 188
property seizure, in war
    on drugs 362–363
public housing, tenant
    ownership and
    control 228, 279, 299

Puerto Rico statehood
    178
Putin, Vladimir 89

Q

Quayle, J. Danforth
    ("Dan") **68–69**
    Roger Ailes and 1
    attempted coup in
        Philippines 3
    election as vice
        president 100*c*
    GHWB and 69
    in GHWB's address
        on administration
        goals 176
    in GHWB's remarks
        on results of the
        presidential
        election 482
    as running mate of
        GHWB xv, 17
    vice presidential
        debate 10, 43

R

racial harmony, in
    presidential debates
    416–417
racial quotas 338
Radio Address to the
    nation on Persian
    Gulf Crisis (January 5,
    1991) **272–273**
Ramos, Fidel 3
Rangel, Charles 26
Rather, Dan 99*c*
"read my lips" xv, 1, 27,
    102*c*
Reagan, Nancy *xiv*
Reagan, Ronald, and
    administration of 99*c*
    Roger Ailes and 1
    Lee Atwater and 4
    James Baker and 7
    William J. Bennett
        and 9
    Nicholas F. Brady
        and 11–12
    Patrick J. Buchanan
        and 13
    Andrew Card and
        21

Reagan, Ronald, and
    administration of
    (*continued*)
      Lauro F. Cavasos,
        Jr., and 22
      Richard G. Darman
        and 27
      Department of
        Veterans Affairs
        28
      détente with
        Gorbachev xxiii
      Elizabeth Hanford
        Dole and 28
      Robert Dole and 29
      education spending
        xviii
      Fahd ibn Abdul
        Aziz and 34
      Barbara Franklin
        and 36
      Robert Gates and
        38
      GHWB as vice
        president xiii
      Al Gore's arms
        control proposal
        43
      Alan Greenspan and
        46
      Peggy Noonan and
        60
      Manuel Antonio
        Noriega and 61
      in the Oval Office
        17
      Colin L. Powell
        and 65
      President's dinner
        xiv
      William H.
        Rehnquist
        nomination as
        chief justice of
        Supreme Court
        70
      and START 18
      John G. Tower and
        84
      Clayton K. Yeutter
        and 89
Reagan-Bush ticket xiii
Reagan Presidential
    Library dedication
    106c

real estate 348
recession xxxi, 11
recognition and awards,
    in Points of Light
    initiative 193
Reform Party 64
Regan, Donald 60
regional security 285
Rehabilitation Act of
    1973 236
Rehnquist, Nan 327
Rehnquist, William H.
    70–71, 101c
Reilly, William K.
    71–72, 72
religion in America 342
Remarks Accepting
    Presidential
    Nomination at the
    Republican National
    Convention (August
    20, 1992) **387–395**
Remarks and Exchange
    with Reporters on
    Iraqi Invasion of
    Kuwait (August 2,
    1990) **237–239**
Remarks and Exchange
    with Reporters on
    Soviet-U.S. Summit
    (May 31, 1990)
    230–235
Remarks Announcing
    Bush-Quayle
    Candidacies for
    Reelection (February
    12, 1992) **355–357**
Remarks Announcing
    Federal Budget
    Agreement (September
    30, 1990) **252–255**
Remarks Announcing
    Proposed Legislation
    to Amend Clean Air
    Act (June 12, 1989)
    187–190
Remarks at Annual
    Convention of
    National Religious
    Broadcasters (January
    27, 1992) **341–345**
Remarks at a White
    House Briefing for
    Conservative Leaders
    (April 26, 1990)
    227–230

Remarks at Maxwell Air
    Force Base War
    College in
    Montgomery, Alabama
    (April 13, 1991)
    289–293
Remarks at Swearing-In
    Ceremony for
    Supreme Court
    Designate Clarence
    Thomas (October 18,
    1991) **326–328**
Remarks at the
    University of
    Michigan
    Commencement
    Ceremony (May 4,
    1991) **297–301**
Remarks at Welcoming
    Ceremony for
    President Vaclav
    Havel of
    Czechoslovakia
    (October 22, 1991)
    329–330
Remarks in Houston on
    the Results of the
    Presidential Election
    (November 3, 1992)
    481–482
Remarks on Civil Rights
    Act of 1991
    (November 21, 1991)
    337–339
Remarks to American
    Society of Newspaper
    Editors (April 9,
    1992) **369–380**
Remarks to Reporters
    on Invasion of Kuwait
    (August 5, 1990)
    239–241
Remarks to UN
    Security Council
    (January 31, 1992)
    352–355
Republican National
    Committee (RNC)
      Lee Atwater 6
      Richard N. Bond
        10–11
      Robert Dole 29
      Robert A.
        Mosbacher 58
      Clayton K. Yeutter
        89

Republican National
    Convention 107c
      Patrick J. Buchanan's
        speech 13
      Frederic Malek 55
      Peggy Noonan 60
      Remarks Accepting
        Presidential
        Nomination
        387–395
Republican presidential
    primaries xiii, 13
Republicans,
    conservative xxiv
Republic of Georgia
    94m, 104c
Republic of the
    Philippines 2–3
research, basic 176
research and
    development 350
Resolution Trust
    Corporation 101c
"Revolving Door"
    advertisement 6, 31
Right in the Old Gazoo
    (Simpson) 77
rights of employees in
    the workplace 71
riots
      Crown Heights
        105c
      Los Angeles xxxi,
        52–53, 77–78,
        107c, 380–383
Roe v. Wade xx, 70, 71
Rogers, Will 229
Romania 22, 94m, 220,
    221
Rook, Susan 468–476
Roosevelt, Franklin D.
    181, 351–352
Roquejeoffre, Michel 284
Rostenkowski, Dan xxii
Rove, Karl 4
Rumsfeld, Donald xiii,
    22–23
Russia 87–89, 346–347,
    370–372
Russian Federation 94m

S
Sadat, Anwar 58
safeguard procedures,
    under NAFTA 386

safety standards, under NAFTA 386
Salinas de Gortari, Carlos (president of Mexico) 383
San Antonio drug summit **357–369**
Sandler, Norman 320
San Francisco earthquake 101*c*
Saudi Arabia xxvi–xxviii, 34–35, 82, 95*m*, 103*c*, 241–243
savings, personal 178
savings and loan crisis xxii, 26, 101*c*, 104*c*, 106*c*
schools, strategy for transformation of 294–297
Schwarzkopf, Herbert Norman xxvi, xxix, **73–75**, *74*, 266, 282
scientific research, in war on drugs 369
Scowcroft, Brent **75–76**
    Robert Gates 38–39
    GHWB, Sununu, and *80*
    in GHWB's remarks at Maxwell Air Force Base War College 290
    in GHWB's remarks on results of presidential election 482
    offensive against Iraq xxvii
    position on expulsion of Saddam Hussein 8
    Colin L. Powell 65
    role in foreign policy xvi
    Margaret H. Thatcher 82
"Scrub Team" 19
SDI. *See* Strategic Defense Initiative (SDI)

Seib, Gerald 326
Senate
    Armed Services Committee 84
    denunciation of David F. Durenberger 32
    Judiciary Committee hearings on Clarence Thomas appointment to Supreme Court xxx, 47
    leadership during Bush administration 109
    message to, returning without approval the Civil Rights Act of 1990 (October 22, 1990) **261–263**
    George Mitchell 57–58
    101st Congress 109–112, 112–114
    102nd Congress 115–117, 117–120
    Alan K. Simpson 77
"Senator Straddle" ad 1, 29
service, in Points of Light initiative 190–191
ServLink Project 192
ServNet Project 192
Sessions, William 99*c*
Shamir, Yitzhak xxvii, xxix, 3–4, **76**
Shaw, Bernard 31
Shevardnadze, Eduard 7–8, 103*c*, 270, 341
Shultz, George 28
Simons, Arthur "Bull" 63
Simpson, Alan K. xxx, **76–77**
Simpson, Carole 423–452

Sisk, B. F. 26
Skinner, Samuel K. xvi, xxx, 21, 54, **77–78**
Slovakia 94*m*, 328–329
Slovenia 104*c*, 105*c*
small businesses 391–392
smoking banned on domestic airline flights 102*c*
Social Security 178, 224–225, 264
Solidarity Union, Poland 101*c*, 226
Somalia xxxii, 412–413, 482–484
Souter, David H. xxi, **78**, 79, 102*c*, 103*c*
South Carolina, and Hurricane Andrew 396
Southern Christian Leadership Conference (SCLC) 50
South Korea 106*c*
Soviet Republics xxiv, 332–334
Soviet Union 94*m*. *See also* Gorbachev, Mikhail Sergeyevich
    in address on administration goals before a joint session of Congress 179
    collapse of 94*m*
    détente with xxiii, xxiv
    domestic problems 234
    Mikhail Gorbachev's resignation 341
    Malta Summit 202–213
    in president's news conferences on attempted coup 311–319, 319–326
    president's news conference with Gorbachev, Moscow **301–311**

    in president's news conference with Gorbachev, Madrid 332–334, 336–337
    reforms 40
    remarks and exchange with reporters on Soviet-U.S. Summit **230–235**
    in remarks at Maxwell Air Force Base War College 290–293
    Brent Scowcroft and 75–76
    secessions from 42
    in State of the Union Address, 1991 276–277
    Margaret H. Thatcher 82
    trade agreement with 231, 232
    U.S. and, in joint statement on Persian Gulf crisis 244–245
    U.S. foreign policy on xxiii–xxv
    U.S. relationship with, under GHWB and Gorbachev 41
space program 101*c*, 176
Speaking the Truth to Power (Hill) 47
Speicher, Joanne 346
Speicher, Scott 346
spending caps 264
spending freeze 390
Spetznaz forces 320–321
Spiegel, Thomas 26
"spin" 5
Starr, Kenneth 100*c*
Statement on Chinese Government's Suppression of Student Demonstrations (June 3, 1989) **187**

Statement on Failure of Senate to Approve Nomination of John Tower as Secretary of Defense (March 9, 1989) **185**
Statement on Flag Protection Act of 1989 (October 26, 1989) **201–202**
Statement on Resignation of Mikhail Gorbachev as President of the Soviet Union (December 25, 1991) **341**
Statement on Signing the Americans with Disabilities Act of 1990 (July 26, 1990) **235–237**
Statement on Signing the Omnibus Budget Reconciliation Act of 1990 (November 5, 1990) **264–266**
State of the Union Addresses 106*c*
    1990 **221–227**
    1991 **276–282**
    1992 **345–352**
    Peggy Noonan 60
staying the course, in presidential debates 458–460
Stewart McKinney Homeless Assistance Act 187
Stockdale, James 43, 107*c*
stock market xxii
Strategic Arms Reduction Treaty (START) 18, 84, 105*c*, 305
Strategic Defense Initiative (SDI) 179–180, 226, 281, 347
Strauss, Annette 351
Strauss, Robert 312–313
student loans, interest on 351

students with special needs 200
sulfur dioxide emissions 187–188, 189
Sullivan, Louis W. xvi, **78–79**, 102*c*
Summit Communication Group 44
Sununu, John H. **79–80**
    George W. Bush and 19
    Andrew Card and 21
    GHWB, Scowcroft, and 80
    on GHWB's domestic policies xvii
    C. Boyden Gray and 44–45
    and 1988 presidential race xiv–xv
    resignation of xxx, 106*c*, **339–341**
Superfund sites cleanup 72
Supreme Court
    abortion rulings 71
    and conservative policy initiatives of GHWB xix–xxi
    justices of 108
    in message to Senate returning without approval the Civil Rights Act of 1990 261–263
    William H. Rehnqist **70–71**
    David H. Souter **78**
    on symbolic value of flag 201
    Clarence Thomas xxx, 47, **82–83**, 326–328
    2000 presidential election 19
Supreme Soviet 333
Swanson, Tim 237
Syria 95*m*

T
Tajikistan 94*m*
targeted growth incentives 252–253
tariff cuts, under NAFTA 384
Task Force on Competitiveness 176
Tate, Sheila xv
taxes
    adoption expense deduction 178
    campaign promise on 18
    capital gains 103*c*, 176, 228, 278, 348–349
    changes in Omnibus Budget Reconciliation Act 264
    credits for child care 178, 228
    credits for research and development 176, 350
    federal withholding tables 348
    gasoline xxii–xxiii, 252
    growth-oriented measures 249
    increase in 102*c*
    Persian Gulf War and increased xxii
    personal exemption 351
    in presidential debates 400–402, 403–404, 476–478
    "read my lips" xv, 1, 27
    in remarks accepting presidential nomination xv, 391–392
Teeter, Robert xv, 482
telecommunications trade, under NAFTA 384
television 382
term limits 435–436

Ter-Petrosyan, Levon 371
terrorist attacks 19, 49, 100*c*, 106*c*
Texas A&M University 39
Texas Rangers 19, 56
Texas v. Johnson xx, 71
textiles, under NAFTA 384
Thatcher, Margaret H. (prime minister of Great Britain)
    GHWB and *81*, **81–82**
    on hostage-taking by Iraq 247
    and Iraqi invasion of Kuwait 239
    and Iraq trade embargo 242
    in president's news conference on Persian Gulf crisis 268
    reelection of 99*c*
    resignation of 103*c*
Thayer Capital Partners 56
Thomas, Clarence **82–83**, 105*c*–106*c*
    C. Boyden Gray and 45
    Anita F. Hill 47
    nomination of xxx
    remarks by GHWB at swearing-in ceremony 326–328
    Alan K. Simpson 77
    John H. Sununu and nomination 79
Thomas, Helen 216, 238, 334–335, 466–478, 468–476
Thompson, James 77
Thornburgh, Richard L. xvi, 10, **82**
Thousand Points of Light 172, **190–193**, 230, 277, 297
Thurmond, Strom 4
Tiananmen Square protest xxiii–xxiv, 76, 100*c*–101*c*

tobacco, smoking of,
banned on domestic
airline flights 102c
tobacco company
advertising 79
Tocqueville, Alexis de
226–228, 230, 372
tolerance, in
administration goals
175
Torrijos, Omar 61
Tower, John G. **83–84**
C. Boyden Gray
and 44
George Mitchell
57
nomination as
secretary of
defense xvi–xvii,
23
nomination as
secretary of
defense rejected
100c
statement on failure
of Senate to
approve
nomination **185**
Tower, Marian 84
Tower Commission 75,
84, 99c
Townsend-Greenspan
and Company, Inc.
45–46
toxic waste 177
trade, foreign. *See also*
North American Free
Trade Agreement
(NAFTA)
Andean Trade
Preference Act
364
China's trade status
xxiii–xxiv, 102c,
104c, 183–184
free trade zone
control in war on
drugs 361–362
General Agreement
on Tariffs and
Trade (GATT)
89, 279, 377, 383,
384
in presidential
debates 424–425

in remarks to
American Society
of Newspaper
Editors 371–372,
376–378
Soviet Union 231,
232, 305
in State of the
Union Address
349
U.S. International
Trade
Commission
(USITC) 385
U.S. Trade
Representative
(USTR) 48
Trade Act of 1974 383
trade embargo, on Iraq
242
training, in war on drugs
369
transition team of
GHWB 44
transportation, land,
under NAFTA 385
transportation bill 348
transportation initiative
287
treatment and
rehabilitation, in war
on drugs 368–369
Trinity International
Partners 80
Truman, Harry S 225,
395
Turkey 95m
Turkmenistan 94m

U
Ukraine 94m, 332–334,
370
Ullman, Owen 317
unemployment benefits,
federal 349
unfunded mandates 351
United Nations (UN)
address to 105c
Convention against
Illicit Traffic in
Narcotic Drugs
and Psychotropic
Substances
360–362

Drug Control
Program 362
and Iraqi invasion
of Kuwait xxvi,
74
member nations in
combat against
Iraq 95m
repeal of "Zionism
Equals Racism"
resolution 106c
sanctions against
Iraq 41–42, 59
in Somalia
482–484
Richard L.
Thornburgh and
83
United Nations (UN)
Security Council
and Iraqi invasion
of Kuwait 237,
242, 247
in president's news
conference on
Persian Gulf
crisis 266,
268–269
in remarks at
Maxwell Air
Force Base War
College 290–293
remarks to
352–355
resolutions 18, 35,
49, 103c–104c,
244–245, 282
*United States v.
Eichmann* 71
United We Stand 64
University of Michigan,
remarks at
commencement
ceremony of
297–301
Uruguay 279, 376–377
U.S. Air Force 241, 483
U.S. Army 483
U.S. Attorney General
83, 265
U.S. Congress. *See*
Congress; House of
Representatives;
Senate
U.S. Foreign Service 33

U.S. International Trade
Commission (USITC)
385
U.S. Marines 483
U.S. Trade
Representative
(USTR) 48
U.S.-Canada Free Trade
Agreement 89
USS *America* (warship)
95m
U.S.-Saudi Joint
Commission on
Economic
Cooperation 34
USS *Finback*
(submarine) 394
USS *Iowa* (warship)
100c
USS *Missouri* (warship)
95m
USSR 105c, 106c. *See
also* Commonwealth
of Independent States;
Russia; Soviet Union
USS *Saratoga* (warship)
95m
USS *Wisconsin* (warship)
95m
Uzbekistan 94m

V
values, in remarks at
annual convention of
National Religious
Broadcasters 342–343
Vanocur, Sander
396–423
Vega, Moises Giroldi 61
Venezuela 357–369
Ventura, Jesse 65
Verner, Liipfert,
Bernhard,
McPherson, and
Hand 58
vetoes xvii–xviii, xxi, 19,
101c
Vietnam 22, 75
Vietnam Syndrome xxvii
Volcker, Paul 46
Volkin (prime minister
of Ukraine) 333
volunteerism, Barbara
Bush and 14

W

Walesa, Lech 222
Wards Cove Packing Co. v. Antonio xxi, 71
war on crime 100*c*, 287, 343, 350
war on drugs. *See also* Declaration of San Antonio; United Nations (UN)
  in address on administration goals before joint session of Congress 176–177
  address to the nation on 193–198
  William J. Bennett as drug czar xviii, 176
  drug crisis 101*c*
  Drug-Free Schools Urban Emergency Grants 186
  drug summits 102*c*, 106*c*, 357–369
  multilateral strategies in 359–366, 368–369
  Office of National Drug Control Policy 9–10
  in presidential debates 414–416
  in remarks accepting presidential nomination 390
  in remarks at annual convention of National Religious Broadcasters 343–344
  in remarks at White House briefing for conservative leaders 229
War Powers Act 24
Warren, Ellen 218
Warsaw Pact 94*m*, 290, 371
Washington gridlock xvii–xviii, 356–357, 392, 432–433
Watkins, James D. xvi, 72, **85**
weapons of mass destruction 285, 288–289, 291–292
Weber, Vin 52
Webster, William H. **85–86,** 99*c*
Webster v. Reproductive Health Services of Missouri xxi, 71
Weed and Seed initiative 343
Welch, Lawrence 24
welfare reform, in State of the Union Address, 1992 351–352
Western Hemisphere, antidrug struggle in 359
White, Byron 328
White House Fact Sheet on NAFTA (August 12, 1992) **383–387**
White House Fact Sheet on Points of Light Initiative (June 22, 1989) **190–193**
White House staff 7–8, 60, 77, 90. *See also* Sununu, John H.
Whitman, Walt 345
Wilmer, Cutler, and Pickering 45
Wilson, Pete 380–381
Wilson, Woodrow 330
Woerner, Manfred (secretary general of NATO) 242
women advisers 469–470, 471–472
women presidential candidates 448–450
worker adjustment programs, under NAFTA 385–387
World Bank 329, 373
World Transformed, A (Bush and Scowcroft) 76
World War I 373
World War II 97*c*
World War II memorial 30
World Wildlife Fund 72
Wright, James B. xvii, 99*c*, 100*c*, 101*c*
Wyoming 76–77

Y

Yarborough, Ralph 98*c*
Yazov, Dmitri T. 320–321
Yeltsin, Boris Nikolayevich **87–89**
  coup denounced by 105*c*
  election to Russian Congress of Deputies 100*c*
  GHWB and 88
  in GHWB's remarks to American Society of Newspaper Editors 371, 373
  in president's news conferences on attempted coup in Soviet Union 311, 313, 319–320, 322–323, 326
  resignation from Communist Party 102*c*
  in State of the Union Address 346–347
Yeutter, Clayton K. xvi, **89–90**
Youth Engaged in Service to America (YES) initiative 180, 191
youth movement, Israel 76
Yugoslavia 40, 94*m*, 304, 306

Z

Zapata Petroleum 15
Zionism 105*c*
"Zionism Equals Racism" resolution 106*c*